THE
WHOLESALE-BY-MAIL
CATALOG™ III

THE
WHOLESALE-BY-MAIL
CATALOG™ III

by
THE PRINT PROJECT

LOWELL MILLER, *Executive Producer*
PRUDENCE McCULLOUGH, *Editor*

St. Martin's Press/New York

The Wholesale-By-Mail Catalog III is a resource for use by the general public. Companies in
this catalog are listed at the sole discretion of the editors, and no advertising fees are solicited
or accepted.

Design by Giorgetta Bell McRee

Library of Congress Cataloging in Publication Data
The Wholesale-by-mail catalog III.
   Rev. ed. of: The New wholesale-by-mail catalog. c1982.
   1. Advertising, Direct-mail—United States.
2. Catalogs, Commercial.   3. Wholesale trade—
United States—Directories.   I. Miller, Lowell.
II. McCullough, Prudence.   III. Print Project.
IV. New wholesale-by-mail catalog.
HF5861.W53   1985   381'.2'02573   85-12536
ISBN 0-312-87076-0 (pbk.)

Contents

Introduction 1
Organization of Listings 3
The Listing Code 5
Charts 8
ANIMAL 19
APPLIANCES, AUDIO, TV, AND VIDEO 31
ART, ANTIQUES, AND COLLECTIBLES 59
ART MATERIALS 69
AUTO AND MARINE 75
BOOKS, MAGAZINES, RECORDS, AND TAPES 89
CAMERAS, PHOTOGRAPHIC AND DARKROOM
    EQUIPMENT, OPTICALS, FILM, AND SERVICES 107
CIGARS, PIPES, TOBACCO, AND OTHER SMOKING NEEDS 125
CLOTHING 133
CRAFTS AND HOBBIES 173
FARM AND GARDEN 197
FOOD AND DRINK 211
GENERAL MERCHANDISE, GIFTS, AND BUYING CLUBS . . 223
HANDCRAFTS, NATIVE PRODUCTS, AND IMPORTS 235
HEALTH AND BEAUTY 243
HOME
    Decor 261
    Furnishings 272
    Kitchen 287
    Linen 293
    Maintenance 303
    Table Settings 309

JEWELRY, GEMS, AND WATCHES 325
LEATHER GOODS 345
MEDICAL AND SCIENTIFIC.............................. 353
MUSIC 361
OFFICE AND COMPUTING............................... 373
SPORTS AND RECREATION............................. 399
SURPLUS.. 421
TOOLS, HARDWARE, ELECTRONICS, ENERGY,
   SAFETY, SECURITY, AND INDUSTRIAL 427
TOYS AND GAMES 445
THE COMPLETE GUIDE TO BUYING BY MAIL 453
   Catalogs, Price Quotes, and Information................... 457
   How to Order 462
   Shipping, Insurance, Handling, Sales Tax, and Duty 474
   Receiving Your Order 483
   Returns, Guarantees, and Warranties 489
   Complaints... 496
Feedback 500
Index.. 501

Introduction

We are very happy to bring you *The Wholesale-by-Mail Catalog III*. This third edition is bigger and better in every way. We've expanded the buying guide, beginning on page 453, to be the most comprehensive primer on mail-order purchasing in print. We've winnowed out the companies in our second edition whose service was below par, as well as those whose prices ceased to represent true discounts. And, as in any field, there were casualties due to deaths, natural disasters, and the Great Recession of 1981–1982. Thanks to help from readers and exhaustive research efforts, this new edition is chock-full of new sources for everything from aids for the disabled to salsa verde.

You can purchase almost anything by mail. And, because mail-order suppliers have low overhead and frequently skip a step or two in the distribution chain, they often offer their goods at cheaper rates. Starting from that premise, we asked ourselves, "Just how much cheaper is it to shop by mail? Can you get prices so low you are actually buying at, or close to, the wholesale price or 30% below retail?"

The answer is Yes. You can avoid the retailer's markup, even if you are an individual desiring only one item, through mail-order purchasing from selected suppliers. If you want to "get it wholesale," this catalog will show you how. Whether it's boots, computers, burglar alarms, cameras, or antiques, you can buy whatever you need for anywhere from 30% to 90% off the price you'd have to pay in a store or nondiscount catalog.

And *that's wholesale*. Though the retail markup varies on different products, the most common figure is about 30%, so we drew our cutoff line at that point. (In fact, markups on many types of products are often in the 50% to 100% range, which accounts for the stupendous discounts you'll find on some goods.) Using the 30% markup as a guideline, you can assume that if a product sells for $10 in a store, the owner paid about $7 for it, maybe a little more or less, depending on the item. Using *The Wholesale-by-Mail Catalog III*, you'll pay what the retailer does *before* the markup. And you won't have to wait for a sale in a store.

Just one more note: Please read our explanation of the listing code and "The Complete Guide to Buying by Mail" before sending for a catalog or placing an order—you'll find it much easier to understand and use this book, and to avoid later problems with all your mail-order transactions.

Happy bargain hunting. We'd love to hear about your experiences with the firms listed in this book. Turn to "Feedback," p. 500, if you'd like to contact us.

THE PRINT PROJECT
Lowell Miller, *Executive Producer*
Prudence McCullough, *Editor*

Organization
of Listings

As you can imagine, organizing a book like this requires many decisions. If a company sells fabric, uniforms, and watches, do we list it in the crafts, clothing, or jewelry section? We asked each firm to designate the product category in which it was strongest in terms of selection. To maintain brevity and minimize confusion, we put the firm's listing—a description of all its goods and services—in that one category. We then *cross-referenced* the firm in every other applicable category.

SEE ALSO: The last page of each chapter of catalogs, headed "See Also," lists firms whose products fall within that category but are filed under their main listing in another chapter. For example, the *See Also* page at the end of the "Animal" chapter shows that Gohn Bros. stocks horse blankets. The firm's main listing is in the "Clothing" chapter, which is where you will find the complete description of the company and its services. Don't overlook the *See Also's*!

PATIENCE: Since companies are constantly revising their catalogs and printing new ones, we ask you to be patient while waiting for literature to arrive. Specifically, please allow *six to eight weeks,* unless the firm's listing indicates a longer possible delay. If the catalog doesn't arrive within the designated period, consult the "Catalogs" section of "The Complete Guide to Buying by Mail" for information on the steps you should take to get it. Note that whenever we were able to determine a firm's schedule of catalog publication, we included this information in the listing. Use this as a guide when sending for catalogs. In addition, remember that some products, such as flower bulbs, can be ordered only at certain times of the year.

PRICE QUOTES: Some firms do not issue catalogs at all. Most of these operate under a price-quote system: You tell them the exact make and model number of the item you want and they give you the price and shipping cost, either by mail or phone. Businesses that operate this way are clearly indicated in the listings. Price-quote firms often have the lowest prices on such goods as appliances, audio and TV components, and furniture; they usually sell well below both the standard manufacturers' suggested list prices and the less formal minimum prices that some manufacturers try to enforce. Before writing or calling for a price quote, or buying in this way, remember to read the "Price Quote" section in "The Complete Guide to Buying by Mail."

MINIMUM ORDERS: In a few cases, the very best buys are available from firms which require a minimum order in dollars or goods (though most of the companies in this book impose no such restriction). Don't be put off by a minimum requirement. If you want something that's a real bargain, chances are you have friends or work associates who'll want it too. Even if you can't find a buying partner, remember that a great bargain can also be a great gift. Stock up on a supply of that special product. This will also keep you one small step ahead of inflation.

A NOTE ABOUT SPECIFIC PRICES: Our criteria for listing companies center on percentage discounts; 30% off today should still be 30% off tomorrow or next year, even if *prices* change—unless profit margins become squeezed. Ordinarily, most sellers set their prices in relation to the rest of the market. When you do see specific prices, please keep in mind that we live in an unstable economic environment. Prices have probably changed in the time it took this book to reach you so they are included only as guidelines.

A CAVEAT: *The Wholesale-by-Mail Catalog III* is compiled as a resource, pointing you to the bargains available by mail. *Never* order goods directly from this book, even if prices and shipping charges are given in the listing. *Always* write to the company first to get a catalog or a current price quote, and be sure to follow specific ordering and payment instructions. All the information in this book is based on our research and fact-checking as of press time, and is subject to change.

The Listing Code

To save space and avoid repetition, we've presented some of the information in the listings in a simple coded form in the boldface columns at the head of each entry. All the factual information is listed and abbreviated as follows:

(1) Company name, address, and phone number(s), including toll-free order numbers.

(2) Literature form: catalog, brochure, flyer, leaflet, price list, etc.; approximate schedule of publication or availability; price; "refundable," "redeemable," or "deductible": cost of catalog refunded or deducted from first order; "SASE": send self-addressed, stamped, business-sized envelope (#10) with request; "information": price quote given by phone and/or letter (specified), or inquiries answered individually.

(3) Discount level: savings you may expect on the suggested list prices or comparable retail of those goods and/or services. Do *not* deduct this percentage from the order total unless so instructed in the listing text or catalog.

(4) WBMC Reader Discount, Bonus, Rebate, or Savings: as explained in the text. Special savings or offers are honored only if requirements (minimum orders, identification of yourself as a WBMC reader, etc.) are met. Do *not* ask firms without such designation for special offers or discounts—no mail-order haggling.

(5) Type of goods sold: name brand, house brand (manufactured by the firm or sold under its label), generic (off-brand or nonbranded goods), custom-made, handcrafted, handmade, second-quality or irregular, imported, domestic, used, surplus, salvage, etc.

(6) Minimum order: if any, in dollars or amount of goods, on credit cards and/or prepaid orders.

(7) Shipping charges and insurance fees (when charged separately), and method of shipment used (applicable to shipments to the the continental U.S. only):

(a) included: shipping cost included in the price of the goods

(b) extra: cost of shipping not included in the price of the goods

(c) UPS: goods shipped by United Parcel Service

(d) PP: goods shipped by Parcel Post or other service of the U.S. Postal Service

(e) FOB: "free on board": goods usually shipped by truck; charges, which are not included in the cost of the goods, are usually collected upon delivery by the carrier

(f) surface mail: goods from overseas firms shipped by boat

(g) airmail: goods from overseas firms shipped by plane

(8) Handling charge: surcharge for packing and/or handling orders, listed separately when not included in shipping and insurance charges.

(9) Sales Tax or Duty, where applicable: if the firm has a business office or outlet in the state in which the goods are delivered, you may have to add sales tax to the cost of the goods and/or services; duty may be charged on goods imported from foreign countries.

(10) Methods of payment: forms accepted for order payments (assume catalog fees must be paid by check or money order unless otherwise stated):

(a) check: personal check

(b) MO: bank or postal money order

(c) certified check: includes cashier's check, bank draft, teller's check, and related bank checks

(d) IMO: bank or postal international money order

(e) IRC: International Reply Coupon, postal voucher used as payment for catalogs from foreign firms

(f) Access: Access credit card

(g) AE: American Express credit card

(h) CB: Carte Blanche credit card

(i) CHOICE: CHOICE credit card

(j) DC: Diners Club credit card

(k) EC: Eurocard credit card

(l) MC: MasterCard credit card

(m) V: VISA credit card

THE DOLLAR CODE: The dollar code symbol ($) represents our opinion of the overall "worth" of the firm to the average bargain-hunter. We take into account the quality of the goods, the quantity of offerings, the depth of discount, and, where information is available, the quality of service. The final judgment is somewhat subjective, but after you've analyzed as many firms as we have, certain ones simply stand out and others fade away.

Four "dollar signs" is a top rating; one is the lowest. *However,* a low rating may only reflect a limited number of products; it doesn't mean that the company is a poor source for those products. There has to be some way of separating the thrilling buys from the merely good. Whenever possible, the ratings reflect our opinion of that firm in comparison to others within the same product category. Comparisons may not apply when the firm's offerings are singular or highly diverse.

A few firms lack dollar-sign ratings. One problem or another made us feel it would be unfair to give them a rating. For example, some firms were unable to supply a catalog for review at the time this book was compiled and could not be assessed properly without it. The lack of a dollar-sign rating should not be considered a "poor" rating of a business. It only means we did not feel qualified to make a judgment. Companies to which we would have had to give a "poor" rating were simply not listed.

THE MAPLE LEAF: If a maple leaf (🍁) appears on the same line as the dollar code, the firm will ship goods to Canada. NOTE: shipping data given in the listings *do not* apply to Canadian deliveries unless specified, and import restrictions may apply to certain goods.

THE COMPLETE GUIDE TO BUYING BY MAIL: In the back of this book you'll find our comprehensive guide to buying by mail. We've tried to anticipate and answer all your questions about ordering, shipping, payment, delivery, warranties, etc. We've carefully screened the vendors and have included only those we feel confident will give you prompt, reliable service. Should a problem arise, however, the information in the guide will provide the most direct route to resolution.

POSTAGE RATES, FEES,

FIRST-CLASS ZONE RATED (PRIORITY) MAIL

Weight over 12 ounces and not exceeding— pound(s)	Local zones 1, 2, and 3	Zone 4	Zone 5	Zone 6	Zone 7	Zone 8
1	$2.40	$2.40	$2.40	$2.40	$2.40	$2.40
2	2.40	2.40	2.40	2.40	2.40	2.40
3	2.74	3.16	3.45	3.74	3.96	4.32
4	3.18	3.75	4.13	4.53	4.92	5.33
5	3.61	4.32	4.86	5.27	5.81	6.37
6	4.15	5.08	5.71	6.31	6.91	7.66
7	4.58	5.66	6.39	7.09	7.80	8.67
8	5.00	6.23	7.07	7.87	8.68	9.68
9	5.43	6.81	7.76	8.66	9.57	10.69
10	5.85	7.39	8.44	9.44	10.45	11.70
11	6.27	7.97	9.12	10.22	11.33	12.71
12	6.70	8.55	9.81	11.01	12.22	13.72
13	7.12	9.12	10.49	11.79	13.10	14.73
14	7.55	9.70	11.17	12.57	13.99	15.74
15	7.97	10.28	11.86	13.36	14.87	16.75
16	8.39	10.86	12.54	14.14	15.75	17.75
17	8.82	11.44	13.22	14.92	16.64	18.76
18	9.24	12.01	13.90	15.70	17.52	19.77
19	9.67	12.59	14.59	16.49	18.41	20.78
20	10.09	13.17	15.27	17.27	19.29	21.79
21	10.51	13.75	15.95	18.05	20.17	22.80
22	10.94	14.33	16.64	18.84	21.06	23.81
23	11.36	14.90	17.32	19.62	21.94	24.82
24	11.79	15.48	18.00	20.40	22.83	25.83
25	12.21	16.06	18.69	21.19	23.71	26.84
26	12.63	16.64	19.37	21.97	24.59	27.84
27	13.06	17.22	20.05	22.75	25.48	28.85
28	13.48	17.79	20.73	23.53	26.36	29.86
29	13.91	18.37	21.42	24.32	27.25	30.87
30	14.33	18.95	22.10	25.10	28.13	31.88
31	14.75	19.53	22.78	25.88	29.01	32.89
32	15.18	20.11	23.47	26.67	29.90	33.90
33	15.60	20.68	24.15	27.45	30.78	34.91
34	16.03	21.26	24.83	28.23	31.67	35.92
35	16.45	21.84	25.52	29.02	32.55	36.93
36	16.87	22.42	26.20	29.80	33.43	37.93
37	17.30	23.00	26.88	30.58	34.32	38.94
38	17.72	23.57	27.56	31.36	35.20	39.95
39	18.15	24.15	28.25	32.15	36.09	40.96
40	18.57	24.73	28.93	32.93	36.97	41.97
41	18.99	25.31	29.61	33.71	37.85	42.98
42	19.42	25.89	30.30	34.50	38.74	43.99
43	19.84	26.46	30.98	35.28	39.62	45.00
44	20.27	27.04	31.66	36.06	40.51	46.01
45	20.69	27.62	32.35	36.85	41.39	47.02
46	21.11	28.20	33.03	37.63	42.27	48.02
47	21.54	28.78	33.71	38.41	43.16	49.03
48	21.96	29.35	34.39	39.19	44.04	50.04
49	22.39	29.93	35.08	39.98	44.93	51.05
50	22.81	30.51	35.76	40.76	45.81	52.06
51	23.23	31.09	36.44	41.54	46.69	53.07
52	23.66	31.67	37.13	42.33	47.58	54.08
53	24.08	32.24	37.81	43.11	48.46	55.09
54	24.51	32.82	38.49	43.89	49.35	56.10
55	24.93	33.40	39.18	44.68	50.23	57.11
56	25.35	33.98	39.86	45.46	51.11	58.11
57	25.78	34.56	40.54	46.24	52.00	59.12
58	26.20	35.13	41.22	47.02	52.88	60.13
59	26.63	35.71	41.91	47.81	53.77	61.14
60	27.05	36.29	42.59	48.59	54.65	62.15
61	27.47	36.87	43.27	49.37	55.53	63.16
62	27.90	37.45	43.96	50.16	56.42	64.17
63	28.32	38.02	44.64	50.94	57.30	65.18
64	28.75	38.60	45.32	51.72	58.19	66.19
65	29.17	39.18	46.01	52.51	59.07	67.20
66	29.59	39.76	46.69	53.29	59.95	68.20
67	30.02	40.34	47.37	54.07	60.84	69.21
68	30.44	40.91	48.05	54.85	61.72	70.22
69	30.87	41.49	48.74	55.64	62.61	71.23
70	31.29	42.07	49.42	56.42	63.49	72.24

Exception: Parcels weighing less than 15 pounds and measuring over 84 inches in length and girth combined are chargeable with a minimum rate equal to that for a 15 pound parcel for the zone to which addressed.

EXPRESS MAIL
NEXT DAY SERVICE

AN OVERNIGHT DELIVERY SERVICE THAT'S FAST, RELIABLE, CONVENIENT AND ECONOMICAL.

Express Mail Service is available 7 days a week, 365 days a year, for mailable items up to 70 lbs. in weight and 108 inches in combined length and girth.

Flat rates: up to 2 lbs., $10.75; over 2 lbs. and up to 5 lbs., $12.85; 6-70 pound rates vary by weight and distance (zones).

Service features include insurance; shipment receipt; and Record of Delivery at the destination post office.

Consult Postmaster or Customer Service Representative for additional information and a copy of your local Express Mail network directory.

The Postal Service will refund, upon application to originating office, the postage for any Express Mail shipments not meeting the service standard except for those delayed by strike or work stoppage.

EXPRESS MAIL
NEXT DAY SERVICE
FIRST-CLASS

LETTER RATES:
1st ounce	22¢
Each additional ounce	17¢

For Pieces Not Exceeding (oz.)	The Rate Is	For Pieces Not Exceeding (oz.)	The Rate Is
1	$0.22	7	$1.24
2	0.39	8	1.41
3	0.56	9	1.58
4	0.73	10	1.75
5	0.90	11	1.92
6	1.07	12	2.09

FOR PIECES OVER 12 OUNCES SEE FIRST-CLASS ZONE RATED (PRIORITY) MAIL RATES

CARD RATES:

Single postal cards sold by the post office.... 14¢ each.

Double postal cards sold by the post office... 28¢ (14¢ each half)

Single post cards........................... 14¢ each.

Double post cards (reply-half of double post card does not have to bear postage when originally mailed)............. 28¢ (14¢ each half)

Presort rate.............................. Consult Postmaster

Business reply mail....................... Consult Postmaster

Note: To qualify for *card rates*, a card may not be larger than 4¼ by 6 inches, nor smaller than 3½ by 5 inches. The thickness must be uniform and not less than 0.007 of an inch.

SECOND-CLASS

(Newspapers and periodicals with second-class mail privileges.)

For copies mailed by the public, the rate is the applicable single piece third or fourth-class rate.

THIRD CLASS

Circulars, books, catalogs, and other printed matter; merchandise, seeds, cuttings, bulbs, roots, scions, and plants, weighing less than 16 ounces.

0 to 1 oz................	$0.22	Over 6 to 8 ozs............	0.98
Over 1 to 2 ozs..........	0.39	Over 8 to 10 ozs...........	1.08
Over 2 to 3 ozs..........	0.56	Over 10 to 12 ozs..........	1.18
Over 3 to 4 ozs..........	0.73	Over 12 to 14 ozs..........	1.28
Over 4 to 6 ozs..........	0.88	Over 14 but less than 16 ozs.............	1.38

BULK RATE
CONSULT POSTMASTER

FOURTH CLASS

(PARCEL POST) ZONE RATES
CONSULT POSTMASTER FOR WEIGHT AND SIZE LIMITS

NONMACHINABLE SURCHARGE:
A parcel mailed to a ZIP Code destination outside the BMC service area for your post office is subject to a surcharge of $0.90 in addition to the rate shown in this table if:
   A. It is nonmachinable according to the standards prescribed in Domestic Mail Manual section 753
      or
   B. It weighs more than 35 pounds.

WITHIN (INTRA-BMC) BMC DISCOUNT:
A parcel mailed to a ZIP Code destination shown below is for delivery within the BMC service area for your post office and is eligible for a discount of $0.16 from the rate shown in this table.
WITHIN (INTRA-BMC) BMC ZIP CODE DESTINATIONS FOR YOUR POST OFFICE ARE:

Weight 1 pound and not exceeding—pound(s)	Local	Zones 1-2	Zone 3	Zone 4	Zone 5	Zone 6	Zone 7	Zone 8
2	1.35	1.41	1.51	1.66	1.89	2.13	2.25	2.30
3	1.41	1.49	1.65	1.87	2.21	2.58	2.99	3.87
4	1.47	1.57	1.78	2.08	2.54	3.03	3.57	4.74
5	1.52	1.65	1.92	2.29	2.86	3.47	4.16	5.62
6	1.58	1.74	2.05	2.50	3.18	3.92	4.74	6.49
7	1.63	1.82	2.19	2.71	3.51	4.37	5.32	7.36
8	1.69	1.90	2.32	2.92	3.83	4.82	5.91	8.25
9	1.75	1.99	2.46	3.13	4.15	5.26	6.49	9.12
10	1.80	2.07	2.59	3.34	4.46	5.71	7.07	10.00
11	1.85	2.13	2.70	3.49	4.71	6.03	7.49	10.82
12	1.90	2.20	2.79	3.65	4.94	6.34	7.89	11.23
13	1.94	2.26	2.89	3.79	5.15	6.63	8.27	11.78
14	1.98	2.32	2.98	3.92	5.35	6.90	8.62	12.30
15	2.02	2.37	3.06	4.04	5.54	7.15	8.94	12.79
16	2.06	2.42	3.14	4.16	5.71	7.39	9.25	13.24
17	2.10	2.48	3.22	4.27	5.88	7.61	9.54	13.87
18	2.14	2.52	3.29	4.38	6.03	7.83	9.81	14.08
19	2.18	2.57	3.36	4.48	6.18	8.03	10.07	14.46
20	2.21	2.62	3.43	4.58	6.33	8.22	10.32	14.83
21	2.25	2.67	3.49	4.67	6.47	8.41	10.56	15.18
22	2.28	2.71	3.56	4.76	6.60	8.59	10.79	15.51
23	2.32	2.75	3.62	4.85	6.73	8.76	11.01	15.83
24	2.35	2.80	3.68	4.94	6.85	8.92	11.22	16.14
25	2.39	2.84	3.74	5.02	6.97	9.08	11.42	16.43
26	2.42	2.88	3.80	5.10	7.08	9.23	11.61	16.72
27	2.45	2.92	3.85	5.18	7.20	9.38	11.80	16.99
28	2.48	2.96	3.91	5.25	7.30	9.52	11.98	17.26
29	2.52	3.00	3.96	5.33	7.41	9.66	12.16	17.52
30	2.55	3.04	4.01	5.40	7.51	9.80	12.33	17.77
31	2.58	3.08	4.07	5.47	7.61	9.93	12.50	18.01
32	2.61	3.12	4.12	5.54	7.71	10.06	12.66	18.24
33	2.64	3.15	4.17	5.61	7.81	10.19	12.82	18.47
34	2.67	3.19	4.22	5.68	7.90	10.31	12.97	18.70
35	2.70	3.23	4.26	5.74	7.99	10.43	13.12	18.91
36	2.73	3.26	4.31	5.81	8.08	10.54	13.27	19.12
37	2.76	3.30	4.36	5.87	8.17	10.66	13.41	19.33
38	2.79	3.33	4.41	5.93	8.25	10.77	13.55	19.53
39	2.82	3.37	4.45	5.99	8.34	10.88	13.69	19.73
40	2.85	3.40	4.50	6.05	8.42	10.98	13.83	19.92
41	2.88	3.44	4.54	6.11	8.50	11.09	13.96	20.11
42	2.91	3.47	4.58	6.17	8.58	11.19	14.09	20.29
43	2.94	3.50	4.63	6.23	8.66	11.29	14.21	20.47
44	2.97	3.54	4.67	6.28	8.74	11.39	14.34	20.65
45	3.00	3.57	4.71	6.34	8.81	11.49	14.46	20.82
46	3.02	3.61	4.76	6.39	8.89	11.59	14.58	20.99
47	3.05	3.64	4.80	6.45	8.96	11.68	14.69	21.15
48	3.08	3.67	4.84	6.50	9.03	11.77	14.81	21.32
49	3.11	3.70	4.88	6.55	9.10	11.86	14.92	21.48
50	3.14	3.74	4.92	6.61	9.17	11.95	15.03	21.64
51	3.17	3.77	4.96	6.66	9.24	12.04	15.14	21.80
52	3.19	3.80	5.00	6.71	9.31	12.13	15.25	21.95
53	3.22	3.83	5.04	6.76	9.38	12.22	15.36	22.10
54	3.25	3.86	5.08	6.81	9.45	12.30	15.46	22.25
55	3.28	3.89	5.12	6.86	9.51	12.39	15.57	22.39
56	3.30	3.93	5.16	6.91	9.58	12.47	15.67	22.54
57	3.33	3.96	5.20	6.96	9.64	12.55	15.77	22.68
58	3.36	3.99	5.23	7.01	9.71	12.63	15.87	22.82
59	3.39	4.02	5.27	7.06	9.77	12.71	15.97	22.95
60	3.41	4.05	5.31	7.10	9.83	12.79	16.06	23.09
61	3.44	4.08	5.35	7.15	9.90	12.87	16.16	23.22
62	3.47	4.11	5.38	7.20	9.96	12.94	16.25	23.35
63	3.50	4.14	5.42	7.24	10.02	13.02	16.35	23.48
64	3.52	4.17	5.46	7.29	10.08	13.10	16.44	23.61
65	3.55	4.20	5.49	7.33	10.14	13.17	16.53	23.74
66	3.58	4.23	5.53	7.38	10.19	13.24	16.62	23.86
67	3.60	4.26	5.57	7.42	10.25	13.32	16.71	23.99
68	3.63	4.29	5.60	7.47	10.31	13.39	16.80	24.11
69	3.66	4.32	5.64	7.51	10.37	13.46	16.88	24.23
70	3.68	4.35	5.67	7.56	10.43	13.53	16.97	24.35

NOTE: If Within (Intra-BMC) BMC ZIP Code destinations for your post office are not shown above, consult your local postmaster and write the ZIP Codes in the space provided.

Consult Postmaster for bound printed matter, special fourth-class, and library rates.

STAMPS, ENVELOPES, AND POSTAL CARDS

ADHESIVE STAMPS AVAILABLE

Purpose	Form	Denomination and prices
Regular postage	Sheets	1, 2, 3, 4, 5, 7, 10, 12,* 13,* 14, 15,* 17, 18,* 19,* 20,* 22, 25, 28,* 29,* 30, 35,* 37, 39, 40, and 50 cents: $1, $2,* and $5
	Books	20 22-cent ($4.40), 5 22-cent ($1.10), 10 22-cent ($2.20), 3 $10.75 ($32.25). 3 $12.85 ($38.55)
	Coils of 100	17-cent, 20-cent,* 22-cent (Dispenser and stamp affixer for use with these coils are also available.)
	Coils of 500	1, 2, 3, 4, 5, 6, 10, 12, 13,* 14, 15,* 17, 18, 20,* 22-cents, and $1
	Coils of 3,000	1, 2, 3, 4, 5, 6, 10, 12, 13,* 14, 15,* 17, 18, 20,* 22, and 25-cents
International Airmail postage	Single or sheet	33, 39, and 44¢

*will be discontinued when stock is exhausted

ENVELOPES AVAILABLE

Kind	Denomination	Selling price each
		Less than 500
Regular..........	22¢	27¢

POSTAL CARDS AVAILABLE

Kind	Selling price each
Single.................	14¢
Reply (14¢ each half)......	28¢

SPECIAL SERVICES — DOMESTIC MAIL ONLY

INSURANCE

For Coverage Against Loss or Damage
Fees (in addition to postage)

Liability	Fee
$0.01 to $25	0.50
25.01 to 50	1.10
50.01 to 100	1.40
100.01 to 150	1.80
150.01 to 200	2.10
200.01 to 300	3.00
300.01 to 400	3.70
400.01 to 500	4.40

REGISTRY For Maximum Protection and Security

Value	Fees in addition to postage	
	For articles covered by Postal Insurance	For articles not covered by Postal Insurance
$0.01 to 100.00	3.60	3.55
$100.01 to 500.00	3.90	3.80
500.01 to 1,000.00	4.25	4.15
For higher values, consult Postmaster		

ADDITIONAL SERVICES

CERTIFIED MAIL.. (in addition to postage)	$0.75

CERTIFICATE OF MAILING...................................... (For Bulk mailings and Firm mailing books, see Postmaster)	$0.45

ADDITIONAL SERVICES FOR INSURED, CERTIFIED AND REGISTERED MAIL

Restricted Delivery*...	$1.25

Return Receipts*
Requested at time of mailing:

Showing to whom and when delivered.....................	$0.70
Showing to whom, when, and address where delivered.......	$0.90

Requested after mailing:

Showing to whom and when delivered.....................	$4.50

*Not available for mail insured for $25 or less

COD

Consult Postmaster for fee and conditions of mailing

SPECIAL DELIVERY FEE (In addition to required postage)

Class of Mail	Weight		
	Not more than 2 pounds	More than 2 pounds but not more than 10 pounds	More than 10 pounds
First Class.............. All other classes........	$2.95 3.10	$3.15 3.60	$4.00 4.50

SPECIAL HANDLING Third and Fourth Class Only (In addition to required postage)

10 pounds and less...	$1.10
More than 10 pounds..	1.60

MONEY ORDERS   For safe transmission of money

$0.01 to 25.00...	$0.75
25.01 to 700.00..	1.00

SIZE STANDARDS FOR DOMESTIC MAIL

MINIMUM SIZE
Pieces which do not meet the following requirements are prohibited from the mails:
a. All pieces must be at least .007 of an inch thick, and
b. All pieces (except keys and identification devices) which are ¼ inch or less thick must be:
(1) Rectangular in shape,
(2) At least 3½ inches high, and
(3) At least 5 inches long.
NOTE: Pieces greater than ¼ inch thick can be mailed even if they measure less than 3½ by 5 inches.

NON STANDARD MAIL
All First-Class Mail weighing one ounce or less and all single-piece rate Third-Class mail weighing one ounce or less is nonstandard (and subject to a 10¢ surcharge in addition to the applicable postage and fees) if:
1. Any of the following dimensions are exceeded:
   Length—11½ inches,
   Height—6¼ inches,
   Thickness—¼ inch, or
2. The piece has a height to length (aspect) ratio which does not fall between 1 to 1.3 and 1 to 2.5 inclusive. (The aspect ratio is found by dividing the length by the height. If the answer is between 1.3 and 2.5 inclusive, the piece has a standard aspect ratio.)

INTERNATIONAL POSTAL RATES AND FEES

LETTERS AND LETTER PACKAGES[1]

Items of mail containing personal handwritten or typewritten communications having the character of current correspondence must be sent as letters or letter packages. Any article otherwise acceptable in postal union mail subject to applicable weight and size limits, may be mailed at the letter rate of postage. Maximum Weight Limit: 4 pounds to all countries.

AIR RATES:

1. Canada and Mexico:

Canada and Mexico*					
Weight Not Over		Rate	Weight Not Over		Rate
Lbs.	Ozs.		Lbs.	Ozs.	
0	1	$0.22	0	11	$2.02
0	2	0.40	0	12	2.20
0	3	0.58	1	0	2.84
0	4	0.76	1	8	3.38
0	5	0.94	2	0	3.92
0	6	1.12	2	8	4.46
0	7	1.30	3	0	5.00
0	8	1.48	3	8	5.54
0	9	1.66	4	0	6.08
0	10	1.84			
Maximum Weight: 4 lbs.					

*Letter class mail to Canada and Mexico receives First-Class service in the United States and airmail service in Canada and Mexico.

2. BAHAMAS, BERMUDA, THE CARIBBEAN ISLANDS, CENTRAL AMERICA, COLOMBIA, ST. PIERRE AND MIQUELON, AND VENEZUELA. Also from American Samoa to Western Samoa and from Guam to the Philippines:

Weight Not Over	Rate	Weight Not Over	Rate	Weight Not Over	Rate
Ozs.		Ozs.		Ozs.	
½	$0.39	16½	$11.13	33	$21.69
1	0.78	17	11.46	34	22.02
1½	1.17	17½	11.79	35	22.35
2	1.56	18	12.12	36	22.68
2½	1.89	18½	12.45	37	23.01
3	2.22	19	12.78	38	23.34
3½	2.55	19½	13.11	39	23.67
4	2.88	20	13.44	40	24.00
4½	3.21	20½	13.77	41	24.33
5	3.54	21	14.10	42	24.66
5½	3.87	21½	14.43	43	24.99
6	4.20	22	14.76	44	25.32
6½	4.53	22½	15.09	45	25.65
7	4.86	23	15.42	46	25.98
7½	5.19	23½	15.75	47	26.31
8	5.52	24	16.08	48	26.64
8½	5.85	24½	16.41	49	26.97
9	6.18	25	16.74	50	27.30
9½	6.51	25½	17.07	51	27.63
10	6.84	26	17.40	52	27.96
10½	7.17	26½	17.73	53	28.29
11	7.50	27	18.06	54	28.62
11½	7.83	27½	18.39	55	28.95
12	8.16	28	18.72	56	29.28
12½	8.49	28½	19.05	57	29.61
13	8.82	29	19.38	58	29.94
13½	9.15	29½	19.71	59	30.27
14	9.48	30	20.04	60	30.60
14½	9.81	30½	20.37	61	30.93
15	10.14	31	20.70	62	31.26
15½	10.47	31½	21.03	63	31.59
16	10.80	32	21.36	64	31.92
Weight Limit — 4 Pounds					

3. ALL OTHER COUNTRIES:

Weight Not Over	Rate	Weight Not Over	Rate	Weight Not Over	Rate
Ozs.		Ozs.		Ozs.	
½	$0.44	16½	$13.07	33	$25.55
1	0.88	17	13.46	34	25.94
1½	1.32	17½	13.85	35	26.33
2	1.76	18	14.24	36	26.72
2½	2.15	18½	14.63	37	27.11
3	2.54	19	15.02	38	27.50
3½	2.93	19½	15.41	39	27.89
4	3.32	20	15.80	40	28.28
4½	3.71	20½	16.19	41	28.67
5	4.10	21	16.58	42	29.06
5½	4.49	21½	16.97	43	29.45
6	4.88	22	17.36	44	29.84
6½	5.27	22½	17.75	45	30.23
7	5.66	23	18.14	46	30.62
7½	6.05	23½	18.53	47	31.01
8	6.44	24	18.92	48	31.40
8½	6.83	24½	19.31	49	31.79
9	7.22	25	19.70	50	32.18
9½	7.61	25½	20.09	51	32.57
10	8.00	26	20.48	52	32.96
10½	8.39	26½	20.87	53	33.35
11	8.78	27	21.26	54	33.74
11½	9.17	27½	21.65	55	34.13
12	9.56	28	22.04	56	34.52
12½	9.95	28½	22.43	57	34.91
13	10.34	29	22.82	58	35.30
13½	10.73	29½	23.21	59	35.69
14	11.12	30	23.60	60	36.08
14½	11.51	30½	23.99	61	36.47
15	11.90	31	24.38	62	36.86
15½	12.29	31½	24.77	63	37.25
16	12.68	32	25.16	64	37.64
Weight Limit — 4 Pounds					

SURFACE RATES:

1. Letters and Letter Packages to all countries except Canada and Mexico:

Weight Not Over		Rate	Weight Not Over		Rate
Lbs.	Ozs.		Lbs.	Ozs.	
0	1	$0.37	1	0	$3.40
0	2	0.57	1	8	4.66
0	3	0.77	2	0	5.92
0	4	0.97	2	8	6.84
0	5	1.17	3	0	7.76
0	6	1.37	3	8	8.68
0	7	1.57	4	0	9.60
0	8	1.77			
Weight Limit — 4 pounds					

**For Canada and Mexico, see Air Rates for Letters and Letter Packages to those countries.

POSTER 51
February 1985

POST AND POSTAL CARDS

Limitations: Only single cards are acceptable in international mail. Reply paid cards and folded (double) cards are not accepted in international mail.

Maximum size   6 × 4¼ inches.
Minimum size   5½ × 3½ inches.

	Surface	Air
Countries other than Canada and Mexico	25¢ each	33¢ each
Canada and Mexico	—	14¢ each

AEROGRAMMES

AEROGRAMMES are air letter sheets that can be folded into the form of an envelope, sealed and sent by air to all countries. No enclosures are permitted with aerogrammes. Aerogrammes bearing imprinted postage are available at post offices for 36¢.

PRINTED MATTER AND SMALL PACKETS [1,2]

Printed matter is paper on which letters, words, characters, figures or images, or any combination thereof, not having the character of actual or personal correspondence, have been reproduced in several identical copies by any process other than handwriting or typewriting.

REGULAR PRINTED MATTER comprises all printed matter other than books, sheet music, and publishers' periodicals.

SMALL PACKETS offer a convenient and economical means for sending small quantities of merchandise, commercial samples, or documents not having the character of current and personal correspondence. The maximum weight limit for small packets vary, consult your postmaster.

OTHER ARTICLES (AO): Includes all printed matter, matter for the blind and small packets.

1. Air Rates for Canada and Mexico*:

CANADA**			MEXICO**			CANADA**			MEXICO**		
Weight not over		Rate	Weight not over		Rate	Weight not over		Rate	Weight not over		Rate
0 lbs.	1 ozs.	$0.22	0 lbs.	1 ozs.	$0.22	4 lbs.	8 ozs.	$ 6.62	4 lbs.	8 ozs.	$ 6.62
0	2	.40	0	2	.40	5	0	7.16	5	0	7.16
0	3	.58	0	3	.58	6	0	8.24	6	0	8.24
0	4	.76	0	4	.76	7	0	9.32	7	0	9.32
0	5	.94	0	5	.94	8	0	10.40	8	0	10.40
0	6	1.12	0	6	1.12	9	0	11.48	9	0	11.48
0	7	1.30	0	7	1.30	10	0	12.56	10	0	12.56
0	8	1.48	0	8	1.48						
0	9	1.66	0	9	1.66	11	0	13.64	11	0	13.64
0	10	1.84	0	10	1.84	—	—	——	12	0	14.72
0	11	2.02	0	11	2.02	—	—	——	13	0	15.80
0	12	2.20	0	12	2.20	—	—	——	14	0	16.88
						—	—	——	15	0	17.96
1	0	2.84	1	0	2.84						
1	8	3.38	1	8	3.38	—	—	——	16	0	19.04
2	0	3.92	2	0	3.92	—	—	——	17	0	20.12
2	8	4.46	2	8	4.46	—	—	——	18	0	21.20
3	0	5.00	3	0	5.00	—	—	——	19	0	22.28
3	8	5.54	3	8	5.54	—	—	——	20	0	23.36
4	0	6.08	4	0	6.08	—	—	——	21	0	24.44
						—	—	——	22	0	25.52

**Direct sack to one addressee (M bag):

	Canada	Mexico
Rate per pound or fraction	$0.97	$0.97

Minimum weight — 15 lbs.; Maximum weight — 66 lbs.

*NOTE: <u>Maximum Weight Limits For Canada and Mexico</u>

	CANADA	MEXICO
Regular printed matter	4 lbs.	22 lbs.
Books and sheet music	11 lbs.	22 lbs.
Catalogs and directories	11 lbs.	22 lbs.

Registered news agents or publishers should consult the postmaster for weight limits and rates for publishers' periodicals.

2. Air Rates for All Other Countries:

WEIGHT NOT OVER	Colombia, Venezuela, Central America, Caribbean Islands, Bahamas, Bermuda, & St. Pierre & Miquelon (Also, from American Samoa to Western Samoa, & from Guam to the Philippines)	South America (except Colombia & Venezuela), Europe (except Estonia, Latvia, Lithuania, & U.S.S.R.), & North Africa (Morocco, Algeria, Tunisia, Libya, & Egypt)	Estonia, Latvia, Lithuania, U.S.S.R., Asia, Australia & New Zealand, Pacific Ocean Islands, Africa (other than North Africa), the Indian Ocean Islands & the Middle East
1 ozs.	$0.58	$0.70	$0.82
2	.89	1.12	1.35
3	1.20	1.54	1.88
4	1.51	1.96	2.41
6	1.82	2.50	3.18
8	2.13	3.04	3.95
10	2.44	3.58	4.72
12	2.75	4.12	5.49
14	3.06	4.66	6.26
16	3.37	5.20	7.03
18	3.68	5.74	7.80
20	3.99	6.28	8.57
22	4.30	6.82	9.34
24	4.61	7.36	10.11
26	4.92	7.90	10.88
28	5.23	8.44	11.65
30	5.54	8.98	12.42
32	5.85	9.52	13.19
2.5 lbs.	7.07	11.68	16.29
3.0 lbs.	8.29	13.84	19.39
3.5 lbs.	9.51	16.00	22.49
4.0 lbs.	10.73	18.16	25.59
Each additional ½ lb. over 4 lbs.	1.22	2.16	3.10
M-Bag: Rate per lb. or fraction	2.20	3.89	5.58

Direct sack of printed matter to one addressee (M bag) weight limit: Minimum — 15 lbs.; Maximum — 66 lbs. Consult your postmaster for preparation requirements for M bags. Weight limits for AO items vary; consult your postmaster.

EXPRESS MAIL INTERNATIONAL SERVICE

Express Mail International Service offers reliable high speed delivery to certain foreign destinations. It also provides document reconstruction insurance at no additional charge, centralized payments for volume mailers, and return service through the foreign postal administration. For rate information and details of services available through Express Mail International Service, please consult your postmaster.

INTERNATIONAL REPLY COUPONS

Individuals may use international coupons to prepay a reply or return of mail from other countries.

INTERNATIONAL MONEY ORDERS

Consult postmaster to find out if service is available to specific countries.

SURFACE RATES:

	REGULAR PRINTED MATTER*		SMALL PACKETS**		
Weight Not Over	Canada and Mexico	All Other Countries	Canada	Mexico	All Other Countries
1 ozs.	$0.22	$0.29	$0.22	$0.22	$0.29
2	.39	.47	.39	.39	.47
3	.56	.65	.56	.56	.65
4	.73	.83	.73	.73	.83
6	.91	1.02	.91	.91	1.02
8	1.09	1.21	1.09	1.09	1.21
10	1.27	1.40	1.27	1.27	1.40
12	1.45	1.59	1.45	1.45	1.59
14	1.63	1.78	1.63	1.63	1.78
16	1.81	1.97	1.81	1.81	1.97
18	1.99	2.16	——	1.99	2.16
20	2.17	2.35	——	2.17	2.35
22	2.35	2.54	——	2.35	2.54
24	2.53	2.73	——	2.53	2.73
26	2.71	2.92	——	2.71	2.92
28	2.89	3.11	——	2.89	3.11
30	3.07	3.30	——	3.07	3.30
32	3.25	3.49	——	3.25	3.49
3 lbs.	3.57	4.19	——	——	——
4 lbs.	3.89	4.89	——	——	——
Each additional 1 lb.	.97	1.22	——	——	——

Direct sack (M bag) to one addressee:

	Canada and Mexico	All Other Countries
Rate per pound or fraction:	$0.87	$1.10

Direct sack of printed matter to one addressee (M bag) weight limit: Minimum — 15 lbs., Maximum — 66 lbs. Consult postmaster for preparation requirements for direct sacks (M bags) of printed matter.

*Weight limits vary — consult postmaster for weight limits for books, sheet music, and publishers' periodicals.
**The maximum weight limit for small packets vary — consult postmaster.

PARCEL POST[2]

AIR RATES

All Countries: Consult postmaster for the air parcel post rates for the specific country that you desire.

SURFACE RATES

1. Canada: From 1 pound up to 2 pounds — $3.35; for each additional pound or fraction — $1.05.
2. Bahamas, Bermuda, the Caribbean Islands, Central America, Mexico and St. Pierre and Miquelon: For the first 2 pounds — $3.70; for each additional pound or fraction — $1.20.
3. All other countries: For the first 2 pounds — $3.90; for each additional pound or fraction — $1.30.

CUSTOMS DECLARATIONS AND OTHER FORMS

At least one customs declaration, either a Form 2966-A, Parcel Post Customs Declaration, or Form 2966-B, Parcel Post Customs Declaration and Dispatch Note, is required for parcel post packages (surface or air) mailed to another country. The multiple part Form 2966-B is used for countries that require more than one customs document. Consult post office.

ENDORSEMENTS

PRINTED MATTER — Mailers must endorse the envelopes or wrappers with the words Printed Matter or Printed Matter - Catalogs when mailing prints at regular printed matter rates, and Printed Matter - Books or Printed Matter - Sheet Music when mailing at special rates provided for that category of prints.

LETTERS OR LETTER PACKAGES — Add the word <u>Letter</u> or <u>Lettre</u> on the address side of letters or letter packages which may be mistaken for another type of mail because of their size or manner of preparation.

SMALL PACKETS — Endorse the envelope or wrapper <u>Small Packet</u> or its equivalent in a language known in the country of destination, e.g. <u>Petit Paquet</u> (French), <u>Packchen</u> (German), or <u>Pequeno Paquete</u> (Spanish).

AIRMAIL — Plainly endorse airmail articles <u>Par Avion</u> or affix a Par Avion label.

SPECIAL DELIVERY — Articles intended for special delivery must bear a Label 57, Expres (Special Delivery), or be marked boldly in red <u>Expres (Special Delivery)</u>.

PARCEL POST — Mailers are <u>not</u> required to endorse parcel post packages with the words <u>Parcel Post</u>.

SPECIAL SERVICES

REGISTRATION (FOR ARTICLES OTHER THAN PARCEL POST)
Available to all countries except Kampuchea (Cambodia) and the Democratic People's Republic of Korea (North).

	INDEMNITY LIMITS	FEE
Canada	$00.01 to $100.	$3.60
	$100.01 to $200.	$3.90
All Other Countries	$20.40	$3.60

RETURN RECEIPT (FOR REGISTERED OR INSURED MAIL)
A return receipt offers the sender proof of delivery. Return receipts may be purchased only at the time of mailing. NOTE: Canada does not provide return receipts for parcels. FEE: $0.70

RESTRICTED DELIVERY (FOR REGISTERED ITEMS ONLY)
Available to many countries. Consult postmaster. FEE: $1.25.

INSURANCE (FOR PARCEL POST ONLY)
Available only for parcel post. Consult postmaster for fees. NOTE: International mail insurance is subject to both United States Postal Service regulations and the domestic regulations of the destination country. *If an insured parcel is received in damaged condition, the addressee must report the damage to the delivering postal administration immediately.*

SPECIAL DELIVERY (FOR ITEMS OTHER THAN PARCEL POST)
Available to most countries. Consult postmaster.

FEES:

Class of mail	Not more than 2 pounds	Over 2 pounds
Letters, letter packages, post and postal cards.	$2.95	$3.15
Other articles.	$3.10	$3.60

CERTIFIED MAIL
Not available for international mail.

C.O.D. MAIL
Not available for international mail.

SPECIAL HANDLING (FOR SURFACE PRINTED MATTER, SMALL PACKETS, AND PARCEL POST)
Entitles article to priority handling between mailing office and United States point of dispatch. FEES: Through 10 pounds - $1.10; over 10 pounds - $1.60.

FOOTNOTES:

1. Letters, letter packages, small packets containing dutiable merchandise, and dutiable printed matter must have the green customs label, Form 2976, Customs-Douane C1, affixed. If the sender prefers, or if the contents exceed $120 in value ($312 effective on January 1, 1986), Form 2976-A, Customs Declaration, must be completed and enclosed with only the upper portion of the green label (form 2976) affixed to the cover of the package. The forms may be obtained at your post office.
2. Consult your postmaster for information and rates to specific countries you desire.

UPS GROUND SERVICE

UPS NEXT DAY AIR

UPS 2ND DAY AIR

WEIGHT NOT TO EXCEED	GROUND ZONES							WEIGHT NOT TO EXCEED	AIR ZONE K	WEIGHT NOT TO EXCEED	48 STATES A	HAWAII D
	2	3	4	5	6	7	8					
1 lb.	$1.23	$1.32	$1.46	$1.52	$1.59	$1.67	$1.74	1 lb.	$11.50	1 lb.	$3.00	$4.53
2 "	1.24	1.34	1.63	1.73	1.87	2.01	2.16	2 "	12.50	2 "	4.00	5.71
3 "	1.32	1.48	1.80	1.95	2.15	2.36	2.57	3 "	13.50	3 "	5.00	6.89
4 "	1.40	1.61	1.97	2.16	2.43	2.70	2.99	4 "	14.50	4 "	6.00	8.07
5 "	1.49	1.76	2.13	2.37	2.70	3.05	3.40	5 "	15.50	5 "	6.50	9.25
6 "	1.57	1.89	2.30	2.59	2.98	3.39	3.82	6 "	16.50	6 "	7.50	10.43
7 "	1.65	2.02	2.47	2.80	3.26	3.74	4.24	7 "	18.00	7 "	8.50	11.61
8 "	1.73	2.14	2.64	3.02	3.54	4.08	4.65	8 "	19.00	8 "	9.50	12.79
9 "	1.82	2.27	2.81	3.23	3.82	4.43	5.07	9 "	20.00	9 "	10.50	13.97
10 "	1.90	2.39	2.97	3.44	4.09	4.77	5.48	10 "	21.00	10 "	11.50	15.15
11 "	1.98	2.52	3.14	3.66	4.37	5.12	5.90	11 "	22.00	11 "	12.50	16.33
12 "	2.06	2.65	3.31	3.87	4.65	5.46	6.32	12 "	23.00	12 "	13.50	17.51
13 "	2.15	2.77	3.48	4.09	4.93	5.81	6.73	13 "	24.00	13 "	14.50	18.69
14 "	2.23	2.90	3.65	4.30	5.21	6.15	7.15	14 "	25.50	14 "	15.50	19.87
15 "	2.31	3.02	3.81	4.51	5.48	6.50	7.56	15 "	26.50	15 "	16.50	21.05
16 "	2.39	3.15	3.98	4.73	5.76	6.84	7.98	16 "	27.50	16 "	17.50	22.23
17 "	2.48	3.28	4.15	4.94	6.04	7.19	8.40	17 "	28.50	17 "	18.50	23.41
18 "	2.56	3.40	4.32	5.16	6.32	7.53	8.81	18 "	29.50	18 "	19.50	24.59
19 "	2.64	3.53	4.49	5.37	6.60	7.88	9.23	19 "	30.50	19 "	20.00	25.77
20 "	2.72	3.65	4.65	5.58	6.87	8.22	9.64	20 "	32.00	20 "	21.00	26.95
21 "	2.81	3.78	4.82	5.80	7.15	8.57	10.06	21 "	33.00	21 "	22.00	28.13
22 "	2.89	3.91	4.99	6.01	7.43	8.91	10.48	22 "	34.00	22 "	23.00	29.31
23 "	2.97	4.03	5.16	6.23	7.71	9.26	10.89	23 "	35.00	23 "	24.00	30.49
24 "	3.05	4.16	5.33	6.44	7.99	9.60	11.31	24 "	36.00	24 "	25.00	31.67
25 "	3.14	4.28	5.49	6.65	8.26	9.95	11.72	25 "	37.00	25 "	26.00	32.85
26 "	3.22	4.41	5.66	6.87	8.54	10.29	12.14	26 "	38.50	26 "	27.00	34.03
27 "	3.30	4.54	5.83	7.08	8.82	10.64	12.56	27 "	39.50	27 "	28.00	35.21
28 "	3.38	4.66	6.00	7.30	9.10	10.98	12.97	28 "	40.50	28 "	29.00	36.39
29 "	3.47	4.79	6.17	7.51	9.38	11.33	13.39	29 "	41.50	29 "	30.00	37.57
30 "	3.55	4.91	6.33	7.72	9.65	11.67	13.80	30 "	42.50	30 "	31.00	38.75
31 "	3.63	5.04	6.50	7.94	9.93	12.02	14.22	31 "	43.50	31 "	32.00	39.93
32 "	3.71	5.17	6.67	8.15	10.21	12.36	14.64	32 "	45.00	32 "	33.00	41.11
33 "	3.80	5.29	6.84	8.37	10.49	12.71	15.05	33 "	46.00	33 "	34.00	42.29
34 "	3.88	5.42	7.01	8.58	10.77	13.05	15.47	34 "	47.00	34 "	35.00	43.47
35 "	3.96	5.54	7.17	8.79	11.04	13.40	15.88	35 "	48.00	35 "	36.00	44.65
36 "	4.04	5.67	7.34	9.01	11.32	13.74	16.30	36 "	49.00	36 "	36.50	45.83
37 "	4.13	5.80	7.51	9.22	11.60	14.09	16.72	37 "	50.00	37 "	37.50	47.01
38 "	4.21	5.92	7.68	9.44	11.88	14.43	17.13	38 "	51.00	38 "	38.50	48.19
39 "	4.29	6.05	7.85	9.65	12.16	14.78	17.55	39 "	52.50	39 "	39.50	49.37
40 "	4.37	6.17	8.01	9.86	12.43	15.12	17.96	40 "	53.50	40 "	40.50	50.55
41 "	4.46	6.30	8.18	10.08	12.71	15.47	18.38	41 "	54.50	41 "	41.50	51.73
42 "	4.54	6.43	8.35	10.29	12.99	15.81	18.80	42 "	55.50	42 "	42.50	52.91
43 "	4.62	6.55	8.52	10.51	13.27	16.16	19.21	43 "	56.50	43 "	43.50	54.09
44 "	4.70	6.68	8.69	10.72	13.55	16.50	19.63	44 "	57.50	44 "	44.50	55.27
45 "	4.79	6.80	8.85	10.93	13.82	16.85	20.04	45 "	59.00	45 "	45.50	56.45
46 "	4.87	6.93	9.02	11.15	14.10	17.19	20.46	46 "	60.00	46 "	46.50	57.63
47 "	4.95	7.06	9.19	11.36	14.38	17.54	20.88	47 "	61.00	47 "	47.50	58.81
48 "	5.03	7.18	9.36	11.58	14.66	17.88	21.29	48 "	62.00	48 "	48.50	59.99
49 "	5.12	7.31	9.53	11.79	14.94	18.23	21.71	49 "	63.00	49 "	49.50	61.17
50 "	5.20	7.43	9.69	12.00	15.21	18.57	22.12	50 "	64.00	50 "	50.50	62.35
51 "	5.22	7.47	9.74	12.06	15.28	18.66	22.23	51 "	64.50	51 "	50.50	62.65
52 "	5.24	7.50	9.78	12.11	15.35	18.75	22.33	52 "	64.50	52 "	51.00	62.94
53 "	5.26	7.53	9.83	12.17	15.42	18.84	22.43	53 "	65.00	53 "	51.00	63.24
54 "	5.28	7.56	9.87	12.22	15.49	18.93	22.54	54 "	65.50	54 "	51.50	63.53
55 "	5.30	7.59	9.91	12.28	15.56	19.02	22.64	55 "	65.50	55 "	51.50	63.83
56 "	5.32	7.62	9.96	12.33	15.63	19.11	22.74	56 "	66.00	56 "	52.00	64.12
57 "	5.34	7.66	10.00	12.38	15.70	19.20	22.85	57 "	66.00	57 "	52.00	64.42
58 "	5.36	7.69	10.04	12.44	15.77	19.29	22.95	58 "	66.50	58 "	52.50	64.71
59 "	5.39	7.72	10.09	12.49	15.84	19.38	23.05	59 "	66.50	59 "	52.50	65.01
60 "	5.41	7.75	10.13	12.55	15.90	19.47	23.16	60 "	67.00	60 "	53.00	65.30
61 "	5.43	7.78	10.17	12.60	15.97	19.56	23.26	61 "	67.00	61 "	53.00	65.60
62 "	5.45	7.81	10.22	12.66	16.04	19.65	23.36	62 "	67.50	62 "	53.50	65.89
63 "	5.47	7.84	10.26	12.71	16.11	19.74	23.47	63 "	67.50	63 "	53.50	66.19
64 "	5.49	7.88	10.30	12.76	16.18	19.83	23.57	64 "	68.00	64 "	53.50	66.48
65 "	5.51	7.91	10.35	12.82	16.25	19.92	23.67	65 "	68.50	65 "	54.00	66.78
66 "	5.53	7.94	10.39	12.87	16.32	20.01	23.78	66 "	68.50	66 "	54.00	67.07
67 "	5.55	7.97	10.43	12.93	16.39	20.10	23.88	67 "	69.00	67 "	54.50	67.37
68 "	5.57	8.00	10.48	12.98	16.46	20.19	23.98	68 "	69.00	68 "	54.50	67.66
69 "	5.59	8.03	10.52	13.04	16.53	20.28	24.09	69 "	69.50	69 "	55.00	67.96
70 "	5.61	8.06	10.56	13.09	16.59	20.37	24.19	70 "	69.50	70 "	55.00	68.25

ANY FRACTION OF A POUND OVER THE WEIGHT SHOWN TAKES THE NEXT HIGHER RATE

ADDITIONAL CHARGES:
For each COD received for collection—$1.90
For each Address Correction—$1.90
For each Acknowledgment of Delivery (AOD)—30 cents
For each package with a declared value
 over $100—25 cents for each additional $100
 or fraction thereof
Weekly service charge—$3.25

WEIGHT AND SIZE LIMITS:
Maximum weight per package—70 pounds
Maximum size per package—108 inches in length and
 girth combined
Minimum charge for a package measuring over 84 inches
 in length and girth combined will be equal to
 charge for a package weighing 25 pounds.

AIR RESTRICTIONS
The maximum value for an air service package
 is $25,000 and the maximum carrier
 liability is $25,000.
No Call Tag service provided in Air Service.
Hazardous materials are prohibited in Air Service.

Some Air Shipments may be via expedited Ground

GROUND SERVICE
ZONE CHART
For Shippers with ZIP Codes 100-01 to 104-99

Service to 48 Continental United States
To determine zone, take first three digits of ZIP Code to which parcel is addressed and refer to chart below.

ZIP CODE PREFIXES	UPS ZONE	ZIP CODE PREFIXES	UPS ZONE	ZIP CODE PREFIXES	UPS ZONE	ZIP CODE PREFIXES	UPS ZONE
010-013	2	267-268	3	470	4	733	7
014	3	270-288	4	471-472	5	734-738	6
015-016	2	289	5	473	4	739	7
017-042	3	290-293	4	474-479	5	740-763	6
043-044	4	294	5	480-496	4	764-765	7
045	3	295-297	4	497-499	5	766-767	6
046-049	4	298-299	5			768-769	7
050-051	3			500-504	5	770-778	6
052-053	2	300-324	5	505	6	779-797	7
054-059	3	325	6	506-507	5	798-799	8
060-089	2	326-329	5	508-516	6		
		330-334	6	520-559	5	800-814	7
100-127	2	335-338	5	560-576	6	815	8
128-136	3	339	6	577	7	816-820	7
137-139	2	342-364	5	580-585	6	821	8
140-147	3	365-366	6	586-593	7	822-830	7
148-149	2	367-375	5	594	8	831-865	8
150-153	4	376-379	4	595	7	870-872	7
154-163	3	380-386	5	596-599	8	873-874	8
164-165	4	387	6			875-877	7
166-169	3	388-389	5	600-639	5	878-880	8
170-199	2	390-392	6	640-649	6	881-884	7
		393	5	650-652	5	890-899	8
200-209	3	394-396	6	653	6		
210-213	2	397-399	5	654-655	5	900-961	8
214-218	3			656-676	6	970-986	8
219	2	400-402	5	677	7	988-994	8
220-238	3	403-418	4	678	6		
239-243	4	420-424	5	679	7		
244	3	425-426	4	680-692	6		
245-253	4	427	5	693	7		
254	3	430-459	4				
255-264	4	460-466	5	700-722	6		
265	3	467-468	4	723-725	5		
266	4	469	5	726-732	6		

See separate charts for UPS Next Day Air (where available), 2nd Day Air and Service to Canada. Air service is provided to all points in Hawaii.

U7232 REV. 1-85

Metric Conversions

WEIGHT

1 gram	0.04 ounce
1 kilogram	2.20 pounds
1 stone (Brit.)	14 pounds
1 ounce	28.35 grams
1 pound	453 grams
1 ton	0.91 metric ton
1 metric ton	1.10 tons

LIQUID

1 pint	0.47 liter	1 liter	2.11 pints
1 quart	0.95 liter	1 liter	1.06 quarts
1 gallon	3.79 liters	1 liter	0.26 gallon

LENGTH

1 inch	25.4 mm
1 inch	2.54 cm
1 foot	0.30 m
1 yard	0.91 m
1 rod (16.5 ft)	5.03 m
1 mile	1.61 km
1 millimeter (mm)	0.04 in
1 centimeter (cm)	0.39 in
1 meter (m)	1.09 yds
1 meter	0.19 rod
1 kilometer (km)	0.62 mile

To convert from kilometers to miles, divide the number of kilometers by 8 and multiply the result by 5.

To convert from miles to kilometers, divide the number of miles by 5 and multiply the result by 8.

CURRENCY EXCHANGE RATES

These values are based on prevailing market rates at the time of printing and may fluctuate. The best place to exchange currency is at a bank or official foreign exchange office.

COUNTRY	UNIT	.50	1.00	5.00	20.00
USA	Dollar Cents	.50	1.00	5.00	20.00
AUSTRALIA *	Dollar Cents	.75	1.50	7.50	30.00
AUSTRIA *	Schilling Groschen	10.08	20.16	100.80	403.20
BELGIUM	Franc Centime	28.50	57.00	285.00	1140.00
CANADA	Dollar Cent	.66	1.32	6.60	26.40
CHINA ** (PEP. REP.)	Renminbi	1.42	2.84	14.20	56.80
CZECHOSLOVAKIA **	Koruna Heller	13.15	26.30	131.50	526.00
DENMARK *	Kroner Ore	5.15	10.30	51.50	206.00
EGYPT *	Pound Piastra	.57	1.15	5.77	23.08
ENGLAND	Pound Pence	.37	.75	3.75	15.00
FINLAND *	Markka Penni	3.02	6.04	30.20	120.80
FRANCE *	Franc Centime	4.36	8.73	43.65	174.60
GREECE *	Drachma Lepta	55.50	111.00	555.00	2220.00
HOLLAND	Guilder Cent	1.62	3.25	16.25	65.00
HONG KONG	Dollar Cent	3.58	7.17	35.85	143.40
HUNGARY *	Forint Filler	26.30	52.60	263.00	1052.00
INDIA **	Rupee Paise	6.53	13.07	65.35	261.40
IRELAND *	Pound Pence	.45	.91	4.55	18.20
ISRAEL *	Shekel Agorot	424.00	848.00	4240.00	16960.00
USA	Dollar Cents	.50	1.00	5.00	20.00
ITALY *	Lire Centesimi	830.00	1660.00	8300.00	33200.00
JAPAN *	Yen Sen	122.00	244.00	1220.00	4880.00
MEXICO	Peso Centavo	119.00	238.00	1190.00	4760.00
MOROCCO **	Dirham Centime	4.98	9.97	49.85	199.40
NORWAY *	Kroner Ore	4.16	8.33	41.65	166.60
PORTUGAL *	Escudo Centavo	65.00	130.00	650.00	2600.00
ROMANIA **	Leu Bani	6.80	13.60	68.00	272.00
SAUDI ARABIA	Riyal Halala	1.74	3.49	17.45	69.80
SOUTH KOREA **	Won Chon	420.00	840.00	4200.00	16800.00
SPAIN *	Peseta Centimo	71.00	142.00	710.00	2840.00
SWEDEN *	Kroner Ore	4.20	8.40	42.00	168.00
SWITZERLAND	Franc Centime	1.20	2.40	12.00	48.00
TAIWAN *	Dollar Cent	18.18	36.36	181.00	727.00
TURKEY *	Lirasi Kuru	178.50	357.00	1785.00	7140.00
U.S.S.R. **	Ruble Kopeck	.44	.89	4.40	17.80
VENEZUELA	Bolivar Centimo	6.06	12.12	60.60	242.40
WEST GERMANY	Mark Pfennig	1.45	2.90	14.50	58.00
YUGOSLAVIA *	Dinar Para	87.50	175.00	875.00	3500.00

* Some restrictions on currency do apply; contact Deak-Perera for further information.
** Import and export of currency prohibited (Official Government Rate)

Deak-Perera does not assume any responsibility for violations of currency import and/or export restrictions, if any, in foreign countries. Please keep yourself informed as to these regulations.

Clothing Sizes

These sizes are meant to be a guide. They often vary from manufacturer to manufacturer. When you shop for clothing, try it on to make sure it fits. If you plan to buy clothing as a gift, carry with you a list of the recipient's measurements and a tape measure.

British measurements are used in Hong Kong, Singapore, and other British-influenced areas. American sizes are used in the Philippines. The cut and dimensions of Japanese clothing differ from those in the U.S., and usually require major alterations.

Women's Dresses & Suits

America	10	12	14	16	18	20	22
Australia	10	12	14	16	18	20	22
Japan	9	11	13	15	17	19	21
England/ New Zealand	32	34	36	38	40	42	44

Men's Suits, Overcoats & Sweaters

America	34	36	38	40	42	44	46	48
Australia	34	36	38	40	42	44	46	48
Japan	S		M		L		LL
England/ New Zealand	34	36	38	40	42	44	46	48

Shirts & Collars

America	14	14½	15	15½	16	16½	17	17½
Australia	36	37	38	39	40	41	42	43
Japan	36	37	38	39	40	41	42	43
England/ New Zealand	14	14½	15	15½	16	16½	17	17½

Women's Shoes

America	6	6½	7	7½	8	8½	9	9½
Australia	6½	7	7½	8	8½	9	9½	10
Japan	23	23¾	24	24½	25	25½	25¾	
England/ New Zealand	4½	5	5½	6	6½	7	7½	8

Men's Shoes

America	7	7½	8	8½	9	9½	10	10½	11	11½
Australia	6	6½	7	7½	8	8½	9	9½	10	
Japan	26		26¾		27½		28		29	
England/ New Zealand	5½	6	6½	7	7½	8	8½	9	9½	10

Hats (Japanese sizes unavailable)

America	6¾	6⅞	7	7⅛	7¼	7⅜
Australia	6⅝	6¾	6⅞	7	7⅛	7¼
England/ New Zealand	6⅝	6¾	6⅞	7	7⅛	7¼

ANIMAL

Livestock and pet supplies and
equipment; veterinary
instruments and biologicals;
live-animal referrals, and
services.

Some doctors are now "prescribing" pets for people who have hypertension, since the simple act of stroking the animal seems to lower blood pressure levels. Most of us adopt animals for less practical reasons, but few of us are aware of the long-term costs of ownership: keeping the average cat or dog for a typical pet lifetime can run upward of $10,000. Many of the companies listed here give you access to significant savings on everything from toys and collars to cages, carriers, and even medication. One company can supply you with a source for virtually any pet-related product. Another sells a liniment developed to treat sore udders, which doubles as a great hand cream. And if you're trying to rid your home or property of pests, you can do it humanely with a device ordered directly from one of the nation's largest manufacturers of box traps. The needs of livestock farmers large and small can also be met by several of these firms, including a British concern that stocks a huge array of self-sufficiency tools and equipment.

One caution when buying animal medical supplies: The FDA requires you swear to the fact that your purchases of hypodermic syringes, needles, and antibiotics are for animal use only; you must also submit your vet's prescription with your order. Be sure to do this whether or not the catalog states this regulation. In addition, before placing your order check with your local health department to see whether local ordinances permit receipt of such materials. And don't forget to keep drugs and medical instruments out of the reach of both pets and small children.

Several of these firms retain veterinarians who can answer questions on products and their use, but they are not permitted to give medical advice. Turn to your own vet for that, and be sure to discuss with him or her your plans to administer any vaccines or medications. Keep handy the number of a 24-hour service that handles medical emergencies, become familiar with symptoms, and know first-aid measures you may have to take in order to transport the sick or injured animal.

Every pet owner should have first-aid information at hand. One of the best booklets we've found is the "Angell Memorial Guide to Animal First Aid," published by the American Humane Education Society and MSPCA. This 22-page guide tells you how to restrain and handle an injured animal, bind a wound, and deal with burns, drowning, heat stroke, problem deliveries, choking, shock, poisoning, and many other problems. Rosters of toxic household substances and plants are included, as well as a list of tips to help prevent accidents and injuries. The booklet costs $1. Request it by title from the American Humane Education Society, 350 South Huntingdon Avenue, Boston, MA 02130.

ANIMAL CITY WHOLESALE

P.O. Box 1076, Dept. W
La Mesa, CA 92041–0318
(619) 469–0188

Catalog: free; pub. twice yearly
Discount: 10% to 50%
Goods: name brand, generic
Minimum Order: $5
Shipping, Handling: $2 on orders under $20;
  included on orders of $20 or more; UPS, PP
Sales Tax: CA deliveries
Accepts: check, MO, MC, V
$$$

When you compute the expenses entailed in keeping a pet, even the smallest kitten (not to mention a horse) can set you back hundreds of dollars a year in visits to the vet, distemper shots, brushes, flea collars, etc. ACW can save you up to 50% (and more with quantity discounts) on just about any product associated with dogs, cats, horses, or fish—antibiotics, wormers, instruments, vitamins, skin treatments, insecticides, grooming aids, horse tack, collars, feeders, books, and more. Goods range from the department-store variety to specialized items sold to vets, groomers, and kennel operators. The catalog also has a number of items pet owners should keep on hand but rarely do, such as "external" thermometers, vitamins and minerals, shampoos, spare leashes and collars, odor removers, and extra toys.

Get together with other dog, cat, fish, bird, or horse owners and save on shipping costs. Animal City Wholesale, a division of PETCO, has been in business since 1965 and guarantees satisfaction with all its goods. Returns on everything except vaccines and instruments are accepted for refund or credit.

**ANIMAL VETERINARY
PRODUCTS, INC.**

P.O. Box 1267
Galesburg, IL 61401
(309) 342–9511: inquiries
and IL orders
(800) 447–8192: orders
except IL

Catalog: free
Discount: (see text)
Goods: name brand, generic
Minimum Order: $10
Shipping, Insurance: extra; UPS
Sales Tax: IL, GA, NV, PA deliveries
Accepts: check, MO, MC, V, AE
$$$

AVP can help your cat or dog "stay healthy, handsome, and contented," at prices that should keep you happy as well. The 84-page catalog presents hundreds of products, including biologicals and medications, dietary supplements, wormers, flea and tick collars and preparations, toys, books, grooming tools and products, cages, feeders, training devices, and much more. The best prices—10% to 50% off list—are on goods bought in quantity, so combine orders with friends to maximize your savings.

DAIRY ASSOCIATION CO., INC.

Lyndonville, VT 05851
(802) 626–3610

Brochure: free
Discount: see text
Goods: house brand
Minimum Order: none
Shipping: included; PP
Handling: 50¢ per order
Sales Tax: VT deliveries
Accepts: check, Mo
$$$$

The Dairy Association Co. has been around since 1889 and is known to generations of herd farmers for its Bag Balm ointment. This lanolin-enriched liniment is formulated to soothe the chapped, sunburned, and scraped udders of cows, but it's also recommended by horse trainers for cracked heels, gauls, cuts, hobble burns, and the like. Others use it on their sheep, goats, dogs, and cats. Even human beings swear by it for weather-beaten, chapped hands. (Apply at night and wear protective cotton gloves, since it stains.) The 10-oz can, sold in other catalogs for over $5, costs only $3 here, and a 4½-lb pail is $20.10. Dilators and milking tubes for injured udders are also available.

Since cracked and dry hoofs can handicap a horse, the Dairy Association Co. has developed an answer to that problem—Hoof Softener. The lanolin, pine oil, and vegetable oils in it help keep the hoof pliable. It sells for $3.50 a pound.

When the leather in your life needs tender loving care, there's Tackmaster. It's a one-step cleaner, preservative, and conditioner that revives everything made of leather (except suede) and helps it last longer. Try it for footwear, clothing, bags, furniture, and tack. A 4-oz bottle is $1.55, pints are $2.80, and quarts are $4.30. Compared to a similar product at $4 a 6-oz bottle, Tackmaster is an excellent buy.

ECHO PET SUPPLIES

Box 145, Dept. WBM
Westland, MI 48185
(313) 425–5293

Catalog: $1; pub. twice yearly
Discount: up to 40%
Goods: name brand, house brand
Minimum Order: none
Shipping, Handling, Insurance: $2.50 per order; UPS, PP
Sales Tax: MI deliveries
Accepts: check, MO, MC, V
$$$ 🍁   (see text)

Echo Pet Supplies, formerly known as Aqua Engineers, offers a wide spectrum of products for the care of tropical and saltwater fish and smaller selections for gerbils, hamsters, guinea pigs, cats, dogs, and birds. Complete aquarium outfits and air pumps, filters, water pumps, heaters, lighting, tank novelties and plants, food, and medicines are stocked. There are cages, shelters, beds, and playthings for birds, rodents, cats, and dogs; and leashes, leads, feeding bowls and devices, grooming implements, and dietary supplements and medications. Prices run to 40% below list or comparable retail, and the monthly sales flyers offer greater savings on selected goods. Flyers are sent on request.

Echo also sells mailing lists of fish clubs by state or for the entire U.S. and Canada, as well as lists of manufacturers of pet products, wholesale suppliers, pet suppliers, and breeders. Echo has been selling fish products since 1963 and under its new management is keeping prices down while expanding inventory.

CANADIAN READERS, PLEASE NOTE: the postage fee on goods sent to Canada is $5 per order. Canadian funds are accepted.

KANSAS CITY VACCINE COMPANY

1611 Genessee St.
Kansas City, MO
64102–5173
(816) 842–5966

Price List: free; pub. twice yearly
Information: price quote by phone or letter with SASE
Discount: up to 33%
Goods: name brand, house brand
Minimum Order: $10
Shipping, Insurance: extra; UPS, FOB Kansas City
Handling: $2 on orders under $10
Sales Tax: MO deliveries
Accepts: check, MO, certified check
$$$

This veterinary-supply firm, established in 1912, carries all sorts of health products for cattle, horses, sheep, hogs, poultry, dogs, and cats. Kansas City Vaccine sells vaccines, antitoxins, flea and tick treatments, grooming tools, wormers, stethoscopes, soaps, tattoo markers, vitamins and dietary supplements, and other related items at prices up to a third less than retail. Among the manufacturers represented are Franklin, Norden, Tylosin, Trax-M, Havoc, Kopertox, Red-Kote, Happy Jack, Chaparral, Lindane, Resco, Ritchey, Oster, and Sunbeam. Kansas City Vaccine sells pet vaccines through the mail where ordinances permit. Excellent savings are available on most products purchased in quantity.

**LIBERTY LEATHER
MANUFACTURERS**

**P.O. Box 213
Liberty, TN 37095
(615) 597-7999**

Brochure: 25¢ and SASE
Discount: to 75% (see text)
Goods: handmade, house brand
Minimum Order: $20 (see text)
Shipping, Insurance: extra; UPS
Sales Tax: TN deliveries
Accepts: check or MO
$$$$

Liberty sells its own handmade bridle-leather dog collars at prices that run to 75% below comparable retail. A sturdy collar, combined with a stout leash, provides much more "breakaway" protection for dogs of the leaping, lunging, bolting variety than do many plastic and chain models.

Liberty offers a variety of weights and styles—plain, studded, etc.—in sizes to fit everything from a miniature to a mastiff. Discounted prices apply to orders of $20 or more. If your needs run short of that, get fellow canine-fanciers to combine orders with you.

**NORTHERN WHOLESALE
VETERINARY SUPPLY, INC.**

**5570 Frontage Rd. N.
Onalaska, WI 54650
(608) 783-0300: inquiries
(800) 362-8025: WI orders
(800) 356-5852: orders
except WI**

Catalog: free
Discount: 15% to 50%
Goods: name brand, generic
Minimum Order: none
Shipping: extra on orders under $20; included on
    orders over $20; UPS
Sales Tax: WI deliveries
Accepts: check, MO, MC, V
$$$

Like the other animal-supply firms listed here, NWV sells a wide range of vaccines, health products, dietary supplements, grooming tools, etc., at savings of up to 40%. Quantity discounts apply to a number of the items. If you have questions, you can consult the staff veterinarian on matters of health and product use.

OMAHA VACCINE COMPANY

3030 L St.
Omaha, NE 68107–0228
(402) 731–1155

Catalog: free; pub. six times yearly
Discount: 33%
Goods: name brand, house brand, generic
Minimum Order: $10
Shipping, Insurance: included on most items; UPS, PP
Handling: $2 on orders under $10
Sales Tax: NE deliveries
Accepts: check, MO, MC, V
$$$

Omaha Vaccine publishes a 128-page catalog of products for livestock, horses, and pets. Biologicals, medications, grooming tools and wormers, dietary supplements, flea and tick products, cages, leads and leashes, horse tack, and many other goods are offered at prices that average 33% below retail or suggested list. Work gloves and boots are also stocked.

Omaha Vaccine was established in 1959, and does most of its business with livestock producers and veterinarians. Some of the pharmaceutical products are available by prescription only.

PBS LIVESTOCK DRUGS

2800 Leemont Ave. N.W.
P.O. Box 9101
Canton, OH 44711–9101
(216) 492–9252
(800) 362–9838: OH orders
(800) 321–0235: orders except OH

Catalog: free
Discount: 20% to 50%
Goods: name brand, generic
Minimum Order: $20
Shipping: included on some items; UPS, FOB Canton or Des Moines
Handling: $2 on orders under $20
Sales Tax: OH and IA deliveries
Accepts: check, MO, MC, V
$$$

If your menagerie consists of livestock rather than pets, you'll find PBS a great source for biologicals and other veterinary products. Commercial dairy, beef, swine, and sheep producers are PBS's principal customers. (Indeed, those unfamiliar with routine livestock care may be somewhat disturbed by the functions of some of the implements and medicines listed in the catalog.) The 64 pages are packed with pharmaceutical products, dietary supplements, ointments, and treatments for all livestock varieties, along with such items as tags, instruments, and much more.

PBS does have some great bargains on items almost anyone can use. Quarts of pure isopropyl alcohol are less than half the drugstore price, and savings on the gallon size are even better. PBS also sells Bag Balm, unrefined wheat germ oil, mineral oil, K-Y jelly, disposable plastic boots and gloves, and work boots, among other items, at great savings. Just remember that the catalog is intended for livestock farmers and not for the squeamish. Your satisfaction is guaranteed.

**SELF-SUFFICIENCY AND
SMALLHOLDING SUPPLIES**

**Priory Rd.
Wells, Somerset BA5 1SY
England
Phone #: 749–72127**

Catalog: $5; pub. biannually
Discount: up to 35%
WBMC Reader Discount: 30% (see text)
Goods: name brand, generic
Minimum Order: none
Shipping, Insurance: 25% of order value (see text); surface mail, airmail
Duty: extra
Accepts: check, IMO, V, Access
$$

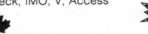

We were tempted to mail a copy of this firm's catalog to PBS, attention: "The Good Neighbors." For those who haven't seen the show, it's a comedy that revolves around the antics of a middle-class couple in Britain who have left the rat race—but not their suburban home—to become self-reliant. If you, too, are tempted to chuck the 9-to-5 routine to raise vegetables and keep pigs and goats in the backyard, don't do it without this resource.

The company, also known as The Countryside Store, was founded in 1975 by two small-scale farmers (smallholders), Alan Buchanan and Richard Collins. Their stock, only part of which is shown in the catalog, is the best and most comprehensive inventory of its kind in the United Kingdom or North America. The 58 pages, filled with drawings and charming illustrations, are divided into sections with cultivation and land-use tools, equipment for livestock care and management, veterinary products, farrier (blacksmith) tools and products for hoof-care and shoeing, poultry-raising goods, household and yard maintenance equipment; and products for dairy farming, butchery, food preparation and storage, wine and beer production, beekeeping, hunting and trapping, pest control, and leather-working. Among the many goods you'll find are saws and machetes, axe handles, cow halters and pig harnesses, salt licks, troughs and buckets, shepherds' crooks, rabbit feeders and water dispensers, hoof knives, incubators, henhouses, egg graders, water hand pumps, milking stools and milk cans, as well as a definitive selection of Sübitas and other cream separators, butter churns, cheese molds and presses, smoking cabinets, Sabatier and Moulinex kitchen tools, grain mills (nonelectric), pie birds, bottle brushes, hops and malt, juice concentrates for wine-making, beehives, decoys and whistles, and mordants. An excellent book list offers reading material on topics of interest to smallholders, but many of the publications—as well as the products—also merit the attention of craftspeople and hobbyists.

Thanks to the strength of the dollar (at this writing), the prices here are more than reasonable: where comparisons could be made, we found savings of up to 35% on equivalent products sold in the U.S. Please note that *all* goods must be paid for in pounds sterling, and the catalog must be purchased by IMO or with ICRs, not by check. The additional WBMC discount of 30% applies only to "bona fide agricultural retailers," so do not request it if you cannot prove you are one. The shipping surcharge is set high purposely to avoid delaying shipment of orders while additional postage is requested. The Countryside Store will refund any overpayment.

TOMAHAWK LIVE TRAP CO.

P.O. Box 323-WM
Tomahawk, WI 54487
(715) 453–3550

Brochure: free; pub. yearly in Jan.
Information: price quote by phone or letter with SASE
Discount: 33% to 50%
WBMC Reader Discount: 10% (see text)
Goods: house brand
Minimum Order: none
Shipping, Insurance: extra; UPS, PP, FOB Tomahawk
Sales Tax: WI deliveries
Accepts: check, MO, certified check
$$$$

Tomahawk makes box traps that capture animals without maiming or killing them. The firm's traps are used by the U.S. Army Medical Corps, state and federal conservation departments, dog wardens, universities, and others who want to catch a critter in a humane way or make sure its pelt and life are not endangered.

Since the business was founded in 1929, Tomahawk has designed traps for everything from mice ($10.11), to large dogs ($136.25), to fish and turtles, birds, and beavers. The models include rigid and collapsible styles, transfer cages, station wagon and carrying cages, and several with sliding doors made for shipping animals. The brochure and price list include dimensions and specifications of each trap and a list of common foods that can be used to lure over 20 animals. The prices on individual traps are a third less than retail, and discounted up to 50% if you buy six or more of the same trap. The reader discount of 10% brings that to 43% to 60%. Be sure to identify yourself as a WBMC reader, both when requesting the brochure and when ordering to qualify, and deduct the 10% from the cost of the goods only.

We recommend both the products and the principle. With prices this low, there's no excuse for setting out dangerous poisoned baits or gruesome spring traps, both of which are potential hazards to animals other than the intended victims. And if you're coping with a mouse problem, be advised that the sticky "hotel" traps are just as ghastly. (If you've ever heard the indescribable screams of a mouse caught in one, you'll probably concur.) If your problem animal is too large or small for a standard trap, write to Tomahawk—special traps are made to order.

**UNITED PHARMACAL
COMPANY, INC.**

3705 Pear St.
P.O. Box 969
St. Joseph, MO 64504
(816) 233–8800

Catalog: free; pub. yearly in Mar.
Discount: 30% to 50%
Goods: house brand, name brand
Minimum Order: $5
Shipping, Insurance: $2 minimum; UPS, PP, FOB
  St. Joseph
Sales Tax: MO and NE deliveries
Accepts: check, MO, MC, V, AE
$$$

UPCO's 128-page catalog can help save you money on thousands of products for dogs, cats, and horses—antibiotics, wormers, instruments, dietary supplements, skin treatments, insecticides, grooming aids, horse tack, collars and leads, feeders, books, etc. You'll reap savings of up to 50% off retail prices and even larger discounts on quantity orders. When you buy distemper vaccine from UPCO and inoculate your dog or cat yourself, you can save up to 80% on the vet's fee. Most people will find the ordinary accessories—flea collars, leashes, toys, feeding dishes and stations, books, brushes, and combs—sufficient for their pets' needs. Professional groomers and those who own vain dogs should note the wide range of ribbons, coat whiteners, nail polish, and similar products. UPCO has been in business since 1952 and accepts returns within 20 days for refund or credit.

WHOLESALE VETERINARY SUPPLY, INC.

P.O. Box 2256
Rockford, IL 61131
(815) 877–0209: inquiries and Rockford-area orders
(800) 892–6996: IL orders
(800) 435–6940: orders except IL

Catalog: free; pub. in May and Nov.
Information: price quote by phone or letter with SASE
Discount: 20% to 50%
Goods: name brand, generic
Minimum Order: $20
Shipping, Insurance: extra; UPS, PP, FOB Rockford
Handling: $2 on orders under $20
Sales Tax: IL deliveries
Accepts: check, MO, MC, V
$$$

A veterinarian has estimated that it costs almost $4,000 to raise an average cat to the age of 11, and over $8,000 for an 80-pound dog. These figures include food, vet expenses, grooming, and licensing. You can cut food bills without compromising quality by buying in bulk from a discount pet-supply outlet or stocking up at supermarket sales or warehouses. And you can save from 20% to 50% on supplies and tools for grooming and even some medical expenses by purchasing through Wholesale Veterinary Supply.

WVS has been doing business since 1971 and stocks over 8,000 products for cats, dogs, rabbits, cattle, and horses. The 104-page catalog is crammed with biologicals, pharmaceuticals, nutritional supplements, surgical instruments, cages and carriers, grooming tools and preparations, leashes and leads, flea and tick treatments, and many other items. You'll also find a large selection of books, leather-care products, flashlights, knives, disinfectants and cleaning products, Georgia and Cedar Crest work shoes, Laredo Western boots, and other goods. Many well-known manufacturers—Sergeant's, Lambert Kay, Oster, Roche, Fortex, Farnam, Absorbine, Holiday—are represented, as well as hard-to-find labels and imports.

WVC retains a professional vet who can answer questions about its products, and the company's management keeps abreast of new developments in research and preventive medicine. Authorized returns are accepted within 30 days.

SEE ALSO:

Gohn Bros. . . . horse blankets . . . CLOTHING
Laurence Corner . . . camel water tanks . . . CLOTHING
Puritan's Pride, Inc. . . . pet vitamins, grooming aids . . . HEALTH
Star Pharmaceutical, Inc. . . . small selection pet vitamins, grooming products . . . HEALTH
Sunburst Biorganics . . . pet vitamins . . . HEALTH
Vitamin Specialties . . . pet vitamins . . . HEALTH
Western Natural Products . . . pet vitamins . . . HEALTH

APPLIANCES, AUDIO, TV, AND VIDEO

Major, small, and personal-care appliances;
sewing machines and vacuum cleaners;
audio components and personal stereo;
TV and video equipment;
tapes, discs, and services.

If it plugs in or runs on batteries, it's probably sold by one, if not many, of the firms listed here. White goods (washers, dryers, refrigerators, and ranges), brown goods (TVs, air conditioners, audio and video equipment, etc.), small kitchen and personal-care appliances, pocket calculators, phone equipment, sewing machines, vacuum cleaners, and floor machines are featured, and many of the companies also sell blank audio and video tapes, luggage, cameras, typewriters, pens, and video games.

Discounts of 30% to 50% are routine, but smart buyers consider more than price when they're shopping. Before you start making inquiries, read the following sections of "The Complete Guide to Buying by Mail": "Cost Comparisons," "Price Quotes," and "Returns, Guarantees, and Warranties."

The Better Business Bureau (BBB) publishes a number of "Booklets on Wise Buying" that can help you make intelligent purchases. Tracts on appliance service contracts, air-conditioning, home computers, microwave ovens, phone purchases, and video equipment are all available. Contact your local BBB to obtain them, or send a SASE for the complete listing of pamphlets and an order form to: Council of Better Business Bureaus, Inc., 1515 Wilson Blvd., Arlington, VA 22209, Attn: Publications Dept.

Sunbeam publishes a 20-page booklet, "Making Less Electricity Do More," that lists the operating costs of many popular electrical appliances and includes a number of recipes. Request the booklet by title from the Consumer Affairs Dept., Sunbeam Appliance Company, Sunbeam Corp., 2001 South York Rd., Oak Brook, IL 60521.

Consumer Reports magazine reviews name-brand products monthly, and publishes summaries of these in its yearly *Buying Guide*. Use the magazine and annual as *adjuncts* to shopping, and note that suggested list and "benchmark" retail selling prices stated with model information may be out of date (this is stated by CR in its guide). *Consumer's Research* also publishes product evaluations and articles of practical interest to consumers.

For additional firms selling appliances and electronics, see "Office and Computing" and "Tools."

AAA-ALL FACTORY, INC.

241 Cedar
Abilene, TX 79601
(915) 677–1311

Brochure: $1 (stamps accepted); refundable to WBMC readers with order; free if requested by phone; pub. spring, summer, fall, winter
Information: price quote by phone
Discount: 35% to 75%
WBMC Reader Bonus: year's supply of belts and bags (see text)
Goods: name brand, house brand
Minimum Order: none
Shipping: FOB Abilene (see text)
Sales Tax: TX deliveries
Accepts: check, MO, certified check, MC, V, C.O.D.

$$$$

AAA has been making the dean's list in the dirt department since 1975— for price, selection, and service, it's at the head of its class. It sells the best latest models in canisters, uprights, convertibles, and minivacuum cleaners: Kirby's "Heritage II," Compact's canister and upright models, Filter Queen's complete cleaning system, the Rexair Rainbow with all the attachments, and both home and commercial lines by Hoover. Eureka's commercial floor buffers/rug shampooers, the Mastercraft wet/dry canister model and heavy-duty floor machines, and the Shelton wet/dry "Jet Vac" are stocked as well. Panasonic, Eureka, and Royal vacuums are available but not listed; you may phone with model information for a price quote. Prices here run from under $23 for the nonelectric Hoky sweeper to $539 for the 20-inch commercial Mastercraft shampooer/polisher. These are compared to list and direct-sales prices which average 50% higher. In addition, most models are up to $10 cheaper when purchased in multiples.

Stay cool while you're vacuuming, shampooing, scrubbing, and polishing with one of All Factory's ceiling fans. These are less than half the cost of their name-brand counterparts. The 36-inch, three-blade model is $21.95, and a 52-inch fan with five cane-inset hardwood blades, three speeds, reversible rotation, and a choice of finishes costs $89.95. Seven light kits are available that fit all but the economy fan.

AAA carries only new products, not seconds or rebuilt models. All machines are covered by the manufacturers' warranties and/or the AAA parts and service contract, and satisfaction is guaranteed (returns are accepted within ten days). On a budget? Put a minimum of $10 down, send at least $10 every 30 days, and your vacuum cleaner or other machine will be sent when you've paid in full—no carrying or finance charges. And if you state that you're a WBMC reader when you order, you will be entitled to a free one-year supply of four belts and 12 paper dust bags (if applicable to your vacuum-cleaner purchase). Phone orders are accepted, but please do not call collect.

**ABC VACUUM CLEANER
WAREHOUSE**

**6720 Burnet Rd.
Austin, TX 78757
(512) 459–7643**

Price Lists: free; pub. Jan., Apr., July, Nov.
Discount: 30% to 50%
Goods: name brand
Minimum Order: none
Shipping: $15 per machine; $30 outside
   continental U.S.; UPS, PP
Sales Tax: TX deliveries
Accepts: check, MO, certified check, MC, V, AE
$$$

This book lists several sources for Hoover and Eureka vacuum cleaners. These machines may receive top ratings from consumer publications, but we're not buying. We know they can do the job, but we believe that you'll get better, longer performance with the sort of machines available at ABC Warehouse.

This company has been selling models by Rexair, Kirby, Filter Queen, and Compact to informed consumers since 1977. Rexair's Rainbow "D3" is under $399 here, although it's sold for up to $1,100 by direct-sales representatives. Instead of dust bags, the Rainbow uses a water-filled tank that "drowns" dust and dirt. The power-nozzle attachment ($139.95) has a motorized beater brush that cleans all rugs from velvet naps to shags. Add the Aqua Mate attachment and your Rainbow becomes a carpet-cleaning extraction unit. Kirby fans will find the "Heritage" upright, complete with wands and hose to convert to tank functions, for $495.95. (It sells for up to $900 from door-to-door salespeople.) The "Rug Renovator" shampoo attachment is also available for $79.95. The Filter Queen is sold here with the power nozzle in both manual and automatic cord-storage models at under $499 (compared to $900 elsewhere). And the Compact, a powerful compact cleaner with "big vac" features that include a motorized power nozzle, costs under $449 here and as much as $880 when bought from a sales representative. Bags and filters are also stocked.

ABC purchases from overstocked distributors and passes along the savings—up to 50%—to you. Further price reductions are offered on quantity purchases and specials. All the machines are new, not rebuilt or second-quality products. ABC honors the manufacturers' warranties and provides parts and service for specified terms. (Policies on all the machines are described in the literature.) Your satisfaction is guaranteed. Returns are accepted within 15 days for refund or credit. If you're budgeting, inquire for information about the layaway plan.

**AMERICAN VACUUM &
SEWING MACHINE CORP.**

2908 Hamilton St.
Hyattsville, MD 20782
(301) 559–6800

Information: price quote by letter with SASE
Discount: 20%
WBMC Reader Discount: 10% (see text)
Goods: name brand
Minimum Order: none
Shipping, Insurance: extra; UPS, PP
Sales Tax: MD deliveries
Accepts: check, MO, MC, V, AE, CHOICE
$$

American offers mail-order shoppers name-brand sewing machines, vacuum cleaners, and accessories and supplies for both. The vacuum brands represented are Eureka, Hoover, Royal, Kirby, and Panasonic. You can get sewing machines by Singer, Necchi, White, Universal, Pfaff, Viking, Elna, Bernina, and New Home.

American discounts everything 20% off the suggested list prices. WBMC readers may deduct an additional 10% from the *discounted* price. (It's easier to deduct a flat 28%, since this is how the discount-on-a-discount computes.) American has been selling vacuum cleaners and sewing machines since 1965 and does business by mail on an inquiry basis. Write to ask whether the model you want is in stock, and include a SASE with your query. American should be able to provide the suggested list on which you base your discount; you can verify this with local shops or the manufacturer.

ANNEX OUTLET LTD.

43 Warren St.
New York, NY 10007
(212) 964–8661

Catalog: free; pub. Jan., May, Sept.
Information: price quote by phone or letter with
   SASE
Discount: 35% to 40%
Goods: name brand
Minimum Order: none
Shipping, Insurance: $4 minimum; UPS, PP
Sales Tax: NY deliveries
Accepts: check, MO, certified check
$$$

Annex Outlet is one of our favorite sources for audio equipment and phone machines. This 13-year-old firm also carries an extensive range of video equipment, including recorders, portable VCRs, cameras, tapes and batteries by Panasonic, RCA, Quasar, JVC, Sharp, Fisher, Hitachi, Vidicraft, Recoton, Can Am, Smith-Victor, Bescor, Maxell, TDK, Scotch, Agfa, BASF, Trimax, Sony, Fuji, Memorex, and other firms. The audio lines include Technics, Sansui, Sharp, Shure, and ADC. Annex carries personal stereo by Aiwa, Sony, and Sanyo, and auto audio by Blaupunkt, Clarion, and Panasonic. You'll find TVs by Sony, Sharp, Hitachi, and other manufacturers, and audio reel-to-reel and cassette tape by TDK, Maxell, Sony, Scotch, Memorex, and Sanyo. You can upgrade your communications equipment with phones from Panasonic, Sanyo, Uniden, Phone-Mate, Electra, and ITT. Let phone machines by Panasonic, Phone-Mate, and Sanyo take messages when you're out. These are just representative listings—Annex carries many more firms, and will give price quotes over the phone and by letter if you include a SASE.

CANADIAN READERS, PLEASE NOTE: Annex imposes a 20% surcharge on goods shipped to Canada.

**ARGUS RADIO &
APPLIANCES, INC.**

**48 E. 21st St.
New York, NY 10010
(212) 505–7080**

Information: price quote by phone or letter with
  SASE
Discount: 20% to 30%
Goods: name brand
Minimum Order: none
Shipping: extra; UPS, FOB NYC
Sales Tax: NY deliveries
Accepts: check, MO, certified check
$$$

Argus stocks white and brown goods (refrigerators, washers, dryers, air conditioners, TVs, video equipment, and audio components) by top manufacturers. The list includes appliances by Amana, Caloric, Frigidaire, Hotpoint, Indesit, Litton, G.E., Maytag, Magic Chef, Tappan, Welbilt, White-Westinghouse, and Whirlpool. There are also TVs and video equipment by Panasonic, Philco, Quasar, RCA, Sanyo, Sony, Sylvania, and Zenith. Call or write (include a SASE) for a price quote.

AUDIO VIDEO CENTER, INC.

4128 S. Florida Ave.
Lakeland, FL 33803
(813) 644–4546

Information: price quote by phone or letter with SASE
Discount: 5% above dealer cost (see text)
WBMC Reader Rebate: $5 on phone orders of $300 or more
Goods: name brand
Minimum Order: none
Shipping, Insurance: extra; UPS
Sales Tax: FL deliveries
Accepts: MO, certified check, MC, V
$$

WBMC Discount

This four-year-old firm sells VCRs and video cameras, TVs, phone machines, portable audio units, and satellite dishes at 5% over dealer cost, which usually works out to 30% to 40% below suggested list prices. Panasonic is represented in every category except satellite dishes (those are by Birdview). There are VCRs, video cameras, and TVs by RCA, Quasar, Sony, and Magnavox; and a range of products from Fuji, Kiwi, Smith-Victor, Marathon, Allsop, and Videolink. If you mention that you're a WBMC reader when placing a phone order of $300 or more, you will be entitled to a $5 rebate or discount on the order total.

BERNIE'S DISCOUNT CENTER, INC.

821 Sixth Ave., Dept.
WBMC
New York, NY 10001
(212) 564–8582, 8758

Catalog: $1 with double-stamped SASE; pub. 4 times yearly
Information: price quote by letter with SASE
Discount: 20% to 50% (see text)
Goods: name brand
Minimum Order: none
Shipping, Insurance: 7% of order value; $5 minimum; UPS, FOB NYC
Sales Tax: NY deliveries
Accepts: check, MO, certified check
$$$

Bernie's was founded in 1948, when good discount stores were more the exception than the rule. Selling products at 8% to 12% above dealer cost ("the best cost," Bernie's tell us, meaning 20% to 50% below list), has established this firm as one of the city's best sources for discounted electronics and appliances. It's no accident—the company shops for the best product/price value when selecting goods from suppliers and tries to carry at least three of the top buys in each product category. Bernie's feels that "quality is critical and so is the company's reputation and service." We found a good proportion of catalog choices were models rated highly in consumer magazines.

The audio department is limited to compact and personal audio by Panasonic, Sony, and Sharp; TVs and video equipment by Sony, Mitsubishi, Panasonic, Toshiba, and Hitachi; blank video tapes from Hitachi, Panasonic, TDK, Fuji, and Sony; video games by Atari and Coleco; phones and answering machines by Panasonic, Sharp, Sanyo, and Phone-Mate; and calculators by Sharp, Casio, and Canon.

Bernie's stocks large appliances but ships within New York City and outlying counties only. Among the goods are washers, dryers, refrigerators, stoves, microwave ovens, and air conditioners by Amana, G.E., Caloric, Gibson, Hotpoint, KitchenAid, Litton, Magic Chef, Maytag, Rangaire, Tappan, Welbilt, White-Westinghouse, Whirlpool, Airtemp, and Friedrich. (Dual-voltage and 220-volt appliances are available.) Smaller household and personal-care appliances can be shipped nationwide, and include the full line of G.E. electronics; vacuum cleaners by Hoover, Eureka, Regina, and Black & Decker; humidifiers, heaters, and air-purifiers from Bionaire, Edison, Corona, Norelco, Oster, and Intermatic; and a range of products by Braun, Clairol, Teledyne (Water Pik), Sunbeam, Remington, KitchenAid, Toastmaster, Presto, Proctor-Silex, Wear-Ever, Norelco, Hamilton Beach, Farberware, Oster, West Bend, Conair, Mr. Coffee, and Panasonic. The ten-page catalog lists popular selections from these firms, and Bernie's invites inquiries on any goods not listed. Write for a price quote and include a SASE with your letter.

BONDY EXPORT CORP.

**40 Canal St.
New York, NY 10002
(212) 925–7785; 7786**

Information: price quote by phone or letter only
  with SASE
Discount: 30% to 50%
Goods: name brand
Minimum Order: none
Shipping, Insurance: extra; UPS, PP, FOB NYC
Sales Tax: NY deliveries
Accepts: check, MO, MC, V, AE
$$$$

Name-brand appliances, cameras, movie and slide projectors, TV and video equipment, vacuum cleaners, phones and answering machines, typewriters, pens, and luggage can all be found at Bondy. The small-appliance lines include G.E., Oster, Hoover, SCM, Clairol, Conair, Braun, Panasonic, Sony, and others. (Note: Bondy sells, but does not *ship,* major appliances.) Bondy also sells G.E. and Amana microwave ovens, Samsonite luggage, Parker pens, Seiko and Casio watches, and discounts Farberware 30% to 50%. Discounts are made on *list prices*—Bondy can't beat your local appliance-store sales prices by 30%. Just get the model or style number of the product you want and write to Bondy for a price quote. Be sure to include a SASE.

CRUTCHFIELD

1 Crutchfield Park, Dept. WH
Charlottesville, VA 22906
(804) 973–1811: inquiries
(800) 552–3961: VA catalog requests and orders
(800) 336–5566: catalog requests except VA
(800) 446–1640: orders except VA

Catalog: free
Discount: up to 60%
Goods: name brand
Minimum Order: none
Shipping, Insurance: included; UPS
Handling: $2 per order
Sales Tax: VA deliveries
Accepts: check, MO, MC, V, AE, CB, DC
$$$$

Crutchfield's beautiful 100-page color catalog of electronics isn't what you'd expect from a discount house. Within its pages, you'll find car stereo components, home audio equipment, and telephone equipment pictured in clear photographs, with specifications and descriptions. Each product section is accompanied by a discussion of new products and technology, definitions of terms, and related advice and recommendations. The current catalog lists car stereo equipment by such top manufacturers as Sony, Pioneer, Concord, and JVC; home stereo by Advent, Sony, Akai, Pioneer, Infinity, and other firms; and name-brand video and telephone equipment.

A highly trained phone staff can advise on component and equipment selection. Charges for delivery via UPS or Parcel Post are included in the prices; air and priority-mail services are offered at an additional fee. Crutchfield guarantees satisfaction and will accept returns within 30 days for exchange, refund, or credit.

DIAL-A-BRAND, INC.

110 Bedford Ave.
Bellmore, NY 11710
(718) 978-4400
(516) 783-8220
(201) 653-6727

Information: price quote by phone or letter with
  SASE
Discount: up to 40%
Goods: name brand
Minimum Order: none
Shipping, Insurance: extra; UPS
Sales Tax: NY deliveries
Accepts: MO or certified check
$$$

Dial-A-Brand has 18 years of experience selling name-brand air conditioners, TVs, video equipment, microwave ovens, and appliances in the New York/New Jersey/Connecticut area. (Deliveries are made farther afield, but the freight charges may offset savings.) Call or write for a price quote on anything in the categories listed that's made by a major manufacturer. Returns are accepted for exchange on defective or damaged goods.

E33 TYPEWRITER & ELECTRONICS

42 E. 33rd St.
New York, NY 10016
(212) 686-1631: inquiries
and NY orders
(800) 223-3201: orders
except NY

Flyer: free with SASE
Information: price quote by phone or letter with
  SASE
Discount: up to 60%
Goods: name brand
Minimum Order: $50
Shipping, Handling, Insurance: 6% of order value,
  $4 minimum; UPS
Sales Tax: NY deliveries
Accepts: MO, certified check, MC, V, AE
$$$

E33 will "meet or beat any advertised price on TVs and VCRs," and that includes Sony! It offers TV and video equipment by that firm as well as Panasonic, RCA, JVC, Sanyo, Quasar, Mitsubishi, Hitachi, Zenith, Toshiba, Sharp, Fisher, and G.E. at savings of up to 60%. The audio department stocks components and personal stereo by Hitachi, Yamaha, Sony, Marantz, JVC, Denon, Sansui, Akai, Technics, Aiwa, and Nakamichi. Name-brand audio and video tapes are also sold at a discount.

E33 is an authorized IBM dealer and it sells typewriters by that company as well as by SCM, Brother, Silver-Reed, Royal, Olympia, Juki, and Sharp. There are computers, peripherals, and software by and for Commodore, Apple, IBM, Atari, Hayes, NEC, Amdek, Juki, Brother, Silver-Reed, and

Epson. You'll find buys on Sharp and Canon copiers; calculators by Canon, Hewlett-Packard, Casio, Sharp, and Sanyo; phones and phone machines by Panasonic, Code-A-Phone, Phone-Mate, Uniden, Record a Call, and Sanyo. Casio musical keyboards and microwave ovens by Panasonic and Sharp are also available. E33 services TVs, video equipment, and typewriters, and can get typewriters in foreign voltage, special keyboard models, and any typeface. PLEASE NOTE: credit cards are accepted on phone orders only.

E.B.A. WHOLESALE CORP.

2329 Nostrand Ave.
Brooklyn, NY 11210
(718) 252–3400, 4000

Information: price quote by phone or letter with SASE
Discount: 5% above cost (see text)
Goods: name brand
Minimum Order: none
Shipping, Insurance: extra; UPS, FOB Brooklyn
Sales Tax: NY deliveries
Accepts: check, MO, certified check
$$$

E.B.A. carries full lines of major appliances, TVs, and video equipment. The firm stocks goods from almost every manufacturer of large appliances, including Amana, Caloric, Frigidaire, G.E., Hotpoint, KitchenAid, Jenn-Air, Magic Chef, White-Westinghouse, and Whirlpool; and air conditioners by Airtemp, Fedders, Carrier, and Friedrich. In addition, E.B.A. carries TV and video equipment by Panasonic, Sony, Sanyo, G.E., Zenith, RCA, Quasar, Sylvania, and Magnavox. The firm charges you 5% above cost on all goods, which amounts to a discount of 10% to 40%, depending on the product. Call or write for a price quote, and include a SASE with your letter.

FOCUS ELECTRONICS, INC.

4523 13th Ave.
Brooklyn, NY 11219
(718) 871–7600: electronics and computer inquiries and NY orders
(800) 223–3411: electronics and computer orders except NY
(718) 436–6262: photography inquiries and NY orders
(800) 221–0828: photography orders except NY

Electronics Catalog: $4, refundable; pub. twice yearly
Photography Catalog: $4, refundable; pub. twice yearly
Information: price quote by phone or letter with SASE
Discount: 20% to 50%
Goods: name brand
Minimum Order: none
Shipping, Handling, Insurance: $4.95 minimum; UPS, PP, FOB Brooklyn
Sales Tax: NY deliveries
Accepts: check, MO, MC, V
$$$ (see text)

Focus has been in the electronics business since 1967 and offers mail-order shoppers the convenience of a 96-page catalog packed with buys on computer hardware and software, audio and video equipment, TVs, and appliances. We found learning and entertainment computers from Atari, Coleco, Commodore, Texas Instruments, and Timex/Sinclair, and an extensive array of accessories and software; home and personal computers by Eagle, NEC, Franklin, IBM, and Tava; peripherals and accessories from those companies and Amdek, Taxan, Zenith, Hayes, Novation, Anchor Automation, EPD, Epson, Brother, Juki, Okidata, and Smith-Corona; computer furniture from PCI and O'Sullivan; and a great selection of programs and blank disks and diskettes by Fuji, Maxell, Memorex, Verbatim, TDK, and IBM. Portable and hand-held computers and calculators from Hewlett-Packard, Texas Instruments, Sharp, Casio, and Canon are also offered.

The TV and video department stocks products by Panasonic, Sony, Sharp, JVC, RCA, Kodak, Kiwi, Recoton, Ambico, TeeGee, and Vidicraft. Focus carries compact and portable audio and components by Fisher, Aiwa, Sony, Panasonic, G.E., and Toshiba; and phones, phone machines, and communications devices from Record a Call, Cobra, ITT, Uniden, TeleConcepts, Muraphone, Webcor, GTE, Phone-Mate, Code-A-Phone, Sanyo, ATC, Zoom Telephonics (Demon Dialer), Electra (Freedom Phone, Bearcat), Panasonic, G.E., and Sony. The appliances include lines by Amana, Thermador, and Sharp (microwave ovens); G.E., Norelco, Remington, Clairol, Conair, Sanyo, Teledyne (Water Pik), Panasonic, Sunbeam, Eureka, Farberware, Moulinex, Presto, and KitchenAid. The Anova modular security system, Casio watches, Parker pens, Sanyo cash registers, Canon copiers, Casio keyboards, Nintendo and Vectrex video games, and Ledu lighting are also available. Planning a trip abroad? Focus carries Franzus adapters and currency-converters and a selection of name-brand electronics in 220-volt models.

The photography catalog was not available for review, but it offers still, movie, and video cameras, darkroom supplies and equipment, and optics by Agfa, Geveart, Berkey, Bosen, Bushnell, Canon, Celestron, Coast, Kodak, Elmo, Fuji, Hanimex, Ideal Photo, Ilford, Kazimar, Kiron, Kiwi, Leitz, Minolta, Nikon, Olympus, Panador, Pentax, Polaroid, Quantum, Ricoh, Smith-Victor, Tamron, Tokina, Vivitar, Yashica, and other manufacturers.

Prices run from 20% to 50% below suggested list or retail prices, and unused returns are accepted within ten days for exchange, refund, or credit. (Computer software cannot be returned.) Since prices fluctuate and what you're buying may be on sale at the time of your order, call or write for a price quote before placing your order.

CANADIAN READERS, PLEASE NOTE: orders are shipped to Canada *freight collect*.

FOTO ELECTRIC SUPPLY CO.

**31 Essex St.
New York, NY 10002
(212) 673–5222**

Information: price quote by letter with SASE
Discount: 30% minimum
Goods: name brand
Minimum Order: none
Shipping, Insurance: extra; UPS, PP, FOB NYC
Sales Tax: NY deliveries
Accepts: check, MO, MC, V, AE
$$$$

Foto has done very little advertising in its 22 years in business because its customers do it all gratis. Foto, which has been written up in almost every New York shopping guide, ships to Europe, Israel, South America, and Canada, as well as all over the U.S. It sells name-brand TVs (Sony, RCA, Zenith, etc.), video equipment, and videotape, and carries the top names in white goods: G.E., Westinghouse, Amana, Whirlpool, Maytag, Magic Chef, Thermador (ranges), and Sub-Zero (refrigerators). Foto also stocks many other name-brand goods—cameras by all the major manufacturers, plus film by Kodak, Fuji, Agfa, and Polaroid. You must *write* with the make and model number of what you need—*prices are not quoted over the phone*.

**HARRY'S DISCOUNTS &
APPLIANCES CORP.**

**8701 18th Ave.
Brooklyn, NY 11214
(718) 236–3507; 5150**

Information: price quote by phone or letter with
 SASE
Discount: 10% to 30%
Goods: name brand
Minimum Order: none
Shipping, Insurance: extra; UPS, FOB Brooklyn
Sales Tax: NY deliveries
Accepts: MO, certified check
$$

Harry's sells audio components, TV and video equipment, video tapes, and large appliances by every major manufacturer. You'll find every Hitachi line, Sony TVs, small appliances and air conditioners by almost every known manufacturer, as well as Fisher audio components, Eureka vacuum cleaners, and much more at Harry's. Large appliances and items that exceed UPS size/weight restrictions are shipped by truck *only* within the five boroughs of New York City, Long Island, and parts of New Jersey. Call or write (include a SASE) for a price quote.

**HUNTER AUDIO-PHOTO,
INC.**

**507 Fifth Ave.
New York, NY 10017
(212) 986–1540**

Video Movie Catalog: free
Product Flyers: free with SASE
Information: price quote by phone or letter with
 SASE
Discount: 20% to 60%
Goods: name brand
Minimum Order: none
Shipping, Handling: extra; UPS
Sales Tax: NY deliveries
Accepts: check, MO, certified check
$$$

Hunter Audio-Photo spells out exactly what it sells via mail, and describes the discounts on each line or manufacturer. Personal stereo (AKA portable audio, or musical earmuffs) by G.E., Sony, Panasonic, and Sanyo are 30% to 40% below list or retail; calculators by Hewlett-Packard, Casio, Texas Instruments, and Sharp are 30% to 45% off; Parker, Cross, and Mont Blanc pens are 30% to 50% below list. Save 20% on Timex watches, 40% on Bulova models, and 50% on Seiko styles. And the popular Ray Ban and Porsche Carrera sunglasses are reduced 30% to 40%. Information on these can be had by requesting a price quote by phone or letter. If writing, include a SASE and ask for any available flyers on that product category.

Hunter's "Video Yesteryear" catalog is a gold mine of old movies, TV shows, cartoons, documentaries, and propaganda—over 600 titles are listed with lively descriptions by Michael Kerbel, an associate professor of cinema at the University of Bridgeport. We found some of our all-time favorites, as well as scores we'd just like to see: the Powell/Lombard version of *My Man Godfrey,* Ella Fitzgerald in concert, Rene Laloux's *Fantastic Planet, Jungle Book* with Sabu as Mowgli, *The Blue Angel, It's a Wonderful Life, The 39 Steps,* Romero's *Night of the Living Dead, Metropolis* (original score), Paddy Chayevsky's "Marty," produced by the Goodyear TV Playhouse, and Harold Lloyd's silent classics. The tapes are sold in VHS and Beta 2 formats; Beta One and ¾-inch U-matic formats are available at an additional charge. Most of the movies are also made in Super-8 film and on PAL system video cassettes.

Hunter Audio-Photo has been in business since 1976 and stocks a much wider selection of goods for its store customers.

ILLINOIS AUDIO, INC.

**12 E. Delaware Pl.
Chicago, IL 60611
(312) 664–0020: inquiries
and IL orders
(800) 621–8042: orders
except IL**

Brochure: free; pub. monthly
Information: price quote by phone or letter with SASE
Discount: pricing 3% to 10% above net cost (see text)
Goods: name brand
Minimum Order: none
Shipping, Insurance: extra; $3 minimum; UPS, FOB Chicago
Handling: $3 on small items
Sales Tax: IL deliveries
Accepts: check, MO, certified check, MC, V
$$$

Illinois Audio has been selling top-of-the-line audio equipment and components since 1973. It carries components by A.D.C., Acoustic Research, Akai, Aiwa, Altec, Audio Control, Audio Pulse, Audio Technica, BASF, Betamax, D.B.X., Discwasher, Dual, Empire, Fuji, Jensen, JVC, Kenwood, Koss, Marantz, Maxell, MXR, Nortronics, Omnisonic, Onkyo, Audio Research, Pickering, Pioneer, Sansui, Sanyo, Scotch, Sennheiser, Shure, Sony, Stanton, TDK, Teac, Technics, and many more. All the goods are brand new and sent in factory-sealed cartons, under manufacturers' warranties. The discounts at Illinois are computed by adding 3% to 10% to the *net cost* of the goods (lower than the dealer cost), which results in 35% to 40% discounts on the suggested list prices. This firm's competitive position is summed up on the order form: "See a Better Price? Let Us Know! We Want Your Business!!"

INTERNATIONAL SOLGO, INC.

1745 Hempstead Tpk.
Elmont, NY 11003
(212) 675–3555: inquiries
and NY orders
(800) 645–8162: orders
except NY

Catalog: $5, refundable (see text)
Information: price quote by phone or letter with SASE
Discount: up to 40%
Goods: name brand
Minimum Order: $25 on prepaid orders; $50 on credit cards
Shipping, Insurance: extra; UPS, FOB Long Island
Sales Tax: NY deliveries
Accepts: check, MO, certified check, MC, V, AE, DC
$$$

International Solgo is one of the pioneers of discounting; it has been in business since 1933 selling goods at low, low prices. Solgo sells appliances, audio components, cameras, jewelry, and luggage, as well as a complete line of TV and video equipment, at discounts of up to 40%. The manufacturers stocked at Solgo include Magnavox, Philco, Quasar, G.E., Zenith, Sony, Panasonic, RCA, and Hitachi. Large, small, and personal-care appliances by Amana, Brown, Eureka, Clairol, Hoover, Charmglo, Garland, Magic Chef, Tappan, Caloric, Admiral, Conair, Hotpoint, Sankyo, Norelco, Mr. Coffee, Maytag, Litton, Rival, KitchenAid, Proctor Silex, Bunn, Norge, Sunbeam, Farberware, and many others are available. There are also several lines of lighters, Cross and Mont Blanc pens and pencils, cameras by Polaroid, Nikon, Minolta, Canon, Yashica, and other firms; audio components by Pioneer, Panasonic, Sankyo, Sanyo, JVC, Audiovox, and others; name-brand luggage, calculators, typewriters, and other office machines, and dual-voltage appliances as well. The discounts are calculated on a cost-plus basis, and Solgo is often found to have the best price in town by New York City bargain-hunters pricing audio components, TVs, or appliances. Current offerings are show cased in the catalog (deductible from purchases of $150 or more), or you can call or write (include a SASE) for a price quote.

JEMS SOUNDS, LTD.

785 Lexington Ave.
New York, NY 10021
(212) 838–4716

Information: price quote by letter with SASE
Discount: 10% to 40%
Goods: name brand
Minimum Order: none
Shipping: extra; UPS
Sales Tax: NY deliveries
Accepts: check, MO, MC, V
$$$

Jems Sounds sells audio components, TVs and video equipment, video games, cameras, calculators, phones and phone machines, and watches. The audio manufacturers represented here include Sony, Panasonic, Sanyo, Toshiba, Onkyo, Teac, Akai, Dual, JBL, Technics, and Marantz. Jems sells TVs and video equipment by Sony, Panasonic, Sanyo, Toshiba, RCA, Zenith, and JVC; video games by Atari; calculators by Sharp, Toshiba, Panasonic, Canon, Texas Instruments, Casio, and Hewlett-Packard; phones and phone machines by Phone-Mate, Record a Call, Sanyo, and ITT; watches by Bulova, Citizen, and Seiko; and cameras by major manufacturers. The discounts run up to 40%, and may go higher if Jems is running a special. Write for a price quote and include a SASE with your letter.

LEWI SUPPLY

15 Essex St.
New York, NY 10002
(212) 777–6910

Information: price quote by letter with SASE
Discount: 20% to 50%
Goods: name brand
Minimum Order: none
Shipping, Insurance: extra; UPS
Sales Tax: NY deliveries
Accepts: check, MO, certified check
$$$$

Lewi sells Brother sewing machines, Olivetti typewriters, Seiko watches, Mikasa china, a complete line of Sony products, and cameras by Yashica, Konica, and Canon. The prices run from 20% to 50% below retail. Write for a price quote, and include a SASE with your letter.

LVT PRICE QUOTE HOTLINE, INC.

Box 444, Dept. W84
Commack, NY 11725–0444
(800) 645–5010: orders,
brochure requests, and
price quotes

Brochure: free
Information: price quote by phone or letter with
  SASE
Discount: up to 40%
Goods: name brand
Minimum Order: $50
Shipping, Handling, Insurance: included on most
  goods (see text)
Sales Tax: NY deliveries
Accepts: check, postal MO, certified check
$$$

LVT gives you instant access to over 4,000 products from more than 110 manufacturers, at savings of up to 40% on suggested list or full retail prices. You can call or write for price quotes on major appliances, microwave ovens, air conditioners, TVs, video equipment and tapes, phones and answering machines, calculators, typewriters, scanners, radar detectors, radios, computers, and peripherals. LVT delivers within the continental United States, and prices include UPS shipping, handling, and insurance charges. Most goods exceeding UPS size/weight limits are delivered free to much of New York, New Jersey, and Connecticut; nonmailable goods sent outside the "local" boundaries are shipped FOB warehouse, freight collect. Complete information on price quotes, ordering, etc. are detailed in the brochure, along with a listing of the brands carried by LVT. PLEASE NOTE: all sales are final, and all goods are sold with valid manufacturers' warranties.

LYLE CARTRIDGES

115 So. Corona Ave.
Valley Stream, NY
11582–0158
(516) 599–1112: inquiries
and NY orders
(800) 221–0906: orders
except NY

Catalog: free with SASE; pub. in the spring and fall
Information: price quote by phone or letter with
  SASE
Discount: up to 75%
Goods: name brand
Minimum Order: $15 on prepaid orders; $25 on
  credit cards
Shipping, Handling, Insurance: $3 minimum; UPS,
  PP
Sales Tax: NY deliveries
Accepts: check, MO, MC, V
$$$$ (see text)

Lyle Cartridges has been in business since 1952 and is one of the best sources we've found for the cartridges, spindles, drive belts, and diamond styli that help make music in your life. If your stereo equipment is by Garrard, BIC, Thorens, Empire, Technics, or similar manufacturers, check Lyle for replacement parts. Lyle carries lines by Shure, Stanton, Audio Technica, Dynavector, ADC, Sonus, Audio Dynamics, Grado, Pickering, B & O, A-static, and Ortofon. Record-care products by Discwasher and LAST and replacement styli from Signet are also available. You can save up to 75% on cartridges and needles here, and Lyle will replace all defective goods.

CANADIAN READERS, PLEASE NOTE: There's a $5 minimum on air parcel post charges, and only U.S. funds are accepted in payment.

MID AMERICA VACUUM CLEANER SUPPLY CO.

666 University Ave.
St. Paul, MN 55104–4896
(612) 222–0763
(800) 622–4017: orders in MN
(800) 328–9430: orders except MN

Catalog: $5, refundable; pub. biannually
Information: price quote by phone or letter with SASE
Discount: 15% to 50%
Goods: name brand
Minimum Order: $15
Shipping, Insurance: extra; UPS, FOB St. Paul
Handling: $2 on orders under $15
Sales Tax: MN deliveries
Accepts: check, MO, certified check, MC, V
$$$

When bad things happen to good machines, you turn to your repair shop for solace and service. All too often, some callous appliance doctor tells you the thingamajig vital to the life of your appliance has been back-ordered for six months and may never arrive. If the appliance in question is a vacuum cleaner, floor machine, blender, coffee maker, iron, mixer, pressure cooker, shaver, or toaster, you may find help in Mid America's 256-page bible of parts and supplies.

This catalog, which is geared to the repair-shop owner, lists thousands of appliance components. More useful to the consumer are the bags, belts, light bulbs, attachments, and other paraphernalia that are usually replaced by the owner. Vacuum cleaners and floor machines dominate, and you can get a full range of parts for models by Airway, Compact, Electrolux, Eureka, Filter Queen, G.E. (Premier), Hoover, Kirby, MagNum, Panasonic, Progress/Colco (Mercedes), RCA/Oreck, Regina, Rexair, Royal, Sunbeam, and Soluvac (vacuum systems). Most of the parts are priced 30% below retail, and quantity discounts are offered. Please remember to consult your appliance manual for guidelines on what you can replace or repair yourself; if you attempt any other repairs you may void the warranty and create an electrical hazard as well. But if you're having the appliance serviced professionally and the part is not available at the shop or is very expensive (some motors are nearly $200), ask whether you can provide it yourself. Bring the catalog to the shop and have the service person show you what's needed— manufacturers' parts numbers won't do, since they're not listed in Mid America's catalog. Before you order, check the catalog date: The big book is published every two years, and price-list updates are issued in between. Request an update if your catalog is over a year old.

When repair bills start to approach replacement costs, it's probably time to retire the old vacuum. Mid America stocks brand-new models by Eureka, Hoover, Kirby, MagNum, Oreck, Panasonic, Progress (Mercedes), Rexair (Rainbow), Royal, Sanitaire, and Shop-Vac. Central vacuum systems are also available. Prices on the machines run from 15% to 50% below list, and some of the brands are difficult to find elsewhere. (We have yet to try any of the sleek Progress/Mercedes machines. If they're as efficient as they are handsome, they'll skew our other "ratings.") The vacuum cleaners and floor machines aren't listed in the catalog; you must call or write for a price quote.

Mid America has been in business since 1952 and guarantees all parts. Unused returns are accepted within 60 days.

ORECK CORPORATION

**100 Plantation Rd.
New Orleans, LA 70123
(504) 733–8761
(800) 535–8810: U.S. orders only**

Catalog: free
Discount: up to 40%
Goods: house brand
Minimum Order: none
Shipping, Handling, Insurance: extra; UPS, PP
Sales Tax: LA deliveries
Accepts: check, MO, MC, V, AE
$$$$

We know vacuum cleaners, because we've tried them all—canister models with water-filled collection receptacles; uprights that beat the rug and restore the nap; power nozzles, centralized systems, rechargeable hand-held units, industrial wet/dry models, "stick" styles, and many more. Each has its problems: price, versatility of function, suction power, weight, ease of storage, cost of repair, etc. Finding a vacuum cleaner that served all our needs and wasn't too large for the hall closet, too heavy to maneuver on the stairs, too difficult to repair, or too pricey seemed impossible, until we heard of the Oreck.

The Oreck XL888 is an upright that weighs just eight pounds, is 48″ tall, and has a powerful motor. The handle drops down without lifting the base off the floor, so it can get all the way under low furniture. It has an effective edge-cleaning device, and a 25-foot cord. Since dirt travels up the handle and drops into the bag, it doesn't block the suction. (This "top-fill" mechanism keeps the vacuum operating at optimum suction until the bag is completely full so efficiency is unimpaired and bags are not wasted.) And the XL888 hangs up neatly, using very little storage space. The price—$239.90—is reasonable for such a machine, but it's usually discounted 31% to $169, or $149 if you buy two or more. The XL888 is backed by a two-year limited warranty; a five-year motor warranty can be purchased for $12.50. In addition, it comes with a trouble-shooting guide and is designed to be repaired by the user. All replacement parts and instructions for installation are available from the firm.

The 32-page color catalog shows a range of other vacuum cleaners, including a four-pound hand-held model; a compact canister style with a cloth dustbag; a stick vacuum that converts to tank style with hose and wands; and several heavy-duty canister models for commercial and institutional use. In addition, Oreck has a 15-pound rug shampooer with a combing action that won't leave swirl marks in your carpet. Oreck also carries power-failure lights, nonelectric carpet sweepers, powerful beam flashlights, and bags to fit Oreck, Hoover, Eureka, Panasonic, Whirlpool, Kenmore, and Electrolux vacuum cleaners (in case lots only). All goods are backed by a 30-day guarantee of satisfaction.

PERCY'S INC.

315 Grove St.
Worcester, MA 01605
(617) 755–5334: inquiries
and orders except MA
(800) 922–8194: MA orders

Information: price quote by phone or letter with SASE
Discount: 3% above dealer cost (see text)
Goods: name brand
Minimum Order: none
Shipping, Insurance: extra; UPS, PP, FOB Worcester
Sales Tax: MA deliveries
Accepts: check, MO, certified check, MC, V
$$$

Percy's has more than 50 years of experience backing its motto, "The difficult we do immediately. The impossible takes a few minutes longer." The firm sells washers, dryers, dishwashers, refrigerators, ranges, standard and microwave ovens, freezers, TVs and video equipment and tapes, dehumidifiers, disposals, and much more. The manufacturers include RCA,

Hotpoint, Panasonic, Maytag, Whirlpool, White-Westinghouse, Caloric, Regency, Jenn-Air, Mitsubishi, Zenith, Frigidaire, Magic Chef, KitchenAid, G.E., Litton (microwave ovens), Sylvania (TVs and video), Waste King, Quasar, and Thermador. The low markups—about 3% above wholesale cost—represent 30% to 50% discounts on list or full retail prices. Call or write for a price quote, and include a SASE with your letter.

S & S SOUND CITY

58 W. 45th St.
New York, NY 10036–4280
(212) 575–0210: inquiries
and NY orders
(800) 233–0360: orders
except NY

Brochure: free; pub. four to five times yearly
Information: price quote by phone or letter with SASE
Discount: 20% to 60%
Goods: name brand
Minimum Order: on blank tapes, six tapes
Shipping, Insurance: extra; UPS, PP, FOB NYC
Sales Tax: NY deliveries
Accepts: check, MO, certified check, MC, V
$$$

S & S has been in business since 1975 selling microwave ovens, air conditioners, audio components, and TV and video equipment. The owners claim to be "the nicest people in town," and will try to get you anything you want. (S & S takes special orders.) There is a complete selection of TVs and video equipment, phone machines, calculators, radios, car audio components, blank and recorded videotapes, and security and surveillance equipment. The TV, video, and audio manufacturers include Zenith, Toshiba, Quasar, RCA, Sanyo, Panasonic, Hitachi, JVC, Emerson, Sony, Akai, Fisher, G.E., Smith-Victor, Ambico, and Vidicraft, among others. There are VCR blanks and movies, phone machines by Panasonic, Record-a-Call, Teletender, AT&T, and Code-A-Phone; Panasonic tape recorders; Sharp security and surveillance equipment, microwave ovens by Sharp, Samsung, Toshiba, Amana, Litton, etc., and more. Call or write (include a SASE) for a price quote. Returns are accepted within seven days.

SALES CITI, INC.

27 Essex St.
New York, NY 10002
(212) 673-8383

Information: price quote by phone or letter with
    SASE
Discount: 10% to 40%
Goods: name brand
Minimum Order: $25
Shipping, Insurance: extra; UPS, FOB NYC
Sales Tax: NY deliveries
Accepts: check, MO, MC, V
$$$

This firm, also known as Sam's Sale Citi, is a real bargain emporium that sells a little of everything at savings of up to 40% on list or retail prices. There are audio components and personal stereo sets by Panasonic and Sony; TV and video equipment by Panasonic, Sony, Sharp, and Zenith; phones and phone machines by Sanyo, Phone-Mate, Code-A-Phone, and ITT; video games by Atari; Samsonite attaché cases; Seiko, Pulsar, Bulova, and Timex watches; and just about everything in small and personal-care appliances. You can call or write for a price quote. Include a SASE with your letter.

SEWIN' IN VERMONT

84 Concord Ave.
St. Johnsbury, VT 05819
(802) 748-3803: inquiries
and VT orders
(800) 451-5124: orders
except VT

Brochures: free
Information: price quote by phone or letter with
    SASE
Discount: 20% to 35%
Goods: name brand
Minimum Order: none
Shipping, Insurance: included on machines; extra
    on parts; UPS
Sales Tax: VT deliveries
Accepts: check, MO, MC, V
$$$

If you're shopping for a name-brand sewing machine but don't want to pay top-of-the-line prices, Sewin' in Vermont has the answer. It carries several of the best American and European brands, including Singer, Pfaff, and Viking, at prices 20% to 35% below list. Sewin' also sells parts for the machines, something to keep in mind when your local service center doesn't have stock or runs its repair department on the extortion principle ($15 for a $2 part to get a $500 machine running again). Sewin' also sells vacuum cleaners made by the best-known firm in the U.S. at very good savings. Advice is given freely over the phone by informed, helpful salespeople.

STEREO CORPORATION OF AMERICA

**1629 Flatbush Ave.
Brooklyn, NY 11210
(718) 253–8888: inquiries
and NY orders
(800) 221–0974: orders
except NY**

Catalog: free; pub. three times yearly
Information: price quote by phone or letter with
   SASE
Discount: up to 10% over cost (see text)
Goods: name brand
Minimum Order: none
Shipping: extra; UPS
Sales Tax: NY deliveries
Accepts: check, MO, MC, V
$$$

SCA, aka Stereo Warehouse/Video Warehouse, has been selling audio components at rock-bottom prices since 1951. There are goods from scores of manufacturers available at SCA, some of which are Teac, BASF, Audio Research, Bose, Onkyo, Technics, Aiwa, Akai, Shure, Pioneer, Yamaha, Sony, ADC, Harman Kardon, Sansui, Maxell, and TDK. The discounts are based on markups on manufacturers' costs, and prices run from cost to 10% above cost. You can interpret that to mean that savings on list prices will be 30% to 60%. To get the best price, call or write with the model or style number, and include a SASE with your letter.

STEREO DISCOUNTERS ELECTRONIC WORLD

**Stereo Equipment Sales, Inc.
6730 Santa Barbara Ct.
Baltimore, MD 21227
(301) 796–5810: customer
service
(301) 796–3980: price
quotes and orders in MD
and AK
(800) 638–3920: price
quotes and orders except
MD and AK**

Catalog: free; pub. twice yearly
Discount: up to 50%
Goods: name brand
Minimum Order: none
Shipping, Insurance: 5% of order value; $1.50
   minimum; UPS, PP, FOB Baltimore
Sales Tax: DE, MD, NJ, PA deliveries
Accepts: check, MO, MC, V, AE, DC
$$$ 🍁   (see text)

Stereo Discounters publishes a 112-page catalog of name brand electronics at savings of up to 50% on suggested list. Over 100 manufacturers are represented, from Allsop to Zenith. Stereo Discounters has an extensive audio department, including car stereo, digital audio, a full range of components, headphones, reel-to-reel decks, studio (recording) products, portable and personal stereo, blank tapes, and record-care products. Video cameras, VCRs, enhancers, games, tapes, cases, and a range of accessories and tape-care products are sold, in addition to phones and phone machines, radar detectors, and related goods. And Stereo Discounters offers a small selection of computers and peripherals, software, diskettes, and maintenance products. O'Sullivan audio, home-entertainment, TV, and computer furniture and work stations and Plateau speaker stands are also sold.

Stereo Discounters is staffed by 14 home-electronics consultants who can recommend components and systems to suit your needs and budget. Authorized returns are accepted. Most deliveries outside the continental U.S. (to Alaska, Hawaii, Puerto Rico, the Virgin Islands, and Canada) are sent freight collect, and shipping charges are quoted on individual orders.

THE VIDEOTIME CORP.

---

48 Urban Ave., Dept. AB26
Westbury, NY 11590
(516) 333–5300: inquiries
and NY orders
(800) 645–2317: orders
except NY

Literature: $1, refundable; pub. six times yearly
Information: price quote by phone or letter with SASE
Discount: 20% to 60%
WBMC Reader Discount: 10% (see text)
Goods: name brand
Minimum Order: $50 on credit cards
Shipping, Handling, Insurance: extra; UPS, PP
Sales Tax: NY deliveries
Accepts: check, MO, MC, V
$$$$

Videotime sells VCRs, cameras, accessories, and tapes by Sony, Panasonic, JVC, Magnavox, Quasar, Hitachi, Toshiba, Sanyo, RCA, and Bogen (tripods). Franklin computers and compatible programs are also available, and all of Videotime's prices are 20% to 60% below suggested list or retail. The company is offering readers of this book a 10% discount on the product prices. When you request the price quote, make sure shipping, handling, and other surcharges are listed separately. Compute the tax, if applicable, on the total, and deduct 10% of the product price from that figure to determine your final price with the WBMC discount.

Videotime has been selling by mail since 1976 and publishes a brochure of specials every other month. Corporate and commercial business is welcome—purchase orders are accepted and the terms are ten days net.

WISAN TV & APPLIANCE INC.

4085 Hylan Blvd.
Staten Island, NY 10308
(718) 356-7700

Information: price quote by phone or letter with SASE
Discount: 10% to 40%
Goods: name brand
Minimum Order: none
Shipping: extra; UPS, FOB NYC
Sales Tax: NY deliveries
Accepts: check, MO, MC, V
$$$

Wisan has been in business since 1946 and has been selling major appliances and TV and video equipment at discount prices by mail for six years. Mr. Wisan tells us that they "shoot straight and try to get the best prices," and says his firm will take special orders for goods not in stock. Some of the appliance manufacturers carried at Wisan are Frigidaire, Hotpoint, G.E., Caloric, Whirlpool, Maytag, Magic Chef, White-Westinghouse, Tappan, Sub-Zero, Amana, Chambers, Waste King, Thermador, KitchenAid, and Jenn-Air. Wisan also stocks TV and video equipment by Zenith, Quasar, G.E., RCA, Sony, Hitachi, and Toshiba.

If you live near New York City, Wisan can service your goods. The firm will ship anywhere, but asks customers outside New York, New Jersey, and Connecticut to note that delivery charges on major appliances tend to offset savings. For the bottom line, call or write for a price quote and shipping estimate.

WISCONSIN DISCOUNT STEREO

2417 W. Badger Rd.
Madison, WI 53713
(608) 271-6889: inquiries and WI orders
(800) 356-9514: orders except WI

Information: price quote by phone or letter with SASE
Discount: 15% to 70%
Goods: name brand
Minimum Order: none
Shipping, Insurance: extra; UPS
Sales Tax: WI deliveries
Accepts: MO, MC, V, AE, C.O.D.
$$$

WDS, which began doing business by mail in 1977, told us it carries "every major brand of electronics—the largest selection in the United States, possibly in the world." Audio components, portable stereo, video equipment, and tapes are available. Call or write for a price quote, and include a SASE with your letter.

IRV WOLFSON COMPANY

3221 W. Irving Park Rd.
Chicago, IL 60618
(312) 267–7828, 9136:
inquiries and IL orders
(800) 621–1468: orders
except IL

Catalog: $4, refundable; pub. yearly in the spring
Information: price quote by phone or letter with SASE
Discount: 7% above cost (see text)
WBMC Reader Discount: 5% above cost on certain goods (see text)
Goods: name brand
Minimum Order: none
Shipping, Insurance: extra; UPS, PP, FOB Chicago
Sales Tax: IL deliveries
Accepts: MO, certified check, MC, V, AE

$$$

If you have friends and relatives in foreign countries or are relocating abroad, you'll find this company's 40-page "Overseas Appliance Catalog" a great resource. Wolfson has been selling 220-volt/50-cycle appliances and electronics for over 30 years, at prices 7% over cost (from 25% to 40% below retail or list prices). Domestic-current goods, as well as some furniture, are also offered.

The foreign-current products include TVs and video equipment, white goods (washers, dryers, refrigerators, stoves, etc.), microwave ovens, air conditioners, audio components and portable stereo, kitchen appliances, vacuum cleaners, personal-care appliances, electric blankets, and power tools. White-Westinghouse, G.E., Amana, Caloric, Roper, Sub-Zero, Thermador, Modern Maid, Gaggenau, Maytag, Zenith, Panasonic, RCA, Sharp, Singer, Black & Decker, Eureka, KitchenAid, Oster, Jenn-Air, and JVC are among the brands represented. "Stepdown" autotransformers, which permit use of domestic appliances on foreign current, are also stocked, as well as current-converters and plug adapters. The catalog includes model information but no prices; call or write for a quote. Wolfson can supply the names of factory-authorized service centers worldwide, and stocks spare and replacement parts for the goods it carries. The company can also convert video tapes from PAL-SECAM to U.S. formats, and vice versa.

Wolfson inventories domestic-current white goods, TVs, audio components, and video equipment, plus furniture by Motif and Carleton at 40% off list, recliners from Catnapper and Berkline, Sealy and Therapeutic bedding, and dinette sets by Chromecraft, Daystrom, Douglas, Dinex, and Kofabco.

Readers of this book are entitled to extra savings on goods by G.E., Caloric, Sub-Zero, and Thermador. If you identify yourself as a WBMC reader, the markup on dealer cost is 5% instead of 7% on products from these companies. Wolfson can answer any questions you might have on sending goods abroad.

SEE ALSO:

American Marine Electronics . . . name-brand marine electronics . . .
AUTO

Comp-U-Card . . . name-brand appliances, electronics . . . GENERAL

E & B Marine, Inc. . . . name-brand marine electronics . . . AUTO

Executive Photo & Supply Corp . . . name-brand personal stereo and video
. . . CAMERAS

The Finals . . . personal stereo, fitness-related electronics . . . CLOTHING

Fiveson Food Equipment, Inc. . . . commercial restaurant equipment . . .
HOME (kitchen)

47st Photo, Inc. . . . name-brand microwave ovens, personal stereo, TV,
video, etc. . . . CAMERAS

Garden Camera . . . name-brand video equipment . . . CAMERAS

Goldberg's Marine . . . name-brand marine electronics . . . AUTO

Greater New York Trading Co. . . . name-brand appliances, TVs,
typewriters, vacuum cleaners, etc. . . . HOME (table settings)

Jilor Discount Office Machines, Inc. . . . name-brand phones, phone
machines, calculators . . . OFFICE

Kaplan Bros. Blue Flame Corp. . . . Garland commercial stoves . . . HOME
(kitchen)

Lamp Warehouse/New York Ceiling Fan Center . . . name-brand ceiling fans
. . . HOME (decor)

Maine Discount Hardware . . . name-brand appliances . . . TOOLS

Mast Abeam . . . name-brand marine electronics . . . AUTO

Olden Camera & Lens Co., Inc. . . . name-brand video equipment . . .
CAMERAS

Opticon Laboratories, Inc. . . . film transferred to video cassettes . . .
CAMERAS

Pearl Brothers Office Machinery & Equipment . . . name-brand typewriters,
office machines, repairs . . . OFFICE

Typex Business Machines, Inc. . . . name-brand typewriters, calculators,
office machines, supplies . . . OFFICE

Warehouse Marine Discount . . . name-brand marine electronics . . . AUTO

West Side Camera Inc. . . . name-brand video cassettes . . . CAMERAS

Whole Earth Access . . . name-brand appliances, electronics . . .
GENERAL

ART, ANTIQUES, AND COLLECTIBLES

Fine art, limited editions,
antiques, and collectibles.

Since antiques and collectibles can be investments as well as objects of pleasure, you should make every effort to buy them at close to wholesale or dealer prices. That way when it's time to sell, you may make money from their appreciation in value in addition to putting the "dealer" markup in *your* pocket. Get to know the market so you can buy wisely. The latest edition of *The Kovel's Complete Antiques Price List* will give you an idea of the price spread among items of similar description and vintage. It doesn't teach you about antiques but it can tell you the going rate for thousands of antiques selling in the U.S. market.

It's best to know what you want when buying by mail, for you're not likely to get more than a photo of the items available. And remember that one-of-a-kind items might be sold out, so give second and third choices, if possible. Don't worry about import duties when buying from the foreign sources—certified antiques and art may be imported duty-free.

ANTIQUE IMPORTS UNLIMITED

P.O. Box 2978
Covington, LA 70434–2978
(504) 892–0014

Price Lists: see text
Discount: 40% to 60%
Goods: antique and antiquated
Minimum Order: varies (see text)
Shipping, Handling, Insurance: extra; PP
Sales Tax: LA deliveries
Accepts: check, MO, certified check, MC, V
$$$$

We've watched this firm move from Ireland (in our first edition) to England (in our second), and now find it stateside in Louisiana (after a run in Nevada). If it were any firm other than Antique Imports, formerly Gand Ltd., we would wonder. But this antiques emporium, which seems to function as the clearinghouse for every Victorian estate in the British Isles, is quite reliable. Prices for its antique collectibles, jewelry, maps, prints, and paintings are much lower here than in antique shops, and Antique Imports supplies dealers whose markups are often 100% or more. Detailed descriptions of each item and its condition are given in the price lists. Because there are no illustrations, it helps to have a sense of imagination and adventure when ordering.

Antique Imports publishes lists for five different categories of antiques. Sample lists are available for $1 each or on a yearly subscription basis. The "Antique and Collectible Jewelry" list (published 10 to 12 times yearly, $12 subscription) includes such items as a Victorian horseshoe-and-leaf motif brooch, c. 1890, for $20, a Georgian mourning ring for $115, and many such bargains. The minimum order from this list is $30. "Antiques and Collectibles" includes Staffordshire pieces, bisque dolls, articles of pewter, brass, and bone; lace collars, clocks, antique bobbins, celluloid dressing sets, and hundreds of other fascinating things. A year's subscription is $5 (three to five lists), and the minimum order is $30. The "Antique Maps, Prints, and Paintings" list costs $5 for three to five issues yearly, and catalogs scores of maps—many of American geography—at a few dollars to several hundred dollars each. The minimum order is $30. "Antiquities," listing products from ancient Egypt, Greece, Persia, Rome, and the British Isles, is truly exotic, with items like an ancient three-strand necklace of beads, Egyptian, ca. 1,500 B.C., at just $50. The subscription is $5 for a year of three to five lists. The minimum order is $30. Curiosity-seekers will relish the lists of "Old Legal Documents," (three to five issues for $5), that describe old indenture papers and wills. Surnames are all noted in the listings; if your family tree includes such names as Shrapnell, Neat, Lazarus, Diggle, or Meatyard, you might come across something of genealogical interest here.

Since antiques are all one-of-a-kind and subject to prior sale, do list second choices. When paying for sample lists, use a check or money order.

GEORGE CHANNING ENTERPRISES

P.O. Box 342
Carmel, CA 93921
(408) 372–0873

Brochure: $3.50, refundable
Discount: 30% to 60%
Goods: house brand
Minimum Order: none
Shipping, Handling, Insurance: $3.50 per order; UPS
Sales Tax: CA deliveries
Accepts: check, MO, MC, V, AE
$$$

The Channing catalog invites you to "discover the treasure of a bygone era," and shows dozens of striking reprints of illustrations that originally appeared over a century ago in *Harper's Weekly*. There's "The Launch of the Atlanta," celebrating a now-forgotten moment; a montage of illustrations on "Law and Moonshine"; a great boating close-up called "Yacht Racing"; and a fashion review, among others. The prices are $10 to $12 a print, and if you order four you'll receive "Mother and Child," a Käthe Kollwitz print, which sells here for $19. Other bonus offers are made on a regular basis.

DECOR PRINTS

---

277 Main St.
P.O. Box 502
Noel, MO 64854
(417) 475–6367

Catalog: $3, refundable; pub. yearly
Discount: 50% (see text)
Goods: house brand
Minimum Order: 15 prints (see text)
Shipping, Insurance: $3.50 on orders under 15
    prints; included on 15 or more; UPS, PP
Sales Tax: MO deliveries
Accepts: check, MO, certified check, C.O.D.
$$$

Decor Prints sells reproductions of well-known oil paintings and Victorian lithographs for $1.50 to $8 each. The color catalog shows each print, from copies of treasures by Gainsborough, Brueghel, Degas, Renoir, and other greats, to the reproductions of nostalgic turn-of-the-century lithographs, advertising posters, and magazine illustrations. A selection of nostalgic themes is also offered on note cards. The prices are already low, but you can deduct 50% if you order 15 prints or more.

EUSTON GALLERY

62/64 Hampstead Rd.
London NW1 2NU
England
Phone #01–388–6811

Leaflet: free
Discount: up to 30%
Goods: original art
Minimum Order: none
Shipping, Handling, Insurance: 20% of order value
Duty: extra (if applicable)
Accepts: check or IMO
$$

In addition to surplus clothing and government goods, Laurence Corner sells art. The Euston Gallery affiliate carries original art—oil paintings, engravings, prints, lithographs, mezzotints, pastels, and more—and will send a leaflet upon request. Past issues have shown paintings from Africa and Australia, Victorian works, and much more. The prices are quite reasonable, and Euston Gallery will advise you of the artist, general condition, and market trends of any pictures that interest you.

THE FRIAR'S HOUSE

Bene't St.
Cambridge CB2 2QN
England
Phone # 223–60275

Price List: free; pub. yearly
Discount: 25% to 60%
WBMC Reader Savings: see text
Goods: name brand
Minimum Order: none
Shipping, Handling, Insurance: included; airmail
Duty: extra
Accepts: check, IMO, MC, V, AE, DC, EC, Access
$$

   The Friar's House sells the exquisite modern paperweight editions by St. Louis, Selkirk Glass, Baccarat, Caithness Glass, and Perthsire, at prices as much as 60% less than those charged in the U.S. The price list does not have illustrations, but the collector who keeps up with new issues will know which is which. The weights are sold with the provision that you may return them if not pleased. The House also sells English hand-painted enamels, "made in the Bilston-Battersea tradition." These include boxes and bibelots by Crummles and Staffordshire. You may request the separate catalog, which is also free.

   In addition, fine china and crystal is available. You can write for prices on lines by Royal Doulton, Minton, Spode, Waterford, Wedgwood, Royal Worcester, Waterford, Edinburgh, Webb Corbett, Royal Brierly, Baccarat, and St. Louis. If you order, be sure to mention that you are a reader of this book, which entitles you to free packing and insurance on your purchases (mailing fees are charged).

A. GOTO

1-23-9 Higashi Shibuya Ku
Tokyo
Japan

Price List: $1, refundable; pub. yearly
Information: inquiries by letter
Discount: up to 75%
Goods: antique, antiquated, new
Shipping, Insurance: extra; surface mail, airmail
Duty: extra (if applicable)
Accepts: IMO
$$$

   While the Victorians were producing the bibelots that fill the lists of Antique Imports Unlimited, the Japanese were creating their own—in a very different spirit. A. Goto's collection of Japanese antiques circa 1850 to 1900 runs from silver acupuncture needles at 60¢ each to wood-block prints for $300.

Goto's price list has no illustrations, but we were sent several photos of ivory and stag horn netsuke ($25 to $60), carved wood netsuke, wood-block print books ($15 to $100), amber netsuke, old Chinese silver pieces, and the scarce ivory inro ($100 to $200). The only less-than-antique pieces we saw were the Burmese jadeite items, identified by an antiques dealer from the photographs as being of recent origin. Even *they* are real bargains, at $2 to $15 each. For the range of netsuke alone—in ivory, wood, black coral, amber, stag horn, hornbill, ivory "nut," and porcelain, as well as "erotic" and "manju" types—this source is a collector's must. Please note: Goto selects the individual items—you indicate the category of goods and materials. There are no returns permitted.

MISCELLANEOUS MAN

P.O. Box 1776
New Freedom, PA 17349
(717) 235–4766

Catalog: $3; $5 for two issues; pub. twice yearly
Discount: 30% plus
Goods: original, antique
Minimum Order: $50 on credit cards
Shipping, Insurance: $3 minimum; UPS, PP
Sales Tax: PA deliveries
Accepts: check, MO, MC, V
$$$

George Theofiles, ephemerologist extraordinaire, is the moving force behind Miscellaneous Man. He trades in vintage posters, handbills, graphics, labels, guides, brochures, and other memorabilia (including a catalog or two), all of which are original—no reproductions or reprints are sold. Among the listings you'll find theater posters, publicity photographs, handbills, promotional giveaways, circus posters and broadsides, advertising posters, and miscellany collected from all over the world. Someone somewhere saved WW II ration books, unused sardine-can labels, old insurance calendars, Army recruiting leaflets, Ku Klux Klan membership applications and other such material, and they're all here at prices that we found to be 30% or more below the going rate. One caution: stock moves very quickly so order as soon as you can. Returns are accepted within 3 days after receipt.

MUSEUM EDITIONS NEW YORK LTD.

105 Hudson St.
New York, NY 10013
(212) 431–1913: inquiries
and NY orders
(800) 221–9576: orders
except NY

Catalog: $4, refundable; free to corporate buyers
Information: price quote by phone or letter with
  SASE
Discount: 10%
WBMC Reader Discount: 20%
Goods: house brand
Minimum Order: none
Shipping, Insurance: extra; UPS, PP
Sales Tax: NY deliveries
Accepts: check, MO, MC, V
$$$

This three-year-old company produces a stunning 32-page catalog listing reproductions of the posters used to announce exhibits in museums and art galleries. If your taste runs to modern and contemporary art, you'll have a field day deciding what to choose for your walls. Among the artists in the catalog we saw were Klee, Pissarro, O'Keeffe, Rothko, Hopper, Hockney, Hiroshige, Glaser, and Randy Green. Prices run from about $10 to $30, and you can deduct 20% if you identify yourself as a WBMC reader. (This offer expires Dec. 1, 1986.) Should you get carried away and order more than 30 posters, Museum Editions will pay the shipping charges. Custom-framing is available; inquire for information. The company is actively soliciting corporate accounts, and its posters would be perfect as incentives and premiums. Inquire for terms.

QUILTS UNLIMITED

P.O. Box 1210, Dept. WBMC
Lewisburg, WV 24901
(304) 645–6556

Catalog and Photographs: $5; $20, year's
  subscription; pub. monthly
Discount: up to 40%
Goods: old, antique, new
Minimum Order: none
Shipping, Insurance: $4 for the first quilt, $2 each
  additional; UPS, PP
Sales Tax: WV deliveries
Accepts: check, MO, MC, V
$$$

You don't have to scour flea markets and country auctions for buys on vintage quilts: This enterprise does it for you. Quilts Unlimited, run by two avid collectors, established a mail-order department to serve the many who live far from good dealers and auctions. Five dollars brings you the booklet listing dozens of quilts; each description includes information on the material used, the number of stitches per inch, whether the work was done by hand or machine, whether signatures or dates are present, estimated age and provenance, the presence of any damage or wear, and size, pattern name, and price. You can find anything here—patchwork, appliqué, stuffed work, tops (the unquilted patchwork or appliqued top fabric without stuffing and bottom fabric; often with unfinished edges), crib quilts, Amish quilts, etc.

The midlevel collector will find a bounty in the $200 to $500 range, and prices do run about 40% less than those charged by antiques dealers for quilts of similar age, size, detail, and condition. Photographs of all the quilts are included with the price booklet, and listings are updated monthly. Returns are accepted within three days for full refund, so don't hesitate about ordering—we're told that half the quilts listed are sold by the end of each month. Quilts Unlimited also offers a number of books of interest to the collector, along with new hand-quilted crib quilts, custom services, and the delightful Barnaby Bear. He's made of nonrestorable patchwork quilt or woven coverlet pieces and costs $35. Reproduction Amish crib and doll quilts should make their appearance in future brochures, as well as quilting materials and supplies.

SAXKJAERS

53 Kømagergade
1150 Copenhagen K
Denmark
Phone # 45–1–11–07–77

Catalog and Brochures: free; pub. in the spring and fall
Discount: 40% minimum
Goods: name brand
Minimum Order: none
Shipping, Insurance: included, surface mail; extra, airmail
Duty: extra
Accepts: check or IMO
$$$

Saxkjaers, a family business founded in 1955, is the definitive source for collectors' plates issued by Royal Copenhagen and Bing & Grøndahl. The yearly issues of Christmas plates will stir even the tamest acquisitive instincts. But don't worry: unless you choose to buy the plates from earlier years, the habit is quite affordable. The brochures show Royal Copenhagen Christmas plates and the cup-and-saucer set, Bing & Grøndahl plates, Mother's Day plates from both firms, and china bells, thimbles, Olympic, and other special issues at savings of at least 40% on the U.S. prices. Back issues of many plates are available. Although prices indicate that appreciation is possible—an 1895 B&G plate is now worth $2,800—common sense cautions against treating limited editions as investments.

In addition to the plate brochures, we were sent a beautiful full-color catalog of Bing & Grøndahl figurines and vases. The selection of porcelain animals, children captured in scores of poses, romantic and character figures, and vases decorated with scenes should help solve many gift dilemmas. A smaller, 24-page color catalog and additional brochures feature the exquisite Mats Jonasson crystal "portraits." Beautifully detailed, lifelike images of animals are carved and etched by hand into irregular blocks of 32% lead crystal. A well-known Fifth Avenue crystal firm sells similar pieces for hundreds to thousands of dollars; at Saxkjaers, they run from $17 to $195, including shipping. Also shown are Royal Copenhagen figurines, vases, and dinnerware; Lladro figures, Bing & Grøndahl dinnerware, Atlantis crystal, Swarovski crystal whimsies; and Danish dolls and wooden toy soldiers. Prices at Saxkjaers include surface postage and insurance, and airmail shipping is available at a nominal surcharge.

The Saxkjaers family runs the entire company. Barely a day goes by when a U.S. visitor doesn't drop in, Mr. Saxkjaers tells us, and the coffee pot is always on for a customer, so drop by if you find yourself in Copenhagen. Saxkjaers is efficient as well as hospitable—letters and inquiries are answered the day they're received, and orders are covered by a money-back guarantee of satisfaction.

SEE ALSO:

Deepak's Rokjemperl Products . . . Indian oil paintings . . . JEWELRY
Dinosaur Catalog . . . collectible pewter and porcelain dinosaurs . . . TOYS
Doll House & Toy Factory Outlet . . . miniatures and collectible toys and dolls . . . TOYS
Dollsville Dolls and Bearsville Bears . . . collectible stuffed bears . . . TOYS
Front Row Photos . . . photos and photo buttons of rock stars . . . BOOKS
Greater New York Trading Co. . . . Lladro, Royal Doulton figurines . . . HOME (table settings)
Guitar Trader . . . vintage fretted instruments . . . MUSIC
Handart Embroideries . . . woven tapestries with animal motifs . . . CLOTHING
Irish Cottage Industries . . . crested Irish spoons . . . CLOTHING
Laurence Corner . . . authentic period theatrical costumes, militaria . . . CLOTHING
Mandolin Brothers Ltd. . . . vintage fretted instruments . . . MUSIC
Prince Fashions, Ltd. . . . oil paintings and copper artcraft on canvas . . . CLOTHING

Rainbow Music . . . vintage guitars and amps . . . MUSIC

Reject China Shops . . . porcelain figurines, collectibles . . . HOME (table settings)

The Renovator's Supply, Inc. . . . reproduction copper weather vanes . . . HOME maintenance

A.B. Schou . . . porcelain figurines, limited issues . . . HOME table settings

Nat Schwartz & Co., Inc. . . . porcelain figurines, collectibles . . . HOME (table settings)

Shannon Mail Order . . . Hummel and Goebel figurines, Peggy Nisbet dolls . . . HOME (table settings)

Albert S. Smyth Co., Inc. . . . porcelain figurines, collectibles . . . HOME (table settings)

Stecher's Limited . . . porcelain figurines, limited editions . . . HOME (table settings)

TAI, Inc. . . . silk-screened military insignias . . . CLOTHING

ART MATERIALS

Materials, tools, equipment,
and supplies for fine and
applied arts.

Name-brand art materials are seldom discounted more than 10% by retail shops unless they're purchased in quantity. But mail-order firms usually offer savings of twice that and also sell "proprietary" products. These are manufactured by lesser-known firms and are much less expensive than their branded equivalents—in fact, we know several working artists who buy nothing but. The firms listed here offer pigments, paper, brushes, canvas, frames, stretchers, pads, studio furniture, vehicles and solvents, silk-screening supplies, carving tools, and many other goods. For related products, see the listings in "Crafts and Hobbies."

DICK BLICK CO.

P.O. Box 1267
Galesburg, IL 61401–1267
(309) 343–6181: inquiries
(800) 322–8183: IL orders
(800) 477–8192: orders
except IL

Catalog: $2
Discount: up to 40%
Goods: name brand, house brand, generic
Minimum Order: $25
Shipping, Handling, Insurance: extra; UPS, FOB Galesburg
Sales Tax: IL, NV, PA deliveries
Accepts: check, MO, MC, V
$$$

Dick Blick lists over 20,000 items in its thick catalog of art supplies and equipment, which is geared to schools but can be used by anyone. Blick has *everything:* Liquitex paints, Shiva pigments, Crayola crayons and finger paints, drawing tables, paintbrushes, Alfac transfer letters, kraft paper, canvas, scissors, adhesives, silk-screening materials, display lighting, printmaking equipment, wood-carving tools, molding materials, kilns, glazes, copper enamels, decoupage, leather-working kits, dyes, macrame material, looms, art slides, blackboards, and *more.* Blick has been in the art-supply business for over 70 years and markets products under its own label at real savings compared to name-brand goods. Quantity discounts are offered, and the selection is unbeatable.

CROWN ART PRODUCTS CO., INC.

90 Dayton Ave., #18
Passaic, NJ 07055
(201) 777–6010

Catalog: free
Information: price quote by phone or letter with SASE
Discount: up to 65%
Minimum Order: none
Goods: house brand
Shipping, Insurance: extra; UPS, PP
Sales Tax: NJ deliveries
Accepts: check, MO, MC, V
$$$

Crown Art is best known to us for its discounts on metal section frames, which are sold here for 65% off suggested list prices. They're available in silver, gold, and black metal, in lengths up to 40 inches. Prices for stock lengths begin at $2.85 and go up to $12. Custom sizes and fractions are available, and assembly hardware is included free. Foam boards and hand-cut mats for mounting are also sold.

Raymond Topple, who runs Crown Art, is also a proficient silk-screen artist and illustrator. He's developed an entire line of supplies for the industry, from textile inks and dyes to unique screen systems, the screens themselves, tools, and other products. If you're a silk-screen artist, be sure to get the catalog just to see what's available, since Mr. Topple may have solved some problem you have with a unique material or tool. His special line of inks and colors is an inspiration in itself. In addition, the firm stocks inks for airbrushing, fabric paints, glass stains, artists' canvas (stretched and on rolls), stretcher bars, acrylic paints, and many other items for artist, student, and hobbyist. Monthly specials on closeouts, new products, and old standbys are offered at savings of 10% to 50%.

JERRY'S ARTARAMA, INC.

P.O. Box 1105W
New Hyde Park, NY
11040–4832
(718) 343–4545: inquiries
and AK, HI, NY orders
(800) 221–2323: orders
except AK, HI, NY

Catalog: $2, refundable; pub. in May and Nov.
Discount: 10% to 70%
Goods: name brand, generic
Minimum Order: $25; $50 on credit cards
Shipping, Handling, Insurance: $4 minimum; UPS, PP, FOB New Hyde Park
Sales Tax: NY deliveries
Accepts: check, MO, MC, V
$$$$

Jerry's Artarama publishes a 154-page compendium of materials, tools, and equipment for sculpture, graphic arts, drafting, calligraphy, block printing, printmaking, fabric painting, sumi-e, scratch art, stained glass, and other arts and avocations. You'll find everything in pigments from fine oils to finger paints, and a comprehensive selection of brushes, vehicles and solvents, studio furniture, lighting, overhead-projection equipment, canvas and framing materials, papers for every purpose, film products, airbrushing equipment, clays and moulage supplies, wood-carving tools, books and manuals, and much more. Depending on the product and the quantity purchased, you can save up to 70% on goods by Grumbacher, Holbein, Rowney, Pelikan, Blockx, Lefrank & Bourgeois, Winsor & Newton, Robert Simmons, Isabey, Caran d'Ache, Higgins, Conte, Koh-I-Noor, Stabilo, Gillott, Speedball, Letraset, Chartpak, Stanrite, Neolt, Ledu, X-Acto, Fredrix, D'Arches, Fabriano, Paillard, Deka, and Iwata, among others. Imported goods seldom sold at a discount are competitively priced. Color charts and additional product information are available upon request. Jerry's backs every purchase with an unconditional guarantee of satisfaction.

PEARL PAINT

---

308 Canal St.
New York, NY 10013
(212) 431–7932: inquiries
and NY orders
(800) 221–6845: orders
except NY

Catalog: $1, deductible; pub. twice yearly
Discount: 20% to 60%
Goods: name brand, house brand, generic
Minimum Order: $50
Shipping, Insurance: extra; UPS, FOB New York
  City
Sales Tax: FL, NJ, NY deliveries
Accepts: check, MO, certified check, MC, V
$$$

Pearl Paint is known throughout New York City as one of the best discount sources for art and crafts supplies. The catalog lists a representative sample, but you can get materials for every possible craft and just about any fine-art material, tool, or piece of equipment from Pearl. A small sampling of the brands stocked includes Grumbacher, Winsor & Newton, Holbein, Bellini, Paasche, Fabriano, and Pelikan, but there are many more. Pearl has been in business for over 50 years, and if the staff can't locate something for you at the store, it can tell you which other art-supply house carries it. Discounts range from 20% to 60%, and specials bring the prices down even further.

STU-ART SUPPLIES, INC.

2045 Grand Ave.
Baldwin, NY 11510–2999
(516) 546–5151: inquiries
and NY orders
(800) 645–2855: orders only
except NY

Catalog and Samples: free
Discount: up to 50%
Goods: name brand
Minimum Order: varies
Shipping, Insurance: extra on orders under $250;
UPS, FOB Baldwin
Sales Tax: NY deliveries
Accepts: check, MO, MC, V
$$$$

Stu-Art carries the well-known Nielson line of metal frames for flat mounting, stretched-canvas mounting, and dimensional-art (deep) mounting. The frames are easily assembled and can be cut to order. They are offered in gold, silver, and six other finishes. The prices run from $1.90 for a pair of 5-inch standard-width segments to $7.50 for two 40-inch segments (two pairs make up one frame). Stu-Art also sells reversible duo-color, acid-free mats in ten colors, regular mats in 18 colors, nonglare or clear plastic for use in place of glass, wood and tenite section frames, and shrink film and dispensers. By putting together your own frames, you can save more than 50% on the cost of packaged frames and have the added advantage of having them cut to order, if desired. If you have an oddly sized or very large picture, you'll be able to save even more, since some shops charge extra for nonstandard sizes.

PLEASE NOTE: don't use the WATS line to request a catalog. If you want to call instead of writing, use the "inquiries" number.

UTRECHT ART AND DRAFTING SUPPLY

33 35th St.
Brooklyn, NY 11232
(718) 768–2525

Catalog: free
Discount: 25% to 50%
Goods: name brand, house brand
Minimum Order: $40
Shipping, Insurance: extra; UPS, FOB Brooklyn
Sales Tax: NY deliveries
Accepts: check or MO
$$$

Utrecht has been selling professional art, sculpture, and printmaking supplies and equipment since 1949, and happens to manufacture some of the best-priced oil and acrylic paints on the market. The products available here include canvas, stretchers, frames, pads, paper, brushes, tools of all kinds, books, easels, tables, pigments, palettes, and much more. In addition to Utrecht's own line, materials by Grumbacher, Eberhard Faber, Chartpak, Strathmore, Pentel, Niji, and other manufacturers are available. The catalog packs over 50 pages with products and information. Utrecht offers discounts of 5% to 20% on the already low prices on certain goods bought in quantity.

SEE ALSO:

Bettinger's Luggage Shop . . . artists' portfolios . . . LEATHER
Carry-On Luggage, Inc. . . . artists' portfolios . . . LEATHER
Innovation Luggage . . . artists' portfolios . . . LEATHER
Thai Silks . . . silk squares for fabric painting . . . CRAFTS
Utex Trading Enterprises . . . silk squares for fabric painting . . . CRAFTS

AUTO AND MARINE

Parts, supplies, maintenance
products, and services.

If you haven't shopped for mail-order auto parts before, you're in for a pleasant surprise. Savings of 30% to 50% are almost routine; because many of the firms are located off the beaten track, they can rent their warehouses for less, stock more, and pass savings on to you. Quick shipment is another feature of many of these firms. They know that if they can't provide a part immediately, the customer will go elsewhere for it. These firms sell everything you could possibly need for your auto, motorcycle, RV, truck, or van (with a few exceptions), including mufflers, shocks, tires, and batteries. Some also stock products for vintage cars as well. And look here for one of the best values around on parts—salvaged goods. Expect savings of up to 70% compared to the price of new parts, and note the guarantees of satisfaction offered by most of these firms. (They wouldn't be around long if their goods didn't survive well.)

If you've spent anywhere from a few hundred to tens of thousands of dollars on a canoe, sailboat, or yacht, you'll want to minimize the upkeep expenses. Save up to 75% on the cost of maintenance products and equipment by buying from these suppliers, who sell every type of coating, tool, and device to keep your vessel afloat. Exhaustive selections of electronics, hardware, instruments, and other goods are offered, as well as galley accoutrements and foul-weather clothing. Even landlubbers should take a look through these catalogs if they're interested in well-designed slickers and oiled sweaters. The handsome teak bath and kitchen fixtures designed for yacht installations are equally useful on terra firma.

If you're interested in purchasing an auto through one of the car-buying services that sell at $125 over dealer price, see the listing for Comp-U-Card in "General Merchandise."

If you do your own mechanical work, you'll find the factory-service manual written for your car an invaluable aid. Manuals for hundreds of models are available for under $15 from Carbook, 181 Glen Ave., Sea Cliff, NY 11579. Request the free catalog, which also lists a range of do-it-yourself books on other topics.

**AMERICAN MARINE
ELECTRONICS**

2 Wilton Ave.
Norwalk, CT 06851
(203) 846–9412: inquiries
and CT orders
(800) 243–0264: orders
except CT

Catalog: free; pub. Jan., May, Sept.
Information: price quote by phone or letter with
  SASE
Discount: 40%
Goods: name brand
Minimum Order: none
Shipping, Insurance: extra; UPS
Handling: $3 per order
Sales Tax: CT deliveries
Accepts: check, MO, MC, V
$$$

American Marine has been in business since 1980 selling *everything* in electronics for sailing vessels. It carries products by scores of manufacturers, running from ACR to Xintex. You'll find depth sounders, compasses, auto-pilots, CB radios, battery chargers, VHF radios, lorans, radar equipment, and much more. We are not sailing people, but one item caught our attention: a fighting chair. The example shown was by Marlin Marine. It resembled a cross between a deck chair and a dentist's seat. Other models are available, and since they're expensive (the one we saw listed for $3,800), be sure to consult American for prices before buying elsewhere. Authorized returns are accepted.

**BELLE TIRE
DISTRIBUTORS, INC.**

Competition Division
12190 Grand River
Detroit, MI 48204
(313) 834–3880

Information: price quote by phone or letter with
  SASE
Discount: 25% to 35%
Goods: name brand
Minimum Order: none
Shipping, Insurance: extra; FOB Detroit
Sales Tax: MI deliveries
Accepts: check or MO
$$

You can buy radial tires here by Michelin, B.F. Goodrich, Goodyear, Pirelli, Uniroyal, and Trams Am, for up to 35% below list prices. Write or call Belle Tire with the model name of the tires you want to get the current price.

**CAPITAL CYCLE
CORPORATION**

**2328 Champlain St. N.W.
Washington, DC 20009
(202) 387–7360**

Catalog: free; pub. yearly
Discount: 20% to 50%
Goods: name brand
Minimum Order: $15 on prepaid orders; $25 on
  credit cards
Shipping: included on orders of $250 or more;
  UPS, PP
Sales Tax: DC deliveries
Accepts: check, MO, certified check, MC, V
$$$

Capital Cycle publishes a 78-page catalog of imported BMW motorcycle parts. The inventory of over 4,000 items includes genuine and original BMW parts manufactured from 1955 through the current year. Catalog prices run up to 50% off list, and quantity discounts are available. If you need repairs on a BMW part, don't hesitate to write—the service department handles these by mail as well.

**CENTRAL MICHIGAN
TRACTOR & PARTS**

**2713 N. U.S. Hwy. 2
St. Johns, MI 48879
(517) 224–6802: inquiries
(800) 292–9233: MI orders
(800) 248–9263, 348–7187:
orders except MI**

Information: price quote by phone or letter
Discount: up to 50%
Goods: used, salvaged
Minimum Order: none
Shipping, Insurance: extra; UPS
Sales Tax: MI deliveries
Accepts: check, MO, certified check, MC, V
$$$

This firm, also known as Tractor Salvage, can save you up to 50% on parts for tractors and combines. It stocks used parts, which are backed by a guarantee of 30 days, and can supply you with anything from starters to cylinder blocks, for machines made by almost any major manufacturer. Some of the goods are reconditioned, and some rebuilt; a rebuilt part is overhauled completely and you can expect it to function as well and for as long as a new one. Call or write with details of what you're looking for. If it's not in stock, your needs can be added to the want-list.

CHERRY AUTO PARTS

5650 N. Detroit Ave.
Toledo, OH 43612
(419) 476–7222: customer service
(800) 472–8639: OH orders and inquiries
(800) 537–8677: orders and inquiries except OH

Information: price quote by phone or letter with SASE
Discount: up to 70% over cost of new parts
Goods: used foreign-car parts
Minimum Order: none
Shipping: extra; UPS, FOB Toledo
Sales Tax: OH deliveries
Accepts: MO, certified check, MC, V
$$$

Why pay top dollar for new car parts if you can get perfectly good ones, used, for up to 70% less? Cherry Auto Parts, "The Midwest's Leading Foreign Car Dismantler," can supply foreign car parts for your Alfa Romeo, Austin, BMW, Datsun, Fiat, Honda, Jaguar, Mercedes, Porsche, Renault, Saab, Toyota, VW, or other auto. New fenders and hoods are also available at a fraction of dealer list price.

Cherry has almost 40 years of experience in the parts business and makes this pledge to its customers: All parts are guaranteed in stock at the time of quotation, and guaranteed to be the correct part and in good condition, as described. Credit-card orders can be shipped the same day (if the order is placed before 12 P.M.), or within 24 hours. Write with a description of the part you need, or call toll-free.

CLARK'S CORVAIR PARTS, INC.

Rte. 2
Shelburne Falls, MA 01370–9748
(413) 625–9776, 9731: information
(413) 625–2558: order recording

Catalog: $4; pub. biannually
Discount: up to 50%
Goods: name brand, generic
Minimum Order: $7
Shipping, Insurance: extra; UPS, PP
Handling: $2 on orders under $7
Sales Tax: MA deliveries
Accepts: check, MO, certified check
$$$ (see text)

Clark's Corvair Parts lists its inventory of over 4,500 Corvair parts in a 400-page catalog that's published every even-numbered year. Between the exhaustive stock and savings of up to 50%, the catalog is an indispensable resource for any Corvair owner. Clark's carries original and replacement GM parts, reproductions, and goods by Chevrolet, TRW, Gabriel, Clevite, as well as over 400 other suppliers. The catalog is completely indexed so you'll have no problem locating what you need. Returns are accepted but a restocking fee may be charged. (Complete terms and sales policy are given in the catalog.)

CANADIAN READERS, PLEASE NOTE: Canadian funds are not accepted. Clark's recommends using a postal money order payable in U.S. funds.

CLINTON CYCLE & SALVAGE, INC.

6709 Old Branch Ave.
Camp Springs, MD 20748
(301) 449–3550: inquiries
and MD orders
(800) 332–8264: orders
except MD

Price List: free
Information: price quote by phone or letter with SASE
Discount: up to 75%
Goods: new, used, salvage
Minimum Order: $15 on credit cards
Shipping, Insurance: extra; UPS
Sales Tax: MD deliveries
Accepts: check, MO, MC, V, AE, CHOICE
$$$

Clinton handles new and used parts for road bikes that are 250cc or larger. Parts for Honda, Suzuki, and Kawasaki cycles are also available. If you need large parts, such as engines, write with details and Clinton will put your name and needs on the want-list. Many of the parts are used and salvaged, so expect a savings of up to 75% compared to the prices of new parts. Clinton also features a large accessories department. Satisfaction is guaranteed.

DEFENDER INDUSTRIES, INC.

255 Main St.
New Rochelle, NY 10801
(914) 632–3001

Catalog: $1; pub. yearly
Information: price quote by phone or letter with SASE
Discount: 25% to 70%
Goods: name brand, generic
Minimum Order: $25
Shipping, Insurance: extra; UPS, FOB New Rochelle
Sales Tax: NY deliveries
Accepts: check, MO, certified check
$$$

Defender defends its claim to have "the largest selection in the USA at the very lowest prices" with a catalog that actually proves it. Its 210 pages are filled with bargains on everything for boat maintenance, sailing, and repairs: coatings, winches, windlasses, communications devices, foul-weather gear, books, tools and hardware, etc. It has an excellent selection of goods for the fiberglass boat and devotes several pages of the catalog to hull finishes. Defender will not be undersold on any item, and will beat any price lower than its own. Defender has earned a reputation for good service and reliability in its 45 years of operation and is one of the best in the business.

DISCOUNT PARTS & TIRES

P.O. Box 43278
Middletown, KY 40243
(502) 491–2400

Catalog: $4
Information: price quote by phone or letter with SASE
Discount: up to 30%
Goods: name brand, generic
Minimum Order: none
Shipping, Insurance: extra; UPS, FOB Middletown
Sales Tax: KY deliveries
Accepts: check, MO, MC, V, AE
$$$

This firm's name says it all. You can get name-brand, high-performance parts, tires, wheels, and accessories from Discount at savings of up to 30%, sometimes more. The brands available include Pirelli, Michelin, B.F. Goodrich, American, Enkei, Gabriel, and Monroe. If you don't see what you're looking for in the catalog, call or write for a price quote.

E & B MARINE, INC.

980 Gladys Ct., Dept. 3048
P.O. Box 747
Edison, NJ 08818
(201) 287–3900

Catalog: free; pub. Feb., June, Oct.
Discount: 20% to 60%
Goods: name brand, generic
Minimum Order: $10
Shipping, Insurance: extra; UPS, PP
Sales Tax: CT, FL, MD, NJ, RI, VA deliveries
Accepts: check, MO, MC, V, AE, CB, DC
$$$

E & B publishes a 132-page catalog with hundreds of goods for sailing, boat maintenance and repair, safety, communications, navigation, and every other possible function. This is one of the "everything and the kitchen sink" discount houses, and it sells at an average of 40% below list. We were told that E & B features around 75 new products in every catalog, also at savings, so it's the place to check for the newest thing at what might be the lowest price. The company has 14 stores throughout the country as well as its mail-order center. Locations are listed in the catalog. Authorized returns are accepted within ten days, and complete terms of the sales policy are stated with ordering information.

EASTERN CYCLE SALVAGE, INC.

87 Park St., Dept. W
Beverly, MA 01915
(617) 922–3707

Information: price quote by phone or letter with SASE
Discount: up to 50%
Goods: used, reconditioned
Minimum Order: none
Shipping, Insurance: extra; UPS
Sales Tax: MA deliveries
Accepts: check, MO, certified check, MC, V
$$$

Eastern Cycle sells used and reconditioned motorcycle parts "at savings of up to 50% retail." Write with your needs or call the company during business hours, Tuesday through Saturday, to see whether the part you need is in stock and to get a price quote.

EURO-TIRE, INC.

567 Rte. 46 West
P.O. Box 1198
Fairfield, NJ 07006
(201) 575–0080: inquiries
and NJ orders
(800) 631–1143: orders
except NJ

Catalog: free
Information: price quote by phone or letter with SASE
Discount: up to 40%
Goods: name brand
Minimum Order: $25
Shipping, Insurance: included; UPS
Handling: $2.50 on orders under $25
Sales Tax: NJ deliveries
Accepts: check, MO, MC, V
$$$

Euro-Tire's specialty is European tires; Michelin, Ceat, Fuida, Dunlop, Conti, Kleber, Pirelli, Phoenix, and Uniroyal (European) are some of the brands represented. Euro-Tire also stocks such items as Hella and Cibie halogen headlamps, Bilstein and Koni shock absorbers, and Rial light-alloy wheels. Prices may run to 40% less than list, and the staff knows its stock. Price quotes are given on goods not listed in the catalog.

GOLDBERG'S MARINE

**202 Market St.
Philadelphia, PA
19106–2877
(215) 829–2200/3719:
inquiries
(215) 829–2214: AK, HI, PA
orders
(800) 523–2926: customer
service except AK, HI, PA
(800) 262–8464: orders
except AK, HI, PA**

Catalog: free; pub. every six weeks
Discount: up to 40%
Goods: name brand, generic
Minimum Order: $25
Shipping, Insurance: extra; UPS, PP
Handling: $2 per order
Sales Tax: PA and NY deliveries
Accepts: check, MO, MC, V, AE, DC
$$$

If it's used for boating, Goldberg's probably has it. This store carries everything from anchors to zinc collars, and lots in between: rope, bilge pumps, rigging, knives, lifeboats, preservers, navigation equipment, fishing tackle, boat covers, winches, and even a kitchen sink. The emphasis is on pleasure-boat equipment, although much of the boating gear—French fishermen's and oiled-wool sweaters, sunglasses, boots, caps, slickers—would appeal to landlubbers, and there are quite a few items that would function well on dry land. Goldberg's also has a "gift boatique," and a selection of stylish galley gear, teak bulkhead racks, and other yacht accessories. The discounts at Goldberg's run around 20% to 40%, although there are many items with greater reductions. The sales catalogs often top these with savings of 50% and more.

MAST ABEAM

6002 Holiday Rd.
Buford, GA 30518
(404) 945–7252

Catalog: $1
Discount: 10% to 30%
Goods: name brand
Minimum Order: $10
Shipping, Handling, Insurance: $2 minimum; UPS, PP, FOB Buford
Sales Tax: GA deliveries
Accepts: check, MO, MC, V
$$$

The 82-page catalog Mast Abeam publishes lists hundreds of items for marine use at discounts of up to 30%. You'll find hardware and navigational equipment, maintenance supplies, lines, anchors, pumps, oars, clothing, and much more. While the prices aren't as low as those of other marine firms we've seen, Mast Abeam does carry a few items we haven't seen elsewhere.

OFFSHORE IMPORTS

3674 E. Noakes St.
Los Angeles, CA 90023
(213) 268–3242: inquiries
(800) 227–9276: CA orders
(800) 421–8561: orders except CA

Catalog: free
Information: price quote by phone or letter with SASE
Discount: 20% to 50%
Goods: name brand
Minimum Order: none
Shipping, Insurance: extra; FOB Los Angeles
Handling: $2 on some shipments
Sales Tax: CA deliveries
Accepts: check, MO, MC, V
$$$

At Offshore you can get Michelin, Pirelli, Yokahama, Semperit, B.F. Goodrich, Goodyear, and Kleber tires at savings of up to 50%. Other car parts are also stocked: wheels by Epsilon, BBS, Carrol Sherby, and Ronaz; car shocks by Koni and KYB; exhausts by Monza and Anza; and steering wheels, suspensions, springs, stabilizer bars, mag wheels, Mercedes wheel locks, and Interpart rear-window louvers—all sold at discount.

SUBTLE DYNAMICS

5119 Westchester Pike
Newton Square, PA 19073
(215) 356–9600: inquiries
and PA orders
(800) 345–1293: orders
except PA

Catalog: $2, refundable
Information: price quote by phone or letter with
 SASE
Discount: up to 30%
Goods: name brand
Minimum Order: none
Shipping, Insurance: extra; UPS
Sales Tax: PA deliveries
Accepts: check, MO, MC, V, AE
$$$

Subtle sells "superior accessories at dramatic discounts" for your foreign car. There are radar detectors by Blaupunkt and Audiobahn, Koni shocks, Bae turbos, Cibie halogen lamps, Recaro seats, Kamei and Foha spoilers, Ansa, Superspring, and Monza exhausts, Momo steering wheels, Ungo alarms, and all sorts of accessories and parts for Porsche, VW Rabbit, and Scirocco autos. If it's not in the catalog, call or write with manufacturer's information for a price quote.

MICKEY THOMPSON TIRES

P.O. Box 227
Cuyahoga Falls, OH 44222
(216) 928–9092

Catalog: free
Discount: up to 50%
Goods: house brand
Minimum Order: none
Shipping, Insurance: extra; UPS
Sales Tax: OH deliveries
Accepts: check, MO, MC, V
$$$

Mickey Thompson carries a unique line of tires it has designed, engineered, and manufactured. It has the widest tires available on the market, and an exclusive lineup of high-performance radials, plus 70–60–50 series sizes with matching heights. Thompson also carries a complete line of on- and off-road RV tires, featuring wraparound tread for extra traction and racing slicks. The materials and workmanship are warrantied, and credits on returned tires are prorated. If you're looking for super-wide, high-performance tires, this is the place to find them. And the prices are up to 50% less than those charged for similar name-brand goods.

TUGON CHEMICAL CORP.

P.O. Box 31
Cross River, NY 10518
(203) 323–3010

Price List and Literature: free; pub. in Jan.
Discount: up to 35%
Goods: house brand
Minimum Order: none
Shipping, Insurance: included; UPS, PP
Sales Tax: NY deliveries
Accepts: check, MO, certified check
$$$ 🍁   (see text)

Tugon Chemical manufactures a line of maintenance products for older wooden boats. These include epoxy primer, caulking, decking, sealant, glue, filler, and rotted-wood aid. Many of the products can be used in low temperatures and on damp or wet wood and still cure effectively. They're formulated to resist water, sun, salt, barnacles, temperature changes, and fuel spills. Tugon's products are more durable, versatile, and of a higher quality than those sold by other firms. If you've tried ordinary compounds and your boat still isn't seaworthy or up to par, write to Tugon with specifics: it will recommend an effective compound that will save you time and money.

CANADIAN READERS, PLEASE NOTE: payment for goods sent to Canada must be made by money order only.

WAREHOUSE MARINE DISCOUNT

P.O. Box 70348
Seattle, WA 98107
(206) 789–3296: inquiries
and WA orders
(800) 426–8666: orders
except WA

Catalog: $2
Discount: 20% to 50%
Goods: name brand, generic
Minimum Order: none
Shipping, Insurance: extra; UPS, FOB Seattle
Sales Tax: WA Deliveries
Accepts: check, MO, MC, V
$$$

Warehouse Marine sells a 200-page catalog with no-nonsense lines of goods for boat maintenance and repairs. Included are finishes, cordage, anchors, windlasses, buoys, horns, seacocks, winches, electronics, communications devices, navigation instruments, lumber, hardware, and more. The catalog also features boating clothes, teak and mahogany furnishings, and a complete line of galley gear. Since scores of these items—from rain slickers to kerosene lamps—are as useful on as offshore, this is one marine catalog landlubbers shouldn't miss.

J.C. WHITNEY & CO.

1917 Archer Ave.
P.O. Box 8410
Chicago, IL 60680
(312) 431–6102

Catalog: $1
Information: price quote by letter with SASE
Discount: up to 60%
Goods: name brand, generic
Minimum Order: none
Shipping, Handling, Insurance: extra; UPS
Sales Tax: IL deliveries
Accepts: check, MO, MC, V
$$$

J.C. Whitney carries just about everything you could want in automotive equipment—accessories, all sorts of parts, maintenance supplies, and even manuals—for foreign and domestic cars, from antique models to the latest from Detroit. All kinds of products for recreational vehicles and motorcycles are available as well. If you don't see what you're looking for in the 200-page catalog (which is unlikely), write for a price quote.

YACHTMAIL CO. LTD.

5–7 Cornwall Crescent
London W11 1PH
England
Phone #
011–441–727–2373

Catalog: $2, refundable
Discount: 30% to 45%
Goods: name brand, generic
Minimum Order: none
Shipping, Handling, Insurance: extra; airmail,
    surface mail
Duty: extra
Accepts: check, MC, V, AE, Access
$$$

Yachtmail specializes in cruiser yacht gear and inflatables, but also sells navigation instruments, winches, pumps, lights, clocks, barometers, and other goods. English brands such as Sowester, Sestrel, and Marpro, are equal or superior to American makes but often hard to find here and then usually expensive; at Yachtmail, prices on goods by these firms are usually 30% below U.S. prices, and sometimes even lower. Smaller items can be shipped at nominal rates so you don't impair your savings. Yachtmail tells us that the most popular items with U.S. buyers are autopilots, life rafts, satellite navigators, echo sounders, log speedometers, and sextants. The company is also often cited for its prices on Avon dinghies, which are usually 30% less than U.S. *discount* prices. If you're about to outfit your yacht or boat, be sure to write for this catalog and check out its prices. Goods are generally shipped by airmail or air freight.

SEE ALSO

Allyn Air Seat Co. . . . air-filled seat liners for cycles, autos, trucks, aircraft seats . . . SPORTS

Annex Outlet Ltd. . . . name-brand auto audio . . . APPLIANCES

Cambridge Wools, Ltd. . . . sheepskin car-seat covers . . . CRAFTS

Caviarteria Inc . . . vintage cars . . . FOOD

Comp-U-Card . . . car-buying service . . . GENERAL

Crutchfield . . . name-brand auto audio . . . APPLIANCES

Danley's . . . marine binoculars . . . CAMERAS

The Finals . . . board sailer . . . CLOTHING

LVT Price Quote Hotline, Inc. . . . name-brand scanners, radar detectors . . . APPLIANCES

Manufacturer's Supply . . . trailer, snowmobile parts . . . TOOLS

Northern Hydraulics, Inc. . . . go-cart, minibike, trailer parts . . . TOOLS

Pagano Gloves . . . deerskin motorcycle jackets . . . CLOTHING

Ruvel and Co., Inc. . . . government-surplus dinghies, etc. . . . SURPLUS

S & S Sound City . . . name-brand auto audio . . . APPLIANCES

Stereo Discounters Electronic World . . . name-brand radar detectors . . . APPLIANCES

BOOKS, MAGAZINES, RECORDS, AND TAPES

Publications of every sort,
cards and stationery,
films, and services.

There's simply no point in paying the cover price for books or full subscription rates for a magazine when you can almost always get them by mail at discounts of 30% to 80%. If you buy only one book a month, you could be saving over $100 per year by purchasing from our sources—and much more if you're currently buying your favorite magazines from the newsstand.

Although they're listed in the "Office" chapter, computer programs are also publications. And there are tens of thousands of them in the public domain, which means they can be copied freely without infringement of copyright (hence the term "free programs"). They're sold at very low prices—often $10 and under—and can be as valuable as protected programs that cost $300 to $900 each. The definitive reference for locating sources and evaluating what's available is Alfred Glossbrenner's *How to Get Free Software,* available in bookstores nationwide.

In addition to books and magazines, you'll find firms listed in this chapter that sell stationery, cards, gift wrapping, ribbon, records and tapes, library embossers, and photos of rock stars.

AMERICAN EDUCATIONAL SERVICES, INC.

419 Lentz Court
Lansing, MI 48917
(517) 371–5550

Information: inquire
Discount: up to 50%
Goods: magazine subscriptions
Minimum Order: none
Shipping: included
Sales Tax: none
Accepts: check or MO
$$$

This magazine service sells subscriptions to students and educators at what it calls the "lowest educational rates anywhere." Over 200 publishers are represented here, with magazines that include *Metropolitan Home, The New Yorker, Road & Track, Time, Teacher,* and *Forbes.* You must be a student or an educator to qualify for these rates—up to 50% off those normally offered by the publishers. Inquire for information.

AMERICAN FAMILY PUBLISHERS

P.O. Box 4824
Chicago, IL 60680
(312) 527-4088

Information: inquire
Discount: up to 50%
Goods: magazine subscriptions
Minimum Order: none
Shipping: included
Sales Tax: none
Accepts: check or MO
$$$$

American Family Publishers is one of several magazine clearinghouses offering subscriptions to dozens of popular periodicals at rates usually much better than those offered by the publishers themselves. AFP combines the magazine offers with bonuses, premiums, and sweepstakes, like those of Publishers Clearing House. Few can resist discounts *and* the chance of winning untold riches. Satisfaction is guaranteed and you can budget your payments over four months without interest charges. We've ordered frequently from AFP with no complaints.

THE AMERICAN STATIONERY CO., INC.

P.O. Box 207, Dept. 8400
Peru, IN 46970-9989
(317) 473-4438

Catalog: free; pub. in Jan. and July
Discount: up to 50%
Goods: custom printed
Minimum Order: none
Shipping, Handling: $1.95 to $3.95; UPS, PP
Sales Tax: IN deliveries
Accepts: check, MO, MC, V
$$$ (see text)

Wouldn't it be nice to have a box full of fresh stationery and postcards, already imprinted with your name and address, sitting beside you right now? It would cut in half the time needed to write a catalog request, and ensure that the catalog reaches your proper address—and your name would be spelled correctly.

American Stationery, founded in 1919, offers a good assortment of personalized stationery at savings of up to 50% on the prices of comparable goods and printing. You will *not* find papers crawling with ladybugs, splashed with arty designs, or cards bordered with fuchsia/lime stripes in the 16-page color catalog. The sheets, envelopes, and cards sold here have the conservative, restrained look of stationery twice as expensive, and the typefaces used are also traditional. The catalog shows deckle-edged and plain sheets and envelopes in white, ivory, and pale blue; heavyweight Monarch sheets, erasable sheets, business envelopes; and "executive" stationery of heavy, chain-laid paper. Large and small personalized memo pads, bill-paying envelopes, and a very attractive collection of bordered postcards and stationery sets are available. Crane's 100% cotton sheets, with matching foil-lined envelopes, are offered with raised-letter printing.

American Stationery approaches current fashion trends with its dove-gray sets, with lettering in darker gray, and beige sheets and envelopes that resemble legal pads. Those who enjoy the tradition of sending handwritten invitations and thank-you notes should see the "hostess" stationery: princess-sized sheets, folded notes, and paneled informals ideal for messages of this length. Your current stock of stationery can be personalized with the three-line embosser sold here, and a good selection of gummed and self-sticking return-address labels is also featured. Satisfaction is guaranteed. Returns are accepted for replacement or refund.

CANADIAN READERS, PLEASE NOTE: The catalog states that American Stationery "cannot ship to foreign countries," but it *will* ship to Canada. Postage costs for orders sent to Canada are higher than the fees stated in the catalog.

BARNES & NOBLE BOOKSTORES, INC.

**126 Fifth Ave.
New York, NY 10011
(201) 440–3336: order inquiries**

Catalog: free
Discount: up to 94%
Goods: books and recordings from major firms and small presses
Minimum Order: $15 on credit cards
Shipping, Handling, Insurance: $2.25 per order
Sales Tax: NJ and NY deliveries
Accepts: check, MO, MC, V, AE
$$$$

Barnes & Noble, founded in 1873, is "committed to a policy of offering you hundreds of new and exciting books at inflation-fighting prices." In addition to great book bargains, it has hundreds of records, tapes, and video cassettes, at discounts of up to 50%—sometimes more when the firm runs a special sale.

The book topics run from Americana to zoology, and include art, cooking, mystery, chemistry, literature, film, medicine, satire, juvenilia, current fiction, linguistics, religion, reference, crafts, photography, and much more. If classical music, jazz, and old radio programs appeal to you, check the records and tapes section. There's also a choice selection of vintage movies—from *Birth of a Nation* to World War II newsreel footage—in Beta and VHS formats. An hour with this catalog of art books, scholarly reprints, quality paperbacks, best-sellers, and publishers' overstock can provide you with something for everyone on your gift list or a summer of worthwhile reading. In addition, the catalog we reviewed offered a place to *put* those books—collapsible beechwood bookshelves—as well as the ubiquitous book embosser, art prints, cassette cases and cabinets, and the Zelco book light. Every item is backed by the Barnes & Noble guarantee of satisfaction. Returns are accepted within 30 days. This firm also offers accounts to libraries, schools, and institutions.

BRIART SERVICES

**P.O. Box 113, Newtown Branch
Boston, MA 02258**

Price List: free with SASE
WBMC Reader Discount: 50%
Goods: name brand
Minimum Order: none
Shipping, Insurance: extra; PP
Sales Tax: MA deliveries
Accepts: check or MO
$$$

Briart sells one thing, and one thing only: Peterson field guides. As New Yorkers, we take an almost voyeuristic interest in nature, and are enthralled by the volumes on animal tracks, Mexican birds, and wildflowers. Should we ever need to know how to handle a bullfrog, the guides will tell us.

These books normally sell for about $7 to $12, but Briart sells them for half their cover prices. Send a SASE for the price list, and be sure to identify yourself as a WBMC reader when you order.

CHESTERFIELD MUSIC SHOPS, INC.

**226 Washington St.
Mt. Vernon, NY 10553–1094
(914) 667–6200**

Catalog: free; pub. quarterly
Information: price quote by letter with SASE
Discount: 30% to 70%
Goods: name brand, generic
Minimum Order: none
Shipping, Insurance: extra; UPS, PP
Sales Tax: NY deliveries
Accepts: check, MO, MC, V, AE
$$$

Chesterfield stocks a staggering range of classical, jazz, popular, and folk LPs and cassettes, and sells them at prices up to 70% off list. Every sort of interest is served, with recordings that run from medieval carols to the classic children's songs rendered by Tom Glazer. Over 100 labels are represented here, including Asylum, Caedmon, Delos, Dictation Disc, Erato, Kicking Mule, Motown, Orion, Painted Smiles, Spoken Arts, and Yazoo. Inquiries are invited for records and tapes not listed in the catalog, but you must write—not call—and include a SASE with your query.

Returns are accepted on records or tapes that have been played only once, and a replacement or catalog credit is given. Chesterfield has done business by mail since 1946, and is regarded as an excellent source for esoteric recordings.

CURRENT, INC.

**The Current Building
Colorado Springs, CO
80901
(303) 593–5990: customer
service**

Catalog: free; pub. twice yearly
Discount: up to 45%
Goods: house brand
Minimum Order: none
Shipping: included on prepaid orders; UPS
Sales Tax: CO deliveries
Accepts: check or MO
$$$

Current's colorful 64-page catalog of holiday and all-occasion cards, notes, stationery, gift wrapping, ribbon, recipe cards and files, calendars, note pads, canning labels, and gifts should save you many trips to the stationery store this year. Current's designs are quite appealing, ranging from animals and nature scenes to quilt and other folk-art motifs. The catalog prices are on a par with those for comparable name-brand goods sold in stores, but if you buy eight items or more, the prices drop about 20%. When your order totals 16 or more items, the discount is 40% to 45%. This is a great source for gifts, and if you buy ahead or combine orders with friends, you'll find it easy to come up with the number of items needed to qualify for the best discount.

DAEDALUS BOOKS, INC.

2260 25th Pl. N.E.
Washington, DC
20018–1404
(202) 526–0058

Catalog: free; pub. five times yearly
Discount: 50% to 95%
Goods: remaindered books
Minimum Order: $10 on credit cards
Shipping, Handling: $3 per order; UPS, PP
Sales Tax: DC deliveries
Accepts: check, MO, MC, V, AE
$$$$ (see text)

How many times have you read a glowing book review, said to yourself, "I'll *have* to read that," and then forgotten about it completely? By the time it's the talk of your literary friends, it will have disappeared from the bookstores.

This is just the sort of reading material that turns up at Daedalus, where fine books from trade publishers and university presses are sold at 50% to 95% off the publishers' prices. Most never became best-sellers and were nosed off bookstore shelves by new arrivals and into the world of remainders. Daedalus turns what some consider a travesty to your advantage—in more ways than in price. For one, it's wonderful to have a catalog that culls the good books from the thousands of available titles: you won't have to weed through the fine print of most remainders catalogs anymore to find the real treasures. And it's great to have a second chance at getting that collection of essays or book of poetry that disappeared all too quickly from the bookstores.

The 40-page catalog we received included many books we've resolved to order *and* read. Among them: Ronald Steel's *Walter Lippmann and the American Century* ($4.98 from $19.95); *A Visit with Magritte,* photographs by Duane Michals ($1.98 from $15); Ruskin's *The Stones of Venice,* edited by Jan Morris; and *Night and Day,* by Tom Stoppard. The categories include literature, general interest, visual and performing arts, philosophy, history, feminism, politics, and social sciences. Stock is limited and moves quickly, so order promptly.

Daedalus has been in business as an independent for just five years, but has already established its presence in the bookselling community, shipping to libraries and bookstores worldwide. Complete terms for institutional and individual orders are stated in each catalog.

CANADIAN READERS, PLEASE NOTE: A $5 shipping fee is imposed on orders sent to Canada, and payment must be made by check or money order in U.S. funds.

D'ELIA'S DESIGNS

217 Putter's Lane
Slidell, LA 70460
(504) 649–0658

Brochure: 25¢ and SASE; pub. in Feb. and Sept.
WBMC Reader Discount: 30%
Goods: stock, hand-finished, custom-designed
Minimum Order: $10
Shipping, Insurance: extra; PP
Sales Tax: LA deliveries
Accepts: check, MO, certified check
$$

You may hate them when they're plastered all over the refrigerator door, but you'll love them on the cards from D'Elia's Designs. They're *fingerprints* —animated with features, limbs, and feelers. D'Elia's cards feature Fingerprint People™ frolicking in the snow on Christmas cards, partying on New Year's greetings, celebrating another year on birthday cards, and just generally making the most of a number of other occasions. Some of the cards are enhanced with coloring, glitter, sequins, and other special effects, hand-applied by the graphic artist who runs the small firm. The cards are almost gifts in themselves and are being offered to WBMC readers at 30% off catalog prices. Identify yourself as a reader when ordering and take the discount on the price of the cards only.

D'Elia's Designs also accepts special orders—custom-designed invitations, announcements, business cards, etc.—which can be embellished with Fingerprint People™ or done in calligraphy. (The WBMC discount doesn't apply to custom work.) The brochure includes details on these services as well as illustrations of the stock cards. Further inquiries are invited.

FRONT ROW PHOTOS

Box 484–W
Nesconset, NY 11767
(516) 585–8297

Catalog: $2, refundable; pub. yearly
Discount: 30% to 50%
WBMC Reader Discount: 10% on first order only
Goods: house brand
Minimum Order: $5
Shipping, Handling, Insurance: $1.50 per order; $4
   on non-U.S. orders; UPS, PP
Sales Tax: NY deliveries
Accepts: check, MO, certified check
$$$

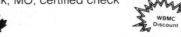

Front Row Photos is a rock fan's dream. It offers thousands of rock-concert photos of the top rock, new wave, and heavy-metal groups from the sixties through today—from AC/DC to ZZ Top. The catalog, which includes two sample photos, lists hundreds of shots of the most popular artists and groups. The one-line descriptions are guaranteed to pique your curiosity. To wit: "Two nice shots of an open-mouthed Elvis at microphone sweating and looking quite angry!" (Elvis Costello), "Bruce singing with hair sopping wet from sweat—Great!" (Springsteen), and "Debbie looking into camera, posing, looking languid" (Blondie), are just a few examples. Since many performers prohibit unauthorized photography during performances, Front Row offers serious fans and photo collectors an easy way to get the shots they missed at the concert without hazarding camera confiscation.

Photos are $1.25 for the 3½″ size and $5.50 for the 8″ × 10″. If you're not satisfied with what you receive, you can return the shots, undamaged, within ten days for an exchange or refund. Front Row also offers bonuses of extra shots and photo buttons with large orders. The WBMC Reader Discount of 10% is available to those ordering for the first time—get your friends together to make the most of your savings and get the bonuses as well.

GREAT AMERICAN MAGAZINES, INC.

Avon Lane
Hampton, VA 23629
(804) 826–2000

Information: inquire
Discount: up to 50%
Goods: magazine subscriptions
Minimum Order: none
Shipping: included
Sales Tax: none
Accepts: check or MO
$$$

A recent mailing from this discount-subscription marketing company included "99 magazine bargains," from *American Health* to *Young Miss*. The publications include both brand-new magazines and old favorites—from newsweeklies to esoteric special-interest bimonthlies. Bonus premiums are usually offered on selected subscriptions. GAM's prices are guaranteed to be the lowest available to the public: if you can find a better offer, GAM will send you the difference. You may pay your bill in three monthly installments, and GAM adds the excitement of a sweepstakes to every order. We've found this firm reliable and prompt in processing orders.

EDWARD R. HAMILTON,
BOOKSELLER

Falls Village, CT 06031

Catalog: free; pub. bimonthly
Discount: up to 90%
Goods: closeout and remaindered books
Minimum Order: none
Shipping, Handling: $3 per order; PP
Sales Tax: CT deliveries
Accepts: check or MO
$$$$

Mr. Hamilton's 36-page tabloid catalog lists *thousands* of bargain books. Every conceivable category is represented—art, humor, poetry, fiction, literature, photography, self-help, reference, business, crafts, psychology, history, film, science, cooking, sports, biography, etc. His regular prices are rock-bottom—usually 50% to 70% off the published prices, and up to 90% off on some books. Past best-sellers show up here frequently. And there are hundreds of books that would be ideal for "stockpiling" for leisurely reads in the future, not to mention gift-giving. Mr. Hamilton guarantees satisfaction and accepts returns.

L & D PRESS

P.O. Box 629
Lynbrook, NY 11563
(516) 593–5058

Literature: free
Discount: up to 45%
Goods: custom printing
Minimum Order: none
Shipping, Handling: included on stationery; UPS, PP, FOB Lynbrook
Sales Tax: NY deliveries
Accepts: check or MO
$$$

L & D has 25 years of experience in printing business cards, envelopes, and stationery. The cards are available in flat and raised thermographic print, at prices starting at $7.95 for 500. Colored stock and inks can be specified at an additional fee, and 18 typefaces are offered. Business letterhead and envelopes are stocked in a variety of styles and sizes, including windowed and airmail envelopes. Logos can be reproduced on the letterhead, and colored inks can be used (both for an additional charge). Imprinted reply messages are sold here at savings of up to 40% compared to virtually identical forms sold by another mail-order firm. L & D also carries personal stationery in princess and monarch sizes, in a choice of ivory, white, or pale blue. Embassy informals and notepads with self-sealing envelopes are shown as well. Accuracy is guaranteed on all printing.

The brochure we received showed Sentry safes, including the fireproof "Survivor" model (an ideal alternative to a safe-deposit box if document storage is needed); the heavy models were 25% off list prices. Full-suspension lateral files in letter and legal sizes with two to five drawers are offered in six colors at about 40% below list prices.

The stock might not be extensive at L & D, but the values are great. Note that the prices on *small* orders of stationery (and in the business world, 500 cards is a small order) are much better than those charged by similar firms.

MAGAZINE BUYERS'
SERVICE

3601 N.W. 15th St.
P.O. Box 8105
Lincoln, NE 68544–8105
(402) 475–1845

Information: inquire
Discount: up to 50%
Goods: magazine subscriptions
Minimum Order: none
Shipping: included
Sales Tax: none
Accepts: check or MO
$$$

Like Publishers Clearing House (see the listing in this section), Magazine Buyers' Service offers a great selection of popular magazines at substantial savings on the regular subscription and single-issue rates. Inquire for information.

MAGAZINE MARKETPLACE
INC.

One Publishers Circle
Peoria, IL 61644

Information: inquire
Discount: up to 50%
Goods: magazine subscriptions
Minimum Order: none
Shipping: included
Sales Tax: none
Accepts: check or MO
$$$

Like Publishers Clearing House and the other subscription agents listed in this chapter, Magazine Marketplace sells subscriptions to general and special-interest magazines at savings of up to 50% on the normal rates, and much more on the single-copy prices. A recent mailing included 96 selections, from *Americana* to *Yankee*. Bonuses, premiums, and sweepstakes are regular features. Magazine Marketplace also pledges a cash bonus—triple the difference—if you can find lower magazine rates elsewhere. And when the bill arrives, you're given the choice of paying in full or in three monthly installments—with no interest charges. Satisfaction is guaranteed, and pro-rated refunds are issued on canceled subscriptions. We've ordered from this firm several times with excellent results.

PUBLISHERS CENTRAL BUREAU

One Champion Ave., Dept. WBMC
Avenel, NJ 07001
(201) 382–7600

Catalog: free; pub. monthly
Discount: up to 80%
Goods: remaindered and out-of-print books
Minimum Order: $10 on credit cards
Shipping, Handling, Insurance: $2.40 per order; UPS, PP
Sales Tax: NJ and NY deliveries
Accepts: check, MO, MC, V, AE
$$$

Publishers Central Bureau is one of the nation's largest clearinghouses for publishers and record manufacturers. PCB has books on every topic—Americana, art and architecture, boating, computers, boxing, trivia, occult and magic, animals, film, humor, crafts, erotica, gardening, diet and beauty, cuisine, and much more. Pop-up books for children, trivia games, posters, library embossers, self-inking stampers, and similar goods have appeared in past catalogs. In addition, PCB has an enormous selection of records and tapes—classical, golden oldies, old radio shows, opera—at great prices. A number of video cassettes were offered in the catalog we received, ranging from *Debbie Does Dallas* (a minor blue classic) to *Do It Debbie's Way* (Ms. Reynolds demonstrating how you, too, can have a flat tummy when you reach a "certain age"). Everything seems to turn up here, and first-rate bargains abound. Returns are accepted within 14 days for refund or credit.

PUBLISHERS CLEARING HOUSE

382 Channel Drive
Port Washington, NY 11050
(516) 883–5432

Information: inquire
Discount: up to 50%
Goods: magazine subscriptions
Minimum Order: none
Shipping: included
Sales Tax: none
Accepts: check or MO
$$$$

If you've never received a communiqué from the fictitious Robert H. Treller of PCH, you may not know that there's no reason to pay full prices for subscriptions to popular and special-interest magazines. Publishers Clearing House acts as an agent for magazine publishers, offering *scores* of subscriptions at savings of up to 50% on regular rates. PCH mailings usually feature bonuses—calendars, watches, buying guides, etc.—offered with selected publications. Most of the magazines aren't limited to new subscribers; in fact, we've found that ordering through PCH and other magazine agents is the best way to renew subscriptions. We save the publishers' renewal notices as they arrive near the end of subscriptions, and then when we receive the next clearinghouse mailing, we compare prices and "resubscribe." When the publishers' computers receive the orders, they usually extend the current subscriptions. (And any snafus caused by discrepancies in the spelling of names can be taken care of by notifying the publisher's subscription department.) The subscription charges are consolidated in one bill from PCH and can be paid in four monthly installments with no finance charges.

PCH guarantees the best new-subscriber deals available to the public, and will send you four times the difference if you find a lower price. But even better than the low PCH rates is the fact that every mailing is part of a sweepstakes drive. Whether you order magazines or not, you have the chance of winning a dream house, fabulous vacation, or tons of cold cash!

STRAND BOOK STORE, INC.

828 Broadway
New York, NY 10003
(212) 473–1452

Catalog: free; pub. bimonthly
Information: inquiries by phone or letter with SASE (see text)
Discount: up to 80%
Goods: new, used, rare, out-of-print books
Minimum Order: $15 on credit cards
Shipping, Handling: $1.75 per order; PP
Sales Tax: NY deliveries
Accepts: check, MO, MC, V, AE
$$$$ (see text)

If you live in New York City and have ever needed an out-of-print book, chances are you headed to Strand. Strand's 40-page catalog of specials lists 900 titles of every sort, from *Coming of Age in Samoa* to Quentin Bell's *Ruskin* to *British Cut and Thrust Weapons*. You'll find critique and commentary, biographies, books on art, architecture, philosophy, crafts, politics, food, drama, and much more, including a lovely group of classic children's books. The catalog represents a fraction of Strand's legendary eight miles of books (two million volumes), including reviewers' copies of new titles that are sold here for 50% off publishers' prices.

Please send your catalog request on a postcard, *not* by letter. And if you don't find what you're looking for in the catalog, write to Strand—the firm states that "particular attention is paid to your special want-lists." If the book is available, the firm will send you a descriptive quotation that includes condition and price. The book is held for two weeks pending your response. Strand also purchases fine collections of "select books." Returns are accepted and institution accounts are welcomed.

CANADIAN READERS, PLEASE NOTE: shipping charges to Canada are $2 for the first book and $1 for each additional volume. Postage overpayments for large orders will be refunded.

TARTAN BOOK SALES

---

500 Arch St.
Williamsport, PA 17705
(717) 326–2461: inquiries
(800) 692–6211: PA orders
(800) 233–8467: orders
except PA

Catalog and Brochure: free; pub. monthly
Information: price quote by phone or letter
Discount: 66% plus
Goods: used books (see text)
Minimum Order: none
Shipping, Handling: $1 for the first book; 35¢ each
    additional; PP, FOB Williamsport
Sales Tax: PA deliveries
Accepts: check, MO, MC, V
$$$$

Many libraries cope with the high demand for current best-sellers and newly published books by *leasing* them from Brodart Co. and in turn *renting* them to readers. When a book's popularity has waned, it's usually returned to Brodart. Tartan Book Sales, a division of Brodart, sells these returned books to stores, institutions, and consumers at a fraction of their published prices. Tartan's staff weeds out any books that have been soiled, stamped by libraries, or otherwise damaged. The books are sold through Tartan's monthly catalogs at a minimum of 66% off list prices.

Only popular hardcover adult fiction and nonfiction books are offered—

no paperbacks, juvenile titles, or reference texts. Shirley MacLaine's *Out on a Limb,* published at $15.95, sells here for $4.98 (the paperback edition lists for $3.95); *Life Extension* is $5.49; Mary Lee Settle's *The Killing Ground* is $4.49; the *Richard Simmons Never-Say-Diet Cookbook* and *Edie* are both $4.98 each. The 24-page catalog we reviewed listed over 200 books, in general fiction, nonfiction, mystery, romance, science fiction, and Western categories. You may buy any listed book in "Flexiweld" binding for $5.98. (This Tartan service includes replacement of the publisher's binding with a more flexible material and application of a clear plastic laminate to the covers.) If you're hard on books or lend them to friends who are, Flexiweld is a good investment.

We also received Tartan's complete 1984 title listing of 2,500 books. These include current releases and popular titles published over the past few years. The books in this catalog are sold to libraries, bookstores, and other firms at 80% and 90% discounts on the publishers' prices. Request this catalog and details on Tartan's sales plans in writing, on company letterhead.

Tartan does not accept returns unless it has made an error in filling your order. If a title is not in stock when your order is filled, Tartan will reprocess the order in 30 days. If the book is still unavailable, you'll be sent a credit slip for the amount paid. This may be used for future orders or returned for a refund check or credit to your account.

**UNITED SUBSCRIPTION
SERVICE**

_____

**100 Pine Ave.
Holmes, PA 19043**

_____

Information: inquire
Discount: up to 50%
Goods: magazine subscriptions
Minimum Order: none
Shipping: included
Sales Tax: none
Accepts: check or MO
$$$

United offers subscriptions to about 50 popular consumer magazines at discount rates, with features similar to those of the other magazine clearinghouses listed in this chapter (bonuses, premiums, sweepstakes, etc.). Inquire for information.

SEE ALSO:

Amity Hallmark, Ltd. . . . offset printing, typesetting . . . OFFICE
Animal City Wholesale . . . books on animals and pet care . . . ANIMAL
Animal Veterinary Products, Inc. . . . books on animals and pet care . . .
   ANIMAL
Sam Ash Music Corp . . . classical and popular records . . . MUSIC
Bailey's, Inc. . . . logging reference books . . . TOOLS
Bike Nashbar . . . manuals on bicycle repairs . . . SPORTS
Bruce Medical Supply . . . small selection of books on health care . . .
   MEDICAL
Buy Direct, Inc. . . . printed business stationery, forms, labels, etc. . . .
   OFFICE
Campmor . . . books on camping, survival . . . SPORTS
Custom Golf Clubs, Inc. . . . manuals on golf-club repair . . . SPORTS
Dinosaur Catalog . . . juvenile and adult reference works on prehistoric
   animals . . . TOYS
Walter Drake & Sons, Inc. . . . stationery, address labels, etc. . . .
   GENERAL
Envelope Sales Company . . . printed business stationery . . . OFFICE
Erewhon Trading Co. . . . books on natural foods and health . . . FOOD
Glorybee Honey, Inc. . . . books on cooking with honey . . . FOOD
Gohn Bros . . . Amish cookbooks, quilting books . . . CLOTHING
Hunter Audio-Photo, Inc. . . . vintage video movies, TV shows, etc. . . .
   APPLIANCES
Jerry's Artarama, Inc. . . . books on fine arts, crafts . . . ART
   MATERIALS
E.C. Kraus . . . books on wine-and beer-making . . . CRAFTS
Lincoln House, Inc. . . . stationery, calendars, cards, etc. . . . GENERAL
Lyle Cartridges . . . record-care products . . . APPLIANCES
The Mexican Kitchen . . . Mexican and Tex-Mex cookbooks . . . FOOD
Paradise Products, Inc. . . . huge selection of party goods . . . TOYS
PBS Livestock Drugs . . . books on livestock care . . . ANIMAL
Regal Greetings & Gifts, Inc. . . . gift wrapping, cards, calendars,
   stationery, etc. . . . GENERAL
Rocky Mountain Stationery . . . handmade stationery . . . HANDCRAFTS
S & C Huber, Accoutrements . . . books on early American crafts . . .
   HANDCRAFTS
Self-Sufficiency and Smallholding Supplies . . . books on crafts, livestock
   raising, small-scale farming, and other self-sufficiency topics . . .
   ANIMAL
Soccer International, Inc. . . . books on soccer . . . SPORTS
Stereo Discounters Electronic World . . . record-care products . . .
   APPLIANCES
Straw Into Gold, Inc. . . . books on textile and other crafts . . . CRAFTS

Sultan's Delight Inc. . . . Greek, Lebanese, Syrian, and Middle Eastern cookbooks . . . FOOD

Terminal Musical Supply, Inc. . . . guitar manuals . . . MUSIC

Turnbaugh Printers Supply Co. . . . comprehensive manual on printing; envelopes, paper stock . . . OFFICE

United Pharmacal Company, Inc. . . . books on animals and pet care . . . ANIMAL

Whole Earth Access . . . books on a wide range of topics . . . GENERAL

Wholesale Veterinary Supply, Inc. . . . large selection books on livestock and pet care . . . ANIMAL

CAMERAS, PHOTOGRAPHIC AND DARKROOM EQUIPMENT, OPTICALS, FILM, AND SERVICES

Equipment, supplies, and services.

Contrary to popular belief, prices on cameras and photographic equipment are, for the most part, better here in the United States than they are in Hong Kong. Even major electronics outlets with small camera departments can probably offer discounts of up to 40% off list prices. The large camera houses carry much more than cameras, bulbs, and film. Some of the specialized goods available include lighting equipment, screens, film editors, splicers, batteries, projection tables, lenses, filters, adapters, cases, darkroom outfits, chemicals, and film-processing services—and they're all sold at substantial discounts.

Even if you don't need custom work done, you can have film processed, enlargements made, slides duplicated, and other services performed by a discount mail-order lab at about half the price a drugstore or retail outlet would charge. One of the firms listed in this chapter can also put your movie film on a video cassette, complete with sound track, at a competitive price.

We'd like to make one strong suggestion regarding camera purchases: Buy American. A foreign-made camera may have been manufactured under different quality-control standards than those followed by the U.S. division of the same company, and it often carries a warranty that is not honored by the U.S. firm. Should the item then need repair, it may have to be sent back to its point of manufacture—which could be Hong Kong or Singapore. Add the expense of mailing to the frustration of waiting possibly months for its return, and the sum total is often a negative experience. Make it a habit to ask whether the product you're pricing is U.S.-made, and whether the warranty will be honored in this country. Consider the risks if you do decide to buy the foreign model.

Beware also the "strip-and-requip" gambit, in which a camera seller takes the outfit as supplied by the manufacturer and *removes* the extra lenses, case, lens covers, flash attachment, and other accessories. Next the seller replaces the components with inferior models (usually termed "famous make" in the ad) and offers the stripped outfit at a very low price. The lens covers, case, attachments, and the original lenses are then offered at a surcharge. When the shopper is through buying the "extras" and "improvements," the price of the original package winds up much closer to list. We've seen far fewer examples of this practice in the last few years since it's been given wide publicity; many firms now make a point of stating that they sell cameras "as outfitted by the manufacturers." The repackaging maneuver and several other less-than-ethical business practices are detailed in the BBB booklet, "Buying Photographic Equipment by Mail." If your local office doesn't have copies, you can order one through the Council's headquarters in Virginia. See the chapter introduction of "Appliances" for the address.

ABC PHOTO SERVICE

Dept. WBMC
1200 Kenmore Ave.
Buffalo, NY 14216
(716) 876–4624

Catalog: free
Discount: up to 50%
Goods: service, name brand
Minimum Order: none
Shipping, Handling: $2.75 per order; PP
Sales Tax: NY deliveries
Accepts: check, MO, MC, V
$$

ABC offers periodic sales on the cost of film developing and enlarging. It stocks a wide range of processing goods at competitive prices as well. Work is done with Kodak paper, and a variety of finishes—glossy, satin, canvas—as well as a full range of sizes and border styles can be ordered.

AD-LIBS ASTRONOMICS

2401 Tee Circle, Suite 106
Norman, OK 73069
(405) 364–0858

Catalog: $1
Information: price quote by phone or letter with SASE
Discount: 10% to 35%
WBMC Reader Bonus: see text
Goods: name brand
Minimum Order: none
Shipping, Insurance: included on prepaid orders delivered within continental U.S.; UPS, PP
Handling: $2 on orders under $25
Sales Tax: OK deliveries
Accepts: check, MO, MC, V
$$$

Ad-Libs sells telescopes and astronomical equipment by the best firms in the business. Its stock includes complete lines for astronomical photography. You can send the company a SASE and receive the one-page list of specials. But the catalog is worth the dollar—it lists pages of equipment by Edmund, Meade, Coulter, Celestron, Questar, Televue, Unitron, Bausch & Lomb, and other firms, and includes lenses, eyepieces, filters, and other accessories. In addition, you'll receive a set of guides to buying the appropriate telescope for your needs, choosing eyepieces and photographic accessories, etc. Complete lists of specifications are included. The prices here are up to 35% off list, so it won't take the moon and stars to get what you want. And if you mention this book when you buy a telescope, you will be entitled to a free atlas of the stars—so don't forget to identify yourself as a WBMC reader.

B & H PHOTO

---

119 W. 17th St.
New York, NY 10011
(212) 807–7479: customer service
(212) 807–7474: inquiries and NY orders
(800) 221–5662: orders except NY

Information: price quote by phone or letter with SASE
Discount: up to 40%
Goods: name brand
Minimum Order: none
Shipping, Insurance: $5.50 minimum; UPS
Sales Tax: NY deliveries
Accepts: check, MO, certified check, MC, V
$$$

B & H sells *everything* for photography—cameras and lenses, darkroom equipment and supplies, bags, projectors, lighting, etc. The top brands are all here, including Nikon, Canon, Olympus, Minolta, Konica, Yashica, Sigma, Bushnell, Pentax, Hanimex, Kiron, Cokin, Vivitar, Kodak, Agfa, Ilford, LowePro, Domke, Slik, Bronica, Hasselblad, Sinar, Omega, Metz, Beseler, Unicolor, and others. The savings run up to 40% on list prices, and returns are accepted within fourteen days with no restocking fee charged.

CAMBRIDGE CAMERA
EXCHANGE, INC.

7th Ave. and 13th St.
New York, NY 10011
(212) 675–8600: inquiries and NY orders
(800) 221–2253: orders except NY

Catalog: free
Information: price quote by phone or letter with SASE
Discount: up to 60%
Goods: name brand
Minimum Order: none
Shipping, Insurance: extra; UPS, PP
Sales Tax: NY deliveries
Accepts: check, MO, MC, V
$$

The manager of this camera emporium told us the firm carries everything you can think of in the way of photographic equipment: cameras, lenses, enlargers, tripods, viewers, cases, bulbs, film, and much more. He read off a dizzying list of camera lines that are available: Nikon, Kodak, Vivitar, Bell & Howell, Leica, Pentax, Elmo, Yashica, Hasselblad, Bolex, Sigma, and Eumig are among a total of over 2,000 brands sold here.

CAMERA WORLD OF OREGON

---

500 S.W. 5th Ave.
Portland, OR 97204
(503) 227–6008: inquiries
(800) 222–6262: all orders

Catalog: $1
Information: price quote by phone or letter with SASE
Discount: 25% to 50%
Goods: name brand
Minimum Order: none
Shipping, Insurance: extra; UPS
Sales Tax: OR deliveries
Accepts: check, MO, certified check, MC, V
$$$

Camera World of Oregon states clearly that "all items are complete with all accessories as supplied by the manufacturer." This tells all who are leery of mail-order camera dealers that Camera World isn't indulging in the old "strip-and-requip" game played by some firms. It also has a great lineup of cameras, lenses, and darkroom equipment by such manufacturers as Canon, Nikon, Pentax, Olympus, Tamron, Kiron, Tokina, Ricoh, Vivitar, Cokin, Kodak, Leitz, Hanimex, Meade, Beseler, Ilford, Agfa, Domke, LowePro, and Tenba. Prices are up to 50% off list, and you can call or write for a price quote. Camera World will accept returns, but they must be authorized, returned within 14 days, and include all the original wrappings. A restocking fee may be charged, depending upon the reason for the return.

COLORCHROME

P.O. Box 25009
Seattle, WA 98125–0509
(206) 364–2485

Brochure: free
Discount: up to 40%
Goods: service
Minimum Order: $5
Shipping, Handling: $3 per order, prints, plus 50¢ each print; 75¢ per roll, film; PP
Sales Tax: WA deliveries
Accepts: check, MO, MC, V, AE
$$$

Colorchrome, founded in 1975, is the mail-order division of a large laboratory that processes film for professional photographers. It can offer you the same quality services at up to 40% below list or comparable prices, and some options not usually available from small processing outfits.

The brochure describes a roster of services that should interest all 35mm-shutterbugs: color film and slide processing, full-frame enlargements, photo calendars, jigsaw puzzles, mounting, and framed prints. The enlargements are made without cropping a portion of the photo (which is done by most processors to make the print fit the old standard sizes), and offered in matte, silk, and canvas textures at no additional cost; they can be coated with a protective "matte spray" to eliminate surface glare for a small fee. Sizes run from 3″ × 5″ to 20″ × 30″. Flush (borderless) mounting is done on ⅛″-thick acid-free board, and the framed prints (flush and done without mounting) are available in silver, gold, black, oak, and "floating" walnut finishes. The calendars, which are sold in 5″ × 7″ and 11″ × 14″ sizes, feature the photo in half the area and the 12-month calendar in the other, and are a great way to turn a good shot into inexpensive gifts for any number of people on your list. Jigsaw puzzles, mounted on ¼-inch thick board, can be cut into 40 to 320 pieces.

The information kit includes a postpaid mailer and current price list, plus a page of coupons that can be used for specials throughout the year. But if you want real savings on such services as standard enlargements, pick up a copy of *Modern Photography* or *Popular Photography*—Colorchrome advertises its lower prices on monthly specials in those publications. Once you become a customer, however, you'll receive quarterly mailings with extra discounts as well. Like most processors, Colorchrome limits its liability to replacement of lost or damaged film with a like quantity of unexposed film.

CANADIAN READERS, PLEASE NOTE: There is a minimum $5 shipping charge on orders sent to Canada.

DANLEY'S

Division of Sporting Optics, Inc.
P.O. Box 1-WM
Ft. Johnson, NY 12070
(518) 842–7853

Information: price quote by phone or letter with SASE
Discount: up to 50%
Goods: name brand
Minimum Order: none
Shipping: included; UPS, PP
Insurance: extra
Handling: $1 on orders under $25
Sales Tax: NY deliveries
Accepts: check, MO, certified check
$$$

Danley's sells sporting optics—complete lines by Bushnell, Bausch & Lomb, Swift, Celestron, Zeiss, Leitz, Nikon, and HPM-Optolyth. We received brochures that showed every kind of binocular made by the firms listed above, including standard and compact models, sports binocs, armored models for field work, giant models, waterproof styles for marine use, zoom lenses, and folding models. Theater glasses, telescopes, and rifle scopes are also available from certain companies. Welt Flip-lock tripods are stocked as well. The prices are at least 20% off list, and usually closer to 40% and 50%. Danley's doesn't have a catalog, but can supply the manufacturer's literature upon request. Call or write for a price quote. Since some of these goods are rarely discounted more than 15%, Danley's represents a real find for the stargazer, spectator, bird-watcher, and hunter. A layaway plan is available, and authorized returns are accepted.

CANADIAN READERS, PLEASE NOTE: Payment for orders sent to Canada must be made in U.S. funds.

EXECUTIVE PHOTO & SUPPLY CORP.

120 W. 31st St.
New York, NY 10001–3485
(212) 947–5290: inquiries and NY orders
(800) 223–7323: orders except NY
(800) 882–2802: computer orders except NY

Information: price quote by phone or letter with SASE
Discount: up to 50%
Goods: name brand
Minimum Order: none
Shipping, Handling, Insurance: $5.95 minimum; UPS
Sales Tax: NY deliveries
Accepts: check, MO, MC, V, AE
$$$

Popular brands and the latest models in cameras, video equipment, computers, phone machines, and other electronics are sold here at up to 50% off list or retail prices. Photography equipment by Nikon, Canon, Hasselblad, Minolta, Olympus, Konica, Vivitar, Tokina, Sigma, Kiron, Pentax, Yashica, Polaroid, Kodak, Contax, and other firms is available. Personal stereo from Sony, Aiwa, Panasonic, Toshiba, Sanyo, and Olympus; video equipment by Panasonic, RCA, Sanyo, and JVC; and blank video tapes from Kodak, Polaroid, Maxell, TDK, and Sony are all stocked here.

Specials on computers and peripherals are run on a regular basis. You can save on products by IBM, Compaq, Sanyo, Apple, AT&T, Columbia, Eagle, Epson, Zenith, Juki, Texas Instruments, Silver-Reed, NEC, Toshiba,

Okidata, Gemini, Brother, Hayes, Taxan, Amdec, and other firms. Executive also stocks Hewlett-Packard calculators, Uniden phones, electronic typewriters by Smith-Corona and Brother, phone machines from Phone-Mate, Panasonic, and Code-A-Phone. Canon copiers, Casio musical keyboards, and Celestron telescopes are available.

Business is done on a price-quote basis; call or write (include a SASE) with model information. Please note that the store is closed on Saturdays and open Sundays, and the WATS lines are for orders only.

47ST. PHOTO, INC.

---

36 E. 19th St.
New York, NY 10003
(212) 260–4415: customer
service
(212) 260–4410: inquiries
and AK, HI, NY orders
(800) 221–7774: orders
except AK, HI, NY

Photography and Darkroom Catalog: $2
General Catalog: $1
Information: price quote by phone or letter with
  SASE
Discount: up to 70%
Goods: name brand
Minimum Order: $35
Shipping, Handling, Insurance: $4.95 minimum;
  UPS
Sales Tax: NY deliveries
Accepts: check, MO, MC, V, AE
$$$

47st. Photo is a circus of audio, video, office, and home electronics, and it also sells cameras and photo equipment. (Computers are sold through 47st. Computing, listed in the "Office" chapter.)

You can experience the Barnum-and-Bailey effect by visiting the firm's main store, which is never, ever, anything but mobbed. Spare yourself the fracas and the waiting on line by doing business by mail and save a bundle—an average of 30% to 50%, and sometimes as much as 70% on specials. Cameras, lenses, tripods, film, light meters, darkroom equipment, photography supplies, lighting, and cases are available. The huge number of manufacturers includes Nikon, Leica, Mamiya, Canon, Eumig, Olympus, Contax, Yashica, Zeiss, Minox, Hasselblad, Minolta, Pentax, Konica, Wein, Gossen, Bronica, Ricoh, Smith-Victor, Beseler, Velbon, Leitz, Schneider, Omega, Soligar, Kiron, Vivitar, Nikkor, Rollei, Tenba, LowePro, Tamron, Sunpak, Sigma, Slik, Kodak, Agfa, Fuji, and Polaroid. Binoculars by Leica, Zeiss, Celestron, and Nikon are stocked, as well as Cometron and Celstron telescopes. If you're shopping for Sony TVs and video equipment from RCA, Panasonic, JVC, Sony, Quasar, or Zenith, you may find your best price here.

47st. carries some personal stereo, along with Casio musical keyboards, and microwave ovens from Litton, Amana, and Sharp. Upgrade your office with a Canon copier or an electronic typewriter from Brother, Silver-Reed, Royal, Smith-Corona, Canon, or Olympia. Dodge calls or make them with answering machines, dialers, and phones by Code-A-Phone, Record a Call, Uniden, Panasonic, Sanyo, Cobra, Webcor ZIP, and other firms.

Although there is a catalog, we recommend that you call or write for the best price. Current specials are listed monthly in *Modern Photography*, and weekly in the Sunday edition of *The New York Times.* 47st. does a large business in used cameras and photography equipment and takes trade-ins. Returns are accepted on everything except photography paper, tapes, and film—within 15 days *if* original wrappings are included and the warranty card has not been filled out.

FRANK'S HIGHLAND PARK CAMERA

**5715 N. Figueroa St.
Los Angeles, CA 90042
(213) 255–0123, 1543, 5151:
inquiries and AK, CA, HI
orders
(800) 421–8230: orders
except AK, CA, HI**

Catalog: $2
Information: price quote by phone or letter with SASE
Discount: up to 50%
Goods: name brand
Minimum Order: $10
Shipping, Insurance: extra; UPS, FOB Los Angeles
Sales Tax: CA deliveries
Accepts: check, MO, MC, V, AE
$$$

You can send for the 96-page discount catalog, or call or write for a price quote on anything by Pentax, Nikon, Canon, Vivitar, Olympus, Kodak, Hasselblad, or any of scores of major manufacturers. Frank (an actual person) will do his best to give you a price that beats all the others you've heard. This is a reputable firm which has been in business for 20 years. It was recommended to us by a WBMC reader who has dealt with Frank's for years and wouldn't shop anywhere else.

GARDEN CAMERA

135 W. 29th St., Dept.
WBMC
New York, NY 10001
(212) 868–1420: inquiries
and NY orders
(800) 223–5830: orders
except NY

Catalog: free; pub. Jan., May, Sept.
Information: price quote by phone or letter with
  SASE
Discount: 5% to 10% over cost (see text)
Goods: name brand
Minimum Order: $45 on credit cards
Shipping, Insurance: $4.95 minimum; UPS, PP
Sales Tax: NY deliveries
Accepts: check, MO, certified check, MC, V, AE
$$$

Garden sells cameras and photography equipment by Nikon, Pentax, Minolta, Olympus, Vivitar, Canon, Mamiya, Hasselblad, Yashica, Contax, LowePro, Bogen, and many other manufacturers. It has Kodak, Agfa, and Fuji film and also stocks all darkroom equipment and accessories.

In addition to cameras, Garden sells calculators by Hewlett-Packard; Canon personal copiers; phones and answering machines by Uniden, GTE, Webcor ZIP, ITT, and Panasonic; personal stereo by Sony, Toshiba, and Aiwa; video equipment by RCA, Panasonic, and JVC; Casio musical keyboards; Bushnell binoculars; and typewriters by Brother, Canon Olivetti, Smith-Corona, and Silver-Reed. Prices are 5% to 10% above dealer cost, which is 30% to 50% below list. Send for the catalog, or call or write for price quotes on specific items.

LION PHOTO SUPPLY, INC.

P.O. Box 14896
Chicago, IL 60614–0896
(312) 281–0869: inquiries
and AK, HI, IL orders
(800) 621–9905: orders
except AK, HI, IL

Catalog: $1, redeemable
Information: price quote by phone or letter with
  SASE
Discount: up to 40%
Goods: name brand
Minimum Order: none
Shipping, Insurance: extra; UPS
Sales Tax: IL deliveries
Accepts: check, MO, MC, V
$$$

This Chicago camera discounter carries all the major brands, including Mamiya, Bronica, Nikon, Canon, Minolta, Vivitar, Metz, Bogen, Kodak, Gossen, Tokina, and Slik, to name just a few. A catalog is available, but we recommend using it only as an introduction to the firm's large stock of lenses, tripods, darkroom equipment, flashes, etc. Call or write for a price quote to get the best deal, since specials are run on a regular basis.

MARDIRON OPTICS

37 Holloway St., Dept. WBM
Malden, MA 02148–5901
(617) 322–8733

Brochures: free
Information: price quote by phone or letter with
   SASE
Discount: up to 40%
Goods: name brand
Minimum Order: none
Shipping, Insurance: included; UPS, PP
Sales Tax: MA deliveries
Accepts: check, MO, certified check
$$$

Mardiron sells top German binoculars and telescopes—by a select group of manufacturers at savings to 40% below list. It offers the Steiner binoculars used extensively by 41 military forces, binoculars and telescopes by Optolyth, and the full range of Swift optics. Mardiron's brochures include recommendations of specific models for different purposes, and list a range of telescope and binocular accessories. We were told that the company is negotiating for the right to carry Hertel & Reuss binoculars, which are on a par with Steiner. If you don't see what you're looking for, call or write with your request.

OLDEN CAMERA & LENS CO., INC.

1265 Broadway, Dept.
WBMC
New York, NY 10001
(212) 725–1234: inquiries
and NY orders
(800) 221–3160: orders
except NY

Catalog: 50¢; pub. yearly
Information: price quote by phone or letter with
   SASE
Discount: 20% to 60%
Goods: name brand
Minimum Order: $50 on credit cards
Shipping, Insurance: $4.95 minimum; UPS, PP
Sales Tax: NY deliveries
Accepts: check, MO, MC, V
$$$$

Olden has one of the most complete inventories of new and used cameras and photographic equipment in New York City. Some of the firms represented here are Konica, Canon, Minolta, Fuji, Omega, Yashica, Hasselblad, Leica, Chinon, Pentax, Mamiya, Hanimex, Kodak, Bronica, Minox, Olympus, Nikon, Rollei, Bogen, Contax, Praktica, Ricoh, and Samigon. Olden stocks a full range of black-and-white and color still and movie film, and self-processing film. In addition, it carries collectors' cameras, underwater photographic equipment and cameras, and books on photography. The highly informative buying guide Olden publishes each year lists specs of many cameras, but it's better to call the firm or write for a price quote when you're ready to buy, since you'll get your best price that way.

In addition to photography equipment, you'll find video cameras and VCRs by RCA, JVC, Elmo, Panasonic, Quasar, Sharp, Magnavox, Vidicraft, and other firms; typewriters by Brother, Smith-Corona, and Canon; phones and phone machines by Uniden, Panasonic, Phone-Mate, Record a Call, and Sanyo; and computers by IBM, Compaq, Apple, and Leading Edge. Call or write for a price quote on goods by these manufacturers.

Olden has been in business since 1937 and has a no-questions-asked guarantee of satisfaction on every purchase—as long as goods are returned within seven days of receipt in the same carton with the same packing materials and the warranty card is *not* filled out. Olden tries to fill orders within 24 hours of receipt.

OPTICON LABORATORIES, INC.

806 Hastings
P.O. Box 2160
Traverse City, MI
49685–2160
(616) 947–4355

Brochure and Price List: free
Discount: 10% to 20%
WBMC Reader Discount: 20% on orders of $100 or more (see text)
Goods: service
Minimum Order: $50
Shipping, Insurance: extra; UPS
Sales Tax: MI deliveries
Accepts: check, MO, MC, V
$$$

Opticon is a service that takes Super-8, 8mm, and 16mm films and converts them to video cassettes in Beta or VHS format. It does this without picking up any "bar" images or harming the original, and it will record sound if sound is present on the original. Opticon Laboratories offers its service at 10% to 20% less than its competitors, and is offering readers of this book an additional 20% discount on all orders of $100 or more—exclusive of shipping charges and tax, if applicable. Please note that this offer *expires November 1, 1986,* and you must identify yourself as a WBMC reader to qualify for the discount. Opticon guarantees its service: if you are not satisfied with the technical quality of the product, the firm will reprocess the order at no cost to you.

**ORION TELESCOPE
CENTER**

**P.O. Box 1158–W
Santa Cruz, CA 95061
(408) 476–8715: inquiries
(800) 443–1001: CA orders
(800) 447–1001: orders
except CA**

Catalog: free; pub. in the spring and fall
Discount: up to 35%
Goods: name brand
Minimum Order: none
Shipping, Insurance: extra; UPS, PP
Sales Tax: CA deliveries
Accepts: check, MO, certified check
$$

We did not receive the catalog from Orion for review, but we were told that the company sells astronomical and terrestrial telescopes, accessories, star charts, and books. You'll find scopes from Meade, Bushnell, Celestron, and other firms at savings of up to 35%. Send for the catalog, or call to see whether the product or line that interests you is stocked.

PRO PHOTO LABS

**P.O. Box 2000
West Caldwell, NJ 07007**

Price List and Mailers: free
Discount: up to 50%
Goods: service
Minimum Order: $5 on credit cards
Shipping, Handling: 75¢ per order: PP
Sales Tax: NJ deliveries
Accepts: check, MO, MC, V
$$$

Pro Photo will develop your 35mm, 110, 126, or disc film for up to 50% less than charged elsewhere. It also handles enlargements, proofs, and prints from slides. The firm says that almost 80% of its business is from repeat orders, and it processes film for many professional photographers. When you write, request the price list and mailers.

SHARP PHOTO

1225 Broadway; Dept. WBM
New York, NY 10001
(212) 532–1733: inquiries
and AK, HI, NY orders
(800) 223–7633: orders
except AK, HI, NY

Catalog: $1.95
Information: price quote by phone or letter with
  SASE
Discount: 30% to 50%
Goods: name brand
Minimum Order: none
Shipping, Insurance: extra; UPS, PP
Sales Tax: NY deliveries
Accepts: check, MO, MC, V
$$$

Sharp Photo's inventory of cameras, photographic equipment, and projectors includes lines by Minolta, Olympus, Canon, Nikon, Pentax, Konica, Yashica, Conta, Bronica, Mamiya, Rollei, Omega, Hasselblad, Rodenstock, Vivitar, Tamron, Tokina, Sigma, Soligar, Chinon, Gossen, Elmo, Eumig, Slik, Fuji, Ilford, Agfa, Beseler, Paterson, and Coast.

Sharp also sells calculators by Texas Instruments, Canon, Sharp, and Hewlett-Packard; Pearlcorder micro-cassettes; Fidelity electronic games; European and American-model Seiko watches; and Panasonic radios and TVs. You can request the catalog and order from it, but we recommend calling or writing for a price quote for the best discount.

SOLAR CINE PRODUCTS, INC.

4247–49 South Kedzie Ave.,
Dept. W
Chicago, IL 60632–2890
(312) 254–8310: inquiries
and IL orders
(800) 621–8796: orders
except IL

Catalog: free (see text)
Discount: up to 40%
Goods: name brand
Minimum Order: $10
Shipping, Insurance: extra; UPS
Sales Tax: IL deliveries
Accepts: check, MO, MC, V, DC
$$$

Solar Cine's catalog is packed cover to cover with all kinds of photographic and processing (slides, movies, reprints, prints) equipment and accessories. It includes listings of cameras, lenses, studio lights, light meters, tripods, and darkroom equipment from Kodak, Elmo, Bell & Howell, Minolta, Sylvania, Smith-Victor, Pentax, Hanimex, Ciro, Soligar, Gossen, and others. There are also scores of books on photography for beginners and professionals, video movies, and other electronics. A sample of Solar Cine's stock is shown in the regular catalog, which is free; a larger catalog, showcasing over 4,000 items, is available for $3.50. If you don't see what you're looking for, you can call or write with your request—it's probably in stock.

WALL STREET CAMERA EXCHANGE, INC.

---

82 Wall St.
New York, NY 10005
(212) 344–0011: inquiries
and AK, HI, NY orders
(800) 221–4090: orders only
except AK, HI, NY

Catalog: $2.95, refundable (see text)
Information: price quote by phone or letter with SASE
Discount: 30% to 70%
Goods: name brand
Minimum Order: none
Shipping, Handling, Insurance: 2% of order value, $5.50 minimum; UPS, PP
Sales Tax: NY deliveries
Accepts: check, MO, MC, V, AE
$$$ CANADA

This firm has been a fixture in New York City's financial district since 1951, and offers the kind of savings that make investors smile—about 40% off on many goods, and even more on specials.

Wall Street Camera carries the comprehensive range of cameras, darkroom equipment, viewers, lenses, and other goods you expect from a major discounter. The firms represented here include Nikon, Rollei, Hasselblad, Mamiya, Omega, Leica, Zeiss, Pentax, Bronica, Olympus, Canon, Gossen, Sinar, Schneider, Beseler, Philips, Paterson, Linhof, Rollex, Rodenstock, and many others. The catalog shows most of the goods, and note that the winter edition is larger and costs $4.95. The price of any of the catalogs is refundable or deductible with orders of $100 or more, and those meeting that minimum will be sent future mailings at no charge. Calling or writing for a price quote is recommended, however, since the firm runs specials and sales on a frequent basis. Used equipment is bought and sold here, and trade-ins accepted as well (by mail and in-store). Returns are accepted within ten days for full refund. Corporate and professional accounts are welcomed.

WEST SIDE CAMERA INC.

2400 Broadway
New York, NY 10024
(212) 877–8760, 8780

Brochure: free with SASE; pub. in Mar. and Sept.
Information: price quote by phone or letter with
  SASE
Discount: 10% to 40% (see text)
Goods: name brand
Minimum Order: $10
Shipping, Insurance: extra; UPS, PP
Sales Tax: NY deliveries
Accepts: check, MO, MC, V, AE
$$

West Side has been selling photography goods since 1976 and carries a full line of name-brand cameras, darkroom supplies and equipment, frames, straps, carrying bags, film, and video tape. Some of the brands offered are Nikon, Canon, Minolta, Ricoh, Olympus, Omega, Paterson, Kodak, Agfa, Ilford, Seal, Bogen, Cokin, Konica, Rollei, Sigma, Vivitar, Kiron, Tokina, Soligar, Dax, Bobby Lee, Hoya, Smith-Victor, Lowel Lighting, and Sprint Chemistry. Hobbyists, take note: West Side emphasizes that it has a comprehensive line of darkroom equipment and supplies. The prices on cameras are 5% to 10% above dealer cost (which amounts to savings of up to 40%), and darkroom supplies are discounted 10%. If you want a price quote, call or write (include a SASE) with the model number and other pertinent information.

THE WORLD OF 35MM

P.O. Box 2945
Paterson, NJ 07509

Price List and Mailers: free
Discount: up to 50%
Goods: service
Minimum Order: none
Shipping, Handling: included
Sales Tax: NJ deliveries
Accepts: check or MO
$$$$

You can have your 35mm film developed, enlargements made, and slides duplicated and printed by World of 35mm at prices that are easily half those charged for the same services by photography shops. Kodak papers and chemicals are used, and production quality is excellent. Send for mailers and the price list.

SEE ALSO:

Annex Outlet Ltd. . . . name-brand video equipment, blank tapes . . .
  APPLIANCES
Berry Scuba Co. . . . name-brand underwater cameras . . . SPORTS
Bondy Export Corp. . . . name-brand still and video cameras, projectors
  . . . APPLIANCES
Central Skindivers of Nassau, Inc. . . . name-brand underwater cameras . . .
  SPORTS
Focus Electronics, Inc. . . . name-brand cameras, darkroom equipment,
  photography supplies . . . APPLIANCES
Foto Electric Supply Co. . . . name-brand cameras, film, video tape . . .
  APPLIANCES
Harry's Discounts & Appliances Corp. . . . name-brand blank video tapes
  . . . APPLIANCES
International Solgo, Inc. . . . name-brand cameras . . . APPLIANCES
Jems Sounds, Ltd. . . . name-brand cameras . . . APPLIANCES
Laurence Corner . . . new, used government-surplus photographic
  equipment . . . CLOTHING
Lewi Supply . . . name-brand cameras . . . APPLIANCES
S & S Sound City . . . name-brand blank video tapes . . . APPLIANCES

CIGARS, PIPES, TOBACCO, AND OTHER SMOKING NEEDS

Cigars, chewing tobacco,
cigarette tobacco, snuff, pipes,
and smoking accessories.

It's not easy being a smoker today, so if you're going to light up and enjoy, you might was well do it at a discount. The companies listed here sell cigars, chewing tobacco, shredded tobacco for cigarette rolling, pipes, and other smoking accessories at savings of up to 75%. If your current smoke is a name-brand cigar, look here for off-brand versions sold at a fraction of the price, and for the famous labels themselves, which are often available at a discount.

You probably know that your right to smoke is being threatened on several levels. The Surgeon General's objective of a "smoke-free society by the year 2000" may never be realized, but local ordinances are being passed all over the country to limit the right to smoke in public and semi-public places. While debates on the ethics of such actions rage on, one fact remains unarguable: smoking poses serious hazards to your long-term health. Millions have quit, aided by everything from hypnosis to nicotine-impregnated gum, but most have done it with something that doesn't cost a cent—sheer willpower.

If you want to overcome nicotine addiction, help is available from many sources. One of the most frequently cited is the American Cancer Society, whose local chapters run "Quit Smoking Clinics." Some chapters charge a small fee for the program, but most offer it free of cost. Contact your local chapter or write to the American Cancer Society, 777 Third Ave., New York, NY 10017 for information. The American Lung Association publishes two booklets, "Freedom from Smoking in 20 Days" and "A Lifetime of Freedom from Smoking." Both are available from local chapters or by writing to the American Lung Association, 1740 Broadway, New York, NY 10019.

As a final note, please remember that tobacco is quite toxic and the residue left in cigarette filters and cigar stubs is potent. Children have been known to eat the contents of ashtrays—with disastrous results. So keep tobacco products and ashtrays out of the reach of children and omnivorous pets.

NURHAN CEVAHIR

Istiklal Caddessi, Dept. W
Bekar sokak 12/4
Beyoglu, Istanbul
Turkey
Phone # 44–41–23

Brochure and Price List: free; pub. biannually
Information: price quote by phone or letter
Discount: 25% to 50%
WBMC Reader Discount: 10%
Goods: handmade
Minimum Order: none
Shipping, Insurance: extra; itemized
Duty: extra
Accepts: IMO or bank draft to Cevahir's bank
$$$$

Nurhan Cevahir sells hand-carved meerschaum cigarette holders and pipes with bowls carved into various shapes whose names are their best descriptions: "Laughing Bacchus," "D'Artagnan," "Cleopatra," and "Tulip," among others. Mr. Cevahir also has a good selection of plain meerschaum pipes, some of which feature etched designs. Four pipe sizes are stocked, and Cevahir's pipes are up to 50% less expensive than similar styles sold in the U.S. Further savings of 10% are offered to customers who identify themselves as WBMC readers. Gift boxes are available at an additional charge, and Mr. Cevahir will dispatch your present directly to the recipient if you wish. He's been shipping goods to customers all over the world for over 20 years and is quite reliable.

FAMOUS SMOKE SHOP, INC.

55 W. 39th St.
New York, NY 10018
(212) 221–1408: inquiries
and NY orders
(800) 672–5544: orders
except NY

Catalog: free; pub. quarterly
Information: price quote by phone or letter with SASE
Discount: up to 30%
Goods: name brand, house brand
Minimum Order: none
Shipping, Insurance: extra, itemized; UPS, PP
Sales Tax: NY deliveries
Accepts: check or MO
$$$

Famous Smoke Shop boasts what may be the country's largest selection of handmade cigars and pipe tobaccos at prices up to 30% below regular retail. Factory arrangements with a number of foreign firms allows it to buy in volume and sell at a discount. Among the famous names, you'll find Macanudo, Bering, Baccarat, Bances, Camino Real, Cohiba, Arturo Fuente,

Canaria D'Oro, Cuesta-Rey, Dannenmann, Don Diego, Don Julio, Don Miguel, El Triunfo, H. Upmann, Hoyo de Monterry, Montecruz, Montesino, Primo del Cristo, Primo del Rey, Punch, Romeo y Julieta, Re-Amo, Dunhill, and many others. Unbranded house cigars, similar in size, shape, length, and taste to their name-brand counterparts, offer the serious smoker even more savings. (Once the ring is off, who's to know the difference?)

The catalog is filled with tips on choosing and enjoying cigars, but let the indecisive be warned: the selection is tremendous. Take the plunge and order—satisfaction is guaranteed. In addition to cigars, you'll find pipe tobaccos, cigarettes, and smoking paraphernalia listed in the catalog, also at good prices. Famous has served finicky New Yorkers for over half a century, and will offer you the same privilege the firm's faithful enjoy: a private charge account.

WALLY FRANK, LTD.

**63–25 69th St.
Middle Village, NY 11379
(718) 326–2233: inquiries
and AK, HI, NY orders
(800) 221–0638: orders
except AK, HI, NY**

Catalog: free; pub. in Apr. and Oct.
Discount: 30%
Goods: name brand, house brand, generic
Minimum Order: none
Shipping, Handling, Insurance: extra on orders
    under $40; included on orders over $40; UPS
Sales Tax: NY deliveries
Accepts: check, MO, MC, V, AE, CB, DC
$$$

Wally Frank has been delighting cigar and pipe smokers for over 50 years with savings of 30% and more on famous-label cigars, tobacco, and privately produced smoke-alikes. There are cigars here for every taste, from extra-mild to full-bodied smokes, including Cuban seed, Jamaican, Dominican, Brazilian, Honduran, Nicaraguan, and U.S. fillers. Selections from Don Diego, Martinez, Lancer, H. Upmann, and other firms are offered at a discount, along with Frank's generic equivalents at lower prices. You can save even more on "irregulars" and closeout specials. Cigar humidors, cutters, holders, and other accessories are shown in the catalog as well.

Half of the 48 pages are devoted to pipe smoking, and a huge number of briar pipes in every bowl shape and stem style are offered at prices beginning at under $5. There are also corn cob and meerschaum pipes, Colibri lighters, pipe-cleaning tools, pouches, racks, and tobacco humidors. Name-brand pipe tobaccos and generic blends are sold at a savings, and loose, plug-chewing, and pinch ("spitless") tobaccos can be procured here at savings when smoking is completely outlawed.

Wally Frank's generous guarantees make trying a lower-priced tobacco or pipe risk-free: smoke up to six Frank cigars or ten pipefuls of Frank Blend and if you're not satisfied, return the remainder for a full refund or credit. Frank's pipes carry a guarantee against bowl burnout for 90 days. If shanks and mouthpieces break, they can be repaired for a moderate charge.

J-R TOBACCO CO.

**100 Sterling Mine Rd.
Sloatsburg, NY 10974
(212) 364–4600: inquiries
and NYC orders
(914) 753–2745: NY State
orders except NYC
(800) 431–2380: orders
except NY**

Catalog: free; pub. quarterly
Discount: to 75%
Goods: name brand, house brand
Minimum Order: $10
Shipping, Handling: $1 per box, 50¢ each
  additional; UPS
Sales Tax: DC, MI, NJ, NY, PA deliveries (if
  applicable)
Accepts: check, MO, MC, V, AE
$$$$

Connoisseurship and warehouse pricing may seem incompatible, but that's the basis for J-R's success. Owner Lew Rothman has been selling fine cigars at a discount since 1971, and we've seen his literature go from a tabloid "riot of bargains" to the 72-page catalog we reviewed. The discounted brand names are still here in force, but half the catalog is devoted to "J-R Alternative Cigars." These are cigars made expressly for J-R by the factories that produce Canaria D'Oro, Don Diego, Don Marcos, Excalibur, Fuente, Fundadore, H. Uppman, Montecruz, Partagas, Primo Del Rey, Pride of Jamaica, Rey Del Mundo, and many other fine smokes. Each of the Alternatives is "the closest product to" a name-brand cigar in size, taste, and origin. The catalog lists the inspiration with its regular retail and J-R's discounted price along with the price (up to 66% less) of the Alternative. These are all handmade, long-leaf cigars. The country of import, ring size, length, and relative body and strength of smoke (very mild to heavy) is given for each one. J-R's best shot at a pre-Castro Cuban smoke-alike can be found in the "Ultimate Cigar," aged one year and produced for J-R by a firm formerly of Havana. *GQ* has given its stamp of approval to this one, and Mr. Rothman considers it his finest.

The catalog is notable for its information on the care and smoking of cigars. Even the ignorant may find it easy to choose gifts by matching the recipient's favorite label with the J-R Alternative or buying the name-brand product itself. Pipe smokers are served with tins of tobacco from Dunhill, Sobranie, Lane's English, MacBarrens, and several other companies, in a choice of blends and package sizes.

J-R has set up shops in several states and even has an outlet in Tel-Aviv. While Mr. Rothman is expanding operations and polishing the catalog, you can still count on his priceless, down-to-earth comments and descriptions. And he guarantees all his cigars "absolutely."

HAYIM PINHAS

P.O. Box 500
Istanbul
Turkey

Catalog: free; pub. every 3 years
Discount: 25% to 50%
WBMC Reader Discount: 10% on orders over
$1,000
Goods: handmade
Minimum Order: 2 pipes
Shipping, Insurance: extra; itemized
Duty: extra
Accepts: check or IMO
$$$$

Turkey, rich in meerschaum, is also rife with pipe carvers. Hayim Pinhas is one of the more prolific, offering over 70 models—from classic designs with smooth bowls to intriguing free-form carvings. He's also captured the visages of Abraham Lincoln, Socrates, and Shakespeare, as well as mermaids, shahs, dogs, skulls, and the *ne plus ultra,* Mickey Mouse himself. The pipes are all fitted with plastic inserts and stems, and are sold here at up to 50% less than similar pipes in the U.S. The catalog includes tips on treating your pipe properly and gives some fascinating facts on meerschaum itself. If your order is over $1000, Hayim offers a discount of 10%, so don't forget to identify yourself as a WBMC reader. This offer expires Oct. 31, 1987.

FRED STOKER FARMS

Rte. 1, P.O. Box 707
Dresden, TN 38225
(901) 364–5419, 3754

Brochure: free; pub. yearly
Discount: up to 70%
Goods: house brand
Minimum Order: none
Shipping: included on local shipments; UPS, PP
Sales Tax: TN deliveries
Accepts: check, MO, certified check
$$$

Mr. Fred "Famous Since 1940" Stoker sells homegrown at down-home prices. He raises tobacco and sells forms and flavors for chewing, smoking, and snuffing, at prices to 70% lower than those of his competitors.

Chewing tobacco is featured prominently. It comes in peach, cherry-apple, wild cherry, wintergreen, mint, cigar, and other flavors, and is packed in flake and plug form, in 1½ to 20lb containers. If you roll your own or pack a pipe, you can save with Stoker's long shredded tobacco for cigarettes, clipping cigar tobacco, and domestic and imported pipe tobacco blends (from $8 to $10 per 1½ lbs); plaid tobacco pouches are $2.50 each. And snuff-lovers can buy their choice of plain or sweet versions of the house No. 1 blend, or snuff flavored with mint, lemon, or cherry.

If your climate's right, you might try your hand at raising a little crop of your own. Stoker sells two varieties of tobacco seeds at $3 and $4 per teaspoonful. And if you're disappointed by the canned sweet potatoes and yams sold in the supermarket, see the list of 16 types Stoker offers. These sweet potatoes are sold in lots of 25 ($5.49) to 1,000 ($34.95), and shipped from April 15 to July 1. With any luck, you could set your holiday table with something quite superior to the tinned orange lumps passed off as tubers. A planting guide is included with each order. Prices are postpaid.

Samples of the tobacco will be sent upon request, and Mr. Stoker offers discounts on quantity orders (inquire for information). Your satisfaction is— if not expressly guaranteed in the literature we received—a high priority.

SEE ALSO:

Shannon Mail Order . . . Peterson of Dublin pipes . . . HOME (table settings)

CLOTHING

Clothing, furs, and accessories
for men, women, and children.

Today, you can buy just about anything to wear by mail—from just about any part of the world. Available are custom-made suits from Hong Kong, sweaters knitted to your design from Ireland, cashmere sweaters from the British Isles, Amish clothing from Indiana, stock underthings to silk lingerie from New York's Lower East Side, swimsuits that have qualified for the Olympics, T-shirts printed with any statement you'd like to make, bridal gowns, large-sized clothing, executive suiting for both sexes, kid's clothes and infants' basics, army-surplus gear, custom-made deerskin coats and jackets, and much more—at savings of up to 90%.

Clothing manufactured in the U.S. is now required to bear care labels that provide specific information on washing, dry cleaning, ironing, drying, etc. The FTC has prepared a booklet that defines all the terms used in the new labeling and answers a number of hypothetical questions. For a copy, request "What's New About Care Labels" from the Federal Trade Commission, Public Reference Office, Washington, DC 20580.

Learning what goes into quality construction of a garment is vital if you're going to shop for name-brand goods by mail. Do your homework while shopping in stores: Identify the manufacturers and designers who maintain high standards of workmanship, and then you'll feel confident about buying those goods without having examined them in person. At least two books can be recommended for the person who wants to get the most out of the least: *Dress Better for Less,* by Vicki Audette (Meadowbrook Press, 1981), and *Good Garb,* by William Dasheff and Laura Dearborn (Delta Publishing Company, Inc., 1980). Both should be available at local libraries.

I. BUSS & CO.

---

738 Broadway
New York, NY 10003
(212) 242–3338, 3339

Catalog: free; pub. yearly
Discount: 30% plus
Goods: surplus
Minimum Order: none
Shipping, Insurance: extra, itemized; UPS
Sales Tax: NY deliveries
Accepts: MO, certified check, MC, V, AE
$$$

This thriving military-surplus firm was founded in 1892 and has just compiled its first catalog. The goods shown represent the "classics" in surplus wear and gear, including a cotton tank top worn by British coal miners ($9.95), khaki cotton-drill pants for men and women, safari hats ($19.95), gray Swiss Army pouches with shoulder straps ($7.95), and the Brittany sailing sweater in cotton knit ($19.95). Especially attractive: a rubber slicker with buckle closures in black or yellow ($20.95), and an authentic French Army rubberized raincoat with slash pockets and half-cape back in pale army green ($28.95). Returns are accepted within ten days on goods with price tags attached.

CHARLIE'S PLACE

**61 Orchard St.
New York, NY 10002
(212) 431–8880**

Information: price quote by phone or letter with SASE
Discount: 20% to 35%
Goods: name brand
Minimum Order: none
Shipping: $3 per order; UPS
Sales Tax: NY deliveries
Accepts: check, MO, MC, V
$$$

Good buys on men's clothing are featured here—name-brand shirts, pants, and outerwear at up to 35% off list prices. The manufacturers stocked at Charlie's Place include Gant, Izod, Arrow, Geoffrey Beene, and London Fog. Business is done on an inquiry basis. Write with the style number or code, size, and color of what you want, and include a SASE with your letter.

CHOCK CATALOG CORP.

**74 Orchard St.
New York, NY 10002–4594
(212) 473–1929**

Catalog: $1; pub. in Apr. and Sept.
Discount: 25% to 35%
Goods: name brand, house brand
Minimum Order: none
Shipping, Handling: $3 per order; UPS
Sales Tax: NY deliveries
Accepts: check, MO, certified check, MC, V
$$$

Louis Chock has been known to bargain-hunting New Yorkers as a great source for unmentionables since it was established in 1921. Chock carries underwear, sleepwear, and hosiery for the entire family, at prices that run from 25% to 35% below list.

For women, there are stockings and panty hose by Mayer, Berkshire, and Hanes; underpants by Vassarette, Jockey For Her, Carter's, and Lollipop; and Vassarette slips and Louis Chock sleepwear. The men's department has boxers and briefs by Hanes, Jockey, and Munsingwear; BVD briefs; Jockey, Hanes, BVD, Munsingwear, and Louis Chock's private label undershirts; pajamas from Knothe, Botany, Oscar de la Renta, and Yves St. Laurent; Munsingwear polo shirts; Jiffies terry scuffs; and sport and dress socks by Interwoven, Burlington, Dior, Supp-Hose, and nonbranded nylon and all-cotton styles. Large and tall men, take note: The catalog has two pages of underwear in sizes running to XXXX (58 to 60).

Chock stocks complete layettes and nursery needs—from waterproof sheets and Curity diapers to a complete line of Carter's undershirts, creepers, gowns, and jamakins. Carter's nightwear and underthings for both boys and girls are listed, as well as Hanes and Jockey underwear for boys and Louis Chock socks.

If you're looking for something by one of the manufacturers mentioned here whose goods are not shown in the catalog, call or write to Chock with the style number—the item is probably available. Returns are accepted within 30 days on unopened packages.

CUSTOM COAT COMPANY, INC.

P.O. Box 69
Berlin, WI 54923–0069
(414) 361–0900

Catalog: free; pub. biannually
Discount: 50% plus
Goods: custom made, house brand
Minimum Order: none
Shipping, Insurance: extra; UPS, PP, FOB Berlin
Sales Tax: WI deliveries
Accepts: check, MO, certified check, MC, V
$$$$

This fall, you can go out and shoot yourself a coat, gloves, mittens, bags, moccasins, and small leather goods. You fell the animals—deer, elk, or moose—and send Custom Coat Co. the tanned or raw hides, and it will turn out your choice of clothing or accessories. Untanned hides can be cured for $1.50 per foot. Skins of odd or mismatched colors can be dyed a uniform dark, russet, or chocolate brown for $4.25 to $10 per hide. If you need tanning done but want to create your own leather goods, you have a choice of four or five colors (depending on the animal) and the charge is $1.50 per foot. Please note that it takes up to ten months to cure elk and moose hides, and no fur work is accepted. Complete details on curing hides, packing for shipping, and a guide to the number of hides needed per garment are provided in the 24-page color catalog.

Custom Coat's charges for creating garments from your leather are at least 50% less than what you'd pay a dressmaker or tailor for the same services—

and chances are neither would have Custom's expertise, acquired from almost 50 years of leather-working. Men's jackets and vests run from $32.25 for a western-style vest with button or zipper closure and rayon lining to $91.50 for a handsome, full-length coat with notched collar, center vent, and satin fleece or pile lining. The same styles made in the company's deerskin are $86.50 and $289.50. Prices on the women's vests and coats cover the same range. The choice of styles is substantial—simple town-and-country jackets and coats, classic wrap coats, safari and bush jackets, fringed styles, western models with scalloped edging and a variety of details, sports coats and fitted riding styles, and motorcycle, bomber, and even zippered sweatshirt-style jackets are available, in addition to a complement of vest designs.

The bags, gloves, and small leather goods represent real bargains, whether you supply the leather or have Custom use its stock deerskin. The bags include tailored envelope styles, fringed pouches, a plain drawstring hobo, a clutch with wrist strap, and some dressy models that cost from $8 to $26.50 ($15 to $52.50 in Custom's leather). The glove department offers mittens with a separate index finger for driving or shooting, an open-palmed style for hunting, all-purpose gloves with elasticized wrists, sturdy mittens for children, and dress gloves with nice details. They're sized for men and women and most can be ordered lined or unlined. And there are change purses, drawstring marble pouches, key cases, billfolds, cigarette cases, golf-club covers, and smooth-soled moccasins in low and laced styles. Gloves in Custom's deerskin are $6.75 to $19 ($4 to $9.75 in your leather); slip-in moccasins are $18.50 ($12, your leather); and many of the accessories are under $5.

Comprehensive measuring directions are given in the catalog, and you may order coats and jackets in larger sizes, longer lengths, with inside pockets, two-tone leather, and pile or fleece linings at an additional fee. Gloves can be ordered in short ("Cadet") or longer finger lengths for a small surcharge. Actual deerskin samples showing each color are provided with the price list.

D & A MERCHANDISE CO., INC.

**22 Orchard St.
New York, NY 10002
(212) 925–4766**

Catalog: free; pub. two to four times yearly
Information: price quote by phone
Discount: up to 33%
Goods: name brand
Minimum Order: none
Shipping: extra; UPS
Sales Tax: NY deliveries
Accepts: check, MO, MC, V
$$$

D & A, established in 1946, sells name-brand lingerie, socks, hosiery, and underwear for men, women, and boys. The men's underwear lines include

Hanes, Jockey, Munsingwear, BVD, Camp, and duofold; socks from Burlington, Interwoven, Dior, Camp, and Wigwam are available. Women can get great buys on underthings by Bali, Carnival, Christian Dior, Do All, Chicas, Lollipop, Exquisite Form, Flexnit, Formfit Rogers, Lillyette, Lily of France, Maidenform, Olga, Playtex, Poirette, Smoothie, Surprise, Vassarette, Warner's, and Danskin. There's hosiery by Burlington, Bonnie Doon, Camp, Trimfit, and Hanes. D & A also carries Hanes and BVD underwear in boys' sizes.

Most of the items are discounted from 25% to 33%, which are excellent reductions on these brands since they're usually sold at list price. Remember: If you don't see what you're looking for in the catalog, call with the style name or number and size for a price quote—it's probably in stock.

THE DEERSKIN PLACE

283 Akron Rd.
Ephrata, PA 17522
(717) 733–7624

Brochure: free, pub. yearly in Sept.
Discount: up to 50%
Goods: house brand
Minimum Order: none
Shipping, Handling: $2 minimum
Insurance: 50¢
Sales Tax: PA deliveries
Accepts: check, MO, MC, V, C.O.D.
$$

Clothing and accessories made of deerskin, sheepskin, and cowhide are offered in this firm's brochure, at prices of up to 50% less than those charged elsewhere for comparable goods. A fingertip-length shearling jacket with full collar and patch pockets is $225; fringed buckskin-suede jackets are $125. Attractive, sporty handbags run from $50 to $80, about a third less than similar styles sold in department stores. A variety of moccasins and casual shoes is offered—from tiny beaded booties at $11.95 to classic soft-soled mocs, sturdy chukka boots, and crepe-soled slip-ons for men and women at under $40. There are also deerskin wallets, clutches, coin purses, and key cases from $2.95 to $22; mittens and gloves for the whole family; beaded belts for $3.95; and a "kiddie coonskin cap" for under $8.

Readers accustomed to full-color catalogs and chatty essays on the glories of natural materials should be advised that this firm offers a bare-bones brochure with (in the example we reviewed) somewhat fuzzy black-and-white product photos. Color availability is specified on some goods and not on others; lining materials for bags and apparel are not generally identified, nor are the types of buttons and hardware used. Don't be put off by the lack of information, though; call or write to the firm *before* you order if you have questions. And bear in mind that The Deerskin Place will accept exchanges and guarantees your satisfaction.

EILEEN'S HANDKNITS

Ardara, Dept. W-3
Donegal
Ireland

Brochure: $2, deductible; pub. biannually
Discount: up to 60%
Goods: handmade, custom-made
Minimum Order: none
Shipping, Insurance: extra; surface mail, airmail
Duty: extra
Accepts: teller's check, MC, AE
$$$

Eileen's sweaters come from the "cottages of Ireland," handmade in patterns that differ from knitter to knitter. The catalog illustrates four styles for women and three for men—cardigans, pullovers, and jackets—but the knitters can create almost any design from traditional patterns and stitches if given complete descriptions of what is wanted. The garments are well-fitting, long-wearing, and classic in styling. Sweaters are under $70, compared to more than $130 in U.S. stores and catalogs. The "steals" here are the tams and mitts, worked in diamond and blackberry stitches; they cost just a few dollars each. Custom work is done for a nominal surcharge, and inquiries are invited. If the sweater doesn't fit when it arrives, it will be altered to suit you or a refund will be made.

EISNER BROS.

76 Orchard St.
New York, NY 10002
(212) 475–6868; 431–8800

Catalog: free
Discount: 30% to 50%
Goods: house brand, name brand
Minimum Order: one dozen of same item (see text)
Shipping, Handling: $5 minimum
Sales Tax: NY deliveries
Accepts: MO or certified check
$$$$

Eisner Bros. has been around for less than 15 years but demonstrates much more selling savvy than some of its third-generation neighbors on New York City's Lower East Side. The Eisners have established themselves as major distributors of T-shirts and other printable items, which they sell to stores, schools, athletic teams, and consumers worldwide. Prices and minimum-order requirements (generally one dozen of the same size and color) are the same for all customers.

The brands represented include Eisner's label, Hanes, Golden Orchard, Screen Stars, Active Sportswear, and Russell. Every style imaginable is shown in the 28-page catalog—"punk" cutoffs, midriff-baring "shimmel" shirts, muscle, long-sleeved, tank, V-neck, French-cut, camisole-style, and children's shirts. Sizes run from six months in the cotton-poly shirt ($13 a dozen) to XXXX (58 to 60) in the Hanes jumbo T-shirt ($42 a dozen), which doubles as a beach coverup or nightshirt. Sweatshirts and pants for children and adults are offered, along with football and baseball jerseys, polo shirts, soccer shirts, extra-long sweatshirts and nightshirts, and halter tops. You'll also find athletic shorts, baseball and coaching jackets, and a large selection of sporting caps and visors. The color range is extensive, and many of the basic items are available in 100% cotton as well as in the popular cotton-poly blend.

Eisner offers you a great way to stock up on men's and boys' underwear at prices of up to 50% less than retail. If you or another family member are a runner or sports enthusiast, note that many of the sweats and "athletic" styles can be ordered in half-dozens. Six pairs of sweat pants and tops will see you through a week of morning runs (you get one day off to do the laundry), and cost $5.25 each at Eisner (compared to *$14* for identical items at New York City stores). And don't keep the savings to yourself. Suggest Eisner as a supplier of athletic wear to your local school board. Consider T-shirts emblazoned with a slogan or logo for civic group fundraising events. Who knows—you might be voted Citizen of the Year!

THE FINALS

---

21 Minisink Ave., Dept. WB
Port Jervis, NY 12771
(914) 856–4456: NY orders
(800) 452–0452: NY orders
and inquiries
(800) 431–9111: orders and
inquiries except NY

Catalog: free; pub. in Mar. and Aug.
Discount: 50% plus
Goods: house brand
Minimum Order: $25 on credit cards
Shipping, Insurance: $3.75 minimum; UPS, PP
Sales Tax: NY deliveries
Accepts: check, MO, MC, V, AE
$$$$

The Finals outfits many American swim teams, and once you've seen its catalog, you'll know why: it offers an unbeatable combination of style, comfort, practicality, and price. The Finals begins with good fabrics (Dupont's Antron nylon and Lycra) and fashions suits designed to provide freedom of movement while minimizing drag in the water.

The swimsuits are sleek and fashionably cut, the women's high on the leg and neck and keyhole backs; the men's are a streamlined minimum. The Lycra in many of the suits ensures a tight fit for competitive use; those competing with the bathroom scale will like the way it smooths out small bulges. The Finals sells swimming aids as well: several types of swimming goggles, latex swim caps, fins, pull buoys, tubes, kick boards, and more.

The catalog also shows shirts, suits, and coverups for lifeguards and surfers; racquetball clothing and shoes; a great collection of running and track gear, and standard shirts, shorts, warm-ups, and sweats. Youthful athletes in the family? Singlets and shorts are $5 to $7 here, in "junior" unisex sizes. And there are Accusplit and Cronus timepieces, Sony's Walkman, and hair and skin products available as well.

This nine-year-old company has enjoyed immense growth over the years. It offers quality goods at great prices—men's swim trunks run from $7 to $12, women's suits from $12 to $25, and most are available in a spectrum of brilliant colors. The other apparel is equally inexpensive.

Your satisfaction is guaranteed or your money back; returns are accepted within 30 days, 90 days on defective goods.

F.R. KNITTING MILLS, INC.

69 Alden St.
Fall River, MA 02723
(617) 678–7553: inquiries
and MA orders
(800) 446–1089: orders
except MA

Catalog: free; pub. yearly
Discount: 40% to 60%
Goods: house brand
Minimum Order: none
Shipping, Insurance: 50¢ per item; UPS, PP
Sales Tax: MA, ME, NH, RI, VT deliveries (if applicable)
Accepts: check, MO, MC, V
$$$ (see text)

Marketing through factory outlets has become a real boon to the small manufacturer, and we're happy to note that many are also setting up direct-mail operations.

Fall River Knitting Mills is part of that trend. The Mill was founded in 1911 when Fall River was a thriving textile center, and the building itself is listed on the National Register. The sweaters produced there are as traditional as the building's six-over-six windows.

The catalog we reviewed showed 16 pages of turtlenecks, crews, V-necks, cardigans, rugby styles, and vests. The classic crewneck in 70% Shetland wool/30% Orlon runs from size six (boys and girls) to men's XL, and costs $9.95 to $11.95. It comes in 26 hues, from heathery wines and browns to bright cherry red and cobalt blue. If you're allergic to wool, you'll appreciate the variety of styles made in acrylic, Wintuk, and Orlon, also offered in a full spectrum of colors. Cotton crews are a steal at $12.95 each, as are the cotton interlock-knit turtlenecks, at less than $9 each. Argyles, snowflake patterns, collegiate stripes, and jacquard designs are executed in all sorts of sweaters and vests. And the "Pride of the Mill" is not to be missed—a cable-front pullover made of Scottish wool, sized for men and women, offered in pastels, gray, natural, and navy. The Mill compares it to others selling for up to $32, but we've seen sweaters of this quality in some catalogs for $45 and $50. Here, it's under $19.

The Mill's monogramming department will personalize your sweater or put that special touch on a gift at an additional cost. Choose from two dozen thread colors and nine styles, including plain script initials and the familiar hearts-and-flowers and anchor motifs.

Department stores command up to twice as much for the *same* sweaters, and none can match the size and color range available to you through the catalog. Your satisfaction is guaranteed on every purchase. Returns are accepted for exchange, refund, or credit. This is a super source for gifts, since *everyone* seems to appreciate another sweater.

CANADIAN READERS, PLEASE NOTE: Payment must be made in U.S. funds, and shipping charges may be higher than those stated in the catalog for orders shipped to Canada.

GOHN BROS.

P.O. Box 111, Dept. WBM-3
Middlebury, IN 46540–0111
(219) 825–2400

Catalog: 25¢; pub. 8 times yearly
Discount: 20% to 60%
Goods: name brand, generic
Minimum Order: none
Shipping, Insurance: 90¢ to $4; UPS, PP
Sales Tax: IN deliveries
Accepts: check, MO, certified check, C.O.D.
$$$$

Reading the Gohn Bros. catalog will take you back to the world where bonnet board, buckram, quilting sheeting, crinoline, and suspender webbing were stock items in the general store. The prices recall better days too, with bow ties at $2.59; 100% cotton Sanforized blue denim in 10 and 13¾-oz weights from $3.29 to $4.69 a yard; muslin at $1.39 a yard; chambray at $1.59 a yard; and quilting thread for 79¢ a spool.

This company is a source for Amish clothing (some of the shirts fasten with hooks and eyes), and the clothes are work-tailored, sturdy, and inexpensive. Men's cotton chambray workshirts are $7.39; broadfall pants (denim) are $12.99; and men's underwear ranges from undershirts at $2.79 each to thermal union suits for $12.69. Men's cotton dress socks, $3.50 in New York stores, are only 79¢ here.

Gohn sells the durable Red Wing shoes for men at 20% off suggested retail prices, and offers rubber galoshes and footwear by LaCrosse and Tingley. In addition, there are work gloves, felt hats, handkerchiefs, diapers and Gerber baby clothing, and—to shade your horse-drawn carriage—a large black buggy umbrella for $12.79.

Gohn's yard-goods department offers such hard-to-find items as all-cotton percale and quilting prints, pillow tubing, 100% cotton sheeting, tailor's canvas, haircloth, mosquito netting, and more. Gohn has batiste at $2.19 a yard, lawn, Swiss organdy, and some double knits. Embroidery floss is 17¢ a skein; wool overcoating under $11 a yard; and there are stiffening, suit lining, and interfacing materials. The prices are about as low as you'll find anywhere, and many of the items Gohn carries are almost impossible to get elsewhere.

Gohn has been doing business since 1906 and proves that practice makes perfect; orders are filled and shipped the day they're received, and satisfaction is guaranteed.

GOLDMAN & COHEN INC.

---

54 Orchard St.
New York, NY 11598–5052
(212) 966–0737

Information: price quote by phone or letter with SASE

Discount: 20% to 60%

Goods: name brand

Minimum Order: none

Shipping, Insurance: $2.50 per order up to $100; $4 on orders of $100 and over; UPS

Sales Tax: NY deliveries

Accepts: check, MO, MC, V, AE

$$$

You can save up to 60% on women's intimate apparel by Bali, Maidenform, Warner's, Playtex, Lily of France, Vanity Fair, Christian Dior, Olga, and other top manufacturers and designers at Goldman & Cohen. (No hosiery is available.)

Although many Lower East Side firms selling the same lines publish price lists or catalogs, Goldman & Cohen has done mail order without one since 1968. You must call or write (include a SASE) for a price quote, and supply style numbers, sizes, colors, etc. when querying. And remember: ordering from a catalog may be more convenient, but the production costs are usually worked into the product markup. This firm repays your small effort of sending or calling for a quote by giving you some of the best buys around on unmentionables.

HANDART EMBROIDERIES

Room #106, Hing Wai
Building
36 Queen's Road Central
Hong Kong
Phone # (5) 235744

Catalog: free; pub. yearly in Jan.
Discount: 30% to 80%; quantity discounts (see text)
Goods: handcrafted, generic
Minimum Order: none
Shipping, Handling, Insurance: included, surface mail; $4 per pound, airmail
Duty: extra
Accepts: check, certified check, IMO, MC, V, AE, Access, EC
$$$$

Handart's catalog—ten photocopied pages illustrating embroidered robes, housecoats, pajamas, handkerchiefs, table linens, sheets, and jewelry—represents just a fraction of the goods stocked by the company. The current listings begin with floor-length cotton robes, or "happy coats," decorated with dragons and other symbols ($8 and up). It ends with hand-embroidered silk ladies' mandarin robes for $40, the type sold in New York City for $80 and more. Handart has satin brocade smoking jackets for "gents" and children's pajamas in brightly colored satin with frog closings, from $8 to $14. The black cotton Kung Fu suits ($14) and shoes ($2.50) are exactly half the price they are in the U.S. Hand-embroidered blouses are available in cotton/poly, polyester crêpe de Chine, and pure silk from $17 to $45 each, less than half the prices commanded for the same goods stateside. There are men's shirts in silk at $20, silk neckties and scarves, and even nightgowns and pajamas in a choice of poly/cotton, rayon, or silk, at no more than $50. Or you can create your own fashions in pongee, raw silk, and satin brocade, all of which cost $7 per 30-inch-wide yard. Spectacular buys can also be found on cloisonné, Taiwan jade, and ivory jewelry and charms.

Drawnwork and embroidered handkerchiefs selling in New York City stores for $5 to $25 run from $6 to $100 *per dozen* at Handart. Hand-embroidered tablecloths and matching napkins begin at $8 for a 36″ square with four napkins and run to $800 for a 6′ × 18′ cloth with 24 napkins. We found similar cloths at a major "discount" house selling for up to four times as much—and that U.S. firm didn't carry as many sizes. Sets of satin (acetate) sheets and pillow cases at Handart cost about as much as *one* sheet of the same size from another popular catalog we consulted.

The savings at Handart are unimpaired by shipping costs since surface mail is included in the prices. Airmail is $4 per pound extra, and billed after the goods are shipped. Handart also offers quantity discounts of 5% on orders over $250 to 25% on those over $1,500. Satisfaction is guaranteed or your money back.

**IRISH COTTAGE
INDUSTRIES LTD.**

44 Dawson St.
Dublin 2
Ireland
Phone # 713039; 713224

Catalog: $1; pub. yearly in Feb.
Samples of Tweeds: $1
Discount: 30% to 60%
WBMC Reader Discount: 10% (see text)
Goods: handmade
Minimum Order: none
Shipping, Handling, Insurance: extra; itemized
Duty: extra (see text)
Accepts: check, IMO, MC, V, AE, DC, Access, EC
$$$

Irish Cottage Industries sends a colorful brochure illustrating Aran sweaters in different patterns and styles. Wool stoles, tweed blouses, scarves, Aran mittens, caps, gloves, place mats, socks, tweed caps, linen handkerchiefs, pewter cups—and even a blackthorn walking stick for about $7—are also listed. Children's sweaters costs about $30 and adults' run up to $70—at least 40% less than comparable goods in the U.S. The "tweeds" sold here are anything but salt-and-pepper dull. Woven in a Disneyland of colors, they are striped, checked, bright, and cheerful. A set of six table mats (about $9) comes in ten colors. The soft, featherweight "gossamer" tweed blouses (under $40) come in solids and stripes of white, brown, pale blue, emerald, and mauve.

The catalog states that "gift parcels under $50" can be sent to the U.S. duty-free, something to remember at Christmas. And don't forget about the WBMC Reader Discount: you may take 10% off the cost of your order, *not including postage costs, if* you pay by check or IMO. (If you make payment with a charge or credit card, you are not eligible for this discount.) Remember to identify yourself as a WBMC reader when you order.

KENNEDY OF ARDARA

Ardara, Co. Donegal
Ireland
Phone # Ardara 6

Catalog: $3, refundable; pub. yearly in Mar.
Discount: to 70%
Goods: handmade
Minimum Order: none
Shipping, Insurance: $9 per garment, surface mail;
    $13, airmail
Duty: extra (see text)
Accepts: check, MO, MC, V, AE, CB, DC, Access,
    EC
$$$

Tucked away in the mountains of Donegal are 900 cottage knitters who create sweaters and accessories of pure, creamy-colored Aran wool in traditional patterns and designs handed down through generations of Irish women. The sweaters pictured in the brochure are classic cardigans and pullovers for both men and women. With good care, they should grow softer with every washing, keep their shape, and not wear out. None costs more than $60; far lower, says Kennedy, than the prices in Lord and Taylor, Saks Fifth Avenue, and Bloomingdale's, where the Kennedy sweaters are sold at retail prices. There are shawls at about $16, Aran mitts for $4.10 per pair, and hats and vests.

Kennedy also sells a number of items not pictured in the brochure: tartan blankets, throws, double-damask tablecloths in seven sizes with matching napkins, mohair scarves and stoles, men's tweed caps, hats, ties, and tweed jackets in six shades; women's tweed capes and jackets, hand-crocheted tray cloths, dressing table sets, coasters, and more. Your inquiries on these goods are invited.

PLEASE NOTE: Duty may not be charged on certain types of goods sold here. Check with your local Customs office for current rates before ordering.

LAURENCE CORNER

62/64 Hampstead Rd.
London NW1 2NU
England
Phone # 01–388–6811

Catalog: $2 via surface mail
Information: price quote by letter
Discount: to 70%
Goods: surplus; new and used
Minimum Order: none
Shipping, Handling, Insurance: extra; surface mail
Duty: extra
Accepts: check, IMO, MC, V, AE, CB, DC, Access, EC

$$$

"A little alteration or attention can turn an ex-Government item of clothing into a highly fashionable article at a fraction of its normal cost." This is the appeal of surplus clothing, summed up by Laurence Corner, London's 33-year-old market for new and used government-surplus clothing and equipment, and odds and ends from all over the world.

The 30-page catalog is a prime example of British humor, illustrated with photos of what is probably the staff, clowning around in bomber jackets, rainwear, greatcoats, underwear, shooting apparel, uniforms from every branch of every service, cowboy hats, and much more. The British surplus business appears to have a unique flavor, stocking World War II hymnals (unused and interdenominational) field operating tables, G.I. pajamas, anti-kerosene jumpsuits, prison handkerchiefs, de Gaulle caps, or periscopes.

New additions to this intriguing catalog are the hospital and restaurant gear (chef's hats and aprons, isolation gowns, etc.), surplus wear for kids (made for cadets), and a line of leather jackets and pants in western styles. Laurence has also established a super theatrical department, and lists c. 1896 costumes from the Imperial Russian Ballet and parasols, tuxedos, sporrans, cudgels, doublets—even Lord Leigh's pith helmet—among the current stock. Some of the costumes mentioned would interest the serious collector, and inquiries are invited on specific items not listed.

The goods are surplus-cheap, and even with duty and the packing and postage charges, there are bargains galore. Remember that Laurence Corner ships both goods and the catalog by surface mail *only,* so allow plenty of time for arrival. And do write *before* ordering if you have questions about an item or its condition or if you're looking for something not shown in the catalog.

In addition to surplus clothing and government goods, Laurence Corner sells art. See the separate listing in the "Art, Antiques, and Collectibles" chapter under the Euston Gallery for more information.

LEE-MCCLAIN CO.

P.O. Box 365
Shelbyville, KY 40065
(502) 633–3823

Brochure: free; pub. yearly in Sept.
Discount: 40% to 50%
Goods: house brand
Minimum Order: none
Shipping: included; UPS
Sales Tax: KY deliveries
Accepts: check, MO, MC, V
$$$

Deciding how to dress for the office has become a process more difficult and anxiety-provoking than managing a million-dollar portfolio or handling a merger—or so "fashion" would have it. Before you go into a dither sponsored by *GQ* or *Working Woman,* remember that the smart money is still on classic clothing: quality fabric, construction, fit, and tailoring never lose impact or real style.

Lee-McClain can supply you with the backbone of a good business wardrobe—suits, jackets, blazers, and coats—at prices 40% to 50% lower than those of comparable garments, and even less than similar styles bearing designer labels. The firm's "Strathmore" clothing line includes men's and women's suits featuring slightly fitted, two-button jackets with flap pockets, moderate lapels, and center vents. The men's slacks are cut straight and full; the women's suit skirts were offered in pinch-pleated and A-line styles in the brochure we received. Fabric choices vary from season to season but include such standards: cashmere and blends, camel hair, wool, worsted, flannel, gabardine, pinstripes, herringbones, glen plaids, hopsacking, and other weaves. The garments are cut and sewn for optimum drape; seams are all matched; and alterations will be done at no additional fee. It's hard to beat $195 for a smashing cashmere sport coat or $250 for a woman's camel hair suit. Wool-worsted slacks for men cost $39, and men's suits in wool flannel are $175.

Lee-McClain will send swatches of fabric for styles made in your size. We recommend noting actual measurements (shoulder width, arm length, waist, and inseam; bust, waist, and hips; height, etc.), instead of standard suit or dress size, to ensure the best fit. Lee-McClain has over half a century of experience in the manufacture of clothing and can answer any questions concerning details not shown or described in the brochure.

L'EGGS SHOWCASE OF SAVINGS

L'eggs Brands, Inc.
Box 1010
Rural Hall, NC 27098
(919) 744–3435: inquiries
(919) 744–3000: orders

Catalog: free
Discount: up to 50% on irregulars
Goods: house brand, name brand; irregular and first-quality
Minimum Order: $20 on credit cards
Shipping, Handling: $1.10 to $2.65; UPS, PP
Sales Tax: NC deliveries
Accepts: check, MO, MC, V
$$$

You know L'eggs—those neat ovoid capsules that line racks in just about every supermarket and variety store in the country. And you know that L'eggs hosiery is reasonably priced, even at full retail. But you can save over 50% on many of your favorite styles by purchasing through the Showcase of Savings catalog, *and* choose from more styles and colors.

We found Sheer Energy, Active Support, Sheer Elegance, Summer L'eggs, knee-highs, Winter L'eggs, and L'eggs Regular in the catalog, as well as the control-top models offered in the different lines. Almost all are available in queen sizes. The color choices include the standard range of nude to off-black and fashion shades in the Sheer Elegance and opaque lines. Note that the hosiery is "slightly imperfect" (irregular), but the catalog promises that it's "perfectly wearable."

The 40-page color catalog also shows slips, half-slips, camisoles, petti-pants, bras, and panties by L'eggs. These are clearly identified as first-quality or imperfect. L'eggs also carries some workout wear—leotards and tights in a shimmering Antron Lycra spandex blend, and a striped leotard and stirrup tights of comfortable cotton/poly/Lycra. Complete measuring guides are provided in the catalog, so you're sure of ordering your proper size.

L'eggs produces four additional catalogs, including Sheer Variety (first-quality hosiery and lingerie), True Delight (larger sizes), L'eggs Stockings (first-quality stockings), and L'eggs Nurse White Hosiery (first-quality products for health professionals). These catalogs may be ordered through the Showcase of Savings catalog.

Have reservations about ordering products with flaws, however insignificant? The L'eggs guarantee of complete satisfaction should reassure you: returns are accepted for replacement, refund, or credit. (Worn items must be washed before returning.)

THE MAIL ORDER BRIDE, INC.

P.O. Box 160
Stilwell, KS 66085

Information: price quote by letter with SASE
Discount: up to 30%
Goods: name brand
Minimum Order: none
Shipping, Insurance: extra; UPS, PP
Sales Tax: KS deliveries
Accepts: certified check, C.O.D. (see text)
$$

The prospective bride who's set the date and begun shopping for her gown soon learns the second meaning of "the big day." That walk down the aisle can easily cost her upward of $10,000, and that's *before* the cousins are flown in from Skokie.

Thanks to The Mail Order Bride, she can save up to 30% on the cost of gowns and dresses for the entire wedding party and spare herself the carnival of bridal-shop consultations. (An afternoon spent gown-shopping in a large bridal salon will test a woman's fortitude—how many anxiety attacks can she suffer before giving in to the Scarlett O'Hara number the saleswoman insists looks simply "ma-a-arvelous" on her?)

Spare yourself. Instead, sit down with current copies of *Bride's* and *Modern Bride* and make your selection from the ads and editorial pages. Then send those pages to The Mail Order Bride, and you'll get a price quote. A deposit of 50% of the gown's retail price is required, along with measurements of each person being outfitted.

Delivery will take about three months, which is typical of bridal salons as well, and orders are shipped C.O.D. Fewer mail-order firms are shipping C.O.D. these days because of the high rate of refusal, but that's unlikely with this company since, once placed, *orders cannot be canceled.* If possible, we recommend seeing the gown in a local store or bridal show before ordering to make sure it's what you really want. If you feel guilty about doing this in your local salon, you can always buy a garter or the ring pillow there to ease your conscience. And if the shop will handle alterations on gowns purchased elsewhere, you can have your dress nipped and tucked there—The Mail Order Bride doesn't offer this service.

NATIONAL WHOLESALE COMPANY, INC.

400 National Blvd., Dept. WBM
Lexington, NC 27292
(704) 249–0211

Catalog: free; pub. Feb., Apr., May, July, Sept., Oct., Dec.
Discount: 30% to 50%
WBMC Reader Bonus: free pantyhose offer to new customers (see text)
Goods: house brand, name brand
Minimum Order: one box (see text); $5 for WBMC Reader Bonus
Shipping, Handling: 95¢ per order; UPS, PP
Sales Tax: NC deliveries
Accepts: check, MO, MC, V, AE
$$$

National Wholesale offers virtually every woman, regardless of height or girth, a chance to save on panty hose. The catalog shows several control-top, support, sheer mesh, and cotton-soled styles, plus a shimmering model of nylon and Lycra. Stockings (support, sheer, garterless) and knee-highs are also available. The hosiery is sized to fit almost any woman, whether she's five feet tall or has 60-inch hips. It's sold by the box (three or six pairs) at prices around 30% below comparable retail. Further savings are possible if you buy a dozen pairs.

In addition to the great hosiery buys, the catalog offers bras, girdles, and body shapers by Glamorise, Sarong, Kayser, Exquisite Form, and Playtex; cotton-knit vests, briefs, and long-leg pants (once referred to as "bloomers"); thermal underwear and pants liners; slips by Pinehurst, Barbizon, and Fig-urefit; and dusters by Swirl. Many of the foundation garments are available in hard-to-find larger sizes.

National Wholesale is offering WBMC readers who have not ordered from the firm previously a bonus offer of a pair of panty hose or knee-highs with orders of $5 or more. Be sure to say that you're a *WBMC reader* and a *new customer* when requesting the catalog and the bonus coupon will be enclosed.

This firm has the endorsement of its local Chamber of Commerce and has been doing business since 1952. Satisfaction is guaranteed or your money back.

PAGANO GLOVES, INC.

3–5 Church St.
Johnstown, NY 12095–2196
(518) 762–8425

Catalog: $1.75, refundable; pub. yearly
Discount: 50% to 75%
WBMC Reader Discount: 10% on orders of $250
  or more
Goods: house brand
Minimum Order: none
Shipping, Handling, Insurance: $3 per order; UPS
Sales Tax: NY deliveries
Accepts: check, MO, certified check, MC, V
$$$

What's butter-soft, improves with age, and looks as good as it feels?

Deerskin. Pagano Gloves has been selling its deerskin clothing, gloves, and footwear since 1946 and offers a large part of its inventory in its 32-page color catalog. Men and women can choose from dozens of coats, jackets, and vests in enduring styles—gored and belted coats, tailored and fringed western models, and classic boxy jackets with notched lapels, to name a few. Motorcyclists are offered an alternative to black leather and rivets in Pagano's streamlined, wind-cutting jackets for men and women. There are also several western-style jackets in sueded cowhide.

Those searching for soft, well-made footwear should consult the catalog for its boots, shoes, and slippers. There are chukka-boot and moccasin styles for men and women, slippers lined with sherpa (synthetic sheepskin), travel slippers, etc. These all make welcome gifts, as do the billfolds, keycases, tobacco pouches, or handbags. Each is simple in design and well constructed.

Science has established the existence of black holes; we have deduced their purpose: to remove, each winter, millions of gloves from the face of the earth. The holes are selective; they take only one glove and it always belongs to a favorite pair. Pagano provides the best consolation—a selection of mittens and gloves in classic styles. Sherpa-lined mitts, perforated golfing and driving gloves, and ribbed-back dress gloves are but a few of the choices. Specialty gloves for shooting, archery, and bowhunting are also available. All unlined gloves are washable.

Pagano's prices represent savings of 30% to 75% compared to those of similar goods in specialty and department stores. As a WBMC reader, you may deduct 10% if your order totals $250 or more. (This discount applies to the cost of the goods only.) Please note that custom services—large sizes, different garment and glove-finger lengths, and pile linings are available at very reasonable surcharges.

THE PETTICOAT EXPRESS

318 W. 39th St.
New York, NY 10018–1407
(212) 594–1276

Flyer: free
Discount: 40% minimum
Goods: house brand
Minimum Order: none
Shipping, Handling, Insurance: $3 per order; UPS,
   PP
Sales Tax: NY deliveries
Accepts: check, MO, certified check
$$$

Most of us get married with the intention of staying that way, but it's the person who has to ante up when the wedding is over who prays hardest for a lifetime match. Now that rules have relaxed, more brides are footing the bill for expenses their parents once assumed, and they're shopping carefully.

Petticoat Express offers savvy brides an easy way to cut 40% off the cost of one unseen necessity—the net and taffeta slips that create the charming silhouette of a full-skirted bridal or attendant's gown. Two styles are offered, in white only: an A-line (#130) for dresses of moderate flare and a flounced, bouffant slip (#640) for full skirts. At $15 and $17 each, a bride could save up to $78 if she were outfitting a party of six. Sizes run from 3/4 to 19/20.

Remember that these petticoats aren't just for weddings—they do wonders for full-skirted evening dresses and costumes. And once you've worn one, you'll be privy to a sound that men of yore found quintessentially feminine, a sound rarely heard today: the muffled rustle of taffeta.

PRINCE FASHIONS LTD.

G.P.O. Box 2868
Hong Kong
Phone #5–780993, 744106

Catalog: free; pub. in Dec. and June
Shirt Swatches and Style Book: free
Suit Swatches and Style Book: $5
Discount: up to 70%
WBMC Reader Discount: 10% (see text)
Goods: name brand, generic, custom made
Minimum Order: None
Shipping: included on some items; $1.20 to $10 on
   others; airmail, surface mail
Duty: extra
Accepts: check, certified check, IMO
$$$

Savvy shoppers have long called Hong Kong the poor man's Savile Row, where it's possible to get custom-made suits and shirts at ridiculously low prices. Prince Fashions makes this service available to mail-order customers worldwide. Bespoken men's suits in fine wool are just $110 and can be made in flannel, cashmere, silk and wool, gabardine, and other fabrics. Shirts are $10.80 in poly/cotton and $18.80 in pure silk. Swatches can be sent (see the information above). A measuring guide is included with both swatch sets.

The color catalog shows pages of women's clothing, including several smart skirts and pants that can be made to your waist/hip/length specifications. Fabrics include wool, cotton velvet, linen, and gabardine, and prices run from $9.40 to $13. There are also classic, well-cut suits and jackets at equally low prices. The other clothing runs the gamut from polyester pantsuits, caftans, and batiked sundresses to hand-embroidered silk blouses ($12.60), satin-lined angora cardigans embellished with embroidery and beadwork, and wool sweaters with cable-knit fronts. Nightwear, much of it oriental in design, is available for every member of the family. Also shown are happi coats and baseball-style jackets; adorable smocked and embroidered dresses for babies and little girls; hostess aprons; satin brocade and needlepoint purse and travel accessories; and embroidered handkerchiefs. Black "Kung Fu" shoes and brocade slippers are sold here at half their U.S. prices. There are reversible leather belts for $4.20, silk ties and scarves, leather handbags, embroidered pillow slips and table linens, Chinese dolls, and oil paintings as well.

Prince also offers a large selection of jewelry, from cloissoné bangles to rings rich with clusters of rubies and sapphires. Again, prices are very low, but you may want to write with questions before ordering. (For example, a catalog note indicates that gold items are plated with five microns of 24K gold. This is heavier than electroplate, but because 24K is pure, hence soft, we wonder how it will wear on rings, which often see constant use.) Quartz-analog watches by Seiko and Casio are available at excellent prices; they're all sold under warranties which are honored worldwide.

This is a prince of a source, and with over 15 years of mail-order experience, the firm knows how to resolve any problems should they arise. Readers of this book are entitled to a discount of 10% on the catalog prices, most of which include shipping. The deduction applies to your *first order only*. Identify yourself as a WBMC reader when ordering, and if you're buying goods for which there are additional shipping charges, *do not* include those fees when you take off the 10%. Please note that the last zero has been dropped from some prices to conserve catalog space, so that "$8.40" becomes "$8.4."

PRISMATEX

**800 Sixth Ave., Dept.
WBMC
New York, NY 10001
(212) 686–7490**

Price List: free with SASE; pub. twice yearly
Discount: 35% to 40%
Goods: name brand
Minimum Order: a dozen items (see text)
Shipping, Handling, Insurance: extra on orders
    under $50; included on orders $50 and over;
    UPS
Sales Tax: NY deliveries
Accepts: check, MO, certified check
$$$

Prismatex is one of many New York mail-order firms that runs a thriving "wholesale" business and offers its most popular products to consumers as well—at considerable savings.

Prismatex sells underwear by Berkshire and Hanes for men and boys, hosiery and panties for women by Berkshire, Mayer panties, and such stock items as tube socks. It's a great source for first-quality basics at up to 40% off, and you can combine any dozen items to meet the minimum-order requirement.

The firm has been in business since 1979 and plans to offer more product lines in its mail-order division in the future.

RACHEL'S FOR KIDS

**4218 13th Ave.
Brooklyn, NY 11219
(718) 435–6875**

Information: price quote by letter with SASE
Discount: 20% to 35%
Goods: name brand
Minimum Order: none
Shipping, Insurance: $2 on the first item; $1 each
    additional; UPS
Sales Tax: NY deliveries
Accepts: check, MO, MC, V
$$$

Our editor's nephew, Thomas, was approached on the playground by a schoolmate who looked him over and declared, "I don't like your clothes." Thomas retorted, "Too bad." The schoolmate replied, "No, it's too bad for you." That the sartorial critique was issued by one five-year-old to another may surprise those who've lost touch with the video generation, but making a fashion/identity statement is just as important to little ones as it is to those of us who pay for it.

You can pay 20% to 35% less for reasonably stylish, comfortable, long-wearing clothing by buying from Rachel's. Among the brands featured here are Oshkosh, Carter's, Billy the Kid, Izod, Dijon, Cutecumber, and Absorba. Sizes run from infant to youth on full lines of separates and activewear. Business is done on a price-quote basis; write with the description or style number, size, and color of the item you want, and include a SASE. Try to get your request to Rachel's as soon as you see the new season's goods arriving in department stores, since you'll have a better selection of colors, fabrics, and styles (stock moves quickly at this popular store). And list second color choices when you order. If Junior insists that wearing blue Oshkosh overalls to school will precipitate trauma and social rejection, you may drop dark hints about how he might *earn* his clothing allowance in the future. This should ensure silence, if not gratitude.

REBORN MATERNITY

**1449 Third Ave.
New York, NY 10028
(212) 737-8817**

Catalog: $2
Discount: 10% to 50%
Goods: name brand, house brand
Minimum Order: $20
Shipping, Insurance: extra; UPS, PP
Sales Tax: CT and NY deliveries
Accepts: check, MO, MC, V, AE
$$$

You can look your best while at your biggest without dipping into Baby's trust fund if you buy from Reborn Maternity, where Jordache, Sasson, J.G. Hook, Belle France, and other famous labels are discounted up to 50%. You can lead a complete life with fashionable swimwear, sportswear, office and dressy clothing, and evening outfits in sizes that run up to 18. The fashions have been chosen to work through your entire pregnancy, in styles that flatter the silhouette at every stage and materials that will be comfortable from one season to the next. Returns are accepted for store or catalog credit.

REIN FURS

**32 New York Ave., Dept.
WC
Freeport, NY 11520
(516) 379-6421**

Literature: free with SASE
Information: price quote by phone or letter with
   SASE
Discount: 10% on sale prices (see text)
Goods: house brand, custom made
Minimum Order: none
Shipping, Insurance: included; UPS, registered PP
Sales Tax: NY deliveries
Accepts: check, MO, certified check
$$$ 🍁   (see text)

"*You can't WEAR high overhead* . . . so why PAY for it?" asks Arthur Rein in his emphatically punctuated brochures. He's ready, willing, and able to create fur garments and accessories for men and women at 10% less than prices charged by his competitors. This includes advertised *sale* prices—which means you can ultimately save 50% to 60% by buying from Rein. (You must provide the dated ad within 30 days of its publication, and the competitor must be selling unrestricted quantities, colors, etc.) You can also send ads and catalog pages showing furs from Neiman-Marcus, Revillon, Ben Kahn, Perry Ellis, and the like and expect a Rein quote for a copy at 30% less.

All furs legal in the U.S. are available here, including Russian sable, lynx, fisher, marten, fox (red, Norwegian blue, silver, etc.), chinchilla, beaver, muskrat, opossum, raccoon, nutria, otter, ermine, coyote, and Blackglama, Emba, and other ranch mink.

Rein has an inventory of ready-made furs, but the custom services he offers are the real core of the business. In addition to coats and jackets of every style, size, and length, you can order stoles, ponchos, vests, hats, boas, scarves, muffs, collars, cuffs, bedspreads, pillow covers, rugs, and just about anything else you want. Fur remodeling—lengthening, stole-to-jacket conversions, color darkening, relining, etc.—is done through Rein's New York City shop, which also houses his showroom. The address and details on the services are given in the literature. Used furs are purchased, and Rein also sells "like-new" garments. Skins and mink scraps, of interest to hobbyists, can also be purchased.

Rein Furs, which may be known to some as "Ada's Custom Fashion Furrier," has been selling furs by mail since 1967. Some coats, jackets, and hats are shown in the literature, but the photographic reproduction is poor. We recommend doing business on an inquiry basis to be sure you get exactly what you want. The procedure for submitting information for a price quote is outlined in Rein's brochures. Every purchase is covered by a guarantee of satisfaction, and returns are accepted within three days for refund. All furs are warranted for a year against defects in workmanship and materials.

CANADIAN READERS, PLEASE NOTE: orders sent to Canada are charged shipping at *cost*.

W.S. ROBERTSON (OUTFITTERS) LTD.

40/41 Bank St.
Galashiels
Scotland
Phone # (0896) 2152

Brochures and Price Lists: $5; pub. in the spring and fall
Discount: 15% (see text)
Goods: name brand
Minimum Order: none
Shipping, Insurance: $3 per item, surface mail; $6, airmail
Duty: extra
Accepts: check, certified check, IMO
$$$

There are cashmere sweaters, and then there are Pringles. Pringle of Scotland has been making fine knitwear since 1815, using natural fibers like cashmere, camel hair, "lamaine" (a Merino wool), lambswool, and Shetland wool. W.S. Robertson sells Pringle's pullovers, cardigans, vests, and polo shirts at savings of about 35% on U.S. prices. (Robertson maintains that the savings are 15%, but our comparisons showed that it had underestimated U.S. markups by about 20%.) Robertson also carries the stylish Lyle & Scott sweaters. Considered as fine as Pringles, they're made in cashmere, lambswool, and Botany wool, and are somewhat less expensive than the comparable Pringle models. The highly regarded knits by Ballantyne and Braemar, in cashmere, lambswool, and Shetland wool, are offered as well.

As long as you're having the goods delivered to an address not in the U.K., you should deduct an additional 15% (the Value Added Tax, not charged on exported goods). The final figure is your purchase price. If you're not paying in pounds, obtain the rate of exchange from your local bank on the day you order and use that figure to convert the pounds to dollars. Remember to add shipping costs *after* you compute the export discount.

ROMANES & PATERSON LTD.

The Edinburgh Woollen Mill
Langholm DG13 OBR
Dumfriesshire
Scotland
Phone # (0541) 80092

Catalog: free
Discount: 20% to 50%
Goods: house brand, name brand
Minimum Order: none
Shipping, Insurance: about $15 per parcel; surface mail
Handling: $5 per order (see text)
Duty: extra
Accepts: certified check, V, AE, Access
$$$

Great Britain's tradition of fine woolens predates the Roman invasion. Scotland's River Tweed, Argyllshire, Cheviot Hills, and Shetland Islands have lent their names to fabrics which have made enduring contributions to the industry.

But you don't have to search the highlands for impeccable skirts and sweaters: a marvelous group of clothing and accessories is available through Romanes & Paterson, the mail-order division of The Edinburgh Woollen Mill. The 32-page color catalog shows dozens of skirts, jackets, and sweaters knitted and woven in the soft, classic styles so popular in the British Isles. There are pleated and A-line skirts and kilts of pure new wool in several weaves, matching jackets and blazers, and sweaters of lambswool and cashmere. The colors are the muted heather blues, greens, mauves, and reliable cream and camel that never go out of style. You'll also find kitten-soft sweaters for women of a lambswool/angora blend in boldly striped patterns and traditional designs, authentic tartan skirts with coordinating sweaters for women and girls, and very heavy sweaters that might double as jackets on chilly autumn days. There are even hand-knitted Aran and Icelandic-design sweaters, scarves, hats, and mittens, and sweater kits in both styles.

In addition to its own label, R&P sells the polished separates of Dalkeith, pretty sweaters of lambswool and cashmere by Glenmac, both sporty and classic sweaters for men and women from Pringle, and several lambswool Lyle & Scott models. The color chart provided at the end of the catalog is vital, since it's impossible to visualize such hues as "petrol," "tern," "bottle," and "mallard." Complete measuring and size information is also given. An embroidery service is available: for about $3, a name or initials can be put on your sweater; custom insignias, crests, and logos may be created to order.

Catalog prices are listed in pounds sterling, and at an exchange rate of $1.50 to the pound they run from 20% to 50% below comparable retail— lambswool sweaters begin at about $15, skirts at $27. Payment made by certified check in dollars must be calculated on the exchange rate prevailing when the order is sent, and you should include $5 for bank processing charges. Your satisfaction is guaranteed. Unworn returns are accepted within 21 days.

A. ROSENTHAL, INC.

**92 Orchard St.
New York, NY 10002
(212) 473-5428**

Catalog: $1; pub. yearly
Information: price quote by phone or letter with SASE
Discount: 20% to 33%
Goods: name brand
Minimum Order: $20 on credit cards
Shipping, Handling, Insurance: $2.50 per order; UPS
Sales Tax: NY deliveries
Accepts: check, MO, certified check, MC, V
$$$

A. Rosenthal has been a fixture on New York's Lower East Side since 1943. This family-run business discounts women's intimate apparel from 25% to 33%, and publishes a catalog that shows a sample of the stock.

Our mailing included an insert listing brands, stock numbers, and discounted prices of hundreds of additional goods. (If you've done your "store work" and copied style numbers and list prices from tags while in the dressing room, you'll be able to shop from this sheet.) You can buy bras, girdles, panties, slips, panty hose, and other goods by Bali, Burlington, Camp Corsets, Dior, Chicas, Chantelle, Danskin, Eve Stillman, Exquisite Form, Formfit Rogers, Flexnit, Goddess, Intimage, Kayser, Lejaby, Lily of France, Lillyette, Lady Marlene, Lollipop, Maidenform, Olga, Playtex, Poirette, Rago, Smoothie, Subtract, Vassarette, Warner's, and other firms at savings of up to 33%. If you don't see what you want in the catalog or on the price sheet, you can call or write (include a SASE) for a price quote. PLEASE NOTE: The shop is closed on Saturdays, and no calls are taken on Sunday.

ROYAL SILK, LTD.

**Royal Silk Plaza
Clifton, NJ 07011
(201) 772-1800: customer service
(201) 340-2400: "fast service" order line
(201) 340-2400: NJ orders
(800) 227-6925: orders except NJ**

Catalog: $2 (13 issues)
Discount: 40% to 60%
Goods: house brand
Minimum Order: none
Shipping, Insurance: $1 to $2 per item; UPS, PP
Sales Tax: NJ and NY deliveries
Accepts: check, MO, MC, V, AE, CB, DC
$$$

In seven years of business, Royal Silk has created the contemporary equivalent of ancient China's famed Silk Road. It offers good-quality silk and silk-blend clothing and accessories for men and women at great prices. Royal Silk can do this because it controls costs on every level—by producing all ads and catalogs "in house," buying fabric from countries with low import restrictions, and dyeing and manufacturing the goods itself.

The sensation of silk against the skin is a luxury no synthetic fabric can reproduce. Silk is also surprisingly practical: absorbent, resilient, and washable (with a few exceptions). Royal Silk includes a fascinating booklet on the history, properties, and care of silk that alone is well worth the $1 subscription fee.

One dollar will also bring you a year of catalogs, featuring shirts, dresses, and accessories for women; work-into-evening dresses; men's shirts and other apparel; sweaters of silk and angora; and stunning evening dresses and accessories. The styling is contemporary, ranging from safari shirts to gorgeous dresses that can go from the office to dinner and the theater. You'll also find bikinis, robes, jewelry, scarves, sashes, jackets, and much more. Women's sizes run from 4 to 20, and some dresses are available in petite lengths for women under 5'4". Shirts and blouses average about $27; dresses run from $49 to $58. Accessories are also inexpensive—30-inch strands of rose quartz, tiger's eye, and amethyst chips were just $15 each in the catalog we reviewed.

Royal Silk guarantees your satisfaction and accepts returns within ten days for refund, credit, or exchange.

RUBENS BABYWEAR FACTORY

Rubens & Marble, Inc.
P.O. Box 14900A
Chicago, IL 60614
(312) 348–6200

Brochure: free with SASE
Discount: 20% to 60%
Goods: house brand; first and second quality
Minimum Order: one package
Shipping, Insurance: $3 minimum; UPS, PP
Sales Tax: IL deliveries
Accepts: check, MO, certified check
$$$

Having a baby? You'll need a layette. When you consider all the other costs ahead of you, it's nice to know you can order most of baby's needs by mail at very low prices.

Rubens & Marble has been supplying hospitals with infants' clothing since 1890 and offers the same goods to you through Rubens Babywear Factory. We consulted *Eastman's Expectant Motherhood* for an expert's advice on outfitting the nursery and compared prices on Rubens and Carter's items. An example: six undershirts, three dozen cloth diapers, and six bassinet sheets cost $41.96 at Rubens; filling the same order with Carter's products cost $83.25 at the suggested list prices. The Rubens baby shirts come in sizes from newborn to 36-months with short, long, and mitten-cuff sleeves, and snap, tie, plain, and double-breasted slipover styles. (These are seconds, with small knitting flaws.) Rubens carries first-quality cotton/wool blend and preemie-sized cotton shirts as well.

You'll also find good buys on fitted bassinet and crib sheets (these are repaired seconds, at about half the cost of first-quality), training and water-proof pants, kimonos, drawstring-bottom baby gowns, and terry bibs. Aren't these the things you hoped to receive at the shower where you netted five teddy bears, a silver rattle, and Aunt Edith's vintage baby bonnet?

SAINT LAURIE LTD.

**897 Broadway, Dept. WBM
New York, NY 10003
(212) 473–0100: inquiries
and NY orders
(800) 221–8660: orders
except NY**

Catalog: $2 for 2 issues; pub. Mar. and Aug.
Swatch Brochure: $10 for 2 issues (includes catalog)
Discount: 33%
Goods: house brand
Minimum Order: none
Shipping, Insurance: $6 for the first item; $3 each additional; UPS, PP
Sales Tax: NY deliveries
Accepts: check, MO, MC, V, AE, CB, DC
$$$

Climbing the corporate ladder? Experts recommend dressing as if you're a couple of rungs above your current level. And Saint Laurie Ltd. makes the dress-for-success strategy possible by making it *affordable*.

Saint Laurie has been manufacturing better suits since 1913 and made its mail-order debut in 1979. The sumptuous color catalog we received showed an equal number of suits and separates (jackets, skirts, and trousers for men). The $2 catalog charge brings you two issues; for $10, you'll receive both the catalogs and complementing swatch brochures with 80 samples. We advise getting the swatch books with the catalogs so you can experience the hand and weight of the cloth before ordering.

The summer catalog shows conservatively styled suits for men and women, and includes information on the structural design and tailoring de-tails that make all the difference: length of belt loops, width of trousers at knee and cuff, type of shoulder, vents, pockets, lapels, etc. All the women's garments and men's jackets are fully lined; the men's pants are sent unhemmed.

You can find Saint Laurie's apparel in retail stores, but you'll save 33% by buying directly from the manufacturer. You'll also have a full selection of fine fabrics, from all-wool worsteds and blends to Italian and Moygashel linens, handwoven silks, gabardines, sharkskin, pinstripes, cotton seersucker, glen plaids, and many more weaves, weights, and fibers. Most of the suits are available in short, regular, long, and extra-long for men; petite, regular, and tall for women. Credits or refunds are given on unworn, unaltered garments returned within two weeks.

PLEASE NOTE: shipping charges are doubled on orders sent to Alaska, Hawaii, and Canada.

7TH HEAVEN FASHIONS, INC.

12125 Rockville Pike
Rockville, MD 20852
(301) 231–9077

Catalog: free
Discount: 20% to 40%
Goods: name brand
Minimum Order: none
Shipping: $2.50 per order; UPS
Sales Tax: DC and MD deliveries
Accepts: check, MO, MC, V
$$$

The glossy 16-page color catalog from 7th Heaven should make shopping for summer playwear and back-to-school clothing a snap. Just hand it over to your child, who'll alert you to what "everybody else has," which is usually what *must* be ordered.

There are dozens of colorful separates for boys and girls by a drove of top manufacturers, including Jet Set, Oshkosh, Levi's, Gitano, Calabash, French Toast, Pierre Cardin, Billy the Kid, and Diane Von Furstenburg. The styling is upbeat, but classic button-down Oxford shirts, subfusc corduroy pants, and Shetland crews are offered for the more conservative tyke. Bonnie Doon tights, knee-highs, and anklets are sold in a choice of luscious colors. Underwear by Hanes and Wundies is available, including "Showtunes," and bikinis and briefs for girls that feature Cabbage Patch Kids and Care Bears. (Break it to her gently—we didn't see a *single* pair of Strawberry Shortcake panties.) But 7th Heaven does have corduroy shoulder bags, lunch totes, backpacks, and umbrellas in eye-popping colors coordinated with the clothing.

Most of the goods are discounted 20% to 25%, but selected items are priced to 40% below list price or comparable retail. And if you spot an item in the current catalog advertised at a lower price elsewhere, include a copy of the ad with your order and 7th Heaven will beat the other price by 10%.

Your satisfaction is guaranteed, and returns are accepted within 30 days for exchange, refund, or credit. Please note that orders to be sent to more than one address must include a $2.50 shipping fee for each additional destination.

---

16 PLUS MAIL ORDER

3250 S. 76th St., Dept. 449
Philadelphia, PA
19153–3291
(215) 492–9619

Catalog: free; pub. Jan., Apr., July, Oct.
Discount: 30%
Goods: name brand, house brand
Minimum Order: none
Shipping, Handling: $1.95 to $4.50; $2 extra to AK, HI, Canada; UPS, PP
Insurance: 75¢ per order
Sales Tax: PA deliveries (if applicable)
Accepts: check, MO, MC, V, AE
$$$

Avoid bright colors, big prints, tiny prints. Never belt a dress with a light-colored sash. Stick to an A-line silhouette. Eschew all manner of frills and ruffles. And never, but *never,* wear anything with horizontal stripes.

The larger woman who lived by those rules finally climbed out of her tent dress and demanded some respect from the fashion industry, and she got it: Some of the biggest names in sportswear, lingerie, and separates have responded with larger-sized lines that are sold in better department stores across the country.

16 Plus® has taken this welcome development a few steps further. It offers everything from queen-sized Berkshire panty hose to after-five dresses by mail, at savings of up to 30% below department-store prices.

The swimsuits, intimate apparel, nightwear, jeans, sportswear, and dresses are all modeled by larger women, so you get a better idea of how the clothing will look on you than if it were worn by willowy size eights. 16 Plus® offers the latest fashions, made by Bonjour, Gitano, Cap Ferrat, Levi's Womenswear, Touche, Fleet Street, Sasson, and other firms. If you're between a 16 and a 52 and have been searching for stylish clothing at affordable prices, 16 Plus® is the answer. Your satisfaction is guaranteed—you have nothing to lose but your caftan!

THE SOCK SHOP

Sweetwater Hosiery Mills
P.O. Box 390
Sweetwater, TN 37874
(615) 337–9203

Price List: free; pub. quarterly
Discount: 33% to 50%
Goods: house brand; first quality, irregular
Minimum Order: none
Shipping, Handling: $2.50 to $6 per order; UPS, PP
Sales Tax: TN deliveries
Accepts: check, MO, MC, V
$$

You can stock up on hosiery for the whole family at The Sock Shop and save at least 33% on comparable retail. The Shop sells sheer and support stockings, knee-high nylons; support, queen-size, control-top, and other panty hose styles; booties, knee-highs, footlets, and anklets. Prices run from 49¢ for crew anklets to $2.25 for argyle knee-highs. The men's department includes tube, crew, and dress socks in cotton, acrylic, nylon, and wool blends. Both first-quality and irregular models are offered, and prices are very low: six pairs of men's tube socks are $3.79, and over-the-calf dress socks are $1.25 a pair in Banlon and $2.75 in zephyr wool/nylon. A similar assortment of dress, crew, and tube socks and anklets, booties, and knee-highs are stocked in sizes for girls and boys.

The Sock Shop also sells underwear—cotton and nylon panties for girls (sizes 2 to 14) and women (sizes 4 to 10); briefs and T-shirts for boys from size 2 to 20; men's brief, boxer shorts, T-shirts, athletic shirts, and golf shirts to size XL; and Olefin ski underwear and "moon boots" (rubber-soled slipper-socks) in all sizes.

The Sock Shop is the factory outlet for Sweetwater Hosiery Mills, in operation since 1896. The company's price list has no illustrations or color charts, so "pecan," "solar beige," "tip taupe," etc. are left to your imagination. Irregular goods are clearly marked as such and are real bargains, but even the first-quality products are up to 50% less than comparable name-brand goods. (The Shop's own estimate of 33% is low.)

SPECIALTY LEATHERS OF
CALIFORNIA

388 Orange Show Lane
San Bernardino, CA 92408
(714) 884–2216: orders and
catalog requests

Catalog: $1, refundable; pub. twice yearly
Discount: 35% to 65%
WBMC Reader Discount: 10% (see text)
Goods: house brand
Minimum Order: $165 for WBMC Reader Discount
Shipping, Insurance: extra; UPS, PP, FOB San Bernardino
Sales Tax: CA deliveries
Accepts: check, MO, MC, V, AE
$$$

Specialty Leathers, established in 1978, offers its line of men's and women's leather clothing accessories by mail through its color catalog. Also available are soft luggage, sport totes, duffles, garment bags, and backpacks in vinyl and nylon.

Glazed lambskin, doe skin, polished calfskin, and cabretta are used in the leather clothing. Prices are excellent: Men's traditional and modified western blazers start as low as $139.45 (with comparable retails at $295 and more, according to Specialty), and women's blazers begin at $124.45 (compared to $250 and up). Vests start at under $50. The size range is as democratic as the pricing—men's from 36 to 54 (there's a 10% surcharge for sizes over 48), and women's from 6 to 20 (with a 10% surcharge for 18 and 20). The garments are fully lined in satin and available in a good choice of colors.

To make the prices even better, Specialty is offering a 10% WBMC Reader Discount on any prepaid orders of $165 or more that are sent to one address. Remember to identify yourself as a WBMC reader when you're requesting the catalog *and* when ordering.

SUNCO PRODUCTS CORP.

P.O. Box 535
Hampstead, NC 28443
(919) 270–3435

Brochure and Price List: free
Information: price quote on quantity orders by phone or letter with SASE
Discount: 30% to 70%
Goods: generic
Minimum Order: twelve gloves (see text)
Shipping, Insurance: extra; UPS, PP
Accepts: check, MO, certified check
$$$

When you've got a job to do, whether it's washing dishes, stripping furniture, or raking the yard, you should protect your hands. You can do it on the cheap by buying from Sunco, where you'll find flock-lined rubber gloves, perfect for household chores, for about 90¢ a pair (compared to $1.50 and more at the supermarket). PVC-impregnated gloves with "pebble finish," perfect for heavier jobs, are sold in other catalogs for $4.95—here they're only $1.35. Suede gloves with elasticized wrists, good for all sorts of tasks, sell for $2.95 to $5.95 a pair, compared to up to $14.95 for similar styles elsewhere. And neoprene-coated, acid-resistant gloves that are $2.95 per pair from Sunco are $8.95 in other catalogs.

You'll also find canvas gloves commonly used by painters and plasterers, terry cloth gloves, and brown jersey gloves. White knit "inspection" gloves are just 30¢ a pair and are identical to the white cotton "cosmetic" gloves sold in drugstores for up to $1. Slip a pair under regular rubber gloves for insulation if you're working with very hot water, and wear them at night if you use a heavy hand cream—they'll protect the bedclothes.

Sunco sells the gloves in lots of one dozen (same size and style), so consider getting friends together to order. And don't forget your gift list. Gardening gloves are always an appreciated present. Your country friends who ruin their good gloves while gathering and chopping wood each winter will thank you for a pair designed for heavy jobs. And every do-it-yourselfer on your list will appreciate leather-palmed work gloves, rubber gloves, and the disposable polyethylene gloves. Prices are excellent, and you can save about 20% more by buying by the case (6 or 12 dozen pairs).

Founded in 1983, Sunco is relatively new to mail order and sells just gloves, plus T-shirts and baseball-style caps that can be printed or embroidered with slogans or logos. We expect this sort of firm to add new lines as business increases and be responsive to requests for specific types of industry-related products.

SUSSEX CLOTHES, LTD.

302 Fifth Ave., Dept. A1
New York, NY 10001
(212) 279–4610

Swatch and Style Brochure: $2; pub. in the spring and fall
Discount: 40% to 45%
Goods: house brand
Minimum Order: none
Shipping, Insurance: $5 for the first garment; $1 each additional
Sales Tax: NY deliveries
Accepts: MO, certified check, MC, V
$$$

The Sussex philosophy is straightforward: offer a man a well-cut suit, sport coat, and slacks in a choice of 40 fabrics, four sizes, and a direct-from-manufacturer price, and you have a customer. This company has over 50 years of experience in making suits for retailers and now offers consumers the same goods through its swatch and style booklet at savings of up to 45%.

The Sussex look is understated. The two-button jacket has a natural shoulder, center vent, flap pockets, moderate lapels, and horn buttons. The trousers are straight leg and have belt loops and quarter-top pockets. Fabrics include wool worsteds in tropical through winter weights, in shades of blue, brown, and gray; pinstripes, glen plaids, tick weaves, wool/polyester blends, and silks. Two-piece suits begin at $179, pants at $55, and a navy worsted blazer with gold buttons is $169 in the single-breasted style. There are sizes to fit men from 5'4" to 6'6".

Full credits or refunds are given on garments returned within two weeks if they're unaltered and unworn and the tickets have not been removed.

TAI INC.

90 Dayton Ave.
Passaic, NJ 07055
(201) 777–6010

Catalog: free
Information: price quote by phone or letter with SASE
Discount: see text
Goods: custom silk-screened designs
Minimum Order: none
Shipping: extra; UPS, PP
Sales Tax: NJ deliveries
Accepts: check, MO, MC, V

 (see text)

TAI offers military insignias hand-screened on aprons, scarves, laundry and duffle bags, T-shirts, pennants, bumper stickers, etc. The catalog shows scores of insignias for Airborne divisions, Special Forces groups, the Marines, Rangers, and the Foreign Legion, among others. Beyond the obvious appeal to current or past members of these groups or aficionados, many of the designs are attractive as pure graphics. There are over 3,500 printed designs available, so if you don't see the insignia you're looking for in the catalog, inquire. Prices are competitive, and quantity discounts are available.

CANADIAN READERS, PLEASE NOTE: only U.S. funds are accepted.

G.M. TRAHOS & SONS, FUR HOUSE

7 Philellinon Str.
105–57 Athens
Greece
Phone # (3228) 256

Catalog: $2; refundable
Information: by letter
Discount: to 75%
WBMC Reader Discount: 10%
Goods: house label, custom made
Minimum Order: none
Shipping, Insurance: extra
Duty: extra
Accepts: check, MO, certified check
$$$

G.M. Trahos & Sons has been crafting fur garments and accessories since

1871 and makes a representative selection available to customers worldwide through its 24-page color catalog. Which is not to say that the Fendis are losing sleep.

The styles shown are, by and large, conservative, and the models have a slightly worn appearance. But there are remarkable bargains to be found here—the prices are, as Trahos tells us, three and four times lower than those commonly charged for similar apparel. Classic single-breasted, notched-collar coats of Persian lamb run from $350 to $450. An Autumn Haze mink cape stole is $375, a Silver Blue fox stole is $275, and a chevron-patterned, double-breasted mink coat is $575. An ankle-length "Black Diamond" mink evening coat, which converts to knee length, is, at $2,000, the costliest item shown. Cloche and derby-style hats are available in mink for under $50. And a fingertip-length, shawl-collared lynx coat for men is also shown, at $450. The prices become yet more attractive with the WBMC Reader Discount of 10%. (Remember to identify yourself as a WBMC reader when ordering to get the discount. The discount does not apply to the cost of the catalog, which is refundable with purchase.)

In addition to offering the pictured clothing, Trahos will reproduce a garment design from photos you supply. The fur selection includes Persian lamb, natural (wild) Greek stone marten, and several sorts of mink. If you want a coat or jacket made to order, write first and include a clear photo of the item to be copied, a description of nonvisible details, and your measurements (use the guide in the catalog). State the fur or furs you'd like used.

PLEASE NOTE: some of the garments are available in "lower grades" of fur at lower prices. Since the prices on the top grades are reasonable, we recommend ordering the best available. (Why buy a luxury if you're going to stint on quality?) In addition, ask Trahos to tell you the country of origin of all furs used in the garment you're ordering, then check with your local Customs office on restrictions and rates of duty on the furs.

WEAR-GUARD WORK CLOTHES

Norwell, MA 02061
(800) 343–4817: customer service
(800) 343–4406: orders

Catalog: $1; pub. twice yearly
Weekend Editions Catalog: free
Discount: 10% to 30%; quantity discounts of 10% to 33%
Goods: house brand, name brand
Minimum Order: varies
Shipping, Handling, Insurance: $3 to $15; UPS, PP
Sales Tax: DE, MA, ME, NJ, PA, RI deliveries (if applicable)
Accepts: check, MO, MC, V, AE
$$$

Wear-Guard supplies more than one million U.S. companies and consumers with work clothing at 10% to 30% below regular and comparable retail prices. (Quantity discounts of 10% to 33% are available on purchases of 24 or more of the same garment.) Wear-Guard's Dacron/cotton men's work shirts are utilitarian, but they come in 18 colors and patterns, with long or short sleeves, in sizes "S" to "XXXXXL," and run from $12.99 to $17.99. There are also T-shirts, polo shirts, chambray shirts, turtlenecks, western and flannel shirts, jeans, Timberland and western-style boots, Durango Wellingtons, work shoes, thermal underwear, and union suits. Wear-Guard features a complete line of outerwear, ranging from jumpsuits and coveralls to Wrangler denim jackets, boat moccasins, varsity-style jackets, and windbreakers. The selection of women's clothing includes work shirts, thermal underwear, work smocks and jumpsuits, sweaters, pants, slickers, and service shoes. Custom designs on patches, emblems, T-shirts, and work shirts are available, as well as your choice of stock logos and lettering.

In addition to clothing, Wear-Guard sells baseball-style caps, web belts, sport sunglasses, Arctic "trooper" hats, gloves and mittens, socks, and a plethora of things handy to truckers and enforcement personnel, including money changers and holsters. The Kel-Lite flashlights are "completely indestructible and unbreakable" and double as clubs ($22 to $28). There are inexpensive first-aid kits, siphon/pumps, tow straps, and other articles to stash in the car for emergency situations as well.

Wear-Guard's "Weekend Editions" catalog has over 60 color pages of selections from the big catalog, including sturdy New England-style separates and footwear for men and women. (Sou'westers, flannel shirts, chinos, buffalo-plaid jackets, stadium coats, and gum shoes are among the offerings.) Prices in this catalog are quite reasonable; it's worth perusing if you like this look.

Wear-Guard has been doing business since 1950 (formerly as Eastern Wear-Guard and Eastern Uniform Co.), and guarantees satisfaction or your money back.

CHARLES WEISS & SONS, INC.

**38 Orchard St.
New York, NY 10002
(212) 226–1717**

Catalog: free with SASE
Information: price quote by phone or letter with SASE
Discount: 20% to 50%
Goods: name brand
Minimum Order: none
Shipping, Handling: $2 per order; UPS, PP
Sales Tax: NY deliveries
Accepts: check, MO, MC, V, AE
$$$

Charles Weiss carries a wide selection of women's intimate apparel and lingerie at low prices with a full guarantee and promises to replace the item or refund your money promptly if you're not completely satisfied with your purchase. You'll find everything here from sport bras to nightwear at savings of up to 50%. Virtually all major brands and designer lines are represented, including Playtex, Dior, Vassarette, Formfit Rogers, Maidenform, Bali, Lily of France, Lilyette, Warner's, Kayser, John Kloss, Barbizon, Olga, Pucci, and Halston. The stock is tremendous and is impossible to list in its entirety in the Weiss catalog. If you don't see what you're looking for, call or write for a price quote.

The Weiss family has been running what may be the largest lingerie emporium in the city for 40 years. If they have the moxie to cope with the demands of discount-hungry New Yorkers day after day, handling your queries and special orders will be a snap. Just remember to include a SASE with any written correspondence.

WORKMEN'S GARMENT CO.

15205 Wyoming Ave.
Detroit, MI 48238
(313) 834-7236

Catalog: $1, refundable
Discount: up to 80%
Goods: new and reconditioned clothing
Minimum Order: $15 on prepaid orders; $20 on credit cards
Shipping, Handling: included; $3 on orders under $15; UPS
Sales Tax: MI deliveries
Accepts: check, MO, MC, V
$$$

As inveterate do-it-yourselfers, we know the costs involved in dressing for work. We've run through countless $6 T-shirts and $13 sweatpants in the course of refinishing floors, stripping woodwork, painting rooms, and reviving furniture. Thanks to Workmen's Garment, we can cut those costs by at least 75%.

This firm's 24-page catalog has great buys on new work clothing and sundry items, including blue and green denim jeans, shop coats (to size 52), coveralls (to size 60 chest), zippered work jackets, shirts (to size XXXXL neck), pants (to size 74 waist), T-shirts, bandannas, towels, cotton and leather work gloves, tube socks, shop aprons, and a selection of Carhartt work clothing, brown duck, blue sail cloth, white sail cloth, etc. These are sold at very competitive prices and are made to stand up to long, hard wear.

But we were drawn by the great prices on the reconditioned clothing. These garments, sold under the "Wear-Again" label, are bought from industrial rental laundries and washed, pressed, and sterilized. They're in good condition and still have considerable wear left in them. Coveralls are as little as $4, leather-palmed work gloves $2, pants and shirts $4 each (large sizes to 50 and XXXL are $5), and there are work jackets, lab coats, etc. Clothing in the "economy line" has seen more wear, but is still quite serviceable. Cleaned and pressed shirts, pants, work jackets, and coveralls are stocked, at prices as low as $2.17 for shirts or pants.

Workmen's has been in business for over thirty years and guarantees satisfaction on the new and reconditioned clothing. (The economy line is sold "as is.") Returns are accepted within ten days for refund or credit. Inquire if you don't find what you're looking for in the catalog—the firm has many other types of work clothing.

SEE ALSO:

Ace Leather Products, Inc. . . . name-brand handbags, attaché cases, small leather goods . . . LEATHER
Altman's Luggage . . . name-brand attaché cases . . . LEATHER
Athlete's Corner . . . name-brand court and running shoes . . . SPORTS
The Austad Company . . . golf and sporting apparel . . . SPORTS
Bailey's Inc. . . . name-brand logging apparel, shoes . . . TOOLS
Beitman Co., Inc. . . . custom-covered buttons, belts, buckles . . . CRAFTS
The Best Choice . . . name-brand apparel, shoes for sports . . . SPORTS
Bettinger's Leather Shop . . . name-brand attaché cases . . . LEATHER
Bike Nashbar . . . bicycling clothing . . . SPORTS
Bowhunters Discount Warehouse . . . camouflage clothing . . . SPORTS
Cambridge Wools, Ltd. . . . Aran sweaters, sheepskin moccasins . . . CRAFTS
Campmor . . . name-brand outdoor clothing, footwear . . . SPORTS
Catherine, S.A. . . . French silk scarves, ties, umbrellas . . . HEALTH
Clothcrafters, Inc. . . . aprons, garment bags, tote bags . . . GENERAL
The Company Store, Inc. . . . name-brand down-filled outerwear . . . HOME (linen)
Custom Golf Clubs, Inc. . . . golf clothing, footwear . . . SPORTS
Cycle Goods Corp. . . . cycling apparel . . . SPORTS
Deepak's Rokjemperl Products . . . cotton and silk kurtas . . . JEWELRY
Defender Industries, Inc. . . . foul-weather wear . . . AUTO
The Down Outlet . . . small selection down-filled outerwear . . . HOME (linen)
Dyker Heights Sports Shop, Inc. . . . football jerseys . . . SPORTS
E & B Marine, Inc. . . . foul-weather wear . . . AUTO
Goldberg's Marine . . . foul-weather wear . . . AUTO
Golf Haus . . . name-brand golf shoes . . . SPORTS
Gurian Fabrics, Inc. . . . crewel tote bags . . . HOME (decor)
Holabird Sports Discounters . . . name-brand court shoes, warmups . . . SPORTS

Hunter Audio-Photo, Inc. . . . Porsche Carrera, Ray Ban sunglasses . . .
   APPLIANCES
Innovation Luggage . . . name-brand handbags, small leather goods . . .
   LEATHER
Las Vegas Discount Golf & Tennis . . . name-brand tennis and golf clothing,
   footwear . . . SPORTS
D. MacGillivray and Coy . . . Scottish clothing . . . CRAFTS
Mass Army & Navy Store . . . new, used military surplus clothing . . .
   SURPLUS
Mast Abeam . . . foul-weather wear . . . AUTO
Omaha Vaccine Co., Inc. . . . work gloves and shoes . . . ANIMAL
Otten & Son . . . clogs and wooden shoes . . . HANDCRAFTS
PBS Livestock Drugs . . . work gloves and boots . . . ANIMAL
Pedal Pushers, Inc. . . . cycling apparel . . . SPORTS
Professional Golf & Tennis Suppliers, Inc. . . . name-brand golf, tennis,
   running shoes, apparel . . . SPORTS
Rammagerdin . . . Lopi sweaters, accessories . . . CRAFTS
Road Runner Sports . . . name-brand running shoes . . . SPORTS
Ruvel and Company, Inc. . . . surplus military clothing . . . SURPLUS
St. Patrick's Down . . . down-filled vests and parkas, Aran sweaters . . .
   HOME (linen)
Shama Imports, Inc. . . . crewel tote bags . . . HOME (decor)
Shannon Mail Order . . . Aran sweaters, tartan skirts, tweeds, etc. . . .
   HOME (table settings)
Ski Warehouse . . . name-brand ski apparel . . . SPORTS
Soccer International, Inc. . . . soccer jerseys, shorts . . . SPORTS
Spiegel, Inc. . . . name-brand clothing for men, women, children . . .
   GENERAL
Sports America, Inc. . . . name-brand tennis, court shoes . . . SPORTS
Squash Services, Inc. . . . name-brand court shoes . . . SPORTS
Sultan's Delight Inc. . . . belly-dancing outfits, Arab headdresses . . .
   FOOD
Michel Swiss . . . French silk scarves, ties, umbrellas . . . HEALTH
Thai Silks . . . embroidered Chinese blouses . . . CRAFTS
Tibetan Self-Help Refugee Centre . . . Tibetan native dress . . .
   HANDCRAFTS
Top of the Line (The Wholesale House) . . . small selection of women's robes
   . . . HOME (linen)
Trade Exchange Ceylon, Ltd. . . . batiked clothing . . . HANDCRAFTS
Warehouse Marine Discount . . . foul-weather gear . . . AUTO
Weiss & Mahoney . . . new, used surplus military clothing . . . SURPLUS
Whole Earth Access . . . name-brand work and functional clothing . . .
   GENERAL

CRAFTS AND HOBBIES

Materials, supplies, tools, and
equipment for every sort of craft
and hobby.

If the high price of crafts supplies is blocking your creative instincts, you'll find this chapter positively inspiring. We've rounded up suppliers for virtually every craft imaginable, including all the needle arts, marquetry, miniatures, quilting, stenciling, wine-making, basketry, clock-making, wheat weaving, quilling, wood carving, spinning and weaving, batiking, decoy-painting, jewelry-making, and many more—and all of them sell at a discount. Greek and Icelandic yarns can be purchased from the source, at a fraction of the prices charged by U.S. firms.

Some of these companies have been in business for generations and specialize in avocations that your local crafts shop may not even know exist. If you have a problem with a material or technique, most can help you solve it by phone or letter. And if your interests run to model trains, cars, planes, and boats, look here for savings of up to 40%. Placing an order from these firms usually guarantees you a spot on the mailing list, and that means you'll receive the sales flyers with savings of up to 70%. Do remember to save your catalogs—they're invaluable for comparison-shopping. They may also be necessary if the company runs promotions or clearances and sends you a leaflet reading "deduct 50% from winter catalog prices on items FA1001 through FX5934," as some do.

For related products that may be of interest, see the listings in "Art Materials" and "Tools."

AMERICA'S HOBBY CENTER, INC.

146 W. 22nd St.
New York, NY 10011–2466
(212) 675–8922

Catalog: $2
Discount: 10% to 40%
Goods: name brand, imported
Minimum Order: none
Shipping: included on deliveries in continental U.S.; UPS, PP
Handling, Insurance: extra
Sales Tax: NY deliveries
Accepts: check or MO
$$$

Mr. Winston, who runs America's Hobby Center, told us his firm carries "every known hobby item by every brand name." There are model airplanes, cars, trains, ships, and boats, as well as the tools, materials, and supplies you'll need to build them and keep them running. The discounts are figured on a legitimate list price, not a grossly exaggerated one, so they represent true bargains. The 160-page catalog has consolidated the specialty books America's used to publish, but sales flyers and bulletins are still sent out—see the information in the catalog and subscribe, because the savings offered in these special offers can be tremendous. The Center has been in business since 1931 and is staffed by avid hobbyists who can offer advice and answer just about any question you may have.

BABOURIS HANDICRAFTS

P. Babouris
56 Adrianou St.
Athens 105 55
Greece
Phone # 32-47-561

Price List and Samples: $2, deductible; pub. every 3 years
Discount: up to 80%
Goods: house brand
Minimum Order: 15kg
Shipping, Insurance: included; airmail
Duty: extra
Accepts: check or IMO
$$$

Babouris sells yarn hand-spun from native wool at up to 80% less than prices charged in the U.S. for the same kind of goods. More than three dozen natural shades and brilliant fast-dyed colors are available, and airmail postage is included in the prices. There's a minimum order of 15kg (about 33 lbs) of yarn, but colors may be mixed to meet this requirement.

BEITMAN CO., INC.

P.O. Box 1541
Bridgeport, CT 06601
(203) 333-7738

Catalog: free
Discount: 10% to 30%
Goods: custom-made
Minimum Order: $5
Shipping, Insurance: extra; PP
Handling: $1 to $2 per order
Sales Tax: CT deliveries
Accepts: check or MO
$$$

Unless you sew a great deal, you may not be aware of the cost of some services usually available only through your local fabric supplier or tailor. Covered buttons, for example, are relatively costly to replace or create. Kits for fabric-covered buttons make the job easy enough for most home sewers, but when heavy material is used it's best to let a professional do it.

Beitman has been supplying home sewers with garment and upholstery buttons, belts, and buckles since 1950. You send the firm your fabric, specify size and style from the many available, and Beitman does the rest. If you want the look of leather, Beitman offers seven shades of synthetic leather at a nominal surcharge. Button sizes range from a ⅓″ ball to a 2⅛″ half-ball, belts from ½″ to 4″ wide. And there are dozens of buckles in coordinating sizes. Screwback earrings and French cufflinks with covered faces can also be made. The upholstery buttons can be ordered in a variety of backing styles—an open nylon hook, standard wire eye shank, nail, prong, threaded nail with washer, and pivot back with tack. The work is excellent and the prices are at least 10% to 30% less than those charged by other services. The price list states all ordering information, and Beitman asks you to send a name tag (a return-address label or your name printed on a piece of paper) that can be affixed to the catalog, to save time in the mail department and expedite your order.

PLEASE NOTE: the color catalog gives 1977 prices, which have been increased by 20% as of this writing. Check the *order blank* for the current increase. Also, Beitman does not ship to Canada, as stated in the previous edition of this book.

BELL YARN CO., INC.

**10 Box St.
Brooklyn, NY 11222
(718) 389–1904**

Price List: free with SASE
Yarn Cards: $2
Discount: up to 50%
Goods: name brand, imported
Minimum Order: none
Shipping: extra; UPS
Sales Tax: NJ and NY deliveries
Accepts: check, MO, certified check
$$$

Happen upon Bell Yarn during a rare lull in business, and you'll probably find the salespeople busy with their own needlework or giving a browser a few pointers on a complex pattern.

Bell has served the nimble-fingered since 1917 and is renowned for its extensive stock of hand-painted French needlepoint canvases. Of broader appeal is the stock of yarn and floss by Columbia, Minerva, Bucilla, DMC, Wonoco, Coronation, Fox, Reynolds, Coats & Clark, Dimension, Pingoin,

Paragon, Margot, Bernat, Berroco, Neveda, and other firms, sold for up to 50% off list prices. Other materials and supplies for knitting, needlepoint, crewel, embroidery, macrame, quilting, rug hooking, and cross-stitch are sold here, also at good prices.

Bell can finish, block, and frame your needlework; prices depend on the project. Send for the price list (include a SASE) and you'll be placed on the mailing list and notified of sales, which offer great bargains on all sorts of goods.

BOYCAN'S CRAFT, ART, NEEDLEWORK & FLORAL SUPPLIES

P.O. Box 897, Dept. WBMC
Sharon, PA 16146
(412) 346–5534

Catalog: $2, partly redeemable (see text); pub. yearly in the fall
Discount: up to 20%
Goods: name brand, generic
Minimum Order: $10
Shipping: $1.85 minimum; UPS, PP
Sales Tax: PA deliveries
Accepts: check, MO, MC, V
$$$

Whether you're a crafts dabbler, dilettante, or devotee, you'll find the Boycan's 104-page catalog a great source for all kinds of crafts supplies. Among the offerings are tools and materials for making candles, lamp shades, hooked rugs, and dolls. Also available are supplies for egg decorating, foliage-drying, tole and paper tole, "Shrink Art," glass staining and engraving, drawing, oil and acrylic painting, wheat weaving, quilling, macrame, crewel, cross-stitch (stamped and counted), knitting, crocheting, flower drying, decoupage, wood-burning, potpourri, stenciling, corn-husk dolls, silk-flower making, basketry, and other arts and diversions.

General crafts supplies are also stocked—crepe paper, craft sticks, woodenware, synthetic fur, musical movements, party favors, a huge collection of ribbon and trimmings, X-Acto knives, color wheels, a complete range of adhesives, felt, styrofoam, magnets, beads, transfer patterns, Puffpaint, and much more. Boycan's lists hundreds of reference texts and pattern books, most of them under $5.

Savings run up to 20% on comparable retail prices, and quantity discounts of 5% to 20% are given on orders of $25 to $100 and over. If you're the "crafty" type, reaching the maximum discount will be easy—the trouble is resisting all those new projects until you've finished what's on your work table. You can redeem half of the catalog cost ($1) with an order of $10 in goods (exclusive of shipping and tax) using the coupon that's printed on the order form. Authorized returns are accepted; claims must be made within ten days of receipt of goods.

CAMBRIDGE WOOLS, LTD.

40 Anzac Ave.
C.P.O. Box 2572
Auckland
New Zealand
Phone # 30–769

Brochure with Samples: $1; pub. yearly
Discount: 30% to 75%
WBMC Reader Discount: 10% on orders over
  $500
Goods: house brand
Minimum Order: none
Shipping, Insurance: included; surface mail
Duty: extra
Accepts: certified check or IMO
$$$$

We priced a popular brand of all-wool worsted knitting yarn at $4.25 per 3½ oz. skein ($1.20 an ounce) in New York City needlework shops. Cambridge sells a virtually identical yarn for 40¢ an ounce—a savings of more than 60%. Cambridge has native New Zealand wool scoured and spun to its specifications. Brightly colored "double knit" (medium-weight) yarn is $7.20 a pound, a "machine" (lighter) weight is $6.40 per pound, and a "bulky knit" in natural creams, grays, and browns is just 30¢ an ounce ($4.80 a pound). The double-knit weight, unscoured (greasy), is 40¢ an ounce, and the machine-weight in natural colors is the same price. The three weights serve the most popular applications: machine-knitting, hand-knitting of light and bulky garments, and weaving.

Scoured spinning wools are sold uncarded in natural shades ($3.50 per pound) and carded in natural and eight rich colors for $4 per pound. The spinning wheels themselves are also here—three Ashford models, from $85 to $200, plus carders, a lazy Kate, and niddy-noddy. Cambridge sells the Ashford products for 30% to 45% less than most U.S. firms.

The color brochure also shows lovely Aran-knit sweaters for the less dextrous, at $50 for the pullover and $55 for the cardigan. Pure wool blankets in several sizes and colors are stocked, as well as sheepskin rugs for bed or floor, ranging from "baby" ($30) to "quarto" ($140) sizes. Infants are actually supposed to sleep better if put to bed on one of these rugs, or so studies show. We all know a sheepskin car-seat cover can ease a long drive; at $40, those sold by Cambridge are about half the price charged by many U.S. firms. The great values available here are not diminished by surcharges for postage—shipping is included in the prices, and goods are sent via surface mail. NOTE: The WBMC Reader Discount expires Oct. 31, 1986.

CRAFT PRODUCTS COMPANY

2200 Dean St.
St. Charles, IL 60174–1098
(312) 584–9600

Clock Kit Catalog: free; pub. in the spring and fall
Clock Component Catalog: $2, refundable; pub. in the summer
Information: price quote by phone or letter with SASE
Discount: up to 50% (see text)
Goods: house brand
Minimum Order: none
Shipping: $1.50 minimum; UPS, PP
Sales Tax: IL deliveries
Accepts: check, MO, MC, V

$ 🍁 (see text)

Craft Products began its business in 1940 with the publication of woodworking patterns and added clock kits in 1950. Clock-making offers the satisfaction of cabinetry and the fascination of clock mechanics; kits provide these same pleasures without demanding much expertise.

The clock kits range from simple plaque styles for beginners to magnificent grandfather clocks. They include "regulator" models, a Gothic wooden wheel clock, tambour, mantel, steeple, bracket, school, and gallery styles. Music-box kits in solid walnut are available, with Swiss movements of 18, 36, and 72 notes, and there are weather stations for wall and desk. Prices for the kits average 50% less than comparable finished products, and if you're resourceful you can save even more. You can shape and rout a piece of leftover lumber and fit it with a set of precision instruments—barometer, hydrometer, and thermometer—for under $13.50.

In addition to kits, Craft Products sells easily applied paste stains and varnishes by the can and as part of "finish kits." Sets of clamps, music and clock movements, and a large selection of flat and bezel dials, hardware, numerals, hands, and other components are available, as well as a book of clock patterns with full-size drawings ($3.50). All of these can be found in the 32-page color "Clock Kits" catalog.

The "Clock Components" catalog shows the *complete* inventory and is easily worth the refundable $2 charge. If you're restoring an old clock, making a jewelry box, or searching for a replacement for a lost part, look here. You'll find the brass finials and rosettes that got knocked off your own clock in the last move; the tiny antiqued knobs three-year-old Junior unscrewed from your silver chest and fed to the dog; duplicates for the long-gone china-hutch key, handsome solid-brass butt and offset hinges; and round convex glass for clocks and antique pictures. Quantity discounts are offered on some products, and the catalogs feature selected specials. Craft Products guarantees your satisfaction and accepts returns within 20 days for refund or credit.

CANADIAN READERS, PLEASE NOTE: a fee of $5 is charged on orders over $100 sent to Canada to cover processing of customs forms.

CRAFTSMAN WOOD SERVICE CO.

1735 W. Cortland Ct.
Addison, IL 60101
(312) 629–3100

Catalog: $1; pub. yearly in Sept.
Discount: up to 40% (see text)
Goods: name brand, house brand, generic
Minimum Order: $10 on prepaid orders; $15 on credit cards
Shipping, Insurance: $2.65 minimum; UPS, PP, FOB Addison
Sales Tax: IL deliveries
Accepts: check, MO, MC, V
$$$ 🍁   (see text)

The Craftsman catalog is 144 pages jammed with the kind of specialty tools and hardware, lumber, veneers, finishes, books, plans, and related products that inspire long workshop retreats. Craftsman has been serving woodworkers since 1930 and offers materials and equipment for marquetry, cabinetry, picture framing, decoys, clock-making, wood burning, upholstery and seat replacement, lamp refurbishing, toy making, and other crafts and hobbies.

The impressive range of veneers and cabinetry-grade lumber includes everything from amaranth to zebra wood, in veneers, planking, turning blocks and squares (for woodenware, chair legs, etc.), carving squares, and musical-instrument stock (for sounding boards, violin backs, violin necks, etc.). A sampler set of 20 different veneers, just $2.25, is a great aid in learning to identify wood species. You can upgrade your shop with the tools and machinery—routers, table saws, lathes, radial drills, honers and sharpeners, clamps, air compressors and sprayers, jointers and planers, engravers, etc.—from such firms as Dremel, Stanley, Wen, Arco, Rockwell, American Machine & Tool, and Surform. Bits, burrs, abrasives, attachments, and accessories are also available. And you'll find stains, adhesives, and finishes by Minwax, Watco, Hope's, Deft, Barrett Coachman, and Trewax as well.

But you don't have to be a woodworker or hobbyist to appreciate the catalog. There are scores of items that anyone doing general home repairs would find useful: hinges, latches, drawer slides, table levelers, chair braces, wood carvings, upholstery tools and materials, suitcase hardware, casters, miniature moldings and hardware, replacement legs for chairs and tables, wood screw-hole plugs, and lazy-Susan bases.

Craftsman's prices run to 40% below comparable retail on certain types of items, but not everything is sold at a discount—shop before you buy. Your satisfaction is guaranteed, and returns are accepted within 30 days for exchange, refund, or credit.

CANADIAN READERS, PLEASE NOTE: The minimum order on goods sent to Canada is $25, and a $3 handling charge is imposed in addition to postage.

FATHER TIME

Clock Specialities Co.
P.O. Box 951
Bradenton, FL 33507
(813) 753-8463

Catalog: $2, refundable; pub. in Feb. and Aug.
Discount: up to 60%
WBMC Reader Bonus: free numerals with each
  clock works
Goods: name brand, generic
Minimum Order: $25
Shipping: included; UPS, PP
Handling: $2.50 on orders under $25
Sales Tax: FL deliveries
Accepts: MO, certified check, MC, V
$$$ (see text)

Father Time sells Seiko quartz and electric clock movements, clock markers, plaques, dials and faces, hands, and coating resins at up to 60% less than comparable goods. The quartz movements carry lifetime warranties against manufacturing defects; the electric movements are covered for one year. There are regular movements in ultrathin, strike, and chime models, and pendulum movements with and without electronic strike and chimes. Most of the movements include a set of hands and hardware. Pendulum rods and bobs and two dozen hand styles in black or brass finish are shown. The hands are 45¢ a pair (less in quantity), and second hands are 20¢ each.

You can face your clock with one of several dials sold here, or choose from among the many predrilled wooden "blanks" and set it with numerals or markers. The wooden backs include free-form, kiln-dried cypress slabs in six sizes; sealed slices of redwood and buckeye burl; and 99 sanded, stained pine blanks cut in the shapes of armadillos, coffee pots, owls, saxophones, sharks, Texas, cats, fire hydrants, razorback hogs, Vermont, and other motifs. There are self-adhesive black styrene markers in Roman and Arabic numerals, Hebraic and Chinese characters, dots, dashes, stars, diamonds, triangles, eyes, the names of states, Masonic emblems, religious symbols, and other decorative designs. Father Time also stocks a variety of redwood plaques that can be used to mount pictures and announcements and then be decoupaged. Glass-Kote resin sealer for the cypress slabs is also sold.

If you order a clock movement, you're entitled to a free set of clock numbers (peel-and-stick) with each movement purchase. Identify yourself as a WBMC reader when you order and indicate your style choice on the form.

GETTINGER FEATHER CORP.

16 W. 36th St.
New York, NY 10018
(212) 695–9470

Price List and Samples: $1.75
Information: price quote by phone or letter with SASE
Discount: 40% to 75%
Goods: generic
Minimum Order: none
Shipping, Insurance: $2 per order; UPS
Sales Tax: NY deliveries
Accepts: MO or certified check
$$$

After 70 years in the trade, the Gettingers have probably heard every feather story ever told. Whether your applications are commonplace or arcane, turn to Gettinger if you need raw or dyed pheasant, turkey, duck, goose, rooster, or peacock feathers. They're sold here loose or sewn (lined up in a continuous row of even length), by the ounce and pound, at prices that begin at $3.50 (loose) and $6 (sewn) per ounce. That's about 40% less than other craft-supply firms by Gettinger's estimate (our comparisons show that the company's prices actually represent savings of up to 75%). Pheasant tail feathers, six to eight inches long, are $13 per hundred, and 25-inch peacock feathers are $19 per hundred. (We've seen these sold in novelty shops for 75¢ to $1 *each*.) Pheasant hides are also stocked ($6.50 and up per skin), plus ostrich plumes and feather boas (sold by the yard).

GREAT TRACERS

3 Schoenbeck Rd.
Prospect Heights, IL 60070
(312) 255–0436

Brochure: 50¢ and SASE; refundable
Discount: up to 50%
WBMC Reader Discount: 20% (see text)
Goods: custom-made
Minimum Order: $5
Shipping, Handling, Insurance: $1 per order; PP
Sales Tax: IL deliveries
Accepts: check or MO
$$$

Great Tracers is a growing firm founded in classic mail-order tradition: it's family-run, offers one product, and sells it at low prices.

That one product is something everyone can use—a personalized stencil. Great Tracers hand-cuts your name and address (or organization or company name, slogan or other message) on stiff oil board. The oil board is laid upon a surface such as plastic, wood, metal, cloth, paper, or concrete, and paint or ink is sprayed, rolled, or brushed over it to leave the ground surface imprinted with the message. The oil board resists absorption of marking media and can be used many times over.

Stencils have almost unlimited applications. Contractors and business people can stencil the company name on machinery and equipment. Stencils can be used for product identification, coding, inventory control, warning labels, hazard markings, parking signs, and the like. Organizations find them useful for making signs announcing special events, campaigns, meetings, sales, etc. The uses around the house are manifold—marking mailboxes, garbage cans, lunch boxes, garden tools, and more. Stencil the undersides of furnishings before a move—it will help in identifying your belongings if they're stolen or misrouted in transit. And of course, using a stencil is a great way to guarantee legible return-address markings on all the packages you mail.

Great Tracers will cut stencils in ⅝" letters with a maximum of 20 characters per line, three lines per stencil, for $5 plus $1 shipping and handling. This is up to 50% less than other firms charge for custom stencils. WBMC readers may deduct $1 from the price of the stencils. Sales tax, if applicable, should be computed on the full price of the stencils and postage added to the final discounted price. You may send for the brochure or order the stencils directly from the firm. Please be sure to send clear, typed or neatly printed copy to avoid errors. Rush orders will be accepted by phone. PLEASE NOTE: this offer expires Oct. 31, 1987.

Great Tracers is busy in the R&D department, working on new products that will make stenciling neat and easy. Look for a selection of paints, applicators, and other supplies in future brochures.

HERITAGE CLOCK AND BRASSMITHS

**Heritage Industrial Park
P.O. Drawer 1577, Dept.
WBM
Lexington, NC 27293–1577
(704) 956–2113**

Catalog: free; pub. in Jan. and Aug.
Information: price quote by phone or letter with
SASE
Discount: 20% to 60%
WBMC Reader Bonus: engraved brass nameplate
with purchase of completed or kit floor clock
Goods: house brand
Minimum Order: $5
Shipping, Insurance: extra; UPS, PP, FOB
Lexington
Sales Tax: NC deliveries
Accepts: check, MO, MC, V, AE, DC

We didn't receive the Heritage catalog but we were told that the company sells a large number of clocks and clock kits, game tables, brassware, and white iron and brass beds. The bonus brass nameplate is offered to WBMC readers who purchase a floor clock in kit (with movement) or finished form. If your order qualifies, remember to identify yourself as a reader of this book and indicate what you'd like engraved on the nameplate.

STAVROS KOUYOUMOUTZAKIS

**Workshop Spun Wools
166 Kalokerinou Ave.
712–09 Iraklion, Crete
Greece
Phone # 284–466**

Price List and Samples: $1
Information: price quote by letter
Discount: up to 80%
Goods: house brand
Minimum Order: 20 pounds (see text)
Shipping: included; airmail
Duty: extra
Accepts: check, certified check, IMO
$$$$

Mr. Kouyoumoutzakis sends out a price list bulging with lush bundles of yarn samples from the wools of Crete and Australia. The wool is suitable for knitting, weaving, and yarn crafts. Cretan yarns in natural (undyed) shades of cream, gray, and dark brown are $4.80 per pound in "thick" and "medium" weights; $5.30 for "thin," and $5.80 for two-ply. The same wools, dyed in brilliant purples, golds, reds, blues, and greens, are $5.80 per pound, in either thick or medium weights. Creamy-colored Australian natural wool, thick or medium, is $5.80 per pound; $6.30 in two-ply. For those who appreciate the unusual, Mr. Kouyoumoutzakis has added goat's hair yarns to the collection. These have the stiff, firmer quality of hair (as opposed to fleece) yarns, and would make superb weaving materials for someone working in natural colors—off-white, salt-and-pepper gray, warm brown, and black are the choices. The single ply is $6.70 a pound; the double, $7.20. Wools of this sort *begin* at about $5 per 4 oz. skein, or $20 a pound, in U.S. specialty stores.

Prices are 10% higher if you order under 20 pounds (still a bargain), and a discount of 3% on the stated prices is given if the order exceeds 100 pounds. The prices include airmail postage, which means delivery within 20 to 30 days after your order is received. Remember to order enough of each color for your intended project, since dye lots are sure to differ. And please consult your customs official before ordering to get the current duty rates.

E.C. KRAUS

Wine & Beer Making Supplies
P.O. Box 7850-WC
Independence, MO
64053–0850
(816) 254–7448

Catalog: free; pub. 4 times yearly
Discount: up to 50% (see text)
WBMC Reader Bonus: see text
Goods: house brand, name brand
Minimum Order: $5 on credit cards
Shipping, Insurance: included; UPS, PP
Handling: 75¢ per order
Sales Tax: MO deliveries
Accepts: check, MO, MC, V
$$$

Here's the way to create your very own "Falcon Crest," without massive real-estate investment, hegemony, or industrial sabotage. E.C. Kraus publishes an illustrated 16-page catalog of supplies and equipment for making your own beer, wine, and liqueurs, and you can save up to half the cost of wine and even more on liqueurs by producing them yourself.

Kraus sells the yeasts you need to begin fermentation, as well as additives, clarifiers to improve wine flavor, purifiers and preservatives, fruit acids, acidity indicators, hydrometers, bottle caps, rubber stoppers, corks and corkscrews, barrel spigots and liners, oak kegs, tubing and siphons, and much more. The Saftborn steam juicer, which extracts and sterilizes juice from fresh or dried fruits and siphons it directly into the bottle, is under $59. Kraus has a good selection of fermenters, a fruit press with a 15-lb capacity, and a grape crusher (which also pulverizes apples, pears, and other fruits). The neophyte vintner or brewer can begin with the "Necessities Box," with supplies for making five gallons of drink, for under $50.

Part of the success of the brew depends on judicious mixtures of flavorings, extracts, and enhancers; the catalog lists dozens of concentrates and dried botanicals as well as recipes for different concoctions contributed by customers. Kraus also supplies Virginia Dare's "Messina" and T. Noirot extracts, which can be combined with hard liquor to produce liqueurs. Armed with a dozen extracts and the *Kitchen Cordials* manual ($1.90), you can cut at least 50% off the cost of after-dinner drinks. Kraus has an excellent bookshelf of manuals and reference texts of interest to the savant and novice alike.

If you identify yourself as a WBMC reader when requesting the catalog, Kraus will send you a coupon for a free copy of the "Winemakers Recipe Handbook," which will be sent with your first order of $5 or more.

LHL ENTERPRISES

Box 241
Solebury, PA 18963
(215) 345–4749

Catalog: $3, redeemable; pub. yearly in the summer
Information: price quote by letter with SASE
Discount: 30% to 40%
WBMC Reader Savings: free shipping on orders of $100 or more
Goods: name brand, generic
Minimum Order: $10
Shipping: extra; UPS, PP, FOB Solebury
Handling: $2.50 on orders under $10
Sales Tax: PA deliveries
Accepts: check, MO, MC, V, AE
$$$ (see text)

Crafts offer all of us an outlet for the tensions of the work day and provide the satisfaction of a tangible product when it is completed. LHL Enterprises sells supplies and equipment for a broad range of crafts and hobbies, at prices that make experimenting with a new interest—or exploring an old favorite—even more appealing.

You'll find materials for embroidery, cross-stitch, candlewicking, macrame, stenciling, painting, quilling, decoy decoration, wood burning, clockmaking, basketry, wheat weaving, potpourri, fabric flowers, jewelry, and other crafts. Among the products are DMC embroidery floss, Charles Craft cross-stitch fabric, Grumbacher pigments and brushes, Liquitex acrylic paints, Stanrite easels, Illinois Bronze spray paints and stains, Adele Bishop stencils, X-Acto implements, Aunt Lydia's rug yarn, Elephant macrame cord, and Fiskars scissors. And there are hundreds of books on almost all of these crafts, from beginners' guides to advanced reference texts.

Savings average 31%, and orders of $100 or more are sent postpaid to readers of this book. To qualify, you must identify yourself as a WBMC reader when ordering; make sure the order is at least $100 *after* deducting the catalog cost (a coupon in included in the catalog) and *before* adding sales tax, if applicable. LHL has packed the 63-page catalog with thousands of products but it doesn't list everything the company carries, so inquire by letter if you don't see what you want. Include the manufacturer's name, product name, stock number, size, and a SASE with your letter. Authorized returns are accepted within five days; books cannot be returned.

CANADIAN READERS, PLEASE NOTE: LHL recommends using Canadian postal money orders payable in U.S. funds for orders. Canadian funds are not accepted.

D. MACGILLIVRAY & COY.

Muir of Aird
Benbecula
Western Isles
Scotland, PA88 5NA
Phone # 0870–2525

Price Lists, Brochures, Swatches: $4; pub. twice yearly
Discount: 30% to 70%
WBMC Reader Discount: 10%
Goods: handmade, custom made
Minimum Order: none
Shipping, Handling, Insurance: extra; surface mail
Accepts: check, IMO, MC, V, AE, EC, Access

$$$$

Four dollars will bring you D. MacGillivray's hodgepodge of price lists, brochures, and swatches. MacGillivray offers everything from Hebridean perfumes to real grouse-claw brooches ($9.50), but is best known for its bargains on woven goods.

The cream of the crop is the selection of authentic clan tartans. Three types of wools and weights are offered—from the acrylic/wool blend at $13 a yard to the all-wool, heavyweight worsted for $24 a yard—in standard, ancient, and reproduction tartan colors. MacGillivray occasionally runs specials on new wool tartans, 54″ wide, for as low as $12 a yard. (The same wool worsted oftens sells for three times as much in Scottish import shops in the U.S.) Also sold are many types of Harris tweeds, Scottish tweeds, suitings, coatings, linings, and dress fabrics, all preshrunk, at $6.80 a yard and up. The muted tweeds are lovely, and the little piles of samples you're sent will give you an idea of the range of colors and textures available. Samples for current specials are enclosed in a separate envelope marked with the exhortation, "Order NOW to obtain a REAL BARGAIN." Samples of the tartans and other fabrics may be ordered from the catalog. Icelandic Lopi wools and sweater kits, and "Shieling" double Harris/Aran, "Croftspun" Shetland, and Falkland Islands knitting wools are available.

Once they're made into garments, you can pair your tweeds with fine sweaters of lambswool, Shetland, or camel hair, available in a palette of colors. The Fair Isle Aran sweaters are offered in jumper (pullover) and lumber jacket (high-necked cardigan) styles, and as jerseys for children, from $17.50 to $34. Hand-knitted Aran sweaters for men and women begin at $60.

There are also berets, shooting stockings, tartan travel rugs and bedspreads, sheepskin rugs, mohair stoles ($20 here, $75 in the U.S.), heraldic wall shields, Harris tweed caps and ties, and hand-tailored kilts. Authentic Highland Dress accessories, from bagpipes and skean dhus to waistcoats and bonnets, can be ordered. On top of this, MacGillivray will tailor clothing or make copies from illustrations, at prices at least 50% less than those charged by most dressmakers.

MacGillivray guarantees satisfaction or your money back, is "always eager to adjust and exchange without any bother," and has been mailing orders to customers worldwide for more than 40 years.

NEWARK DRESSMAKER SUPPLY, INC.

P.O. Box 2448, Dept. WM
Lehigh Valley, PA
18001-2448
(215) 837-7500

Catalog: free
Discount: up to 50%
Goods: generic, name brand
Minimum Order: none
Shipping, Insurance: extra; UPS, PP
Sales Tax: PA deliveries
Accepts: check, MO, MC, V
$$$$

Newark Dressmaker carries a full line of sewing and crafts supplies. There are 48 pages of ribbons, trims, appliqués, scissors, bias tapes, piping, braid, twill, gadgets, supplies for making dolls and bears, bobbins, rhinestones, name tapes and woven labels, buttons, thread, floss, and hundreds of other items. Newark, in business since 1930, guarantees fast service and satisfaction with every purchase.

RAMMAGERDIN H.F.

P.O. Box 751
121 Reykjavik
Iceland
Phone # 354–1–11122

Catalog and Yarn Cards: $1; pub. yearly in May
Discount: 30% plus
WBMC Reader Discount: 10% off orders over
$200 (knitting yarn only)
Goods: name brand, handcrafted
Minimum Order: 8 to 10 skeins on yarn (see text)
Shipping, Insurance: included except on yarns
(see text)
Duty: extra
Accepts: check, IMO, MC, V, AE, CB, DC, EC,
Access

$$$

The Lopi wool that creates the soft, soft Icelandic sweaters and accessories available in many catalogs can be purchased here by the skein, at prices much lower than those charged in specialty yarn stores in the U.S.

Rammagerdin sells three kinds of Lopi in the undyed shades of cream, gray, and brown, for which the wool is known, and also in a bevy of muted, dyed colors. The types of yarn include Lopi regular, the triple-ply most often used in sweaters; Lopi light, double-ply; and Lopi lyng, a loosely twisted double-ply. All are pre-washed and mothproofed. The natural colors are as appealing as ever and combine beautifully in the traditional sweater designs, but the dyed shades are poetic—heathery rose, moss, slate blue, gold, seafoam, etc. They could serve as the accent color to the Icelandic designs or stand alone beautifully. Lopi regular, $2 per 100g skein (3½ ozs), costs $4.59 in U.S. shops. Shipping charges are $3.85 (surface) for eight skeins which is the minimum order for Lopi regular or lyng (the minimum on Lopi light is ten skeins). If you buy in bulk for several projects, you'll save on shipping (postage on 46 skeins is under $10, surface), and if your goods total exceeds $200 you can deduct 10%. Identify yourself as a WBMC reader if you take the discount, and remember that it applies to *yarn only*. Pattern books are $5.85 each, and a dozen sweater kits are offered as well.

Rammagerdin also sells completed sweaters and accessories. There are cardigans, pullovers, ponchos, vests, and zippered jackets for men and women; full-length coats and delicate shawls for women; socks, slippers, caps, scarves, mittens, and blankets of Lopi; and cardigans for children. Many incorporate the snowflakes and geometrics of classic Icelandic patterns, but there are quite a few contemporary designs. Prices are routinely half the cost of the same goods in the U.S. The 24-page color catalog shows the clothing to great effect and also pictures Icelandic figures, free-form vases and lamps, and seafood samplers packed with the best of Iceland's waters. Airmail postage is included in the prices of everything but the yarns.

No return policy is given in the catalog, but Rammagerdin has done business honorably for 35 years and can be relied upon to continue in the same fashion.

ROMNI WOOLS AND FIBRES LTD.

3779 W. 10th Ave.
Vancouver, B.C. V6R 2G5
Canada
(604) 224-7416

Catalog: $1, refundable (see text); pub. twice
  yearly
Information: price quote by phone or letter
Discount: 20% to 50%
Goods: house brand, name brand, generic
Minimum Order: none
Shipping, Insurance: extra; PP
Handling: $1 per carton
Duty: extra
Accepts: check, MO, certified check, V
$$$

Romni is one source no spinner, weaver, or knitter should overlook. The 12-page, hand-printed catalog lists one of the best selections of unspun tops, fibers, and yarns you'll find anywhere, and the prices are 20% to 50% below comparable retail.

New Zealand fleece is sold in natural colors, carded and uncarded, greasy and scoured. Acrylic, Orlon, nylon, cotton, flax, hemp, jute, a variety of silks, alpaca, angora, cashmere, mohair, camel hair, goat's hair, and yak tops are available for spinning. The yarns and cords, suitable for weaving, embroidery, knitting, tapestry-weaving, crocheting, and rug-making include single through four-ply standards and bouclés, tweeds, loops, slubs, hand-spuns, metallics, and other textures in a comparable range of fibers. And Romni offers a broad range of dyes, mordants, and chemicals, including natural dyes (annato seed, cochineal, indigo, madder, etc.) and Deka and Dylon products.

You won't have to look elsewhere for equipment, either. Several spinning wheels are shown, including castle, traditional, folding, and electric models, and drum and hand carders, card cloth, pickers, looms, warping boards, umbrella swifts, ball winders, reeds, shuttles, shed sticks, crochet hooks, and tapestry beaters and needles. Romni also sells buttons of abalone, yew, rosewood, bubinga, tulip wood, and zebra wood.

A book list of over 300 titles on various textile arts may be ordered for $1 (Canadian readers should send 50¢ and a SASE). Quantity discounts of up to 25% are offered on certain yarns and fibers. If you're planning to buy a substantial amount, request the "Discount Sheet." Samples are available at prices listed in the catalog; we recommend ordering "The Works," samples of all the yarns and fibers stocked, which costs $10. When you place your first catalog order, be sure to request reimbursement for the $1 fee so your refund isn't overlooked.

The prices are in Canadian dollars, and you should be sure to check the conversion rate before ordering—at this writing, the Canadian dollar is worth about 75¢ in U.S. funds. Customs charges and higher shipping costs will offset some of these savings for U.S. customers. Romni accepts authorized returns on most goods. Terms of the policy are detailed in the catalog.

ROUSSELS

107–2340 Dow.
Arlington, MA 02174–7199
(617) 643–3333

Catalog: 25¢; pub. twice yearly
Discount: 20% to 80%
Goods: generic, overstock
Minimum Order: $12
Shipping, Insurance: extra; UPS, PP
Sales Tax: MA deliveries
Accepts: check, MO, certified check
$$$$

Roussels carries a full line of hobby and craft supplies, markets overruns, odd lots, and discontinued items through its brochure. We've seen some *very* inexpensive jewelry and lapidary materials here—earrings, necklaces, rings, chains, findings, polished stones, sharks' teeth, display materials and gift boxes, and much more. Most of the items are sold by the dozen or gross, but you can sample a little of everything through "trial offers." In addition to great savings on closeouts, Roussels invites inquiries on regular hobby and crafts supplies. Call or write with your requests.

STRAW INTO GOLD, INC.

3006 San Pablo Ave., Dept.
WBM
Berkeley, CA 94702
(415) 548–5247

Catalog: SASE
Updates and Flyers: free with SASE (see text)
Discount: up to 70% (see text)
Goods: name brand, house brand, imported
Minimum Order: $20 on credit cards
Shipping, Insurance: extra; UPS, PP
Handling: up to $2.50 per order
Sales Tax: CA deliveries
Accepts: check, MO, certified check, MC, V
$$$

Straw Into Gold is a highly regarded mail-order source for textile crafts supplies and equipment. The roster of fibers available for spinning includes several types of silk, cotton (including pima), flax, wools (from New Zealand and domestic sheep), mohair, camel hair, goat's hair, and yak tops. The complete line of Ashford spinning wheels and tools is also available although not sold at a discount. Natural and synthetic dyes, thickeners, and additives are stocked, as well as fabric-painting supplies. The range of yarns is equally comprehensive; Chatelaine from France, Crystal Palace, yarns from Japan and Europe in silk, cotton, linen, and wool, etc. An extensive collection of coned silks, cottons, and wools for weavers and machine knitters is also stocked.

You may also find basketry materials in the catalog—reed, sea grass, fiber rush, and pigtail (natural) raffia. Dozens of Folkwear patterns are listed, and books on spinning, weaving, dyeing, and other crafts. And there are rubber stamps; sheep dominate, though there are weaving motifs, some generic symbols, a renegade dinosaur, and an aardvark or two.

Many of the catalog offerings are priced at list or retail, but quantity discounts of up to 30% are given on a large number of products. In addition, specials on fibers, yarns, books, and other goods appear regularly in flyers, and savings on these run up to 70%. The catalog—an unbound set of pages and brochures—may include some of these fliers, but to guarantee regular mailings, you should become an "Envelope Person." Send the company four long, self-addressed envelopes with enough postage for two ounces (or two IRCs for each envelope), and you'll receive the specials flyers, supplementary catalog pages, and other information as it becomes available. Fiber samples and yarn cards may be requested; details are given in the literature. Straw Into Gold, founded in 1971, is run by true professionals sure to have an answer to your questions on textile crafts.

CANADIAN READERS, PLEASE NOTE: payment for orders sent to Canada must be made in U.S. funds by check or money order only.

THAI SILKS

252-W State St.
Los Altos, CA 94022
(415) 948–8611

Brochure: 50¢; pub. in Feb. and Aug.
Information: price quote by phone or letter with SASE
Discount: 30% to 50%
Goods: imported
Minimum Order: one half yard on fabrics
Shipping: $2 minimum; UPS, PP
Sales Tax: CA deliveries
Accepts: check, MO, MC, V, AE
$$$

Silk is beautiful, comfortable, and surprisingly durable when properly maintained. It's also quite affordable at Thai Silks, where the home sewer, decorator, and artist can save 30% to 50% off retail on yardage and piece goods.

The company was founded in 1964, and since then the proportion of silks it actually imports from Thailand has dwindled to 2%—the rest come from China, India, Italy, and Japan. The stock ranges from the sheerest chiffons and China silks to upholstery-weight silks and includes jacquard weaves, crepe de Chine, pongee, silk satin, raw silk, brocades and tapestry weaves, silk taffeta, woven plaids, Dupioni silk, and other weights, weaves, and textures. The hand-hemmed scarves in chiffon, crepe de Chine, and China silk are ideal for painting and batik and come in several sizes. Javanese and Malaysian batiked cotton and cotton shirting and lawn, poplin, georgette from China and India are also listed. Samples are available for a fee that is refunded if they're returned within 30 days. Closeouts aren't listed in the catalog, but a $2 deposit brings you prices and samples of about two dozen materials being discontinued or sold out.

In addition to yard goods, Thai Silks usually stocks Chinese embroidered handkerchiefs, embroidered blouses in silk, and embroidered tablecloths, placemats, and napkins from China at prices usually half those charged in import shops and department stores. Quantity discounts are offered to firms and professionals (dressmakers, artists, etc.) who include a business card with their orders. Savings run from 10% on orders of $30 to 25% on $200 orders, but do not apply to specials or sale goods. The brochure includes some useful tips on sewing with and caring for silk. Thai Silks guarantees your satisfaction and accepts returns for refund or credit.

UTEX TRADING ENTERPRISES

**710 Ninth St., Suite 5
Niagara Falls, NY 14301
(716) 282–4887; ext. 18**

Price List: free with SASE; pub. twice yearly
Discount: up to 50%
Goods: imported
Minimum Order: $20
Shipping, Insurance: $3 minimum; UPS, PP
Sales Tax: NY deliveries
Accepts: MO, certified check, teller's check
$$$

Utex trades in silk—yard goods, scarves for batik and hand-painting, silk thread, floss, and yarn. The brochure lists over 100 weights, weaves, and widths of shantung, pongee, taffeta, twill, Habotai, peau de soie, lamé, suiting, and much more. Sets of samples are available on a deposit basis. Utex includes a roster of specific fabrics recommended for wedding dresses, blouses, lingerie, kimonos, and other apparel, which should help the home sewer who might otherwise be overwhelmed by the selection. Prices begin at under $5 a yard, and quantity discounts up to 25% are offered on quantity purchases.

YANKEE INGENUITY

P.O. Box 26-W
Thompson, CT 06277–0026
(203) 923–2061

Catalog: $1, refundable; pub. yearly in the fall
Information: price quote by phone or letter with SASE
Discount: 30% to 70%
WBMC Reader Discount: 5%
Goods: house brand
Minimum Order: none
Shipping, Insurance: $1.50 minimum; UPS, PP
Sales Tax: CT deliveries
Accepts: check, MO, MC, V
$$$

Clock hobbyists who supply the Ingenuity can buy their materials here at thrifty Yankee prices of up to 70% less than comparable retail. Compact quartz mechanisms, complete with mounting hardware and your choice of hands, cost $3.50 to $8.75 each, depending on the quantity purchased. Brass-faced, disk-shaped digital movements and other quartz movements are available, as are a range of hand styles, self-adhesive dial markers, dial templates that assure accurate layouts, steel clock bases for desk or shelf display, and sawtooth hangers for wall-hung models.

Yankee Ingenuity is offering WBMC readers a 5% discount on all purchases. Be sure to identify yourself as a reader when ordering. Compute shipping and tax, if applicable, on the price of the goods *before* you take the discount. Your satisfaction is guaranteed, and undamaged returns are accepted within 30 days for refund or credit.

SEE ALSO:

A.E.S. . . . Makita power tools . . . TOOLS
The Airborne Sales Co. . . . surplus hobby and crafts supplies . . . TOOLS
American Discount Wallcoverings . . . name-brand decorator fabrics . . .
  HOME (decor)

American Vacuum & Sewing Machine Corp. . . . name-brand sewing machines and attachments . . . APPLIANCES

The Bevers . . . wooden toy wheels, balls, etc. . . . TOOLS

Dick Blick Co. . . . wide range of crafts supplies . . . ART MATERIALS

Crown Art Products . . . silk-screening materials . . . ART MATERIALS

Deepak's Rokjemperl Products . . . lapidary equipment, mineral specimens . . . JEWELRY

Del-Mar Co. . . . resin-embedded gold cabochons . . . JEWELRY

Doll House & Toy Factory Outlet . . . dollhouse kits and assembly supplies . . . TOYS

The Fabric Center . . . name-brand decorator fabrics . . . HOME (decor)

Gohn Bros. . . . hard-to-find, natural-fiber yardage, thread, floss, notions, quilt frames . . . CLOTHING

Gold N' Stones . . . jewelry findings . . . JEWELRY

Good 'N' Lucky Promotions . . . closeout crafts supplies . . . JEWELRY

Gurian Fabrics, Inc. . . . crewel fabrics . . . HOME (decor)

Handart Embroideries . . . silk yard goods . . . CLOTHING

Hong Kong Lapidaries . . . gemstones . . . JEWELRY

International Import Co. . . . cut precious and semiprecious gemstones . . . JEWELRY

Kountry Bear Company . . . stuffed bears in kits, patterns . . . TOYS

Plastic BagMart . . . zip-top plastic bags . . . HOME (maintenance)

Protecto-Pak . . . zip-top plastic bags . . . HOME (maintenance)

Rein Furs . . . mink scraps . . . CLOTHING

Robinson's Wallcoverings . . . decorator fabrics . . . HOME (decor)

S & C Huber, Accoutrements . . . American period crafts supplies, equipment . . . HANDCRAFTS

Samarth Gem Stones . . . jewelry findings, stones, beads . . . JEWELRY

Sanz International, Inc. . . . name-brand decorator fabrics . . . HOME (decor)

Ginger Schlote . . . jewelry findings . . . JEWELRY

Self-Sufficiency and Smallholding Supplies . . . dyes, mordants, textile chemicals, leather tanning, dyeing products, beekeeping equipment . . . ANIMAL

Sewin' in Vermont . . . name-brand sewing machines, attachments . . . APPLIANCES

Shama Imports, Inc. . . . crewel fabric . . . HOME (decor)

Trade Exchange Ceylon, Ltd. . . . native batiked fabrics . . . HANDCRAFTS

World Abrasives Co., Inc . . . fine abrasives for wood, stone, metal . . . TOOLS

FARM AND GARDEN

Seeds, bulbs, live plants,
supplies, tools, and equipment.

If you buy your plants at the local florist or nursery, you're probably going to find the same varieties everywhere, and the prices will be about the same across the board. But if you go the mail-order route, you'll have your choice of rare varieties of bulbs, plants, flowers, herbs, and other growing things. And plants and seed packages make lovely gifts for your horticultural friends. But do make sure, when you're ordering, that the plant will survive in your climate or home environment—a delicate woods flower specimen will not last long in an eastern exposure or an overheated house.

Although we're interested in saving you money, improvements in your landscaping can also *make* you money. A well-planned investment of $50 to $100 in "environmental improvement" can increase the value of your property by as much as $500, especially if you've got something unusual for your locality. Remember that the same cautions about plant survival apply here, perhaps more strongly. "Hostile" soil will take its toll until the gardener gets wise and has it tested, only to find that it can support only certain types of growth. Investigate *before* you order and you'll save yourself time, labor, and money.

For related products, see the listings in "Tools."

BEAR MEADOW FARM

---

23 Wall St.
North Adams, MA 01247
(413) 663–9241

Catalog: $1, refundable; pub. in Mar. and Oct.
Discount: 20%
WBMC Reader Discount: 15% (see text)
Goods: organically cultivated
Minimum Order: on plants
Shipping: 15% of order value; $2.50 minimum;
 UPS, PP
Handling, Insurance: $1
Sales Tax: MA deliveries
Accepts: check, MO, MC, V
$$$

Bear Meadow Farm sells live, organically cultivated herbs, geraniums, and "exotic house plants" in 3″ and 5″ pots for $1.85 and $2.75 respectively. Hundreds of plants are available, from agrimony to yerba buena. The price list includes hints on the cultivation and use of herbs. Part of the harvest from the Farm is featured in the catalog as dried herbs and potpourri. The cooking and medicinal herbs range from alder buckthorn bark to zahtar and cost from about 9¢ an ounce for sea salt to $5.49 per ounce for powdered goldenseal.

The catalog also lists fruit-flavored teas, potpourris, bath herb mixes, essential oils, pomander balls, spice ropes, sachet bags, herb wreaths, kitchen witches, and even herbal vinegars, jellies, and jams. Chutneys, marmalades, pickles, relishes, honey, fruit jams, jellies and butters, and books on herbs and gardening complete the catalog.

The prices of these goods run about 20% less than those charged elsewhere for the same plants and handcrafts, and Bear Meadow is offering WBMC readers an additional 15% off all orders over $10, exclusive of shipping, handling, and insurance. Calculate shipping and tax charges on the *undiscounted* total and be sure to identify yourself as a WBMC reader when you order.

BRECK'S

**6523 N. Galena Rd.
Peoria, IL 61632
(309) 691–4616**

Catalog: $1
Discount: up to 50% (see text)
Goods: house brand, imported
Minimum Order: none
Shipping, Handling: extra; UPS
Sales Tax: IL and OH deliveries
Accepts: check, MO, MC, V
$$

Breck's has been "serving American gardeners since 1818" with a fine selection of spring flower bulbs. Breck's imports its bulbs directly from Holland and offers discounts of up to 50% on orders placed by July 31 for fall delivery and planting. The Breck's tulip, crocus, daffodil, hyacinth, iris, anemone, delphian, and windflower bulbs are culled from the best of the crop and yield flowers of breathtaking color and size. All specifications—blooming period, height, color and markings, petal formation, and scent—are given in the catalog descriptions.

In addition to early-order discounts and savings on bulb collections, Breck's also offers bonuses of free bulbs on orders totaling $25 or more. You are guaranteed satisfaction with your bulbs or blooms, and returns are accepted for exchange, replacement, refund, or credit.

CAPRILAND'S HERB FARM

Silver St.
Coventry, CT 06238
(203) 742-7244

Brochure: free with SASE; pub. yearly
Discount: up to 50%
Goods: house brand, generic
Minimum Order: none
Shipping: extra; UPS
Sales Tax: CT deliveries
Accepts: check, MO, certified check
$$

Capriland's grows over 300 kinds of herbs and scented geraniums, as well as roses and other flowers. Many are offered in two-inch grow pots for under $2 each, or to 50% less than prices charged by other specialty sources. All the standard culinary herbs and less common varieties are listed, such as Egyptian onions, rue, wormwood, mugwort, monardas, and artemisia. You can enhance your garden borders with santolinas, germander, lamb's ears, and nepetas, or plant an unusual ground cover with ajuga, camomile, woodruff, and thyme, among others. Plants are shipped between March 1 and October 31.

The brochure should intrigue anyone interested in medicinal and arcane uses for herbs; the book list has several titles along those lines, and charm necklaces and rite materials are sold as well. Capriland's also sells the harvest from its farm in a variety of forms—sachet pillows, dolls, and loose potpourri materials. Half-pounds of rose buds and lavender are a third less than what they cost in New York City stores, and lemon verbena, frankincense and myrhh are also available. And don't miss the costumed collectors' dolls, which are quite reasonably priced.

DE JAGER BULBS, INC.

188 Asbury St.
South Hamilton, MA 01982
(617) 468-1622

Catalog: free
Discount: up to 50% (see text)
Goods: house brand, imported
Minimum Order: none
Shipping: extra; UPS
Sales Tax: MA deliveries
Accepts: check, MO, MC, V
$$

De Jager imports its bulbs directly from nurseries in Holland, so it's able to offer them at excellent prices. If you order by July 1 for fall delivery and planting, you can save almost 50% on the cost of tulip, narcissus, hyacinth, daffodil, crocus, and other bulb varieties, compared to the cost of the same type of bulb sold by other mail-order houses or garden centers.

De Jager's selection is super. There are pages of tulip bulbs in every possible color and petal formation, bulbs for forcing and indoor cultivation, and collections of De Jager's best-sellers at great savings. The color catalog gives both common and botanical names of the flowers, and describes the color, scent, optimum growing conditions, blooming period, and approximate height of the mature plants. De Jager ships the bulbs in mid-September through December, guarantees your satisfaction with the bulbs (not the flowers), and accepts returns for exchange, refund, or credit.

De Jager's spring planting catalog has similar savings on tubers and seeds for begonias, dahlias, creeping flowering plants, peonies, African violets, berries, vegetables, fruits, common garden flowers, and roses.

DUTCH GARDENS INC.

Dept. Z2091N
P.O. Box 400
Montvale, NJ 07645–0400
(201) 391–4366

Catalog and Price Lists: free; pub. in Dec. and Apr.
Discount: up to 60%
Goods: house brand, imported
Minimum Order: $20 on credit cards
Shipping: included; UPS
Sales Tax: NJ deliveries
Accepts: check, MO, certified check, MC, V
$$$$

This is, quite simply, the most beautiful bulb catalog we've ever seen—over 60 color pages of flower "head shots" that are breathtaking in their perfection. And the prices charged by Dutch Gardens are, surprisingly, some of the lowest anywhere—up to 60% less than other mail-order firms and garden-supply houses.

You'll find old friends and new varieties among the Dutch-grown tulip, hyacinth, daffodil, narcissus, crocus, anemone, iris, snowdrop, allium, amaryllis, and other spring-flower bulbs. The tulips alone include hybrid Greigii, Emperor, Darwin, Triumph (the Apricot Beauty is exquisite), single, double, fringed, parrot, lily, and peony types. Wood hyacinths, pure white amaryllis, double narcissi, and darling dwarf irises are a few that we quite liked, though it's hard to play favorites.

Each flower is identified by its common and botanical name. The size of the bulb, the height of the fully grown plant, planting zones, blooming period (very early, early, middle, or late season), and appropriate growing situations are also listed. The catalog includes a zone chart, a guide to the depth bulbs should be planted, and helpful instructions on terrace plantings, indoor growing, and forcing. Those looking for bulbs suitable for rock or miniature gardens and for naturalizing should check both the selections and planting suggestions to obtain the optimum effects. All gardeners should consider using the Bulb Booster 9–9–6 fertilizer, which is said to produce bigger, longer-lasting flowers and better bulb reproduction in successive years. A pound costs under $2 and covers 25 square feet.

Dutch Gardens prefers to receive orders by July 15, but will accept them as late as September 25 for northern states and October 15 for southern areas. The catalog is sent with ten order forms, so you can combine orders with friends and neighbors. If, all totaled, they amount to $70 or more, you're entitled to a 10% bonus in the bulbs of your choice or a 10% discount. The bulbs are shipped, postpaid, to the primary purchaser who in turn distributes the individually wrapped and labeled orders to each person who ordered. Delivery is made for the planting time in your area, so it's inadvisable to solicit orders from Aunt Mabel in Louisiana if you live in Wisconsin. All bulbs are guaranteed to bloom, provided planting instructions have been followed correctly.

GLORYBEE BEE BOX, INC.

1015 Arrow St.
Eugene, OR 97402–9121
(503) 584–1649

Brochure: free; pub. quarterly
Discount: 30%
Goods: name brand, house brand, generic
Minimum Order: none
Shipping, Insurance: extra; UPS, PP, FOB Eugene
Sales Tax: OR deliveries (if applicable)
Accepts: check, MO, MC, V
$$$

Glorybee sells a complete line of equipment and supplies for keeping bees, including live bees and assembled hives. Glorybee even gives courses covering the essentials of beginning beekeeping and "pays the highest prices" for beeswax. This firms sells all the equipment you'll need to set up a hive: foundations, hive frames, hardware, extracting equipment, an observation hive, queen and drone traps, honey dabbers, veils, gloves, tools, smokers, escapes, excluders, repellents, bee feed and stimulants, and honey pumps. The prices are excellent, about 30% less than those charged by retail outlets. And if you have any bee-related questions, give the firm a call—the people who run it have been in the bee business for years and can help you out of just about any sticky situation that might arise.

J.E. MILLER NURSERIES, INC.

5060 W. Lake Rd.
Canandaigua, NY 14424
(716) 396–2647: inquiries
(800) 452–9601: NY orders
(800) 828–9630: orders
except NY

Catalog: free; pub. in the spring and fall
Discount: up to 50%
Goods: house brand, generic
Minimum Order: $10 on credit cards
Shipping, Handling: extra; UPS
Sales Tax: NY deliveries
Accepts: check, MO, MC, V, AE
$$

You'll be ready to dig up your lawn and fill in the swimming pool to plant fruit trees and arbors when you see the luscious-looking offerings in Miller's nursery catalog. The problem will be in choosing from the russet apples, golden plums, black grapes, red raspberries, indigo blueberries, ruby cherries, fat strawberries, and dozens of other fruit and nut trees. If it's shade you need, there are poplar, locust, maple, and ash trees, some of which are said to grow house-high in just three years. Miller also carries asparagus, grapes, and rhubarb, and some common flower bulbs. All the trees and shrubs are sent as plants and are guaranteed to grow or will be replaced. Prices are guaranteed to win you over, too; especially those in the half-off catalog sales.

OREGON BULB FARMS

Dept. W-3
39391 S.E. Lusted Rd.
Sandy, OR 97055–9595
(503) 663–3133

Catalog: $2, refundable; pub. yearly in the
　　summer
Discount: 30%
Goods: house brand
Minimum Order: $25 on credit cards
Shipping, Handling: extra; UPS, PP
Sales Tax: OR deliveries (if applicable)
Accepts: check, MO, MC, V
$$

Oregon Bulb Farms, founded in 1929, develops and sells the stunning Jan de Graaff (Jagra) lilies. These are hybrid lilies, many of which resemble more glorious versions of the tiger lilies sold in florists' shops. They have the impact of orchids and other exotic blossoms but are easier to cultivate and guaranteed to bloom. Over 70 types were available at this writing, though new varieties are developed yearly and added to the catalog.

Asiatic and Oriental hybrids are offered in upright-flowering, outward-facing, pendant, and trumpet formations. The lilies include plain, freckled, and color-streaked varieties in white, every shade of pink and orange, yellows, and combinations. Most are scented and the blossoms, which appear from June to September, can reach up to 20″ in diameter, depending on the variety. Oregon Bulb has developed a line of genetic dwarf lilies especially for indoor cultivation, which can be transplanted to the garden where they should continue to flower for years.

The bulbs offer the amateur gardener an opportunity to raise showy flowers without the fuss and careful tending "exotics" usually require. The prices—$2.35 to $4.20 a bulb—represent savings of up to 30% on similar varieties sold at garden shops. Savings of about 13% more may be realized on orders of a dozen or more of the same bulb; collections are offered at up to 40% less than the cost of bulbs purchased separately. For each $35 in bulbs you order, you'll be sent one free bulb (Oregon's choice). Complete planting and cultivation instructions are included with every order.

**PRENTISS COURT
GROUND COVERS**

P.O. Box 8662
Greenville, SC 29604–8662
(803) 277–4037

Brochure: 25¢; pub. yearly in the spring
Discount: 30% to 40%
Goods: house brand
Minimum Order: 50 plants of the same variety
Shipping, Insurance: included; UPS
Sales Tax: SC deliveries
Accepts: check, MO, certified check, MC, V
$$$

We became ground-cover converts after years of labor and much money spent nursing a Manhattan courtyard into a semblance of lawn proved fruitless, and one of our neighbors stick a few Boston ivy plants into the mud and scrub. They took off like wildfire, apparently responding to those factors that had defeated the grass—a good amount of shade and water. Every habitat is different, but ground cover plants often succeed where grass seedings and turfings fail. Ground cover offers the further advantages of reduced maintenance and a more interesting display, and people who tramp heedlessly across a beautiful expanse of grass will hesitate before treading upon vines and flowers.

You can buy any number of ground covers from Prentiss Court, from several varieties of ajuga to Vinca major. Crownvetch, day lilies, Boston ivy, Euonymus fortunei, fig vine, English ivy and other Hedera helix, Japanese honeysuckle, St. Johnswort, jasmine, phlox, and liriope and sedum are offered. Many of the plants are shown in line drawings in the brochure, so you may want to consult other catalogs or a botanical reference text for color plates and data on individual species. Prentiss Court gives planting instructions in the brochure along with a guide to spacing plants for given areas of coverage. Most of the plants are available bare-root and potted; potted prices are higher but are still at least 30% to 40% less than the same varieties bought from a garden center. Remember that you must order a minimum of 50 plants of the same variety, but at an average bare-root price of 50¢ each, this is quite reasonable. If those plants are spaced a foot apart, they'll cover 50 square feet—and you'll never have to mow again.

RAINBOW GARDENS
NURSERY & BOOKSHOP

P.O. Box 721-W5
La Habra, CA 90633-0721
(213) 697-1488

Catalog: $1, refundable; pub. yearly in Nov.
WBMC Reader Discount: see text
Goods: plants and books
Minimum Order: $10 on plants; $15 on credit cards
Shipping: $4 per plant order; $1.50 for the first book, 50¢ each additional book; UPS, PP
Insurance: 50¢ per order on books
Sales Tax: CA deliveries
Accepts: check, MO, MC, V
$$ 🍁   (see text)

WBMC Discount

Rainbow Gardens Nursery & Bookshop sells plants—epiphyllums (orchid cactus) and other rain-forest cacti—and close to 200 books and magazines on cacti, succulents, bromeliads, epiphyllums, ferns, and greenhouse care and propagation. We've listed Rainbow Gardens because it offers an excellent selection of certain types of plants and gives readers of this book a special discount on plant orders.

Many of the orchid cacti (epiphyllums) and rain-forest cacti (epiphytes) are shown in color photographs throughout the 24-page catalog; the blooms are spectacular, brilliantly colored specimens with pointed petals and sepals and stamens that dangle like tendrils. A four-page guide to cultural care and planting is included with every order or provided upon request if you send a SASE. Most of the plants are sent as rooted 6″ to 8″ cuttings, at prices from $2.50 to $10. A dozen collections are offered, including a group of miniatures and several for the beginner.

The catalog of books includes excellent reference texts and picture books that should enhance your cultivation efforts and inspire further collecting. Among the titles are *Pineapple Top Growers Handbook, Cacti of the United States and Canada, Colour Encyclopedia of Succulents,* and *Gardening Under Artificial Light.*

The reader discount of 10% applies to first orders only, with a minimum $50 purchase excluding shipping, handling, and sales tax. You must order within the calendar year in which you receive the catalog and identify yourself as a WBMC reader when ordering to qualify for the discount.

CANADIAN READERS, PLEASE NOTE: the minimum order on goods shipped to Canada is $50 (U.S. funds only), plus additional shipping and handling charges. There is also a $6.50 fee for a phytosanitary certificate (agricultural inspection). You're asked to make sure importation of such plants is permitted by Canadian law and to file any necessary permits before ordering.

FRANZ ROOZEN B.V.

Vogelenzangseweg 49
2114 BB Vogelenzang
Holland
Phone #: 02502–7245

Catalog: free; pub. yearly in June
Discount: 10% to 30%; quantity discounts
WBMC Reader Discount: 10% on catalog prices
Goods: house brand
Minimum Order: $22
Shipping, Handling, Insurance: included
Duty: extra
Accepts: check, certified check, IMO, EC
$$$

The Roozen color catalog informs us that the Roozen family has been growing bulbs since 1789. Mr. Franz Roozen and his son are still busy improving stock bulbs and developing new varieties, especially what they term "strong-flowering garden tulips."

Of the more than 1,000 different bulbs grown in the Roozen fields, hundreds are available by mail. Price are, on the average, about the same as those offered by U.S. discounters who import bulbs directly from Holland. Some prices are notably lower—the Allium giganteum and Red Riding Hood tulip bulbs are about half the U.S. price. Savings aren't consistent, though, and prices on a few goods are about 20% higher at this firm than in the U.S. But don't overlook Roozen when pricing and ordering bulbs, because shipping, handling, and insurance charges are included in the prices. In addition, there are large bulb assortments offered at good prices, and quantity discounts of 3% to 10% are available on orders of $75 to $250 and over. The WBMC discount of 10% furthers your savings. Be sure to identify yourself as a reader and meet the minimum-order requirements in the catalog. Get together with neighbors or show the catalog to your community-beautification committee and take advantage of all the discounts.

U.S. orders are accepted no later than September 15 (Canadian orders, September 1), and deliveries are made from October through November. Complete planting instructions are included with each order.

ROYAL GARDENS INC.

P.O. Box 588
Farmingdale, NJ 07727
(201) 780-2713

Catalog: free; pub. yearly in the spring
Discount: up to 40% (see text)
Goods: house brand, imported
Minimum Order: $15 on credit cards
Shipping, Handling: extra; UPS
Sales Tax: NJ deliveries
Accepts: check, MO, MC, V, AE
$$$

Royal Gardens publishes a gorgeous 64-page catalog literally blooming with glorious color shots of its spring flowers. Tulip, lily, crocus, hyacinth, narcissus, daffodil, amaryllis, anemone, iris, and other bulbs and plants are shown, all of which are sold at up to 40% less than regular prices if ordered by July 31.

The Royal Gardens stock is all Dutch-grown and features extensive selections of favorite spring flowers. You'll find over a dozen categories of tulips, lots of daffodils, giant bearded irises (sold as plants), including a delicate pink-and-cream variety and the stunning cinnamon/violet "Wild Apache"; fragrant double peonies with blooms up to ten inches across, bleeding hearts, beautiful dangling white snowflakes tipped with green, giant allium, several sorts of anemones, grape and giant hyacinths, distinctive fritillaria, and many others. Dwarfs and miniatures, hybrids, and varieties suitable for naturalizing, rock gardens, and forcing are all available. Collections are sold at extra savings, and a bonus of eight tulip bulbs is sent with orders of $25 or more. Your bulbs are delivered in the fall, and planting instructions are included with each order. Royal Gardens guarantees that every bulb and plant will grow and bloom and accepts returns for replacement, exchange, refund, or credit.

VAN BOURGONDIEN BROS.

245 Farmingdale Rd.
P.O. Box A
Babylon, NY 11702
(516) 669-3523: inquiries
(800) 832-5689: NY orders
(800) 645-5830: orders
except NY

Catalog: free; pub. in the spring and fall
Discount: up to 40%
Goods: house brand, imported
Minimum Order: none
Shipping, Handling: extra; UPS, PP
Sales Tax: NY deliveries
Accepts: check, MO, MC, V, AE, DC
$$$

The spring and fall catalogs from Van Bourgondien supply a wealth of house plants, flowers, shrubbery, berries, ground cover, herbs, fruit trees, and more. Both 64-page editions offer Hosta and hybrid lilies, ground cover (periwinkle, alyssum, sedum, etc.); Oriental poppies, wild flowers (including lady's slippers, larkspurs, bluebells, and others); and a wide range of irises, amaryllis, phlox, gypsophilia, and other flowers. Supplies and tools are also offered—fertilizers, knee pads, grow lights, composters, garden carts, and more.

The fall catalog pictures an excellent group of spring-flower bulbs, including tulip, daffodil, hyacinth, crocus, narcissus, anemone, allium, fritillaria, and other selections. There are collections and assortments of perennials, geraniums, delphiniums, shasta daisies, lavender, flowering house plants, foxtails, black-eyed Susans, and many other plants, bulbs, and roots.

The spring catalog shows a wide variety of pleasures for garden and home, including house plants, herbs, carnivorous plants, begonias, dwarf fruit trees, shade trees and shrubbery (including Japanese cherry trees, wisteria, dogwood, hydrangeas, azaleas, etc.); strawberries, cherries, raspberries, grapes, nut trees, rhubarb, shallots, artichokes, cranberries, and many others.

Van Bourgondien's prices are generally to 40% less than those charged by garden-supply centers, and collections are offered at greater savings. Shipping schedules are given in the catalog. All bulbs, plants, and root cuttings are guaranteed to be "as described" and in perfect condition at the time of shipment.

SEE ALSO:

Arctic Glass Supply, Inc. . . . passive solar greenhouse panes . . . HOME (maintenance)

Clothcrafters, Inc. . . . knee pads, gardening aprons . . . GENERAL

Central Michigan Tractor and Parts . . . salvaged, rebuilt, reconditioned tractor and combine parts . . . AUTO

Maine Discount Hardware . . . lawn and garden machinery parts . . . TOOLS

Manufacturer's Supply . . . garden tractor, lawn mower, trimmer parts . . . TOOLS

Northern Hydraulics, Inc. . . . lawn and garden machinery parts; Jacobson tractors . . . TOOLS

Self-Sufficiency and Smallholding Supplies . . . gardening and farming implements . . . ANIMAL

Southeastern Insulated Glass . . . passive solar greenhouse panels . . . HOME (maintenance)

Fred Stokes Farms . . . sweet potato plants, tobacco seeds . . . CIGARS

Sunco Products Corp. . . . protective gloves . . . CLOTHING

Whole Earth Access . . . gardening tools, rototillers, etc. . . . GENERAL

Zip-Penn, Inc. . . . lawn mower parts . . . TOOLS

FOOD AND DRINK

Foods, beverages, and
condiments.

Herbs, spices, coffee, and tea are mail-order naturals, and all are available through the firms listed here. But these sources also offer you the best cheese buys in New York City, freshly baked whole-grain breads, caviar, Italian truffles, Mexican and Syrian foods, giant pistachio nuts, Vermont maple syrup, and much more, at savings of up to 80%.

When ordering, be mindful of the weather. Don't order such highly perishable or temperature-sensitive foods as chocolate, soft cheeses, fruits, vegetables, and uncured meats during the summer unless you have them shipped express and plan to eat them right away. (Most catalogs include caveats to this effect. Some firms will not ship certain goods during the summer under *any* circumstances.)

Don't overlook these food and drink firms when making out gift lists. Whether it's one package of rare herbs or a year of gustatory delights provided by an "of-the-month" program, you can choose presents that will be remembered long after they're consumed, and many of these companies offer the convenience of direct shipment to the recipient.

CAVIARTERIA INC.

29 E. 60th St.
New York, NY 10022
(212) 759–7410: inquiries
and AK, HI, NY orders
(800) 221–1020: orders
except AK, HI, NY

Catalog: free; pub. yearly; updated with quarterly newsletters
Information: price quote by phone or letter with SASE
Discount: up to 50%
Goods: house brand, name brand, imported
Minimum Order: $25 on credit cards
Shipping, Handling, Insurance: included on some items; $5 to $10 per order on others; UPS, PP
Sales Tax: NY deliveries
Accepts: check, MO, MC, V, AE, DC
$$$ (see text)

Caviarteria is something of a paradox. It's run by the Sobols, two of the friendliest, most down-to-earth people in mail order, which is not what one expects from purveyors of some of the rarest gourmet fare on the face of the earth.

Caviarteria is the largest distributor of caviar in the U.S. It offers several grades of Caspian Beluga and Sevruga (generally considered the finest caviars), and American sturgeon, whitefish, and salmon caviars at prices that run from $10 an ounce for Kamchatka bottom-of-the-barrel vacuum-packed eggs to $100 for a 3½ oz. jar of Imperial Beluga, the best available. U.S. caviars are less expensive, and we found other gourmet shops selling the same delicacies for up to twice what Caviarteria charges. The catalog also features whole sides of smoked Scottish salmon (two pounds unsliced, $45), and Norwegian gravlax; fresh patés, foie gras, and fresh whole French goose livers ($100 a pound, Cryovac-packed); tinned white and black Italian truffles, French morels and cepes; the heavenly Belgian Lèonidas crème fraiche chocolates (which we've seen sold nowhere else in the U.S.); French glacé fruits, candied chestnuts, and other delectables—all of which are offered at competitive prices.

The catalog concludes on a thoroughly upmarket note—with a listing of classic cars. These are being sold by a younger member of the Sobel clan and include a 1956 Bentley SI Fastback for $45,000, a 1960 Jaguar Mark II, a Daimler V8 250S, and various Rolls-Royces and Bentleys. Even the cars are sold on a "direct-import" basis and represent "exceptional values." The models mentioned here may have already been sold, but if you're interested in similar collectors' cars, direct your written inquiries to Bruce Sobel at Caviarteria.

CANADIAN READERS, PLEASE NOTE: only nonperishable foods and other items can be shipped to Canada.

CHEESE OF ALL NATIONS

153 Chambers St.
New York, NY 10007
(212) 732–0752; 964–0024

Catalog: $1; pub. in Apr. and Sept.
Information: price quote by phone or letter with
  SASE
Discount: 20% to 40%
Goods: imported and domestic
Minimum Order: varies
Shipping, Insurance: extra; UPS, PP
Sales Tax: NY deliveries (if applicable)
Accepts: check, MO, AE
$$$

This firm has been selling cheese for more than 40 years and is known for its selection and prices. The former consists of hundreds of different sorts of cheese from "all nations"; the latter includes the best discounts we've seen on cheese.

Cheese of All Nations sells to New York City's restaurants, and wholesales to other stores, but it will sell cheese to you too. The people who staff this firm know and love fromage, so you won't find yourself a victim of inexperience or indifference, as you might at the hands of other mail-order cheese operations. (It's sheer ignorance or sloppiness that accounts for cutting a cheese long before it's about to be shipped.) If you've been put off cheese by what's arrived in the mail from other firms, give Cheese of All Nations a try. And don't forget your cheese-loving friends—give them a year of international flavor through the Cheese of the Month Club, and they'll never forget *you*.

EREWHON TRADING CO.

**Erewhon Mail Order, Dept. WBMC
236 Brookline, MA 02146
(617) 738–4516: inquiries and MA orders
(800) 222–8028: orders except MA**

Catalog: free
Discount: 10% on quantity orders
Goods: house brand, name brand
Minimum Order: $25 on credit cards
Shipping: extra; UPS
Sales Tax: MA deliveries
Accepts: check, MO, MC, V
$$$

Erewhon is one of the best-known names in the health-food business. It distributes all over the U.S., and virtually every natural-food store in the country has at least a few Erewhon products on its shelves. The 12-page catalog also lists goods by Dr. Bronner, Nature's Gate, Hain, Health Valley, Kendall, Arrowhead Mills, Pure & Simple, Chico-San, Del Verde, Marusan, Essene, Baldwin Hill, and other firms. The huge range of products includes nut butters, oils, grains, beans, seeds, nuts, flours, Japanese goods, pasta, granola, natural cosmetics, toiletries, cooking utensils, books, and many other goods. A kosher line is also marketed. Quantity discounts of 10% are offered on case and bulk purchases.

GLORYBEE HONEY, INC.

**1006 Arrowsmith St., Dept. WMC
Eugene, OR 97402–9121
(503) 584–1649**

Brochure: free; pub. quarterly
Discount: 30%
Goods: name brand, house brand
Minimum Order: none
Shipping, Insurance: extra; UPS, PP, FOB Eugene
Sales Tax: OR deliveries (if applicable)
Accepts: check, MO, MC, V
$$$

Glorybee Honey has opened a separate food division in its apiary-supply business that features the firm's gourmet line of honey and beeswax candles, honey pots, honey candy, and such items as recipe boxes, honey and spice racks, cookbooks that include a guide to canning with honey, bee pollen, and propolis. Prices average about 30% below retail, and quantity discounts are offered on bulk purchases. How sweet it is!

LYNN DAIRY, INC.

Rte. 1, Box 177
Granton, WI 54436
(715) 238–7129

Price List: free with SASE
Discount: up to 50%
Goods: house brand
Minimum Order: none
Shipping: extra; UPS
Sales Tax: WI deliveries
Accepts: check or MO
$$$

When you're making a special cheese sauce or souffle, you probably get the critical ingredient from a well-stocked fromagerie. But when all you need is a chunk of cheddar or mozzarella for burgers, grilled-cheese sandwiches, or chili garnish, you probably opt for the convenience of buying a prepackaged block from the supermarket. And you pay for that convenience.

If you use cheddar, Colby, or mozzarella on a regular basis, you can save up to 50% on the cost-per-pound of these cheeses by buying them from Lynn Dairy. This firm manufactures 15 "basic" cheeses, from several ages of cheddar to Swiss, caraway, salami, and onion cheese. Twelve-ounce jars of sharp cheddar spread are available in 11 flavors, including plain, jalapeño pepper, brandy, and garlic. Combine with slices of beef summer sausage (sold in 12oz sticks) and a supply of crackers, and you've got the beginnings of a great party.

The prices are very good—Lynn's medium and two-year-old, extra sharp cheddar are 35% to 45% cheaper than their supermarket equivalents; the mozzarella is 50% less. But it's not really fair to compare these to the jaundiced hunks in the dairy case, because the flavor and texture of Lynn's products are far superior. Since shipping is extra, ordering from Lynn becomes cost-effective when the amount runs over a few pounds. Combine orders with friends for the best savings, or assemble your own food gifts at holiday time. Lynn Dairy will also do this for you, packing your selection in artificial grass, at a surcharge of $1.25.

PLEASE NOTE: Lynn does not accept orders for shipment to Alaska, Hawaii, or Canada.

THE MEXICAN KITCHEN/LA COCINA MEXICANA

P.O. Box 213
Brownsville, TX
78520–0213
(512) 544–6028

Price List: free; pub. in Jan. and July
Discount: up to 50%
WBMC Reader Offer: 30% off chile-sauce package (see text)
Goods: name brand, generic, imported
Minimum Order: none
Shipping, Handling, Insurance: $1.25 minimum; UPS
Sales Tax: TX deliveries
Accepts: check, MO, certified check
$$$

The fire and spice of real Mexican food can be yours through The Mexican Kitchen without a foray south of the border. It sells authentic ingredients, hard-to-find seasonings, and cookbooks full of recipes for Mexican and Tex-Mex favorites.

The Kitchen, also known as La Cocina Mexicana, offers eight kinds of El Comal dried whole chile pods, ground chile powders, herbs and spices used in Mexican cooking, prepared seasonings (including a salt-free line, chorizo and taco flavorings, and many others); and canned chiles. Some of the goods stocked here are very hard to find elsewhere, and prices are up to 50% less than those charged by other specialty suppliers. Piloncillo (cones of brown sugar), Ibarra chocolate (with almonds and cinnamon), achiote, Bueno mole poblano, nopalitos (diced cactus pads), dried corn husks for tamales, and chile chipotle (smoke-dried jalapeño peppers) aren't to be found at the A&P. And chances are the cookware selection at your local department store won't yield tortilla presses, lava mortar and pestles, flan molds, wooden molinillos (chocolate beaters), tortilla baskets, or many of the other Mexican kitchen utensils available at the Mexican Kitchen.

The standard prices here are good, but check the closeout sections of the price lists for further savings of up to 30%. As a WBMC reader, you're also entitled to a special introductory offer on a set of eight different 7-oz cans of chile sauces—30% off the regular prices. Identify yourself as a WBMC reader *when you request the price list,* which should include details on the special. (This offer expires Oct. 31, 1986.) Do note that these chiles are the real thing and much hotter than supermarket varieties, so use them judiciously. And be sure to scrub your hands well after handling chile pods and powders, since even tiny amounts of the potent oils released in the cutting and grinding can be irritating to the skin and cause hours of discomfort if accidentally rubbed in the eyes. (We speak from personal experience here.) Some cooks wear thin, disposable latex gloves while working with chiles, which solves the problem effectively.

MR. SPICEMAN

615 Palmer Rd., Dept. W3
Yonkers, NY 10701–5769
(914) 576–1222: inquiries
(warehouse)
(914) 961–7776: orders
(office)

Catalog: $1, deductible; pub. Feb., June, Oct.
Discount: up to 94%
WBMC Reader Discount:10% off first order only
  (see text)
Goods: name brand, generic
Minimum Order: $10 on prepaid orders; $25 on
  credit cards
Shipping, Insurance: $1.70 minimum via UPS;
  included on orders over $75; $1 extra via PP;
  20% extra to AK and HI
Handling: $1.50 on orders under $10
Sales Tax: NY deliveries (if applicable)
Accepts: check, MO, MC, V
$$$$ 🍁   (see text)

Charles A. Loeb, Jr., aka Mr. Spiceman, publishes a catalog that runs—literally—from soup to nuts, but he's best known for his seasonings. Mr. Loeb supplies herbs and spices to restaurants, delis, fine food outlets, and consumers at astoundingly low prices.

He quoted savings of 40% to 60%; we did extensive price checking and found possible savings of up to 94% (on bay leaves, bought in 1 lb bulk packaging). Comparing prices on ground allspice, cayenne pepper, ground cumin, curry powder, paprika, and other commonly used herbs and spices, we computed savings of 60% to 75%—again, well above Loeb's estimate. (Per-pound prices on the 5 lb bags are even lower than those of the 1 lb bags we used to make the comparisons.) The stock includes all the basics, and such unusual and hard-to-find seasonings as achiote, guaram masala, juniper berries, pâté spices, and freeze-dried shallots—over 130 in all.

And that's just the beginning. Mon Cheri chocolates, candy for Easter and Christmas, Xylitol gum, Tic Tac mints, crystallized ginger, and hard candies represent some of the "Candy Store" selections. Sun Giant California Snacks and Combos are also available in bulk at prices well below supermarket levels. The lines of Knorr bouillon, Gravy Master flavoring, Panni mixes, 4C products, French's mixes, Virginia Dare extracts and flavorings, and sausage-seasoning mixes are helpful when restocking the pantry. Tea drinkers can choose from many herbal blends and the Earl Line teas, four variations on Earl Grey. Savings are best on "bulk" sizes—a pound of cut and sifted orange-spice tea costs over 50% less than the same tea bought in 30-bag boxes. The catalog ends with several pages of food-preparation tools. While thoughtfully chosen, these items are *not* discount-priced.

Mr. Loeb is offering a WBMC Reader Discount of 10% on your first order. Deduct 10% from the total item cost *before* you add shipping and tax charges. You must identify yourself as a WBMC reader to qualify for the discount. Pass the catalog around among your friends and combine orders—

you'll save on postage and by buying in bulk. And if you've never thought of herbs and spices as gifts, think again. Whether the recipient is just learning to cook or already turns out four-star meals nightly, he or she will appreciate generous refills of frequently used items or a selection of unusual seasonings. (Repack in attractive containers and include a few recipes featuring some of the herbs or spices you're giving—an inexpensive but thoughtful present!)

CANADIAN READERS, PLEASE NOTE: Loeb cannot ship meat products to Canada.

SIMPSON & VAIL, INC.

P.O. Box 309
Pleasantville, NY
10570–0309
(914) 747–1336

Catalog: free; pub. yearly
Discount: 10% to 15%
WBMC Reader Discount: 10% on first order only
Goods: connoisseur-grade, house brand
Minimum Order: none
Shipping: $2.25 minimum; UPS, PP
Sales Tax: NY deliveries (if applicable)
Accepts: check, MO, MC, V
$$$

WBMC Discount

Simpson & Vail sells gourmet coffees at prices from 10% to 15% below those charged by other coffee stores in New York City and then adds another discount of 10% for WBMC readers. S&V carries American (brown), French, Viennese, and Italian roasts, water-processed/decaffeinated brown roast and espresso, Kenya AA, Tanzanian Peaberry, Kona, and other straight coffees and blends. All beans are ground to order.

Simpson & Vail also offers a full line of classic teas and blends, and naturally flavored connoisseur teas redolent with rum, almond, lotus, coconut, etc. Tea "accessories" like caddies, infusers, filters, teapot cozies, and tea bricks are also available. Their coffee and tea selections in canisters make wonderful gifts.

Be sure to mention WBMC when you request the catalog *and* when you order so you'll qualify for the 10% WBMC discount. And remember that it's offered on your first order only, so make that one count. Once you've ordered, you'll receive the quarterly sales flyers with specials, so the savings will keep coming.

SULTAN'S DELIGHT INC.

P.O. Box 253
Staten Island, NY
10314–0253
(718) 720–1557

Catalog: free; pub. in Feb. and Sept.
Discount: up to 50%
WBMC Reader Discount: 10% on first orders over $25
Goods: name brand, generic, imported
Minimum Order: $15
Shipping, Insurance: extra; UPS, PP
Sales Tax: NY deliveries
Accepts: check, MO, MC, V
$$$

When struck by cravings for hummus, baba ghannouj, or falafel, reach for the catalog from Sultan's Delight. This five-year-old firm sells Middle Eastern food specialties, nuts, beans, spices, dried fruits, confections, coffee, cookware, cookbooks, gifts, and even accessories for the belly dancer, at prices up to 50% less than those charged by gourmet and import stores. Near East and Sahadi products are also featured. The catalog includes canned tahini, couscous, tabouleh, fig and quince jams, stuffed grapevine leaves, bulghur and other grains, semolina, green wheat, orzo, fava and other beans, Turkish figs, pickled okra, stuffed eggplant, several kinds of olives, herbs and spices, jumbo pistachios and other nuts, roasted chick peas, halvah, Turkish delight, marzipan paste, olive oil, Turkish coffee, fruit leather, filo, feta cheese, Syrian breads, and much more. Cookbooks with recipes for traditional dishes from Greece, Lebanon, Syria, and the Middle East are available. Also listed are Turkish coffee pots and cups, falafel molds, couscous pots, and other utensils. After your feast, you can slip into a Sultan's sequined bra and pantaloons and belly dance a few hundred calories away to the tunes of *The Best of Belly Dancing* or many other records and tapes. Authentic musical instruments—derbakkeh, finger cymbals, inlaid tambourines, and ouds—are sold, as well as backgammon sets, hassocks, Arab headdresses, and water pipes.

You can deduct an additional 10% from your first order if you identify yourself as a WBMC reader and if your order totals at least $25 without tax or shipping charges. Sultan's Delight stocks and can obtain other items, so call or write if you're looking for a Middle Eastern food or gift specialty not listed in the catalog.

TASTEFULLY YOURS

899 Francisco Blvd. E.
San Rafael, CA 94901
(415) 485–0643

Catalog: free
Discount: 20% to 30%
Goods: house brand
Minimum Order: $30
Shipping, Insurance: included; UPS, PP
Sales Tax: CA deliveries
Accepts: check, MO, certified check
$$ (see text)

In the past few years an entire food industry has developed for people whose primary concerns are convenience, calorie control, and flavor. Tastefully Yours offers another option in the same category: Yurika Foods "gourmet" entrees packed in retort pouches. The pouches aren't frozen, don't need refrigeration, and take only a few minutes to heat. Pouch-packaged foods have a shelf life of five years, equal to or longer than those of many canned and frozen products, and they are ideal alternatives to the powdered foods used by campers.

Over a dozen entrees are currently available, including chicken breast with white wine, beef stroganoff, chicken cacciatore, shrimp creole, sweet-and-sour pork, and several others. They're made without preservatives or additives, and most are well under 300 calories. The entrees are competitively priced at $2 to $3.66 each, up to 30% less than similar retort-packaged products. Tastefully Yours also offers the Yurika "inches away" meal-replacement drink mix, reduced-calorie chocolate mousse mix, and a coffee additive of powdered minerals that is supposed to double the brewed yield and enhance its flavor as well.

We haven't sampled any of the foods so we can't say whether they live up to their descriptions, but they look quite tempting in the color photographs. You can try them at no risk, since satisfaction is guaranteed or your money back.

ELBRIDGE C. THOMAS & SONS

Rte. 4, Box 336
Chester, VT 05143
(802) 263–5680

Brochure: 50¢; pub. yearly in the spring
Discount: up to 50% (see text)
Goods: grade A syrup
Minimum Order: none
Shipping, Insurance: extra; PP
Sales Tax: VT deliveries (if applicable)
Accepts: check, MO, certified check
$$$

Mr. Thomas makes and sells the nectar of New England—pure, grade A Vermont maple syrup. We compared prices charged by at least a dozen "sap farmers." His not only beat these by up to 50%, but also came in ahead of the non-Vermont grade A syrup sold in our local supermarkets by up to 30% (on gallon prices). Vermont syrups are considered superior since the state's grading guidelines are stricter than U.S. standards. They require a heavier density product and accurate labeling, and they prohibit the addition of preservatives. Vermont's soil and climate conditions provide the optimum environment for the half-million hard-rock maples that are tapped each year. All this contributes to that special flavor that distinguishes real Vermont maple syrup.

You don't have to know that one gallon of syrup requires 40 gallons of sap, "a log as big as a man," and weeks of work, to appreciate what it does for pancakes and waffles—but don't limit yourself to breakfast. The brochure lists many ways to use maple syrup in favorite foods—maple milk shakes, candied maple sweet potatoes, maple ham, pie, frosting, and baked beans are just a few examples.

Mr. Thomas sells his syrup in half-pint, pint, quart, half-gallon, and gallon tins; he also offers maple sugar in cakes. A 10% discount is given on orders of any 12 items sent to the same address, so you can sweeten the lives of a dozen people on your gift list and save even more money.

ZABAR'S

2245 Broadway
New York, NY 10024
(212) 787–2000: inquiries
and NY orders
(800) 221–3347: food
orders except NY

Catalog: free; pub. in Oct.
Discount: up to 50%
Goods: name brand, imported, house brand
Minimum Order: $10
Shipping, Insurance: $5 minimum; UPS
Sales Tax: NY deliveries
Accepts: check, MO, MC, V, AE, DC
$$$

Zabar's has been characterized as New York City's ultimate deli; after years of tentative steps into the world of direct-mail, Zabar's has finally brought out a catalog that should earn it the title of caterer to the nation. A little of every department is featured in the 48-page issue, which lists smoked Scottish salmon, plum pudding, peppercorns, brie, Bahlsen cookies and confections, pâtés, mustards, crackers, escargot, Lindt and Ghiradelli chocolates, Tiptree preserves, Dresden stöllen, extra-virgin olive oil, savory prosciutto, and many other temptations. The prices run to 35% less than those charged by other specialty-foods catalogs, and the stock is the freshest around.

Zabar's also sells several excellent cookware lines, including Mauviel hotel-weight copper pans from France, Le Creuset, Farberware, and Revere Ware cookware, Krups and Simac machines, Braun coffee-makers, Robot Coupe food processors, Mouli kitchen tools, and much more. Prices on these goods are as much as 50% below list. The catalog is published in October for holiday orders, so don't expect to receive one out of season. The cookware is available throughout the year. Call or write for availability information and price quotes.

SEE ALSO:

E.C. Kraus . . . wine- and beer-making supplies, flavorings . . . CRAFTS
Protecto-Pak . . . zip-top food-storage bags . . . HOME (maintenance)
Puritan's Pride, Inc. . . . herbal teas . . . HEALTH
Rammagerdin . . . Icelandic seafood samplers . . . CRAFTS
RSP Distributing Co. . . . survival foods . . . GENERAL
Self-Sufficiency and Smallholding Supplies . . . beer and wine production supplies, butchery tools . . . ANIMAL
Star Pharmaceutical, Inc. . . . herbal tea . . . HEALTH
Sunburst Biorganics . . . small selection herbal tea, natural foods . . . HEALTH
Vitamin Specialties . . . herbal tea . . . HEALTH

GENERAL MERCHANDISE, GIFTS, AND BUYING CLUBS

Buying clubs and firms offering
a wide range of goods and
services.

This is, as usual, a potpourri of firms selling everything from toweling to silver fox jackets. Some of the companies are here because they *are* buying clubs and general merchandisers; others because they defied easy classification. All offer excellent savings, including the three mail-order giants—Best Products, Spiegel, and Sears. Only Best Products can be considered a discount house in the strictest sense of the term, but if you place regular orders with Spiegel and Sears, you'll receive sales catalogs with savings of up to 60% on many of the goods they carry. Their service departments are first-rate, so buying and delivery are a breeze. Go through the other listings carefully—there are some real finds here and countless answers to the question of what to give for Christmas, birthdays, anniversaries, Mother's Day. . . .

BEST PRODUCTS CO., INC.

P.O. Box 25031
Richmond, VA 23260
(804) 261–2197: inquiries
(800) 552–9841: VA orders
(800) 446–9827: orders
except VA

Catalog: $1
Discount: up to 50%
Goods: name brand, house brand, generic
Minimum Order: varies
Shipping, Insurance: extra; UPS, FOB warehouse
Sales Tax: charged in many states
Accepts: check, MO, MC, V
$$$

Best Products is a catalog showroom operation with over 100 outlets across the country. Over 8,000 items, from tools to jewelry, are shown in the 500-plus page catalog, which should be noted for its discounts on name brand toys. Best Products has been in business since 1957 and has outlasted many other showroom chains because it offers excellent service and real discount prices.

CLOTHCRAFTERS, INC.

Elkhart Lake, WI 53020
(414) 876–2112

Catalog: free; pub. yearly in Sept.
Discount: up to 40%
Goods: house brand, generic
Minimum Order: none
Shipping, Insurance: included; UPS, PP
Handling: $2 on orders under $15
Sales Tax: WI deliveries
Accepts: check, MO, MC, V
$$$

This firm sells "plain vanilla" textile goods of every sort, from cheesecloth by the yard to flannel gun-cleaning patches (about two hundred for $2). Most of the products are made of pure, white cotton—no logos, idiotic mottos, or fussy designs. For the kitchen, there are pot holders and pan handlers (50¢ each); taffeta toaster covers ($1); dish towels, chefs' hats, and other goods. You can make bouquet garni with your own herbs and spice and these bags (12 for $2) and save up to half the cost of packaged seasonings. Salad greens bags, *sans* lettuce illustration and definition, are less than 60¢ each, compared to $5.95 for the "gourmet" variety. There are denim place mats, plain cotton napkins, hot pads, aprons, cotton duck shower curtains, laundry bags, tote bags, shoe totes, woodpile covers and firewood carriers, garment bags, cider-press liners, and more. Mosquito netting is just $3.50 per 90″-wide yard, and the netting head bag is $1.50—compared to $5.95 in another catalog. The lightweight cotton terry towels are ideal for beach and summer house, and they dry more quickly than the heavier versions. Clothcrafters also sells a full range of Portuguese cotton flannel sheets, pillowcases, and liners for sleeping bags at prices to 35% less than those charged elsewhere for identical goods.

Clothcrafters has been in business since 1936 and is known for its good service. All purchases are covered by a guarantee of satisfaction, and returns are accepted for exchange, refund, or credit.

COMP-U-CARD

777 Summer St.
Stamford, CT 06901
(800) 252–4100:
membership, price quotes,
and orders

Information: inquire
Discount: up to 50%
Goods: name brand
Minimum Order: none
Shipping, Handling, Insurance: included; UPS
Sales Tax: included, if applicable
Accepts: check, MO, MC, V
$$$$

For $25, you can get a year's membership in Comp-U-Store, the nation's largest buying computerized shopping service and join over a million customers saving up to 50% on a wide range of products and services.

Membership entitles you to a year of unlimited toll-free calls for price quotes from Comp-U-Card's database of more than 60,000 name-brand items—appliances, VCR's, table settings, computers, jewelry, furniture, and much more. You'll also receive regular mailings of the company's "Best Buys" newsletter and catalogs, which feature specials and buying tips. Membership gives you access to the CUC car-buying service, through which you can purchase an auto for as little as $50 over dealer cost,(plus destination charges from Detroit). Arrangements made with National and Avis enable you to save on car rentals, too. Prescription drugs and dietary supplements can be bought for less through a pharmacy affiliate. Details of all these services are given in the literature. Comp-U-Card has computer "tie-ins" with manufacturers and distributors, which it finds and offers such low prices. Membership is covered by a money-back guarantee of satisfaction.

WALTER DRAKE & SONS, INC.

**Drake Building
Colorado Springs, CO
80940
(303) 596–3854**

Catalog: 25¢; pub. 7 times yearly
Discount: up to 40%
Goods: house brand
Minimum Order: none
Shipping, Handling: extra; UPS
Sales Tax: CO deliveries
Accepts: check, MO, MC, V
$$$$

Walter Drake publishes a catalog featuring a wide variety of goods at very low prices. Drake's return-address labels are one of the all-time bargains—still $1.29 for 1,000—their cost three years ago. Drake has developed its stationery line with other well-priced labels, notepads, business cards, correspondence paper and envelopes, and other useful goods for the home office.

The catalog offers other goods as well, most of which are under $10: kitchen gadgets, Christmas decorations, personalized accessories, grooming tools, toys, party goods and novelties, pet products, household organizers, energy savers, and more. Drake's products are usually of a better quality than those sold by other low-price houses, and delivery and other services are quite good.

GRAND FINALE

P.O. Box 819027
Farmers Branch, TX 75381
(214) 934–9777

Catalog: $2, year's subscription; pub. 10 times
  yearly
Discount: up to 75%
Goods: name brand, generic
Minimum Order: none
Shipping, Handling, Insurance: extra; UPS
Sales Tax: TX deliveries
Accepts: check, MO, MC, V, AE
$$$$

If you've ever coveted something from the Horchow Collection or Trifles but passed it up because you couldn't afford it, you may have a second chance with the Grand Finale. This Horchow affiliate publishes a 32-page catalog stocked with clearances and closeouts from the Collection and Trifles catalogs and from other gift houses and respected manufacturers. *Anything* can show up here: diamond earrings, hand-embroidered nightgowns, leather desk sets, cashmere mufflers, electric pasta machines, Christmas decorations, antique chinoiserie, personalized stationery, side tables, toys, sheets, Mikasa china, silk ties, and Halston bags are just a few of the notables that have appeared in previous Grand Finales, at up to 75% less than they were sold previously.

Since the savings are spectacular and quantities are usually limited, orders are filled on a first-come, first-served basis. Refunds, *not* substitutions or back orders, are made on products that have sold out. This is one catalog you shouldn't miss when doing your holiday shopping.

HANOVER HOUSE

Hanover, PA 17331
(717) 637–1600

Catalog: free
Discount: up to 75%
Goods: generic
Minimum Order: none
Shipping, Handling: extra; UPS
Sales Tax: PA deliveries
Accepts: check, MO, MC, V
$$

Hanover House is the budget end of a chain of catalog houses that includes PL-Premium Leather, Pennsylvania Station, and Adam York. Hanover House is strong on low-priced gifts, accessories, and useful household items. Everything from the practical to the highly improbable has appeared in the pages of a HH catalog at some point, but the draws are the items once sold in the upmarket catalogs that sometimes appear here at savings of up to 75%. On the basis of these bargains alone, this is a good catalog to peruse when you're looking for low-priced gifts.

LINCOLN HOUSE, INC.

**2015 Grand Ave., Dept.
WBMC-3
Kansas City, MO 64141
(816) 842–3225**

Catalog: free; pub. in the spring and fall
Discount: 30%
WBMC Reader Discount: 10% (see text)
Goods: house brand, generic
Minimum Order: 6 items for WBMC discount (see text)
Shipping, Insurance: included; UPS
Handling: $1 per order
Sales Tax: MO deliveries
Accepts: check, MO, MC, V
$$$

Lincoln House publishes a 96-page catalog of candles, gifts, and stationery items. Outstanding offerings in the current catalog include a fabric magazine rack, brass candlesticks, terra-cotta bread baskets, an auto organizer, spice-scented draft stoppers, recipe files, stationery, gift wrappings, and Christmas ornaments. The holiday items are noteworthy, especially the collection of handmade ornaments, candles, decorated cookie tins, and gift bags. Prices are up to 30% less than comparable retail, and if you buy six items (any assortment), you can take an additional 10% off the prices. Just deduct the 10% from the goods total and write "WBMC Reader Discount" across the order form. Add handling to the sum *after* taking the discount and calculate sales tax (if applicable) on the full value of the goods. Your satisfaction is guaranteed, and returns are accepted.

**REGAL GREETINGS &
GIFTS, INC.**

**2221 Niagara Falls Blvd.
Niagara Falls, NY 14304
(716) 731–9001**

Catalog: free; pub. twice yearly
Discount: up to 30% (see text)
Goods: house brand, generic
Minimum Order: none
Shipping, Handling, Insurance: $2.95 minimum; UPS
Sales Tax: NY deliveries
Accepts: check, MO, MC, V
$$$

If you were forced to do all of your holiday shopping from one catalog, the 80-page winter edition from Regal would probably provide you with a gift for everyone on your list, along with tags, wrappings, and ribbons for tying it all up—at prices up to 30% less than comparable retail.

In addition to seasonal wrapping collections, cards, address labels, and stationery, Regal offers a wide range of other goods: household organizers, kitchen helps, vases and candlesticks, napkin rings and table linens, bathroom accessories, candles, jewelry boxes, and lots of toys and novelties. The most recent catalog included a handsome brass candle-holder center-piece, revolving spice racks, a gingerbread house kit, crib activity centers and playthings, letter racks, perfume atomizers, au gratin dishes, clothing hampers, Christmas wreaths and ornaments, stickers and albums, model cars, book lights, shower caddies, scented drawer liners, garment bags, wooden alphabet blocks, and collectors' dolls, among other things. The prices are generally competitive, and some items—especially the gift-wrapping collections—are real bargains. Each catalog we've received has included a "take 25% off every price" offer, making the buys that much better. Satisfaction is guaranteed. Returns are accepted on everything except personalized goods within 30 days for exchange, refund, or credit.

RSP DISTRIBUTING CO.

P.O. Box 2345
Redondo Beach, CA 90278
(213) 542–0431

Catalog: $1, refundable; pub. in Oct., updated monthly

Information: price quote by phone or letter with SASE

Discount: 40% to 90%

Goods: generic, closeouts

Minimum Order: $25

Shipping, Insurance: extra; UPS

Handling: $2.50 on orders under $25

Sales Tax: CA deliveries

Accepts: check, MO, certified check

$$$

Anyone who's familiar with the current offerings in gift and novelty catalogs will find the photocopied pages from RSP Distributing real eye-openers. The sheets we received showed the same toys, jewelry, household organizers, and gift items we'd seen in slick four-color catalogs listed here at 50%, 75%, and even 90% less. Book lights and boxed sets of burner covers were selling for $4; cloisonné hair clips for $2.25 (regularly $5.95 and more); a darling stuffed fox for $4.50 (from $11); a metal doll stand for $1 (seen elsewhere for $3.95); sterling rings set with semiprecious stones for under $8; and die-cast model sports cars for $13.80 a dozen (compared to $1.95 and more each). These goods were pictured; bigger savings were available on closeouts of similar products that were listed without illustrations. Many were sold by the dozen and were the type of goods ideal for the flea-market vendor or adventurous consumer.

In addition to closeouts, RSP also sells "plain-label food products," which have shelf lives of up to ten years. Packed in #10 cans, they include flours and grains, peanut butter powder, beans and rice, dehydrated banana slices, vegetable stew, green beans, corn, potato slices, mashed potato granules, nonfat milk, and other staples. Prices run from $2.60 for white flour to $16.20 for the corn and beans. This represents savings of up to 70% compared to similar products sold by camping and survivalist suppliers. Discounts of 5% are offered on all prepaid orders of $100 or more. Returns are accepted within ten days for exchange or refund.

SEARS, ROEBUCK AND CO.

925 S. Homan Ave.
Chicago, IL 60607

4640 Roosevelt Blvd.
Philadelphia, PA 19132

General Catalog: $4, redeemable; pub. twice yearly
Discount: up to 60% (see text)
Goods: name brand, house brand, generic
Minimum Order: see text
Shipping, Insurance: extra
Sales Tax: charged on deliveries to many states
Accepts: check, MO, SearsCharge
$$$$

Does a direct-mail legend whose annual sales account for over 1% of the GNP really *need* an introduction? Sears, Roebuck and Co. publishes two Big Books (1,514 pages) a year, and they stock everything from lingerie to the kitchen sink. Sears also offers 19 "Specialogs," smaller catalogs that feature lines of uniforms and work clothing, carpeting, toys, crafts supplies, and other goods. Orders of mailable goods under 25 pounds can be delivered directly to your home or office, saving you the trip to the pickup depot.

We've listed Sears here because the company runs sales on a regular basis, with savings of up to 60% on a wide range of goods. This includes the famous Craftsman line of power and hand tools, which are usually given top ratings in consumer product reviews. If you place two orders of $30 or more every six months you'll receive many of the sales catalogs as well as the new Big Books. The catalog can be ordered directly from either address listed here for $4; it includes a coupon good for $4 on purchases of $20 or more on store or catalog purchases. You can order any of the Specialogs through the catalog for $1 each, or pick them up at no cost in any Sears store.

SGF

Box 819068
Dallas, TX 75381–9068
(214) 385–2722

Catalog: $2, year's subscription redeemable; pub. 4 times yearly
Discount: 30% to 60%
Goods: name brand, generic
Minimum Order: none
Shipping, Handling, Insurance: extra; UPS
Sales Tax: TX deliveries
Accepts: check, MO, MC, V, AE
$$$$

This is the newest addition to the Horchow empire—a catalog offering Savings on Gifts and Furnishings to the tune of 30% to 60%. It's a posh version of the Grand Finale catalog and features more furnishings, home accents, and luxury merchandise. Furs, diamond jewelry, fine china and flatware, and home accoutrements have appeared in the past few issues. This is less an outlet for discontinued Horchow goods than an off-price venture in mail-order luxe. The same policy concerning order fulfillment applies, however, and both SGF and the Grand Finale accept returns within 30 days on everything except personalized and custom-ordered goods.

SPIEGEL, INC.

1515 W. 22nd St.
Oak Brook, IL 60521
(800) 523–3100: IL orders
(800) 345–4500: orders
except IL

Catalog: $3, refundable; pub. twice yearly with supplements
Discount: up to 50%
Goods: name brand
Minimum Order: none
Shipping, Insurance: extra; UPS, FOB point of departure
Sales Tax: IL and PA deliveries
Accepts: check, MO, MC, AE
$$$

The once-dowdy Spiegel revamped its image and inventory about five years ago and now sets the pace for fashion trends in middle America. Spiegel carries stylish women's wear and clothing for men and children; home furnishings and decorative touches; and some appliances and electronics. Three dollars brings you the big seasonal catalogs, but when you place an order you'll receive "private sale" catalogs with the same goods at prices cut up to 50%. Cookware sets, cashmere sweaters, classic skirts and blazers, phone answering machines, and draperies are among the things we've ordered at an average of 40% below list prices. The catalogs overlap, so Spiegel is, in effect, running a constant sale. If you haven't seen the catalog in a couple of years, invest $3—you'll be surprised, seduced, and delighted.

TRADE-MARK BUSINESS BARTER EXCHANGE OF NEW YORK

**P.O. Box 175, Box 10-C
Baldwin, NY 11510
(516) 868–6407: inquiries in NY
(800) 547–8820: inquiries except NY**

Brochure: free with SASE
Information: inquiries by phone or letter with SASE
Discount: 33% on memberships
Goods: bartered products and services
Minimum Order: none
Shipping, Handling, Insurance: not usually applicable
Sales Tax: see text
Accepts: check or MO

Bartering is the world's oldest method of transacting business, and it's been revived recently in the form of organized bartering services. Trade-Mark Business Barter Exchange is one such network, created "for business owners doing business with each other on a part cash, part trade dollar basis." An enrollment fee may be charged for membership (details were not included in the information we received). Membership entitles you to several free listings in TMBBE's regional barter directory, computerized accounting of all transactions, newsletters highlighting new business entries and offers, and more. You can barter for any number of products and services: roofing, interior design, catering, plants, hypnosis therapy, office supplies, wood stoves and firewood, advertising and printing, hotel stays, security systems, and dry cleaning, to cite but a few samples. Transactions are based on your regular selling price, and you can negotiate 20% to 80% of the sale in cash.

Before joining any barter service, you should consult your accountant regarding the IRS and state sales tax regulations that may apply to such transactions. This firm is a licensee of Trade-Mark Business Barter Exchange, which has other regional branches. If the branch listed here doesn't serve your area, request the address of your network from Trade-Mark Business Barter Exchange, 9045 S.W. Barbur Blvd., Portland, OR 97219.

WHOLE EARTH ACCESS

2950 7th St.
Berkeley, CA 94710
(415) 845–3000

Catalog: $3; pub. yearly in the fall
Discount: up to 60%
Goods: name brand, generic
Minimum Order: $20
Shipping, Insurance: extra; UPS, PP, FOB Berkeley
Handling: $3 on orders under $20
Sales Tax: CA deliveries
Accepts: check, MO, MC, V
$$$

While this firm has no affiliation with Stewart Brand's enterprises, it's conceived in the same spirit. Whole Earth Access, a 270-page general-store-by-mail, offers a wide range of goods chosen for performance and durability at up to 60% below list or comparable retail. General product categories include food preparation, clothing, health, energy, outdoor living and recreation, gardening and homesteading, and carpentry and construction.

The "knives" section of food tools includes useful information on evaluating materials and construction, and pointers on care and sharpening. Similar service pieces are included with many of the listings. Individual products are discussed in depth and most are accompanied by photographs. The catalog we reviewed offered food processors by Cuisinart and KitchenAid, the professional Hamilton Beach blender, crank grinders, Henckels and Russel Harrington cutlery, the Acme juicer and several lever models, and coffee and espresso devices by Melior and Melitta. Also listed were sprouters, tortilla presses, Vollrath stockpots, paella pans, pot racks, Wolf commercial ranges, stemware, Levi's and Lee clothing, Oshkosh and Carhartt overalls, Frye and Timberline boots, negative ion generators, water stills and filters, Fuchs hair and tooth brushes, olive-oil soap, Homelite chain saws, heaters, Aladdin oil lamps, Hunter ceiling fans, generators, bedding, Sea Eagle inflatable rafts and canoes, Gerber sport knives, gloves, Celestron and Nikon optics, rototillers, a full range of hand and power tools, and books on every topic. This is just a small sample of the goods and brands stocked at Whole Earth; we were told that audio, video, camera, computer, calculator, and typewriter lines are being added, as well as a department devoted to goods for infants and children.

Whole Earth Access has been in business since 1969 and invites your suggestions and comments on the catalog and products. Customers are sent updates on new additions and sales, and the firm will accept returns with prior authorization for exchange, refund, or credit.

SEE ALSO:

Ace Leather Products, Inc. . . . travel clocks, gifts . . . LEATHER
Gohn Bros. . . . Amish "general store" goods . . . CLOTHING
Good 'N' Lucky Promotions . . . closeout merchandise, novelties . . . JEWELRY
Laurence Corner . . . new, used government surplus . . . CLOTHING
Paradise Products . . . party goods . . . TOYS
Plastic BagMart . . . plastic bags for every purpose . . . HOME (maintenance)
Plexi-Craft Quality Products Corp . . . Lucite ® and Plexiglas ® furniture, accessories, and gifts . . . HOME (furnishings)
Rapidforms, Inc. . . . gift boxes, wrapping, ribbon, packing and shipping supplies . . . OFFICE
Roussels . . . closeouts and overstock goods . . . CRAFTS
Stecher's Limited . . . name-brand timepieces, pens, lighters . . . HOME (table settings)

HANDCRAFTS, NATIVE PRODUCTS, AND IMPORTS

Imported and handcrafted
goods.

There is simply no way to resist the astounding bargains in "imported" goods or the handcrafts of a region or country. You can buy eighteenth-century American crafts from Connecticut, bibles inlaid with mother-of-pearl from Israel, piñatas from New Mexico, wooden shoes from Holland, rugs from Tibetan refugees living in India . . . the list goes on and on.

Because most of the goods are handmade, there may be delays in shipment if stock has run out, especially if you order during the holiday rush. So send for catalogs as soon as possible—via airmail—and order early. Don't count on anything you're ordering from overseas to reach you by a certain day, even when having goods shipped airmail. When ordering from overseas sources, be sure to read the relevant sections in "The Complete Guide to Buying by Mail" in the back of this book—it will aid you in every aspect of your transaction.

GOOD SHEPHERD'S STORE

George T. Abu Aita and Brothers
P.O. Box 96
Bethlehem
Israel
Phone # 74229

Catalog: $3
Discount: 20% to 40%
Goods: handcrafted
Minimum Order: $30
Shipping, Insurance: extra
Duty: extra
Accepts: check or IMO
$$$

The Good Shepherd's Store publishes a 16-page catalog of religious and gift articles made of olivewood and mother-of-pearl. There are carvings of Moses, Mary, the flight to Egypt, the Saviour, and beautiful Nativity sets, all in olivewood. The store carries olivewood camels connected with little chains to form a caravan, for between $1 and $16. There are also lovely olivewood vases, candlesticks, egg cups, salad sets, jewelry boxes, and bibles. The items finished in mother-of-pearl—striking jewelry boxes, bibles, crosses, and jewelry—cost about twice as much as those in olivewood. This firm is over 25 years old and is quite experienced in shipping goods to countries worldwide.

LA PIÑATA

No. 2 Patio Market, Old Town
Albuquerque, NM 87104
(505) 242-2400

Price List: free with SASE
Discount: up to 50%
Goods: house brand
Minimum Order: $10
Shipping, Insurance: extra; UPS
Sales Tax: NM deliveries
Accepts: check, MO, certified check, MC, V
$$$

La Piñata, run by the Sanchez family, is our favorite source for piñatas—hollow papier-mâché animals and characters traditionally filled with candy and prizes and broken by a blindfolded party guest. Although scrambling for the treats may be the best part of having one, it always seems a shame that the piñata must be broken to get them—especially when it's pretty or novel, as are those sold at La Piñata. Fortunately, the prices here are so low that you can afford to buy two—one to break and one to keep.

The selection is about the best you'll find outside Mexico itself. There are Sesame Street characters, including Big Bird, Cookie Monster, and Oscar; superheroes like Batman and Superman; springing cats, pumpkins, Santa, snowmen, witches, stars, reindeer, and other seasonal characters; and all sorts of animals, including bears, burros, cats, elephants, frogs, pigs, kangaroos, penguins, and more. Prices begin at under $5, and there are three sizes from which to choose. Please don't ask for a discount—the prices are already cause for celebration!

CANADIAN READERS, PLEASE NOTE: orders can be sent only to those areas of Canada served by UPS.

OTTEN & SON

P.O. Box 55655
1007 ND Amsterdam
The Netherlands
Phone #: 20-629724

Catalog: $1, deductible
Information: inquire by letter
Discount: up to 20%
WBMC Reader Discount: 10%
Goods: handcrafted
Minimum Order: none
Shipping, Handling, Insurance: $4.40 minimum; surface mail
Duty: extra
Accepts: check, IMO, MC, V, AE, EC, Access
$$$

Wooden shoes, or "klompen," are still worn in Holland by gardeners, fishermen, butchers, and dairy workers. Otten & Son sends out a charming brochure on the history and manufacture of wooden shoes. In one part of Holland it tells us, a boy courting a girl would give her carved wooden shoes decorated with her initials. The "klompen" have even affected the language—there are several Dutch words derived from the sound made by walking in the shoes.

Otten makes seven models, including souvenir shoes with windmills carved on the toes. Most of the shoes are painted lively colors, and there is a low-cut model that is easier to walk in than the traditional style. Otten also sells wooden clogs with leather uppers, much like those made by Olof Daughters of Sweden. Prices begin at $5.02 for white shoes in a child's size 4 and go up to $13.04 for souvenir shoes in a man's size 14. The leather and wooden clogs are about $21 a pair. Prices are further reduced by the WBMC discount of 10%. *Be sure to mention WBMC both when requesting the catalog and when ordering.* And note that there is a surcharge of about $3 for payments made by check. Quantity discounts of 20% are given on orders of 25 pairs.

Don't overlook the uses for these shoes—the large sizes can be used as doll beds, letter holders, planters, lamp bases, even pencil holders. They make wonderful gifts, too.

ROCKY MOUNTAIN STATIONERY

11725 Co. Rd. 27.3
Dolores, CO 81323
(303) 565–8230

Brochure; Samples, Price List: free with SASE
Discount: up to 50%
WBMC Reader Discount: 30% (see text)
Goods: handcrafted
Minimum Order: none
Shipping, Insurance: included; PP
Sales Tax: CO deliveries
Accepts: check or MO
$$$$

Rose Ruland is an artist who takes flowers and leaves from her garden and the surrounding wilds of the Rockies, presses them, and uses them to create note cards. She also does small oil paintings on notes, and each is unique. Both the "Nature" and "Just a Note" series are sold in collections of 12 cards of assorted colors with envelopes. We have seen individual cards of similar description selling in local card shops for $2 and up; her price is just $7.95 for 12—a little more than 66¢ a card. And if you identify yourself as a WBMC reader, you may buy them for $3 less—just $4.95, or two collections for $9. Your satisfaction is guaranteed. Returns are accepted. Please remember to enclose a SASE when requesting the price list and samples.

S & C HUBER,
ACCOUTREMENTS

82 Plants Dam Rd.
East Lyme, CT 06333
(203) 739–0772

Catalog: $1.50; pub. yearly
Discount: up to 30%
Goods: handmade, generic
Minimum Order: none
Shipping, Insurance: extra; UPS, FOB East Lyme
Sales Tax: CT deliveries
Accepts: check or MO
$

The Hubers' center for "early country arts" maintains the spirit of the eighteenth and nineteenth centuries: They run their business from a farm that predates the Revolutionary War, and the crafts products and finished goods listed in their 32-page brochure are just as authentic.

Spinners and weavers can purchase tools—a castle spinning wheel, table loom, niddy-noddies, carders, shuttles, and spindles—and fibers, including fleece, flax, cotton, silk, cashmere, camel hair, and llama tops. Natural dyes and mordants are also listed. A variety of yarn is stocked in wool, cotton, linen, and silk. Reproduction sampler kits, linen and Williamsburg yard goods, floor cloths, herbs, potpourri, reproduction redware and combware, woodenware, beeswax candles and tin lighting fixtures, period stencils and supplies, basketry materials, bandboxes, reproduction Shaker baskets and boxes, and an excellent list of books on these crafts are all stocked as well. To be fair, prices are not "discount," but we found a few crafts supplies sold here at up to 30% less than prices charged by other mail-order firms.

TIBETAN REFUGEE SELF
HELP CENTRE

Havelock Villa
65 Gandhi Rd.
Darjeeling 734101
West Bengal, India
Phone # 2346

Catalog: $2 (see text)
Discount: up to 80%
Goods: handcrafted
Minimum Order: none
Shipping, Insurance: extra
Duty: extra
Accepts: check, IMO, teller's check (see text)
$$$$

The Tibetan Refugee Self Help Centre was established in 1959 when Tibet was taken over by Communist China. The Centre provides not only a surrogate homeland for hundreds of Tibetans, but also a means of preserving their cultural heritage and generating income by the production of native handcrafts.

The small black-and-white catalog gives you an idea of the craftsmanship and design of the goods. The Centre's specialty is carpet-making, and the catalog illustrates 23 rugs, which cost $162 or $174.60 each, depending on the complexity of the design. The rugs are all 6 by 3 feet handwoven with vegetable-dyed Tibetan sheep's wool. The designs are striking: dragons, birds, a snow lion and lotus, birds and flowers, lucky signs, and an unusual lotus and bat motif, to name a few. The Centre's artisans will weave your own designs for only 5% more than the stock prices and execute rugs in your own choice of colors. (The traditional colors are rich and subtle, like those of good dhurries.)

The Centre also sells chair cushions in similar motifs and color schemes. Other home accoutrements include: multicolored table mats and brass candlestands; an ornate brass soup stove for $58; carved wooden good-luck symbols and picture frames; carved and painted low tables from $27.50 to $135.50; and ornate brocaded religious scrolls.

The apparel is equally appealing: rustic, handwoven wool shawls worked with Tibetan designs; hand-knitted pullovers and cardigans for $25; hand-knitted six-foot fringed mufflers for $10; and Tibetan-style cotton shirts for $3.45 to $4.50. Best of all are the hats, lavishly trimmed with fur, sold for no more than $25 here (compared to $60 and more in the U.S.); and the boots, made of wool and leather and decorated with appliquéd leather designs and embroidery, that cost $12.50 to $20.75 These make exotic slippers-cum-leg warmers for scuffing about the house on winter nights, but since most are designed for outdoor use, it's a shame to keep them inside.

The Centre also sells a potpourri of such items as bookmarks, pincushions, handmade stationery, greeting cards, and even Tibetan Apso dogs, which it breeds.

Charges for packing and postage aren't included in the prices. We advise you to send the full payment for the goods with your order and then ask the Centre to send an estimate of packing and postage costs immediately, so you can pay them and avoid a delay in shipping. *Make all payments by bank or postal IMO, including those for the catalog,* to "Tibetan Refugee Self Help Centre, Darjeeling," and send them by *registered mail.* The Centre is not for the impatient; surface mail can take months to arrive, and if stock is depleted, your order may be further delayed until it's replenished. The goods, however, are worth the wait.

**TRADE EXCHANGE
(CEYLON), LTD.**

**72 Chatham St.
Colombo 1
Sri Lanka
Phone # 25521**

Catalog: $5
Discount: up to 80%
Goods: handmade
Minimum Order: $1,000
Shipping: FOB Sri Lanka
Duty: extra
Accepts: check
$

Trade Exchange sells batiked fabric created by the traditional wax-dyeing methods. The firm makes the fabric into clothing, bedspreads, lamp shades, and hangings, and markets them under the "Laklooms" label. The clothing comes in Eastern styles, primarily full-length dresses that make use of the spectacular patterns produced by batiking. The sarees are distinctly ethnic and quite flamboyant, but there are also western styles in brilliant colors and border prints.

The prices are up to 80% less than those charged in import shops for the same goods, but do note the minimum order. We've included this company especially for businesses, but it's always here if and when you need several hundred yards of cheesecloth or want to redo the house in handwoven cotton.

SEE ALSO:

Babouris Handicrafts . . . native Greek yarns . . . CRAFTS
Caviarteria Inc. . . . imported foods . . . FOOD
Nurhan Cevahir . . . hand-carved Turkish meerschaum pipes . . . CIGARS
Deepak's Rokjemperl Products . . . Indian carvings, brassware, paintings . . . JEWELRY
D'Elia's Designs . . . hand-finished greeting cards . . . BOOKS
George and Son's Co. . . . Korean-design cabinets . . . HOME (furnishings)
Gold N'Stones . . . native Alaskan jewelry . . . JEWELRY
Handart Embroideries . . . wide variety handcrafted Oriental goods . . . CLOTHING
Hong Kong Lapidaries, Inc. . . . carved stone, shell jewelry, cloisonné . . . JEWELRY
House of Onyx . . . cloisonné, soapstone, ivory, onyx objets d'art . . . JEWELRY
Irish Cottage Industries, Ltd. . . . hand-knitted Aran sweaters, accessories . . . CLOTHING
Kennedy of Ardara . . . hand-knitted Aran sweaters, accessories . . . CLOTHING
Kountry Bear Company . . . the "original Kountry Bear" stuffed toy . . . TOYS
Stavros Kouyoumoutzakis . . . native Greek yarns . . . CRAFTS
Leather School . . . handmade Venetian-style leather goods . . . LEATHER
D. MacGillivray & Coy. . . . Scottish woven goods, Highland dress accessories . . . CRAFTS
The Mexican Kitchen . . . Mexican foods, cooking utensils . . . FOOD
Hayim Pinhas . . . hand-carved Turkish meerschaum pipes . . . CIGAR
Prince Fashions Ltd. . . . Oriental handcrafts . . . CLOTHING
Rama Jewelry Ltd., Part. . . . traditional Thai rings . . . JEWELRY

Rammagerdin . . . Icelandic Lopi clothing . . . CRAFTS

W.S. Robertson (Outfitters) Ltd. . . . fine Scottish knitwear . . . CLOTHING

Romanes & Paterson Ltd. . . . fine Scottish knitwear, woolens . . . CLOTHING

Samarth Gem Stones . . . carved agate objets d'art . . . JEWELRY

Shannon Mail Order . . . Irish crystal, linens, jewelry . . . HOME (table settings)

Shibui Wallcoverings . . . handcrafted oriental wallcoverings . . . HOME (decor)

Sultan's Delight Inc. . . . Middle Eastern foods and gifts . . . FOOD

Thai Silks . . . Chinese, Indian, Italian silk yardage . . . CRAFTS

HEALTH AND BEAUTY

Cosmetics, perfumes, and toiletries;
vitamins and dietary supplements;
wigs and hairpieces.

You can save up to 90% on your cosmetic and beauty needs and still get the name brands featured in beauty emporiums and department stores. You can also save on imported luxury fragrances by importing them yourself, directly from France. "Copycat" scents are manufactured by three firms listed here—shop them all to see whose version comes closest to the real thing, and save up to 90% on the cost of the original.

Beauty comes from within, which is the reason you'll find firms selling vitamins and dietary supplements listed here. Countless books and magazines focus on what, if anything, you should take to augment your diet. We can't fully recommend any of these: Too many are fonts of unscientific advice and undocumented claims; many tend to pander to the universal fears of aging and cancer, and tout the unrealistic belief that one product or exercise can guarantee good health and sex appeal in 24 hours to 30 days. *Jane Brody's Guide to Personal Health* is a good general reference on topics of wide interest; *The Harvard Medical School Health Letter, Medical Abstracts Newsletter, American Health,* and *Prevention* are all accessible and informative. But don't rely on one alone—periodical X may give rave reviews to a newly synthesized enzyme while periodical Y explains why it won't cure your ulcer and can interfere with iron absorption. After reading *both* you'll be in a much better position to judge whether to add it to your regimen. Don't miss the government pamphlets available through local departments of health, and the commonsense health guides published by Consumers Union. Last but not least, do not attempt self-cures if you have serious symptoms or a chronic medical problem. Consult a physician if such conditions exist or develop.

For more firms selling related products, see the listings in "Medical and Scientific."

BAZAAR'S BEAUTY COLLECTION

P.O. Box 1725
Sandusky, OH 44870

Information: see text
Discount: up to 80%
Goods: name brand
Minimum Order: $10 on credit cards
Shipping, Handling: $2 per order; PP
Sales Tax: OH deliveries (see text)
Accepts: check, MO, MC, V, AE
$$$

Some of the best buys on top scents and expensive skin-treatment and hair-care products are found not in catalogs but in *magazines.* The September and October issues of *Harper's Bazaar* and *Town & Country* usually feature collections of such goods, including full and sample sizes at savings of up to 80%. In the past, we've seen scents from Galanos, Anne Klein, Christian Dior, Giorgio, Lagerfeld, Guy Laroche, Molinard, Armani, Jean-Louis Scherrer, Caron, Balmain, and other well-known houses and designers, as well as treatments from Charles of the Ritz, Sebastian, Clientele, Georgette Klinger, Leslie Blanchard, Milopa, Nexxus, etc. The products are listed in the magazines, and ordering information and a bound-in-form are included.

We've ordered repeatedly from Bazaar's collection, which has the largest number of products (usually 50 or more), with good results. Orders from both collections are handled by a fulfillment house in Ohio, but you *can't order directly from that source.* Wait for the issue of either magazine featuring the promotion and order from that. (We've included the address for those who place an order, misplace the magazine, and then have questions and don't know where to write.) Please note that you're asked to allow up to eight weeks for delivery; our orders have usually taken six to seven weeks to arrive. Although sales tax would normally be charged on goods sent to Ohio addresses, it's not requested in the ordering information.

BEAUTIFUL BEGINNINGS

**Spencer Building
Atlantic City, NJ 08411
(800) 222–0252: NJ orders
(800) 222–0053: orders
except NJ**

Catalog: free; pub. fall, winter, spring
Discount: 50% to 85%
Goods: name brand
Minimum Order: $2; $10 on credit cards
Shipping, Handling: $1.25 to $3.15; PP
Insurance: 45¢ per order
Sales Tax: on deliveries to 42 states
Accepts: check, MO, MC, V, AE
$$$$

The 80-page Beautiful Beginnings color catalog is packed with all kinds of name-brand cosmetics, skin treatments, bath products, perfumes, jewelry, and accessories. Brands represented in the current catalog include Coty, Lanvin, Revlon, Max Factor, Frances Denney, Prince Matchabelli, Helena Rubinstein, Diane Von Furstenberg, Yves St. Laurent, Germaine Monteil, Jōvan, Village, Elizabeth Arden, Hermès, Charles of the Ritz, Stagelight, Dana, Scandia, Stendhal, Bonne Bell, and Orlane, among others. You'll also find a variety of grooming aids, vanity organizers, costume jewelry, and bath products for children. The discounts run up to 85%; bonuses and special offers for phone customers are routine.

Beautiful Beginnings is a division of Spencer Gifts, which has been in business since 1947. It backs all sales with an unconditional guarantee of satisfaction or your money back (refund or credit).

BEAUTIFUL VISIONS, INC.
_____

**810 Hicksville Rd., C.S.
4001
Hicksville, NY 11802–9877**
_____

Catalog: free; pub. bimonthly
Discount: 40% to 85%
Goods: name brand
Minimum Order: none
Shipping, Handling, Insurance: $1 to $2.55; UPS
Sales Tax: NY deliveries
Accepts: check, MO, certified check, MC, V
$$$

Imagine hundreds of name-brand beauty products–at up to 85% off list prices! The Beautiful Visions catalog offers almost 50 pages of beauty essentials from top manufacturers: L'Oreal, Aziza, Barielle, Revlon, Almay, Elizabeth Arden, Max Factor, Vidal Sassoon, Jōvan, and other firms. The products are all full-sized and available in current "fashion" colors, not just last year's shades. Prices in the current catalog begin at 25¢ for eyebrow/eyeliner pencils. There's something here for part of every beauty regimen, from Helena Rubinstein's shampoo to Jovan's buffer and lotion for feet. Beautiful Visions also offers "Jackpot Specials," surprise packages ranging from $3.95 for a $15-plus value to $19.95 for an assortment worth $150. The catalog helps you beat not only the high cost of cosmetics but also the hit-or-miss quality of beauty-club packages.

BEAUTY BUY BOOK
_____

**65 E. Southwater
Chicago, IL 60601
(312) 977–3740**
_____

Catalog: free; pub. Jan., Apr. July, Sept.
Discount: 30% to 90%
Goods: name brand
Minimum Order: none
Shipping, Handling, Insurance: $1.75 to $3.35;
    UPS
Sales Tax: IL deliveries
Accepts: check, MO, MC, V, AE
$$$$

Before paying top dollar for cosmetics, skin-care products, perfumes, costume jewelry, and accessories, see the 40-page, full-color Beauty Buy Book. It can save you up to 90% on products by Prince Matchabelli, Max Factor, Germaine Monteil, Jōvan, Yves St. Laurent, Bonne Bell, Lancaster, Halston, Diane Von Furstenberg, Orlane, Yardley, Countess Isserlyn, Charles of the Ritz, Aziza, Rachel Perry, Elizabeth Arden, and other manufacturers.

Unlike many beauty-bargain firms, this one sells current goods in fashionable shades, as well as a wealth of practical items: cosmetic sponges, powder puffs, cosmetic cases and vanity organizers, totes, atomizers, and makeup brushes, at varying savings. The catalog offers surprise packages of cosmetics at 75% below regular retail prices. Those "gifts" and "purchase-with-purchase" bonuses used as promotions at beauty counters often show up here, but you don't have to buy anything at full retail price to get them.

Beauty Buy Book's parent company, GRI Corp., has been in business for almost 30 years and guarantees satisfaction or your money back.

BEAUTY BY SPECTOR, INC.

Dept. WBMC–85
McKeesport, PA
15134–0502
(412) 673–3259

Catalog: free; pub. 4 times yearly
Discount: up to 50%
Goods: house brand
Minimum Order: none
Shipping, Insurance: $3 per order; UPS, PP
Sales Tax: PA deliveries
Accepts: check, MO, certified check, MC, V
$$

The use of wigs and hairpieces dates back to ancient Egypt and has seen periods of great popularity, especially during the eighteenth century. But the fantastic creations worn by the court of Louis XV—crimped, powdered, scented, and sometimes stiffened with plaster of Paris—are a far cry from today's wigs.

Beauty by Spector offers dozens of stylish wigs and hairpieces at savings of about 50% over salon prices. The catalog shows wiglets, cascades, and falls ideal for dressy or special occasions. At $15, some cost less than one styling at a beauty salon. The full wigs for women range from neat, softly curled heads to "Showgirl," two feet of wavy glamour. The catalog we received offered two hairpieces for men: the popular "Royal Gold" with a thermal-conductive base for comfort and natural growth patterns ($99.95); and "Macho," a wavy, no-part mesh-based piece ($125).

Almost half the styles are made with 100% human hair; the others of frizz-free modacrylic fiber. Everything shown is available in a choice of 54 colors. If you provide a hair sample, the piece or wig you order will be matched to its closest shade. Spector is preparing a color catalog that should be available in 1985. It will show designer styles for women, "unisex" styles, and "celebrity toupees."

The firm has been doing business by mail for 20 years and will gladly recommend products to best suit your individual needs. We're told that premiums are sometimes offered to new customers, and a special effort will be made to give WBMC readers attractive offers. So remember to identify yourself as such when you send for the catalog.

CATHERINE, S.A.

6, Rue de Castiglione
75001, Paris
France
Phone # 260–81–49

Brochure: free; pub. in the spring
Discount: 40% to 60%
Goods: name brand
Minimum Order: none
Shipping, Insurance: $7 per 2 pounds, surface;
  $11, airmail
Duty: extra
Accepts: check, IMO, V, AE
$$$$ (see text)

Catherine, like the other Parisian boutiques accepting orders from overseas, sells a huge array of perfumes, toilet water, and skin-care products, as well as gifts. The firms represented here include Azzaro, Balenciaga, Balmain, Jean-Charles Brosseau, Capucci, Caron, Cartier, Carven, Chanel, Couturier, Desprez, Dior, Prince D'Orléans, Fath, Givenchy, Grès, Gucci, Halston, Hermès, Jacomo, Jourdan, Lagerfeld, Lancôme, Lanvin, Laroche, Leonard, Missoni, Molinard, Morabito, Patou, Piguet, Paco Rabanne, Oscar de la Renta, Révillon, Nina Ricci, Rochas, Sonia Rykiel, Yves St. Laurent, Jean-Louis Scherrer, Schiaparelli, Ungaro, Valentino, Van Cleef & Arpels, and Worth.

Catherine also carries 32 scents for men in the form of toilet water. The selection of beauty products and skin treatments includes full lines from Orlane, Stendhal, Dior, Lancôme, Chanel, Yves St. Laurent, and Paco Rabanne (for men), as well as bath oils in a few select fragrances. Rigaud candles, Per Spook and Yves St. Laurent silk ties and scarves, and handmade French umbrellas complete the catalog.

You can save up to 60% on the prices of the same items bought in the U.S., and since postage charges are little more than you might spend on sales tax, the only surcharge you incur is duty (which Catherine says is charged rather erratically).

Catherine is an actual person, the head of this family firm. She gives you the benefit of her 26 years of experience in personal service, good advice, and such amenities as free gift wrapping and card enclosures.

CANADIAN READERS, PLEASE NOTE: parcels sent to Canada are limited to *one pound* shipping weight.

J.W. CHUNN PERFUMES

43, Rue Richer
75009, Paris
France
Phone # (1) 824–42–06

Price List: free; pub. yearly in the summer
Discount: 30% to 60%
Goods: name brand
Minimum Order: none
Shipping, Insurance: extra; minimum $4, surface; $5.50, airmail
Duty: extra
Accepts: check, certified check, IMO
$$$ (see text)

J.W. Chunn was founded in 1925 and is the oldest of the French perfume shops listed here. Like the other firms, Chunn told us you could save 30% to 40% on the scents and beauty products it sells. We did our comparisons, and found that, ounce for ounce, you can save over 50% on most of the perfumes. Some, such as Mystère and Infini, are 60% less than the same scents sold in the U.S.

The designers and fragrance houses represented include Azzaro, Balenciaga, Balmain, Jean-Charles Brosseau, Capucci, Caron, Carven, Courrèges, Couturier, Desprez, Dior, Fath, Givenchy, Grès, Halston, Hermès, Jourdan, Lagerfeld, Lancôme, Lanvin, Ted Lapidus, Laroche, Le Galion, Missoni, Molinard, Molyneux, Orlane, Patou, Piguet, Paco Rabanne, Révillon, Nina Ricci, Rochas, Yves St. Laurent, Van Cleef & Arpels, Weil, and Worth. Products for men are not listed but may be available; write for information. Rigaud candles are sold here at less than half the U.S. prices, and extensive lines of skin-care products by Lancôme and Orlane are available.

Prices are based on the rate of exchange at the time the brochure was printed and are guaranteed to fluctuate. Chunn will credit your account (and presumably send you a reimbursement check if you prefer) if the rate runs in the favor of the dollar when your order is processed. If the franc has improved, you'll be billed for the difference. (Please remember that all of the French perfume shops retain the right to calculate prices on the basis of the dollar-to-franc rate in force when your order is received.)

CANADIAN READERS, PLEASE NOTE: Postage charges on goods shipped to Canada are higher than the rates stated in the catalog, and the size of shipments may be limited. Before ordering, write and ask for mailing costs on the goods you want.

ESSENTIAL PRODUCTS CO., INC.

**90 Water St.
New York, NY 10005–3501
(212) 344–4288**

Price List and 5 Perfumed Cards: free with SASE
Discount: up to 90% (see text)
Goods: house brand
Minimum Order: $18
Shipping, Handling, Insurance: $2 for the first
  bottle; 50¢ each additional; $2 extra for airmail;
  UPS, PP
Sales Tax: NY deliveries
Accepts: check, MO, certified check, IMO
$$$$ 🍁   (see text)

Essential's owner says it best himself: "We offer our versions of the world's most treasured and expensive ladies' perfumes and men's colognes, selling them at a small fraction of the original prices."

Essential doesn't sell the actual name-brand perfumes, but very good reproductions, which are marketed under the brand name "Naudet." "Naudet 3" is similar to Bal à Versailles; "Naudet 39" is like Patou's "1,000", and "Naudet 71" is quite like Eau Sauvage. In all, there are 43 different copies of costly perfumes like L'Air du Temps, Arpege, Opium, and Joy; 14 colognes for men are listed, from Aramis to Zizanie. A 1 oz bottle of ladies' perfume is $18 ($10.50 the half); 4 ounces of any men's cologne cost $9.

The general consensus among professionals in the fragrance field is that "copycat" scents are usually successful in capturing the top notes, or initial impression of just-applied perfume, but the base notes, or lingering medley, may differ from or be weaker than the original. Since the evaluation and appreciation of any scent is a subjective matter, you will have to try them yourself to see if the copies are right for you.

Essential Products was established in 1895 and has been annoying prestigious perfume firms and delighting customers for quite a while. The essence of its success is the product. Essential is so sure you'll like its perfume, it offers a guarantee of satisfaction or your money back and accepts returns within 30 days. Once you become a customer, you'll receive the firm's regular mailings in March and October.

CANADIAN READERS, PLEASE NOTE: shipping and handling charges are doubled for shipments outside the U.S.

HARVEST OF VALUES

Hillestad Corp.
1545 Berger Dr., Dept. WC
San Jose, CA 95112
(408) 298–0998

Catalog: free; pub. in Jan. and July
Discount: 20% to 40%
WBMC Reader Discount: 10% (see text)
Goods: house brand
Minimum Order: none
Shipping, Insurance: included; UPS, PP
Handling: $1 on orders under $15
Sales Tax: CA deliveries
Accepts: check, MO, certified check, MC, V
$$$$

When it comes to buying vitamins and minerals, we're difficult customers. We're put off by "miracle" enzymes, firms that tout megadoses, and catalogs that don't disclose ingredients.

But not Harvest of Values. The easy-to-read catalog reprints the label information—the number of units of each vitamin or mineral, the percentage of the U.S. RDA they represent, and the sources from which the ingredients are extracted. The multi-vitamin-and-mineral supplements are formulated in low levels, with the recommendation that you take a specific number per day. This permits you to tailor the dosage to your own needs. (Taking small amounts of supplements several times a day ensures more constant levels in the body and a better chance that fat-soluble vitamins will be absorbed properly.) Harvest of Values sells a multi for adults and a chewable version for children; vitamins E, A, C, and B-complex; a stress formula, chelated iron, bone meal, lecithin, and alfalfa. If you like to take several supplements, take the hassle out of rounding up your daily dose with "Pick-A-Pill." This cylinder has seven smoke-colored plastic compartments, sits on shelf or table, and dispenses your selection gumball-style. It's $11.49.

Some people swear by topical applications of vitamin E to fade scars; Harvest sells an E cream with aloe vera ($2.95 for two ounces), and there's a similar formula in hand and body lotion. The catalog also shows a pH-balanced cream rinse, conditioning shampoos, a liquid "soapless" soap, and an all-purpose, biodegradable, phosphate-free cleanser for dishes, hand-washables, and general cleaning. Everything is guaranteed against defects in manufacturing. Returns are accepted on unused products within 30 days.

The prices of the supplements and toiletries are 25% to 40% below those of comparable products, but you can save more: Harvest of Values is giving WBMC readers a 10% discount on their orders. Deduct the 10% from the cost of the goods only, *before* you add handling and sales tax, if applicable. You must identify yourself as a WBMC reader to qualify for the special discount.

PARFUMERIE GRILLOT

10, Rue Cambon
75001, Paris
France
Phone # 260–76–35

Price List: free; pub. yearly
Discount: up to 60%
Goods: name brand
Minimum Order: none
Shipping, Insurance: extra
Duty: extra
Accepts: check or IMO
$$$$ (see text)

Grillot's list of perfumes and toilet waters includes fragrances by Balenciaga, Balmain, Caron, Carven, Courrèges, Desprez, Dior, Givenchy, Grès, Lagerfeld, Laroche, Molyneux, Patou, Piguet, Paco Rabanne, Nina Ricci, and Worth. "Infini," $100 an ounce in the U.S., is $40.50 at Grillot; "Chloé," usually $120 an ounce, costs $54.55 here; Balmain's "Ivoire," bought by many at $150 an ounce, can be found here for only $76.30. Grillot also sells skin-treatment products by Dior, bath oils by Weil and Desprez, and Rigaud candles. There were no men's fragrances listed in the brochure we received, but they may be available—inquire for information. Shipping charges are assessed per package and are nominal. Grillot has been selling by mail since 1952 and is a highly reputable firm.

CANADIAN READERS, PLEASE NOTE: you must pay in *U.S. dollars* instead of converting the listed prices to your dollar equivalents and paying in Canadian funds.

PURITAN'S PRIDE, INC.

105 Orville Dr.
Bohemia, NY 11716
(800) 832–1111: NY orders
(800) 645–1030: orders
except NY

Catalog: free
Discount: up to 75%
Goods: house brand
Minimum Order: $12 on credit cards
Shipping, Handling, Insurance: included; UPS, PP
Sales Tax: NY deliveries
Accepts: check, MO, MC, V
$$$ (see text)

You'll find hundreds of nutritional supplements in the 72-page Puritan's Pride catalog, at prices up to 75% less than similar formulations sold by other firms. Vitamins, minerals, amino acids, natural diet aids, glandular extracts, and related miscellany—brewer's yeast, alfalfa tablets, herbal tea, ginseng, bee pollen—are offered in a choice of potencies and formulations. Both synthetic and naturally derived supplements are sold, and most of them are free of starch and sugars. Special formulations for geriatric needs, stressful living, pets, children, men, women, and hair are listed—most with complete disclosures of the content of each tablet or capsule and its RDA proportion.

A good selection of beauty products is offered, including soaps, creams, lotions, shampoos, conditioners, sun screens, toothpaste, analgesic balms, and lipstick. Most are enriched with jojoba, aloe vera, vitamin E, fruit extracts, etc. Well-priced thermometers, heating pads, electric foot massagers, and sphygmomanometers are also shown. Puritan's Pride has been in business for over 23 years and guarantees complete satisfaction on all your purchases. Returns are accepted for refund or credit.

CANADIAN READERS, PLEASE NOTE: A $3 surcharge for shipping and handling is imposed on orders sent to Canada, and only U.S. funds are accepted.

J. RICHELLE PARFUMS LTD.

**603 Bedford Ave.
Brooklyn, NY 11211
(718) 387–7961**

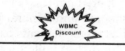

Brochure: free
Discount: up to 90% (see text)
WBMC Reader Bonus: 2 free bottles perfume with each 6 ordered (see text)
Goods: house brand
Minimum Order: none
Shipping, Handling, Insurance: $2 for the first item; 50¢ each additional; UPS, PP
Sales Tax: NY deliveries
Accepts: check, MO, certified check
$$$

Established in 1982, J. Richelle is one of the most recent entries in the flourishing "copycat" fragrance industry. Like the other firms marketing interpretations of famous scents, its products sell for a fraction of the originals. They're not *identical,* but the copies of Chanel No. 5 and Shalimar that we tested were *very* close. If you like the Richelle version as much as the genuine article, you'll save up to 90% by buying the former.

Copies of Bal à Versailles, Chanel No. 5, Chloé, Halston, Joy, L'Air du Temps, Opium, Oscar de la Renta, Shalimar, Youth Dew, Anais Anais, Armani, First, and Ivoire are available for women at this writing; "interpretations" of Aramis, Eau Sauvage, Paco Rabanne, and Polo for men. Richelle charges $9.50 for a half-ounce bottle of women's perfume and the same price for two ounces of men's eau de toilette. WBMC readers who order six bottles of perfume can choose two additional bottles of perfume (the bonus does not apply to the toilet water). PLEASE NOTE: this offer expires Oct. 31, 1986

If you'd like to sample the scents before investing in the half-ounce bottles, you can order a set of .75ml vials. There are four collections, ranging from seven perfumes to a sample of every Richelle fragrance at $9.99. Ask your friends to try the Richelle versions of their favorites—if they like them, your gift problems are solved!

STAR PHARMACEUTICAL, INC.

11 Basin St., Dept. WBMC
Plainview, NY 11803
(516) 938–9220; 822–4621:
customer service
(800) 645–7171: KY orders
(800) 262–7827: orders
except KY, NY

Catalog: free; pub. Jan., Apr., June, Sept.
Discount: up to 60%
WBMC Reader Discount: 10% on first orders of
    $25 or more
Goods: house brand, name brand
Minimum Order: $15 on credit cards
Shipping, Insurance: included: UPS, PP
Handling: $2 on orders under $10
Sales Tax: NY deliveries
Accepts: check, MO, MC, V
$$$

WBMC Discount

Star has 30 years of experience in the manufacture of vitamins, minerals, and supplements. Most of the 48-page catalog is devoted to these; after poring over the cornucopia, we can't imagine anyone faulting Star on its inventory. It sells standard and mega-strength multi-vitamins and minerals, and formulations for athletes, women, children, your hair, families, senior citizens, dogs, and cats. You'll find just about every vitamin and mineral in every useful form, strength, and combination, as well as trace elements and miscellany—kelp, bran, brewer's yeast, alfalfa, RNA/DNA, bee pollen, and amino acids, to list a few. Star sells supplements comparable to Theragran-Z, Micebrin-T, Chocks, Ferro Sequels, Stresstabs, and other name-brand products at prices up to 60% less. The firm also offers the national brands themselves—at a discount. Most of Star's products are sugar and starch free, all are fresh, and the supplements are packed in tamper-resistant containers.

The second half of the catalog is really an armchair drugstore without the pharmacy. There's a wide assortment of "natural" toiletries enriched with vitamin E, aloe vera, jojoba, henna, collagen, and elastin. Also listed are diet aids, pet grooming products, and Celestial Seasonings teas. The "Star Medicine Chest" carries hundreds of name-brand products and Star formulations: cold, cough, and allergy remedies, laxatives, deodorants, shaving products, contact-lens solutions, dentifrices, contraceptives, hair-care and body products, soaps, acne medications, bandages, sleeping pills, asthma relievers, motion-sickness pills, baby products, foot preparations, rubs and liniments, suntan lotions, and much more. Clinistix and glucose tablets for use by diabetics, as well as heating pads, oral thermometers, and sphygmomanometers complete the section.

Star is offering a discount of 10% to readers of this book who order $25 or more. Identify yourself as a WBMC reader when you order and deduct the 10% *before* adding sales tax, if applicable. (Shipping is included.) This offer applies to first orders only.

Prices are best on the Star brand, but if your local drugstore doesn't stock a name brand product you need, you may find it easier to order it from Star than go to the next town for it—you'll save money on gas, at any rate. Star guarantees your satisfaction and accepts returns within 30 days.

SUNBURST BIORGANICS

**838 Merrick Rd., Dept. W-3
Baldwin, NY 11510
(516) 623–8478: inquiries
and NY orders
(800) 645–8448: orders
except NY**

Catalog: free; pub. every 6 to 8 weeks
Discount: 25% to 70%
Goods: house brand
Minimum Order: $15 on credit cards
Shipping, Insurance: included; UPS, PP
Handling: $1 on orders under $10
Sales Tax: NY deliveries
Accepts: check, MO, certified check, MC, V
$$$ (see text)

Sunburst, established in 1972, carries a complete line of vitamins, minerals, beauty aids, pet vitamins, and digestive aids under the Sunburst label. The vitamins and supplements are formula equivalents of standard name brands, and Sunburst's exclusive formulations are also featured. The products contain no sugar, starch, salt, or preservatives. The prices are 25% to 70% below those charged for comparable products. Sunburst will send customers free gifts with every purchase and often includes a coupon good for a $1 discount on orders of $25 or more in the catalog.

CANADIAN READERS, PLEASE NOTE: a surcharge of 10% on your total order or $5, which ever is greater, is made to cover special handling costs.

MICHEL SWISS

**16, Rue de la Paix
75002, Paris
France
Phone # (1) 261–61–11**

Catalog: free; pub. yearly in the fall
Discount: to 60%
Goods: name brand
Minimum Order: none
Shipping, Insurance: extra; $4 minimum, surface;
    $6 minimum, airmail
Duty: extra
Accepts: check or IMO
$$$$

Not only are perfumes usually half as expensive when bought directly from France, but—since most French firms use finer cutting oil and alcohol, and blend the perfume in higher concentrations—the quality of the French product is usually higher than that of its domestic counterpart.

Michel Swiss, which has been doing business by mail for over 35 years, offers scores of scents at savings of up to 60%. Most of the classics can be found here, as well as perfumes so new they're not yet marketed in the U.S. Our most recent catalog listed fragrances from Azzaro, Balenciaga, Balmain, Cardin, Caron, Cartier, Carven, Jean Couturier, Courrèges, Jean D'Albret, De Rauch, Desprez, Dior, Gucci, Hermès, Jourdan, Lancôme, Lanvin, Laroche, Le Galion, Leonard, Molinard, Molyneux, Morabito, Patou, Piguet, Paco Rabanne, Révillon, Nina Ricci, Rochas, Sonia Rykiel, Jean-Louis Scherrer, Torrente, Valentino, Versace, Weil, and Worth. The fragrances are available as perfume, toilet water, soap, bath oil, talc, body cream, and even bubble bath. Michel Swiss also sells skin-care products by Orlane and Lancôme at excellent prices.

Men's fragrances are well represented, from Azzaro to Worth for Men. Toilet water and after-shave by Dana, Alain Delon, and Roger & Gallet are offered, as well as products by many of the perfume manufacturers listed previously. The catalog also mentions that other luxuries—crystal Sèvres animals, Limoges and Marcel Franck purse accessories, French umbrellas, scarves by Lanvin, and silk ties—are available. Inquiries are invited on these goods.

TULI-LATUS PERFUMES, LTD.

146–36 13th Ave.
P.O. Box 422
Whitestone, NY 11357–0422
(718) 746–9337

Brochure with Perfume Card: free; pub. Feb., Apr., July, Oct.
Discount: up to 86% (see text)
WBMC Reader Discount: $5 on perfumes (see text)
Goods: house brand
Minimum Order: $15 on credit cards
Shipping, Handling, Insurance: $1 per item; $5 maximum; UPS, PP
Sales Tax: NY deliveries
Accepts: check, MO, MC, V, AE
$$$

Would you pay $250 for something if you could get a similar product for $40? Tuli-Latus has built 14 years of business on the obvious answer to that question. This firm makes "exquisite renditions" of some of the world's finest, most expensive perfumes.

The catalog we received listed 33 women's scents, including copies of Joy, Shalimar, L'Air du Temps, Chloé, Opium, Lauren, Ivoire, and Patou's "1,000." The self-assured male may choose from "New Mown Hay," or the house versions of Russian Leather, Gucci For Men, and Guerlain's Le Mouchoir de Monsieur. (He should be sure of himself and the fragrance he chooses because the men's scents, like the women's, are sold as perfumes. These make stronger and more lasting olfactory impressions than colognes.)

Tuli-Latus offers its perfumes in a choice of bottles, including French glass and lead crystal with glass stoppers. Refillable purse atomizers with funnel and pouch are shown for $8. This firm also produces Biocare facial cream, lotion cleanser, and body lotion. The creams contain collagen and vitamin E; the brochure says the products are identical to others selling abroad for four times as much.

As if this weren't attractive enough, Tuli-Latus is adding the inducement of a WBMC Reader Discount of $5, which applies to orders of perfume only (excluding shipping, handling, and applicable sales tax). Remember to identify yourself as a WBMC reader to qualify for this discount.

VALRAY INTERNATIONAL, INC.

739 N.E. 40th Ct.
Ft. Lauderdale, FL
33334–3037
(305) 563–8411

Brochure: free
Discount: 20% to 70%
Goods: house brand
Minimum Order: none
Shipping, Insurance: $2 per order; UPS, PP
Sales Tax: FL deliveries
Accepts: check, MO, MC, V
$$ (see text)

Valray markets "Rejuvenation" skin treatments and cosmetics under its house label, Maximilian. The brochure lists products developed for mature skin; some are fortified with collagen and jojoba oil. They cost from $8 to $13 per 4 oz container. Those who avoid soap might like the cleansing lotion that's part of that line; it's $6 for four ounces.

If your skin is on the oily side, you may find the "Scrub Plus" helpful as part of a program to control oil and breakouts. The facial mask can be used once a week for toning and deep cleaning. Follow cleansing procedures with "Herbal Skin Freshener" to remove any lingering traces of makeup or cleanser. Valray's eye and throat cream, wrinkle-smoother, and bleaching cream can help with specific beauty problems.

In addition, Valray offers a selection of makeup—foundation, powder, blush, lipstick, cover stick, mascara, and eyebrow pencil, all at reasonable prices. Valray has been in business since 1974 and guarantees your complete satisfaction. Full refunds are made on goods returned within 30 days.

CANADIAN READERS, PLEASE NOTE: payment for orders sent to Canada must be made in U.S. funds only.

VITAMIN SPECIALTIES CO.

8200 Ogontz Ave.
P.O. Box 401
Wyncote, PA 19095
(215) 885–3800: inquiries
and Philadelphia orders
(800) 822–3972: PA orders
except Philadelphia
(800) 523–3658: US orders
including AK, HI, PR, VI;
except PA

Catalog: free; pub. twice yearly
Discount: 40% to 60%
Goods: house brand
Minimum Order: $15 on prepaid orders; $15 on
   credit cards; $25 on orders to Canada
Shipping, Insurance: included (see text); UPS, PP
Handling: $1 on orders under $15
Sales Tax: PA deliveries
Accepts: check, MO, MC, V
$$$ (see text)

Vitamin Specialties sells its own brand of vitamins, minerals, dietary supplements, and nonprescription drugs for 40% to 60% less than the comparable name-brand products.

You'll find megas, multis, singles, and "natural" vitamin and mineral formulations in tabs, caps, syrups, sublingual tablets, and powder. There are special formulations for the needs of adolescents, senior citizens, pregnant women, children, people under stress, and vegetarians. Dietary supplements—amino acids, RNA/DNA, natural whole glandular products, enzymes, etc.—are offered as well. If you'd like to save money on over-the-counter cold remedies, laxatives, antibacterial ointments, acne medications, sleep inducers, and antacids, you'll find a good selection in the 82-page catalog. We found you could save considerably by buying the Vitamin Specialties product instead of the "comparable" name brand. (Ten Contac capsules cost $2.59 in a local drug store, 50 Acton caps cost $2.15 at Vitamin Specialties.) But please note: The formulas are listed as "comparable," and differences may be significant to some users. For example, the name-brand Contac capsule contains 75mg phenylpropanolamine hydrochloride (PPL HCL) and 8mg chlorpheniramine maleate. One Acton cap has 50mg PPL HCL, 4mg chlorpheniramine maleate, and .2mg belladonna alkaloids. Even the vitamin/mineral formulaic equivalents may differ. Centrex, which "contains the exact potencies of all ingredients present in Centrum," doesn't quite: Centrum has 25mcg selenium and 7.7mg potassium, while Centrex has 15mg and 7.5mg, respectively. These minor discrepancies will be inconsequential to most people, and those who care can always compare ingredient disclosures on the name brand product to the information in the VS catalog before ordering.

The catalog doesn't stop here: You'll find books on nutrition and health, pet vitamins, herbal teas, diet aids, shampoos, soaps, skin lotions and oils, and other toiletries, all at discount prices.

This firm hasn't been in business since 1948 without knowing the ropes vis-à-vis mail order. So while its refund policy (returns accepted within 30 days on goods with unbroken seals) appeared odd at first, we learned that it reflected proper adherence to new regulations concerning such products. VS pays postage on orders (via UPS or Parcel Post) sent within the continental U.S., and (via PP) to Alaska, Hawaii, Puerto Rico, and the Virgin Islands.

CANADIAN READERS, PLEASE NOTE: The minimum order to Canadian addresses is $25, and a 20% surcharge is imposed on your order if you pay in Canadian funds.

WESTERN NATURAL PRODUCTS

511 Mission St.
P.O. Box 284-W3
South Pasadena, CA 91030
(818) 441-3447

Catalog: free; pub. yearly in the winter
Discount: 30% to 50%
WBMC Reader Discount: $2 off first order
Goods: house brand
Minimum Order: none
Shipping, Insurance: included on orders over $12; UPS, PP
Sales Tax: CA deliveries
Accepts: check, MO, MC, V
$$$

This 14-year-old firm supplies health supplements that are formulaic equivalents of name-brand products but sell for 30% to 50% less. They are also "natural," meaning that natural sources are used for the ingredients. Parents take note: the chewable vitamins are sweetened with honey or fructose, not sucrose or saccharin.

A comparison with Theragran showed that Western's "Plan 1" multi-vitamin had twice as much vitamin E and B-6 as Theragran, more B-12, and included folic acid, which Theragran lacked. Plan 1 is $4.25 for 100 capsules, compared to pharmacy prices of $11 and more for Theragran 100s. In addition to vitamins, minerals, enzymes, and other dietary supplements, Western sells Nature's Gate products for skin and hair; such items as kelp, ginseng, and pet vitamins are also available.

As an incentive to new customers, Western is offering WBMC readers a discount of $2 off their first orders. Identify yourself as a reader when ordering and deduct the $2 from the cost of the *goods* only. Western's no-questions-asked, money-back guarantee should convince those hesitant about abandoning Myadec, Z-Bec, Stress Tabs, and One-A-Day that they have nothing to lose and savings to gain.

SEE ALSO:

Dairy Association Co., Inc. . . . Bag Balm liniment . . . ANIMAL
Erewhon Trading Co. . . . natural cosmetics and toiletries . . . FOOD
The Finals . . . small selection hair- and body-care products, vitamins . . .
   CLOTHING
Good 'N' Lucky Promotions . . . discount cosmetics . . . JEWELRY
D. MacGillivray & Coy. . . . Hebridean perfumes . . . CRAFTS
Shannon Mail Order . . . French perfumes . . . HOME (table settings)
Tastefully Yours . . . calorie-controlled meals, diet drinks . . . FOOD
Whole Earth Access . . . massagers, Fuchs brushes . . . GENERAL

HOME

Decor

Floorcoverings, wall and
window treatments, lighting,
upholstery materials, tools, and
services.

**AMERICAN DISCOUNT
WALLCOVERINGS**

1411 Fifth Ave.
Pittsburgh, PA 15219
(412) 471–6941: inquiries
and PA orders
(800) 245–1768: orders
except PA

Information: price quote by phone or letter with
 SASE
Discount: 10% to 40%
WBMC Reader Discount: 30% to 50% on selected
 grass cloths and "string" wallpapers
Goods: name brand, imported
Minimum Order: none
Shipping, Insurance: extra; UPS
Sales Tax: PA deliveries
Accepts: check, MO, MC, V
$$

American Discount, established in 1905, offers savings of up to 40% on
wall coverings, window treatments, and decorator fabrics by a number of
well-known firms. Custom window treatments are discounted 25% to 40%
and include Levolor miniblinds, woven woods, soft-light shades, and mini-

blinds by Del Mar, Joanna, and Kirsch. Products by Verosol, Nanik, Flex-alum, and Bali are also available.

Wall coverings are discounted 15% to 20%; fabrics are discounted 10% to 20%. The impressive roster of manufacturers and lines includes Advent, Artex, Birge, Comark, Decorator's Walk, Eisenhart, Greeff, Imperial, Judscott, Laura Ashley, Marimekko, Quadrille, Sanitas, Scalamandré, Schumacher, United, Walltex, York, and Zumsteg. If you're looking for grass cloth or "string" wallpaper, remember that American Discount will give you special savings of 30% to 50% on selected styles if you identify yourself as a WBMC reader. Request samples and prices of what's available.

All business is done on a price-quote basis. You're asked to give the name of the manufacturer, line or pattern-book title, model or stock number, and amount needed of the blinds, wallpaper, or fabric you're pricing. All goods are first quality, and returns are accepted within 20 days under terms stated on the order form. Be sure to request this form when you call or write for a price quote.

THE FABRIC CENTER

---

519 Electric Ave.
Fitchburg, MA 01420
(617) 343–4402

Price List: free
Information: price quote by phone or letter with SASE
Discount: 25% to 50%
Goods: name brand
Minimum Order: none
Shipping, Insurance: 25¢ per yard; UPS, PP
Sales Tax: MA deliveries
Accepts: check, MO, MC, V
$$$

You can add life to old furniture with new slipcovers or upholstery, and revive the look of your home with fresh draperies. But even if you supply the labor, you'll need a good deal of fabric, and, at an average of $10 to $20 a yard, this can amount to a tidy sum.

Save up to 50% at The Fabric Center on the very same material sold at fabric and decorating stores. The Center stocks goods by Covington, Schumacher (including Waverly Fabrics), John Wolf, Robert Allen, George Harrington, Andrea Dutton, Fabricade, Emmess, Paul Barrow, American Textile, and other well-known firms. The price list is a lengthy roster of fabrics identified by name and stock number and is by no means comprehensive. If you don't see what you're looking for, call or write (include a SASE) for a price quote. The Fabric Center has been in business since 1933 and guarantees your satisfaction.

GURIAN FABRICS INC.

**276 Fifth Ave.
New York, NY 10001
(212) 689–9696: inquiries
and NY orders
(800) 221–3477: orders
except NY**

Brochure: $1; pub. yearly
Discount: 40%
WBMC Reader Discount: 10%
Goods: handcrafted
Minimum Order: $25 on credit cards
Shipping: extra; UPS, PP
Sales Tax: NY deliveries
Accepts: check, MO, MC, V
$$$

Gurian sells crewel fabric and home accessories that are "handmade at the foot of the Himalayas in fabled Kashmir." Crewel, an old needle art, is embroidery done with loosely twisted wool yarn instead of floss. Gurian's fabrics are worked in the stylized flower-and-vine designs of traditional crewel and include multi-colored patterns, white-on-white, and green and blue, brown and gold, rust and gold, and reds. The embroidery is done on hand-loomed 52″ wide Indian cotton, which resembles homespun. The material can be washed by hand or dry cleaned.

Prices run from $12 to $26 per yard; chair seats, pillow covers, tote bags, bedspreads, and tablecloths are also stocked. The price list gives the repeats for each pattern and shows the most popular design used to cover a chair and upholster an entire room—walls, blinds, banquette, and ceiling. Ordering actual samples ($1 each) is recommended, since the color of the photographs in the 12-page brochure may not be entirely true. If you identify yourself as a WBMC reader, you can take 10% off the purchase price of anything except samples, exclusive of shipping and tax charges. Quantity discounts of 10% are also given on purchases of full bolts. Gurian's guarantees your satisfaction and accepts returns within 15 days.

**KING'S CHANDELIER
COMPANY**

**P.O. Box 667
Eden, NC 27288
(919) 623–6188**

Catalog: $2; pub. yearly
Discount: up to 50% (see text)
Goods: house brand, name brand
Minimum Order: $100 on credit cards; $15 on
    chandelier parts
Shipping, Handling, Insurance: included on fixture
    shipments east of Mississippi River; 3% on
    deliveries west and to AK, HI, PR; $5 on
    chandelier parts; UPS, PP
Sales Tax: NC deliveries
Accepts: check, MO, MC, V
$$$

There is nothing quite like the confection of light created by a crystal chandelier to add presence to a home. The Kings have been designing and producing chandeliers since 1935 and offer much of their stock in the 96-page black-and-white catalog. It shows chandeliers, candelabras, and wall sconces in a range that should satisfy every taste and budget.

There are designs to suit Victorian decor and, for the "Colonial," fixtures that run from an austere one-light sconce in brass ($65) to a chandelier with 18 curving, solid-brass arms and the classic brass ball at bottom ($1,500 with clear glass shades). The majority of the catalog is devoted to the fantastic creations that make a feast of refraction: chandeliers and candelabra dripping with prisms, pendalogues, faceted balls, and ropes of crystal buttons. The variation in styles is tremendous, from the simple Berkeley models with curved arms and no hanging crystals to the Schonbrunn, a masterwork of Strass crystal with 18 lights. This achievement is 44 inches wide, 5 feet long, and costs $9,000. You might need a palace to justify the latter, but many of the fixtures sold here are scaled for houses of more modest proportions. And they work with so many decorating modes. Even contemporary decor can be enhanced by the drama of a classic chandelier—the juxtaposition of the dramatic chaos of light and color against the clean, spare lines of modern furniture can be quite pleasing.

Catalog prices are up to 50% less than those charged by other firms for fixtures of similar design and materials. King's also offers you such options as different finishes on the metals, hurricane shades or candelabra tapers, candelabra or standard sockets, and candle or bulb bases on many of the styles. The fixtures are U.L.-approved and shipped partially disassembled. Spare parts—glass shades, drops, crystal buttons, chandelier bulbs, bobeches, and wire prism pins—are also offered.

Satisfaction is guaranteed on all lighting fixtures. Your purchase price will be refunded or credited on goods returned, *postage and insurance paid,* within five days. PLEASE NOTE: Do *not* deduct the cost of the catalog or the "discount" from the prices unless King's includes a special offer with your catalog, and do not ask for a reader discount.

LAMP WAREHOUSE/NEW YORK CEILING FAN CENTER

**1073 39th St.
Brooklyn, NY 11219
(718) 436–8500**

Information: price quote by phone or letter with SASE
Discount: 10% to 30% plus
Goods: name brand
Minimum Order: none
Shipping, Insurance: extra; UPS, PP, FOB Brooklyn
Sales Tax: NY deliveries
Accepts: check, MO, MC, V, AE
$$$

Lamp Warehouse sells virtually any American-made lamp available today, including desk, table, swag, hanging, wall, pole, and ceiling. The brands include Stiffel, Quoizel, American Lantern, and comparable firms. Track lighting is also available.

A related concern, the New York Ceiling Fan Center, offers a full line of Casablanca and Hunter ceiling fans, also at discount. Neither company has a catalog, but they will give price quotes over the phone or by letter (include a SASE). If you're phoning, please note that both firms are closed on Wednesdays. Lamp Warehouse was established in 1954 and is notable for its comprehensive inventory.

N. PINTCHIK, INC.

**478 Bergen St.
Brooklyn, NY 11217
(718) 783–3333**

Information: price quote by phone or letter with
    SASE
Discount: up to 40%
Goods: name brand, imported
Minimum Order: none
Shipping, Insurance: extra; UPS
Sales Tax: NY deliveries
Accepts: check, MO, MC, V, AE, DC
$$$

When the Manhattan Bridge needed a new coat a few years ago, the city turned to Pintchik for the paint. When the Landmarks Preservation Commission wanted an authentic brownstone paint, it asked Pintchik to oversee the production. And when thousands of New Yorkers need cabinet fixtures, paint, wall coverings, window treatments, floor finishes, and other decorative accessories, they, too, count on Pintchik.

The company was founded over 70 years ago by Nathan Pintchik and is run by the third generation of the family. The Pintchiks offer every major brand of wallpaper and stock over 2,000 patterns in their stores and warehouses. You can even have wallpaper made to order with your own pattern or logo custom-printed, in a choice of colors (with a minimum of six rolls). Levolor blinds are sold at 40% off list, and Louverdrape verticals are also available at a discount. Pintchik can also have the verticals laminated in your choice of fabric or wallpaper. If you can't find the paint you need at your local supplier, try Pintchik; it stocks lines by Pratt & Lambert, Benjamin Moore, Pittsburgh Paints, Luminall, Emalj, Red Devil, and other firms. Color chips are available upon request. Flooring by Armstrong, Hartco, Kentile, Lees, and other companies is also stocked. Call or write for a price quote, and note that while returns are accepted within three weeks, a 20% restocking fee is imposed. Inquiries from institutions and businesses are welcome, and special discounts are given on commercial orders.

**ROBINSON'S
WALLCOVERINGS**

**Dept. J27
225 W. Spring St.
Titusville, PA 16354
(814) 827–1893**

Catalog and Samples: $1; pub. yearly in Jan.
Discount: up to 50%
Goods: name brand, generic
Minimum Order: $10 on credit cards
Shipping: extra; UPS
Sales Tax: PA deliveries
Accepts: check, MO, MC, V, AE
$$$

Robinson's Wallcoverings went into business in 1919, and the catalog prices look as if they haven't risen much in the intervening years. They begin at around $2 a roll, and the stock includes paper, scrubbable vinyl, and flocked wall coverings. Many of the prints are on the sedate side, but there are many handsome patterns that would complement all sorts of decorator styles—pastel powder-room prints, designs for the kitchen and den, and a wide variety suitable for bedrooms and living rooms. Don't miss the J.G. Hook collection of paper and borders, or the selection of GEAR designs for children's rooms.

All the papers are pretrimmed and most are prepasted. Robinson's includes a guide to the number of rolls needed per room in the catalog, and offers all the tools and supplies you'll need to hang the paper. Matching fabrics are available for some patterns; other home accessories—pillows, lighting, and curtains—are also stocked. Satisfaction is guaranteed, and returns are accepted within 30 days.

**SANZ INTERNATIONAL,
INC.**

**P.O. Box 1794
High Point, NC 27261
(919) 883–4622; 882–6212**

Flyers: free
Information: price quote by phone or letter with
    SASE
Discount: 30% to 90%
Goods: name brand, imported
Minimum Order: none
Shipping: included; UPS, PP
Sales Tax: NC deliveries
Accepts: check, MO, certified check
$$$

Sanz offers the home decorator an easy way to save 20% to 30% on name-brand wallpapers and fabrics, and 50% to 90% on grass cloth *without* compromising on selection. Sanz accepts orders for goods made by virtually every major manufacturer, including many "to the trade" firms that usually deal with decorators exclusively. Lines by Schumacher (including Waverly), Brunschwig & Fils, Scalamandré, York Imperial, Greeff, Color House, United, and over 500 other companies are available. Business is done on a price-quote basis—by phone or letter—and Sanz places your order with the manufacturer, who ships the goods directly to you. (The return policy and warranties are those stated by the manufacturer in the sample book.) Be sure to state the number of rolls needed when requesting prices, since quantity discounts may apply. Shipping is included in the prices.

Imported grass cloth is listed but not described in the flyers; request additional information and samples if you're interested. And note that Sanz can offer High Point discounts on furnishings, lamps, carpeting, and other home accoutrements. Again, little information is given in the flyer, but you can call or write with your inquiries. In business since 1977, this firm is also associated with The Hang It Now stores, Greensboro Wallcoverings, Wallpaper Now, and Interiors by Sanz.

SHAMA IMPORTS, INC.

P.O. Box 2900, Dept.
WBM–85
Farmington Hills, MI 48018
(313) 553–0261

Brochure: free; pub. yearly
Discount: 50%
Goods: handcrafted
Minimum Order: none
Shipping: extra; UPS, PP
Sales Tax: MI deliveries
Accepts: check, MO, MC, V
$$$

Shama Imports sells crewel fabrics, embroidered in India and worked in wool on hand-loomed cotton. These employ the serpentine flower-and-vine motifs of classic crewel in a variety of colors and patterns, as well as several distinctive designs not seen elsewhere. There are two which feature plumed birds, one with an arrangement of spring flowers that's reminiscent of American folk art, and a beige-on-white design that's ideal for more neutral decorating schemes. The crewel runs from $12 to $28 per yard, can be washed by hand or dry cleaned, and is 52″ wide. Bolts (about 50 yards) are sold at a 10% discount. The plain background fabric is $6 per yard. Chair and cushion covers, tote bags, bedspreads, and tablecloths are also available.

The 8-page color brochure shows every design and the price list gives the repeats, but you should get samples of the fabrics you like before ordering because colors of the goods may differ from those pictured. Large samples may be ordered for $1 each, and pieces showing one quarter of the complete pattern are $5 each, refundable. Shama guarantees your satisfaction, and accepts uncut, undamaged returns within 30 days for refund or credit.

SHIBUI WALLCOVERINGS

P.O. Box 1638
Rohnert Park, CA 94928
(707) 526–6170: inquiries
and CA orders
(800) 824–3030: orders
except CA

Brochure and Samples: $2, redeemable
Discount: 50%
Goods: handcrafted
Minimum Order: none
Shipping, Insurance: included; UPS, PP
Handling: $7.80 on orders under $100
Sales Tax: CA deliveries
Accepts: check, MO, MC, V
$$$

If you've been looking for something different in wall coverings, search no more. Shibui offers intriguing wallpaper made by Japanese and Korean firms, an unusual alternative to prepasted vinyls and flocks. Two dollars will bring you samples from current stock, which includes jute-fiber grass cloth, rush cloth, cork, "foliage" papers, textured weaves, and a bamboo design on linen. Prices are about 50% less than those charged for comparable goods elsewhere.

The coverings are created of open-weave cloth, jute, rush, paper-thin sheets of cork, and leaves applied to colored papers. The foliage wallpapers are especially dramatic; they're created with leaves that are boiled and bleached until almost translucent, then dyed, and pasted by hand on white, burgundy, and copper-colored paper. If upholstering your walls in linen or slubbed silk is beyond your budget, see the textured weaves—one in particular has all the quiet elegance of this decorator treatment at a fraction of the price.

The wallpaper rolls are priced singly but sold in triple-roll bolts, 3-by-36 feet, and cost from $9.80 to $19.80 per roll. (Single and double rolls can be cut, but these are not returnable.) If the small samples sent with the price list are not enough to judge the effect, you may request larger samples. A paper-hanging tool kit, adhesives, and protective coating are available as well. Shibui has been doing business by mail for 20 years and backs all its wall coverings with an unconditional guarantee of satisfaction. Returns are accepted within 30 days.

SILK PLANTS LTD.

P.O Box 19896, Airport
Facility
Columbus, OH 43219
(614) 471–8178

Catalog: $1; pub. twice yearly
Discount: up to 50%
Goods: house brand
Minimum Order: $20 on credit cards
Shipping, Handling: extra; UPS, PP
Sales Tax: OH deliveries
Accepts: check, MO, MC, V
$$

Many of the plants and floral arrangements you see in lounges, offices, and other places of business are creations of fabric and wire of the type sold by Silk Plants. These clever impostors have far more subtle coloring and detail and a more lifelike appearance than their plastic counterparts and cost about as much as real plants. Prices here are up to 50% less than those charged by other firms for similar plants and arrangements.

The 24-page color catalog includes everything from single vines at a few dollars each to a 7½-foot ficus tree with 1,464 leaves at $190. There are palms and hanging ferns, scheffleras, philodendrons, spider plants, violets, begonias, mums, fuchsia stems, apple blossom trees, "cut" spring flowers, and many others. Most are sold without pots, so you don't pay for a container that doesn't complement your decor. In addition to arranging them in baskets, pots, and vases, you can weave the vines into trellises for an attractive wall display. Silk Plants sells floral clay, moss, pins and clips, and "Sahara" (foam blocks used in professional arrangements to anchor stems). A guide to potting, arranging, and cleaning the foliage is included with each order. Satisfaction is guaranteed, and returns are accepted *in the original cartons* within ten days for refund or credit.

WELLS INTERIORS INC.

7171 Amador Plaza Rd.,
Dept. WBM–5
Dublin, CA 94568
(415) 829–2121: inquiries
and orders
(800) 547–8982: inquiries
and orders

Catalog, Color Card, Price List: $4
Information: price quote by phone or letter with SASE
Discount: up to 60%
Goods: name brand
Minimum Order: none
Shipping: included on most items; UPS, PP, FOB Dublin
Sales Tax: CA and OR deliveries
Accepts: check, MO, MC, V
$$$$

Wells Interiors carries name-brand window treatments—slat and vertical blinds, woven woods, pleated shades, and translucents—at up to 60% off list prices. Levolor's Riviera, Thrifty Custom, and vertical lines can be ordered in any of the fabrics, materials, colors, and options Levolor offers at 50% off. Additional discounts are given on quantity purchases. Louverdrape verticals, Roc-Lon "sew-it-yourself" Roman insulated shades, Del Mar woven woods, wooden blinds, Softlight shades, and metal blinds and verticals are all sold at half the suggested retail.

The catalog you're sent as part of the $4 literature package is the Kirsch "Window Shopping" book, a beautiful, 128-page color guide to a full range of window treatments. It should be quite helpful in making decisions about which window treatments suit your needs and decor; the many photographs of room settings are especially valuable as idea material and will aid in coordinating curtains and blinds with the rest of your decorating scheme. Kirsch's full lines of drapery rods and hardware, woven woods, pleated shades, decorator roller shades, verticals, and miniblinds are shown in the book as well. Complete instructions on measuring windows for different installations and a guide to the available patterns and colors are also included.

Wells Interiors guarantees "the lowest prices" on the products it sells and will beat any other dealer's price down to cost. Prices on blinds include postage. The price list gives the suggested retail cost of many of the lines; call or write for a price quote on goods not mentioned. Please note that phone orders are accepted, but written confirmation is required before they're processed.

SEE ALSO:

Barnes & Blackwelder, Inc. . . . name-brand lamps, wall coverings, carpeting . . . HOME (furnishings)

Barnes & Noble Bookstores, Inc. . . . Zelco book lights . . . BOOKS

Blackwelder's Industries, Inc. . . . name-brand clocks, lamps, carpeting . . . HOME (furnishings)

Cambridge Wools, Ltd. . . . sheepskin rugs . . . CRAFTS

Catherine, S.A. . . . Rigaud scented candles . . . HEALTH

Cherry Hill Furniture, Carpet & Interiors . . . name-brand lamps, carpeting, etc. . . . HOME (furnishings)

J.W. Chunn Perfumes . . . Rigaud scented candles . . . HEALTH

Craft Products Company . . . clock kits . . . CRAFTS

Deepak's Rokjemperl Products . . . inlaid rosewood panels . . . JEWELRY

The Deerskin Place . . . sheepskins for floor or bed . . . CLOTHING

Edgar B. Furniture Plantation . . . wall coverings, decorator fabrics . . . HOME (furnishings)

The Gailin Collection . . . Strass crystal chandeliers . . . HOME (table settings)

Heritage Clock and Brassmiths . . . brassware and clocks . . . CRAFTS

D. MacGillivray & Coy. . . . sheepskin rugs . . . CRAFTS

Parfumerie Grillot . . . Rigaud scented candles . . . HEALTH

Quality Furniture Market of Lenoir, Inc. . . . name-brand lamps, clocks, mirrors, rugs, etc. . . . HOME (furnishings)

Regal Greetings & Gifts, Inc. . . . vases, candlesticks, decorative items . . . GENERAL

Rein Furs . . . custom fur bedspreads, pillow covers, throws, rugs . . . CLOTHING

The Renovator's Supply, Inc. . . . reproduction light fixtures, bathroom fittings, curtains, clocks, etc. . . . HOME (maintenance)

James Roy Furniture Co., Inc. . . . name-brand carpeting . . . HOME (furnishings)

S & C Huber, Accoutrements . . . floor cloths . . . HANDCRAFTS

A.B. Schou . . . Waterford lamps . . . HOME (table settings)

Stuckey Brothers Furniture Co., Inc. . . . name-brand lamps, mirrors, clocks . . . HOME (furnishings)

Thai Silks . . . upholstery-weight silks . . . CRAFTS

Tibetan Refugee Self Help Centre . . . hand-woven Tibetan rugs and accents . . . HANDCRAFTS

Furnishings

Household furnishings of all types,
including outdoor furniture.

**BARNES &
BLACKWELDER, INC.**

**1804 Pembroke Rd.
Greensboro, NC 27408
(919) 373–8504: NC
inquiries
(800) 334–0234: inquiries
except NC**

Brochure: free
Information: price quote by phone or letter with
 SASE
Discount: 30% to 43%
Goods: name brand
Minimum Order: none
Shipping, Insurance: included; FOB Greensboro or
 manufacturer
Sales Tax: NC deliveries
Accepts: check, MO, certified check, V, MC
$$$

This firm, a division of the well-known company of John Barnes Interiors, was founded by Mr. Barnes and Wayne Blackwelder in 1972 to offer "fine furniture at affordable prices." They've exceeded their goal in both departments, with savings of up to 43% and lines of lamps and home accessories, wall coverings, and rugs and carpeting offered in addition to furniture.

You'll save from 40% to 43% on furniture, carpeting, and accessories by such firms as Hickory Chair, Henredon, Sligh, American Drew, Ficks Reed,

Mt. Airy, White of Mebane, Madison Square, Baker, Hickory Mfg., Serta, Wildwood Lamps, La Barge, Lee Woodard, Young Hinkle, Dixie, Barcalounger, Century, Thomasville, Henry Link, Statton, Herschede Clocks, Gulistan (J.P. Stevens), Pande Cameron, Karastan, and many others. Decorator fabrics and wallcoverings are discounted 30%, and include lines by Greeff, Brunschwig & Fils, Payne, David & Dash, Clarence House, Lee/Jofa, Scalamandre, Westgate, Katzenbach & Warren, Schumacher, and other companies.

The brochure includes a partial listing of the manufacturers represented, but because orders can be taken on goods by other firms, call or write for a price quote even if you don't see the brand listed. The literature also describes the sales policy: orders must be completed in writing, and a 30% deposit is required on furniture (full payment on fabrics and wallcoverings). After you place the order, Barnes & Blackwelder will send you a copy of the order, followup questions, a sample swatch of the upholstery fabric, the estimated date of shipment to Barnes from the manufacturer, and a second notice requesting balance due when the order is ready to ship. Barnes & Blackwelder has arrangements with a delivery service that will oversee your order through uncrating and setup. Claims for damages incurred in transit should be filed with the delivery service, but Barnes & Blackwelder "will always accept final responsibility to insure that you will be another satisfied customer."

Whether writing or calling for a price quote, remember to provide the manufacturer's name, stock number, and fabric number, grade, and stock number on upholstered pieces.

THE BEDPOST, INC.

795 Bethel Rd.
Columbus, OH 43214
(614) 459-0088

Catalog: $2.50; pub. yearly
Information: price quote by letter with SASE
Discount: 20% to 50%
Goods: name brand, house brand
Minimum Order: none
Shipping, Insurance: extra; UPS, PP, FOB Columbus
Sales Tax: OH deliveries
Accepts: check, MO, MC, V
$$$

The Bedpost sells water beds and frames, liners, tape, heaters, and other accessories, plus hot tubs, saunas, spas, and bedroom furniture. The manufacturers represented include Bassett, Stanley, Burlington, America the Elegant, Broyhill, Trendwest, Pacific Frames, and Avery. Prices run to 50%

below list and comparable retail, and The Bedpost occasionally offers additional discounts on selected items. If you don't see what you're looking for in the catalog, write and ask whether the item is stocked (include a SASE with your letter).

BLACKWELDER'S INDUSTRIES, INC.

RR 12–390
Statesville, NC 28677
(704) 872–4491, 8291:
inquiries and orders
(800) 438–0201: inquiries
and orders

Catalog and Brochures: $5, refundable; pub. every 18 months
Information: price quote by phone or letter (see text)
Discount: 30% to 50%
Goods: name brand, house brand
Minimum Order: none
Shipping, Insurance: extra; UPS, FOB Statesville
Sales Tax: NC deliveries
Accepts: check, MO, certified check, MC, V
$$$$

Norris Blackwelder founded his company in 1938 to allow the average consumer to buy better furniture. His son John, now president, has carried on the tradition of excellence in price, selection, and service that makes Blackwelder's one of North Carolina's best furniture discounters.

Blackwelder's handsome 72-page catalog features over 1,500 items from prominent manufacturers but is just a sample of the available home and office furnishings, grandfather clocks, pianos, Oriental rugs, and lamps. In addition to the master catalog, there are nine others that showcase designs of different periods and styles, pianos, clocks, carpets, and Blackwelder's Leather Limited, the house line of classic and contemporary leather-upholstered seating. These are listed on the price/brochure/master catalog worksheet, a self-mailer which lists the over 140 brands stocked by Blackwelder's and includes a section for requesting price quotes on any item made by those firms. Blackwelder's offers: furniture by American of Martinsville, Barcalounger, Bassett, Brown Jordan, Casa Bique, Century, Drexel, Habersham Plantation, Henredon, Hickory, Kittinger, Lane, Madison Square, Sligh, Stanley, Thayer-Coggin, Tropitone, White of Mebane, and many others; lamps from Ainsley, Stiffel, Sunset, and Wildwood; brass beds by Swann, J.B. Ross, Dresher, and Brass Bed of America; pianos by Kimball, Chickering, Masson Hamil, and Bösendorfer; office furnishings by Myrtle and Miller; and rugs and carpets from Pande Cameron, Karastan, Bigelow, Milliken, and others.

You'll save from 30% to 50% on the list prices of just about everything you buy from Blackwelder's, and 3% more if you join the "Share the Secret" Club. Pay $25 to join and receive ten catalogs and a package of materials to distribute among friends and co-workers. You keep a roster of these people, and each time they make a purchase, you receive 3% of their total purchase price as a discount on your next order. (There is no increased cost to your friends.) If an organization joins the Club, its members can have their purchases applied to the group's "account" to achieve real savings on office or lounge furniture, carpeting, pianos, etc. Information on the Club is included with the master catalog.

If you have your order delivered outside North Carolina, the shipping costs may be less than the sales tax you'd have paid if you'd purchased the same goods at higher prices in your own state. Delivery is made by UPS (when size and weight permit), common carrier (truckers who usually make sidewalk deliveries), and North American Van Lines, a household goods moving firm that will uncrate your order and set it up. The van delivery may be more expensive than standard trucking charges, but it has a real advantage: You can inspect the furniture while the movers are uncrating it and file a claim for damages, and the van line will pay all repair costs. Blackwelder's uncrates, inspects, and recrates all goods sent by the van line before they're sent on to you to ensure that no manufacturing defects are present. The common carrier only accepts claims that prove damage was caused *in transit*. You may pay a surcharge for delivery inside your home.

Blackwelder's guarantees your satisfaction and accepts returns (freighted at your expense) within 30 days; the 20% restocking fee may be applied to another purchase if made within 90 days. Price-quote requests from all 50 states and the Bahamas, Bermuda, Puerto Rico, and many areas of the West Indies are accepted over the toll-free lines. To get an accurate price, remember to include all finish and fabric-grade information and the name of the line or collection as well as that of the manufacturer in your request.

A BRASS BED SHOPPE

12421 Cedar Rd., Dept. W
Cleveland Heights, OH
44106
(216) 371–0400

Catalog and Price List: free; pub. twice yearly
Information: price quote by letter with SASE
Discount: 50%
Goods: name brand
Minimum Order: none
Shipping, Insurance: extra; FOB Cleveland
  Heights
Sales Tax: OH deliveries
Accepts: check, MO, MC, V, AE
$$$

Old brass beds were all the rage about fifteen years ago, and even truly inferior models of rolled sheet-brass were commanding top dollar. Today, you can pay less for a better-quality product in a choice of styles and sizes, thanks to A Brass Bed Shoppe.

This firm publishes a 12-page catalog that shows 20 different designs, some in white iron with brass accents, at prices that start at $120 for a twin headboard ($232 for the complete bed). A number of the styles incorporate classic serpentine designs and scrolls and ball finials, but there are as many in spare, straight-post styles and a few fresh interpretations. All of the beds sold here are made of solid brass, not sheeting, and finished in a baked epoxy. Post diameters and the height of headboards and footboards are listed in the catalog. A Brass Bed Shoppe stocks hundreds of beds by nationally known manufacturers, and welcomes price-quote requests on models not shown.

If you'd prefer a water bed to a standard mattress, check here: "flotation systems" are offered at savings of up to 50%. Standard and "waveless" (no-motion) beds are stocked, and complete sets include the mattress, foundation, fill kit, water conditioner, and instructions; the beds are covered by a 15-year warranty. Heaters are available separately, as well as heavy-duty frames. (Frames are included at no charge with the purchase of a headboard and footboard.)

Brass Bed Shoppe states that parts and workmanship are "guaranteed to meet with your satisfaction," and returns are accepted for replacement or refund. Safe delivery is also guaranteed. A "bridal layaway" plan permits you to hold your choice with a minimum $25 deposit and pay $25 per month with no charges or interest fees. The offer doesn't appear to be limited to prospective brides, so we assume that anyone can use the plan to budget a purchase.

CANNONDALE'S

Rte. 113 S., Drawer 1107
Berlin, MD 21811
(301) 641–4477: inquiries
and MD orders
(800) 522–1776: orders
except MD

Brochures: free; pub. in Jan. and June
Discount: up to 50%
Goods: house brand
Minimum Order: none
Shipping, Insurance: extra; FOB Berlin
Sales Tax: DE and MD deliveries
Accepts: check, MO, certified check, MC, V
$$$

If you've always coveted a *real* brass bed—solid brass, not plate—but have been put off by the price, you'll be glad to know about Cannondale's. Its beds are constructed of .032 gauge solid brass in turn-of-the-century styles. Prices are excellent: Complete beds start at under $275, and headboards are available separately at about half the cost of the complete beds. Most of the beds have been given a lacquer finish; some are simply polished. Handsome antique replicas in white iron are also sold, beginning at under $225 for a complete bed. (Specify the "white iron" or "brass" brochure when requesting literature.) Cannondale's offers a no-questions-asked, money-back guarantee and accepts authorized returns within 30 days. A layaway plan is also available if you want to budget your purchase.

CHERRY HILL FURNITURE, CARPET & INTERIORS

P.O. Box 7405,
Furnitureland Sta.
High Point, NC 27264
(800) 328–0933

Catalog: $3, refundable
Portfolio of Catalogs: $3, refundable
Brands List: free
Information: price quote by phone or letter with SASE
Discount: 40% to 50%
Goods: name brand
Minimum Order: none
Shipping, Insurance: extra; FOB High Point
Sales Tax: NC deliveries
Accepts: check, MO, certified check
$$$$

Cherry Hill, founded in 1933, makes shopping for home and office furniture, rugs and carpeting, and accessories both easy *and* rewarding. All calls for price quotes, inquiries, and orders are taken over the WATS line, and there's no limit to the number of products you can "cost out" at one time. Discounts are substantial—an average of 45% off list. The Contract Division offers special volume discounts for business owners, developers, architects, purchasing directors, and others coordinating the furnishing and decoration of an office or residential complex. Deliveries are made via common carrier or van line, depending on your choice and/or your delivery area. And Cherry Hill represents over 500 of the best names in furnishings and accessories. The office lines include selections by Alma, Baker Contract, Condi, Cartwright, Hardwood House, Steelcase, Knoll, Myrtle, OSI, Thonet, Vecta, and many others; carpeting and rugs by Alexander, Smith, Bigelow, Cabin Crafts, Courtistan, Karastan, Lees, Mohawk, Pande Cameron, and other firms are available; and just about every manufacturer of home furnishings and accessories is also represented.

The "Portfolio of Catalogs" showcases new selections from well-known manufacturers, and is well worth the $3 (refundable) charge if you're still comparing styles and designs. The other catalog is "Living with Drexel

Heritage," a 96-page book of beautifully photographed rooms; it can be quite helpful in coordinating colors and decorative accessories to complement different furniture styles. The brochure, available upon request, lists a fraction of the available brands and describes the selling terms. But if you're ready to buy and have the model and stock numbers of the item you want, just call—the sales representatives will give you all the information over the phone.

EDGAR B. FURNITURE PLANTATION

P.O. Box 849
3550 Hwy. 158
Clemmons, NC 27012
(919) 766–7321: inquiries
and NC orders
(800) 334–2010: orders
except NC

Catalog: $3; pub. yearly
Brands List: free with SASE
Information: price quote by phone or letter with SASE
Discount: 40%
Goods: name brand
Minimum Order: none
Shipping, Insurance: extra; FOB Clemmons
Sales Tax: NC deliveries
Accepts: check, MO, certified check, MC, V
$$$

You can rely on Edgar B. for a choice group of furnishings, accessories, and wallpaper and decorator fabrics from about 50 manufacturers, and savings of about 40% off list. This firm was founded by the Broyhill family and sells lines by Thomasville, Henredon, Century, Davis, Hickory, Drexel, and other top companies. We did not receive the catalog, but learned that the firm offers complete decorating services and has arrangements with a private furniture-moving firm that will see your order through uncrating and setup (as well as common carrier service for areas not served by the moving company). Send a SASE for the brochure listing the available brands, or write or call for a specific price quote. Edgar B. was founded in 1979, and has earned an excellent reputation for good service and prices.

THE FURNITURE BARN OF FOREST CITY, INC.

P.O. Box 609, Bypass 74
Forest City, NC 28043
(704) 287–7106, 7, 8

Brand List: free
Information: price quote by phone or letter with SASE
Discount: 40% to 50%
Goods: name brand
Minimum Order: none
Shipping, Insurance: extra; FOB Forest City
Sales Tax: NC deliveries
Accepts: check, MO, MC, V, CHOICE
$$$$

Furniture Barn offers lines by scores of manufacturers at up to 50% below list prices; furniture, bedding, and accessories are all available, and goods are shipped by common carrier or van line (depending on your choice or area).

If you're pricing an item by Lane, American Drew, Bassett, Bernhardt, Broyhill, Caro-Craft, Casa Bique, Clark Casual, Cox, D & F Wicker, Freeman & Co., Habersham Plantation, Continental Chair, Henredon, Hibriten, Keller, Maddox, Park Place, Regency House, Sligh, Stanley, Southwood, Thayer Coggin, Sorenti, Thomasville, Tropitone, White of Mebane, Young Hinkle, or any other well-known manufacturer, call or write for a price quote. A deposit of one third is required before orders are placed with the manufacturer, and the balance is due before shipment. This firm was established in 1970 and has been doing business by mail since 1979; it was recommended by a reader for its prompt handling of her order and excellent delivery service.

GEORGE AND SON'S CO.

**125–2 Wu-Fu 2nd St.
Kaohsiumg, Taiwan
Republic of China
Phone # 2012772**

Information: see text
Discount: up to 70%
Goods: handcrafted
Minimum Order: none (see text)
Shipping, Insurance: included; surface mail
Duty: extra
Accepts: check, MO, certified check
$$

George and Son's Co. is the renamed Sion-Fuk Enterprises, the company noted in previous editions of this book for its hand-carved rosewood and teak screens, tables, desks, and chairs. George and Son's has narrowed its focus to gift items and small pieces of furniture. We didn't receive a catalog, but we were sent a photograph of one of the most popular items, a Korean design cabinet constructed of plain and burl woods and fitted with ornate brass hinges, latches, and decorative hardware. These cabinets are the perfect size for night stands or end tables and cost just $110 each. (Similar cabinets sell for $250 to $350 in local import shops.) Because they're small enough to be mailed, George and Son's can send them directly to your home—you won't have to hassle with having the order trucked from the dock or airport terminal. If you're interested, write to the company and request a photograph of the "Korean-design chest" mentioned in WBMC. Commercial accounts are welcomed.

**MURROW FURNITURE
GALLERIES, INC.**

P.O. Box 4337, Dept. WBMC
Wilmington, NC 28406
(919) 799–4010: inquiries
and NC orders
(800) 334–1614: orders only
except NC

Brochure: free
Information: price quote by phone or letter with
    SASE
Discount: 30% to 50%
Goods: name brand
Minimum Order: none
Shipping, Insurance: extra; FOB Wilmington
Sales Tax: NC deliveries
Accepts: check, MO, MC, V
$$$$

Murrow was founded in 1979, and represents over 500 manufacturers offering lines of furnishings, lamps, and bedding. Among the brands available here are Thomasville, Drexel, White of Mebane, Baker, Henredon, Sligh, Hickory, Broyhill, Casa Bique, Dixie, Ficks Reed, National of Mt. Airy, Barcalounger, Hekman, American Drew, John Widdicomb, LaBarge, Madison Square, Gilliam, Harden, Hickory, Sherrill, Thayer Coggin, Unique, Wildwood Lamps, Stiffel, Bernhardt, Century, Stanley, Mastercraft, Link Taylor, Henry Link, Young Hinkle, Emerson Leather, Bennington Pine, Knob Creek, Lane, Vanguard, Woodmark, Tropitone, Greeff, Mobel, and Stanton Cooper, but this is only a partial listing—request the brochure for a complete roster, or call or write for a specific price quote. A deposit is required when the order is placed, and the balance is due prior to shipment. Delivery options and terms of sale are detailed in the literature. The deep discounts and extensive selection make this one of the best sources around, so be sure to call or write for a quote even if you think you've already gotten the lowest possible price elsewhere.

**PLEXI-CRAFT QUALITY
PRODUCTS CORP.**

514 W. 24th St.
New York, NY 10011
(212) 924–3244

Catalog: $2
Information: price quote by phone or letter with
    SASE
Discount: up to 75%
Goods: house brand, custom-made
Minimum Order: none
Shipping, Insurance: extra; UPS, FOB, NYC
Sales Tax: NY deliveries
Accepts: check, MO, MC, V
$$$

Plexi-Craft manufactures its own line of Lucite® and Plexiglas® goods, including pedestals, cubes, shelving, computer stands, étagères, wine racks, valets, desk accessories, magazine racks, towel holders, bathroom fixtures, chairs, album holders, and occasional, coffee, and dining tables. These goods all cost up to 75% less at Plexi-Craft than they do when bought in department and specialty stores. Plexi-Craft also does custom work; send a picture with dimensions of the item you want made, and Plexi-Craft will give you a price quote.

QUALITY FURNITURE MARKET OF LENOIR, INC.

**2034 Hickory Blvd. S.W.
Lenoir, NC 28645
(704) 728–2946**

Brands List: free with SASE
Information: price quote by phone or letter with SASE
Discount: up to 50% (see text)
Goods: name brand
Minimum Order: none
Shipping, Insurance: extra; FOB Lenoir
Sales Tax: NC deliveries
Accepts: check, MO, certified check
$$$$

The next time you're traipsing through the furniture showroom of your local department store, checking to see whether they've reduced the price on that $1,500 Thomasville breakfront that was just *made* for your dining room, consider this sobering fact: Even if the price is slashed by 20%, you're going to be paying *double* the actual cost of the piece.

The markup on Thomasville goods is usually 120% over cost, and the industry range is 110% to 125%. This shocking piece of news came to us from Quality Furniture Market, where the savings are computed on a cost-plus basis. Quality's markup is just 15% to 20%, which means it could sell you the breakfront for just $750. Since the shipping charges are often less than the sales tax charged on a purchase made locally, the overall savings are even greater. Quality, which has been in business since 1954, offers indoor and outdoor furniture, bedding, lamps, clocks, mirrors, and area rugs by hundreds of firms. Lines by American Drew, Art Flo, Artisan Brass Beds, Barcalounger, Bassett, Boling Chair, Brady, Brandt Cabinet Works, Broyhill, Burlington House, Capitol Victorian, Chatham Country, Century, Cochrane, Colonial Clocks, David Morgan, Dixie, Dresher, Emerson Leather, Flair, Gilliam, Grand Manor, Habersham Plantation, Henredon, Hekman, Homecrest, Jeffco, Knob Creek, Kingsdown, Lawnlite, Levolor, Lyon-Shaw, Miller Desk, Molla, Morris Greenspan Lamps, Nettle Creek, Plantation Patterns, Rachlin, Schumacher, Sealy, Selig, Serta, Shoal Creek, Stanley, Swan Brass Beds, Taylor Woodcraft, Tropitone, Venture, Waverly Fabrics, Young Hinkle, and many other companies are available.

Business is done on a price-quote basis, and full payment is required before the order will be placed with the manufacturer. Shipment is made by common carrier (dump delivery), so you must arrange for uncrating and setup yourself. Be sure to keep the original carton and packing materials until you've inspected the piece, and file claims for damages incurred in transit with the trucking firm. The terms and other conditions of sale are stated clearly on the brands list. Quality is proud of its reputation as well as its prices, and invites you to check its ratings with Dun and Bradstreet and the Lyons listing, as well as the Lenoir Chamber of Commerce.

ROBERTS BRASS COMPANY

24 Park Lane Rd., Dept. WMI
New Milford, CT 06776
(203) 354–6142

Catalog: $1; pub. in Sept.
Discount: up to 40%
WBMC Reader Discount: 20%
Goods: house brand, handcrafted
Minimum Order: none
Shipping, Insurance: extra; FOB New Milford
Sales Tax: CT deliveries
Accepts: check, MO, MC, V
$$$$

The modern equivalent of the Princess and the pea is the purist who simply can't fall asleep in a lacquered brass bed. Roberts Brass respects that sensibility, proclaiming that "we do not cover our products with artificial coatings!" While a lacquered bed may eventually tarnish and require recoating if the finish is nicked or worn off, an uncoated bed requires nothing but an occasional polishing. (The brochure says this is needed two or three times a year, but city dwellers and heavy smokers may find that cleaning is needed more frequently to maintain the glow.)

The six-page color catalog shows a delightful selection of traditional beds embellished with curving brass and ball finials as well as more restrained styles that would complement almost any decorating scheme. Most of the beds are offered in the four standard sizes, and each is made of solid brass. All beds, except those with rounded headboards and footboards, can be ordered with either cannonball or mushroom finials at no extra cost. The values are as solid as the products; we compared one model to an identical bed in another catalog and found the Roberts bed was *$950 less* than the other firm's (at regular prices) and $150 below its sale price. If you identify yourself as a WBMC reader, you can deduct 20% from the catalog prices, which makes this an unbeatable source for an unlacquered bed.

Each bed comes complete with the headboard, footboard, and steel side rails, and headboards are available separately. Satisfaction is guaranteed, and returns are accepted within 30 days if packed in the original carton. Roberts will also help you with your budget; deposit half the purchase price when you order and pay the balance before the bed is shipped in four to six weeks, or put 25% down and pay the rest in monthly installments over a year.

JAMES ROY FURNITURE CO., INC.

15 E. 32nd St.
New York, NY 10016
(212) 679–2565

List of Brands: free; updated quarterly
Information: price quote by phone or letter with SASE
Discount: 33% minimum
Goods: name brand
Minimum Order: none
Shipping, Insurance: extra; FOB NYC or manufacturer
Sales Tax: NY deliveries
Accepts: check, MO, certified check, MC, V (see text)
$$$$

James Roy guarantees at least one third off manufacturers' suggested retail prices on an impressive list of over 180 nationally known brands of furniture (including office furnishings), mattresses and springs, and carpeting. The manager stresses that the discount of at least 33% is made on the true manufacturers' suggested list prices.

Roy carries Drexel, Henredon, Heritage, Broyhill, Lane, Stiffel, Thayer Coggin, Sealy, Thomasville, Simmons, Pennsylvania House, and Stanley, to name just a few. There is no catalog—you must write or call for a price quote. Roy's stock is on display in the New York City showroom, but you can send for the manufacturer's brochure or catalog of current lines to look over the selection and get style or model numbers, finish options, fabric choices, etc. (Don't request these from Roy—see the introduction to this section for more information.) Furniture is delivered directly from the manufacturer or from James Roy's warehouse. Shipping charges depend on the mile-per-pound rate.

Please note that James Roy accepts credit cards on deposits only. Final payments must be made by check, certified check, or money order. This firm has 25 years of experience in mail order and can be trusted to handle your order efficiently.

SHAW FURNITURE GALLERIES

P.O. Box 576
Randleman, NC 27317
(919) 498–2628: NC
inquiries and orders
(800) 334–6799: inquiries
and orders except NC

Brochure: free
Information: price quote by phone or letter with
SASE
Discount: 40% plus
Goods: name brand
Minimum Order: $100
Shipping, Insurance: extra; FOB Randleman
Sales Tax: NC deliveries
Accepts: check, MO, MC, V

$$$

The Shaw family has been selling furniture at a discount since 1940, growing from a small firm serving the needs of Randleman to a well-established company that ships across the U.S. and to Canada. The roster of firms represented by the Shaws numbers over 300, including American Drew, Bassett, Baker, Binswanger Mirrors, Brass Beds of America, Broyhill, Burlington, Butler, Carsons, Chaircraft, Council Craftsmen, Davis Cabinet, Directional, Dresher, Ficks Reed, Flexsteel, Gilliam, Hekman, Habersham Plantation, Henredon, Henry Link, Nickory, Hitchcock Chair, Link-Taylor, Madison Square, Null, Pulaski, Ross, Selig, Sealy, Serta, Seth Thomas, Schoonbeck, Sherrill, Stanley, Stuart, Stiffel, Tropitone, Unique, Vaughan, White of Mebane, and many others.

Price quotes can be given over the WATS line, and although Shaw appreciates having the manufacturer's data, if you're having trouble finding the information the sales staff will be happy to help by sending brochures and providing advice. You have a choice of common carrier shipment (dump delivery) or "in-home" delivery service, which includes uncrating and setup. We recommend the latter, since you can inspect for damages before the truckers leave your home or office and file claim on the spot. (This is more a matter of peace of mind than probability, since properly handled goods are not often damaged in transit.)

The brochure lists about half the firms carried by Shaw, so if you don't see the manufacturer noted, write or call anyway. Greensboro residents should call 275–0938; High Point residents can call 889–5704.

**STUCKEY BROTHERS
FURNITURE CO., INC.**

Rte. 1, P.O. Box 527
Stuckey, SC 29554
(803) 558–2591

Information: price quote by phone or letter with
  SASE
Discount: 30% to 40%
Goods: name brand
Minimum Order: none
Shipping, Insurance: extra; FOB manufacturer or
  Stuckey
Sales Tax: SC deliveries
Accepts: check, MO, V
$$$

This firm may be South Carolina's answer to High Point—it sells a full line of furniture and accessories at North Carolina prices, represents over 300 manufacturers, and has been handling mail orders since 1948.

If you're looking for savings on anything by Hickory, Thomasville, Broyhill, Dixie, Stanley, Hekman, Ficks Reed, Fairfield, Drake Smith, Craftique, Madison Square, Nichols & Stone, Ridgeway Clocks, Singer, Stiffel, Thayer Coggin, Vogue Rattan, Westwood Lamps, La-Z-Boy, Bassett, Serta, Sealy, American Drew, Lane, Samsonite, or other prominent manufacturers, call or write for a price quote. In addition to the standard lines of furniture, Stuckey features a good selection of nursery furnishings, bedding, lamps, clocks, and mirrors. Those who've searched in vain for good patio and outdoor furniture at a discount should stop here—Stuckey carries Finkel, Lyon-Shaw, Meadowcraft, Molla, Plantation Patterns, Tropitone, Winston, and Woodard, among others.

Call or write for a price quote, and request shipping information (type of carrier and approximate charge) before ordering.

**RICHARD P. ZARBIN AND
ASSOCIATES**

225 W. Hubbard St.
Chicago, IL 60610
(312) 527–1570

Information: price quote by phone or letter with
  SASE
Discount: 40%
Goods: name brand
Minimum Order: none
Shipping, Insurance: included; UPS, FOB
  manufacturer
Sales Tax: IL deliveries
Accepts: check, MO, certified check
$$$

Zarbin sells name-brand furniture, carpeting, and bedding at discounts of up to 40% on suggested list prices. All the top manufacturers are represented: Drexel, Directional, Baker, Century, Broyhill, Dixie, Thomasville, La Barge, Hickory, Gilliam, Lane, Harden, Stiffel, Flexsteel, La-Z-Boy, Selig, American of Martinsville, Barcalounger, Henredon, Heritage, Henry Link, Karpen, Link-Taylor, Sealy, White of Mebane, Lees, Salem, Galaxy, Monticello, Masland, Burlington, Armstrong, and many others.

Zarbin was founded in 1969, and runs an excellent mail-order department. Business is done on a price-quote basis, and goods are generally shipped from the manufacturers' warehouses to the trucker, freight collect. Call or write for a price quote and shipping estimate, and remember to include the manufacturer's name, style number of the article, and fabric and grade numbers, if applicable.

SEE ALSO:

Alfax Mfg. . . . office, institutional furnishings . . . OFFICE
Barnes & Noble Bookstores, Inc. . . . folding beechwood bookshelves . . .
  BOOKS
Beitman Co., Inc. . . . custom-covered upholstery buttons . . . CRAFTS
Bloom & Krup . . . name-brand bedding, Childcraft cribs . . .
  APPLIANCES
Business & Institutional Furniture Company . . . office, institutional
  furniture . . . OFFICE
Buy Direct, Inc. . . . computer furniture . . . OFFICE
Frank Eastern Co. . . . office furniture . . . OFFICE
The Gailin Collection . . . English solid cast brass beds . . . HOME (table
  settings)
Grayarc . . . small selection office chairs, work stations . . . OFFICE
Heritage Clock and Brassmiths . . . white iron, brass beds . . . CRAFTS
Laurence Corner . . . government-surplus trestle tables, chairs . . .
  CLOTHING
Sanz International, Inc. . . . name-brand furnishings . . . HOME (decor)
Sierra Fitness Distributors . . . posture chairs . . . SPORTS
Stereo Discounters Electronic World . . . home entertainment, audio, TV
  furniture . . . APPLIANCES
Irv Wolfson Company . . . small selection name-brand bedding, recliners,
  dinette sets . . . APPLIANCES

Kitchen

Cookware, bakeware,
restaurant equipment, and
food storage.

A COOK'S WARES

**3270 37th St. Ext.
Beaver Falls, PA 15010
(412) 846–9490**

Catalog: $1; pub. yearly
Discount: 20% to 50%
Goods: name brand, generic
Minimum Order: none
Shipping, Insurance: extra; UPS
Sales Tax: PA deliveries
Accepts: check, MO, certified check, MC, V, AE
$$$

It's nice to save 20% to 50% on kitchenware, but it's even better when the selection is geared for serious cooks and includes only the best of what's available.

That's what A Cook's Wares is all about. Byron and Gail Bitar, serious cooks themselves, run this mail-order firm and publish a catalog full of useful information on what they're selling and why they've chosen to sell it. No Mongolian spices or pink peppercorns here.

You *will* find the All-Clad lines, Le Creuset, Leyse (including Leyson), and Vollrath cookware. The Bitars also stock the Mauviel collection from France—3mm thick, hotel-weight tinned copper pots and pans sold at competitive prices. Bakeware includes selections from Pillivuyt (for which there are also serving pieces), Isabelle Marique Blue Steel, and Chicago Metallic's Village Baker, and Bakalon lines.

The bulk of the 12-page, black-and-white catalog is devoted to cutlery, food-preparation equipment, and related products. There are Peacock copper and brass pot racks, a Bron mandoline, Chambord infusion coffee makers, Braun grinders, J.K. Adams wooden knife blocks, Taylor Woodcraft work tables and cutting boards, Mouli kitchen tools, and Atlas pasta machines. Large groups of cutlery and implements from Wustof-Trident, Henckels, F. Dicks, Forschner Solingen, and Victorinox are shown as well as Le Prix bistro flatware, William Bounds salt and pepper mills, fine copper and china double boilers by B. Waldow; Norton and other sharpening stones and steels; Sparta pastry, vegetable, and cleaning brushes; and lettuce spinners from Copco, Cogebi, and Mouli. And there are scores of little things—strainers, food mills, larding needles, linen kitchen twine, fat separators, garlic presses, tongs, whisks, whips, molds, parchment paper, and much more.

Prices and savings vary considerably. New products and specials are featured in catalog inserts at discounts of up to 50%. Before buying nonsale items, be sure to make price comparisons. The Bitars guarantee your complete satisfaction and will accept goods returned within 30 days for exchange or refund.

FIVESON FOOD EQUIPMENT, INC.

324 S. Union St.
Traverse City, MI
49684–2586
(616) 946–7760: inquiries
and MI orders
(800) 632–7342: orders
except MI

Catalog: free with SASE (two stamps); pub. spring, summer, fall, winter
Information: price quote by phone or letter with SASE
Discount: 40%
WBMC Reader Savings: free freight on utensil orders over $500
Goods: name brand
Minimum Order: none
Shipping, Insurance: extra; UPS, PP, FOB Traverse City
Sales Tax: MI deliveries
Accepts: certified check, MC, V
$$$

Fiveson has been selling restaurant equipment to the food-service industry since 1937. If you're in the market for anything by Hobart (commercial), Garland, Gold Medal, Libbey, or other major manufacturers, you'll probably find it here.

The tabloid catalog we received showed pizza ovens, popcorn machines, commercial refrigerators, Garland ranges, ice machines, Hamilton Beach bar mixers, Univex deli slicers and mixers, steam tables, griddles, Belgian waffle irons, coffee brewers, Libbey glassware, Pyrex and Corning china, food-storage units, and restaurant furnishings. Savings average 40% on list prices. Call or write for a price quote.

If you order over $500 in utensils (and you'd have to buy a lot, because they're quite inexpensive here), you're entitled to free shipping on the order if you mention that you're a WBMC reader.

KAPLAN BROS. BLUE FLAME CORP.

523 W. 125th St.
New York, NY 10027–3498
(212) 662–6990

Brochure: free with SASE
Information: price quote by phone or letter with SASE
Discount: 50%
Goods: name brand
Minimum Order: none
Shipping, Insurance: extra; FOB factory
Sales Tax: NY deliveries
Accepts: check, MO, certified check
$$$

You probably know the Garland stove by sight even if you've never been in a restaurant kitchen—it's the commanding fixture shown in many shelter magazine features on high-tech design. A commercial gas stove built to withstand decades of heavy professional use, it has much larger burner areas and oven cavities than most appliances made for the consumer market. Buying a Garland makes sense for the chef who does a lot of cooking and baking, but be warned that it throws off much more heat and is much heavier (400 to 800 lbs.) than standard appliances. (Before buying, check to make sure your floors can support one, make sure there is enough insulation in the walls adjacent to it, and upgrade your exhaust system.)

The most popular Garland stove for the home is the six-burner model, which lists for over $1,400. You can get it from Blue Flame for 50% less. The firm also sells Garland fryers, ovens, griddles, and salamanders. It will send the Garland brochure upon request and give price quotes on anything the company makes. Blue Flame has been in business since 1945. We know several people who've ordered from the firm and they've all had the same treatment: prompt service and excellent discounts.

M.A. KNUTSEN INC.

P.O. Box 65095
West Des Moines, IA 50265
(515) 279–9075

Manufacturers' Brochures and Price Lists: $2,
   refundable
Discount: 30%
Goods: name brand
Minimum Order: $20
Shipping, Insurance: extra; UPS, PP
Sales Tax: IA deliveries
Accepts: check, MO, MC, V
$$$

Finding cookware at a discount is easy if you're buying a packaged set, but you usually have to hold out for a sale if you want open stock. If you're shopping for Cuisinart's Stainless Cookware or Calphalon, wait no longer, go straight to Knutsen and save 30% on almost everything these manufacturers carry. This includes the Cuisinart food-preparation machines, attachments, and cookbooks. Knutsen offers the same savings on Wustof Trident knives and the Baker's Advantage black steel bakeware, and will be adding more lines in the future. These are all first-quality products, for which Knutsen guarantees satisfaction and accepts returns within 30 days for exchange, refund, or credit.

PARIS INTERNATIONAL INC.

Paris Bread Pans
500 Independence Ave. S.E.
Washington, DC 20003
(202) 544–6858

Price List: free
Discount: up to 50%
Goods: house brand
Minimum Order: none
Shipping, Insurance: included
Sales Tax: DC deliveries
Accepts: check, MO, certified check
$$$$

These French bread pans are a great buy. They were designed by Clyde Brooks (the Little Old Bread Man) so he could duplicate the bread he'd eaten in France. The pans have become quite popular and are recommended in *The Cook's Catalogue*. They're made of nonstick quilted aluminum and Mr. Brooks (and a flock of his customers) assures us there is "nothing as good" for baking French bread. One set of 18″ pans makes four loaves and costs $9.95, compared to up to $20 for bread pans sold in gourmet stores.

Mr. Brooks has designed and now manufactures two other very useful items. One is the large, 18″ double-trough bread pan that holds two Italian loaves, two French bâtards, or two loaves of San Francisco sourdough bread. Mr. Brooks includes a recipe booklet that's no less than a treatise on sourdough along with the pan; the recipe alone would be worth the price of the pan ($8) to a home baker frustrated by the temperamental nature of sourdough. And you'll get more cookies into each batch if you use the "Whole Oven Baking Sheet," sized large (16″ × 20″) for 30″ stoves and smaller (16″ × 17″) for wall ovens. Any of these would make a super, inexpensive gift for someone who loves to bake.

WORLD'S FARE

P.O. Box 5678, Dept. WBM
Smithtown, NY 11787
(516) 231–0353: inquiries
(800) 972–5855: IL orders
(800) 621–5199: orders
except IL

Catalog: free; pub. Jan., Mar., Sept.
Discount: up to 20%
Goods: name brand, generic
Minimum Order: $15 on credit cards
Shipping, Insurance: $1.90 minimum; UPS
Sales Tax: NY deliveries
Accepts: check, MO, MC, V
$$

The World's Fare publishes a glossy 28-page catalog of cookware and gourmet gifts. A recent issue showed copper kitchen accents and serving pieces, aluminum stockpots and stainless fish poachers, mixing bowls, clay bakers, wok sets, the Atlas pasta machine, cappucino machines, mugs, molds, wine racks, and more. The prices are competitive and satisfaction is completely guaranteed. Returns are accepted within 30 days.

SEE ALSO:

Bondy Export Corp. . . . . Farberware cookware . . . APPLIANCES
Chanute Iron & Supply Co., Inc. . . . . Insinkerator garbage disposers . . .
   HOME (maintenance)
Clothcrafters, Inc. . . . . dish towels, pot holders, coffee filers, etc. . . . .
   GENERAL
Erewhon Trading Co. . . . . cookware . . . FOOD
Landis House . . . Pfaltzgraff bakeware . . . HOME (table settings)
The Mexican Kitchen . . . Mexican cookware . . . FOOD

Mr. Spiceman . . . cookware and kitchen gadgets . . . FOOD

Regal Greetings & Gifts, Inc. . . . kitchen helpers . . . GENERAL

Robin Importers, Inc. . . . name-brand kitchen cutlery, knife blocks, pepper mills, etc. . . . HOME (table settings)

Self-Sufficiency and Smallholding Supplies . . . kitchen implements and cookware, grain and coffee mills . . . ANIMAL

Simpson & Vail . . . tea-brewing utensils, teapots . . . FOOD

Spiegel, Inc. . . . name-brand cookware . . . GENERAL

Sultan's Delight Inc. . . . utensils for Middle Eastern cooking . . . FOOD

Whole Earth Access . . . name-brand cookware, kitchen appliances . . . GENERAL

Zabar's . . . name-brand counter appliances, cookware . . . FOOD

Linen

Bed, bath, and table textiles,
accessories, and services.

EZRA COHEN CORP.

307 Grand St.
New York, NY 10002
(212) 925–7800

Catalog: free; pub. yearly
Information: price quote by phone
Discount: 25% to 60%
Goods: name brand
Minimum Order: none
Shipping, Insurance: extra; UPS, PP
Sales Tax: NY deliveries
Accepts: check, MO, MC, V, AE
$$$$

Cohen has been selling bed and bath linens for over 50 years, and publishes a catalog for its mail-order customers. Bed linens by Wamsutta, Stevens, Martex, Cannon, Burlington, and Springmaid are available here, plus the designer lines by Dior, Katja, Laura Ashley, Bill Blass, etc. Towels by Fieldcrest, Martex, and Cannon are carried, as well as Northern Feather pillows, Dyne comforters, Dakotah bedspreads, bath carpeting, and closet organizers. Cohen offers well-priced custom services, and can make shams, dust ruffles, and sheets for round and oddly shaped beds to order.

If you don't see the product, line, size, or color you're looking for in the catalog, call for a price quote.

THE COMPANY STORE INC.

1205 S. 7th St., Dept. S
La Crosse, WI 54601
(608) 784–9522: customer service
(608) 788–9910: AK and HI orders
(800) 356–9367: orders except AK, HI

Catalog: free; pub. Jan., Mar., Aug.
Information: price quote by phone or letter with SASE
Discount: up to 50%
Goods: name brand, house brand, custom-made
Minimum Order: none
Shipping, Handling, Insurance: $2.50 and $5 per item; UPS, PP
Sales Tax: MN and WI deliveries
Accepts: check, MO, MC, V, AE
$$$

Would you believe that Gloria Vanderbilt and Bill Blass have their clothes made here? Strictly speaking, it's true—they have down jackets, coats, and robes made here which later appear in department stores for up to 50% more. The Company Store sells these, as well as down comforters and pillows, at similar savings. And the goods have quality features that bear mention.

First of all, the down *is* down, and not just feathers or a mix (unless otherwise labeled). The "loft power" is excellent—a warm 450 to 550 cubic inches per ounce. Second, the bedding fabric is a downproof cotton/polyester blend. Third, the sewing is done by machine but guided by hand, which results in a better-looking, better-made product. And the channel comforters are actually channel-stitched, a process which entails more fabric and labor but creates a bed covering relatively free of cold spots. (We know the importance of this since our editor recently purchased—and returned— a "channel-look" comforter. The channels appeared to be welded together. The fine print in the ad said the "unique process" used to create this effect was called "fusing;" we figured an acetylene torch had been employed by a blindfolded worker—the cold spots that occurred every three inches as a result of the "fusing" process were an inch wide, and the work was shoddy. The editor won a refund, as well as a time-consuming lesson in careful shopping.)

You'll have no such problems at The Company Store, the factory outlet for Gillette Industries, founded in 1911. The 20-page color catalog shows several down-comforter styles—box, channel, and ring—plus a lovely star patchwork pattern and a spring-weight comforter. Complementing pillows in baby/boudoir, butterfly, neckroll, Continental, standard, queen, and king sizes and shapes are also available.

Since washing and even dry cleaning eventually breaks the down into fiber and reduces its lofting power, you should always slipcover your comforter in a duvet to protect it from soil. The Company Store has eyelet, shirred, and classic two-color reversible duvets, with matching pillow shams to complete the ensemble.

In addition, the catalog shows a down-filled mattress pad, crib-sized comforter, and a down-filled "baby sac" with drawstring hood. Zippered vinyl storage bags, priced at $5, protect your comforter and other bedding through the summer. The Company Store is responsive to consumer needs and offers customers in frigid climates a vital service: it will add extra down to its comforters at a cost of $2 per ounce (the price as of this writing). Satisfaction is unconditionally guaranteed.

THE DOWN OUTLET

Pine St. Extension
P.O. Box 451
Nashua, NJ 03060
(603) 883–9024

Brochure: free
Discount: 25% to 35%
Goods: house brand
Minimum Order: none
Shipping, Handling, Insurance: $3.75 per order; UPS, PP
Sales Tax: MA, NH, PA deliveries
Accepts: check, MO, MC, V
$$$

After years of having manufactured down-filled products for specialty shops and department stores, The Down Outlet has gone retail. You can get the same well-made, high-quality comforters (under the "Nimbus" label) and outerwear, and save up to 35% by ordering directly from the factory.

The comforters are made in twin, full/queen, and king sizes, in regular fill for rooms kept above 62 degrees and "super" for chillier environments. They're channel-constructed in downproof ecru cotton and finished with piped edges. Every comforter is guaranteed for ten years against defects in construction or workmanship. Zippered cotton/poly duvets are available in two reversible color combinations, from $37 to $59 each.

Take the warmth with you when you get out of bed with the Down Outlet's vest ($39), Taslan pullover ($29), and heavy-duty parka. Each is made in an assortment of colors and sizes.

The Down Outlet guarantees your satisfaction and will accept returns within 30 days for exchange, refund, or credit.

DOWN TOWN

P.O. Box 271
Kenilworth, IL 60043
(800) 323–6556: IL orders
(800) 942–6345: orders
except IL

Catalog: free
Discount: 10% to 50%
Goods: generic
Minimum Order: none
Shipping, Insurance: extra; UPS, PP
Sales Tax: IL deliveries
Accepts: check, MO, MC, V
$$

Down Town stocks the things you need to make your long winter nights soft and cozy. Down-filled pillows and comforters, and Portuguese flannel sheets are all available at prices up to 50% less than those charged in department stores for comparable products. Satisfaction is guaranteed.

**DREAMY DOWN
FASHIONS, INC.**

287 W. Butterfield Rd.
Elmhurst, IL 60126
(312) 941–3840: inquiries
and IL, AK, HI orders
(800) 222–3696: orders
except IL, AK, HI

Catalog: free; pub. 4 times yearly
Discount: 45% to 55%
WBMC Reader Savings: free shipping on U.S.
  deliveries
Goods: house brand
Minimum Order: none
Shipping, Insurance: $3.50 to $7; UPS, PP
Sales Tax: IL deliveries
Accepts: check, MO, MC, V, AE (see text)
$$

If you've ever shopped seriously for a down comforter, you know that the range of fills, fabrics, and construction methods, and the consequent variations in price, can be bewildering. It's often hard to determine whether the price comparisons made in ads are really legitimate.

Dreamy Down sells comforters, pillows, and bed linens at prices 45% to 55% below comparable retail. Having evaluated the products by description, we concur with the firm's estimate: these pillows and comforters can be fairly compared to those by Dyne and other good labels.

The "Elan" style is filled with white goose down (38 ounces, full size; 550-plus fill power) and has an all-cotton cover of 200-plus threads-per-square-inch, tightly corded edges, etc. It's $249, with a comparable value of $390. The "Aristocrat," filled with duck down, has 450-plus fill power, and is covered in box-stitched, downproof poly/cotton. "Naturally" is described as a "feather bed, a European tradition." It's an all-cotton, channel-stitched comforter filled with a feather-down mix. (The brochure shows this being used as a covering; however, the traditional feather bed was slept *upon,* with a down or eiderdown comforter on top.) Other styles and fills are shown in the 16-page catalog; most are offered in a range of tasteful colors. Pillows with the same kinds of fills are offered, as well as shams, dust ruffles, and duvets. The stunning hand-painted duvets, shams, and accessories by Louise Justin shouldn't be missed.

Past catalogs have included some interesting asides on the history and care of quilts. One of the most intriguing is the recommendation that you air your comforter after a summer thunderstorm. It's believed that the ozone in the air restores the lanolin around the down, which keeps it from drying out and breaking down. It's certainly worth a try.

The comforters carry warranties of three to ten years (terms unspecified), and all purchases are covered by a guarantee of satisfaction. Returns are accepted within 30 days for full refunds. If you're having goods delivered within the continental U.S., you are entitled to free shipping. You must identify yourself as a WBMC reader to qualify for these savings. And if you're having your order delivered by Parcel Post, you must pay by check or money order—not by credit card.

CANADIAN READERS, PLEASE NOTE: Payment must be made by check or money order, and you must pay shipping charges.

ELDRIDGE TEXTILE CO.

**277 Grand St.
New York, NY 10002
(212) 925–1523**

Information: price quote by phone or letter with SASE
Discount: 30% to 40%
Goods: name brand
Minimum Order: none
Shipping: extra; UPS
Sales Tax: NY deliveries
Accepts: check, MO, MC, V
$$$

Knowing you can get them at discounts of 30% to 40% makes sheets seem somehow smoother, towels fluffier, pillows softer. Eldridge can provide a complete range of bed, bath, and table lines at these savings, from top manufacturers. The list includes Cannon, Fieldcrest, Martex, Dakotah, Jabara, Utica, Sunweave, Springmaid, Croscill, Dan River, Crowncrafts, Wamsutta, Curtron, Burlington, Howard, Jackson, Saturday Knight, and many others. Wallpaper and window treatments are also stocked. Call or write (include a SASE), stating the manufacturer's name, style number, color, and size of what you want for a price quote. Returns are accepted on unused items for refund or credit. Eldridge has been selling soft goods and housewares since 1939, and takes special orders for items not in current stock.

HARRIS LEVY

278 Grand St.
New York, NY 10002
(212) 226–3102: inquiries
and NY orders
(800) 221–7750: orders
except NY

Information: price quote by phone or letter with SASE
Discount: 25% to 40%
Goods: name brand, imported, custom made
Minimum Order: $15 on credit cards
Shipping: extra; UPS
Sales Tax: NY deliveries
Accepts: check, MO, MC, V
$$$

Levy is one of the plums of New York's Lower East Side—a firm that sells the crème de la crème of bed, bath, and table linens at savings of up to 40%.

The discounted luxe includes Egyptian percale and linen sheets, Belgian crash towels, Irish damask tablecloths, and bed coverings from Switzerland, England, France, and Italy of a quality usually reserved for trousseaux. The major mills are also represented in the bed and bath departments—Springmaid, Dan River, Martex, Wamsutta, Fieldcrest, Burlington, and Stevens are among the brands stocked. Levy's is also known for its custom services, which include monogramming, special sizing or shaping of sheets, and tablecloths, dust ruffles, curtains, pillow cases, and similar goods made to order in the sheeting of your choice or your own fabric.

If you'd like a price quote on goods from a major manufacturer, call or write, and give the name of the mill, style number, color, size, etc. If you want to know Levy's prices on imported goods, either describe what you're looking for, or, if you've seen the item in another catalog, send the page with your inquiry. Levy is purveyor to a number of New York's rich and famous as well as to countless mortals who crave the best for less. It can be relied upon to deliver quality goods at the right price.

RUBIN & GREEN INC.

290 Grand St.
New York, NY 10002
(212) 226–0313

Information: price quote by phone or letter with SASE
Discount: 30% to 40%
Goods: name brand
Minimum Order: $5
Shipping, Insurance: extra; UPS
Sales Tax: NY deliveries
Accepts: check or MO
$$$

Rubin & Green carries a wide selection of bed, bath, and table linens by Wamsutta, Burlington, Martex, and Springmaid at discounts of up to 40%. The firm also sells bath carpeting by Carter, shower curtains from Bloomcraft, pillows, Faribo blankets, comforters, napkins, tablecloths, and more. Call or write (include a SASE) for a price quote; be sure to state the manufacturer, line, color or pattern, and size of the goods you're pricing.

ST. PATRICK'S DOWN

St. Patrick's Mills
Douglas, Cork
Ireland
Phone # 21–931110

Catalog: $1; pub. in the spring and fall
Discount: up to 70%
Goods: house brand, handcrafted
Minimum Order: none
Shipping, Insurance: extra, itemized; fastmail
Duty: extra
Accepts: check, IMO, MC, V, AE, DC, Access
$$$

It's taken St. Patrick's Mills over 200 years to assemble a catalog, but that's probably because the craftspeople who run the firm have been too busy working to fuss with layout or negotiate with printers. The catalog is one of the quainter stock lists we've seen in a while, embellished as it is with softly colored family scenes, lambs, robins, wisteria, and shamrocks.

Perhaps the most impressive article here, from an engineering standpoint, is the Honeycomb Quilt, a channel comforter with interior *latitudinal* baffles which help keep the down from shifting to the ends of the quilt. (This is a problem with standard channel design.) They're anchored within the quilt to one side only, so they're not airtight cubes of down—this would reduce the lofting power and consequently the warmth. Three fill choices are offered— feather and down, duck down, and goose down—and four sizes. Prices range from $68 (twin, feather/down fill) to $227 (king, goose down). Summer-weight and crib-sized comforters are also available. The comforters are made of all-cotton cambric; duvets in a linen/cotton blend are offered in several muted color combinations. A stunning log-cabin patchwork comforter and coordinating wall hangings, throw pillows, and other accents are shown, as well as linen-blend sheets, down pillows, nightshirts, feather beds and wool underlays (for sleeping *upon*), table linens, Aran sweaters, and down-filled sleeping bags, anoraks, and vests.

When the catalog was reviewed, St. Patrick's Down was offering several bonuses with orders of certain lines; a patchwork duvet, Cross pen or pencil, and Aran sweater (sold for $85) were the incentives. A friend who ordered from the company's first catalog received such a gift, so the program may be still in existence—but if it isn't mentioned in the catalog you receive, please don't request it. The prices are excellent, and some items—the feather beds, linen blend sheets, and crib-sized down comforters with duvets—are not easily found in the U.S. PLEASE NOTE: Do not ask for special discounts!

J. SCHACHTER CORP.

115 Allen St.
New York, NY 10002
(212) 533–1150, 1151, 1152

Catalog: $1, refundable; pub. yearly
Information: price quote by phone or letter with
 SASE
Discount: 20% to 50%
Goods: name brand, house brand, custom-made
Minimum Order: $35 on credit cards
Shipping, Insurance: extra; UPS, PP
Sales Tax: NY deliveries
Accepts: check, MO, MC, V, AE
$$$

Schachter has been making comforters and pillows for the bedding industry, and recovering old comforters for private customers since 1919. The services and custom-made goods are its mainstay. They include comforters, coverlettes, bed ruffles, pillow shams, duvets, and shower curtains. ("Coverlettes" are slightly longer and wider than comforters, and lighter as well—warmer than a blanket cover but lightweight enough for summer use.)

The 16-page color catalog lists prices for sizes and fillings for the bed covers. Filling choices include lambswool, polyester, white goose down, and Neither Doun polyester (a nonallergenic, synthetic alternative to down). All prices for the C.O.M. (customer's own material) goods are exclusive of fabric charges.

In addition to custom services, Schachter sells finished goods—sheets from Wamsutta, Cannon and Martex bath linens, Carter cotton bath rugs and accessories, Northern Feather pillows and Dyne comforters, Hudson

Bay blankets, goods by Dan River and Avanti, Schachter's own comforters and accessories, and more.

For prices on goods or services not listed in the catalog, call or write for a price quote. Include a SASE with your letter.

SHORLAND TEXTILE CO.

274 Grand St.
New York, NY 10002
(212) 226–0228

Information: price quote by phone or letter with SASE
Discount: 25% to 40%
Goods: name brand
Minimum Order: none
Shipping: extra; UPS
Sales Tax: NY deliveries
Accepts: check, MO, MC, V
$$$

Shorland has been selling domestic linens for 63 years, and offers bed and bath linens by Fieldcrest, Springmaid, Martex, Wamsutta, Dan River, and other major mills at prices up to 40% below suggested retail. Price quotes are given by phone or letter (include a SASE), and returns are accepted on unused goods for refund or credit.

SEE ALSO:

Cambridge Wools, Ltd. . . . wool blankets, sheepskin bed covers . . . CRAFTS
Clothcrafters, Inc. . . . cotton place mats and napkins, flannel sheets, towels, shower curtains . . . GENERAL
Gohn Bros. . . . sheets, blankets, towels . . . CLOTHING
Gurian Fabrics Inc. . . . crewel tablecloths, bedspreads . . . HOME (decor)
Handart Embroideries . . . hand-worked table linens, towels, bed linens, satin sheets . . . CLOTHING
Irish Cottage Industries Ltd. . . . tweed table mats, throws, cushions . . . CLOTHING
Kennedy of Ardara . . . tartan blankets, throws, double-damask table linens, etc. . . . CLOTHING
Laurence Corner . . . government-surplus blankets, sheets . . . CLOTHING
D. MacGillivray & Coy. . . . Scottish wood bedspreads . . . CRAFTS
Prince Fashions Ltd. . . . hand-worked table linens . . . CLOTHING

Quilts Unlimited . . . antique, old, custom-made quilts . . . ART, ANTIQUES

Rammagerdin . . . Lopi blankets, throws . . . CRAFTS

Robin Importers . . . Carefree table linens . . . HOME (table settings)

Rubens Babywear Factory . . . bassinet, crib sheets . . . CLOTHING

Shama Imports, Inc. . . . crewel tablecloths, bedspreads . . . HOME (decor)

Shannon Mail Order . . . wool blankets, plaid throws, damask and lace table linens . . . HOME (table settings)

Thai Silks . . . embroidered Chinese table linens . . . CRAFTS

Whole Earth Access . . . wool blankets, down comforters . . . GENERAL

Irv Wolfson Company . . . foreign-current electric blankets . . . APPLIANCES

Workmen's Garment Co. . . . small selection Cannon, generic bath and dish towels . . . CLOTHING

Maintenance

Hardware, tools, equipment, supplies, and materials.

ARCTIC GLASS SUPPLY, INC.

Rte. 1-W, Box 157
Spring Valley, WI 54767
(715) 639–3762

Catalog: $2, refundable; pub. in the spring and fall
Discount: 40% to 60%
WBMC Reader Discount: 5% to 10% on quantity
  prices (see text)
Goods: name brand, seconds
Minimum Order: none
Shipping, Insurance: extra; FOB Spring Valley
Sales Tax: WI deliveries
Accepts: MO, certified check, MC, V
$$$$

Before you begin any construction job, you sit down and cost out the materials, right? When Joseph Bacon began building his passive solar greenhouse six years ago, he overlooked one expense—the double-glazed thermopane panels. Mr. Bacon and his family had already framed the greenhouse when he started pricing the glass, and he was shocked to learn that the bill would be close to $3,000. He finally located the factory that manufactures glass for Marvin and Andersen patio doors, and purchased second-quality panels for a total of $900. They filled the bill, and Mr. Bacon realized that what had worked for him could work for others with the same needs, and Arctic Glass Supply was born.

Although the glass is actually replacement patio door panels, it's been used for everything from underground homes to gas stations to solar outhouses. Arctic sells double and triple panes with ¼″ air spaces, and sometimes stocks panels with ½″ spaces (these have a 10% better U value than the ¼″ space panels). The fact that the glass is second-quality doesn't affect its performance—all panels are guaranteed against leakage or failure for ten years. They're constructed of ³⁄₁₆″ glass and double-sealed, so you won't be looking at the world through a fog in five years as you might with single-seal glass. Information on installation is included in the brochure, plus full details on the manufacturers' warranties.

The prices here are up to 60% less than those charged for first-quality panes. The Bacons offer quantity discounts of 5% on purchases of 20 panes or more; 10% on orders of 40 or more. If you identify yourself as a WBMC reader when ordering, you can deduct an additional 5% and 10%, respectively, for the same number of panes. Crating charges to major cities are listed in the brochure. The Bacons guarantee your satisfaction and accept returns within 30 days for refund or credit. This is an excellent way to save hundreds of dollars if you're remodeling or building, and you'll wind up using better-quality materials for a fraction of the price. Arctic's panes are also ideal alternatives to costly solar panels, and the brochure includes particulars on retrofitting and installations that will help you decide whether they're suitable for your needs.

CHANUTE IRON & SUPPLY CO., INC.

402 N. Malcolm
Chanute, KS 66720
(316) 431–9290

Information: price quote by phone or letter with SASE
Discount: 25% to 50%
Goods: name brand
Minimum Order: none
Shipping, Insurance: extra; UPS, PP, FOB Chanute
Sales Tax: KS deliveries
Accepts: check, MO, certified check
$$$

You can save up to 50% on a variety of plumbing supplies, fixtures, and tools through Chanute Iron & Supply, which has been in operation since 1941. Chanute carries Delta faucets, Insinkerator garbage disposers, Wayne pumps, Miami Carey medicine chests and accessories, Aqua Glass whirlpools and fiberglass tubs and showers, Crane fixtures, swimming pool supplies and chemicals, and tools by Rigid, Kline, and the professional line by Black & Decker. Replacement parts for every type of faucet are also stocked. Get the manufacturers's model number or the name of the item you're pricing, and call or write Chanute for a quote.

PLASTIC BAGMART

400 Maple Ave.
Westbury, NY 11590
(516) 997–3355

Price List: free; pub. yearly
Information: price quote by letter with SASE
Discount: 40% to 60%
Goods: generic
Minimum Order: none
Shipping, Insurance: $2 per case west of the
   Mississippi River; UPS
Sales Tax: NY deliveries
Accepts: check, MO, certified check
$$$

What was life like before plastic bags? We don't remember, and can't imagine coping with leftovers or trash without them. Suffice it to say plastic bags have wide applications in homes, offices, and industries, so saving some money on these frequently used items can add up to significant sums in the long run. The Plastic BagMart carries bags in sizes that run from 2″×3″ to 43″×46″ and are stocked in one to four mil thicknesses. (The brochure states that evaluating bags on the basis of the number of mils may not be accurate, since new high-stretch plastics provide the strength of a higher mil measurement in a thinner product.) In any case, there are garbage and trash cleanup bags, kitchen and office wastebasket bags, food-storage bags, large industrial-type bags, "zip" top styles, and plastic shopping bags. Prices run to 60% lower on per-bag costs than those charged by supermarkets and office-supply firms. You'll have to buy by the case, which may be 100 to 1,000 bags, depending on the size. It may seem like a lot if you've been buying them in packs of 15 and 20, but don't let that keep you from saving some money; remember, you'll use them eventually. All of BagMart's products are covered by a money-back guarantee. Returns are accepted within 15 days for exchange, refund, or credit.

PROTECTO-PAK

P.O. Box 5096, Dept. A
Longview, TX 75608
(214) 297–3985; 757–6092

Price List and Sample: $2, refundable; pub. in
   June and Dec.
Information: price quote by letter with SASE
Discount: 35%
Goods: house brand
Minimum Order: $10
Shipping, Insurance: $1.50 minimum; UPS
Sales Tax: TX deliveries
Accepts: check, MO, certified check
$$$

Protecto-Pak manufactures "zip" top heavy-duty plastic bags in stock sizes from $2'' \times 3''$ to $13'' \times 15''$. Because the seal makes them relatively airtight, they're great space-saving alternatives to bulky containers and heavier storage units. We store our herb and spice reserves in this kind of bag; packed in a light-proof tin, they occupy a fraction of the cabinet space of half-filled jars and canisters. The zip-top bags are also useful for storing crafts supplies (yarns and flosses stay pristine and untangled in them), spare parts from furniture kits, polished silverware (wrapped in cloth), buttons and surplus trims for different garments, tobacco, daily doses of vitamins and dietary supplements, office supplies, photographs, hosiery (nylons stay snag-free in suitcases and drawers), hardware, and so on. Special sizes and thicknesses are available, and Protecto-Pak can have bags printed to order (minimum 10,000). All the bags are approved for food storage and quantity discounts are given on case purchases (1,000 bags).

THE RENOVATOR'S SUPPLY, INC.

5503 Renovator's Old Mill Millers Falls, MA 01349 (413) 659–3773

Catalog: $2; $5, 3-year subscription; pub. Jan., May, July, Sept., Nov.
Discount: up to 70%
Goods: name brand, house brand, generic
Minimum Order: none
Shipping, Insurance: included on orders over $20; UPS, PP
Handling: $2 on orders under $20
Sales Tax: CT, MA, NY deliveries
Accepts: check, MO, MC, V
$$$

If you've ever had to outfit an old home with new hardware, or wanted fixtures and brasses that didn't *look* new, you know why Renovator's Supply is a source cherished by many homeowners. Renovator's carries everything from the front doorbell to the back-door bolt, at prices that can run to 70% less than comparable retail, depending on the quantity purchased.

The current catalog shows iron, brass, and porcelain bath hardware and plumbing fixtures; oak bathroom accessories; drawer, window, and door hardware of every era in brass, porcelain, and iron; lighting fixtures of every sort; glass lamp shades; wall plates; copper lanterns and weathervanes, wrought-iron door knockers and latches, hinges, screws, sash hardware, bolts, fireplace tools, grills, candle holders, and even candle molds; as well as things like tin and copper matchboxes, pierced tin lamp shades and candle boxes, brass candlesticks, and embossed leather replacement chair seats.

Since it's not likely that you'll purchase a dozen brass-and-porcelain bathroom faucets or 500 fleur-de-lis cabinet knobs at one time, you should combine orders with friends and neighbors to get the best quantity prices possible. If you need just one item, console yourself with the thought that single-item prices at Renovator's are a good 10% to 20% below those charged by other firms for the same type of goods. Satisfaction is guaranteed, and returns are accepted within 30 days for refund or credit.

SOUTHEASTERN INSULATED GLASS

**6477B Peachtree Ind. Blvd.
Atlanta, GA 30360
(404) 455–8838: inquiries
and GA orders
(800) 841–9842: orders
except GA**

Catalog: $1, refundable; pub. yearly
Discount: 50%
Goods: house brand
Minimum Order: none
Shipping, Insurance: extra; FOB Atlanta
Sales Tax: GA deliveries
Accepts: check, MO, certified check, MC, V
$$

Southeastern manufactures insulated (thermopane) glass panels and skylights, and can sell them to you at factory-direct prices 50% below list. The panels, ⅛″ tempered glass with ¾″ air spaces, can be used for greenhouses, grow frames, porch enclosures, storm windows, etc. They are sold sealed and unframed, in sizes running up to 46″ × 90″. The skylights are sold completely assembled in aluminum frames, ready for installation. Both the panels and the skylights are stocked in plain and bronze-tinted glass, and butyl flashing tape, glazing tape, butyl caulking compound, and setting blocks are also available.

Southeastern's literature includes illustrations of existing applications and installation details for a solarium roof and window wall. The panels and skylights are warrantied, but improper installation or use of incompatible sealants will void the guarantee. Read the material carefully and make sure you'll be able to comply with the warranty conditions before you order.

SEE ALSO:

AAA All Factory, Inc. . . . name-brand vacuum cleaners, floor machines, rug shampooers, ceiling fans . . . APPLIANCES

ABC Vacuum Cleaner Warehouse . . . name-brand vacuum cleaners . . . APPLIANCES

Alfax Mfg. . . . trash can liners . . . OFFICE

American Vacuum & Sewing Machine Corp. . . . name-brand vacuum cleaners, supplies . . . APPLIANCES

The Bedpost, Inc. . . . hot tubs . . . HOME (furnishings)

Bondy Export Corp. . . . name-brand vacuum cleaners . . . APPLIANCES

Clothcrafters, Inc. . . . mosquito netting, flannel polishing cloths . . . GENERAL

Grayarc . . . trash bags, wipes, door mats, etc. . . . . OFFICE

Greater New York Trading Co. . . . Hoover, Eureka vacuum cleaners . . . HOME (table settings)

Great Tracers . . . custom-made name stencils . . . CRAFTS

Harry's Discounts & Appliances Corp . . . name-brand vacuum cleaners . . . APPLIANCES

Mid America Vacuum Cleaner Supply Co. . . . name-brand vacuum cleaners, floor machines, parts, attachments; small appliance parts . . . APPLIANCES

Oreck Corp. . . . Oreck vacuums, floor machines . . . APPLIANCES

Percy's Inc. . . . name-brand garbage disposals . . . APPLIANCES

R.D. Associates . . . energy-saving devices . . . TOOLS

Sewin' in Vermont . . . name-brand vacuum cleaners . . . APPLIANCES

Sunco Products Corp. . . . protective gloves . . . CLOTHING

Table Settings

China, crystal, glass, flatware, woodenware, and related goods.

A. BENJAMIN & CO., INC.

**80–82 Bowery
New York, NY 10013
(212) 226–6013**

Information: price quote by phone or letter with SASE
Discount: 25% to 75%
Goods: name brand
Minimum Order: $50 on some types of goods
Shipping: extra; UPS
Sales Tax: NY deliveries
Accepts: check, MO, certified check
$$$

A. Benjamin has been selling top brands in china, glassware and crystal, flatware (stainless to sterling), and giftware since 1944. (Benjamin also sells diamonds and jewelry, though not by mail.) A sample of the extensive list of brands carried includes Noritake, Mikasa, Franciscan, Gorham, Reed & Barton, Wallace, Lunt, International, Oneida, Towle, and Supreme.

All of Benjamin's mail-order business is done on a price-quote basis, and the owner asks that you mention WBMC when you call or write. Since the firm stocks so much merchandise, if you're shopping for anything in the way of name-brand stemware, china, silver, or giftware you should call or write to see whether it's stocked and get a price quote. Don't forget to include model or style numbers, suite or pattern names, piece descriptions or measurements, and colors when you write. And be sure to enclose a SASE with the letter.

CANADIAN READERS, PLEASE NOTE: Benjamin tells us it will ship to you if you give a U.S. address (presumably for forwarding). We suggest that you write to the firm for information if you're serious about ordering.

EMERALD

---

184 High St.
Boston, MA 02110
(617) 423–7645
Ballingeary
County Cork
Ireland

Catalog: free; pub. several times yearly
Discount: up to 50%
Goods: name brand, generic, handcrafted
Minimum Order: $20 on credit cards
Shipping, Insurance: extra; itemized
Duty: extra
Accepts: check, MO, MC, V, AE, Access
$$$

Irish whimsy taken to the ultimate power could produce a Celtic cross of compressed Irish peat. At Emerald, it can and does—but this source should really be noted for its prices and selection in the china and crystal departments.

The focus at Emerald is on things Irish, including Waterford crystal, walking sticks, and an extensive line of Belleck china in a variety of place settings and decorative pieces. Wedgwood and Royal Doulton are stocked as well. Emerald carries the Beswick Beatrix Potter figurines by Royal Doulton, Aynsley's Teddleybears nurseryware, Wedgwood's Peter Rabbit lamps and table settings, and the beloved Bunnykins line by Royal Doulton. Figurines by Goebel, Border Fine Arts, Royal Doulton, Irish Dresden, Lladro, Belleek, and Hummel were shown in the 16-page color catalog we received.

The best buys are on Waterford stemware and decorative pieces, and the aforementioned lines of gifts and collectibles. Prices run to 50% less than those charged in U.S. department stores. What's more, most of Emerald's prices have remained constant or have dropped from last year's catalog, and adjustments are made for the stronger dollar. (This is not done in any U.S. catalogs we've seen—in fact, prices have *risen* on the same imported goods by up to 20% in domestic catalogs.)

Emerald has established a "Collectors' Club," a real bonanza of benefits that are well worth the $10 membership fee. Among other things, you'll receive newsletters filled with bargain offers and information, advance copies of the catalogs and mailings, and $50 in discount coupons to be applied against orders. Details are given in the catalog.

Although orders are sent from Ireland, Emerald has an agent in Boston who dispatches catalogs and forwards orders (saving you a little postage). As always, your satisfaction is guaranteed. Returns are accepted but must be authorized; procedures are outlined in package enclosures. Emerald has been doing business by mail since 1963, and has been recommended for its service and low prices by a number of readers.

FORTUNOFF

Direct Sales Division
P.O. Box 1550
Westbury, NY 11590
(212) 671–9300: inquiries
and NY orders
(516) 294–3300: inquiries
and NY orders
(800) 344–3449: orders
except NY

Catalog: $2, pub. twice yearly
Information: price quote by phone
Discount: up to 50%
Goods: name brand
Minimum Order: none
Shipping, Insurance: extra; UPS, PP
Sales Tax: NJ and NY deliveries
Accepts: check, MO, MC, V, AE, CB, DC
$$$

Those who know this company may well ask why Fortunoff is listed here rather than with other jewelry firms since it is renowned for its staggering array of costume, fine, and fashion jewelry. Fortunoff does indeed sell jewelry and features a tempting selection at competitive prices in its catalogs. Intermittent flyers highlight specials and sales. But it's listed here because the company runs a continuous sale on fine flatware and has boasted that its sterling prices are "unbeatable."

If you're planning to take the investment plunge or are shopping for silver plate or stainless-steel flatware, you'll find savings of up to 50% (and more when there's a special sale) on lines by Oneida, Towle, Reed & Barton, Kirk-Stieff, Lunt, International, and other companies. Serving pieces and giftware by these firms are also stocked. The catalogs devote most of their pages to jewelry. We recommend calling for a price quote on the flatware for your best price.

THE GAILIN COLLECTION

P.O. Box 53921
Fayetteville, NC 28305
(919) 864–7372: NC price
quotes
(800) 334–5698: price
quotes except NC

Information: price quote by phone or letter with
 SASE
Discount: 35% to 55%
Goods: name brand
Minimum Order: varies on goods; $200 on credit
 cards
Shipping, Insurance: extra; UPS, PP, FOB, U.S.
 port
Sales Tax: NC deliveries
Accepts: check, MO, MC, V
$$ 🍁

Gailin tells us that "nobody in the country can match our prices" on English and French china and crystal, or Strass chandeliers from Germany. Gailin doesn't *stock* goods; it acts as an agent, placing your order with European suppliers who ship the goods directly to you. Because Gailin actually processes the payment, it is considered the "seller," and this subjects your transaction to protective laws that don't apply to your dealings with foreign firms.

China by Coalport, Aynsley, Crown Staffordshire, Royal Crown Derby, Minton, Spode, Royal Worcester, Wedgwood, and Haviland, Raynaud, Bernardaud, and Parlon Limoges is available; crystal from Baccarat, St. Louis, Waterford, Edinburgh, and Stuart can be ordered. Gailin can also save you about 33% on Strass crystal chandeliers, and offers English brass beds. These are reproductions of antiques made of solid cast brass, and Gailin feels they "could not be found in this country at twice the price."

You may call or write for prices on the products you want, and Gailin will send you a complete, written price quote which includes shipping costs. The quotes are valid for ten days. Complete ordering, payment, shipping, and liability terms are given with the order form. Please note that beds are delivered to the port of your choice, and sent overland freight (collect) to you. Gailin charges $75 to clear customs for you, asks you to prepay duty, and then sees that the goods are freighted to you. (If you live near or in the port city, you may want to assume these responsibilities yourself and save the clearance fee.)

Returns of the "second thoughts" variety are not accepted. Goods are guaranteed to be first-quality, and breakage and damage are compensated by the carrier's insurance. Defective beds will be repaired or replaced, as Gailin sees fit.

GERED

173/174 Piccadilly
London W1V OPD
England
Phone # 734–7262

Catalog: free
Discount: up to 50%
Goods: name brand
Minimum Order: none
Shipping, Insurance: extra; surface mail, airmail
Duty: extra
Accepts: check, IMO, MC, V, AE, DC
$$$

Gered is the source of choice for anyone setting a table in Wedgwood or Spode china. This company carries full lines by both firms, a sampling of which is shown in the 12-page color catalog. The accompanying price list catalogs the remainder of the inventory. With savings running up to 50% on an incomparable selection, Gered is the place to check prices before buying elsewhere.

GREATER NEW YORK TRADING CO.

81 Canal St.
New York, NY 10002
(212) 226–2808; 2809, 8850

List of Brands: free with SASE; pub. twice yearly
Information: price quote by phone or letter with SASE
Discount: 20% to 60%
Goods: name brand
Minimum Order: on some items
Shipping, Handling, Insurance: extra; UPS, PP
Sales Tax: NY deliveries
Accepts: check, MO, certified check
$$$

If you're shopping for a large or small appliance, TV, typewriter, vacuum cleaner, or china, crystal, or flatware, write or call the Greater New York Trading Co. This firm carries appliances by Amana, G.E., Hotpoint, Frigidaire, Kitchenaid, Tappan, Magic Chef, Litton, Roper, Whirlpool, White-Westinghouse, and Caloric; TV and video equipment from Sony, Zenith, Panasonic, Hitachi, Toshiba, RCA, Quasar, Sylvania, G.E., and M.G.A.; typewriters by Olivetti, SCM, Olympia, Adler, and Hermes; and vacuum cleaners by Hoover and Eureka.

Greater New York is also known for its extensive tableware department. The china lines run from Aynsley to Wedgwood, and include Bernardaud Limoges, Franciscan, Ginori, Hutschenreuther, Lenox, Mikasa, Minton, Portmeiron, Rosenthal, Spode, the Royals—Copenhagen, Doulton, and

Worcester—and more. Crystal from Avitra, Baccarat, Val St. Lambert, Galway, Kosta Boda, Stuart, Orrefors, and other firms is available. Silverware (from stainless to sterling) by Christofle, Kirk-Stieff, Lunt, Oneida, Towle, Tuttle, Wallace, Reed & Barton, Georg Jensen, International, Gorham, Rogers, and other companies is offered as well. And if you or someone on your gift list collects figurines by Lladro or Royal Doulton, don't buy elsewhere before getting a price quote from this firm.

Greater New York Trading has flourished on the business of shrewd New Yorkers, who know a discount (up to 50%) when they see one. A half-century in business has taught the owners that you don't waste time or money on frills, like expensive catalogs. The somewhat inky list of brands they sent us does not state prices—you must call or write (include a SASE) for a quote. Be specific in indicating the *quantity* of goods you're planning to purchase, as well as the standard pattern, suite, piece, and color information.

LANDIS HOUSE

**132 E. Main St., Dept. A
Palmyra, PA 17078
(717) 838–6134**

Brochures: $1, refundable
Discount: 20% to 39%
Goods: name brand
Minimum Order: $15 on credit cards
Shipping, Insurance: $2.50 to 8% of order value;
   20% on orders to AK and Canada; 30% to HI;
   UPS, PP
Sales Tax: PA deliveries
Accepts: check, MO, MC, V
$$

Pfaltzgraff produces the sort of tableware and crockery we think of as "user-friendly"—simple, traditional designs in sturdy, thick stoneware that won't have you praying every time the children clear the table. The Pfaltzgraff company is planted in the heart of Pennsylvania Dutch territory and has been turning out pottery since 1811. Its current production includes dinnerware, glassware, serving pieces, bakeware, and a range of accessories and decorative pieces. The designs are inspired by Americana, from the salt-glaze look of "Yorktowne" to "The Americana Collection," which combines the coloring of yelloware with sponged quilt motifs and decorations. There are several other patterns, including an appealing Christmas-tree design, and the all-white "Heritage." The latter echoes the shape of antique serving pieces, but is simple enough to work with just about any style and decor.

All designs and glazes are hand-applied, and the stoneware is chip-resistant and safe in the dishwasher, microwave, and conventional oven. Each piece is warranted by Pfaltzgraff for one year against defects in workmanship or materials.

Landis House sells first-quality Pfaltzgraff at 20% off list prices. The color brochures show all the pieces for each line, and a complete list of suggested retail prices is included. If you buy dinnerware sets at the Landis discount, you're actually saving up to 39% on the suggested list prices of the individual pieces. Landis backs the Pfaltzgraff warranty with its own guarantee of complete satisfaction.

PLEASE NOTE: shipments to Alaska, Hawaii, and Canada are charged 20% or 30% on the value of the goods.

REJECT CHINA SHOPS

**13 Silver Rd., Wood Lane
London W12 75G
England
Phone # 01–749–9191**

Catalog: $3; pub. yearly
Information: price quote by phone or letter
Discount: 25% to 70%
Goods: name brand
Minimum Order: none (see text)
Shipping, Insurance: included on most goods (see text)
Duty: extra
Accepts: certified check, IMO, MC, V, AE, CB, DC, Access
$$$$

No bargain-hunter's trip to London is complete without a stop at one of the Reject China Shops. We've been to the store in the posh Knightsbridge section and can tell you that there is a better selection in the mail-order department! Now that you've just saved yourself round-trip air fare, why not use the money to treat yourself to a new set of china? And with the funds you've saved on *that,* how about some choice crystal stemware?

You don't have to use "I Love Lucy" logic to justify buying here—Reject's prices are a good 25% to 70% below U.S. list. (Reject's own estimate was 25% to 50%; our comparisons showed savings of up to 70% on some items, though most are priced 30% to 55% below domestic retail.) The handsome color catalog shows bone china, porcelain, stoneware, dinnerware and gifts by Belleek, Caverswall, Price & Kensington, Portmeirion, Adams, Aynsley, Burgess and Leigh, Coalport, Denby, Masons, Gien, Hornsea, Johnson Brothers, Bernardaud Limoges, Midwinter, Palissy, Paragon, Poole Pottery, Royal Albert, Royal Grafton, Royal Worcester, Spode, T.G. Green, and Villeroy & Boch; and crystal giftware and stems by Waterford, Webb Corbett, Tyrone, Atlantis, Baccarat, Daum, Edinburgh, St. Louis, and Stuart. This is not a complete list, and the catalog shows just a sampling of the patterns and suites made by these firms.

Shipping and insurance charges are included in the cost of dinnerware and stemware if you order a minimum of four place settings or eight glasses (smaller orders are assessed a $10 surcharge). Most of the giftware and other items are charged an additional shipping fee. Prepaid orders must be made in pounds sterling, and all goods are sent on a final-sale basis. (Replacements are given for items broken in transit.) The firm says that its "worldwide reputation is your guarantee of satisfaction." PLEASE NOTE: All exported goods are first-quality.

ROBIN IMPORTERS, INC.

510 Madison Ave.
New York, NY 10022
(212) 752–5605; 753–6475:
inquiries and NY orders
(800) 223–3373: orders
except NY

Brochure: free with SASE; pub. in the spring and fall
Information: price quote by phone or letter with SASE
Discount: 20% to 60%
Goods: name brand
Minimum Order: none
Shipping: extra; UPS
Sales Tax: NY deliveries
Accepts: check, MO, MC, V, AE, CB, DC
$$$$

Don't buy a fork, snifter, soup bowl, or paring knife before checking with Robin. In addition to offering an exhaustive stock that includes the best names in fine china, stoneware, 18/8 stainless-steel flatware, crystal and glass stemware, and kitchen cutlery, Robin sells at 20% to 60% off the suggested retail prices.

The color brochures we received showed examples of the lines—place settings, flatware patterns, stemware, figurines, cutlery, serving utensils, and gadgets—but are only representative of stock. China by Adams, Arabia, Arita Arzberg, Bernardaud Limoges, Block, Coalport, Denby, Fitz and Floyd, Franciscan, Giraux Limoges, Heinrich, Hornsea, Hutschenreuther, Lenox, Mikasa, Queensware, Rauchart, Raynaud Ceralene Limoges, Rosenthal, Royal Worcester, Spode, Stonehenge, Thomas China, and Villeroy & Boch is available; the crystal department includes lines by Sasaki, Orrefors, Kosta Boda, Daum, Lalique, Baccarat, Littala, Wedgwood, Waterford, Galway, Atlantis, and Val St. Lambert. Robin sells sets and individual pieces of flatware by Yamazaki, Boda Nova, Dalia, Georgian House, Gorham, Hachman, Henckels, International Silver, Lauffer, Lunt, Mikasa, Northland, Oneida, Rebacraft, Washington Forge, Stanley Roberts, Towle, Supreme Cutlery, Wallace, and W.M.F. Fraser. In addition, the brochures showed a potpourri of such related goods as Sadek Bakeware, Lladro figurines,

Swarovski crystal whimsies, Wilton Armetal, Vannes Le Chatel crystal vases, and other gift items. Robin also carries kitchen cutlery and steak knives by Sabatier, Henckels, and Wustof Trident, plus Tommer wooden knife blocks, Melior Chambord coffee makers, Cole and Mason salt and pepper mills, the Screwpull, the Crystal Saver, and Carefree cotton/Dacron tablecloths and napkins in all sizes and colors.

Discounts vary from line to line; some of the china and crystal brands are seldom offered on sale, much less discounted year round. Robin periodically offers month-long specials on selected groups of goods at even greater savings. Since the brochures don't mention these sales and don't include prices on the illustrated items, you must call or write for a price quote.

PLEASE TAKE NOTE: all requests for brochures and all written price-quote requests must include a SASE (long envelope). The WATS line is only for orders outside New York. If you're calling for a price quote or ordering within New York, use the other phone lines. Goods are shipped via UPS— no deliveries to Alaska, Canada, or elsewhere outside the continental U.S.

ROGERS & ROSENTHAL, INC.

**105 Canal St.
New York, NY 10013
(212) 925–7557**

Price List: free with SASE
Information: price quote by phone or letter with SASE
Discount: to 65%
Goods: name brand
Minimum Order: none
Shipping: extra; UPS
Sales Tax: NY deliveries
Accepts: check or MO
$$$

The inventory at Rogers & Rosenthal consists of china, crystal, glassware, and flatware, at savings of up to 65% off retail prices. A sampling of the well-known brands carried includes International, Gorham, Towle, Reed & Barton, Wallace, and Lunt. The price list is free, and you can also call or write for a price quote (include a SASE with your written correspondence) if you don't see what you're looking for in the listing.

RUDI'S POTTERY, SILVER, & CHINA

178A Rte. 17 N.
Paramus, NJ 07652
(201) 265–6096: inquiries
and NJ orders
(800) 631–2526: orders
except NJ

Leaflet: free; pub. in May and Sept.
Information: price quote by phone or letter with
    SASE
Discount: 20% to 60%
Goods: name brand
Minimum Order: none
Shipping, Insurance: extra; UPS, PP
Sales Tax: NJ deliveries
Accepts: check, MO, MC, V
$$$

Rudi's has built up an extensive line of brands in the 20 years it's been in business, and can answer almost every need and taste in table settings. You can get china, stemware, and flatware here at up to 60% off list prices—and choose from some of the finest manufacturers around.

The list includes Gorham, Lunt, Towle, Wallace, International, Kirk-Stieff, Bucellati, Lenox, Royal Doulton, Spode, Baccarat, Waterford, Tiffin, Val St. Lambert, Christofle, Galway, Mikasa, Orrefors, Kosta Boda, Lalique, Daum, Sèvres, Bernardaud and Ceralene Limoges, Minton, Rosenthal, Georg Jensen, Royal Copenhagen, Royal Worcester, Coalport, Belleek, Noritake, Stuart, Arzberg, Fitz and Floyd, Reed & Barton, Wedgwood, Tuttle, Ginori, and Adams.

Although the firm has a leaflet, you should call or write (include a SASE) for a price quote on goods from the firms listed above. Include the name of the pattern or suite, colors when applicable, names or descriptions of the pieces you want. Ask for the shipping costs before ordering.

A.B. SCHOU

4 NY Østergade
DK–1101 Copenhagen
Denmark
Phone # (45) 1–13–80–95

Porcelain Catalog: $4, redeemable; pub.
    biannually
Stemware Catalog and Brochures: $3
Crystal Catalog: $2, redeemable
Discount: 30% to 55%
Goods: name brand
Minimum Order: none
Shipping, Handling, Insurance: included; airmail,
    surface mail
Duty: extra
Accepts: check or IMO
$$$$ (see text)

Founded in 1920, A.B. Schou sells fine European crystal and porcelain. The beautiful porcelain catalog shows a wide range of vases, figurines, candlesticks, bonbonnières, and a limited range of dinnerware and serving pieces. The firms represented include Royal Copenhagen, Bing & Grøndahl, Florence, Kronberg, Lladro, NAO, Royal Doulton, Wedgwood, Royal Worcester, Villeroy & Boch, Goebel, Hummel, Aynsley, Herend, Kaiser, and Spode. Schou's prices, which *include* postage (surface), are superb: a five-piece place setting of Royal Copenhagen's "Blue Fluted," full lace, is $390 list but $183 here. Lladro figurines are about 45% below retail. If you're shopping for dinnerware or limited issues, send for the separate catalog and brochures, which show the entire range of stock.

A few pieces of crystal are shown in the porcelain catalog, but the complete collection is pictured in the crystal catalog, available separately. In addition to the most comprehensive listing of Waterford stemware, vases, and giftware we've seen anywhere, Schou sells decorative and service pieces by Atlantis, St. Louis, Sèvres, Kosta Boda, Lalique, Nachtmann, Marcolin, Swarovski, Waterford, Baccarat, and Orrefors. Price comparisons of the Waterford stemware show that it sells at about 30% below list price at Schou. And we've found the Bavarian hock glasses by Nachtmann selling in import shops for twice as much as they cost here.

Specials are sometimes featured in separate brochures, and offerings on seconds (clearly marked as such) have been made in the past.

CANADIAN READERS, PLEASE NOTE: a 10% surcharge is imposed on payment made in Canadian funds.

NAT SCHWARTZ & CO., INC.

549 Broadway
Bayonne, NJ 07002
(201) 437–4443: NJ price quotes and orders
(800) 526–1440: price quotes and orders except NJ, AK, HI

Catalog: free; pub. yearly
Information: price quote by phone or letter with SASE
Discount: up to 65%
Goods: name brand
Minimum Order: none
Shipping, Insurance: $3 minimum; UPS
Sales Tax: NJ deliveries
Accepts: check, MO, MC, V
$$

We received a beautiful 48-page color catalog from Schwartz filled with fine china, crystal, flatware, jewelry, and gifts. Schwartz has been in business since 1959 and has an extensive inventory of goods, a fraction of which is shown in the catalog. The firm carries china and giftware by Lenox, Wedgwood, Minton, Royal Doulton, Royal Crown Derby, Coalport, Royal Worcester, Oxford, Aynsley, Spode, Haviland Limoges, Bernardaud Limoges, Pickard, Gorham, Mikasa, Belleek, Edward Marshall Boehm, and Lladro. Crystal stemware and gifts by Waterford, Val St. Lambert, Galway, Stuart, Wedgwood, Gorham, Lenox, Queen Lace, and Mikasa are offered. You'll find sterling, silver plate, and stainless flatware and holloware from Towle, Gorham, Wallace, Tuttle, Reed & Barton, International Silver, Lunt, Kirk-Stieff, Oneida, Georgian House, Lauffer, and Mikasa.

The catalog lists about half the stock at full retail prices, but reductions on the "sale" goods run up to 65%. And just because something is listed as full price doesn't mean Schwartz isn't selling it at a discount. You can get the current selling price for a catalog item or find out availability on goods not shown by calling (WATS-line inquiries are accepted) or writing (include your phone number on all correspondence). Don't order silver directly from the catalog, since prices may fluctuate—call or write for the current quote.

Schwartz will help you select gifts and even coordinate china, crystal, and flatware selections. The firm's "Ship-A-Gift" service includes free gift wrapping and card enclosures and shipment to the recipient, and both bridal and gift registries are maintained. Every purchase is covered by the Schwartz guarantee of satisfaction, and returns are accepted on unused goods for exchange, refund, or credit. Please note that the 20% deposits required on special orders are not refundable.

SHANNON MAIL ORDER

**Shannon Free Airport
Ireland
Phone # 353–61–62610**

Catalog: $1; pub. 3 to 4 times yearly
Discount: 10% to 70%
Goods: name brand, handcrafted
Minimum Order: $25 on credit cards
Shipping, Insurance: extra; itemized
Duty: extra
Accepts: check, bank IMO, MC, V, AE
$$$ (see text)

Shannon's Airport Shop is probably the best-known of the "duty-free" shops abroad. ("Duty-free" is a deceptive term; you're usually charged duty on all dutiable goods you order, regardless of the policies of the shop. However, consumers who order regularly from overseas firms report that duty is often not charged at all on small parcels.)

Shannon has been doing business by mail for over 30 years. Its catalog features china and crystal, with French perfumes, clothing, table linens, and gifts and collectibles rounding out the 56 color pages.

The china firms represented in the current catalog include Belleek, Royal Tara, Noritake Ireland, Spode, Minton, Royal Albert, Royal Doulton, Beswick, Wedgwood, Coalport, Royal Worcester, Aynsley, and Limoges. The emphasis is on giftware—vases, candy dishes, ring stands, cachepots—but select place settings and serving pieces are also offered. Savings, without the shipping or duty included, are usually more than 30% on the U.S. retail prices and are often more substantial. For example, a five-piece place setting of Spode's "Christmas Tree" is regularly $65; at Shannon it's $34.25. Wedgwood's "Runnymede Dark Blue" is $89.25 in this catalog; elsewhere, it's $195. And one of Princess Diana's bridal selections, "Evesham" by Royal Worcester, costs about twice as much in New York City department stores as it does at Shannon.

The flash and fire of 24% lead crystal by Galway and Waterford can be had at savings of up to 40% off list prices. Several suites are available, as well as serving and decorative pieces. In addition, Shannon carries Anri figurines, Royal Doulton character mugs, Royal Doulton's Bunnykins figures, Wedgwood's Beatrix Potter nursery accoutrements, Goebel and Hummel collectibles, Mullingar pewter, Victorinox knives, Peggy Nisbet dolls, Peterson pipes, and lovely Claddagh jewelry in traditional motifs. Aran sweaters, tartan skirts, tweed caps, Jimmy Hourihan capes and jackets, and stylish accessories from Iceland, England, and Germany are available as well.

Genuine bargains can be found among the Irish linen handkerchiefs, Nottingham lace tablecloths and bedspreads, and damask table linens. The "satin band" damask cloth shown here is *identical* in description and appearance to one we saw in a catalog from an upscale firm in the U.S. The 72" × 108" size is $93.30 at Shannon and $290 in the other catalog; the 72" × 144" size is $130.45 here, and $400 from the upscale firm; and a set of six 22" napkins is $40.50 at Shannon, and $120 in the luxury catalog. With these savings of almost 70%, we wouldn't be surprised to see a return to formal dining!

Shannon's other strong suit is perfume, available here at heady discounts of over 50%. A sample of the designers and houses includes Yves St. Laurent, Halston, Hermès, Dior, Karl Lagerfeld, and Balenciaga. Compare Shannon's prices to those of the French firms in the "Health and Beauty" chapter before you buy.

Satisfaction is guaranteed, and returns are accepted within thirty days for refund, credit, or exchange.

CANADIAN READERS, PLEASE NOTE: shipping charges listed in the catalog are valid on orders sent to Canada. Prices are given in U.S. dollars, but Canadian funds are accepted. Use the rate of exchange in force on the day you order.

ALBERT S. SMYTH CO., INC.

25 Aylesbury Rd.
Timonium, MD 21093
(301) 561–2417: customer service
(800) 638–3333: orders

Catalog: $1, year's subscription; pub. in the spring and fall
Information: price quote by phone or letter with SASE
Discount: up to 50%
Goods: name brand, generic
Minimum Orders: $100 on special-order china patterns
Shipping, Handling, Insurance: $3.50 minimum; UPS, PP
Sales Tax: MD deliveries
Accepts: check, MO, MC, V, AE, CB, DC, CHOICE
$$

All that gleams and glitters may be found here at savings of up to 50%—from diamond bracelets to fine crystal and china. The fall catalog concentrates on jewelry, offering a fine selection at prices that begin under $20 and run into the thousands. We saw distinctive gold bracelets and bangles, several versions of the again fashionable circle pin, strands of polished semiprecious beads, timeless gem solitaires and gold dome rings, pearls, cameos, and a group of gold-filled jewelry about a fourth the cost of the same styles in solid 14K gold. The collection of pierced earrings and jackets is exceptional in terms of style; watches by Citizen, Seiko, and Pulsar are carried as well.

If you're seeking a gift for the home, consider the selection of clocks from Seiko, Citizen, and Howard Miller; or pewter candlesticks, coffee sets, punch bowls, and other items from Kirk-Stieff. Smyth's stock of giftware, dinnerware, and stemware by Lenox, Wedgwood, Noritake, Royal Doulton, Spode, Waterford, Reed & Barton, Towle, Gorham, and Wallace is always available, whether shown in the current catalog or not. Savings run up to 50% on the suggested list or comparable retail prices.

A whole menu of special features is offered, including bridal registry, gift consultations, wrapping and card enclosures, engraving, and bonus gifts. Your satisfaction is guaranteed. Returns are accepted on everything except personalized or custom-ordered goods within 30 days for replacement, refund, or credit.

STECHER'S LIMITED

27 Frederick St.
Port-of-Spain
Trinidad, W.I.
Phone # (62) 32585, 6

List of Brands: free
Information: price quote by phone or letter
Discount: 25% to 50%
Goods: name brand
Minimum Order: none
Shipping, Insurance: extra
Duty: extra
Accepts: check or IMO
$$$$

Here in Trinidad is one of the world's greatest sources of luxury goods at fabulous discounts. Stecher's carries the best of the best in tableware, watches, clocks, pens, and lighters, at savings of up to 50%.

The stock includes crystal by Waterford, Baccarat, Lalique, Daum, St. Louis, Sèvres, Orrefors, Kosta Boda, Iittala, Riedel, Holmegaard, Val St. Lambert, Swarovski, and Rosenthal. Place settings, gifts, and figurines from Royal Crown Derby, Royal Albert, Wedgwood, Royal Doulton, Minton, Royal Worcester, Spode, Coalport, Aynsley, Belleek, Bing & Grøndahl, Rosenthal, Hutschenreuther, Limoges (Bernardaud, Haviland, and Ceralene), Arabia, Lladro, Capodimonte, and Kaiser are available. The flatware lines include Georg Jensen and Wallace, among others.

This is an impressive list, but Stecher's is more frequently cited for its bargains on watches, clocks, jewelry, pens, and lighters. Again, only primo goods: timepieces by Patek-Philippe, Cartier, Piaget, Giraud-Perregaux, Seiko, Consul, Borel, Heuer (chronographs), Audemars Piguet, and similar firms are offered, in addition to pens and lighters from Dupont, Dunhill, Cartier, Lamy, Cardin, Waterman, Scheaffer, and Cross, plus a wide variety of fine jewelry (including cultured pearls) and leather goods.

Stecher's has no catalog, but will send a list of brands and lines of merchandise currently available. The firm invites inquiries concerning specific goods and manufacturers, and will send specific brochures and prices upon request. The much recommended Stecher's, established in 1946, has satisfied the whims of such shoppers as Marlene Dietrich and Lena Horne.

TREASURE TRADERS LTD.

P.O. Box N-635
Nassau, Bahamas
(809) 322–8521

Price List: free
Manufacturers' Brochures: free; sent upon request
Discount: to 40%
Goods: name brand
Minimum Order: $100
Shipping, Insurance: included
Duty: extra
Accepts: check or MO
$$$$

Treasure Traders is justly named. Located in the sunny Bahamas, it sells highly coveted china and crystal from the finest companies. In china, choose from Royal Worcester, Coalport, Rosenthal, Ginori, and Wedgwood, also at 40% off. Crystal by Stuart, Royal Brierly, St. Louis, Kosta Boda, Daum, Orrefors, and Baccarat is available at similar savings.

We did not receive an updated brochure, but past lists have not included product photos. We recommend that you request manufacturers' brochures if you're not familiar with the goods described in the price list. This is a superb source for top brands; it leaves you with no excuse for buying flatware, china, or crystal at list prices locally—unless time is of the essense. Please note that delivery from Treasure Traders ranges from six weeks to a year from the time you order your goods, so you must be patient. But when your dinnerware finally arrives, you'll have saved a bundle—and bought the best.

SEE ALSO:

A Cook's Wares . . . Pillivuyt porcelain serving pieces, pepper mills . . . HOME (kitchen)

Deepak's Rokjemperl Products . . . brass tableware . . . JEWELRY

The Friar's House . . . name-brand British crystal, china . . . ART, ANTIQUES

Irish Cottage Industries, Ltd. . . . small Irish pewter beakers . . . CLOTHING

Laurence Corner . . . government-surplus mess kits, tableware . . . CLOTHING

Lewi Supply . . . Mikasa china . . . APPLIANCES

Rama Jewelry Ltd., Part. . . . silver and bronze tableware, candlesticks . . . JEWELRY

Saxkjaers . . . small selection Danish tableware . . . ART, ANTIQUES

JEWELRY, GEMS, AND WATCHES

Fine, fashion, and costume jewelry;
loose stones, watches, and services.

This book gives you access to firms that offer everything from flea market neck chains for pennies to diamond and emerald collars costing close to $200,000. Before you buy in the "high end," you must know and understand terms and industry standards to determine what offer represents the best value. We could use this space to tell you the difference between rolled and filled gold, what "GIA-certified" signifies, and the meanings of "chatoyant," "rutile," "dichroic," and other interesting words used in gemology. Instead, we are going to cite references and urge you to read all the publications mentioned here. They'll help you become an educated consumer.

But becoming a *wise* consumer takes a different kind of knowledge. Before you buy a piece of jewelry, you should know *why* you're buying it. You're in the clear if all you want is a bit of color to enhance an outfit, since you're not going to insist on the perfect Burmese ruby. You're probably still on safe ground if you're buying for the sake of having a specimen—a strand of semiprecious beads or a small diamond (and we mean small).

You enter the danger zone when you approach gems and jewelry, armed with large amounts of money, ignorance, and wishful thinking. Wishful thinking is what leads uninformed consumers to believe they can get the better of dealers who've been in the business for 20 years and know exactly what they're selling. It leads people to buy as "investors" on the basis of undocumented appreciation figures, expect similar rates of return on their stones or jewelry, and eventually experience disappointment. (Buying an "investment-grade" piece does not an investor make.) Wishful thinking is believing an appraisal value equals a resale value. Don't mistake an appraisal value for the amount of money you could get for your gems or jewelry; it's a measure of the market value of stones, which may be as high as three to four times the resale value. Since inflated appraisals may also cost you extra insurance premium dollars, make sure your valuations are realistic. Protect yourself by getting at least two, preferably by GIA-trained jewelers or dealers.

There are many worthwhile publications on gems and jewelry; one we found quite useful is *All About Jewelry: The One Indispensable Guide for Buyers, Wearers, Lovers, Investors* by Rose Leiman Goldenberg. The book covers precious and semiprecious stones, pearls, metals, and other materials used in jewelry, and includes color plates. (Arbor House Publishing Co., 1983, $6.95, paper. It may be available in your local library.)

The BBB publishes a pamphlet called "Jewelry," which is available from local offices or by mail. See the chapter introduction to "Appliances" for the address and information.

The FTC has established guidelines for the jewelry trade and publishes pamphlets for consumers that discuss the meaning of terms, stamps, and quality marks, etc. Request "Gold Jewelry," "Bargain Jewelry," and "Guides for the Jewelry Industry" from the Federal Trade Commission, Public Reference Office, Washington, DC 20580.

The GIA can tell you what should appear on a GIA report and confirm whether an appraiser has been trained by the organization. You can write to the Gemological Institute of America, Inc., 1180 Ave. of the Americas, New York, NY 10036 for information. There is also a GIA office in Santa Monica, CA.

The Jeweler's Vigilance Committee can tell you whether your dealer is among the good, the bad, or the ugly. This trade association monitors the industry and promotes ethical business practices. It can be reached by writing to The Jeweler's Vigilance Committee, 1180 Ave. of the Americas, 8th Fl., New York, NY 10036.

DEEPAK'S ROKJEMPERL PRODUCTS

61, 10th Khetwadi
Bombay 400 004
India
Phone # 38 80 31

Price List: free; pub. in Jan.
Illustrated Catalog: $1 or 4 IRCs
Discount: up to 80%
WBMC Reader Discount: 5% on orders of $50 or more
Goods: handcrafted
Minimum Order: $25 from any catalog section (see text)
Shipping, Insurance: included
Duty: extra
Accepts: certified check, postal IMO, AE
$$$$

Astounding bargains can be found here on jewelry, gemstones, Indian handcrafts, and clothing. About half the unillustrated price list covers stones and jewelry, including cut, tumbled, and rough (specimen) precious and semiprecious stones, silver filigree pieces, and others of carved bone ivory, sandalwood, buffalo horn, and mother-of-pearl.

Deepak's is a treasure trove for the jewelry crafter with its staggering range of cabochons, faceted stones, drilled and undrilled beads in many shapes and sizes, and a variety of stones cut and drilled for pendants and earrings. You'll find everything here from amethysts to zircons, including Burmese rubies, sapphires of several colors, lapis lazuli, malachite, garnets, and agates. Deepak's has most of the tools and supplies you'll need to turn out finished pieces—jeweler's pliers, saws, files, tweezers, scoops, loupes, stone sieves, scales, gauges, vises, trays, boxes, and more—at discount prices.

Strung necklaces in several bead cuts and shapes are available, from as low at $1.55 for a 16″ agate necklace. Carved plates, snuff bottles, vases, small figures, eggs, key rings, marbles, and belt buckles of amethyst, smoky topaz, aventurine, and other semiprecious stones are also stocked.

Deepak's offers a better selection of handcrafts than import shops here do, and at much better prices. Bone-ivory elephant bridges are just $1.75 to $5.15; sandalwood magic balls are $8.05 to $18.75; horn animals begin at $2.85; and rosewood elephants are as little as 65¢ each. Brass artware, cloth dolls in traditional dress, paintings on pipal leaves, and embroidered kurta shirts ($5 cotton, $10 silk) are listed. Though not mentioned in the catalog, Deepak's sells Chinese freshwater "rice" pearls and printed cotton fabric.

Mineral collectors shouldn't miss the rough gem and mineral specimens, listed in the catalog under "Shah's Rock Shop." Specimens of moonstone, garnet, sunstone, turquoise, ruby (in matrix), and amethyst are among the offerings.

Deepak's was established in 1964 and is quite experienced in exporting to businesses and consumers. In addition to its price list and catalog, it sends out special-offer flyers in April and August, with great buys on select lots from the catalog. The minimum order is just $25, but that applies to *each lettered section* of the catalog or price list—you can't combine 100 jasper marbles ($20) from section F with a sandalwood fan ($5.15) from section G to meet the minimum. Readers of this book are entitled to a 5% discount on orders of $50 or more *if* they provide a photocopy of this listing with the order. A schedule of further quantity discounts, based on dollar value and units, is given in the catalog. PLEASE NOTE: WBMC and quantity discounts do not apply to orders from the special-offer flyers. Returns are accepted but must be authorized.

DEL-MAR CO.

**705 Frisco
Houston, TX 77022−9990
(713) 695−0158**

Catalog: refundable; pub. biannually in June
Discount: up to 50%
Goods: houses brand, generic
Minimum Order: none
Shipping, Handling: 10% on orders under %50;
    included on orders of $50 and more; UPS, PP
Sales Tax: TX deliveries
Accepts: check, MO, certified check
$$ (see text)

Del-Mar sells unusual jewelry—necklaces, earrings, belt buckles, tie tacks, and bolo ties—of "pounded gold." Gold nuggets are melted down and any impurities removed. Then the gold is pounded thin and combined with resin and gold flakes to form a new nugget of 23K gold, after which it's cut and polished. The result looks somewhat like a tumbled gold-flecked mineral. The random patterning is quite attractive and shown to best advantage against the black backing material (red, white, and blue backgrounds are also used). Some pieces are further enhanced with small bits of turquoise or copper; a few use the same embedding technique with abalone and silver.

The 16-page color catalog pictures a number of lovely pendants—heart, teardrop, and diamond shapes—and pierced and drop earrings, as well as a group of undrilled "stones" that the hobbyist can use in all sorts of creations. But most of Del-Mar's catalog is given to pounded-gold cabachons designed to be set in a choice of western belt buckles, bolo ties, and money clips. Del-Mar will take the stone of your choice, set it in the accessory of your choice, and box it for you. Most of these cabochons are embedded with gold or cloisonné figures or emblems. These range from golden cowboy boots and saddles to logos for the Knights of Columbus, Masons, Shriners, and Elks, not to mention bears, ducks, Mercury dimes, eagles, bowling pins, armadillos, dice, trout, slot machines, a stagecoach and others too numerous to list.

Finished necklaces and earrings are as little as $9 each, bolo ties begin at $12, and buckles and money clips at $20. Undrilled stones and belt-buckle cabochons run from $1.25 to $8.50 each. Del-Mar tells us that some stores sell the same goods for three times as much, which may interest you if you have a resale number—write or call for wholesale prices.

CANADIAN READERS, PLEASE NOTE: the shipping charge on orders to Canada is 15% of the order value.

**DIAMONDS BY RENNIE
ELLEN**

**15 W. 47th ST., Rm. 401
New York, NY 10036
(212) 896–5525**

Catalog: $2
Discount: 50% to 75%
Goods: stock jewelry, custom made
Minimum Order: none
Shipping, Handling, Insurance: $6 minimum; UPS
Sales Tax: NY deliveries
Returns: within 5 working days
Accepts: check, MO, certified check
$$$$

It's hard to believe that you can buy diamond engagement rings whole-sale, but that's Rennie Ellen's business. She claims to sell at 50% to 75% below retail, which gives you some idea of the standard retail markup on precious gems. Rennie Ellen is one of the few female diamond cutters in the business, and she will personally cut and set diamonds of any shape, size, and quality to order, in platinum or gold. She also buys diamonds and you can call her for price quotes. The 12-page color catalog shows a sample of her diamond artistry, and includes a good selection of well-designed jewelry—rings, pendants, and earrings—set with rubies, sapphires, emer-alds, amethysts, tourmalines, pearls, and opals.

Rennie Ellen is part of a vigilant effort to keep New York City's diamond district free from disreputable dealers, earning her the title of "Madame Mayor" of 47th Street. If you live in or are visiting New York Ctiy, call and make an appointment to see her. She'll show you her wares, give you a rundown on some of the unsavory tricks of the trade practiced on her street, warn you about the extreme sales tactics used by other jewelers, ánd explain the significance of the colored lighting many of them use in their windows. If you buy jewelry from Ms. Ellen, it will be accompanied by a detailed bill of sale, something few catalog firms offer. We recommend Rennie Ellen as a paragon of integrity as well as a good jeweler.

GOLD N' STONES

**Box 636
Sterling, Ak 99672
(907) 262–9713**

Catalog: $1, refundable; pub. late fall
Discount: 10% to 40%
Goods: house brand
Minimum Order: $25
Shipping, Insurance: included on most items
Handling: $1 on orders under $10
Sales Tax: AK deliveries
Accepts: check, MO, certified check
$$$

Jade jewelry is the strong suit at this firm, which was established in 1972. You'll find it in pendants of every conception, from bezels filled with polished chips to classic balls, hearts, and crosses, and even one shaped like the 49th state. Jade bead necklaces and bracelets, earrings, rings, and stickpins are also offered. Tumbled Alaskan garnets, hematite, and walrus ivory are used in a variety of jewelry and accessory pieces. And gold nuggets, recalling Alaska's pre-Pipeline era, can be had in acrylic presentation boxes or in bezels on pendants and earrings. Prices are quite reasonable—from $1 for jade worry stones to $50 for the gold-nugget pendant. Jewelry is guaranteed against damage for five years, and repairs or replacements are made within that period.

In addition to what's shown in the catalog, Gold N' Stones sells bulk jade, soapstone, jasper, and agate, and some jewelry set with non-Alaskan semiprecious stones—amethysts, opals, coral, peridots, aquamarines, and more. Craftspeople should inquire if interested in findings, bolo cord, and gift boxes, since these are also available.

**GOOD 'N' LUCKY
PROMOTIONS**

**P.O. Box 370
Henderson, NV 89015
(702) 564–3895**

Price List: $1, refundable; pub. four times yearly
Information: price quote on volume orders by phone or letter with SASE
Discount: 40% to 70%
WBMC Reader Discount: 10% off catalog prices
Goods: generic
Minimum Order: $30
Shipping, Insurance: included; UPS, PP
Sales Tax: NV deliveries
Accepts: check, MO, certified check, MC, V
$$$

You never know what you'll find at Good 'N' Lucky. X-ray glasses at $6.80 a dozen, sterling silver rings for $2.95, survival foods, and sewing notions were offered in the catalog we reviewed, along with hundreds of other closeouts, overruns, bankruptcy goods, customs seizures, and the like. The catalog is geared for the flea-market or swap-meet operator, and emphasizes "quick sale" items of every sort. Many are available in lots under a dozen. Anyone looking for a source for party favors, novelties, stocking stuffers, and last year's fad should look here.

We saw enameled butterfly pins (four for $2.50), birthstone rings, olivewood cross pendants, gold-plated meile leaves, chains, jade necklaces, cubic zirconia rings (three for $4), 16″ strands of tumbled amethyst, tiger's eye, and rose quartz for $10.80 each, copper bracelets for $8.60 a dozen, tie tacks, children's jewelry, men's rings, and much more.

But that's not all. The catalog included Chinese fans, sunglasses, porcelain knickknacks, steak knives, whoopee cushions, Elvis posters, rain bonnets, sealing tape, old *Playboy* magazines, fish hooks, bandannas, arrowheads, clock motors, wind chimes, and strawberry-scented erasers—all at a fraction of the prices they cost in stores.

And there's more. Good 'N' Lucky has separate catalogs of adult novelties ($1), jewelry ($2), and name-brand cosmetics ($3), which should be ordered from the general catalog. Phone orders over $50 are discounted by $2, and readers of this book are offered a 10% discount on their purchases. Be sure to identify yourself as a WBMC reader and meet the minimum order requirement of $30.

HONG KONG LAPIDARIES, INC.

c/o Zarlene
31 W. 47th St., 2nd Floor
New York, NY 10036
(212) 221–3247: inquiries
and NY orders
(800) 223–7814: orders
except NY

Catalog: $1; pub. Jan. and July
Discount: 10% to 35%
Goods: generic
Minimum Order: $25
Shipping: $3 per order; UPS, PP
Handling: $3 on orders under $25
Sales Tax: NY deliveries
Accepts: check, MO, MC, V
$$

Hong Kong Lapidaries (a New York firm) sells a wide range of precious and semiprecious stones in a variety of forms—cabochons, beads, loose faceted and cut stones, strung chips, and more. The choice of sizes and shapes is also excellent. In addition to several types of pearls, garnets, amethyst, onyx, abalone, and the dozens of other stones offered by similar firms, you'll find Egyptian clay scarabs of recent vintage, coral, cameos, cubic zirconia, yellow jade, and cloisonné jewelry, and objets d'art.

The 32-page color catalog should delight jewelry hobbyists, but it has a number of items that would interest other craftspeople. There are lovely square and disc inlays in intaglios that would be stunning if used to decorate a jewelry box or create a game-board pattern. If you make clothing, don't miss the tigereye and onyx buckles and stone buttons. And if you're all thumbs but have admired the asymmetrical open hearts sold by a famous Fifth Avenue jewelry emporium, you'll be glad to know you can get similar hearts here at a fraction of the price. Just thread a chain through the hole, and you have a necklace.

Catalog prices run from 10% to 35% below comparable retail and quantity discounts are offered on some goods. Hong Kong Lapidaries was founded eight years ago and guarantees satisfaction on all purchases. Returns are accepted within 12 days.

HOUSE OF ONYX

**120 Main St.
Greenville, KY 42345
(502) 338–0661: inquiries
and KY orders
(800) 626–8352: orders
except KY**

Catalog: free; pub. six times yearly
Discount: 40% to 60%
Goods: generic, imported
Minimum Order: $25
Shipping, Handling, Insurance: $4 minimum; UPS,
  PP, FOB Greenville
Sales Tax: KY deliveries
Accepts: check, MO, MC, V
$$$$

Opening the House of Onyx catalog is like walking into Woolworth's and finding Tiffany's instead. The 56-page tabloid usually shows one of its current specials on onyx, soapstone, or cloisonné on the cover, so it's something of a surprise to open the catalog and find reports on the gem industry and listings of diamonds and other precious stones. But it's nothing new to any of the 50,000 clients worldwide who know the House and rely on it for investment stones and jewelry at fair prices.

The handcrafts merit your special attention; Aztec onyx chess sets, onyx ashtrays, bookends, vases, desk sets, statuettes, jewelry boxes, candlesticks, earrings and necklaces, and Mexican dyed onyx fruit have appeared in past mailings. The House sells real ivory necklaces, bracelets, netsuke, and gift items. The ivory is obtained from elephants who died natural deaths, so you're not contributing to the extinction of a species by buying it, and it's not the "bone" ivory often sold by Oriental firms. The cloisonné ranges from beads at $1 each to a pair of 30″ vases at $9,000. The soapstone carvings of animals and other figures are much finer than those we've seen in other catalogs, and the prices are up to 75% less. There are also exceptional Oriental carvings in rose quartz, tigereye, lapis lazuli, turquoise, and agate.

The jewelry runs from better grades of semiprecious bead necklaces and strands of freshwater pearls to cultured pearls and diamond rings, earrings, and pendants. At this writing, House of Onyx sells the "rainbow" bracelet of approximately 40 square-cut semiprecious stones set in 14K gold for $900. Compare that to $1,895 to $3,600 in other catalogs. It's not that the House uses inferior materials or the workmanship is poor; it just takes a smaller markup.

Those shopping for investment stones should review their needs and call House of Onyx to discuss availability and price. Discounts of 50% and 60%

are given on parcels of $2,000 to $12,500. Your satisfaction is guaranteed on all purchases, and returns are accepted within five days. The investment parcels are also covered by the House "buy-back" policy. Details will be provided when you discuss your prospective purchase.

But the House of Onyx tabloid is more than a catalog; it's a forum. In it, owner Fred Rowe talks shop, and then some. His perspectives and commentary on the world of high finance, business, and international politics are fascinating. We've read a lot of "editorialog" over the years, and find his to be some of the most refreshing, accurate, and entertaining. And his references, which include banks, the local Chamber of Commerce, the BBB, and others, are all listed. You can call them yourself and verify the fact that he does business with integrity and honor. He's a gem among dealers.

INTERNATIONAL IMPORT CO.

P.O. Box 747
Stone Mountain, GA
30086–0747
(404) 938–0173; 939–8168

Catalog: free; pub. yearly in Oct.
Information: price quote by phone or letter with SASE
Discount: see text
Goods: cut and polished stones
Minimum Order: $10
Shipping, Insurance: extra; PP
Sales Tax: GA deliveries
Accepts: check, MO, certified check, IMO
Resale Number, Letterhead: necessary for trade discounts

$$$

International lists about 3,000 different cut precious and semiprecious stones in its 56-page catalog, only a fraction of the firm's inventory of over 100,000 stones. Everything from actinolites to zircons can be found here, at prices that run from a few dollars to tens of thousands. Each gem is cut (no rough stones are sold), and weight, size, shape, and color specifications are listed. There are no illustrations, and all purchases are made on an approval basis. You must send a deposit of 50%, and you have five days to decide whether to keep or return the stones.

International Import is geared for the collector or jeweler, and is a top-notch source for investment-grade stones. The company has been doing business for 35 years and is highly respected in the gem trade. The stones are listed at dealer prices, which are generally at least a third lower than what the same goods cost at retail. But because the *quality* of the stones is generally superior to that of gems sold by other firms, the prices may seem high. That's why everything is sent on approval—so you may judge for yourself. If you've been looking for a reliable source with extensive stock at competitive prices, International is the answer.

J B JEWELRY

P.O. Box 04458
Milwaukee, WI 53204
(414) 242–4822

Catalog: $1; pub. yearly in Sept.
Discount: 40% (see text)
WBMC Reader Discount: 50% (see text)
Goods: name brand
Minimum Order: none
Shipping, Handling, Insurance: $2.50 to $7; UPS, PP
Sales Tax: WI deliveries
Accepts: check, MO, certified check, MC, V
$$$

Ever wonder who supplies your local jeweler with those diamond solitaires, emerald pendants, and gold chains? It may very well be Hallmark, a manufacturer of classic rings, earrings, and bracelets.

You can get that same Hallmark jewelry from John Balog, who runs J B Jewelry. You'll know it's the same because the catalog he sends you is the 18-page Hallmark Collection, complete with the manufacturer's prices for comparable pieces. While many jewelers sell at or near these prices, J B lets you take 40% off the cost. Mr. Balog is offering readers who order by February 1, 1986 an extra 10% discount—that's a 50% reduction! (After that date, the standard 40% discount applies.) Identify yourself as a WBMC reader when you send for the catalog and when you place your order, and take the discount on the cost of the goods only (not shipping charges or sales tax).

The Hallmark Collection includes a good selection of diamond solitaires and wedding bands, diamond slides and studs, beautiful styles set with rubies, sapphires, and emeralds, and freshwater and cultured pearls. There are some charming pendants and earrings that would make ideal gifts for the young girl who appreciates the real thing; many of them cost under $100 with the discount. Men's rings, including the onyx and diamond favorites, are shown as well as birthstone jewelry and a group of very affordable rings, bracelets, and pendants set with opals, cubic zirconia, aquamarines, garnets, "polar" star sapphires, amethysts, and smoky topaz quartz. Everything is gift-boxed, and your satisfaction is guaranteed. Returns are accepted within 30 days on everything except goods that have been worn, personalized, or special-ordered.

LOVE'S, INC.

Love's Plaza
P.O. Box 3086, Dept. D603
Rock Hill, SC 29731–3086
(803) 366–8391: inquiries
and SC orders
(800) 845–6151: catalog
requests and orders except
SC

Catalog: $1, refundable; pub. Mar. and Sept.
Information: price quote by phone or letter with
 SASE
Discount: 25% to 50% plus
Minimum Order: none
Shipping, Handling, Insurance: $2.50 to $7; UPS
Sales Tax: SC, NC deliveries
Accepts: check, MO, MC, V, AE
$$$

The 16-page color catalog from Love's shows some real buys on jewelry for every taste and budget. Pierced earrings in 14K gold can be had for as little as $9.88 (with a comparable retail of twice that price), and a one-carat brilliant-cut diamond solitaire is $2,950. The emphasis is on the classic— anniversary bands, gold ropes and chains, shell earrings, shrimp rings, signet rings—but you'll also find savings on contemporary styles selling for 25% to 50% less than prices charged in fashion and gift catalogs. The sales flyers published between catalogs offer even better discounts.

Love's has an attractive group of tricolored gold and silver jewelry, ropes of gold balls and semiprecious stone beads that can be combined to complement your clothing, diamond-studded men's rings, and Mikimoto cultured pearls in necklaces and bracelets. Cubic zirconia earrings, rings, and pendants are sold at prices at least 30% lower than those seen for the same styles in other catalogs. Seiko, Pulsar, and Concord watches are not shown but are available (write for a price quote on these).

Love's has 18 years of experience selling jewelry and guarantees your satisfaction on every purchase. Diamond solitaires are sold with a lifetime trade-in privilege. Returns are accepted within 14 days of receipt. We recommend calling or writing before you order if you have questions on a prospective purchase, especially an investment-level diamond, since grading information isn't given in the catalog descriptions.

M & I HABERMAN, INC.

**122 E. 42nd St., Rm. 521
New York, NY 10168
(212) 697-5270**

Catalog: $3, refundable; pub. in Feb.
Information: price quote by phone or letter with
  SASE
Discount: up to 50%
WBMC Reader Bonus: jewelry polishing cloth with
  orders over $25
Goods: name brand, generic
Minimum Order: none
Shipping, Insurance: extra; UPS
Sales Tax: NY deliveries
Accepts: check, MO, MC, V, AE, CB, DC
$$$ (on watches)

Haberman's gorgeous, 162-page color catalog shows every kind of jewelry imaginable—from gold charms and chains to a bracelet set with over 50 carats of diamonds and emeralds that costs $193,435. You can deduct 50% from the catalog prices of gold jewelry (unless the market price of gold rises above $450, in which case the discount is adjusted); and the sterling silver and gold-filled jewelry is 30% off. As stated in other listings, it's difficult to compare genuine value on gold jewelry when the total weight of the piece is not given; two pairs of shell earrings identical in appearance may differ in price by hundreds of dollars if one is hollow and the other solid. But all in all, Haberman's jewelry prices seem high, even with the discounts. We recommend getting the catalog and deciding for yourself.

Haberman's watch department, on the other hand, is a sure thing; savings of up to 50% can be had on the best timepieces. Seiko, Rolex, Wittnauer, Longines, Movado, Piaget, Lorus, Corum, Rado, Heuer, Lasalle, Pulsar, Omega, Accusplit, Minerva, Caravelle, Bulova, Citizen, and Timex watches are all available. Clocks from Seiko and Linden are also offered. None of the timepieces is shown in the catalog; you must call or write (include a SASE) with model information to get a price quote. Remember to specify details, since manufacturers often offer choices in face and strap color, case finish, size, etc.

Loose diamonds and colored stones may be purchased by mail, and specific inquiries are invited. If your order is over $25 and you state that you're a WBMC reader, Haberman will send you a jeweler's cloth. Use it to coax the highest luster from your pieces (except pearls) between washings. Haberman was founded in 1918 and can supply answers to any questions you have concerning your jewelry or watch purchase.

P & J COMPANY

740 N. Plankinton Ave.
Suite 824
Milwaukee, WI 53203
(414) 271–5396

Catalog: $1, refundable; pub. twice yearly
Information: price quote by phone or letter with
  SASE
Discount: 30% to 60%
Goods: house brand
Minimum Order: none
Shipping, Insurance: included; UPS, PP
Sales Tax: WI deliveries
Accepts: check, MO, MC, V
$

P & J, founded just two years ago, manufactures 400 gold and silver products, which it sells to jewelers. The firm offers the same goods to consumers through a catalog (not available at the time of review). We have seen three examples of P & J's line, however—a grape-cluster ring, horseshoe tie tack/pin, and a duck in flight. Each is available in sterling silver or 14K gold, at prices 30% or more below comparable retail.

P & J backs each sale with an unconditional guarantee of satisfaction, and accepts returns within 30 days.

PIZAZZ, INC.

337 W. Concord Pl.
Chicago, IL 60614
(312) 266–7776

Brochure: $2 and SASE, refundable; pub. in Jan.
  and Sept.
Information: price quote by phone on quantity
  discounts
Discount: 40% to 75%
Goods: house brand
Minimum Order: none (see text)
Shipping, Insurance: 3% of order value; UPS, PP
Sales Tax: IL deliveries
Accepts: check, MO, certified check
$$$

Pizazz sells just that—a little zip and fanfare for your waist, ears, and throat, at prices that will leave you lighthearted. Over two dozen cloisonné belt buckles are offered in well-executed motifs, from butterflies to modern geometrics. The buckles are sold with adjustable leather belts and cost about $10 each. There is a smashing assortment of drop and post earrings in brilliant colors. These are kiln-fired enamels with electroplated silver or gold over the base metal, which look much more expensive than their $4 to $6 price tags. These are done in simple modern designs—a disc of color set in a rectangle, a slash of enamel across a triangle, etc. Pizazz also sells 36″ lengths of synthetic pearls, coral, and turquoise; and genuine agate, rose quartz, amethyst, jasper, and other semiprecious stones. Most are strung with 4mm beads, and can be twisted together to form a rope effect and caught with one of the decorative clasps ($2 to $4). The ropes are $6 to $21 per strand, depending on the stone or material used.

The catalog we received was written for the wholesale buyer, and listed a minimum order of $100. This does not apply to retail buyers. Large quantity orders are welcomed. Call for discounts.

PROFESSIONAL MARKETING CONSULTANTS

P.O. Box 1057
Poway, CA 92064
(619) 451–1610

WBMC Discount

Pearl Catalog: free
Information: price quote by phone or letter with SASE
Discount: 30% to 40% (see text)
WBMC Reader Discount: 10% on pearl purchases
Goods: name brand, generic
Minimum Order: $100 to $3,000 (see text)
Shipping, Insurance: included; PP (registered)
Sales Tax: CA deliveries
Accepts: check, MO, certified check

PMC, founded in 1977, sells investment-grade diamonds, colored stones, and pearls. You're sent the 12-page pearl catalog, which shows Akoya, Mastoloni, and South Seas pearls, plus pins, necklaces, pendants, and rings set with cultured round, Biwa, baroque, Mobe, and seed pearls. The prices run from under $50 for a pair of 6mm stud earrings to $80,000 for an 18″ strand of large round Burma South Seas pearls.

The jewelry is exquisite, but we are unable to say whether the pearl prices are "low" since there is no real standardized grading system in the industry. But whatever the value, it's improved by the reader discount of 10%. There's a $100 minimum-order requirement on pearl purchases ($1,000 on pearl necklaces) and you must identify yourself as a WBMC reader to get the discount.

PMC advertises that it won't be undersold on GIA-certified diamonds and that its prices are 10% above wholesale. They begin at about $3,000 for a one-carat stone. Colored stones, precious and semiprecious, are also sold at "30% to 40%" below retail, and there is a minimum order of $500 on these. You can call or write for a price quote if you're shopping for a particular stone. PMC is geared for the investment buyer, so make sure you understand the dynamics of the "hard assets" market before you exchange your C.D.'s for a packet of fire and ice.

RAMA JEWELRY LTD., PART.

987 Silom Rd.
P.O. Box 858
Bangkok 10500
Thailand
Phone # 234–7521

Brochure and Price List: free
Discount: 30% plus
WBMC Reader Discount: 10%
Goods: handmade
Minimum Order: $50
Shipping, Insurance: included
Duty: extra
Accepts: certified check, bank draft
$$$

Rama's lovely color brochures show photographs of about 500 pieces of gem-studded jewelry, chiefly rings. The range of styles is truly comprehensive, from classic solitaires and pearls in simple settings to the fabulous Princess Rings for which this 25-year-old firm is known.

Princess Rings are traditionally set with opals, rubies, sapphires, pearls, and onyx, but Rama offers many interpretations of this fetching style, including many set with just one type of stone. A score of handsome men's rings, colorful pins, bracelets, earrings, and pendants are offered as well. Most of the pieces can be ordered in white or yellow 14K gold, sterling, and gold or silver plate. The stones shown include diamonds, emeralds, amethysts, topaz, jade, garnets, aquamarines, and turquoise. In addition, Rama sells sterling silver rings and pendants, silverware, and bronzeware.

Our brochure did not include a current price list, but past comparisons have shown you'll save at least 30% by buying from Rama. Save an additional 10% when you order by identifying yourself as a WBMC reader. Quality and workmanship are guaranteed.

R/E KANE ENTERPRISES

Division of Rennie Ellen
P.O. Box 1745
Rockefeller Plaza
New York, NY 10185
(212) 869–5525

Catalog: see text
Discount: 50% plus
Goods: stock and custom made
Minimum Order: none
Shipping, Handling, Insurance: minimum $6; UPS
Sales Tax: NY deliveries
Accepts: check, MO, certified check
$$$

If you have diamond taste but a rhinestone budget, consider the best alternative to the natural stone—cubic zirconia. C.Z. has the fire and dazzle of a diamond, but costs a fraction as much. A synthetic stone, it's harder than "paste" (rhinestones, made of glass) and zircons, which are natural stones sometimes heat-treated to achieve the appearance of diamonds. Indeed, C.Z. is such a successful impostor that few can distinguish it from the diamond without the aid of specialized tools.

Rennie Ellen, the eminently trustworthy diamond cutter listed in this section, offers C.Z. jewelry at the very low price of $10 per carat. Carat is a measure of weight, and C.Z. weighs 80% more than diamonds. So if you want your jewelry to look as if it's set with a one-carat diamond, you should order a 1.8 ct. C.Z., or two carats, to make the computations easier.

SAMARTH GEM STONES

P.O. Box 6057
Colaba, Bombay 400 005
India
Phone # 213512

Price List: $1, refundable
Discount: to 75%
Goods: rough and polished stones
Minimum Order: $50
Shipping: $6 minimum; surface and air mail
Insurance: 1.75% of order value
Duty: extra
Accepts: certified check, bank draft, IMO
$$$

Samarth sells cut and rough gemstones, most of which are from Indian and Brazilian mines. The bulk of the stock is semiprecious stones: agate, garnet, amethyst, citrine, quartz, lapis lazuli, peridot, onyx, bloodstone, moonstone, aquamarine, tigereye, jasper, and tourmaline predominate. Rubies, sapphires, and emeralds are also sold as strung beads and loose stones. (The latter may be purchased on an approval basis.) Samarth is a great source for the sorts of necklaces that are priced much higher in gift and department store catalogs. An 18″ strand of lapis lazuli was listed in Samarth's stock at $40. Twisted six-strand ropes of garnets are $30 at Samarth, compared to over $100 at department stores. Strings of amethyst are $5 and $10, an 18-inch string of peridot chunks costs $8, and a length of faceted bloodstone beads is just $5.

In addition to the wide choice of stones, you can choose from many shapes—smooth and faceted balls, triangles, barrels, ovals, octagons, cubes, rectangles, discs, and tumbled chunks. Samarth will string your necklace on a nylon thread without clasp, on a knotted string with a clasp, and with gold or silver-plated balls or "semi-cultured" pearls as spacers—all at the same price.

Jewelry-makers will be interested in the large assortments of cabochons, beggar's beads, drilled agate charms, earring drops, and pendants. There are also ashtrays, paperweights, carved bottles, and eggs.

The price lists are minimally descriptive and have no illustrations, so you should consult a gemstone reference guide if you're unsure of a stone's characteristics and color. Meeting the $50 minimum order should be easy, and quantity discounts of 5% to 40% are offered on large orders.

GINGER SCHLOTE

Box 19523M
Denver, CO 80219
(303) 934–1168

Catalog: free; pub. yearly
Discount: up to 60%
Goods: house brand
Minimum Order: none
Shipping: included; PP
Sales Tax: CO deliveries
Accepts: check, MO, certified check
$$

Ginger Schlote's firm is only five years old, but she's had many years of experience working with her father in his jewelry business.

Mrs. Schlote sells inexpensive chains, findings, and some finished jewelry. A few items are sterling silver or gold filled, but most are made of a base metal with a white (silver) or yellow (gold) colored finish. Chains, of which there are over two dozen styles, begin at 49¢ each, up to 40% less when bought in quantity. There are also many novel pendants, rings, keyrings, bolas and cord tips, and tack pins.

Jewelry hobbyists looking for rock-bottom prices on findings and supplies should check the catalog for earring wires and clips, pendant mountings, bell caps, jump rings, clutchbacks, pushnuts, cement, and presentation boxes. Bonus offers are listed in flyers accompanying the catalog. Mrs. Schlote guarantees your satisfaction and will accept returns within ten days.

A. VAN MOPPES & ZOON
(DIAMANT) B.V.

P.O. Box 52535
1007 HA Amsterdam
Holland
Phone # (020) 761242

Catalog: $5, refundable; pub. yearly
Discount: 20% to 40%
Goods: house brand
Minimum Order: none
Shipping, Insurance: included; airmail
Duty: extra; refunded (see text)
Accepts: check, IMO, MC, V, AE, CB, DC, EC
$$$

Past Van Moppes catalogs have showcased the breathtaking, extravagant creations that have garnered the firm several jewelry design awards. The current mailing, 30 color plates of rings, pendants, and earrings, concentrates on more understated and affordable pieces. Most of the jewelry is set with diamonds in 18K white or yellow gold, and there are several pendants and earrings embellished with rubies and sapphires. The designs are classic: Tiffany-set solitaires, simple "eternity" rings, heart motifs, gorgeous cocktail rings, and similar styles dominate. Men who lament Tiffany's ban on pinky rings needn't go unadorned. Van Moppes has a select group of unobtrusive jewelry that's a vast improvement on the flashy hardware usually seen in this category.

Prices run from $100 to $22,365, but most pieces are in the $200 to $1,500 range—from 20% to 40% less than what's charged by U.S. firms for jewelry of similar styling and carat weight. Van Moppes offers more than good prices, though. Established in 1828, it's a family-run concern that provides a written guarantee on all purchases (including a trade-in provision). Returns are accepted within ten days for replacement or refund. Official appraisals are available without cost on items up to .35 ct., and for $10 on larger gems. Engraving is offered free of charge. Van Moppes will even refund U.S. duty charges. After you've paid, send a photocopy of the bill or receipt to the firm and you'll receive reimbursement.

The quality of the jewelry itself is superb. The gold used in the settings is 18K, purer than the 14K that dominates the U.S. market. The cutting is excellent—even the tiny diamonds used to accent a larger stone are given the full 57 facets of a brilliant cut. This maximizes the dazzle of the gem so even the smallest stones have the fire characteristic of diamonds. (Look closely at the photos of similar jewelry in other catalogs and you'll find many of the stones look flat and dull, lacking the flash that comes from painstaking cutting and polishing.) In addition to the catalog selection, Van Moppes sells loose diamonds and will work from your designs to create custom jewelry.

SEE ALSO:

Antique Imports Unlimited . . . antique jewelry . . . ART, ANTIQUES
Beautiful Beginnings . . . small selection costume jewelry . . . HEALTH
Beautiful Visions, Inc. . . . small selection costume jewelry . . . HEALTH
Beauty Buy Book . . . small selection costume jewelry . . . HEALTH
Berry Scuba Co. . . . name-brand diving watches . . . SPORTS
The Best Choice . . . chronograph sports watches . . . SPORTS
Bondy Export Corp. . . . Seiko and Casio watches . . . APPLIANCES
Central Skindivers of Nassau, Inc. . . . name-brand diving watches . . . SPORTS

The Finals . . . sports watches . . . CLOTHING

Fortunoff . . . fine, fashion, costume jewelry . . . HOME (table settings)

Handart Embroideries . . . Oriental cloisonné, jade, bone-ivory jewelry . . . CLOTHING

Hunter Audio-Photo, Inc. . . . Timex, Seiko, Bulova watches . . . APPLIANCES

Jems Sounds, Ltd. . . . name-brand watches . . . APPLIANCES

Lewi Supply . . . Seiko watches . . . APPLIANCES

D. MacGillivray & Coy. . . . Scottish brooches . . . CRAFTS

Prince Fashions Ltd. . . . Oriental jade, bone-ivory, jewelry, pearls, watches . . . CLOTHING

Royal Silk, Ltd. . . . small group fashion jewelry . . . CLOTHING

RSP Distributing . . . closeout jewelry . . . GENERAL

Sales Citi, Inc. . . . name-brand watches . . . APPLIANCES

Nat Schwartz & Co., Inc. . . . small selection fine jewelry . . . HOME (table settings)

Shannon Mail Order . . . Irish Claddagh jewelry . . . HOME (table settings)

Albert S. Smyth Co., Inc. . . . fine and costume jewelry, watches . . . HOME (table settings)

Stecher's Limited . . . name-brand watches, clocks . . . HOME (table settings)

LEATHER GOODS

Small leather goods, briefcases,
handbags, attaché cases,
luggage, trunks, and services.

When we were researching the first edition of this book several years ago, we were asked to keep mum about the brands these firms carried. We asked why, and were told that if a major department store stocking these products and selling them at full retail noticed a discounter getting publicity—and sales—it would threaten to pull its account with the manufacturers unless supplies were cut off to the discounter. Fortunately, in the past few years there's been a tremendous boom in off-price shopping, and manufacturers know that positive brand identification doesn't depend on association with a flashy retailer. It's the discounters who have the clout now, and it's because *you* have insisted on bargains. Strike one blow against vertical price fixing!

The firms listed here stock everything you'll need to tote your effects to the office, around town, and around the world. In addition to handbags, briefcases, suitcases, steamer and camp trunks, and small leather goods, some companies also stock cases for musical instruments and portfolios for models and artists.

Note the firm selling Italian leather goods—great workmanship, materials, and prices—but remember that these are bargains only as long as the dollar/lire rate is favorable.

If you're buying luggage, consider the number of different materials available and the pros and cons of each before making your purchase. Molded plastic is almost indestructible, but it's heavy and scuffs easily. Rip-stop nylon is the lightest material widely available, but it's easily punctured and affords the contents little protection against hard knocks or rain. Soft-sided vinyl and reinforced fabric luggage can be punctured and torn, but aren't as heavy as the molded type. Leather is luxurious and can be quite durable, but usually shows scuffs and makes a great target for thieves working baggage areas at airports. You can add to this list on your own; consider your own needs and buy accordingly.

One last tip: Don't buy luggage with attached wheels. Baggage handlers say the wheels often jam in conveyor systems and are usually ripped off by the time you've taken a few trips. Collapsible luggage carriers, which can be taken with you as hand baggage, solve the problem of getting bags around in huge, porterless terminals.

Additional listings of firms selling small leather goods and handbags can be found in "Clothing."

ACE LEATHER PRODUCTS, INC.

2211 Ave. U
Brooklyn, NY 11229
(718) 891–9713; 645–3534:
inquiries and NY orders
(800) 342–5223: orders
except NY

Catalog: free with SASE; pub. in Oct. and June (see text)
Information: price quote by phone or letter with SASE
Discount: 20% to 40%
Goods: name brand
Minimum Order: none
Shipping, Insurance: extra; UPS, PP
Sales Tax: NY deliveries
Accepts: check, MO, MC, V
$$$

There's nothing like a brand-new attaché or briefcase to make that work you're taking home from the office seem less dreary, or a smart two-suiter to guarantee first-class treatment on your business trips. You can upgrade your image on the cheap at Ace, where name-brand goods are up to 40% off list prices.

The luggage department features American Tourister, Ventura, Boyt, Lark, French, Samsonite, and Andiamo, at 30% to 40% savings. You needn't *pay* executive to *look* it—the attaché and briefcases by Schlesinger, Lion, Yale, Grace, Atlas, Michael Scott, and Scully are 20% off list. Women heeding corporate fashion dictates can hide their Meyers, Etienne Aigner, Liz Claiborne, Stone Mountain, or Dooney & Bourke handbag from Ace in the aforementioned briefcase and put the 30% savings toward a management seminar. Or invest the money in a travel alarm by Seiko, Bulova, or Linden, also offered at Ace—you'll never miss an important business meeting because your wake-up call came an hour late. And when you close the deal, sign the papers in style with a Cross pen—they're 20% off list price at Ace.

The company is committed to low prices and good service, which account for its longevity—sixty years in the business. Ace deals primarily on a price-quote basis, but publishes a Christmas catalog in October, and *sometimes* another one in June.

ALTMAN LUGGAGE

135 Orchard St.
New York, NY 10002
(212) 254–7275

Information: price quote by letter with SASE
Discount: 20% to 50%
Goods: name brand
Minimum Order: none
Shipping, Insurance: extra; UPS
Sales Tax: NY deliveries
Accepts: check, MO, MC, V, AE, DC
$$$

Here's an easy way to cut your carrying costs: buy your luggage, briefcase, backpack, or attaché case at Altman. Hartmann, Samsonite, Lark, Schlesinger, Atlas, Michael Scott, and other well-known brands are stocked here at up to 50% off list prices.

Altman doesn't have a catalog, so you must write for a price quote (include a SASE). State the model number, color or design (if applicable), and other particulars when querying.

A TO Z LUGGAGE CO., INC.

4627 New Utrecht Ave.
Brooklyn, NY 11219
(718) 435-2423

Catalog: free; pub. in Nov. (see text)
Information: price quote by phone or letter with SASE
Discount: 20% to 60%
Goods: name brand
Minimum Order: none
Shipping, Insurance: extra; UPS, PP
Sales Tax: NY deliveries
Accepts: check, MO, MC, V, AE, CB, DC
$$$

You could probably afford another vacation this year if you had bought your luggage from A to Z. This 45-year-old firm sells only first-quality luggage from the top firms: Samsonite, Hartmann, American Tourister, Amelia Earhart, Lark, Ventura, and others. It carries everything from small totes and overnight bags to steamer trunks.

The catalog is available in November for Christmas shopping. If you're not buying during that season, you'll have to get a price quote. Salespeople at A to Z will do their best to answer questions over the phone, but since they're usually busy with store customers, the firm prefers that you write for a price quote, including manufacturer, model number, color, and a SASE with your letter.

BETTINGER'S LUGGAGE SHOP

80 Rivington St.
New York, NY 10002
(212) 475-1690; 674-9411

Information: price quote by phone or letter with SASE
Discount: 30% to 50%
Goods: name brand, generic
Minimum Order: none
Shipping, Insurance: extra; UPS, PP
Sales Tax: NY deliveries
Accepts: check, MO, MC, V, AE
$$$

Bettinger's has been helping New Yorkers pack up and go since 1914, and the proprietors know their goods. For its selection alone, this source deserves your attention: Oleg Cassini, Skyway, Atlas, Andiamo, Boyt, Ventura, Lark, Wings, Fulton, American Tourister, Samsonite, and several other firms are featured here. There are attaché cases, instrument cases, artists' portfolios, sample cases, and camp and steamer trunks. All this is enough to make you want to hit the road, especially when you're saving 30% to 50% on the list prices. Be sure to include model number, color, and size information when you ask for a price quote, and include a SASE if you're writing.

CARRY-ON LUGGAGE, INC.

97 Orchard St.
New York, NY 10002
(212) 226–4980

Information: price quote by phone or letter with SASE
Discount: 30% to 50%
Goods: name brand
Minimum Order: none
Shipping: extra; UPS
Sales Tax: NY deliveries
Accepts: check, MO, MC, V
$$$

Carry-on is where you can carry off great bargains on suitcases, attaché cases, and other leather goods, by such firms as Ventura, Lark, Samsonite, Tumi, Wings, Amelia Earhart, St. Thomas, Anne Klein, Christian Dior, Diane Von Furstenberg, Invicta, Pierre Cardin, Verde, Harrison, Michael Scott, Rolfs, and Rona. If you're looking for a portfolio of the sort that models and artists tote, just inquire—these are also stocked. Write or call (include a SASE) for a price quote, and include the style number and color of the product you want.

INNOVATION LUGGAGE

487 Hackensack Ave.
River Edge, NJ 07661
(201) 487–6000: inquiries and NJ orders
(800) 631–0742: orders except NJ

Brochure: free
Information: price quote by phone or letter with SASE
Discount: 20% to 50%
Goods: name brand
Minimum Order: $15
Shipping: extra; UPS
Sales Tax: NJ and NY orders
Accepts: check, MO, MC, V, AE, DC
$$$

Innovation's stock of luggage, portfolios, briefcases, attaché cases, handbags, and small leather goods represents the most popular brands in this country at savings that inspire getaways: up to 50% off suggested list or retail prices.

This firm is the largest independent Samsonite dealer in the U.S. It also offers products by Amelia Earhart, Tumi, Lark, American Tourister, Ventura, Hartmann, Skyway, Invicta, Land, and many other firms and designers. Stock changes regularly and specials are run frequently, so we recommend ordering on a price-quote basis for your best deal. The ten-page brochure is most easily obtained in the holiday season and shows an array of gift suggestions as well as stock items. Innovation has 15 stores in New Jersey and New York where you can save even more on discontinued lines and one-of-a-kind styles.

LEATHER SCHOOL

Monastery of Santa Croce
Piazza S. Croce, 16
Florence
Italy
Phone # 244533

Catalog: 5 IRCs or $5
Discount: up to 75% (see text)
Goods: house brand
Minimum Order: none
Shipping, Insurance: included on orders over
  $100, air mail
Duty: extra
Accepts: check or IMO
$$$$

The Leather School was founded by an order of Franciscan monks to perpetuate the art of Florentine leather-work. The traditions are carried on by young boys apprenticed to the master artisans who work at the Monastery.

The products of the School can be compared quite fairly to those of "status" leather-goods shops, some of which were also founded in Italy. But the Leather School sells nothing of vinyl-impregnated canvas or initial-ridden fabric—all the goods are made of fine polished and nappa leathers.

Among the products offered in the color flyleafs are wallets, eyeglass cases, handbags, attaché cases, desk sets, and belts. Because the School exports to stores worldwide, it offers both fashionable and traditional designs. Striking tricolor shoulder bags in soft, nappa leather were *more* stylish than many boutique offerings we'd seen and were outrageously inexpensive at under $15 each. Larger town-and-country styles ran about $60 to $90, still quite reasonable.

But it's the more structured bags and other goods of polished calf that demonstrate fully the artisans' skills. A simple gusseted envelope model with gold-plated closure and adjustable strap is under $65; a leather-lined reproduction of the bag Kate Hepburn carried in *Summertime* costs under $75. The small leather goods are bargains by any standard: a woman's billfold with change purse is $24.50 at the School, while an almost identical "status" version cost $70. That same retail company sells its folding bill holder for $45; the School has a look-alike for $3.40. A practical reversible men's belt that fetches $65 to $70 in other catalogs is just $13.20 here. The attaché cases and desk sets are beautifully made and outfitted; try finding a leather-lined attaché case with English brass corners, combination locks, two interior file pockets, and slots for cards and pens at $160 elsewhere. Venetian-style finishing is also done at the School; the leather is stamped in patterns of gold and hand-painted in contrasting colors. Mirrored lipstick cases are 90¢, leather-topped compacts $1.80, key cases up to $3.80, and coin purses, French purses, and cosmetic cases $2 to $13.

If you'd like something made to order, write to the School with a complete description and you'll get a price quote. If you'd like a plain bag gilded, add $1 to the price. Gold initials are stamped free of charge. And note that some goods are offered in "all colors," but no color chart is provided. We recommend using other illustrations as a guide, and sending a clipping of the desired color taped to your order. We also ask that you include an additional $3 if your order is under $50 to cover the currency-conversion fee that will be charged to the School.

NORTH COUNTRY LEATHER

1 Front St.
P.O. Box 25
East Rochester, NH 03867
(603) 332–0707

Brochure: $2, refundable
Discount: up to 50%
Goods: house brand
Minimum Order: none
Shipping: extra; UPS
Sales Tax: NH deliveries
Accepts: check, MO, MC, V
$$$

North Country sells the kind of bag that is destined to spend very little time in the closet. The company offers over two dozen handbag and shoulder bag styles of rich, durable cowhide in a variety of classic colors. The bags are made to last, down to the solid brass hardware that won't turn silvery after a few months of wear. And the scuffing and hard knocks, which drive most bags into retirement or a refinisher's hands, only give the cowhide "character." North Country's prices are as down-to-earth as its products—to 50% less than comparable goods—from about $40 to $100. The six-page brochure is illustrated with line drawings, and returns are accepted.

SEE ALSO:

Bondy Export Corp. . . . Samsonite luggage . . . APPLIANCES

Custom Coat Co. . . . gloves, moccasins, bags, small leather goods . . . CLOTHING

Dairy Association Co., Inc. . . . Tackmaster leather conditioner . . . ANIMAL

The Deerskin Place . . . leather wallets, shoulder bags . . . CLOTHING

The Finals . . . nylon getaway, duffle bags . . . CLOTHING

Holabird Sports Discounters . . . racquet bags . . . SPORTS

International Solgo, Inc. . . . name-brand luggage . . . APPLIANCES

Laurence Corner . . . government-surplus toiletries kits, duffle bags, suitcases . . . CLOTHING

Pagano Gloves . . . deerskin and cowhide wallets, keycases, handbags . . . CLOTHING

Prince Fashions Ltd. . . . leather handbags . . . CLOTHING

The Renovator's Supply, Inc. . . . trunk hardware . . . HOME (maintenance)

Sales Citi, Inc. . . . Samsonite attaché cases . . . APPLIANCES

Specialty Leather of California . . . nylon and vinyl duffle bags, sport totes, garment bags . . . CLOTHING

Sunco Products Corp. . . . suede and cowhide work gloves . . . CLOTHING

MEDICAL AND SCIENTIFIC

Prescription drugs, hearing aids,
contact lenses and eyeglasses, and
post-surgery supplies and equipment.

Buying your medications by mail is convenient and often much less expensive than having prescriptions filled at the local drugstore. Even the prices of generic drugs are lower by mail, affording you savings of up to 60% on some commonly prescribed remedies. You can also save up to half the cost of hearing aids, contact lenses, eyeglasses, breast forms, and products for the ostomate and convalescent patient by ordering them from the firms listed here.

Wonder what to do with your old eyeglasses? Help others who can't afford them see more clearly—send them to New Eyes for the Needy, P.O. Box 332, Short Hills, NJ 07078.

Want to keep up with government news on medicine and regulatory matters? Subscribe to *FDA Consumer,* published ten times yearly. Rate information and order forms are included in the "U.S. Government Books" catalog, available free upon request from the Superintendent of Documents, U.S. Government Printing Office, Washington, DC 20402, Attn: Books Catalog.

For related products, see the listings in "Health and Beauty."

BRUCE MEDICAL SUPPLY

411 Waverly Oaks Rd.
Dept. WBM
P.O. Box 9166
Waltham, MA 02254
(617) 894–6262: inquiries
(800) 342–8955: MA orders
(800) 225–8446: orders
except MA

Catalog: free; pub. 4 times yearly
Discount: 20% to 60%
Goods: name brand, generic
Minimum Order: none
Shipping, Insurance: extra; UPS, PP
Handling: $1.50 per order up to 50 pounds
Sales Tax: MA deliveries (if applicable)
Accepts: check, MO, MC, V
$$$$

The Bruce Medical Supply catalog has 40 pages of products for diabetics and ostomates—people who have had tracheostomies, colostomies, ileostomies, and urostomies—as well as general supplies for the convalescent or incontinent person. Several lines of pouches are shown, and related supplies include dressings, adhesives and removers, disks and seal rings, irrigators, lubricants, cleansing products, deodorants, disinfectants, and other goods. Bathtub safety benches, tub grips, decubitus (bed sore) protection, wheelchairs, canes, crutches, magnifying glasses, sphygmomanometers, stethoscopes, compresses, and other health-care products are all stocked.

Bruce also sells a line of fitness equipment—jogging machines, treadmills, rowers, cycles, and multigyms. All prices are discounted—sometimes by as much as 60%—and most of the goods are manufactured by well-known medical-supply firms. Several books on related topics are also offered. Goods are shipped in unmarked boxes, and your complete satisfaction is guaranteed.

RIC CLARK COMPANY

9530 Langdon Ave.
Sepulveda, CA 91343
(818) 892–6636

Catalog: free
Discount: 50% plus
Goods: name brand
Minimum Order: none
Shipping, Insurance: included
Sales Tax: CA deliveries (if applicable)
Accepts: check or MO
$$$$ (see text)

Ric Clark publishes a polished little catalog featuring his six hearing aid models. All the models are photographed next to another object to give you an idea of the relative size. There are models for hearing losses that range from mild to severe, including an in-the-ear model and "compression" aids that are said to "cushion" sudden loud noises. You may pay a $10 deposit on any of the aids and try one for a month—batteries included—and if you decide against purchasing at the end of the 30-day trial period, simply return it and Mr. Clark will refund your money.

A budget plan is offered for those who want to spread payments; you can pay $20 a month (with a 10% finance charge) until the aid is purchased. If you pay in full, the aids cost from $209.49 to $279.49—about half the prices charged by hearing aid dealers. You have to send Mr. Clark a note from your doctor stating that you may need a hearing aid, or sign the waiver section of the order form if you want to purchase or try one. We're pleased that Mr. Clark recommends you see a doctor to make sure hearing loss isn't related to another physical problem before buying an aid. It is excellent advice. All the aids are guaranteed, and repairs are available at nominal rates for aids no longer under warranty.

CANADIAN READERS, PLEASE NOTE: payment must be made in *U.S.* funds.

**DUK KWONG OPTICAL
CENTRE**

**27 Cameron Rd., 4th Fl.
Tsimshatsui, Kowloon
Hong Kong
Phone # 668019**

Price List: free; pub. in Jan.
Discount: 30% to 80%
Goods: prescription, house brand
Minimum Order: none
Shipping, Handling, Insurance: $3 per pair, airmail
Duty: extra
Accepts: check, MO, certified check, MC, V, AE,
   EC, Access
$$$

Duk Kwong sells stylish eyeglass frames and sunglasses at low prices—$4 to $40 for the frames, with prescription lenses beginning at $13. There is a good range of styles, including aviator models, folding frames, lorgnettes, and fashionable and conservative models. Duk Kwong also sells hard and soft contact lenses, made from your prescription or duplicated from your own lenses. Clear and tinted hard lenses are $45; soft lenses are $100. The eyeglass lenses are available in tinted plastic, safety lenses, and photochromic types, for single, bifocal, and trifocal vision correction. You can deduct 10% if you buy two pairs of glasses; deduct 15% if you order three or more. You're bound to find a frame to suit your tastes here, and the prices are excellent. Be sure to send your most recent prescription when you order.

**FEDERAL/GETZ
PHARMACY SERVICE**

**Second and Main Sts.
Madrid, IA 50156
(515) 795–2450: IA orders
(800) 247–1236: orders
except IA**

Catalog: free
Information: price quote by phone or letter with
   SASE
Discount: up to 60%
Goods: house brand, generic
Minimum Order: $5
Shipping, Insurance: included; UPS, PP
Handling: 75¢ per order
Sales Tax: IA deliveries
Accepts: check, MO, MC, V
$$$

Federal/Getz sells vitamins and dietary supplements, over-the-counter remedies, generic prescription drugs, beauty aids, and much more. You can save up to 50% on vitamins and supplements by buying the house brand and up to 60% on prescription drugs by ordering the generic equivalents. To prove there's no difference in quality, Federal includes the formulas for the vitamins and nonprescription drugs in the catalog, so you can see that identical ingredients are used in the branded and proprietary products. The vitamins and supplements include formula equivalents of Theragran, Myadec, Geritol, Stresstabs, Unicap, and other nationally known products. The drugs are listed with their trade names, list prices, chemical names, and the lower generic prices. Be sure to ask your doctor to specify the generic name on the prescription or it can't be filled with the lower priced product. Everything sold here is backed by the firm's unconditional guarantee of satisfaction, and returns are accepted within 30 days.

LINGERIE FOR LESS

11075 Erhard
Dallas, TX 75228
(214) 324–9135

Information: price quote by phone or letter with SASE
Discount: up to 75%
Goods: house brand
Minimum Order: none
Shipping, Insurance: extra; UPS
Sales Tax: TX deliveries
Accepts: check or MO
$$$$

This lingerie shop sells the "Soft Touch Breast Form," a molded gel breast form for mastectomy patients, comparable to others selling for more than three times as much. It's available in seven sizes, costs under $40, and is designed to fit all kinds of brassieres. To get the current selling price and shipping charge, call or write (include a SASE) and state your size. The form is unconditionally guaranteed for one year.

**NATIONAL CONTACT LENS
CENTER**

838 Fourth St.
Santa Rosa, CA 95404
(707) 542–3404

Catalog: 25¢
Information: price quote by phone or letter with SASE
Discount: up to 50%
Goods: name brand
Minimum Order: none
Shipping, Insurance: extra; UPS, PP
Sales Tax: CA deliveries
Accepts: check, MO, MC, V

The Santa Rosa Optometry Center runs this lens-by-mail service that can save you up to 50% on your next pair. The catalog was not available for review, but the company sells "all" hard and soft lenses, including Hydrocurve, Bausch & Lomb, Flexlens, Aquaflex, and any other major brand or line made. You can call National Contact with your prescription to see whether it can be filled in your brand choice, and to obtain the price. We can't recommend this for people being fitted for the first time, (medical supervision is advisable for them), but anyone who has worn lenses and has a recent prescription should have no problems.

PHARMACEUTICAL SERVICES

126 W. Markey Rd., Dept. WBMC
Belton, MO 64012
(816) 331-0700

Price List: free
Discount: 20% to 60%
Goods: name brand, house brand, generic
Minimum Order: none
Shipping, Insurance: free on prescription drugs;
  $1 on nonprescription drugs under $20; UPS
Sales Tax: MO deliveries (if applicable)
Accepts: check or MO
$$$

You can save up to 60% on your next prescription if you make sure your doctor okays its generic equivalent and you have it filled by Pharmaceutical Services. We found the prices of generics lower at this source than at local drug stores, and the selection superior. You can save an additional 10% on all your purchases here by paying a $12 yearly fee, and at the end of each year Pharmaceutical will send you a printout of all the prescriptions you ordered—a real help when preparing tax returns. Pharmaceutical also sells over-the-counter remedies, vitamins, dietary supplements, and other goods—all of which are competitively priced. Orders are shipped promptly.

PRESCRIPTION DELIVERY SYSTEMS

136 S. York Rd.
Hatboro, PA 19040
(215) 674-1565: AK, HI, PA orders and inquiries
(800) 441-8976: orders and inquiries except AK, HI, PA

Brochure: free
Information: price quote by phone or letter with SASE
Discount: up to 40%
Goods: generic, name brand
Minimum Order: none
Shipping, Insurance: extra; UPS, PP
Sales Tax: PA deliveries
Accepts: check, MO, MC, V
$$$

Prescription Delivery sells branded pharmaceuticals, generic over-the-counter remedies and vitamins, and other products. Over 50,000 drugs are stocked, and you may use the WATS line to call for a price quote on your needs. Savings on the drugs can amount to 40% on the list prices, but most are sold at 10% and 15% below drugstore prices. If your prescription is not available in generic form or you don't want to use generics, this is an easy way to save—after getting the quote and making sure what you need is in stock, mail in the prescription and Prescription will send your order and bill you. Orders of $100 or more must be prepaid, and satisfaction is guaranteed.

RITEWAY HAC

P.O. Box 59451
Chicago, IL 60659
(312) 539–6620

Brochure: free
Discount: 50% plus
Goods: name brand
Minimum Order: none
Shipping, Insurance: extra; UPS, PP
Sales Tax: CA deliveries
Accepts: check or MO
$$$

A $10 deposit will buy you a 30-day trial of all but one of Riteway's eight hearing aids, which are manufactured by Royaltone and Danavox. If you decide to buy the aid, you can pay a third of the cost up front and the rest in $20 monthly installments with no finance charges. The aids run to $249.50 for the deluxe, in-the-ear model. There are three over-the-ear models, the customized style for nearly invisible sound enhancement, and a power body model for severe hearing losses. The specifications for frequency, range, and battery type and life are included. Riteway's policy is especially convenient because of the small deposit and the 30-day trial policy, but please note that the $10 ($40 for the in-the-ear model) is not refunded if you decide against buying the aid. Satisfaction is guaranteed on every purchase.

SEE ALSO:

Ad-Lib Astronomics . . . name-brand telescopes . . . CAMERAS
Allyn Air Seat Co. . . . . air-filled wheelchair seat liners . . . SPORTS
Animal Veterinary Products, Inc. . . . . animal biologicals, medications . . .
ANIMAL

Bailey's, Inc. . . . first-aid kits, ImmunIvy, ImmunOak . . . TOOLS

Comp-U-Card . . . prescription drugs . . . GENERAL

Danley's . . . name-brand telescopes . . . CAMERAS

Executive Photo & Supply Corp. . . . Celestron telescopes . . . CAMERAS

47st Photo, Inc. . . . Celstron, Cometron telescopes . . . CAMERAS

Harvest of Values . . . nutritional supplements . . . HEALTH

Kansas City Vaccine Company . . . livestock and pet biologicals, medications . . . ANIMAL

Laurence Corner . . . government-surplus medical, dental, optical equipment . . . CLOTHING

Mardiron Optics . . . name-brand telescopes . . . CAMERAS

Northern Wholesale Veterinary Supply . . . animal biologicals, dietary supplements . . . ANIMAL

Omaha Vaccine Co., Inc. . . . biologicals, pharmaceuticals for livestock . . . ANIMAL

Orion Telescope Center . . . name-brand telescopes . . . CAMERAS

PBS Livestock Drugs . . . livestock biologicals, instruments . . . ANIMAL

Plastic BagMart . . . zip-top plastic bags . . . HOME (maintenance)

Puritan's Pride, Inc. . . . nutritional supplements, thermometers, heating pads, sphygmomanometers . . . HEALTH

Self-Sufficiency and Smallholding Supplies . . . veterinary instruments, animal pharmaceuticals . . . ANIMAL

Star Pharmaceutical, Inc. . . . nutritional supplements, OTC remedies, sphygmomanometers . . . HEALTH

Sunburst Biorganics . . . nutritional supplements . . . HEALTH

United Pharmacal Company, Inc. . . . biologicals, instruments for animal care and treatment . . . ANIMAL

Vitamin Specialties Co. . . . nutritional supplements, OTC remedies . . . HEALTH

Wear-Guard Work Clothes . . . lab coats . . . CLOTHING

Western Natural Products . . . nutritional supplements . . . HEALTH

Wholesale Veterinary Supply, Inc. . . . biologicals, veterinary surgical supplies . . . ANIMAL

MUSIC

Instruments, supplies, and services.

We are based in New York City, so we know that professional musicians don't pay full price for their fine instruments. Odds are they buy them from one of the sources included here. Our listees sell top-quality music products, and while these outlets usually serve the knowledgeable, they will be perfectly happy to work with you even if you're a rank neophyte. You can save hundreds of dollars on top-rate equipment; if you're equipping a band, you might even save enough money to buy the van and pay the roadies.

When buying instruments, go for quality—they can last a lifetime or even several, and the resale market for quality pieces is good. Buy wisely today and 20 years down the road you may be selling your "vintage" axe to Guitar Trader for several times what you paid!

A.L.A.S. ACCORDION-O-RAMA

**16 W. 19th St.
New York, NY 10011
(212) 675-9089**

Catalog: free
Information: inquiries by phone or letter
Discount: 20% to 40%
WBMC Reader Discount: 2% to 5% (see text)
Goods: name brand
Minimum Order: none
Shipping, Insurance: extra; UPS, PP, FOB NYC
Sales Tax: NY deliveries
Accepts: check, MO, MC, V
$$$

Accordion-O-Rama *is* accordions. This company has been in business for 35 years and is an authorized dealer and factory-service center for Dellape, Hohner, Pollytone, Excelsior, Arpeggio, and Avanti. It also sells Cordovox, Paolo Soprani, Iorio, Elka, Cintioli, Nunzio, Sano, Serenelli, and Scandalli accordions. The catalog, cards featuring individual models with color photos attached, gives you an idea of the beauty of these instruments. Prices for these deluxe models are 20% to 40% below list, and you can reduce that by an additional 2% to 5% with the WBMC reader discount. (Identify yourself as a reader when you order and ask for the discount that applies to the model you're buying.) Accordion-O-Rama also sells accordion synthesizers, accordion speakers, organ-accordions, and an accordion stand and invisible accordion strap by Bandoleer, both of which are exclusives. The company does repairs, will overhaul your accordion completely, sells reconditioned models, and accepts trade-ins.

SAM ASH MUSIC CORP.

124 Fulton Ave.
Hempstead, NY 11550–3755
(718) 347–7757: inquiries
and orders in New York
City
(800) 632–2322: orders in
NY State
(800) 645–3518: orders
except NY

Catalog: free (see text)
Information: price quote by phone or letter with
SASE
Discount: 30% to 50%
Goods: name brand
Minimum Order: $15
Shipping, Insurance: extra; UPS, PP
Sales Tax: NY and NJ deliveries
Accepts: check, MO, MC, V, AE
$$$

In 1924, a violinist and bandleader named Sam Ash set up shop in Brooklyn at the behest of his wife, Rose. What began as a modest musical instruments business became a seven-store empire offering instruments, sound systems, recording equipment, specialized lighting, and repairs to ordinary people, superstars and aspirants, schools, and the military. And it's still a family business.

Sam Ash carries hundreds of manufacturers, including Acoustic, Alembic, Altec, Ashly, Bach, BGW, Biamp, Bose, Buffet, Bundy, Casio, Cerwin-Vega, Crumar, Deagan, Delta Lab, Electro-Voice, Ensonia, Fender, Gemeinhardt, Getzen, Gibson, Gretsch, Guild, Hohner, Holton, Ibanez, JBL, King, Korg, LeBlanc, Loft, Ludwig, Marshall, Martin, Mic Mix, Moog, Multivox, Musser, Ovation, Paiste, Pearl, Peavey, QSC, Ramsa, Rhodes, Roland, Samson, Selmer, Shure, Siel, Slingerland, Studiomaster, Tama, Tangent, Tapco, Tascam, Teac, Washburn, Wurlitzer, Yamaha, Zildjian, etc. Instrumental, vocal, band, and orchestra sheet music are also available at the Sam Ash stores.

Discounts average 40%, and all merchandise is covered by Sam Ash and/or the manufacturers' warranties. Ash is developing a catalog, "printing a section at a time," we're told. Because the section available at the time you write may not include what you're looking for, remember that you can call or write for a price quote (be sure to include a SASE with your letter). Since at any given moment the firm will be offering select equipment at 50% off, be sure to call here before you buy elsewhere.

CARVIN

1155 Industrial Ave., Dept.
W-85
Escondido, CA 92025
(619) 747–1710

Catalog: free
Discount: up to 40%
Goods: house brand
Minimum Order: $10
Shipping, Insurance: extra; UPS, FOB Escondido
Sales Tax: CA deliveries
Accepts: check, MO, certified check
$$$

Carvin manufactures an excellent line of music equipment—mixers, amps, mikes, monitor systems, and electric guitars. Most of the latter are look-alikes for classics like the old Les Pauls but cost much less. Carvins are more than just good-looking; they've earned the endorsement of at least one rock luminary. And you can test them for yourself because Carvin gives you a ten-day free trial period. If you're not completely satisfied you can return the equipment for an immediate refund. This guarantee covers all the Carvin products.

The smashing color catalog lists specifications, features, and individual guarantees with the description of each item. After paging through the catalog, one musician remarked that "any company that can promise no buzz on an action 1/16″ from the neck is making a really *fine* guitar." In other words, Carvin guarantees a superior product. All servicing and performance testing under the warranty is done free of charge. Warranties range from one to five years, depending on the item.

**CASCIO MUSIC COMPANY,
INC.
(Interstate Music Supply)**

P.O. Box 315
New Berlin, WI 53151
(414) 786–6210

Catalog: free
Discount: 20% to 50%
Goods: name brand, house brand
Minimum Order: $25
Shipping, Insurance: extra; UPS, PP, FOB New
  Berlin
Sales Tax: WI deliveries
Accepts: check, MO, MC, V
$$$

This firm has 40 years in the music business. It can supply you with instruments, electronics, recording equipment, and accessories from such manufacturers as Ludwig, Fender, Yamaha, Gibson, Martin, Selmer, Armstrong, and Besson. The Cascios also have their own line, marketed under the Interstate Music Supply moniker. Savings run up to 50%, and the selection is vast—even the 96-page catalog doesn't cover it all. If you don't see what you're looking for, give Cascio (IMS) a call—the item is probably in stock.

FRED'S STRING WAREHOUSE

212 W. Lancaster, Dept. WM
Shillington, PA 19607
(215) 777–3733

Catalog: $1; pub. Jan., Apr., Sept.
Discount: 40%
Goods: name brand, house brand
Minimum Order: none
Shipping, Insurance: extra; UPS, PP
Sales Tax: PA deliveries
Accepts: check, MO, MC, V, CHOICE
$$$

You can improve your sound and save up to 40% on list with Fred's catalog of steel, brass, and bright and phosphor bronze strings for every type of guitar, as well as a full range of strings for pedal steel, mandolin, bass, banjo, violin, sitar, autoharp, bouzouki, and other instruments. The brands include Martin, Vega, Darco, D'Addario, Savarez, Ernie Ball, GHS, Guild, John Pearse, Dr. Thomastik-Infeld, Gibson, Aranjuez, Fender, and Black Diamond, among others. Picks, cables, harmonicas, Di Marzio pickups, Ibanez effects boxes, the Crybaby, mikes, and capos can also be found here at savings of up to 40%. Authorized returns are accepted within five days.

FREEPORT MUSIC

41 Shore Dr.
Huntingdon Bay, NY 11743
(516) 549–4108

Brochure: $1, refundable; pub. 9 times yearly
Information: price quote by phone or letter with SASE
Discount: 20% to 60%
Goods: name brand
Minimum Order: $10 on prepaid orders; $25 on credit cards
Shipping, Insurance: $2.75 minimum; UPS, PP, FOB Huntingdon Bay
Sales Tax: NY deliveries
Accepts: check, MO, MC, V
$$$$

Freeport has been in business since 1921 and will probably be here in 2021 because you can't beat great prices and a good selection. This firm carries Ludwig drums at 40% off list prices; drums and sets by Pearl, SlingerLand, and Tama; guitars by Dobro, Guild, Martin, Yamaha, and Gibson; Kawai pianos and organs; Morley, Roland, Boss, Earth, Ampeg, Marshall, and Fender amps and electronics; DiMarzio pickups, Shure mikes, Franz metronomes, and more. There are woodwind instruments from Selmer, King, LeBlanc, and Buffet; Selmer brasses, Leigh woodwind accessories, Armstrong flutes, Moog electronics, Hohner harmonicas; and strings, reeds, valve oil, cases, music stands, guitar straps, picks, and disco lighting and stage effects for rock groups. Look no further for musical saws, piano tuning kits, FM wireless transmitters for guitars and mikes, and used instruments—they're all here.

Freeport's discount policy is summed up in its brochure: "We will not be undersold. If you get a legitimate lower price from any music store or mail-order house on any item we sell, call or write to us. We will beat that price and then some. We will make it 'worth it to you' to do your business with Freeport Music." So don't buy an instrument or another set of strings before you get a price quote from this firm.

GUITAR TRADER

---

12 Broad St.
Red Bank, NJ 07701
Attn: Bugs
(201) 741–0771

Vintage Guitar Bulletin: $20, year's subscription of 12 issues; $35, 2 years; refundable
Information: price quote by phone or letter with SASE
Discount: 40%
WBMC Reader Bonus: see text
Goods: name brand
Minimum Order: none
Shipping, Insurance: $20 per instrument; UPS, PP
Sales Tax: NJ deliveries
Accepts: check, MO, MC, V
$$$ (see text)

If you did a double take at the price of this firm's catalog, it's understandable. But this is really a magazine for the guitar collector, complete with a Q&A column, restoration clinic, and blast-from-the-past features on now-rare guitars. The listings include both used and vintage guitars. Prices can top $10,000, but many are below $500, so this group is worth a look if you appreciate the quality of older guitars but don't want to make a major investment. The vintage department also stocks violins, banjos, mandolins, ukeleles, amps, and other electronics.

New acoustic and electric guitars and some electronics are offered—several Ovation lines, Martin, Guild, Washburn, Gibson, Honda, Dean, Kramer, Hofner, BC Rich, Rickenbacker, Fender, and Di Marzio pickups—all at a discount of about 40%. Back issues of the Bulletin are available, and you can charge the subscription to your credit card. Readers spending more than $200 on an instrument are entitled to the bonus book, *Guitar Identification*.

CANADIAN READERS, PLEASE NOTE: Higher shipping charges are assessed on orders sent to Canada, and payment is accepted for the subscription and/or goods in U.S. funds only.

**KENNELLY KEYS MUSIC
AND DANCE, INC.**

**5030 208th St. S.W.
Lynnwood, WA 98036
(206) 771–7020: inquiries
(800) 562–6558: WA orders
(800) 426–6409: orders
except WA**

Catalog: free; pub. yearly in Feb.
Information: price quote by phone or letter with
  SASE
Discount: 30% to 40%
Goods: name brand
Minimum Order: none
Shipping, Insurance: extra; UPS, PP
Sales Tax: WA deliveries
Accepts: check, MO, certified check, MC, V, AE
$$$

Marching bands, student musicians, guitarists, take note: Kennelly has an excellent selection of instruments and equipment for all of you. Woodwinds, brass, percussion instruments, guitars, speakers, amps, tuners, effects boxes, autoharps, mikes, stage lighting, mike cords, snakes—they're all here, at prices that sometimes run more than 40% below list. Kennelly stocks goods from virtually every manufacturer, including Armstrong, Artley, Bach, Benge, Buffet, Bundy, Deagon, Fender, Gemeinhardt, Getzen, Gibson, Electro-Voice, Korg, Larilee, LeBlanc, Ludwig, Ovation, Pearl, Polytone, Rico, Roland, Selmer, and Vito. The repair department does business by mail. Authorized returns are accepted.

MANDOLIN BROTHERS LTD.

629 Forest Ave.
Staten Island, NY 10310
(718) 981-3226

Catalog: free; pub. twice yearly
Information: price quote by phone or letter with
 SASE
Discount: 37½%
Goods: name brand
Minimum Order: none
Shipping, Insurance: $20 minimum on instruments;
 UPS, PP, FOB Staten Island
Sales Tax: NY deliveries
Accepts: check, MO, MC, V, AE
$$$

Every guitarist we know has dreams of owning a vintage axe—a guitar made before 1969, when better materials and more handcrafting were used in production. Beyond the aesthetic and investment considerations, many musicians believe that the sound quality of vintage instruments is much finer than that of the new ones.

Mandolin Brothers sells vintage fretted instruments—guitars, mandolins, banjos—at good market prices, and offers select new, name-brand guitars, mandolins, banjos, and electronics at discount prices. Stanley Jay, president of the company, tells us his basic discount is 37½% off list prices on Martin, Ovation, and Guild instruments. You can order from the catalog or call for a price quote.

MANNY'S MUSICAL INSTRUMENTS & ACCESSORIES, INC.

156 W. 48th St.
New York, NY 10036-1578
(212) 819-0756

Information: price quote by phone or letter with
 SASE
Discount: 30% to 50%
Goods: name brand
Minimum Order: none
Shipping, Insurance: extra; UPS, FOB NYC
Sales Tax: NY deliveries
Accepts: check, MO, MC, V
$$$

Manny's has been selling musical instruments for over 50 years, and it's hard to go into the store without seeing a famous face from the world of rock and roll. *Everything* is available at Manny's, from rock electronics to fine woodwinds and brass instruments. You can call or write with requests on just about any musical instrument, and if it's not in stock it can probably be ordered. Savings run to 50%, and there are regular sales on selected goods which bring prices down even further.

MOGISH STRING CO.

P.O. Box 493-W
Chesterland, OH 44026
(216) 729–3470

Catalog: free; pub. twice yearly
Information: price quote by phone or letter with
 SASE
Discount: 51%
Goods: name brand
Minimum Order: none
Shipping, Insurance: $1.85 minimum; UPS, PP
Sales Tax: OH deliveries
Accepts: check, MO, certified check
$$$

Jim Mogish began his business selling guitar strings and accessories, and eight years later has a 20-page catalog of "fretted instruments and accessories for the discriminating musician." He still has strings, including lines by Martin, D'Addario, Vega, GHS, Guild, Gibson, Fender, S.I.T., Ernie Ball, Savarez, La Bella, Dr. Thomastik, Prim, Piastro, and other firms, along with picks, capos, straps, and other accessories. Shure mikes, Di Marzio pickups, and guitars by Guild, Yamaha, Gibson, and Fender are sold as well. Discounts run up to 51%. If you need any advice on strings, Mr. Mogish is the man to ask.

NATIONAL EDUCATIONAL MUSIC COMPANY, LTD.

1181 Rte. 22
Box 1130-WM
Mountainside, NJ 07092
(201) 232–6700: inquiries
and AK, HI, NJ orders
(800) 526–4593: orders
except AK, HI, NJ

Catalog: free; pub. in Mar. and Aug.
Information: price quote by phone or letter with
 SASE
Discount: up to 50%
Goods: name brand
Minimum Order: none
Shipping, Insurance: extra; UPS, PP, FOB
 Mountainside
Sales Tax: NJ deliveries
Accepts: check, MO, MC, V, AE
$$$$

NEMC has been supplying school bands with instruments since 1959 and offers you the same equipment at savings of up to 50% on list prices. Brass, woodwind, and percussion instruments by Armstrong, Signet, LeBlanc, Selmer, Bundy, Vito, King, Gemeinhardt, Yamaha, Artley, Conn, Schreiber, Holton, Benge, Musser, Bach, Ludwig, Slingerland, Mirafone, Gill, Sabian, Roth, DEG, and many other firms are listed. If you don't see what you're looking for in the 21-page catalog, call or write for a price quote—it's probably stocked.

RAINBOW MUSIC

Poughkeepsie Plaza Mall
Rt. 9
Poughkeepsie, NY 12601

Catalog: free; pub. quarterly
Information: price quote by phone
Discount: 40%
Goods: name brand
Minimum Order: none
Shipping, Insurance: $3 minimum; UPS, PP
Sales Tax: NY deliveries
Accepts: check, MO, teller's check, MC, V, AE
$$$

The pot of gold at the end of this Rainbow is the choice selection of vintage guitars and amps, priced as low as business sense permits. The catalog we received included a large number of Gibson electrics and arch-tops, Fender electric and bass guitars and amps, and special issues and collectors' instruments by Rickenbacker, Ibanez, Peavy, Kramer, and others.

Rainbow also sells new equipment by Fender, Gibson, Hamer, Alembic, Rickenbacker, Steinberger Sound, Kramer, Ovation, Yamaha, Martin, Alvarez-Yairi, and Adamas, and amps from Legend, Roland, Marshall, Fender, and Music Man. Effects boxes, pickups, strings, keyboards, speakers, equipment cases, mixers, tape decks, and other equipment are all stocked at savings of up to 40%. Rainbow buys used guitars and amps and accepts trade-ins. If you don't see what you're looking for in the catalog, call to see whether the item is in stock.

SILVER & HORLAND, INC.

170 W. 48th St.
New York, NY 10036
(212) 869–3870

Information: price quote by phone or letter with
    SASE
Discount: 30% to 50%
Goods: name brand, generic, used, vintage
Minimum Order: $15
Shipping, Insurance: extra; UPS, PP
Sales Tax: NY deliveries
Accepts: check, MO, certified check
$$$$

Silver & Horland carries just about everything in the way of musical equipment and supplies and has been selling it all by mail since 1935. It offers new, used, and vintage instruments and carries all the top names: Seiko, Yamaha, Takamine, Gibson, Fender, Guild, Martin, Selmer, Armstrong, etc. However, no percussion instruments or harps are available. S & H does have Moogs, guitars, brass instruments, and supplies—reeds, picks, mouthpieces, and strings. Call with the model number or brand and a description of whatever you need for a price quote, and include a SASE. Repair service is available, and old equipment is purchased.

SUPERSAVE MUSIC

P.O. Box 944
Morganton, NC 28655

Catalog: $1; pub. yearly in Jan.
Discount: 30% plus
Goods: name brand
Minimum Order: none
Shipping, Insurance: extra; UPS, PP
Sales Tax: NC deliveries
Accepts: check, MO, certified check
$$

SuperSave publishes a 33-page catalog of instruments, accessories, stands, picks, drum heads, bongo cowbells, harmonicas, violin bridges, effects boxes, and much more in the "this 'n' that" line of musical equipment and sundries, at savings of up to 45%. There are products by all the major manufacturers: Schaller, Yamaha, Shure, Vega, Darco, Gibson, LaBella, D'Addario, Fender, Guild, and many more. This catalog is a great resource for the goods most music-supply houses don't include in their catalogs, such as cleaning equipment, drum keys, amp corners and glides. This is a *mail*-order firm: No phone orders are taken, and the prices in the catalog stand from one issue to the next.

TERMINAL MUSICAL SUPPLY, INC.

166 W. 48th St.
New York, NY 10036
(212) 869–5270

Information: price quote by phone or letter with SASE
Discount: up to 40%
Goods: name brand
Minimum Order: none
Shipping, Insurance: extra; UPS
Sales Tax: NY deliveries
Accepts: check, MO, MC, V
$$$

Terminal Music began its life as a pawnshop and is now a fixture on "musican's row," or West 48th Street in New York City. It carries a full range of instruments, including classical, band, fretted, string, keyboard, percussion, and Latin. All the major brands are available, as well as some of the hard-to-find: Madeira and Suzuki guitars, for example. Instruction manuals, metronomes, and other accessories are also sold. Although the company does a brisk trade in used instruments, it sells nothing but new equipment by mail. Call or write for a price quote.

SEE ALSO:

Bettinger's Luggage Shop . . . instrument cases . . . LEATHER
Blackwelder's Industries, Inc. . . . name-brand pianos . . . HOME (furnishings)
Executive Photo & Supply Corp. . . . . Casio musical keyboards . . . CAMERAS
Focus Electronics, Inc. . . . . Casio musical keyboards . . . APPLIANCES
47st Photo, Inc. . . . . Casio musical keyboards . . . CAMERAS
Laurence Corner . . . bagpipes . . . CLOTHING
Sultan's Delight Inc. . . . . esoteric musical instruments . . . FOOD

OFFICE AND COMPUTING

Office machines, furniture, and supplies;
computers, peripherals, and software;
printing and related services.

Want to score points with the company? Move your own venture into *Fortune's* golden circle? Get hardheaded about office expenses. Chances are good that you're not getting the best possible prices on supplies, printing, furnishings, and the countless items needed to keep the workplace running. You should shop as diligently for correction film and daisy wheels as you do for computer systems and word processors.

An important link in the budgetary chain is the office manager, who's often responsible for ordering supplies. You should know what that person's up against—if your company doesn't place regular orders, it's common practice for the supplier to send a sales rep around to apply a little charm to the hapless manager. The pressure tactics are often effective, since it's difficult to turn down a person who only wants to help restock the storeroom. You can begin a cost-control program by having the person you delegate as purchaser send for the catalogs listed here, so you can build up a file of discount sources for all your needs.

On computers: if you're a first-time buyer or are seeking to upgrade your system, the best advice we can give you is to read, read, and read some more. Attend demonstrations of new products. Watch colleagues at work with different hardware or programs. And ask questions—don't assume that everything does what it's claimed to do, as quickly, as easily, or as neatly as the ads would have you believe. Develop a vigorous skepticism for the term "compatible," and make sure you understand the limitations of such hardware and software before you buy. At some point, the industry will have to standardize, but until then it's "caveat emptor."

The reading material we recommend includes everything Peter A. McWilliams has written (especially for those just learning about computers); *The Whole Earth Software Catalog,* the quarterly update, *Whole Earth Software Review,* and *How to Buy Software* by Alfred Glossbrenner. These books include reviews of a number of prominent and obscure periodicals and can serve as a starting point. They're available in most bookstores and are updated regularly. The quarterly is $18 per year (four issues) from Whole Earth Software Review, P.O. Box 27956, San Diego, CA 92128. There are thousands of books on the market to guide you through the purchase of hardware and software and the use of specific systems, and many of them merit your attention. Don't limit yourself to what we've listed— they're cited because we found them accessible and their authors honest. In addition to books, there are scores of magazines and newsletters that cover every facet and name in computing. Once you're beyond the neophyte stage of computer literacy, you may find some of these helpful in getting the most use from your system.

The firms listed here can save you thousands of dollars on computer costs.

There's even one that offers discounts of up to 50% on the tool you'll need when the circuits blow from hardware overload: a pen.

ALFAX MFG.

**431 Canal St.
New York, NY 10013
(212) 966–6830: inquiries
and NY orders
(800) 221–5710: orders
except NY**

Catalog: free
Discount: 25% to 50%
Goods: house brand, name brand
Minimum Order: none
Shipping, Insurance: extra; UPS, FOB factory (see text)
Sales Tax: NY deliveries
Accepts: check, MO, MC, V, AE
$$$

How would you like to help your company, day-care center, club, or school save some money? It's easy—just have a copy of the Alfax catalog sent to the person who purchases supplies and equipment.

You'll find everything from nursery-sized stacking chairs and play tables to lounge ensembles in oak and Brazilian leather-look vinyl upholstery at Alfax. Every type of basic institutional furnishings is here: a variety of folding chairs and tables, molded plastic and padded stackable chairs; hardwood tables, lecterns, chairs, and bookcases; conference tables, a range of files and literature-storage units, and luxury appointments for the executive office. If you're looking for nursery mats, chalk and bulletin boards, P.A. systems, solar shades, trash can liners, trophy cases, carpet mats, lockers, hat racks, park benches, heavy steel shelving, prefabricated offices, or computer stations and work equipment, the 56-page Alfax catalog is the source. Although geared for the commercial-institutional buyer, many of the products are easily adapted to home use.

Alfax has been in business since 1949 and backs all purchases with an unconditional guarantee of satisfaction. Goods are shipped from the factory nearest you (Cincinnati, Dallas, Ft. Smith, Chicago, Philadelphia, Charlotte, Boston, or Los Angeles). Alfax will establish accounts with commercial buyers and bid for contracts. A design professional is on staff to recommend furnishings for offices, meeting rooms, classrooms, etc., and will provide you with a free layout to meet your needs.

AMITY HALLMARK, LTD.

**149–44 41st Ave.
Flushing, NY 11355
(718) 939–2323**

Brochure: free; pub. yearly
Information: price quote by phone or letter with
  SASE
Discount: up to 60%
Goods: custom printing
Minimum Order: $20
Shipping: included on orders to 15 states; 75¢ to
  $2 per ream to others; UPS, PP, FOB Flushing
Sales Tax: NY deliveries
Accepts: check, MO, certified check
$$

Amity's prices on some of its offset printing beat those of the printer who beat those of the printer who beat those of the printer who beat those of our local copy shop. In other words, some of the prices are quite low—up to 60% less than those of the same services offered by other discount printers. The savings apply chiefly to long runs (over 10,000) and special papers. The best prices were found on the 11" × 17" size.

Amity can print paper in the sizes cited above, and in 3½" × 5½" cards, five sizes of envelopes (plain and windowed), and carbonless sets. A full complement of special services and papers is listed in the brochure—colored, heavy, and card stock, gummed labels, cutting, colored inks, reductions and enlargements, halftones, folding, punching, padding, collating, and numbering. Raised-print business cards in a choice of colored inks are available from $19 per 1,000.

The firm, which has 35 years of printing experience, has upgraded its equipment and can now offer an extensive range of faces, point sizes, and special effects in its typesetting department. Prices for these services begin at $7.50 for a letterhead and $30 for an 8½" × 11" circular.

Although some of Amity's prices are not competitive, it does offer some real bargains. The next time you're pricing a job, be sure you include Amity in your estimates. Note that shipping is free on orders to 15 local states, and 75¢ to $2 per 1,000 8½" × 11" sheets to other states, including Alaska and Hawaii.

**BUSINESS &
INSTITUTIONAL
FURNITURE COMPANY**

611 N. Broadway
Milwaukee, WI 53202
(414) 272–6080: customer
service
(800) 242–7200: WI orders
(800) 558–8662: orders
except WI

Catalog: free; pub. in Jan. and July
Information: price quote by phone or letter with
  SASE
Discount: 30% to 40%
Goods: name brand, house brand
Minimum Order: none
Shipping, Insurance: extra; UPS, PP, FOB
  manufacturer
Sales Tax: WI deliveries
Accepts: check, MO, MC, V, AE
$$$

Business & Institutional Furniture sells just that: desks, chairs, files, bookcases, credenzas, and all kinds of office furniture and machines. It carries every type of file imaginable, from corrugated transfer files to beautifully finished, full-suspension fireproof lateral files. There are storage cabinets, folding and stacking chairs, lockers, handtrucks, carts, stools, folding tables, data and literature storage units, computer work stations, waste cans, mats, announcement boards, shelf units and organizers, outdoor furniture, prefabricated offices and partitions, energy-saving devices, and much more.

B & I offers a range of machines and products to fill the needs of offices large and small. The color catalog shows desktop 3M copiers, check writers, coin sorters, collaters, paper folders, duplicators, addressers, cordless phones, dialers, dictating machines, time clocks, key safes, calculators, etc. Although these products are designed primarily for commercial use, many are easily adapted to household applications. The industrial shelving is perfect for basement storage. Folding chairs, at little more than one-time rental cost when bought in quantity, provide the ideal solution to seating problems at parties. Olefin mats installed at the back door help keep mud in its place. Solar-control shades can be hung anywhere to minimize light and heat transmission. You can save up to 40% by buying from B & I, more if you buy in quantity. The "three-year, no-risk guarantee" is unbeatable.

BUY DIRECT, INC.

216 W. 18th St., Dept. WBMC
New York, NY 10011
(212) 255-4424

Catalog: $2, refundable; pub. yearly in Dec.
Information: price quote by phone or letter with
  SASE
Discount: 15% to 40%
Goods: name brand, generic
Minimum Order: $50 to open business account
Shipping, Insurance: extra; UPS, FOB NYC
Sales Tax: NY deliveries
Accepts: check, MO, certified check
$$$

Supplies for both sides of the office world—paper and electronic—are sold here at savings of up to 40%. The 144-page catalog features products for computers, word processors, copiers, and microfiche systems. Disks, ribbons, typing elements, print wheels, correction film, storage units, cleaning kits, copier supplies, labels, envelopes, forms and many other goods, are offered by IBM, Qume, Diablo, Burroughs, Wang, NEC, GP Technologies, Camwil, Ko-Rec-Type, Verbatim, 3M, Maxell, Nashua, Certron, Wilson Jones, Acco. A wide range of computer stands, work stations, data files, and related furniture is stocked, along with acoustical panels, ergonomic seating, computer cables and connectors, voltage regulators, lighting, collators, copiers, calculators, pocket and portable computers, electronic typewriters, and much more. The catalog doesn't show everything Buy Direct stocks, so call or write with inquiries if you don't see what you're looking for. Authorized returns are accepted; a restocking fee may be charged.

CALIFORNIA DIGITAL

17700 Figueroa St.
Carson, CA 90248
(213) 217-0500: inquiries
and CA orders
(800) 421-5041: orders
except CA

Information: price quote by phone or letter with
  SASE
Discount: up to 50%
Goods: name brand
Minimum Order: none
Shipping, Insurance: $3 minimum; UPS, PP
Sales Tax: CA orders
Accepts: check, MO, MC, V
$$$ (see text)

Hardware and software and technical advice are available here—the advice given freely. You can call or write for a price quote on computers, modems, terminals, printers, monitors, diskettes, and other computer-related goods by Teac, Tandon, Juki, Remex, Apple, Okidata, NEC, Epson, Amdek, Princeton Graphics, Wyse, Silver-Reed, Diablo, Sanyo, IBM, Eagle, Ampro, Dysan, Maxell, Memorex, Scotch, Verbatim, and other firms. Expect savings of up to 50%. Returns are accepted on defective merchandise, and repairs are also made.

CANADIAN READERS, PLEASE NOTE: The shipping charge on goods sent to Canada is 10% of the order value, and any overcharges will be refunded.

COMPUTER CONNECTION

**12841 S. Hawthorne Blvd.
Hawthorne, CA 90250
(213) 514–9019: inquiries
and CA orders
(800) 732–0304: orders
except CA**

Information: price quote by phone or letter with
  SASE
Discount: up to 50%
Goods: name brand
Minimum Order: none
Shipping, Insurance: $4 minimum; UPS
Sales Tax: CA deliveries
Accepts: check, MO, MC, V
$$$

Computers, peripherals, and software are sold here at savings of up to 50% off list. And you can call the Connection if you see a lower advertised price and the company will probably beat it. If you're shopping for printers, modems, computers, monitors, disk drives, and accessories by IBM, Apple, Kaypro, Sanyo, Okidata, Riteman, Qume, Star Micronics, Tava, Sanyo, NEC, Compaq, Tandon, Panasonic, Epson, C-Itoh, Brother, Dynax, Juki, Toshiba, AST Research, Quadram, Hayes, or Princeton Graphics, be sure to get a quote from the Computer Connection.

**COMPUTER HUT OF NEW
ENGLAND, INC.**

**101 Elm St.
Nashua, NH 03060
(609) 889–0666: inquiries
and NH orders
(800) 525–5012: orders
except NH**

Price List: free
Information: price quote by phone or letter with
  SASE
Discount: 15% to 50%
Goods: name brand
Minimum Order: none
Shipping, Insurance: 3% of order value; $5 to $8
  minimum; UPS, PP
Sales Tax: NH deliveries
Accepts: check, MO, certified check, MC, V
$$

We've finally found Electronic Village, better known as Nashua, New Hampshire. While it may not have a Mainframe Street, Software Shack, or Disk Drive, it does have the Computer Hut. Under its thatched eaves you'll find personal computers, peripherals, and software from a variety of manufacturers.

There are disk drives by Tandon, Panasonic, Shugart, Teac, Maynard Electronics, Quadram, AST Research, Tecmar, Hercules, Fredericks Electronics, Amdek, Microlog, and USI; hard-disk systems from Mountain, Maynard, and Tallgrass; printers by Epson, Brother, Dynax, C-Itoh, Star Micronics, NEC, Okidata, Toshiba, IDS, Daisywriter, and Silver-Reed; modems by Hayes and Novation; Amdek and PGS monitors; and computers from IBM, Eagle, Columbia, Corona, Tava, and NEC. Some software is also available. Prices run from 15% to 50% below list, with an average discount of 30%. Authorized returns are accepted, and goods can be sent to APO and FPO addresses for a 12% shipping fee.

COMPUTER WAREHOUSE

Dept. PF
2222 E. Indian School Rd.
Phoenix, AZ 85016
(602) 954–6109: inquiries
(800) 528–1054: orders

Information: price quote by phone or letter with SASE
Discount: 35% to 50%
Goods: name brand
Minimum Order: none
Shipping, Handling, Insurance: $8 per order; UPS, PP
Sales Tax: AZ deliveries
Accepts: check, MO, certified check, MC, V, AE
$$$

We asked every firm listed in this book when it was founded; Computer Warehouse was the only company to spell it out to the day: July 7, 1980. (Several years of work with exacting information-processing systems tend to engender precise thought—up to a point.)

Computer Warehouse sells micro systems, peripherals, and software. Computers and systems by Sanyo, Commodore, Quadram, Epson, Altos, NEC, Eagle, Northstar, Televideo, and Zenith; printers from Juki, NEC, Okidata, Qume, IDS, Epson, Inforunner, Silver-Reed, Star Micronics, Diablo, C-Itoh, and other makers; and ADDS, Altos, Hazeltine, Qume, Televideo, Wyse, and Zenith video terminals were available as of this writing. (This is a highly volatile industry whose manufacturers trace meteoric paths on their sales charts one month and nose dives the next.) Computer Warehouse also carries Rana disk drives; monitors from Amdek, Princeton

Graphic, Sanyo, Taxan, and Zenith; and diskettes by Maxell, Scotch, and Elephant.

The prices here are 35% to 50% below list, and you can call or write for a price quote. You'll get the best idea of what's available by checking the Computer Warehouse ads in *Personal Computing, PC Magazine, Byte Magazine*, and *Popular Computing*.

CONROY-LAPOINTE, INC.

12060 S.W. Garden Pl.
Portland, OR 97223
(503) 620–9877: inquiries
and Portland orders
(503) 620–9878: order
information
(800) 451–5151: OR orders
(800) 547–1289: orders
except OR

Information: price quote by phone or letter with SASE
Discount: 20% to 80%
Goods: name brand
Minimum Order: none
Shipping, Insurance, Handling: 3% of order value; $5 minimum; UPS, PP
Sales Tax: CA, OR, WA deliveries
Accepts: check, MO, certified check, MC, V, AE
$$$$ 🍁 (see text)

Conroy-LaPointe, which has been selling computers and electronics since 1958, lays claim to the title of "world's largest computer mail-order firm." In this case, bigger spells better—Conroy has good business references and excellent recommendations from consumer publications.

Computers, peripherals, software, diskettes, and accessories by scores of manufacturers are stocked, including IBM, Apple, Amdek, Alloy, Control Data, Concorde, Teac, Rana, Hewlett-Packard, Princeton Graphic, Quadram, Zenith, Hayes, Novation, Epson, Juki, Tally, Okidata, Maynard, ComX, Koala, Microsoft, Magnum, Tecmar, Titan, Plantronics, Dysan, Fuji, Maxell, Generik, Verbatim, CDC, and others. Most of the prices are 30% to 50% below list, but savings on closeouts, specials, and overstocked models can run up to 80%. Selected goods are featured in ads run monthly in *Byte* and *PC World*.

The catch to this bonanza? Conroy won't hold your hand while you agonize over computer selection. The company's slogan says it best: "Low prices for professionals who know what they want and know how to use it!" All sales are final, and returns are accepted only when goods are defective or the firm has erred in shipment. There's no shoulder to cry on if you make a bad decision, so *read* the buying guides, *attend* demonstrations of new products, and exhaust your "computerate" friends with *questions* before you commit yourself financially.

CANADIAN READERS, PLEASE NOTE: if you're having goods shipped to parts of Canada not served by UPS, call or write for a separate shipping quote.

FRANK EASTERN CO.

Dept. PC105
599 Broadway
New York, NY 10012
(212) 219–0007: inquiries
and NY orders
(800) 221–4914: orders
except NY

Catalog: free; pub. in Jan. and May
Information: price quote by letter with SASE
Discount: 30% to 50%
Goods: name brand, house brand
Minimum Order: $75 on credit cards
Shipping: extra; UPS, FOB NYC
Handling: $3 on orders under $40
Sales Tax: NY deliveries
Accepts: check, MO, MC, V
$$$$

Frank Eastern carries everything you need for your business or home office at discounts of 30% to 50%. You can stock up on office sundries from 3M-Scotch, Swingline, BIC, Rubbermaid, and other name-brand manufacturers—pens, Flair markers, tape, files, envelopes, corrective typing aids, word-processing accessories, stands—etc. We'd be lost without Eastern's "Tidi-Files," (corrugated-cardboard files for publications storage), and the firm's transfer and sturdy standard suspension files.

Entire offices can be and have been furnished through Eastern. The catalog shows executive and clerical seating, a range of desks in wood and steel, conference seating, handsome wood bookcases appropriate for home use, conventional filing cabinets, space-saving lateral files in wood and steel, fireproof Sentry safes, literature and magazine racks, computer work stations, data-reference storage equipment, desktop work organizers, folding chairs, and a wide range of institutional furniture. Eastern's ergonomic, task, and clerical chairs are designed to minimize the back strain associated with long desk hours and are offered at typical Eastern prices of 30% to 50% below comparable retail. Try to talk your boss into one for your office—pain is inversely related to productivity. Whether you run an office or are just trying to organize, this catalog should prove helpful. Frank Eastern has been in business for over 40 years, and guarantees satisfaction. Returns are accepted for refund or credit.

ECONOMY SOFTWARE

**2040 Polk St.
San Francisco, CA 94109
(415) 845–2651: inquiries
and CA orders
(800) 227–4780: orders
except CA**

Price List: free; pub. quarterly
Information: price quote by phone or letter with
  SASE
Discount: 30% to 50%
WBMC Reader Discount: see text
Goods: name brand
Minimum Order: none
Shipping, Insurance: extra; UPS
Sales Tax: CA deliveries
Accepts: check, MO, MC, V, AE

$$$$

If you're looking for good prices on popular word-processing and spreadsheet programs, check with Economy before buying elsewhere. It carries software by Alpha, Anderson Bell, ASI, Continental, Digital Research, Hayes, IMSI, Lifetree Systems, Micropro, Microsoft, Perfect Software, Visicorp, Wang, and many other firms at savings of up to 40%. Identify yourself as a WBMC reader if your order totals $100 or more (excluding shipping, handling, and sales tax) and you may deduct $5. (This offer expires Sept. 30, 1986.) Quantity discounts are offered, and all goods are guaranteed against defects.

800-SOFTWARE INC.

**940 Dwight Way, Suite 14
Berkeley, CA 94710
(415) 644–3611: inquiries
and CA orders
(800) 227–4587: orders
except CA**

Brochure: free
Information: price quote by phone or letter with
  SASE
Discount: 30% to 50%
WBMC Reader Discount: see text
Goods: name brand
Minimum Order: none
Shipping, Insurance: extra; UPS
Sales Tax: CA deliveries
Accepts: check, MO, MC, V, AE

$$$$

800-Software was recommended to us by a computer buff who has access to every discount source in New York City but buys from 800 instead. Software by ALS, Amdek, Ashton-Tate, AST, Continental, Digital Research, Fox & Geller, IUS, Micropro, Microsoft, Perfect Software, Visicorp, and many other firms is available at 30% to 50% savings. In addition to programs for IBM-PCs and compatibles, the firm offers Amdek monitors, Maxell and Memorex diskettes, and *advice*. Corporate and dealer accounts are welcomed. All goods are backed by the 800-Software guarantee against defects. The company publishes a listing of products, but call or write for a price quote before buying since specials are run on a frequent basis. If your order totals $100 or more (excluding shipping, handling, and sales tax) you may deduct $10 from the total. Be sure to identify yourself as a WBMC reader when you order. (This offer expires Sept. 30, 1986.)

ENVELOPE SALES COMPANY

Normandy, TN 37360
(615) 857–3333

Brochure: free
Discount: up to 60%
Goods: custom printed
Minimum Order: none
Shipping: extra; FOB Normandy
Sales Tax: TN deliveries
Accepts: check or MO
$$$$

This company offers mailers in a broad range of sizes, weights, styles, and colors, at prices the firm says should save you "up to 40%." Our estimates are closer to 60%, based on rates charged by discount suppliers.

Envelope Sales sends a full-color brochure that shows windowed and plain envelopes in sizes from 6¾ to 12, privacy-tinted bill-payers, both plain and windowed envelopes in seven colors, and business-reply and return envelopes. Brown kraft mailers, with and without clasps, are available printed and unprinted in nine sizes. And you can order business letterhead and matching envelopes in any of ten type styles, in watermarked bond (20 and 25 pounds). Logos can be reproduced and colored inks used at an additional fee.

Most of the stationery is sold in minimum lots of 1,000. Prices include printing—up to four or six lines, depending on the item. The brochure is extremely easy to read and provides photographs and exact measurements of all the envelopes. The prices are excellent, especially for quality stock and printing, but shipping is extra—include the postage charges to find your actual cost.

47ST. COMPUTING

36 E. 19th St.
New York, NY 10003
(212) 260–4415: customer
service
(212) 260–4410: inquiries
and AK, HI, NY orders
(800) 221–7774: orders
except AK, HI, NY

Information: price quote by phone or letter with
  SASE
Discount: up to 50%
Goods: name brand
Minimum Order: $35
Shipping, Insurance: $4.95 minimum; UPS
Sales Tax: NY deliveries
Accepts: check, MO, MC, V, AE
$$$

This is the computer division of 47st. Photo, one of New York City's largest camera and electronics discounters. Like the parent company, it carries a huge range of products at savings of up to 50%. Computers, peripherals, and software by IBM, Apple, Kaypro, Compaq, Hyperion, Datamac, AT&T, NEC, Epson, Sharp, Hewlett-Packard, Panasonic, Sanyo, Olivetti, Texas Instruments, Hayes, Teac, Taxan, Princeton Graphic, Novation, Comrex, Okidata, Silver-Reed, Juki, Qume, Brother, Toshiba, Atari, and other companies are available along with diskettes from Fuji, Nashua, IBM, Maxell, 3M, and Verbatim. See the listing for 47st. Photo, Inc. in the "Appliances" chapter for more information on terms of sale.

GRAYARC

Greenwoods Industrial Park
P.O. Box 2944
Hartford, CT 06104–2944
(203) 379–9941: customer
service
(800) 243–5250: orders

General Supplies Catalog: free
Computer Forms Catalog: free
Discount: 15% to 50%
Goods: house brand, name brand
Minimum Order: none
Shipping, Insurance: extra; FOB shipping point
Handling: 95¢ per order
Sales Tax: CT and TX deliveries
Accepts: check, MO, MC, V
$$$

Grayarc's business forms, machines, and office supplies are priced to save your company money and designed to expedite all kinds of business procedures.

The general catalog has 60 pages of multiple forms, stationery, labels, office supplies, machines, furniture, shipping materials, storage equipment, and other goods. Reply messages, purchase orders, work proposals, invoices, statements, sales slips, insurance memos, bills of lading, receiving reports, and credit memos are among the available forms, many of which are offered in a choice of carbon and carbonless sets. Plain and windowed correspondence envelopes in several sizes and colors are stocked, along with inter-office envelopes, Tyvek, brown kraft, and white paper mailers, and padded and air-bubble shipping bags. A variety of letterhead styles and paper weights, business cards, and memos are shown, and labels for every need. Grayarc's custom department can provide copy, artwork, logos, embossing, and special ink colors and can even make forms to your specifications—at competitive prices.

The catalog we received included printing calculators from Royal, Seiko, and Unitrex, the latest Brother electronic typewriter, a 3M compact copier, cash registers, time clocks, and supplies. Literature racks and shelving, parts bins, and storage files are sold, as is a small selection of office chairs and work stations. And there are postal scales, rolls of air-bubble packing material, several types of sealing tape and strapping materials, trash bags, pens and pencils, self-inking stampers, and much more.

Grayarc's prices are up to 50% less than those charged for similar goods in other catalogs, but savings depend on the product and quantity ordered. (Compare before you buy, because we found near-retail prices on some items.) A sampling of computer forms, stationery, and supplies (printer ribbons, print wheels, diskettes) is shown in the general catalog, but request the computer-forms catalog for the full inventory. Include the make and model of your computer or word processor when you write. Satisfaction is guaranteed. Returns are accepted within 30 days for refund or credit—contact Grayarc's customer-service department for procedures.

HABER'S

---

33 Essex St.
New York, NY 10002
(212) 473–7007

Information: price quote by phone or letter with SASE
Discount: 33% to 50%
Goods: name brand
Minimum Order: none
Shipping, Insurance: extra; UPS, PP
Sales Tax: NY deliveries
Accepts: check, MO, MC, V

$$$$

Haber's sells the crème de la crème of pens at up to 50% off suggested retail prices. Mont Blanc, Dupont, Aurora, Waterman, Cross, Parker, Sheaffer, Lamy, and Elysée are the available brands. If you're shopping for a fountain or ballpoint pen or mechanical pencil made by one of these firms, call or write (include a SASE) for a price quote. We've found that a good pen is a wonderful gift and is indispensable in the office; when the computers shut down, the pens emerge and carry on.

HARDWARE, SOFTWARE, ANYWARE

**10 Coles St.
Brooklyn, NY 11231
(718) 596–3592**

Price List: free
Information: price quote by phone or letter with
  SASE
Discount: up to 50%
Goods: name brand
Minimum Order: none
Shipping, Insurance: extra; UPS, PP
Sales Tax: NY deliveries
Accepts: check or MO
$$$

HSA sells computers and peripherals by such firms as Apple, Atari, and Texas Instruments, at savings of up to 50% on list prices. Software is also available. Call or write for a price quote and request the price sheet that lists additional products made by the same manufacturer.

JILOR DISCOUNT OFFICE MACHINES, INC.

**1020 Broadway
Woodmere, NY 11598
(516) 374–5806**

Information: price quote by phone or letter with
  SASE
Discount: 20% to 50%
Goods: name brand
Minimum Order: see text
Shipping, Insurance: extra; UPS, PP, FOB
  Woodmere
Sales Tax: NY deliveries
Accepts: check, MO, certified check
$$

Jilor's line of office electronics includes typewriters, calculators, dictation equipment, telephones, answering machines, and floppy disks. There are typewriters by Smith-Corona, Olympia, Brother, Olivetti, and Silver-Reed; calculators from Sanyo, Sharp, Canon, and Texas Instruments; and dictation equipment by Sanyo, Olympus, and Panasonic. One- and two-line telephones by Uniden, Webcor, Teleconcepts, Panasonic, ITT, and ATC are available, as well as answering machines, dialers, speaker-phones, and related accessories by major manufacturers. Don't rely on the brochure for current prices or a complete listing of available goods; you're better off calling or writing (include a SASE) for a price quote.

Jilor has been selling by mail for ten years and runs its mail-order department in the following fashion: It ships on a C.O.D. basis if the item you're ordering is in stock and will order something not in stock after receiving payment via certified check. You must include a SASE with any correspondence if you want a response. If the item you order is defective, write to Jilor and describe the problem. Request authorization to return the item. When you receive it, send the item insured with *return receipt requested*. (This advice applies to all firms dealing on a price-quote basis and also to catalog firms that don't print return policies and procedures in their catalogs or include same with shipments.)

Jilor has a repair department that can probably get your cranky IBM Selectric or other machine working smoothly again. Call or write for information, stating brand, model, and problem. A sample of what the dysfunctional machine produces (besides your expletives) should also be included if it demonstrates the problem.

**LYBEN COMPUTER
SYSTEMS**

**1250 Rankin, Bldg. E
Troy, MI 48084
(313) 777–7780**

Catalog: free
Information: price quote by phone or letter with
    SASE
Discount: up to 50%
Goods: name brand
Minimum Order: none (see text)
Shipping, Insurance: $2 per order (see text); UPS
Sales Tax: MI deliveries
Accepts: check, MO, MC, V
$$$

Save up to 50% on disks, diskettes, printer paper, and other supplies through Lyben. Memorex, Dysan, Verbatim, and other brands are offered, and products are sold by the box. The shipping fee of $2 per order applies to everything except bulk shipments of paper. Call or write for a price quote—there's always a special on something here.

MICRO MART, INC.

**Technology Corporate
Campus
3159 Campus Dr.
Norcross, GA 30071
(404) 449–8089: inquiries
and GA orders
(800) 241–8149: orders
except GA**

Information: price quote by phone or letter with
   SASE
Discount: up to 60%
Goods: name brand
Minimum Order: none
Shipping, Insurance: extra; UPS
Sales Tax: FL, GA, LA, MD, KY, NC, TN deliveries
Accepts: check, MO, MC, V
$$$$

Micro Mart offers savings of up to 60% on an excellent selection of computers, peripherals, and software for business applications. Disk drives, hard disks, multifunction boards, modems, monitors, printers, plotters, chips, CRTs, programs, keyboards, diskettes, mice, and many other types of products are stocked by manufacturers including IBM, Apple, Epson, Smith-Corona, Orchid, Toshiba, Star Micronics, Tandon, Peachtree, Lotus, Fox & Geller, Norton, ATI, Borland, Lattice, Microsoft, Hercules, Quadram, Amdek, Wyse, Dysan, Maynard, C-Itoh, Qume, Diablo, and Digital Research. Micro Mart also offers advice and technical support. If you're looking for the latest in corporate networking and protocol conversion equipment, be sure to call or write for a price quote, since Micro Mart keeps pace with the newest technology in this area.

**NATIONAL BUSINESS
FURNITURE, INC.**

**222 E. Michigan St.
Milwaukee, WI 53202
(414) 276–8511: inquiries
(800) 558–9803: customer
service
(800) 242–0030: WI orders
(800) 558–1010: orders and
inquiries except WI**

Catalog: free; pub. in May and Nov.
Information: price quote by phone or letter with
   SASE
Discount: 35% to 40%
Goods: name brand, generic
Minimum Order: none
Shipping, Insurance: extra; UPS, FOB Milwaukee
Sales Tax: WI deliveries
Accepts: check, MO, MC, V
$$$

Furnish your office for less by using the 48-page NBF catalog, where you'll find desks, conference tables, chairs of every description, files and storage units, computer work stations furniture, and other office staples at savings of up to 40% on suggested list prices. The manufacturers represented here include Jefsteel, Hon, La-Z-Boy, Indiana Desk, Cole, Samsonite, Globe, Cosco, Dolly Madison, Raynor, Allied, Hunt Litning, Edsal, AVM, Meco, Davenport, Miller, Sidex, Regal, Lifeline, PFI, Posturecraft, and Springer Penguin. Authorized returns are accepted; a restocking fee is charged.

PACIFIC EXCHANGES

P.O. Box 12310
San Luis Obispo, CA
93406–0172
(805) 453–1037: customer
service
(800) 592–5935: CA orders
(800) 235–4137: orders
except CA

Price List: free with SASE
Information: price quote by phone or letter with
SASE
Discount: 33% to 45%
Goods: name brand
Minimum Order: box of 10 disks
Shipping: included: UPS
Handling: $2 per order
Sales Tax: CA deliveries
Accepts: check, MO, MC, V
$$$

Pacific Exchanges sells computer software and disk-storage units. There are diskettes by Dysan, Memorex, BASF, 3M-Scotch, Maxell, TDK, Nashua, Wabash, and Verbatim. A floppy-disk saver kit, head-cleaning diskettes, and file boxes for storing the floppy disks are also available. In addition to giving quantity discounts, Pacific runs specials on the storage products with the purchase of disks.

**PEARL BROTHERS OFFICE
MACHINERY & EQUIPMENT**

476 Smith St.
Brooklyn, NY 11231
(718) 875–3024, 3063

Brochure: free with SASE
Information: price quote by phone or letter with
SASE
Discount: 25% to 40%
Goods: name brand
Minimum Order: none
Shipping, Insurance: extra; UPS, PP
Sales Tax: NY deliveries
Accepts: check, MO, certified check
$$$$

We've given Pearl a top rating because of the favorable reviews it's received from readers in the past. In one instance, a couple living in Maryland bought an IBM Selectric for their son, a new student at Columbia University. Pearl tried to deliver but the building manager didn't know which apartment the son had taken. On his second attempt, the delivery man got the apartment number but encountered a broken elevator, so he climbed 11 flights of stairs to complete his mission.

Pearl combines 37 years of this kind of service with discounts of 25% to 40% on typewriters, check writers, calculators, word processors, and cash registers. The available brands include IBM, Royal-Adler, Max, Casio, TEAL, Sharp, Paymaster, Olympia, Towa, and Hermes. Call or write for a price quote and include a SASE with your letter.

RAPIDFORMS, INC.

**501 Benigno Blvd.
Bellmawr, NJ 08031−2554
(609) 933−0480: inquiries
(800) 582−7633: customer
service in NJ
(800) 322−5587: NJ orders
(800) 257−5287: customer
service except NJ
(800) 257−8354: orders
except NJ**

Business Forms Catalog: free; pub. in July and Dec.
Computer Forms Catalog: free
Retail/Service Forms Catalog: free
Discount: up to 40%
Goods: house brand
Minimum Order: $10
Shipping: included on prepaid orders; UPS, PP, FOB point of shipment on account orders
Handling, Insurance: $2 on account orders
Sales Tax: NJ deliveries
Accepts: check or MO
$$

This firm's name describes several aspects of its business. First, it sells business forms. The stock includes blanks, invoices, and scores of other forms designed for every commercial purpose which are formatted to expedite transactions at the processing and receiving ends. And Rapidforms ships quickly—within 48 hours on unprinted goods and in six to nine days on imprinted forms.

The general business-forms catalog includes statements, invoices, order forms, work orders, estimate and price-quote forms, sales slips, credit/debit memos, blanks, phone records, memos, checks, personnel notices, and a comparable range of continuous (computer) forms.

Business cards and stationery, several types of envelopes—large mailers, Tyvek, bubble-pack—and labels for every purpose, trash can liners, packing materials and sealing tape, polyethylene storage bags, and disposable wipes for food-service, auto-shop, and assembly-line use are shown as well.

The retail/service catalog lists the same forms described in the general catalog and also offers shopping bags, gift boxes, wrapping paper, ribbon and bows, sales flyers and sign-making kits, gift certificates, and labels and label guns. We didn't receive the catalog of computer forms but were told it offers a complete stock of continuous forms and stationery.

Rapidforms was established in 1940 and guarantees unconditional satisfaction or your money back. Savings differ depending on the product and quantity ordered, but our comparisons showed that Rapidforms prices some goods up to 40% less than competitors. Quantity discounts on large orders (1,000 to 2,000) of the same item bring the savings up to 70%.

CANADIAN READERS, PLEASE NOTE: shipping is not included on prepaid orders sent to Canada.

TRIPLE A SCALE & MFG. CO.

2945 Southwide Dr. Memphis, TN 38118 (901) 363–7040

Flyer: free; pub. in Jan. and June
WBMC Reader Discount: 30%
Goods: house brand
Minimum Order: none
Shipping: included; PP
Sales Tax: TN deliveries
Accepts: check or MO
$$$$

The handy little "Triple A Precision Ounce Postal Scale" sold here measures up to four ounces (in gradations of one fourth up to two ounces), and comes in a pocket-sized case that includes a current chart of postal rates and a copy of the five-year guarantee. It usually sells for $6, but is only $4.20 to WBMC readers. Triple A Scale also sells brass test weights ranging from one gram to four ounces. The scale is guaranteed to perform "accurately and properly" for five years and will be accepted for repair or replacement within that time.

Several functions are suggested: postage determination, food measurement, lab use, craft and hobby needs, and weighing of herbs. We have used ours for several years, for the obvious and the arcane, and rely on it completely. It's flat and light enough to carry with you, but you can also hang it up by the finger ring so you always have it handy. When you order the scale, be sure to mention WBMC to get the 30% discount. (The weights are not discounted.)

TURNBAUGH PRINTERS SUPPLY CO.

**104 S. Sporting Hill Rd.
Mechanicsburg, PA 17055
(717) 737–5637**

Printer's Bargain News: 50¢; pub. biannually in Oct.
Discount: see text
Goods: name brand, generic; new, used
Minimum Order: $15
Shipping: extra; UPS, PP
Sales Tax: PA deliveries
Accepts: check or MO
$$$

Despite the application of computer technology in almost every phase of typesetting and printing, the traditional methods are still widely used. Turnbaugh offers printers working in the manner of Gutenberg new and used presses, type, and related equipment and supplies. Stock is listed in *Printer's Bargain News,* a 16″ × 22″ broadside packed with buys on printing presses (hand, treadle, and power), offset machines, paper cutters, stapling machines, folders, booklet stitchers, punching machines, and numbering machines. Most of the equipment is used, and descriptions include general condition, bed dimensions of the presses, and the way each press is equipped. Among the brands and types of machinery often available are Chandler & Price, Kelsey, Baltimore, and Gordon—though anything and everything, including antique hand presses, eventually turns up at Turnbaugh.

Enormous numbers of type, leads, slugs, rules, leaders, quoins, keys, spacers, gauge pins, printers' saws, and composing sticks are listed, as are brayers, cold padding cement, inks, type cleaner, rollers, galley locks, type cabinets and cases, engraving tools, bone paper folders, embossing powder, and scores of other items necessary to printing. The broadsides we received also offered paper stock, which may interest those outside the trade: Dennison shipping tags, coated 100-pound cover stock, bristol board, bond, business envelopes, offset and book-quality paper, business cards, gummed tape and labels, and more.

Savings on used machinery run to 70% on the cost of new; the other equipment and supplies are competitively priced. (We haven't listed a discount level in the core information because these machines are not rebuilt and can't be compared fairly to new equipment.) Turnbaugh has been in existence since 1931 and, as long as lasers don't supplant lead entirely, should continue to serve the small printing shop. Seeing the range of typefaces printed out on the price sheets may inspire some to take up printing as a hobby; you can get an idea of what this might involve by reading *The Practice of Printing,* a 300-page manual on typesetting, layout, and offset printing ($16.75).

Please note that Turnbaugh does not *do* printing. And you'll observe that the lists do not include shipping charts—you're asked to "include plenty for postage." If you're unable to approximate the cost, ask Turnbaugh to give you a quote.

**TYPEX BUSINESS
MACHINES, INC.**

**23 W. 23rd St.
New York, NY 10010
(212) 243–2500: inquiries
and NY orders
(800) 221–9332: orders
except NY**

Price List: free with SASE
Information: price quote by phone or letter with
  SASE
Discount: 30% plus
Goods: name brand
Minimum Order: none
Shipping, Insurance: extra; UPS, PP
Sales Tax: NY deliveries
Accepts: check, MO, MC, V
$$$

Looking for a typewriter, calculator, disk drive, copier, cash register, or supplies for same? They're all stocked at Typex in a choice of brands that includes SCM, Silver Reed, Royal, Olympia, Juki, Sierra, Hermes, Olivetti, Brother, Nikkam, IBM, Sharp, Canon, Casio, Panasonic, and Texas Instruments. Foreign-language typewriters may be found here. When repairs are needed on your typewriter, contact the firm—service is offered in the New York-metropolitan area.

Typex has been around since 1935, when monster Underwoods, carbon paper, and typing pools were the backbones of most businesses. (It's hard for us to imagine life without Xerox machines or typewriters that do everything but make coffee.) You'll help speed your replies and keep prices at 30% to 50% below list by sending a SASE with all your correspondence and including make and model numbers with your price-quote requests.

**UNITED STATES POSTAL
SERVICE**

**U.S. Stamped Envelope
Agency
Williamsburg, PA
16693–0500
(814) 832–3229**

Information: see text
Discount: up to 60% (see text)
Goods: custom-printed
Minimum Order: 500 envelopes
Shipping, Insurance: included; PP
Sales Tax: see text
Accepts: check or MO
$$$$

One of the best buys on printed envelopes is available through the USPS, which works through the U.S. Stamped Envelope Agency. You can order envelopes with embossed stamps (postage) in windowed or plain styles, size 6¾ or 10, with up to seven lines of printing (maximum 47 characters per line). The printing is clean and clear, and the envelopes of good quality; we're surprised more small businesses and consumers don't know about the service. The price is excellent: a box of 500 plain #10 envelopes is $109.85 at this writing. That's $100 for first-class postage and $9.85 for the envelopes and printing. Considering the fact that a box of envelopes costs that alone at discount, it's like getting the printing free. (Our local printer charges $25 for 500 #10 envelopes printed in the same fashion, so the USPS prices can represent savings of up to 60%.)

The U.S. Stamped Envelope Agency processes the orders, but to get order forms and information, see your local post office. Ask for PS Form 3203, "Printed Stamped Envelopes Order," and Notice 18, which describes the printing options and shows samples of the typeface used.

WINDFALL LISTS

**Lindsey Plaza
P.O. Box 268
Lyman, SC 29365–0268
(803) 439–3442**

Brochure: free; pub. monthly
Discount: up to 40% (see text)
WBMC Reader Discount: 30%
Goods: proprietary
Minimum Order: $10
Shipping: included
Sales Tax: NC deliveries
Accepts: check, MO, certified check, MC, V

If your business is moving into direct mail, you're probably shopping for lists. These are simply names and addresses of potential customers rented or sold by list brokers or other firms. Your smartest list dollars generally go toward names of active buyers who, for any number of reasons, would be likely to purchase your goods or services.

Windfall Lists sells names on pressure-sensitive labels in sequential ZIP codes at "factory-direct prices," which are indeed low—$3 for 50 names, $25 for 1,000, to $150 for 10,000 names. The WBMC reader discount of 30% brings prices down to the lowest we've seen anywhere.

The lists are names of "fresh opportunity seeking buyers" who have responded to direct-mail offers within the last three months and spent an average of $25 each. Further classifications include "book /information buyers" and "multilevel enthusiasts." Satisfaction is guaranteed and ten free names are supplied for each undeliverable listed name. Free samples are offered to those who send a SASE. If you'd like to know more about the lists, inquire, and remember to identify yourself as a WBMC reader so you can take advantage of the discount.

**WOLFF OFFICE
EQUIPMENT CORP.**

**1841 Broadway
New York, NY 10023
(212) 581–9080**

Information: price quote by phone or letter with
  SASE
Discount: 5% to 40%
Goods: name brand
Minimum Order: $100
Shipping: extra; UPS or FOB NYC
Sales Tax: NY deliveries
Accepts: check, MO, MC, V
$$$

Wolff has an extensive inventory of office machines and furniture and is known locally for its well-staffed service and repair department. The stock here includes typewriters, calculators, check writers, dictation machines, and phone machines by SCM, Olivetti, IBM, Sharp, Sanyo, Olympia, Osborne, Royal-Adler, Remington-Rand, Hewlett-Packard, Texas Instruments, Victor, and Phone-Mate. Savings run up to 40%, and price quotes are given over the phone or by letter (include a SASE). Returns are accepted for refund or credit, but note that there is a 15% restocking fee. Be sure to get authorization before sending anything back.

SEE ALSO:

The American Stationery Co., Inc. . . . custom-printed stationery, note
  pads, envelopes . . . BOOKS
Annex Outlet, Ltd. . . . name-brand phones, phone machines . . .
  APPLIANCES
Bernie's Discount Center, Inc. . . . name-brand phones, phone machines
  . . . APPLIANCES
Blackwelder's Industries, Inc. . . . leather and name-brand office furniture
  . . . HOME (furnishings)
Bondy Export Corp. . . . name-brand typewriters, phones, phone machines,
  Parker pens . . . APPLIANCES
Cherry Hill Furniture, Carpet & Interiors . . . name-brand office furniture
  . . . HOME (furnishings)

Crutchfield . . . name-brand phones, phone equipment . . . APPLIANCES

Executive Photo & Supply Corp. . . . name-brand computers, peripherals, calculators, phone machines, typewriters, Canon copiers . . . CAMERAS

Focus Electronics, Inc. . . . name-brand computers, peripherals, software, phones, phone machines, Parker pens, Canon copiers . . . APPLIANCES

47st Photo, Inc. . . . name-brand phones, phone machines, typewriters, Canon copiers . . . CAMERAS

Garden Camera . . . name-brand phones, phone machines, typewriters . . . CAMERAS

Greater New York Trading Co. . . . name-brand typewriters . . . HOME (table settings)

Great Tracers . . . custom-made name stencils . . . CRAFTS

Hunter Audio-Photo, Inc. . . . name-brand calculators, pens . . . APPLIANCES

International Solgo, Inc. . . . name-brand pens, calculators, typewriters . . . APPLIANCES

Jems Sounds, Ltd. . . . name-brand calculators, phones, phone machines . . . APPLIANCES

L & D Press . . . imprinted business cards, stationery, lateral files, Sentry safes . . . BOOKS

Leather School . . . fine Italian leather desk sets . . . LEATHER

Lewi Supply . . . Olivetti typewriters . . . APPLIANCES

LTV Price Quote Hotline, Inc. . . . name-brand computers, peripherals, calculators, typewriters, phones, phone machines . . . APPLIANCES

Maine Discount Hardware . . . office furniture, electronics . . . TOOLS

Olden Camera & Lens Co., Inc. . . . name-brand phones, phone machines . . . CAMERAS

Oreck Corp. . . . Oreck commercial, institutional vacuum cleaners, floor machines, air purifiers . . . APPLIANCES

Plastic BagMart . . . plastic trash can liners . . . HOME (maintenance)

James Roy Furniture Co., Inc. . . . name-brand office furniture . . . HOME (furnishings)

S & S Sound City . . . name-brand calculators, phones, phone machines . . . APPLIANCES

Sales Citi, Inc. . . . name-brand phones, phone machines . . . APPLIANCES

Sharp Photo . . . name-brand calculators, Pearlcorder microcassettes . . . CAMERAS

Stecher's Limited . . . name-brand pens . . . HOME (table settings)

Stereo Discounters Electronic World . . . name-brand phones, phone machines, computers, peripherals, software, accessories . . . APPLIANCES

Trade-Mark Business Barter Exchange of New York . . . business barter network . . . GENERAL

Turnkey Material Handling, Inc. . . . office, commercial equipment and furniture . . . TOOLS

The Videotime Corp . . . Franklin computers, software . . . APPLIANCES

Whole Earth Access . . . name-brand office electronics . . . GENERAL

SPORTS AND RECREATION

Equipment, clothing, supplies,
and services for all sorts of
sports and recreational
activities.

If the high price of recreation equipment seems unsporting to you, you've turned to the right place. Discounts of 30% are standard among many of the suppliers listed here, who sell clothing and equipment for cycling, running, golfing, skiing, aerobics, tennis and other racquet sports, skin and scuba diving, camping, hunting, hiking, basketball, triathaloning, soccer, and other pleasures. Racquet stringing, club repair, and other services are usually priced competitively as well. Buying your gear by mail may well be the only sport that repays a nominal expenditure of energy with such an enhanced sense of well-being.

We'd like to thank the Printing House Racquetball & Squash Club of New York City for assistance in obtaining material for preparation of this chapter.

ALLYN AIR SEAT CO.

18 Millstream Rd.
Dept. WMBC
Woodstock, NY 12498
(914) 679–2051

Fliers: free; pub. yearly
Information: price quote by phone or letter with SASE
Discount: up to 20% (see text)
WBMC Reader Discount: 30% (see text)
Goods: house brand
Minimum Order: none (see text)
Shipping, Insurance: included; UPS, PP
Sales Tax: NY deliveries
Accepts: check, MO, certified check
$$$ (see text)

Allyn Air sells several items that should help you go the distance in comfort, whether you're traveling by bike, car, plane, truck, or wheelchair.

Cyclists numbed by long hauls on hard saddles can't afford to miss the Bicycle Air Seat. It's a heavy-duty, air-filled slipcover for racing seats that absorbs road shocks and prevents soreness, and costs just $11. The motorcycle model and a full-sized Air Seat that fits standard and bucket auto seats, aircraft seats, wheelchairs, and trucks are just $30 each. All of Allyn's Air Seats are guaranteed for one year, and are installed quite easily.

Allyn also sells an adjustable rearview mirror that fits into the end of most handlebars ($8), a nylon gear bag that fits within the triangular space of a closed-frame bicycle ($15), nylon panniers, and Lexan leg fairings (splatter shields) for motorcycles. The prices are listed as "retail" in the literature, but we've seen similar products selling for up to 20% more elsewhere. You can buy at retail, but if your order totals $100 or more, you're entitled to the reader discount of 30%. Identify yourself as a WBMC reader when ordering, compute sales tax (if applicable) on the *retail* prices, and add that figure to the discounted total.

CANADIAN READERS, PLEASE NOTE: additional shipping fees may be charged on orders sent to Canada.

ATHLETE'S CORNER

P.O. Box 16993
Plantation, FL 33318
(305) 475–0327: inquiries
and FL orders
(800) 327–0346: orders
except FL

Price List: free
Information: price quote by phone or letter with SASE
Discount: 10% to 30%
Goods: name brand
Minimum Order: none
Shipping, Insurance: extra; UPS
Sales Tax: FL deliveries
Accepts: check, MO, MC, V
$$

The Athlete's Corner sells professional tennis racquets at discount prices. The manufacturers carried include Prince, Head, Kennex, Donnay, Wilson, Dunlop, and Yamaha, among others. There is also a good selection of court and running shoes by Asahi, K-Swiss, Nike, Adidas, New Balance, and Ektelon. Everything is sold at a discount, and stringing services are available. Returns are accepted and exchanges made on unused goods.

THE AUSTAD COMPANY

Dept. WBM
P.O. Box 1428
Sioux Falls, SD 57101
(605) 336–3135: inquiries
and SD orders
(800) 843–6828: orders
except SD, AK, HI

Catalog: free; pub. Jan., Mar., June, Oct.
Discount: up to 40%
Goods: name brand, house brand
Minimum Order: none
Shipping: $1.75 to $7.50 on orders to U.S. ZIP-coded areas; UPS, PP
Sales Tax: SD deliveries
Accepts: check, MO, MC, V, AE
$$$

Austad discounts a variety of sports and leisure equipment, but the color catalog devotes most of its 62-plus pages to golf.

Whether your game is nine holes on Sunday or a threat to Tom Watson, you'll find the playing equipment and apparel you need here—all at great prices. The clubs include sets and singles by Wilson and MacGregor, as well as Senator (the house brand), for male, female, and junior players. Balls by Wilson, Titleist, Top Flite, Pinnacle, and Senator are offered, as well as wooden and plastic tees, gloves, grips, club-head covers, a range of bags and carts, and umbrellas. Austad's footwear ranges from a running-shoe style to the classic fringe-tongued models in vinyl and leather, and there are rain shoes for diehards. The firm's cardigan sweaters, shirts, pants, socks, and hats will take you from the green to the clubhouse in respectable if not riveting fashion. Other sports and leisure activities are represented by basketball (Converse Pro Stars and MacGregor balls), running (New Balance, Nike, and Etonic shoes), and workout equipment for the home (a rower, minitrampoline, collapsible gym, and stationary bicycle).

The bottom line is price, and Austad's prices are routinely 15% to 40% below suggested list or comparable retail, sometimes less when the firm holds a special sale. Don't miss the real buys—"X'd out" golf balls, potluck shoe styles, overstocked clubs—or the golf tips peppered throughout the catalog. Austad's selling policy is as good as its discounts: It offers a no-questions-asked, money-back guarantee; ships 98% of the orders the same day they're received; will ship outside the U.S. and its possessions, and states that its prices are *not* subject to change without notice! Returns are accepted within 30 days of receipt, and all goods are unconditionally guaranteed against defects for one year.

CANADIAN READERS, PLEASE NOTE: Shipping charges are quoted separately on each order, and shipments are subject to size limitations.

BERRY SCUBA CO.

Dept. WBMC
6674 N. Northwest Hwy.
Chicago, IL 60631
(312) 763–1626: inquiries
(800) 621–6019: orders

Catalog: free; pub. twice yearly
Information: price quote by phone or letter with SASE
Discount: up to 30%
Goods: name brand
Minimum Order: $25 on credit cards
Shipping, Insurance: extra; UPS, PP
Sales Tax: FL, GA, IL deliveries
Accepts: check, MO, certified check, MC, V, PADI Card, AE

$

Berry told us that it's the oldest, largest, and best-known direct-mail scuba firm in the country. It carries a wide range of equipment and accessories for diving and related activities, including regulators, masks, wet suits, fins, tanks, diving lights, strobes, underwater cameras and housing, Seiko diving watches, pole spears, and much more. Among the manufacturers represented are Ikelite, Seatec, Sherwood, Dacor, Fisher, Wenoka, Poseidon, Pennform, and U.S. Divers. We did not receive the catalog for review, but recommend calling or writing for a price quote before ordering from it because Berry runs regular specials and you may get a better price. The 64-page catalog is free; Berry will send you the 256-page compendium for $2, or $4.50 via first-class mail.

THE BEST CHOICE

P.O. Box 13-X
Hershey, PA 17033
(800) 222–1934: PA orders
(800) 233–2175: orders
except PA

Catalog: free; pub. in Feb. and Nov.
Discount: up to 35% (see text)
Goods: name brand, generic
Minimum Order: none
Shipping, Insurance: $2.25 minimum; UPS, PP
Sales Tax: PA deliveries
Accepts: check, MO, MC, V, AE, CB, DC, CHOICE
$$

You wouldn't expect to find a great source for running, tennis, aerobics, biking, racquetball, and basketball gear in the town that produces *trillions* of calories a year, but here it is. The Best Choice, (formerly known as T.B.C.), publishes a catalog of running gear that includes shoes by Adidas, Brooks, Etonic, Nike, New Balance, and Reebok, all listed by name with size ranges and discount prices. The running apparel is strictly serious; singlets, jackets, shorts, all-weather suits, Gore-Tex clothing, winter mitts; other items by Adidas, Sub 4, Nike, New Balance, Frank Shorter, Bill Rodgers, GUTS, and Pro-Togs are carried. The Best Choice also sells TracPac stash pockets, jogging bras and athletic underwear, Spenco and Sorbothane insoles and heel stabilizers, Eternal Sole and Shoe Goo, socks and peds, and even chronograph watches.

The Best Choice has an extensive line of tennis gear that includes shoes by Adidas, Bata, Brooks, Puma, Fred Perry, K-Swiss, Le Coq Sportif, Nike, Reebok, Asahi, Tretorn, Soma, New Balance, and Diadora. There are racquets by Head, Prince, Wilson, Dunlop, Donnay, Kennex, Snauwert, Yonex, and Yamaha; Prince tennis bags; clothing by Adidas and Le Coq Sportif; even great plain all-cotton polo shirts. The serious player will appreciate the court equipment: ball hoppers, Rol Dri water removers, and the

Prince ball machines. There are also racquet repair supplies—gut, nylon strings, grips, tapes, and string savers.

The Best Choice also sells lines of apparel for hiking, biking, aerobics, swimming, and triathaloning, and carries Nike basketball shoes. The firm will resole tennis, running, and basketball shoes, and will restring tennis racquets. The 48-page color catalog is a real boon to athletes tired of going through ten price-quote firms to find one with the right shoes in stock, and is an inspiration to less committed sports and workout mavens. But please note that most of the goods are sold at near-retail prices. We've listed The Best Choice because it offers an excellent selection and prompt service (most orders are shipped within 48 hours of receipt). There are usually a few things in each catalog priced 30% to 35% below list, but don't expect pages of bargains. Replacements are made for defective goods, and wrong sizes may be exchanged if returned unworn within ten days.

BIKE NASHBAR

215 Main St., Dept. WBM
New Middletown, OH 44442
(216) 542–3671: inquiries
(800) 654–2453: OH orders
(800) 345–2453: orders
except OH

Catalog: 50¢; pub. Feb., May, Aug., Oct., Dec.
Discount: 20% to 50%
Goods: name brand, house brand, generic
Minimum Order: none
Shipping, Insurance: $1.95 minimum; UPS, PP
Sales Tax: OH deliveries
Accepts: check, MO, MC, V
$$$

Bike Nashbar, formerly known as Bike Warehouse, is one of the country's top sources for the serious bicyclist. It sells road, touring, dirt, and racing bikes, as well as parts, accessories, frames, clothing, books, and much more. The 56-page catalog is stocked with such items as Colnago and Guerciotti frames, Campagnolo parts, a range of tires by several companies, saddles by Brooks, Avocet, and other firms; toe clips and straps, brakes, Bike Porter car racks, helmets, skin shorts, jerseys, cycling gloves and shoes by Detto Pietro, Bata, and other companies; water bottles, air pumps, Kryptonite and other locks, and much more. Bike Nashbar guarantees you the lowest prices on these top-notch goods; if you can locate lower published prices elsewhere (excluding closeouts and special orders), Bike Nashbar will beat them by 5¢. In addition to selling gear for the cyclist, the firm also sells tents and camping equipment. If you don't see what you want in the catalog, call or write, since it may be in stock.

Satisfaction is guaranteed, and returns are accepted within ten days for refund or credit on all goods except used items, specials, and closeouts. If you place an order for goods, you can also order a catalog subscription for $1.50, which will bring you five issues over the course of a year.

BOWHUNTERS DISCOUNT WAREHOUSE, INC.

P.O. Box 158
Zeigler Rd.
Wellsville, PA 17365
(717) 432–8651: inquiries
(717) 432–8611: orders

Catalog: free; pub. quarterly
Discount: up to 30%
Goods: name brand
Minimum Order: $10
Shipping, Insurance: extra; UPS
Sales Tax: PA deliveries
Accepts: check or MO
$$$

Bowhunting, archery, and hunting equipment are available here at prices to 30% below list. The catalog features bows, arrows, bow sights, quivers, targets, game calls, camping equipment, camouflage clothing, firearms, shooting equipment, and other products by Connecticut Valley Arms, Browning, Martin, Jennings, Bear, Euston, PSE, and other manufacturers. Authorized returns are accepted and a restocking fee is imposed.

CAMPMOR

P.O. Box 999
Paramus, NJ 07652
(201) 445–5000: inquiries
and NJ orders
(800) 526–4784: orders
except NJ

Catalog: free; pub. 3 times yearly
Discount: 20% to 50%
Goods: name brand, generic
Minimum Order: $20 on phone orders
Shipping, Insurance: extra; UPS
Sales Tax: NJ deliveries
Accepts: check, MO, MC, V
$$$

Campmor's 112-page catalog is full of great buys on all sorts of name-brand camping goods, bike touring accessories, and clothing. Just about anything you might need for a stay in the woods can be found here at savings of up to 50% on the prices of the same or comparable goods bought from other firms. The famous Swiss Victorinox knives are sold here at up to 30% less than elsewhere. Comparable bargains are available on Woolrich, Thinsulate, and Borglite Pile clothing; Duofold and Polypro underwear; Timberland boots and Eureka tents; Wenzel, Coleman, and Bristlecone Mountaineering sleeping bags; backpacks by Wilderness Experience, Kelly Camp Trails, and Lowe Alpine Systems; Coleman cooking equipment, Buck knives, Silva compasses; and books on every aspect of the great outdoors. There are many camping accessories with broader applications, such as first-aid kits, Frost-Guard protective cream, and windchill gauges. Campmor has been going strong since 1946 and prides itself on sending orders out within 24 hours of receipt. Returns are accepted for exchange, refund, or credit.

CENTRAL SKINDIVERS OF NASSAU, INC.

2608A Merrick Rd.
Bellmore, NY 11710
(516) 826–8888

Catalog: free
Discount: up to 40%
Information: price quote by phone or letter with SASE
Goods: name brand
Minimum Order: $50 on prepaid orders; $75 on credit cards
Shipping, Insurance: included on some items; UPS, PP
Sales Tax: NY deliveries
Accepts: check, MO, certified check, MC, V, PADI Card

$$

Central has been in business since 1970, and sells name-brand diving gear at savings of up to 40%. It carries tanks from U.S. Divers, Dacor, and Sherwood; jackets from U.S. Divers, Seaquest, Seatec, and Dacor; a full range of regulators, and watches and timers from Tekna, Seiko, Chronosport, and Heuer. This is just a sample of what is available; the catalog shows the full selection and you're invited to call for information on products not listed—they may be in stock.

CUSTOM GOLF CLUBS, INC.

10206 N. Interregional Hwy. 35
Austin, TX 78753
(512) 837–4810
(800) 252–8108: TX orders
(800) 531–5025: orders except TX

Accessories Catalog: free; pub. yearly in Feb.
Repair Catalog: free; pub. yearly in Feb.
Discount: 30% to 50%
Goods: house brand, name brand
Minimum Order: $10
Shipping, Insurance: extra; UPS, PP, FOB Austin
Handling: $2 on orders under $10
Sales Tax: TX deliveries
Accepts: check, MO, certified check, MC, V
$$$

Golfers looking for clubs with custom features should check this company's private line of Golfsmith woods, irons, wedges, and drivers. Every club sold here can be made to the customer's specifications. Options include left- and right-handed models, men's and women's styles, five degrees of flexibility, and your choice of length, weight, color, and grip size. The prices are lower than those charged for some standard name-brand clubs, and far below what you'd pay for custom features elsewhere. The Golfsmith clubs and the company's lines of clothing, footwear, bags, carts, gloves, manuals, balls, club covers, and other goods are shown in the Accessories Catalog.

The Repair Catalog offers 92 pages of pro-shop products—replacement club heads, shafts, grips, refinishing supplies, tools, manuals, and many other goods. Custom Golf Clubs runs a mail-order repair department and lists the services it offers in the Repair Catalog. The next time you need work done on your clubs, check Custom's rates against those of your local pro shop—chances are you'll get a better deal here.

CYCLE GOODS CORP.

2735 Hennepin Ave. So.
Minneapolis, MN 55408
(612) 872–7600: inquiries and MN orders
(800) 328–5213: orders except MN

Catalog: $3; $4 overseas, refundable (see text); pub. yearly
Information: price quote by phone or letter with SASE
Goods: name brand, generic
Minimum Order: none
Shipping, Insurance: extra; UPS, PP
Sales Tax: MN deliveries
Accepts: check, MO, MC, V, AE, CB, DC
$$$

The Cycle Goods Corp., formerly Cycl-Ology, publishes a 175-page catalog of parts, tools, clothing, and accessories for the cyclist, including product information, and valuable tips for improved performance and maintenance. We were told that it sells "any item stocked or unstocked relating to the industry." The roster of brands is staggering: TTT, Peugeot, Ciöcc, Suntour, Campagnolo, Sergal, Cycle Pro, Bata, Protogs, Avocet, Detto Pietro, Sugino, Cinelli, Nadax, Vetta, Omas, Atom, Maillard, Columbus, Reynolds, Kryptonite, Bendix, Gitane, Berec, Citadel, Araya, Fiamme, Mavic, Weinmann, Rigida, Michelin, Brooks, Messinger, Stewart Warner, Tailwind, Carlisle, and Kingsbridge are among the firms represented. Savings run up to 40%, and you're asked to call or write if you don't see what you're looking for, since it's probably stocked or can be ordered. This is a firm no serious cyclist should miss.

DYKER HEIGHTS SPORTS SHOP, INC.

8304 13th Ave.
Brooklyn, NY 11228
(718) 833–8877

Brochure: free; pub. quarterly
Information: price quote by phone or letter with SASE
Discount: up to 30%
Goods: name brand, generic
Minimum Order: none
Shipping, Insurance: extra; UPS
Sales Tax: NY deliveries
Accepts: check, MO, MC, V
$

This is "Joe Torre's" Brooklyn shop, where you can buy jerseys, caps, and duffles bearing the logos of any NFL team, plus pennants, the official NFL football by Wilson, and other goods. The brochure doesn't show the name-brand sporting goods—equipment for football, baseball, softball, basketball, and other popular sports by Rawlings, Wilson, Majestic, Jesco, Empire, Felco, Koho, and other firms—which are sold at savings of up to 30% on list prices. Call or write for a price quote.

GOLF HAUS

700 N. Pennsylvania
Lansing, MI 48906
(517) 489-8842

Brochure: free; pub. bimonthly
Information: price quote by phone or letter with
  SASE
Discount: 20% to 60%
WBMC Reader Bonus: see text
Goods: name brand
Minimum Order: $30
Shipping, Insurance: included; UPS, PP
Sales Tax: MI deliveries
Accepts: check, MO, MC, V
$$$

Golf Haus has the "absolute lowest prices on pro golf clubs" anywhere. It offers every possible manufacturer, including Ping, Titleist, Wilson, Ram, Lynx, Spalding, MacGregor, Hagen, Powerbilt, Dunlop, and all the Proline clubs, bags, balls, putters, etc. Golf Haus has Bag Boy carts, Etonic and Foot Joy shoes, and accessories like gloves, umbrellas, spikes, scorekeepers, visors, rainsuits, tote bags, socks, and much more. As if savings of up to 60% weren't enough, Golf Haus will give readers of this book a free set of 1-3-4-5 club covers worth $15 with the purchase of a set of clubs. Be sure to identify yourself as a WBMC reader when you're ordering to claim this bonus.

HOLABIRD SPORTS DISCOUNTERS

Holabird Industrial Park
6405 Beckley St.
Baltimore, MD 21224
(301) 633-3333, 8200

Price List: free; pub. 5 to 6 times yearly
Information: price quote by phone or letter with
  SASE
Discount: 30% to 35%
Goods: name brand
Minimum Order: none
Shipping, Insurance: $2.75 per order; UPS, PP
Sales Tax: MD deliveries
Accepts: check, MO, MC, V, CHOICE
$$$

Buy here and you get the "Holabird Advantage": prices up to 35% below list on tennis, racquetball, squash racquets and accessories; service on manufacturers' warranties; prompt shipment, and free stringing on all racquets (with tournament nylon), plus covers.

The selection of tennis racquets includes lines by AMF Head, Adidas,

Davis, Donnay, Dunlop, Durbin, Fila, Kennex, Kneissl, Le Coq Sportif, Match Mate, Prince, Rossignol, Slazenger, Snauwaert, Spalding, Wilson, Yamaha, Bard, Yonex, Fox, and Bancroft. Balls from Wilson, Penn, and Dunlop are offered at discount. Also available: the Prince ball machine, and shoes by Adidas, Converse, New Balance, Nike, Foot Joy, AMF Head, K-Swiss, Le Coq Sportif, Etonic, Fred Perry, Puma, TBS, Tretorn, Asahi, and Diadora.

If racquetball is your game, try Holabird for racquets by AMF Head, Wilson, Ektelon, AMF Voit, Leach, and Kennex. Shoes by Foot Joy, Bata, Adidas, AMF Head, Patrick, and Nike. Racquetball balls are also stocked.

Now that squash is no longer strictly Ivy League, we're seeing more racquets and supplies offered by discounters. Holabird has some of the lowest prices we've seen on a number of models. It carries lines by AMF Head, AMF Voit, Bancroft, Donnay, Dunlop, Kennex, Slazenger, Manta, and Wilson. Buy your eye protection here (don't play without it); you can choose from eye guards made by AMF Voit, Rainbow, Ektelon, and Leader Hogan. Bags by Head, Prince, Wilson, AMF Voit, and Ektelon are offered for all the racquet sports. If you supplement your game with workouts, check Holabird for savings on Nike running shoes and aerobic shoes by Nike, Etonic, and Foot Joy. Not listed in the brochure but in stock are warm-ups by Paul Sullivan, Fila, and Adidas; and racquetball gloves from Champion, Saranac, AMF Voit, and other firms.

The racquets come prestrung, but custom stringing with any of 18 types of gut or synthetic strings is offered. Authorized returns are accepted within five days on everything but used goods. If you don't see what you're looking for in the listing, it's probably available—call or write for information and a price quote.

LAS VEGAS DISCOUNT GOLF & TENNIS

4813 Paradise Rd.
Las Vegas, NV 89109
(702) 798–6300: inquiries
and NV orders
(800) 634–6743: orders
except NV

Catalog: free
Discount: 25% to 40%
Goods: name brand
Minimum Order: none
Shipping, Insurance: extra; UPS, PP
Sales Tax: NV deliveries
Accepts: check, MO, MC, V, AE, CB, DC
$$$

Las Vegas sells name-brand gear for tennis, golf, racquetball, and jogging at savings of up to 40%. The firm carries golf equipment by Wilson, DDH, Stan Thompson, Spalding, Ram, Lynx, Ben Hogan, Powerbilt, Ping, Tiger

Shark, Browning, Dunlop, MacGregor, Toney, Titleist, and PGA—clubs, drivers, putters, wedges, chippers, bags, and balls. If you're looking for golf clothing by Izod, Turfer, Lamode, or Foot Joy, Las Vegas probably has it.

Las Vegas offers tennis racquets by Head, Wilson, Donnay, Prince, Dunlop, Kennex, Bancroft, Yamaha, Davis, and Spalding. There are nylon, gut, and synthetic-gut strings from several firms; tennis balls by Penn, Wilson, Dunlop, and Tretorn; shoes by Tretorn, Fred Perry, Adidas, Head, Asahi, Nike, Foot Joy, and K-Swiss; and clothing by Bogner, Fila, Adidas, Ellesse, Tacchini, Tail, and Izod. Racquetball players looking for a price-break on racquets by Head, Ektelon, or Wilson should stop here. You can pick up eye guards, footwear, Voit jump ropes (to help pass time while waiting for a court) and other goods, all at excellent prices.

PEDAL PUSHERS, INC.

1130 Rogero Rd.
Jacksonville, FL 32211
(904) 725-3444: inquiries
(800) 342-7320: FL orders
(800) 874-2453: orders
except FL

Catalog: free; $4 to Canada; pub. three times yearly
Information: price quote by phone or letter with SASE
Discount: 10% to 40%
Goods: name brand, house brand
Minimum Order: $15
Shipping, Insurance: $2.95 minimum; UPS, PP
Sales Tax: FL deliveries
Accepts: check, MO, MC, V, AE, CB, DC
$$$

Pedal Pushers offers 48 pages of frames, parts, accessories, maintenance supplies, tools, and clothing for the bicyclist. Look here for products by Cinelli, Phil Wood, Avocet, Sun Tour, Campagnolo, Zefal, Rigida, Mavic, Weinmann, Ambrosio, Shimano, Brooks, and Dura-Ace; tires by Wolber, Michelin, Clement, or Cycle Pro; frames and parts by Masi, Woodrup, Holsworth, Ciöcc, Gios Torini, Guerciotti, and Rossini; Jim Blackburn racks, and Cannondale bags and panniers. If you don't see what you want, call or write—the item may be in stock but not listed. Prices are 10% to 40% below list and regular retail, and sometimes even lower if Pedal runs a sale or special.

PROFESSIONAL GOLF & TENNIS SUPPLIERS, INC.

7825 Hollywood Blvd.
Pembroke Pines, FL 33024
(305) 981–7283: customer service
(800) 432–0158: FL orders
(800) 327–9243: orders except FL

Brochure: free with SASE; pub. 4 times yearly
Information: price quote by phone or letter with SASE
Discount: 30% to 50%
WBMC Reader Bonus: see text
Goods: name brand
Minimum Order: none
Shipping, Handling, Insurance: included on most items; UPS, PP
Sales Tax: FL deliveries
Accepts: check, MO, MC, V, AE, CB, DC, Access, EC

$$$

This firm actually represents several businesses. Professional Golf Suppliers, Inc., carries pro-golf sets and single clubs by Acushnet, Titleist, Ben Hogan, Browning, Dunlop, First Flight, Hagen, Jerry Barber, Lynx, Mac-Gregor, PGA, Ping, Pinseeker, Powerbilt, Ram, Rawlings, Sounder, Spalding, Stan Thompson, Taylor Made, Tiger Shark, Tony Penna, and Wilson. In addition, Professional offers name-brand golf gloves, bags, shoes, balls (including rewashed), and carts (Bag Boy and Kangaroo Katty), as well as related miscellany—golf caps, wooden tees, head covers, socks, and the like. Repairs are also available.

Professional Tennis Suppliers carries tennis racquets by Bancroft, Davis, Donnay, Dunlop, Durbin, Fila, Fischer, Head, Kennex, Kneissl, Le Coq Sportif, Match Mate, P.D.P., Pro Group, Prince, Rossignol, Slazenger, Spalding, Scepter, Snauwaert, Volkl, Wilson, Yamaha, and Yonex. There are running and tennis shoes by Adidas, Bata, Brooks, Converse, Diadora, Foot Joy, Fred Perry, Head, K-Swiss, Le Coq Sportif, Lotto, New Balance, Nike, Pro-Keds, PTS, Puma, Sauconey, Tretorn, and Yamaha. Custom stringing with a choice of two dozen types of nylon and gut strings is available. Pro Tennis Suppliers carries balls by Penn, Wilson, and Dunlop, grips, nets, ball-throwing machines, hoppers, stringing machines, bags, and things like Tourna Grip, String-A-Lings, Shoe Goo, as well as other playing aids.

Professional Tennis Suppliers has expanded its stock to include squash racquets by Donnay, Dunlop, and Head. And a new division, Professional Racquetball Suppliers, Inc., provides racquets from Ektelon, Leach, Head, AMF, Voit, and Wilson; shoes by Adidas, Foot Joy, Bata, Asahi, and Head; bags from Ektelon, Head, Leach, Wilson, and Voit; and name-brand balls, gloves, eye-protection gear, clothing, and more.

Even looking good is less expensive at Professional. Choose your wardrobe from Fila, Ellesse, Sergio Tacchini, Head, Fred Perry, Izod, Top Speed, Boast, Tail, Wilson, Adidas, and other brands of designer sportswear. You must call with style numbers for a price quote, since these items aren't listed in the brochure. And you can get more life out of your boat and deck shoes with Professional's resoling and repair service.

If the savings of up to 40% aren't incentive enough, Professional throws in a free "professional" golf or tennis T-shirt with each order of over $75 in equipment. Remember to identify yourself as a WBMC reader if you want the shirt.

PLEASE NOTE: Professional imposes a surcharge of 3% on the total cost of orders charged to a MasterCard or VISA account. Also, we advise you to comparison shop carefully—we found a few items listed in the brochure at full retail prices.

**PROFESSIONAL GOLF
SUPPLIERS, INC.**

**7825 Hollywood Blvd.
Pembroke Pines, FL 33024
(305) 981–7283**

For information on this firm, see Professional Golf & Tennis Suppliers, Inc., in this section.

**PROFESSIONAL
RACQUETBALL
SUPPLIERS, INC.**

**7825 Hollywood Blvd.
Pembroke Pines, FL 33024
(305) 981–7283**

For information on this firm, see Professional Golf & Tennis Suppliers, Inc., in this section.

ROAD RUNNER SPORTS

1431 Stratford Ct.
Del Mar, CA 92014
(800) 227–7375: CA orders
(800) 841–0697: orders
except CA

Price List: free; pub. in May and Sept.
Information: price quote by phone or letter with
  SASE
Discount: 10% above cost (see text)
WBMC Reader Savings: free shipping
Goods: name brand
Minimum Order: none
Shipping, Insurance: $2 per order (see text); UPS,
  PP
Sales Tax: CA deliveries
Accepts: check, MO, MC, V, AE
$$$

Road Runner boasts "the absolute lowest running shoe prices," selling at a 10% markup on wholesale cost, or up to 35% below list prices. The brands available include Nike, New Balance, Saucony, Brooks, Tiger, Adidas, Etonic, and Mazuno. If you identify yourself as a WBMC reader when you order, you can save the $2 shipping fee. If you don't see the style you're looking for in the price list, call or write—it's probably in stock.

**SIERRA FITNESS
DISTRIBUTORS**

**155 Glendale #15
Sparks, NV 89431
(702) 356–8471, 8472:
inquiries and NV orders
(800) 722–0398: orders
except NV**

Brochure: free
Discount: 50%
Goods: name brand
Minimum Order: none
Shipping, Insurance: extra; FOB Sparks
Sales Tax: NV deliveries
Accepts: check, MO, MC, V
$$

Sierra sells two products that have become quite popular among health and fitness freaks: the "postural" chair and the gravity-inversion machine. The BackSaver chair is said to provide relief from backaches caused by hours of slumping in a conventional seat; the model sold here is made of birch and upholstered in a choice of fabrics. We saw two prices listed—$109 and $179—and have seen chairs of identical design and similar construction selling for up to $250 in gift catalogs. Three Backswing inversion machines are offered, including the economy model ($149), the home model ($179), and the professional Backswing ($279). It's wise to try this first on a machine at a health club to make sure you like the sensation, and please note the medical cautions listed in Sierra's literature. (There are some who shouldn't use the machine no matter how much they enjoy it; or as Sierra puts it: "a small minority of persons should never become inverted.") Sierra guarantees your satisfaction, and accepts returns within 30 days for refund or credit.

SOCCER INTERNATIONAL, INC.

P.O. Box 7222, Dept. WBMC
Arlington, VA 22207
(703) 524–4333

Catalog and Bumper Sticker: $1; pub. biannually
Discount: 20% to 33%
WBMC Reader Discount: 10% (see text)
Goods: name brand, generic
Minimum Order: $10
Shipping, Insurance: $3 minimum; UPS, PP
Sales Tax: VA deliveries
Accepts: check, MO, certified check
$$$ 🍁 (see text)

Soccer International was founded in 1976 by a soccer enthusiast who approaches the sport with a sense of humor. The 12-page color catalog gives as much space to patches, soccer-design pillows, soccer "croquet," and soccer night-lights, clocks, and radios, as it does to English and Umbro jerseys, shorts, and hosiery, balls from Brine, Mikasa, Mitre, and Umbro, PVC leg shields and ankle guards, duffle bags, ball inflators, nets, and practice aids. There's also a well-chosen list of books on every aspect of this game.

Prices run up to a third less than list on some items, and you can take an additional 10% off if you identify yourself as a WBMC reader and order at least $25 in goods. Quantity discounts are available on bulk purchases of individual items. Inquire for information.

CANADIAN READERS, PLEASE NOTE: orders can be shipped to Canada from January to September only.

SPORTS AMERICA, INC.

P.O. Box 26148
Tamarac, FL 33320
(305) 742–2021: customer
service
(800) 327–6460: orders

Price List: free; pub. spring, fall, winter
Information: price quote by phone or letter with
  SASE
Discount: 30% to 40%
Goods: name brand
Minimum Order: none
Shipping, Insurance: $2.90 per item; UPS, PP
Sales Tax: FL deliveries
Accepts: check, MO, MC, V, AE, CB, DC
$$$ 🍁 (see text)

Sports America sent us a red, white, and blue "hot list" of tennis and racquetball gear, full of racquets, balls, shoes, and other necessities priced as much as 40% below list or retail. In the tennis "racket riot" we saw equipment by Head, Snauwaert, Yonex, Dunlop, Durbin, Slazenger, Avante Garde, Prince, Rossignol, Wilson, Match Mate, and Kennex. They were offered in a choice of two kinds of string at no extra charge, or a selection of gut, graphite, and synthetic materials at $7 to $21 per racquet. The racquetball "racquet rampage" included prestrung goods by Head, AMF Voit, Ektelon, Leach-DP, Kennex, and Wilson. Several squash racquets by Head, Dunlop, and Ektelon were also listed.

Sports America carries shoes by Nike, Adidas, Reebok, Head, Asahi, New Balance, and K-Swiss; bags by Prince, Ektelon, Kennex, Head, Yonex, Snauwaert, and Match Mate; Prince ball machines, a wide range of strings, and eyeguards, gloves, socks, Tourna Grip, Shoe Goo, Babolat racquethead tape, tennis nets, Prince ball machines, and more. Sports America sells only first-quality goods, and accepts authorized returns within 30 days on everything except used, custom-made, or personalized items.

SQUASH SERVICES, INC.

P.O. Box 491
Richboro, PA 18954
(215) 364–4999: inquiries
and PA orders
(800) 356–9900

Information: price quote by phone or letter with SASE
Discount: up to 35%
Goods: name brand
Minimum Order: none
Shipping, Insurance: $2.75 per order; UPS
Sales Tax: PA deliveries
Accepts: check, MO, certified check, MC, V
$$$

Good squash racquets are not cheap—they begin at $50 *without* custom stringing—and a competition player can go through several a month. That's why the pros we know buy from discount suppliers. Squash Services ranks with the best. Tennis enthusiasts are also served.

The company carries lines by Pro Kennex, Goudie, Gray's, Manta, Slazenger, Dunlop, AMF Head, Spalding, Century Sports, and Donnay. Most of the racquets are prestrung, but custom services and a choice of strings are available. Squash Services also sells court shoes by Nike, Pro Kennex, Foot Joy, Tretorn, and Adidas, along with Tourna Grip, eyeguards, gloves, bags, and other accessories. The tennis department stocks racquets by Wilson, Pro Kennex, Head, Slazenger, Prince, and Dunlop, and shoes by Adidas, Nike, Foot Joy, Kennex, and Converse. Call or write for a price quote.

**STUYVESANT BICYCLE &
TOY INC.**

349 W. 14th St.
New York, NY 10014
(212) 254–5200; 675–2160

Catalog: $2.50; pub. every 2 to 3 years
Information: price quote by phone or letter with
  SASE
Discount: 10% to 30%
Goods: name brand
Minimum Order: none
Shipping, Insurance: extra; UPS, PP, FOB NYC
Sales Tax: NY deliveries
Accepts: check, MO, certified check
$$$

Stuyvesant has been selling bicycles, cycling equipment, and supplies since 1939, and mailing them since 1946. The firm's stock runs from children's bicycles to top-notch track and racing bikes (a specialty), and includes everything in between: tandems, city bikes, used bikes, touring bikes, specials, and closeouts. You'll find parts, helmets, jerseys, shoes, toe clips, pumps, locks, water bottles here as well. The brands carried include Cinelli, Atala, BMX, Raleigh, Huffy, Bianchi, Ross, Corso, Puch, and Bottechia, and there are parts and components by Campagnolo, Suntour, Cinelli, Regina, and Tipiemme, among others. Top-of-the-line Simoncini frame sets and Sergal clothing are also offered. The Stuyvesant staff is helpful and experienced in every aspect of cycling, and can answer just about any question you might have.

THE TENNIS CO.

26441 Southfield Rd.
Lathrup Village, MI 48076
(313) 557–3570: inquiries
and MI orders
(800) 521–5707: orders
except MI

Information: price quote by phone or letter with
  SASE
Discount: up to 35%
Goods: name brand
Minimum Order: none
Shipping, Insurance: $2.75 per order; UPS
Sales Tax: MI deliveries
Accepts: check, MO, certified check, MC, V
$$$

Come out a winner before you set foot on the court by buying your racquets at discount. The Tennis Co. sells tennis and squash equipment at savings of up to 35% on list prices. The tennis department includes lines of racquets by Head, Wilson, Prince, and Kennex, which can be custom-strung in a choice of synthetic gut or nylon. Squash players are offered racquets by

Spalding, AMF Head, Dunlop, Kennex, Donnay, Manta, and Slazenger. Many of these racquets come prestrung from the manufacturers, but The Tennis Co. also offers stringing in natural and synthetic gut. Merco 70+ squash balls are available as well. Call or write for a price quote.

SEE ALSO:

Bruce Medical Supply . . . small selection fitness equipment . . . MEDICAL

I. Buss & Co. . . . . military-surplus sleeping bags . . . CLOTHING

Chanute Iron & Supply Co., Inc. . . . . swimming pool chemicals, supplies
. . . HOME (maintenance)

Clothcrafters, Inc. . . . . flannel gun-cleaning patches, mosquito netting . . .
GENERAL

Custom Coat Co. . . . . custom tailoring and dyeing of deer, elk, and moose
hides . . . CLOTHING

Danley's . . . name-brand rifle scopes . . . CAMERAS

Eisner Bros. . . . . athletic apparel . . . CLOTHING

The Finals . . . athletic, swimming apparel, fitness equipment . . .
CLOTHING

47st Photo, Inc. . . . . name-brand binoculars . . . CAMERAS

Laurence Corner . . . backpacks, rucksacks, ammo boxes, targets,
government-surplus camping equipment . . . CLOTHING

Mass Army & Navy Store . . . camping supplies, equipment . . . SURPLUS

Pagano Gloves . . . deerskin gloves for hunters and archers . . .
CLOTHING

A. Rosenthal, Inc. . . . . running bras, dance leotards, swimsuits . . .
CLOTHING

Ruvel and Company, Inc. . . . . camping supplies, equipment . . . SURPLUS

St. Patrick's Down . . . down-filled sleeping bags . . . HOME (linen)

16 Plus Mail Order . . . women's larger size swimwear, running apparel . . .
CLOTHING

Tastefully Yours . . . retort-packed entrees for camping, etc. . . . . FOOD

Weiss & Mahoney . . . camping supplies, equipment . . . SURPLUS

SURPLUS

Surplus and used goods
of every sort.

Surplus was probably the original genetic type of "bargain" merchandise, and as you can see from our listings there are still plenty of surplus goods around to make bargain hunters happy. This is the world of military overstock, obsolete electronics, and the 90% discount. It hasn't happened, but we know that one day we're going to graduate from mess kits and heavy-duty flashlights and buy one of those legendary "under $100" G.I. jeeps!

THE AIRBORNE SALES CO.

P.O. Box 2727
Culver City, CA 90230
(213) 870–4687

Catalog: $1, refundable
Discount: up to 90%
Goods: surplus
Minimum Order: $10
Shipping, Insurance: extra; UPS, FOB Culver City
Sales Tax: CA deliveries
Accepts: check, MO, MC, V
$$$$

The Airborne Sales Company has been in business since 1946 and is still going strong, selling all kinds of government surplus at tremendous savings. The goods are described in the catalog as "hobbyist and do-it-yourself materials," and include generators, starters, and motors for airplane and marine use, plus model cars, boats, planes, and trains. In addition, there is an extensive selection of hydraulics, hardware, tools, and the strange and unique items found only, it seems, in surplus catalogs. Authorized returns are accepted; a restocking fee is imposed.

HARBOR FREIGHT SALVAGE CO.

3491 Mission Oaks Blvd.
P.O. Box 6010
Camarillo, CA 93011–6010
(805) 388–2000: customer
service
(800) 222–6138: customer
service
(805) 388–3000: orders
(800) 423–2567: orders

Catalog: free
Discount: up to 50%
Goods: name brand, generic
Minimum Order: $50
Shipping, Handling: $1.50 per item on orders
   under $50; included on orders over $50; UPS,
   PP
Insurance: 75¢ per order
Sales Tax: CA and KY deliveries
Accepts: check, MO, certified check, V, MC
$$$

Every mailing we've received from Harbor Freight has featured tools and hardware and little else, but we're not complaining: it's a great way to pick up drill and auger bits, a replacement Stanley measuring tape for the workshop, a complete set of Pittsburgh Forge socket wrenches, mildew-proof tarps with brass-plated grommets, a cordless Black & Decker drill (handy when we've misplaced all the extension cords), pipe sealing tape so we can save on plumbing repairs, and an extra camp knife or two. Past brochures have also featured work benches, saw blades, wood lathes, heavy-duty bench grinders and disc sanders, drill presses by Central Machinery, and similar shop equipment. The prices run up to 40% off list and comparable retail, and the range of all-purpose and specialty tools and hardware make this a valuable source for all do-it-yourselfers.

MASS ARMY & NAVY STORE

895 Boylston St.
Boston, MA 02115
(617) 267–1692; 1559:
inquiries and MA orders
(800) 343–7749: orders
except MA

Catalog: free; pub. in Mar. and Sept.
Discount: up to 40%
Goods: new, surplus
Minimum Order: none
Shipping, Handling: extra; UPS, PP
Sales Tax: MA deliveries
Accepts: check, MO, MC, V, AE
$$

The 30-page color catalog from Mass Army & Navy is a far cry from the grubby price lists published by most surplus centers, but much of the stock is new. You'll find a wealth of genuine and reproduction government issue apparel, including camouflage clothing, French Foreign Legion caps, pith helmets and leather pilots' caps, U.S. Air Force sunglasses, Canadian battle pants, Vietnam jungle boots and a range of casual and heavy-duty footwear, and knapsacks and sundry items. There are printed T-shirts, sleeping bags, air mattresses, backpacks, camping gear of all sorts, night sticks, handcuffs, duffle bags, insignia and patches, camping knives, gloves, mess kits, compasses, Lee and Levi jeans, emergency candles and fire sticks, bandannas, bomber jackets, pea coats, and cotton turtleneck sweaters for men and women in 29 vivid colors for just $8.75 each.

Mass Army swears that it will not be undersold; if you find the same item offered elsewhere at a better price, tell Mass Army and it will refund the difference. Returns are accepted for exchange, refund, or credit.

RUVEL AND COMPANY, INC.

3037 N. Clark St.
Chicago, IL 60657
(312) 248–1922

Catalog: $2
Discount: up to 70%
Goods: surplus
Minimum Order: none
Shipping, Insurance: extra; UPS, PP
Sales Tax: IL deliveries
Accepts: MO, certified check, MC, V
$$$

Ruvel specializes in U.S. Army and Navy surplus goods, although the catalogs shows much more: G.I. duffle bags, high-powered binoculars, leather flying jackets, Justrite carbide and electric lamps, strobe lights, mess kits, dinghies, government surplus mosquito netting, nightsticks, snowshoes, Primus campstoves, and toxicological aprons are just a few of the various things that have turned up at Ruvel. This is a great source for camping gear and accessories—the G.I. goods were built to endure wars—and the price is right: up to 70% less than non-surplus goods of comparable quality. When you order, be sure to list second choices since stock is almost always limited and bargains like these move fast.

THE SURPLUS CENTER

1000–15 W. O St.
P.O. Box 82209
Lincoln, NE 68501
(402) 474–4366

Catalog: free
Discount: up to 50%
Goods: new, surplus
Minimum Order: none
Shipping, Insurance: extra; UPS
Sales Tax: NE deliveries
Accepts: check, MO, certified check, MC, V
$$$

The Surplus Center was established in 1940, and offers an excellent array of tools and hardware, some of which is priced 50% below list or original selling price. You'll find blowers, compressors, hand tools of all kinds, electrical equipment and supplies, plumbing equipment and tools, grinders, and a range of products suited for commercial and industrial use. The Burdex line of security and surveillance equipment is carried, as well as generic security and safety hardware and systems components.

WEISS & MAHONEY

142 Fifth Ave.
New York, NY 10011
(212) 675–1915

Catalog: $1
Discount: up to 75%
Goods: name brand, surplus
Minimum Order: $10 on credit cards
Shipping, Insurance: extra; UPS
Sales Tax: NY deliveries
Accepts: check, MO, MC, V, AE
$$

Weiss & Mahoney's catalog is filled back to back with new and recycled uniforms, insignia, accessories, parade and camping equipment, trophies, flags, and goods of a similar sort. Everything turns up here, from Brasso and Snow-Proof to Eureka and Kirkham tents and Coleman stoves to new and used military clothing. Past catalogs have shown athletic socks and shorts, swim trunks, denim jeans and overalls, watch caps, balaclavas, sneakers, used tuxedo jackets, overcoats, and a large group of camouflage clothing.

Weiss can also supply you with custom-made indoor presentation and parade flags, stock foreign and American flags, flagpoles, and holders. It has all sorts of military medals, emblems, and other collectibles, plus such items as gun holsters, badge holders, handcuffs, and night sticks. The store of camping gear and supplies is extensive, ranging from the basics—tents, sleeping bags, and knapsacks—to plastic egg holders, folding shovels, and portable commodes. Note that the bargains are found in recycled surplus, and discounts on new, name-brand goods are modest.

SEE ALSO:

I. Buss & Co. . . . . military-surplus clothing . . . CLOTHING
Laurence Corner . . . new and used government surplus . . . CLOTHING

TOOLS, HARDWARE, ELECTRONICS, ENERGY, SAFETY, SECURITY, AND INDUSTRIAL

Materials, supplies, equipment, and services.

This section offers the do-it-yourselfer, hobbyist, logger, and small-time mechanic a wealth of tools and hardware, some of it at rock-bottom prices. Repair and replacement parts for lawn mowers, trimmers, garden tractors, snowmobiles, snow throwers, blowers, go-carts, minibikes, and even plumbing and electrical systems are available from these companies. The tools run from pocket screwdrivers and fine wood chisels to complete workbenches and professional machinery; the hardware includes hard-to-find specialty items as well as stock nuts, bolts, nails, etc.

When you're working, be sure to observe safety precautions. Use goggles, dust masks, respirators, earplugs, gloves, and other protective gear as indicated. Make sure blades are sharp and electrical cords are in good repair, and keep tools, hardware, and chemicals out of the reach of children. If you're using a chain saw, make sure it's fitted with an approved antikickback device. Most of the firms selling chain-saw supplies should be able to provide one to fit your model.

For more tools and related products, see "Crafts and Hobbies," "General," "Home (maintenance)," and "Surplus."

A.E.S.

P.O. Box 1790-WC
Ft. Bragg, CA 95437
(707) 964–6661: inquiries
(800) 336–8665: CA orders
(800) 331–8665: orders
except CA

Catalog and Price List: $1
Information: price quote by phone or letter with SASE
Discount: 20% to 40%
WBMC Reader Discount: 10% on tool accessories (see text)
Goods: name brand
Minimum Order: $10
Shipping, Insurance: extra: UPS, PP
Sales Tax: CA deliveries
Accepts: check, MO, MC, V
$$

If you're in the market for power tools by Makita or Jet, A.E.S. is your source. It discounts complete lines from these two firms from 20% to 40%, and is offering readers of this book additional savings of 10% on all tool *accessories* (not the tools themselves). The catalog you receive is the manufacturer's literature on Makita goods. It includes complete listings and specs on the cordless line, saws (jig, circular, miter, PVC, and chain), drills, routers, trimmers, planers, jointers, sanders, nibblers and shears, polishers, grinders, concrete planers, drywall screwdrivers, and accessories. The price list includes both the retail and A.E.S. discounted prices. Inquiries are accepted by phone or mail on the Jet tools. A.E.S. (which stands for Appropriate Energy Solutions) may add more manufacturers in the future, so if you're buying power tools be sure to see what's currently stocked.

ALL ELECTRONICS CORP.

**905 S. Vermont Ave.
Los Angeles, CA 90006
(213) 380–8000: inquiries
(800) 258–6666: CA orders
(800) 826–5432: orders
except CA**

Catalog: free; pub. 3 times yearly
Information: price quote by phone or letter with SASE
Discount: up to 70%
Goods: generic, surplus
Minimum Order: $10
Shipping, Handling, Insurance: $2.50 minimum; UPS, PP
Sales Tax: CA deliveries
Accepts: check, MO, MC, V
$$$$

All Electronics sells surplus electronics for up to 70% less than their original value, and sometimes even more. The catalog is full of things that should interest electronics hobbyists: semiconductors, lamps, heat sinks, sockets, cables and adaptors, fans, connectors, plugs, switches, solenoids, relays, capacitors, wire, fuses, resistors, transformers, potentiometers, keyboards, computer fans, P.C. boards, joysticks, and many other items. There are things here as well that everyone can use, including replacement phone cords at less than half the cost of new cords, screwdrivers, socket wrenches, multiple outlet strips, surge suppressors, battery chargers, and replacement knobs for electronics. All parts are guaranteed to be in working order and authorized returns are accepted within 15 days. The catalog is indexed for easy reference.

BAILEY'S, INC.

Western Division:
Hwy. 101
P.O. Box 550
Laytonville, CA 95454
(707) 984–6133: inquiries,
CA orders, orders under
$50
Southern Division:
1520 S. Highland
P.O. Box 9088
Jackson, TN 38314
(901) 422–1300: inquiries,
TN orders, orders under
$50

Catalog: $1; pub. Jan., May, Sept.
Information: price quote on volume orders by letter
  with SASE or nonWATS phone
Discount: 20% to 70%
Goods: name brand, house brand, generic
Minimum Order: none
Shipping, Handling, Insurance: $3 minimum; UPS,
  PP
Sales Tax: CA and TN deliveries
Accepts: check, MO, MC, V
$$$$

Bailey's, our favorite source for chain saws, parts, logging gear, and related goods, came through the 1982 recession with flying colors. In fact, there's now a second Bailey's in Jackson, Tennessee. (Customers in the East and South can order from that office and save on shipping costs.)

The Bailey's 74-page catalog lists all kinds of Oregon chain reels and bars by McCulloch, Pioneer, Stihl, Husqvarna, and Homelite. Bar and chain oil, bar wrenches, files, Simington chain grinders, spark plugs, tape, and guide bars are also available. Logging is treacherous work and requires firm footing, and Bailey's stocks calked and heavy-duty boots by Wesco, Chippewa, and Buffalo, plus tree saddles and belts, leg pads, and climbing spurs. There are tree-marking paints and crayons, Duerr log splitters, Alaskan saw mills, Lewis winches, wire rope, Duff-Norton tree jacks, and hard hats.

You don't have to be a logger to love this firm. Bailey's regularly offers such universally useful items as boot dryers, eye and head-protection gear, E.A.R. plugs and headset noise mufflers, lightweight axes, and the classic Safety Yellow rain jacket (so classic in fact that Ralph Lauren has issued a designer version, at a price that makes us wonder whether status rain is next). If you chop your own firewood, you'll want to take a look at the Woodlander Sawbuck (a folding, 12½-lb aluminum sawbuck for $42 that holds logs up to 16″ across); splitting mauls and replacement handles, and wedges. The Bailey's safety equipment includes several stretchers and a first-aid kit that Bailey's says is a popular item—it tells the user how to treat emergency situations directly and is magnetized so it's readily available in your truck or car. The 14-oz aerosol fire extinguisher ($5) is used for dousing chain-saw fires; you can put one in your workshop and bring another along on camping trips. Equally useful: mink-oil leather conditioner, all-cotton heavyweight T-shirts (printing available), Lee dungarees, Five Brothers cotton flannel shirts, work gloves, Filson jackets and pants, and traditional red suspenders. And the kids won't let you overlook the Tonka Toys—cranes, dump trucks, bulldozers, and more, from $14 to $20.

Most of the goods at Bailey's are discounted from 20% to 60%, but the sale catalogs offer specials at up to 70% off list prices. Members of the National Timber Fallers Association are entitled to extra discounts. All orders are shipped the same day they're received, and Bailey's will ship to Hawaii and Alaska via USPS. Mr. Bailey and his staff are very friendly people who stand ready to help with all your logging-related needs and questions.

THE BEVERS

P.O. Box 12
Wills Point, TX 75169
(214) 272–8370

Catalog: $1, refundable; pub. yearly
Information: price quote by letter with SASE
Discount: up to 50%
Goods: name brand, generic
Minimum Order: none
Shipping, Handling: extra; UPS, PP
Sales Tax: TX deliveries
Accepts: check, MO, certified check, MC, V
$$$

The Bevers sells very useful hardware and equipment for woodworking, construction, household repairs, and any number of other purposes. In the past, we've needed many of the screws and bolts sold here for different projects and seldom found them at the local hardware store. For example, the catalog lists steel and brass wood screws in many sizes with round and flat heads, lock and flat washers, a full range of eye bolts and squared screw hooks, Tap-Lok threads, machine screws (with slotted round and flat heads, plus pan and hex heads), hex heads and carriage bolts, lag screws, clamps (picture frame, "C," and gluing), doweling drill bits, countersinks, and rotary and sandpaper drums for drills. There's a good selection of wooden parts for making toys and repairing furniture, including wood balls, toy wheels, Shaker pegs, game pieces, golf tees, screwhole buttons, knobs and pulls, and turned finials and balusters. We priced several items and found savings of up to 50% compared to our local hardware stores, but let us pass on Mr. Bever's comments on the whole business of discounting: "I give no discounts—we offer good quality merchandise at the best price we can with a *full count.* I have no use for discount firms that make up their prices by shorting their customers." We hadn't realized that firms might do this, but few customers are going to sit down and count an order of 1,000 screws to make sure they're all there. Since 950 will probably look like the full amount to most eyes, Mr. Bever's claims should alert those of you buying from other suppliers. Take the time to make sure you're getting what you ordered if you buy elsewhere.

CAMELOT ENTERPRISES

P.O. Box 65, Dept. W
Bristol, WI 53104–0065

Catalog: $1, redeemable; pub. quarterly
Information: price quote by phone or letter with SASE
Discount: 30% to 60%
WBMC Reader Discount: 5% on orders over $50 (see text)
Goods: name brand, generic
Minimum Order: none
Shipping, Handling: extra; UPS
Sales Tax: WI deliveries
Accepts: check, MO, certified check, MC, V
$$$

Camelot sells "quality fasteners, hardware, and tools direct to the craftsman" at savings of 30% to 60% on comparable retail. You'll find a full range of nuts (hex, K-lock, wing, stop, etc.); bolts (hex-head, machines, carriage); screws (wood, lag, machine); washers, thread fittings, cotter pins, anchors, and other hardware, plus Mayhew wood chisels, offset screwdrivers, and punches. Other hand tools by Rockford, Campbell-Hausfeld, GAM, Chicago Pneumatic, Stanley, Makita, Ram Tool, and Bush Lake Industries are available but not shown in the catalog. You can request a flyer on any line produced by these companies, or write for a price quote (include a SASE) on specific models. If your order totals $50 or more (excluding shipping and sales tax), you're entitled to the WBMC reader discount of 5%. Identify yourself as a reader when you order to qualify. And don't miss the specials and coupon offers usually inserted in the catalog—they're often good for additional savings of 10% on selected lines or items. Satisfaction is guaranteed, and returns are accepted within ten days for replacement, refund, or credit.

D.R.I. INDUSTRIES, INC.

**11300 Hampshire Ave. S.
Bloomington, MN
55438–2498
(612) 944–3530**

Catalog: free; pub. quarterly
Discount: up to 60%
Goods: house brand, name brand, generic
Minimum Order: none
Shipping, Handling: extra; UPS
Sales Tax: MN deliveries
Accepts: check, MO, MC, V, AE, CB, DC
$$$

D.R.I. bills itself as "the hardware store in your mailbox." It's a great source for fasteners, parts bins and workshop cabinets, and hand and power tools. One of D.R.I.'s most popular lines is the Work-Shops collection of complete hardware sets. These are organized assortments of rivets, snaps, anchors, nails, terminals and connectors, hole plugs, nuts and bolts, power-drive fasteners, threaded inserts, O-rings, plumbing-repair hardware, hose clamps, washers, spacers, thumb screws, frame-hanging parts, hitch and cotter pins, half-moon keys, and many other bits and pieces. They're sorted by size and type, and packed in clear plastic boxes, carry cases, cabinets, or bins. You can order the collections by type or buy the "Dream Work-Shop," a set of 20 of the most-used individual assortments. It has over 13,500 pieces and costs $399.99, compared to over $1,100 for the same goods bought piecemeal at retail. The Work-Shops represent savings on several levels: They're up to 60% less expensive than similar assortments assembled from other sources; they include hard-to-find sizes and parts, so you're spared a lengthy search when you need a nonstandard item; they save trips to the hardware store for frequently used items. Since it's easy to see what's running low, you can reorder specific parts *before* you run out—the D.R.I. catalog has 38 pages of fasteners sold in bulk (among them items not included in the Work-Shops). A guide to the selection and use of fasteners is included in this section.

D.R.I. also sells a range of tools and equipment—bicycle-repair sets, lug wrenches, auto-body repair tools, a portable oxy-propane torch, folding sawhorses, a great collection of hardware cabinets and organizers, several Makita power tools, a variety of hand saws, socket wrenches, clamps, dovetailing guides, calipers, tile nippers, screwdrivers, files, pliers, honing tools, a compact vacuum/blower, cord reels, drill bits, and much more. Satisfaction is completely guaranteed on every purchase, and returns are accepted for replacement, refund, or credit.

ECOTECH, INC.

P.O. Box 9649-W
Washington, DC 20016
(202) 244–3858

Catalog: $1, refundable; pub. yearly
Information: price quote by phone or letter with SASE
Discount: 30% to 50%
WBMC Reader Offer: see text
Goods: name brand, house brand, generic
Minimum Order: none
Shipping, Insurance: included on some items; UPS, PP
Sales Tax: DC deliveries
Accepts: check, MO, MC, V

WBMC Discount

We didn't receive Ecotech's catalog, but were told it features over 300 products designed to save energy in the house and on the road, and it includes goods for commercial applications. Novan and Arco solar systems and products, Thermar instant hot-water heaters, Conserv Energy equipment, Palona "constant flo" heaters, and many other items are offered at 30% to 50% below list or comparable retail.

Ecotech is offering WBMC readers a special price on the Ultra Showerhead, which cuts water flow to about two gallons a minute (compared to six to ten with conventional heads) without reducing the shower to a drizzle. The unit is self-cleaning, easy to install, has a five-year warranty, and is selling for under $10, postpaid. You can call or write for the current price and, if you order, you're entitled to a free copy of the catalog plus a coupon good for $5 off a future order of $50 or more. Remember to identify yourself as a WBMC reader when you request the price or send for the catalog, since you may be offered other specials as well. Satisfaction is guaranteed, and returns are accepted within 30 days for refund or credit.

ETCO ELECTRONICS CORP.

Rte. 9 N.
Plattsburgh, NY 12901
(518) 561–8700

Catalog: $1; pub. every 6 to 8 weeks
Discount: up to 70%
Goods: name brand, generic
Minimum Order: $10
Shipping, Handling, Insurance: extra; UPS, PP
Sales Tax: NY deliveries
Accepts: check, MO, MC, V
$$$$ 🍁 (see text)

ETCO's "great catalog of electronic things" will gladden the hearts and enrich the workshops of all electronics buffs. The 16-page tabloid is jammed with name-brand electronics sold at savings of up to 70% off original and list prices. Current offerings include Winegard satellite dishes, all sorts of telephones, amps, parabolic microphones, VCRs and parts, speakers, headsets, door chimes, dummy TV cameras for "security purposes," tuners, microphones, adaptors, condensers, loudspeakers, terminals, hardware, modulators, resistors, TV picture tubes, and *thousands* of other things. Whether you're a hobbyist or simply looking for great buys on electronics, you can't afford to miss this catalog.

CANADIAN READERS, PLEASE NOTE: ETCO welcomes orders from Canadian customers, and includes information on shipping and handling charges assessed on orders shipped to Canada in the catalog. At this writing, ETCO has a store in Pointe Claire, Quebec, as well as its Plattsburgh center.

FIXMASTER INC.

P.O. Box 49511
Atlanta, GA 30359
(404) 633-2210

Price List: free with SASE; pub. in the spring and fall
Discount: 40% to 50%
Goods: name brand
Minimum Order: none
Shipping, Handling, Insurance: $3 per order; UPS
Sales Tax: GA deliveries
Accepts: check or MO
$$$$

If your repairs or home-improvement projects call for abrasives and band-saw blades, call on FixMaster. This firm carries 3M, Norton, and Carborundum abrasives—sanding belts from 3″×21″ to 6″×48″, sandpaper sheets, sanding discs, emory cloth, and rolls of aluminum-oxide sandpaper. FixMaster also sells Nickelson band-saw blades—165 sizes are stocked, and the inventory exceeds 8,000 blades. The blades can cope with wood, soft metals (brass, copper, and aluminum) and ferrous metals (iron and steel).

Savings on both abrasives and blades can be as great as 50%, and even more if you're buying in volume. FixMaster lists only a fraction of what's stocked. If you don't see what you want, write and ask whether it's available.

MAINE DISCOUNT HARDWARE

P.O. Box 6074-W
Falmouth, ME 04105
(207) 781-2509

Catalog: $4.95, refundable (see text); pub. yearly in Mar.
Discount: 20% to 40%
WBMC Reader Discount: 30% on some goods (see text)
Goods: name brand, generic
Minimum Order: $20; $50 for WBMC Reader Discount
Shipping, Insurance: included on small orders; UPS, PP, FOB Falmouth
Handling: $2 on orders under $20
Sales Tax: ME deliveries
Accepts: check, MO, MC, V
$$$

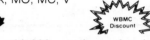

Maine Discount Hardware carries over 10,000 products for industry, farm, office, and home, and they're showcased in the hefty 1,122-page catalog. There are motors for every conceivable application, plus capacitors, blowers, switches, mounts, and related products; relays, starters, solenoids, alternators, generators, compressors, terminals, and outlets; hand and power tools, safety equipment, loading equipment, industrial storage units, office and institutional furnishings and supplies, office electronics, home and institutional appliances, farm and garden equipment, heating and cooling devices, and systems for home and institution, and many, many other types of goods. Each catalog stock number is listed in the separate "suggested list prices" book; you find the Maine Discount price by locating the suggested list for the product you want and deducting 23% from that—with the exception of tools by Black & Decker, Skil, and Milwaukee, on which you deduct 33%. And if you cite this book as your reference when ordering, you can deduct *30%* from the list prices of Dayton electric motors and air tools, Teel pumps, and Speedaire air compressors, instead of the standard 23% discount. Over 20 pages of the catalog are devoted to a valuable terminology/technology guide that tells you how to evaluate lighting, heating, cooling, and other needs in industrial and commercial installations. The catalog price is refunded with your first purchase of $25 or more.

MANUFACTURER'S SUPPLY

P.O. Box 157, W-4
Dorchester, WI 54425
(715) 654–5821: inquiries
(800) 472–2360: WI orders
(800) 826–8563: orders
except WI

Catalog: $1 pub. yearly
Discount: up to 40%
Goods: name brand, generic
Minimum Order: none
Shipping, Insurance: extra; UPS, FOB Dorchester
Sales Tax: WI deliveries
Accepts: check, MO, MC, V
$$$

One of the unwritten laws of mechanics states that anything that works now will break down eventually. Your chain saw, lawn mower, motorcycle, snowmobile, three-wheel vehicle, snow-thrower, trimmer, trailer, and rototiller are not immune to problems; when they need repair you can turn to the 144-page bible of parts from Manufacturer's Supply.

Keep your chain saw running smoothly with the Supply's sprockets and nose assemblies, chains, grinders, files, air filters, T-wrenches, starter springs, carburetor parts, and guide bars (stocked for 18 saw brands). There are things to help you chop wood—wedges, axes, log splitters, and parts—and things to help you burn it. BK and Hot Shot wood-burning furnaces, Magic Heat air circulators for your furnace, stove, or fireplace, Aqua Siphon hot-water heaters that are used with wood stoves and furnaces, and Neuman chimney cleaners and brushes are also available.

Whizz-Witch lawn trimmers and replacement filament, Hoffco scythes, and a range of parts for standard and riding lawn mowers are stocked, plus semipneumatic tires for mowers and shopping carts, wheelbarrows, and hand trucks. If you own a motorcycle, see the catalog for pistons, Metzeler tires, wheels, batteries, roller chain, "Hot Hands" handlebar heaters, spark plugs, contacts, clutch parts, drive belts, and more. Manufacturer's sells wheels, hubs, bearing kits, roller chains, sprockets, clutches, belts, and other goods for trailers, minibikes, go-carts, riding mowers, snow-throwers, rototillers, garden tractors, and three-wheelers. And the snowmobile owner will find a wealth of tracks, cleats, lubricants, studs, slides, pistons, piston rings, bearings, gaskets, oil seals, fan belts, carburetors, fuel filters, ignition coils, wear rods, suspension springs, windshields, and engines for a full range of models.

In addition, the catalog lists Briggs & Stratton winches, screws of every sort, nuts, hitch and cotter pins, washers, O-rings, locknuts, springs, wing nuts, half-moon keys, terminals, thread-repair kits, clutch pullers, and many other items that can mean the difference between a do-it-yourself repair job and a costly visit to a service center. The products themselves are priced to 40% below list or comparable retail, and authorized returns are accepted within 30 days.

NORTHERN HYDRAULICS, INC.

P.O. Box 1219
Burnsville, MN 55337
(612) 894–8310: inquiries
and MN orders
(800) 533–5545: orders
except MN

Catalog: free; pub. in Mar. and Sept.
Information: price quote by phone or letter with
 SASE
Discount: 20% to 60%
Goods: name brand, house brand, generic
Minimum Order: none
Shipping, Insurance: extra; UPS, PP
Handling: $1 per order
Sales Tax: MN and SC deliveries
Accepts: check, MO, MC, V
$$$

Northern Hydraulics makes it easy to save up to 60% on hydraulics, gas and electric engines, logging equipment, trailer parts, air tools and compressors, winches, hand tools, lawn and garden equipment, and much more. The copiously illustrated 104-page catalog is indexed and well organized.

You'll find a good selection of log splitters, wedges, Homelite chain saws, Oregon chain and bars, files, and other logging equipment. There are Prince, Parker, Webster, Viking, Williams, and other hydraulic pumps, Orbmark motors, valves for all kinds of motors, mounting brackets and couplings, hydraulic tanks, filters, strainers, hoses, and other parts and equipment. Also shown are gas engines for use with log splitters, lawn and riding mowers, rototillers, and other machines, plus vertical and horizontal-shaft models by Briggs & Stratton and Tecumseh, and replacement mufflers and starters. The catalog has a whole section devoted to go-carts, parts, and accessories; minibike parts, ATV tires and wheels, pneumatic tires, amp starters and other electrical supplies; halogen tractor lamps, generators, sandblasting equipment and pressure washers, air compressors, the Aqua Siphon water heater, propane tanks, pulleys, air tools and accessories, and hand tools.

The lawn and garden equipment can make tending everything from a modest plot to several acres much easier; there are string trimmers, cultivators, Jacobsen garden tractors, agricultural pumps, mower tires, blowers, sprayers, tillers, insecticides, and other aids. And Century welders, airless sprayers, hypro pumps, vehicle winches, trailer jacks and parts, tarps, and many other products are also available from Northern, at very competitive prices. If you don't see what you're looking for in the catalog, inquire— it may be stocked.

R.D. ASSOCIATES

P.O. Box 99
New Rochelle, NY 10804
(914) 636–8699: inquiries
and orders

Catalog: $1, refundable; pub. yearly
WBMC Reader Discount: 30%
Goods: name brand, generic
Minimum Order: $15 on credit cards
Shipping, Handling: extra; UPS
Sales Tax: NY deliveries
Accepts: check or MO
$$

The "Energy Savers" catalog from R.D. Associates is just that—44 pages filled with all kinds of equipment designed to cut down on home energy costs. The catalog also includes an explanation of the U.S. Energy Tax Act and its applications.

R.D. Associates sells insulating jackets for water heaters, Heat Fins that convert part of the heat lost in your flue pipe to radiant heat, automatic timers for hot water heaters, quartz and kerosene heaters, outlet insulators, radiator heat-reflectors, light dimmers, water-conserving shower heads, window and door weather stripping, thermal drapery liners, solar tea-makers, gas matches, emergency candles, and many other gadgets designed to save energy dollars. You can take 30% off the price of everything in the catalog if you identify yourself as a WBMC reader when you order. Satisfaction is guaranteed and returns are accepted for replacement, refund, or credit.

SAW CHAIN
H & H MANUFACTURING &
SUPPLY CO.

P.O. Box 692
Selma, AL 36702
(205) 872–6067

Price List: free
Discount: 33% to 50%
Goods: house brand
Minimum Order: none
Shipping, Handling: $2 per order: UPS
Sales Tax: AL deliveries
Accepts: check, MO, certified check
$$$

H & H Manufacturing can offer you savings of up to 50% on saw chain, guide bars, and sprockets for chain saws by Homelite, Pioneer, Husqvarna, McCulloch, Lombard, Craftsman, Remington, Poulan, Stihl, Echo, John Deere, Jonsereds, Olympic, and other firms. Chain is sold in a range of pitches and gauges, and both gear-drive and direct-drive sprockets are stocked to fit all models. When you order these, be sure to include all the information requested on the form—saw make and model, chain pitch, gauge, number of drive links, type of bar, length, etc—so H & H can provide the proper chain, bar, or sprocket.

This company, which does business by mail as "Saw Chain," also sells Swedish double-cut files and can supply wire rope in all sizes and lengths, logging chokers, slings, and other logging equipment. Inquiries are invited on goods not described in the price list. All chain, bars, files, and sprockets are unconditionally guaranteed to "last as long or longer than any other make," and replacements are issued for any parts that do not live up to this promise.

THE TOOL WAREHOUSE

Willow Park Center, Dept. WBMC
Farmingdale, NY 11735
(516) 420–1420: inquiries and NY orders
(800) 645–9166: orders except NY

Catalog: $1, year's subscription; pub. in May and Nov.
Information: price quote by phone or letter with SASE
Discount: 10% to 50%
Goods: name brand, generic
Minimum Order: $20
Shipping, Handling, Insurance: extra; UPS, PP, FOB Farmingdale
Sales Tax: NH and NY deliveries
Accepts: check, MO, certified check, MC, V
$$$

How many times have you tackled some home repair or improvement project, only to find yourself stymied by a design problem or stopped because you lack an expensive tool? The solution usually lies not in altering plans or investing a lot of money in special equipment, but in getting the *right* kind of hinge, screw, drill bit, or tool attachment. Find out what's at your disposal with the catalog from The Tool Warehouse. It carries everything from pocket screwdrivers to sawbucks—rasps, lathes, vises, hammers, saws, chisels, gouges, calipers, razors, clamps, air compressors, wrenches, jacks. A sample of the manufacturers stocked includes Stanley, Milwaukee, Rockwell, Bosch, Porter Cable, Makita, Hitachi, Ryopi, Channelock, SK, Crescent, Lufkin, Weller, Wiss, Campbell-Hausfeld, Speedaire, Chicago Pneumatic, and Ingersoll Rand. While many of the tools are shown in the 78-page catalog, you can call or write for a price quote on models that aren't listed. Whether you're just starting to assemble a workshop or have a lifetime of tools and experience, be sure to get this catalog before you begin another project—doubtless you'll find many things to make the job easier, and you'll save up to 50% in the bargain.

**TURNKEY MATERIAL
HANDLING, INC.**

**36 Letchworth St.
Buffalo, NY 14213
(716) 885–0155: inquiries
and NY orders
(800) 828–7540: orders
except NY**

Catalog: free; pub. 3 times yearly
Discount: up to 50%
Goods: name brand, generic
Minimum Order: $20
Shipping, Insurance: extra; UPS, PP, FOB
 manufacturer
Sales Tax: NY deliveries
Accepts: check, MO, MC, V, AE
$$$

You don't have to live "high-tech" to appreciate the fact that many goods manufactured for industrial use are superior in design and durability to those produced for the consumer market. Turnkey stocks commercial shelf units that illustrate this perfectly: They're made of 22-gauge steel, sold in open and closed styles, stronger and more stable than the same kind of shelving sold in housewares departments, and they cost about the same.

Turnkey carries heavy-duty units, metal storage-bin units, and stainless steel wire shelving as well as the standard shelves. The 112-page catalog also has the largest selection of steel storage cabinets and parts bins we've seen anywhere, from small units perfect for hardware to 108-drawer wall cabinets in steel, and a huge number of plastic bin-and-frame arrangements. These are all ideal for home use, in the workshop, kitchen, children's rooms, and anywhere else your decor permits. Turnkey also offers a better selection of mats and runners than many other firms, including antifatigue, cocoa-fiber, antistatic, rubber tire, and indoor/outdoor coverings. The catalog shows computer work stations, printer stands, stainless steel rolling carts, office and folding chairs, suspension and insulated files, lockers, flat and roll files, moving pads, canvas tarps, security gates, hoists, ceiling fans, hand trucks, rolling ladders, heavy-duty delivery bicycles, trash cans, hydraulic lifts, first-aid kits and protective gear, power-failure lights, pumps, and many other product lines.

Turnkey has been in business since 1946, gives quantity discounts on specified products, and offers a ten-day free trial guarantee on standard catalog items. Authorized returns are accepted, and a 20% restocking fee is imposed on goods returned after the trial period.

**U.S. GENERAL SUPPLY
CORP.**

100 Commercial St.
Plainview, NY 11803
(516) 349–7275: inquiries
(516) 349–7282: orders

Catalog: $1, refundable
Discount: up to 40%
Goods: name brand, generic
Minimum Order: $10 on credit cards
Shipping, Insurance: extra; UPS, FOB
 manufacturer
Sales Tax: NY deliveries
Accepts: check, MO, MC, V
$$$

This company stocks over 6,000 items at "rock bottom prices." The bulk of the stock is comprised of tools, machinery, and hardware, but telephones, car maintenance supplies, filing cabinets and chests, scales, binoculars and opticals, lawn and garden-care supplies, all kinds of scissors, sphygmomanometers, collectors' coins, fishing tackle, magnifying glasses, and BB guns have all appeared here as well. Most of the tools and hardware shown in the 194-page catalog are well-known brands: Black & Decker, Stanley, Unibraze, Skil, Rockwell, Arco, Milwaukee, Wen, Electro, Dremel, Toolkraft, and more. Almost every item is illustrated by a line drawing, and specifications are included in the descriptions. Both the suggested retail and discounted prices are listed, so you can figure out your savings. Quantity discounts are also available.

**WORLD ABRASIVES CO.,
INC.**

1866 P Eastern Parkway
Brooklyn, NY 11233
(718) 495–4300

Catalog: free; pub. in the spring
Information: price quote by phone or letter with
 SASE
Discount: 35% to 50%
WBMC Reader Discount: 10% (see text)
Goods: house brand
Minimum Order: none
Shipping, Insurance: $1.75 minimum; UPS
Sales Tax: NY deliveries
Accepts: check, MO, certified check
$$$

World Abrasives sells all kinds of sanding products and related goods: cloth sanding belts for wood, metal, and plastic; waterproof belts for wet grinding of wet glass and ceramics; sanding discs, sheets, rolls of sanding material, and grinding discs. It also specializes in hard-to-find sizes and types of abrasives. Belts are sold in lots of ten, discs in lots of 25, sheets in packages of 25, and specialty items and rolls in individual lots. The prices are good—a solid 35% to 50% below those charged by hardware stores and do-it-yourself centers, and quantity discounts are offered. You may also deduct 10% from the price of the goods, but you must identify yourself as a WBMC reader when you order to qualify. World Abrasives offers an advisory service to help with all your sanding problems, and urges you to write if you need something that isn't listed, because it's probably made for one of World's industrial customers.

ZIP-PENN, INC.

P.O. Box 15129
Sacramento, CA 95851
(800) 952–5535: CA orders
(800) 824–8521: orders
except CA

Catalog: free
Discount: up to 40%
Goods: name brand, generic
Minimum Order: none
Shipping, Handling, Insurance: extra; UPS
Sales Tax: CA, FL, PA deliveries
Accepts: check, MO, MC, V
$$$

If you're a chain-saw owner, you may already know about Zip-Penn. The firm is one of the country's best sources for chain-saw parts—chains, bars, sprockets, carburetors, and more. Parts are available for David Bradley, Dolmar, Echo, Frontier, Homelite, Husqvarna, Jobu, John Deere, Jonsereds, Lombard, Massey Ferguson, McCulloch, Partner, Pioneer, Poulan, Remington, Craftsman, Skil, and Wards saws; inquiries regarding parts for other brands are invited. In addition to replacement and repair parts, Zip-Penn sells tools and machines for filing and grinding, log lifters, wedges, chain-saw oil, "mini-mills," and protective clothing and accessories such as leggings, chaps, goggles, hats, safety visors, noise guards, and dust masks.

When summer comes and the winter's wood is seasoning in the shed, Zip-Penn anticipates your next move—mowing the lawn. If the mower breaks down, fix it yourself and save money with the aid of Zip-Penn's mufflers, air filters, starter rope and handles, fuel lines and filters, points, condensers, and other parts. Zip-Penn offers a "no quibble" guarantee against defects in materials and workmanship on all the products it sells, as well as prompt delivery and goods service.

SEE ALSO:

The Airborne Sales Co. . . . hydraulics, tools . . . SURPLUS

Arctic Glass Supply, Inc. . . . replacement thermopane patio door panes, passive solar panels . . . HOME (maintenance)

Business & Institutional Furniture Company . . . handtrucks, carts . . . OFFICE

Chanute Iron & Supply Co., Inc. . . . Kline, Rigid, Black & Decker power tools . . . HOME (maintenance)

Clothcrafters, Inc. . . . shop aprons, woodpile covers, tools holders . . . GENERAL

Craft Products Company . . . small selection tools, finishes . . . CRAFTS

Craftsman Wood Service Co. . . . wood-working, power tools . . . CRAFTS

Frank Eastern Co. . . . industrial and institutional supplies, furnishings . . . OFFICE

Great Tracers . . . custom-made name stencils . . . CRAFTS

Harbor Freight Salvage Co., Inc. . . . hardware, tools, parts, shop equipment . . . SURPLUS

L & D Press . . . Sentry safes . . . BOOKS

Oreck Corp. . . . beam flashlights, power-failure lights . . . APPLIANCES

Plastic BagMart . . . plastic trash can liners . . . HOME (maintenance)

Protecto-Pak . . . zip-top plastic bags . . . HOME (maintenance)

The Renovator's Supply, Inc. . . . reproduction house hardware, brasses . . . HOME (maintenance)

S & S Sound City . . . Fanon surveillance, security equipment . . . APPLIANCES

Sears, Roebuck and Co. . . . Craftsman tools . . . GENERAL

Southeastern Insulated Glass . . . double-insulated skylights, glass panels . . . HOME (maintenance)

Sunco Products Corp. . . . heavy-duty protective gloves . . . CLOTHING

The Surplus Center . . . tools, hardware, security equipment . . . SURPLUS

Tugon Chemical Corp. . . . wood epoxies, resins . . . AUTO

Wear-Guard Work Clothes . . . work clothes, accessories, tools, security apparel, enforcement equipment . . . CLOTHING

Whole Earth Access . . . name-brand hand, power tools . . . GENERAL

Workmen's Garment Co. . . . new and reconditioned work clothing, gloves . . . CLOTHING

TOYS AND GAMES

Juvenile and adult diversions.

For every parent who eagerly turned to this section only to find less than a wealth of sources, we offer our sympathies and apologies. After years of research, we've finally come to the conclusion that the market is not conducive to discounting. Aside from the large discount chains, there are very few firms selling toys at savings of 30% or more. Why?

Because it's a seller's market and no one is forced to discount to remain competitive. While we continue our search for discount toy sources, we urge parents to sit down and talk with their children about what's on the gift lists they've drafted. All too often they seem to be rosters of what's been run on the TV commercials. We believe that there are ways of discussing the manipulative effects of advertising without turning your children into cynics, crushing the holiday spirit, or jeopardizing the myth of Santa Claus. You might be aided by *Penny Power,* published by Consumers Union. It's written for those eight-to-thirteen-year-olds, and includes product reports, juvenile money management, entertainment, and tips on wise shopping. A year (six issues) at $9.95 can be ordered from Penny Power, Subscription Dept., Box 2859, Boulder, CO 80321. Good luck!

DINOSAUR CATALOG

P.O. Box 546
Tallman, NY 10982

Catalog: $1; pub. biannually
Discount: up to 35% (see text)
Goods: name brand, generic
Minimum Order: none
Shipping, Handling, Insurance: $2.95 minimum; UPS, PP
Sales Tax: NY deliveries
Accepts: check, MO, MC, V
$$ 🍁 (see text)

Obsessions with dinosaurs seem to afflict prepubescent boys so frequently that one is led to wonder whether there's a "prehistoric-interest" hormone released by the pituitary at some critical stage in development. Girls are not immune either, and there's no guarantee anyone will outgrow the fixation. If you haven't, you'll wonder how you lived without the Dinosaur Catalog.

This is a colorful, beautifully produced treasure: 20 pages of dinosaur models, rubber stamps, posters, stationery, T-shirts, mobiles, books, and much more. The selection is unparalleled: Exact-scale replicas from the British Museum, glow-in-the-dark dinosaurs, porcelain beasts, plastic dinosaurs sold by the pound, hand-painted cast-stone and flexible vinyl models, dinosaurs with removable tails that can be used as small storage units, and large "Hong Kong" killer styles are among the listings on just two pages. The catalog shows the "wood fossil" series of glue-free models, which are stocked in three sizes and a simple version for children. The German skeleton assembly kits of white, glow-in-the-dark plastic are a real thrill. The Dinosaur Catalog offers two lines of fine, hand-finished pewter models and even a dinosaur demitasse spoon, as well as goods for children that include plush stuffed dinosaurs, cubes that become dinosaurs when dropped in water, soft-sculpture toys that zip out of their own self-contained eggs, a variety of wood and board jigsaw puzzles, a dinosaur party set, stickers, and posters. You can communicate on British postcards that have realistic depictions of dinosaurs, or notecards, or create distinctive stationery with any number of stamps—from a dancing triceratops to the fanged head of a T.rex. Templates for outline tracing, dinosaur cookie cutters, identification/rummy cards, dinosaur bingo, erupting volcanos, soft rocks, dinosaur ties and jewelry, and many other wonderful things are offered. The prices are competitive, compared to those charged for the same goods by toy stores and gift shops, and we found savings of over 30% on a few items.

CANADIAN READERS, PLEASE NOTE: a $3 surcharge is imposed on orders sent to Canada.

DOLL HOUSE & TOY FACTORY OUTLET

---

325 Division St., Dept. WBM-85 Boonton, NJ 07005 (201) 335–5501

Catalog: $2; pub. yearly in Aug.
Discount: 15% to 75%
WBMC Reader Bonus: free dollhouse accessory or toy miniature (see text)
Goods: house brand, name brand
Minimum Order: $25 on credit cards
Shipping, Insurance: 10% of order value; $2 minimum; UPS, PP
Handling: $1 on orders under $10
Sales Tax: NJ deliveries
Accepts: check, MO, MC, V, AE
$$$$

These days, any firm selling toys, dolls, dollhouses, and miniatures by mail at discount prices should qualify as a national treasure. Doll House & Toy Factory Outlet fills the bill with a color catalog packed with dollhouse kits and miniatures in 1"-to-1'-scale, plus name-brand toys and dolls. (Some ½"-to-1'-scale house kits and accessories are offered as well.)

The dollhouse styles include a "timbered" Tudor, grand Southern plantation/estate house, turreted Victorian mansions, classic clapboard American Colonial and farmhouse with a wraparound porch, stately Southern Colonial with dormers and two-story columns, and a Victorian home with widow's walk and a "secret" tower room. A "corner sweet shop," general store, firehouse, and brick-faced townhouse are available to small-scale developers. All the assembly and finishing supplies you'll need—glues, wood putty, stains, paints, wallpaper adhesive, rubber clamps, knives, and construction tools—are sold separately.

Since the urge to alter, improve, and renovate strikes every homeowner, Doll House Factory Outlet supplies room and porch additions, gingerbread trim, a terrific group of windows and doors, moldings, clapboard, brick, roofing and shake shingles, dormers, staircases, hardware, newel posts, pilasters, brackets, and many other architectural elements and trim. And there are pages and pages of furnishings and accessories (with the requisite "families"), from pickle barrels and chocolate cake for the bakery to electrified fireplaces and lighting fixtures, modern kitchens, nurseries complete with porcelain babies, a billiard table, several bathroom sets, lighted Christmas trees, and even "attic" paraphernalia.

The prices run from 15% to 75% below comparable retail, with most items tagged at 35% less than those in other miniatures catalogs. And you can save at least 20% on European wooden toys, Steiff stuffed toys, Effanbee dolls, and other desirable collectibles and playthings. You're entitled to a free miniature accessory or toy (of the Outlet's choice), valued up to $1.98, provided your order totals $20 or more, excluding shipping and tax. There's a limit of one per household, and you must identify yourself as a WBMC reader to receive the bonus. Doll House Factory Outlet has been in business since 1969 and backs all purchases with a guarantee of satisfaction. Returns are accepted within ten days for exchange, refund, or credit.

CANADIAN READERS, PLEASE NOTE: You may pay for the catalog with IRCs, and should contact the firm before ordering to get shipping costs on goods sent to Canada.

DOLLSVILLE DOLLS AND BEARSVILLE BEARS

373 S. Palm Canyon Dr.
Palm Springs, CA 92262
(619) 325–2241

Catalog: $2, redeemable
Discount: up to 30% (see text)
Goods: house brand
Minimum Order: none
Shipping, Insurance: extra; UPS
Sales Tax: CA deliveries
Accepts: check, MO, MC, V, AE
$$$

If you buy your bears by the dozen, you'll save 30% off retail prices by ordering from Dollsville/Bearsville. The 20-page catalog gives you almost 200 choices, with Teddy bears the strong suit and character bears for collectors. The catalog will delight the many who've never outgrown this childhood love, as well as discerning bear connoisseurs. Discounts are given on smaller orders—20% for six to eleven bears, and 10% for three to five—but considering the popularity of this stuffed toy, you'll have no trouble finding friends and neighbors who can't live without a classic brown bear or "Humphrey Beargart." So combine orders to get the 30% discount. And if you can bear to part with them, they do make wonderful gifts for young children.

G. HENCKE AND CO.

4793 Büren
West Germany-RFA

Catalog: $3
Discount: see text
Goods: house brand
Minimum Order: 500 DM
Shipping: FOB West German port
Insurance: extra
Duty: extra
Accepts: certified check

$$

Hencke sells such classic board games as backgammon, dominoes, go, mah-jongg, mikado, and chess, at up to 50% less than prices commonly charged for comparable goods. The lovely color catalog features chess sets and boards which range from a tiny travel game to a set of "Ming Dynasty" pieces in ivory with a five-inch king. There are two basic chess-piece styles: plain chess symbols and figure sets. The "symbols" are available in many different designs, from a traditional set in plastic to an abstract "Picasso" group in macassar wood. There are more traditional sets with pieces represented as figures or characters. The minimum order is 500DM (about $180 at this writing), so get your friends together or buy several sets for gift-giving.

**KOUNTRY BEAR
COMPANY**

**P.O. Box 6214
Spartanburg, SC 29304**

Catalog: free
Discount: 50% (see text)
Goods: house brand, handcrafted
Minimum Order: 5 items (see text)
Shipping, Insurance: 10% of order value; included
    on orders over $200; UPS
Sales Tax: SC deliveries
Accepts: check or MO
$$

The cover of this catalog shows the whole Kountry Bear family assembled on the steps of a rural home. This is an unusual species, native to South Carolina, distinguished by the big, black button eyes and jointed limbs, also finished with buttons. There are three sizes, 9″, 14″, and 19″, which can be purchased finished ($9 to $16) or as kits with everything except the stuffing ($6 each, in the 14″ size only). The bears are made of colorful wool plaids; those who cherish the furry variety can buy the special Kuddle Bear, a limited edition priced at $50. You may also send your own fabric and have the Kountry Bear sewers create your own bespoke bear—patchwork patterns suit this animal particularly well, so you might consider sending quilt pieces.

Every Kountry Bear is handmade, and the finished bears come with registered name tags. Patterns for the bears are also available at just $2.25 each. The prices listed here apply to orders of five or more of the same item; the cost is doubled if you order fewer. These bears are quite distinctive, a must-have for the serious collector and a special gift for a child. And don't forget to order enough so you can keep one yourself.

**PARADISE PRODUCTS,
INC.**

**P.O. Box 568
El Cerrito, CA 94530
(415) 524–8300**

Catalog: $2; pub. yearly in Jan.
Discount: 25% (see text)
Goods: house brand
Minimum Order: $30 net
Shipping, Insurance: 10% (surface mail) to 15%
    (airmail) of order value; minimum $5 or $7.50;
    UPS, PP, FOB point of shipment
Handling: $4 on orders under $30
Sales Tax: CA deliveries
Accepts: check, MO, MC, V
$$$$

There is no way to give a calm, rational description of the goods Paradise

Products carries. Any catalog that pictures thousands of favors, decorations, and costumes for more than 120 kinds of parties should be given to certifiably adult, practical people only, since it may incite childlike souls to riot.

Four pages are devoted to Oktoberfest goods alone—steins, Alpine cow horns, Tyrolean hats, Kaiser helmets, wigs, lederhosen, records of beer-drinking music, streamers, signs, paper goods, posters, lamps, bunting, and many other items are offered. Every conceivable country and traditional theme is represented, including the Gay Nineties, Roaring Twenties, St. Patrick's Day, safari, "Las Vegas Night," Yugoslavia, Hawaiian luau, Central America, Monaco, football, the circus, and all-purpose patriotism, to name just a few. Supplies for the generic bash—balloons, streamers, tissue balls and bells, glassware, party hats, banquet table paper, crepe paper streamers and rolls, garlands, pennants,—are also offered.

Many of the products in the 72-page color catalog are competitively priced, and you deduct 25% from the printed prices in order to find the amount you pay. Goods are guaranteed to be as represented in the catalog, and shipments are guaranteed to arrive in time for the party date. (Allow extra time for products shipped from the manufacturer, as noted in the copy; be sure to provide the date of your event and the time of day if ordering fresh orchids.) This party heaven has been in business since 1952, and offers quantity discounts to those throwing mammoth wingdings.

TOY BALLOON CORP.

204 E. 38th St.
New York, NY 10016
(212) 682–3803

Price List: free with SASE
Discount: 30% to 70%
Goods: house brand
Minimum Order: none
Shipping: extra; UPS
Sales Tax: NY deliveries
Accepts: check or MO
$$$

Instead of buying balloons every time you're throwing a party, why not plan ahead, order a gross or two, and save some money? You end up spending from 10¢ to 25¢ for each balloon when you buy them in small packages at the five-and-ten or local party-supply store. At Toy Balloon, the prices on the same sort of balloons are up to 70% less, bought by the gross. The selection is fabulous: There are round balloons from 6″ to 18″ in diameter; long balloons, round balloons in silver, gold, clear, black, purple, and brown; marbleized and polka-dotted balloons; novelty shapes, and more. Toy Balloon also sells blo-pumps, shower nets, string, a vacuum-cleaner attachment for inflation, metal hand pumps, ribbon, and clips to seal the balloons. Imprinting is available at a nominal surcharge. If you're celebrating something extra special, you might want the large display balloons—at four and six feet across, they're for the serious party.

SEE ALSO:

America's Hobby Center, Inc. . . . model planes, boats, trains, cars, etc. . . . CRAFTS

Bailey's, Inc. . . . Tonka Toys . . . TOOLS

Bernie's Discount Center, Inc. . . . name-brand video games . . . APPLIANCES

Best Products Co., Inc. . . . name-brand toys . . . GENERAL

Deepak's Rokjemperl Products . . . sandalwood chess sets, Indian cloth dolls . . . JEWELRY

Focus Electronics, Inc. . . . name-brand video games, computer games . . . APPLIANCES

Good 'N' Lucky Promotions . . . toys, novelties for adults and children . . . JEWELRY

Handart Embroideries . . . Chinese dolls . . . CLOTHING

House of Onyx . . . onyx chess sets . . . JEWELRY

Jems Sounds, Ltd. . . . Atari video games . . . APPLIANCES

La Piñata . . . piñatas . . . HANDCRAFTS

Prince Fashions Ltd. . . . Chinese dolls in traditional dress . . . CLOTHING

Quilts Unlimited . . . patchwork bear . . . ART, ANTIQUES

Rammagerdin . . . Icelandic dolls . . . CRAFTS

Regal Greetings & Gifts, Inc. . . . toys, games, novelties . . . GENERAL

RSP Distributing Co. . . . closeout toys, novelties . . . GENERAL

S & S Sound City . . . name-brand video games . . . APPLIANCES

Sales Citi, Inc. . . . Atari video games . . . APPLIANCES

Saxkjaers . . . Danish dolls, wooden toy soldiers . . . ART, ANTIQUES

Shannon Mail Order . . . Peggy Nisbet dolls . . . HOME (table settings)

Stereo Discounters Electronic World . . . name-brand video games . . . APPLIANCES

THE COMPLETE GUIDE
TO BUYING BY MAIL

I. CATALOGS, PRICE QUOTES, AND INFORMATION....... 457

    A-*Catalogs* 457
        1-Refundable Catalogs.................................. 458
        2-Sending for Catalogs................................. 458
        3-Catalogs from Foreign Firms 458
        4-Receiving Catalogs 459
        5-Delayed Shipment of Catalogs........................ 459
        6-Catalog Shipment Conditions of WBMC Firms 460

    B-*Price Quotes* 460
        1-Finding the Information.............................. 461
        2-Price Quotes by Letter............................... 461
        3-Price Quotes by Phone 461

    C-*Requesting Information* 461

II. HOW TO ORDER..................................... 462

    A-*Cost Comparisons*................................... 462

    B-*Ordering*... 462
        1-Second Choices and Substitutions 463
        2-WBMC Reader Offers................................ 463
        3-Redeeming the Cost of the Catalog 463

    C-*Phone Orders* 463
        1-WATS Lines.. 463
        2-Ordering 464
        3-The Pros and Cons of Phone Orders 465

    D-*Ordering from Foreign Firms*........................ 466

    E-*Payment* 467
        1-Prepaid Orders 467
        a-personal checks 467

b-certified checks.................................... **467**
c-bank money orders **467**
d-postal money orders **467**
e-bank international money orders **468**
f-postal international money orders **468**
g-bank drafts **468**
h-cable transfers.................................... **468**
2-Credit, Charge, and Debit Cards.................... **468**
a-MasterCard **470**
b-VISA **470**
c-American Express **470**
d-Diners Club..................................... **471**
e-Carte Blanche................................... **471**
f-CHOICE **471**
g-Access **471**
h-Eurocard **471**
3-Paying for Goods from Foreign Firms **471**

F-*Return Policies*..................................... **472**

G-*Resale Numbers and Letterhead*........................ **472**

H-*Canceling Your Order* **473**

III. SHIPPING, INSURANCE, HANDLING, SALES TAX,
AND DUTY **474**

A-*Shipping* **474**
1-Shipping Computations **474**
a-Postpaid... **474**
b-Itemized... **474**
c-Numeric... **474**
d-Flat Order Fees **475**
e-Free **475**
f-Sliding Scales **475**
g-Tables... **475**
2-Saving on Shipping Costs **475**
3-Carriers **476**
a-UPS **476**
b-USPS—PP....................................... **477**
c-Private Trucking Firms............................ **477**

B-*Shipments from Foreign Countries* **478**
1-Mailable Orders.................................... **478**
a-Airmail.. **478**
b-Surface Mail **478**
c-Accelerated Surface Mail **478**
2-Nonmailable Orders **479**

a-Air Freight 479
b-Sea Freight 479

C-*Handling Charges* 479

D-*Insurance* 480

E-*Sales Tax* 480

F-*Duty* 481
1-Assessment of Duty 481
2-Prohibitions and Restrictions 482
3-Obtaining Information 482

IV. RECEIVING YOUR ORDER............................... 483

A-*Accepting Deliveries from U.S. Firms* 483

B-*Delayed Shipments from U.S. Firms*.................. 484
1-The FTC Mail Order Rule 484
a-General Terms of the Rule 484
b-The Option Notice 485
c-The Renewed Option Notice........................ 486
d-The Rule and Refunds 486
e-The Rule and Phone Orders........................ 486
f-The Rule and the Truth............................ 487

C-*Deliveries from Foreign Firms* 487

D-*Delayed Shipments from Foreign Firms* 488

V. RETURNS, GUARANTEES, AND WARRANTIES 489

A-*Returns* 489
1-Obtaining Authorization 489
2-Restocking Fees..................................... 489
3-Sending the Item.................................... 490
4-Refunds and Credits................................. 490
5-Exchanges... 490
6-Postage Reimbursement.............................. 490

B-*Guarantees and Warranties* 490
1-The Magnuson-Moss Warranty—Federal Trade
Commission Act 490
a-Full Warranties..................................... 491
b-Limited Warranties 491
c-Other Provisions 492
2-Implied Warranties 492
a-The Warranty of Merchantability.................... 492
b-The Warranty of Fitness for a Particular Purpose 492

3-Consequential Damages *492*
4-Evaluating Warranties *493*
5-Complying with Warranty Terms *493*
6-Obtaining Service *494*

VI. COMPLAINTS *496*

A-*Complaint Procedures* *496*
1-The Complaint Letter *496*

B-*Obtaining Help* *496*
1-Consumer Action Panels (CAPs) *496*
a-FICAP *496*
b-MACAP *496*
2-Better Business Bureau (BBBs) *496*
3-Direct Marketing Association (DMA) *497*
a-Mail Order Action Line (MOAL) *497*
4-The Federal Trade Commission (FTC) *497*
a-The Fair Credit Billing Act (FCBA) *497*
5-The United States Postal Service *498*
6-Bankruptcy Courts *499*

C-*Complaints about Foreign Firms* *499*

The Complete Guide
to Buying by Mail

If you don't know UPS from PP, or what "FOB factory" means, this section will prove an invaluable tool in untangling the web of confusion that ensnares many mail-order shoppers. Armed with knowledge and endowed with patience, you'll be prepared to conquer the world of mail-order bargains and emerge victorious—a satisfied customer reaping huge savings.

Read this section before you order a catalog or call for a price quote. It will save you time, and may save you even more money.

CATALOGS, PRICE QUOTES, AND INFORMATION

CATALOGS: Most mail-order firms publish price lists, leaflets, brochures, or catalogs. These can range in volume and sophistication from mimeographed, one-sheet price lists to lavish books with hundreds of color photographs and detailed descriptions. Some firms send just one issue of their catalogs; others add your name to their mailing lists for a number of issues; and others offer their catalogs on a subscription basis, like magazines.

A diminishing number of catalogs are sent free of charge; most firms now request a fee, usually $1 to $5. Sometimes, instead of a charge, firms will request a business-sized (#10), self-addressed, stamped envelope (SASE). Some firms request both a SASE and a nominal fee. The U.S. Postal Service offers a valuable service—stamps and stamped envelopes by mail. These are the ordinary variety you'd get at the post office (not the philatelic line). Ask your postmaster or carrier for PS Form 3227, "Stamps by Mail," or request it from the Consumer Advocate, U.S. Postal Service, Washington, DC 20260–6320. Orders are usually delivered within a few days. Please note: the November 1981 form lists a 40¢ order-processing fee, which has been dropped. If you receive the old form, omit the surcharge from your payment.

"Refundable" Catalogs. Some firms allow you to recoup the cost of the catalog when you order; this is indicated by the word "refundable," "deductible," or "redeemable" following the price of the catalogs listed in this book. Procedures for reimbursement vary: The catalog may come with a coupon

tucked or printed inside with instructions to enclose it with your order and *deduct* the amount from the total (the same as *redeeming* the coupon). You may be asked to include the coupon with your order without deducting the amount, and wait for a *refund* check from the firm. Often, there is no such coupon in the catalog, in which case you should include a letter requesting your refund check with your order. Don't deduct the catalog fee from your order unless so instructed, and be sure you meet minimum-order requirements when you make your purchase.

Sending for Catalogs. When you send for a catalog, write a complete letter stating which catalog you want (some firms have several), and *always include your return address, printed clearly, in the letter*. Please refer to WBMC as your source, since it may qualify you for special discounts. Mention all enclosures so they're not overlooked. Keeping a separate mail-order "calendar" of dates on which catalog requests and orders were sent, inquiries made, and orders received is an excellent idea if you shop by mail frequently. Just remember that keeping complete records of all mail-order correspondence will prove very important if anything goes wrong.

If a catalog costs less than $1, send coins taped securely between thick pieces of cardboard. For catalogs costing $1 or more, send a check or money order unless you're dealing with a foreign firm (see below). *Never* send stamps unless the firm specifies, and don't use a credit card to pay for a catalog or a subscription to a series of catalogs unless the listing states that this is permitted.

Catalogs from Foreign Firms. When sending for a catalog from a foreign firm, use an international money order (IMO), personal check, or International Reply Coupons (IRCs). Money orders can be purchased at a bank or post office. If you send a personal check, it's a good idea to add about $3 to the payment. This will cover the currency-conversion charge the firm has to pay to change your dollars to pounds, francs, marks, or rupees. It's a considerate gesture, but not mandatory.

IRCs are certificates that can be exchanged for units of surface postage in foreign countries. They are available at the post office for 65¢ each. Use IRCs when they are requested or when the catalog costs 50¢ or less.

While you can use one of these conventional methods of payment, you can save handling charges if the catalog is under $5 by sending cash through the mail. Technically it's risky and should be used only when you're dealing with dollars, not change, but there's a foolproof way to conceal the money and enclosures completely, and remain within the half-ounce weight limit of a 44¢ stamp. Get a piece of black flint paper from your local art-supply store. Cut the paper into pieces that just fit inside the envelope you're using. Place the money within the folded letter, and the letter and piece of flint paper inside the envelope. Voilà! Complete privacy! Note: Letters sent to India containing any payment should be sent by registered mail, and it's inadvisable to try to correspond with—much less order from—firms in countries that are in political disarray or at war. In all cases, remember to mention your enclosures of cash, coupons, money order, or check in the accompanying letter.

When a foreign firm offers a catalog at airmail and surface-mail rates, spend a little more and get it sent by airmail. Surface mail can take a long, long time—sometimes two months or more—to arrive, and the catalog may be out of date by the time it gets to you. Send your catalog request or order by airmail too, to avoid these delays.

Receiving Catalogs. Catalog publication schedules vary. Some firms publish new price lists weekly, while others bring out massive catalogs every ten years. When firms run out of catalogs, are between printings, or issue catalogs seasonally, there can be a delay of months before you receive your copy. Some firms will notify you by letter or postcard when this occurs. Most will not. Compounding the problem is the fact that every time a firm is mentioned in an article or book such as this, it may receive hundreds, thousands, even tens of thousands of catalog requests over the course of a few weeks. Small firms are often swamped with bags of mail, and the fulfillment process is further slowed. If the catalog supply is exhausted, it may take weeks to get a print order filled, labels prepared, and catalogs sent. The delays are troublesome not only for the firm, which may lose sales to other catalogs that arrive quickly, but also for the potential customer who needs an item by a certain date. Unfortunately, many of the delays are also illegal.

Delayed Shipment of Catalogs. According to the FTC Mail Order Rule (also known as the "30-Day Rule"), a firm must ship goods ordered by mail within 30 days after receiving a properly completed order. The Rule doesn't apply to catalogs for which you send absolutely nothing except the request, or subscriptions to catalogs (except the first issue of the subscription), but it does apply to all others.

If a firm asks you to send anything to obtain the catalog—10¢, a SASE, $5, a page number clipped from this book, etc.—it must abide by the Rule and ship your catalog within 30 days after receiving the properly completed order. (For a definition of "properly completed" and a discussion of "shipping" vs. "delivery," see "The FTC Mail Order Rule," p. 474.) If the shipment is delayed, the firm is obliged to take certain steps, which are detailed in "The Option Notice," p. 485. *However,* the 30-Day Rule is amended when the firm states clearly in its advertisement or, as in this book, in an unpaid listing, that customers must allow a longer period to receive the catalog (often seen as "allow six to eight weeks for delivery"). And if a firm lists its publication schedule, that also constitutes a clear indication of availability. For example, if Acme Inc. (a fictitious firm) issues catalogs in September and April, customers cannot reasonably expect delivery in periods immediately preceding those months.

But even this straightforward publication schedule can cause problems for customers. Since many mail-order firms publish catalogs two or three times yearly, Acme can be used as an example to help you understand how complications might arise. Assume that, like many of its actual counterparts, Acme Inc. issues catalogs that supercede each earlier edition. This means that the September edition should be valid until the April edition is published. But if the firm sells seasonal goods (gifts, clothing, seeds and bulbs, etc.), much of the stock shown in its September catalog may be exhausted by the end of January. Knowing this, the firm may decide to hold orders for catalogs received in January and February until spring and send the April catalog when it's available. Result: the customer waits up to 12 weeks to receive anything.

Catalog Shipments of WBMC Firms. The previous illustration is just one example of how a delivery delay could occur, even when the firm is acting in good faith. Since it's impossible to anticipate and circumvent every problem surrounding catalog delivery, we can offer only general precautions. First, allow six to eight weeks for shipment of any nonfree catalog or literature ordered from a firm listed in this book. Second, if a firm's catalog publication schedule is listed, do not order more than *one month before* or *three months after* the nearest date. (Catalogs published yearly are an exception; these should be available year round unless they're published for seasonal business.)

If you follow the guidelines above, and your catalog is not delivered and you don't hear from the firm, consult "The FTC Mail Order Rule," p. 474, for information on what steps to take.

On a happy note: ordering from a company on a regular basis is an almost surefire way to guarantee that you'll receive its catalogs in the future. And unless you ask the firm to omit your name from the mailing lists it rents and exchanges with other firms, you'll also receive literature from other mail-order companies.

PRICE QUOTES: Certain firms offer their goods on a price-quote basis. These firms almost invariably sell name-brand goods that can be identified by manufacturer's name, stock or model number, and color or pattern name or code. Cameras, appliances, audio and TV/video components, china, furniture, and sporting goods are commonly sold by discounters on a price-quote basis.

A price quote is simply the statement of the cost of that item from that firm. The company may guarantee that price for a limited period of time, or until stock is depleted. Some firms include tax, shipping charges, insurance, and handling in their price quotes, giving you one figure for the final cost. Don't accept such a price quote—make sure each fee or surcharge is itemized separately. The importance of this will become apparent if you have to return the item for a refund, in which case you probably won't be reimbursed for the shipping and handling charges.

Finding the Information. Before writing or calling for a price quote, you'll need to know the manufacturer's name, product code (model or style number or pattern name), and size and color information, if applicable. This data can be found on the factory cartons and tags of goods in stores, and in manufacturers' brochures. (Obtain the latter by writing to the customer service department of the manufacturer and requesting a brochure or specification sheet on the product or line.) If you're pricing an item you found in a catalog, remember to look for the manufacturer's data, not the catalog code numbers which are usually listed next to the item price. If you're using a buying guide or magazine as a source for information, be cautioned that the material may be out of date and errors may occur in printing, so verify the information before requesting price quotes.

Price Quotes by Letter. Most of the firms listed in this book will give quotes over the phone, but a letter is usually cheaper and simpler, and it gives you a record of the quote. When you write requesting price quotes, include all the available information about the items. Leave blanks next to each item so the person giving the quote can enter the price, shipping cost or estimate, and any related charges. Ask the firm to note how long it will honor the given prices. Request prices on no more than three items at a time. (Retailers tell us that they relegate photocopied sheets requesting 20 price quotes to the wastebasket, since the sender appears to be doing a survey rather than serious shopping.) And you *must* include a SASE with your request.

Price Quotes by Phone. If you phone for a price quote, be sure to have all the information in front of you when you call. *Don't* make collect calls, and don't use the "800" numbers for price quotes unless the listing states specifically that inquiries are permitted on those lines. To avoid problems later, ask to speak to someone in a position of authority, preferably the manager. Take down his or her complete name and tell the person you're making a note of all the information given you. Treat phone calls as seriously as letters; the notes you take may be the only tangible record you will have.

NOTE: If you make a purchase using a credit card, certain aspects of the transaction are not protected by the laws that regulate mail orders. For more information, see "The FTC Mail Order Rule," p. 484

REQUESTING INFORMATION: A small percentage of mail-order firms offer services or custom-made products, and conduct business on an *inquiry* basis. When you contact such a firm, your request for information must be specific. Whether you want your linens monogrammed in Gothic letters or want to add to your vintage Märklin collection, your letter must include all the information that could possibly help the company to serve you. First, read the WBMC listing carefully. Send an article for repair, restoration, or to be matched *only* when the listing so indicates—otherwise, write to the firm with a description of the article you're looking for or want matched (include rubbings, drawings, or photographs if appropriate) or describe the article and its conditions, and what repairs or alterations or services you need. When sending any item, include a cover letter describing what you want done (even if you're already stated this in a previous letter—correspondence is often mislaid). Insure the package, and send return postage and insurance by separate cover, in case the firm can't do the work or you decide against having it done. (In such an event, be sure your cover letter includes a request to the firm to insure the item and check with your home-insurance carrier to see whether loss or damage to the item will be covered under your policy before sending valuables or antiques.) Allow at least a month for the firm to evaluate the job and send you an estimate—many specialty shops are run by just one or two people and tend to have backlogs.

HOW TO ORDER

You may think you're ready to order, but are you sure? If you haven't done your cost comparisons, do them now and make certain you're really getting the best deal.

COST COMPARISONS: Your chief consideration is the *delivered* price of the product. Gather all your price quotes and/or catalogs and compute this price. Next, compare the figure to the *delivered* cost of the item if purchased from a local supplier. To be accurate, you must place a monetary value on the time it takes to order vs. going to a retailer, purchasing the item, and bringing it home or having it sent to you. You must also consider, if applicable, such costs as mileage (from 13¢ to 19¢ a mile, depending on the car), duty on orders from foreign countries, sales and use tax, shipping and trucking, installation, parking costs, etc. If you're purchasing a gift, you may also have to compare the costs of having the catalog house wrap the item and send it to the recipient to your own time, materials, and mailing costs. Last, you must weigh the intangibles—the various return policies, the prospect of waiting for a mail delivery vs. getting the item immediately, the guarantees offered by the retailer and mail-order firm, etc. After contemplating costs and variables, you'll have arrived at the bottom line and will be ready to order, if that's your choice.

ORDERING: Locate the order blank in the catalog and use it. If supplied, use the self-sticking address label on the catalog as requested. If there is no order blank, try to find one in another catalog to use as a guide to format. Transcribe all pertinent information—code numbers, name of item, number of items ordered, units, prices, tax, shipping and handling charges—onto a separate piece of paper. Include your name, address, phone number, the firm's name and address, and appropriate information if you're having the order sent to another address. Observe minimum-order requirements. If the catalog is more than six months old, order from a new edition (unless the listing indicates the catalog is published once a year). Remember that prices can change without notice. While some firms can guarantee all prices in a catalog to a certain date, the best most can do is guarantee a price as of the order date. You may find yourself billed for the difference between the old price and the new if you order from an out-of-date catalog, or when you order from foreign firms pricing in dollars. (This is because of the fluctuations of the exchange rate.) Make a copy of the order, and file it with the catalog.

*Second Choices and Substitutions. When the firm advises it and you're willing to accept them, give *second choices*. These usually refer to differences in color, not product. If you will accept *substitutions* (which may be different products that the firm considers comparable to what you ordered), you must give permission in writing on the order form. Making substitutions without written authorization from the buyer is unlawful. If you will not accept second choices in color and want to be sure the firm knows this, write "NO SECOND CHOICES OR SUBSTITUTIONS ACCEPTED" in red on the order form.

*WBMC Reader Offers. If you wish to take advantage of a WBMC Reader Discount, Rebate, Bonus, or other special, be sure to comply with the conditions stated in the listing. Unless otherwise indicated, deduct any discounts from the total cost of the *goods only,* not from the total that includes shipping, handling, insurance, and tax.

*Redeeming the Cost of the Catalog. If the listing states that the catalog cost is refundable, redeemable, creditable, or deductible, consult p. 458 for information on reimbursement procedures.

PHONE ORDERS: Many of the firms listed in this book take orders over the phone and have toll-free "800" numbers that enable you to order without incurring costs. Understanding what these numbers are and how they work is part of becoming an informed shopper. It will help you understand and evaluate some of the claims made for and against them.

*WATS Lines. The phone numbers with "800" area codes are WATS (Wide Area Telecommunication Service) lines. When you call a firm on its 800 line, no charge is made to your phone bill, even though the call *originated* from your phone. Instead, the cost of the call is billed (in terms of prepriced minutes) to the 800 number, where the call *terminates*.

A firm wishing to offer WATS to its customer chooses the calling areas it want to serve from seven bands that include the continental U.S., Hawaii, Alaska, Puerto Rico, and the Virgin Islands. (AT&T's rumblings about overseas WATS lines may have become reality by the time this is printed, thus furthering the scope considerably.) Sometimes WATS includes all bands but exempts the state in which the 800 number terminates from service. In order to offer in-state customers a toll-free order or response mechanism, a firm may have a separate 800 number to be used by callers in that state exclusively. It may also have a branch office in another state handle those calls, or ask in-state customers to use its toll lines. Some firms electing to use the last method accept collect calls on those non-800 lines from in-state callers as a compromise.

Another option available to the mail-order firm is the vendor. While operating "in-house" or "proprietary" lines works well for some companies, others choose to have a specialist (also known as a "telemarketer") handle the orders, inquiries, and complaints. Telemarketers offer companies new to phone-selling an opportunity to test the power of an 800 number without investing in line installation and operator training. You can sometimes identify firms using a telemarketing service by the presence of a WATS line to be used by customers of a state other than the one in which the firm is located. For example, a catalog from a firm in Pennsylvania has one "call toll-free 1-800 . . ." line, and in smaller print, "In Illinois, call . . ." Illinois is the locus of a large telemarketing firm; Nebraska is headquarters for several. When you see second WATS lines for residents of those states in a catalog or listing and the firm is located in another state, chances are good that the phone lines are being handled by an outside vendor.

All of which brings us to the burning issue: Is there any reason to *care* whether your order is handled in-house or by a telemarketing service?

Well, some writers on consumer issues advise against placing an order through a telemerketing service. Their arguments hinge on the belief that a vendor's operators might not be able to supply product information not given in the catalog, state the shipping cost of the item, tell the customer whether the item is in stock, or give an estimated delivery date, etc. Implicit in the argument is the assumption that in-house operators can answer these questions.

Neither opinion, we feel, has been sufficiently documented to justify a wholesale ban or endorsement. Each selling situation is unique. Whereas most in-house operators may be able to tell you if an item is out of stock, they probably can't if the firm's operations aren't computerized. Nor are they necessarily guaranteed immediate access to additional information about the products. Every telemarketing representative should be able to give you the order total, including shipping and tax (it's one of the lines that appears on the CRT screen when the order is keyed in and finalized). No operator, anywhere, can tell you the *delivery* date of an item. An operator with stock information can only tell you when an item will be *shipped;* from there on, it's in the hands of the carrier. (Most telemarketing operators, when asked about delivery, will ask you to allow four to six weeks.) A good telemarketing service will have a statement of the firm's return policy in its data bank. Do not order from a firm whose operator or service representative cannot describe the terms of the policy. And do not order when you're told that no returns are accepted under any circumstances, unless you're willing to take the gamble.

Ordering. Before picking up the phone to place your order, follow this procedure:

(1) Have your credit card ready;

(2) Make sure the card is accepted by the firm and hasn't expired;

(3) Have the delivery name, address, and ZIP code available;

(4) Have the ordering information—catalog code numbers, units, colors, sizes, etc.—written down in front of you;

(5) Have the catalog from which you're ordering at hand—the operator may ask for encoded information on the address label.

When you place the call, ask the operator these questions:

(1) What is your name or operator number?

(2) Are any of these items out of stock?

(3) When will the order be shipped?

(4) Will any of the items be shipped separately?

(5) What is the total, including shipping and tax, that will be charged to my account?

(6) What are the terms of the return policy?

Every operator should answer questions one, five, and six. Only those operators with stock information will be able to answer question two, and, in all likelihood, only in-house operators can answer three and four.

Please note that many operators are instructed to ask for your home phone number, and sometimes your office number as well. This is done for your protection, so they can verify that you are the person placing the order and not a criminal who's obtained your card information from a carbon slip or stolen card. Since the firm may have to absorb the losses arising from fraud, it may choose to refuse an order from you if you won't divulge your phone number, especially if you're buying certain types of goods and your order total is high.

While you're on the phone, the operator may try to sell you more goods. This may be an "upsell," in which you're induced to buy tennis balls if you've purchased a racquet, a sweater if you've bought pants, etc. Beware of this technique if you're trying to stick to a budget. On the other hand, you may be offered a real bargain on goods the firm is clearing out: When a company has too few of an item to run it in a catalog, it's sometimes put "on sale" to phone customers; when this occurs, the company's loss is your gain. Just make sure you really want the item—a bargain you'll never use is no bargain at all.

Once the transaction is completed and you've noted the operator's name or number, checked off the items you ordered, struck off those you didn't, entered the billing amount, and noted the time and date of the call, put this record in your file. It may prove valuable later if you have problems with your order.

The Pros and Cons of Phone Orders. Phone orders have certain advantages to mail orders. They're usually processed more quickly and, when the phone operator has stock information, you can know immediately whether an item is available or not. However, there are disadvantages, which relate to regulations governing shipment of goods. For more information, see "The FTC Mail Order Rule," p. 484.

ORDERING FROM FOREIGN FIRMS: Despite the fact that the world is supposed to be switching to the metric scale, many of the catalogs from Europe and elsewhere use the U.S. system—inches and pounds—in measurements. Converting metric measurements to U.S. equivalents is easy, though. Use the chart on p. 8.

There are fundamental and confusing differences in sizing systems, color descriptions, and generic terms in different countries. Sizes fall into three categories: U.S., British, and Continental. The sizing chart on p. 8 can be used as a general guide to size equivalents. Always measure yourself before ordering clothing, and list the measurements on the order form if you're unsure of the proper size.

Color descriptions and terms can leave you with more questions than answers. Is "emerald" a deep or pale shade of green? Will the "Provençal pink" speak of shy blushes or apoplexy? Color charts can resolve these questions, but you must allow for variations between photographic reproduction and the product itself. When the descriptive terms in a noncolor catalog leave you in doubt as to the shade, write to the firm and ask for samples *before* you order. Never try to match the color of an item you already have without the actual material (and even then, allow for subtle differences from one dye lot to another). These caveats apply to all orders, domestic and foreign.

There are some words used in Great Britain that have different meanings in the U.S.. For example, the trunk of a car is called the "boot" in England; the hood is the "bonnet." A "jumper" is not a sleeveless dress worn over a blouse, it's a pullover sweater. Woven "rugs" are usually blankets sized to cover the top of a bed; a "torch" is a flashlight; a "spanner" is a wrench; a "beaker" is often a large cup, rather than a lab flask; a "cot" is a baby's crib. Note these differences, and write to the firm before ordering if you have questions about a term.

The majority of foreign firms listed in this book state prices in U.S. dollars. If they do not, you'll have to convert the firm's currency to dollars when you order. First, compute the total, including shipping, insurance, and other charges (but do *not* include duty). Next, convert this figure to dollars using the rate of exchange prevailing on the day you send the order. You can get the rate from most banks or your nearest American Express office. We have included a currency-conversion chart on p. 8 as a general guide to foreign currency values. You can get the most recent issue of the table by requesting the "Currency Guide" from Deak-Perera; 41 E. 42nd St., New York, NY 10017.

Before you order, be sure to determine the rate of duty you'll be charged when the goods arrive, as well as any shipping or transportation costs not included in your order total. See these sections for more information: "Paying for Goods from Foreign Firms," p. 471; "Shipments from Foreign Countries," p. 478; "Duty," p. 481; and "Deliveries from Foreign Firms," p. 487.

NOTE: orders sent to India, South America, and Africa should be dispatched via registered mail.

PAYMENT. There are many ways to pay for your order; at times, the differences among them can be confusing. This section represents an effort to define terms, explain procedures, and correct some misconceptions brought to light in the course of our research. For the purposes of this book, we've developed two classifications for payment methods: "prepaid" and "charge, credit, and debit cards." We've made this distinction based on the rules that apply to refunds under the FTC Mail Order Rule, but we stress that some methods have characteristics of both categories.

Prepaid Orders. Some of these payment methods apply to orders sent within the U.S., some to orders sent to foreign countries, and some are applicable to both.

PERSONAL CHECKS are accepted by most firms, are cheap and inexpensive, and can be sent without a visit to the bank or post office. Since some firms wait until your check has cleared before sending your order, shipment may be delayed as much as two weeks (U.S. firms) to a month (foreign firms) when you pay by check. (The increasing implementation of electronic transmittal systems and centralized banking should reduce this lag in the future.) Paying by check has the added advantage of providing you with a receipt, the canceled check, which is returned to you with your monthly statement. If, in the future, U.S. banks adopt the policy in force in some banks in England and retain your canceled checks, make sure you request them. If you have to pay a surcharge for this, consider switching to a bank that offers the service free of charge.

CERTIFIED CHECKS are guaranteed personal checks. You bring your check to the bank on which it's drawn, and pay a fee of about $4. The bank marks the check "certified" and freezes that sum in your account. Every firm that accepts personal checks will accept a certified check, and the guarantee of funds should preclude the delay for clearance. The canceled certified check is returned with the other canceled checks in your statement. A certified check is also known as a *bank check,* a *teller's check,* and a *cashier's check.*

BANK MONEY ORDERS can be obtained at any bank for a fee ranging from 50¢ to $1.50. You ask the teller for an order in the desired amount and fill in the firm's name, and your name and address. If the order isn't dated mechanically, insert the date. Most come with a carbon receipt; some have stubs which should be filled in on the spot before you forget the information.

Bank money orders are accepted by U.S. firms and generally treated as certified checks (i.e., no waiting for clearance). If necessary, you can have the order traced, payment stopped, and a refund issued. You'll find this vital if your order is lost in the mail, since there's always a chance it's been intercepted and an unauthorized party will attempt to cash it.

POSTAL MONEY ORDERS, sold at the post office, are available in amounts up to $500 and cost from 75¢ to $1.55. They're self-receipting and dated, and can be replaced if the order is lost or stolen. Copies of the cashed money order can be obtained through the post office for up to two years after it's paid. This can prove quite helpful in settling disputes with firms that claim nonreceipt of payment. And, like stamped envelopes and stamps, money orders can be bought through postal carriers by customers on rural routes or with limited access to the post office.

BANK INTERNATIONAL MONEY ORDERS, issued by banks, are used to pay foreign firms. You complete a form and, if the catalog prices are listed in foreign currency, the bank computes the amount in dollars based on the day's exchange rate. These orders cost from $2.50 to $4.00, and are receipted. Like domestic money orders, you send them to the firm yourself with the order. They are usually treated as immediate payment.

POSTAL INTERNATIONAL MONEY ORDERS are used to pay foreign firms and cost from $1.30 to $1.80, depending on the amount of the order. The ceilings on amounts to different nations vary from $200 to $500, and postal IMOs cannot be sent to every country. Amounts of $400 or more must be registered. When you buy a postal IMO you fill out a form stating your name and address, and the name and address of the firm, and pay the order amount and surcharge. The post office forwards the data to the International Exchange Office in St. Louis, Missouri, which sends a receipt to you and forwards the money order, in native currency, directly to the firm (or to the post office nearest it, which sends it on). We're told the entire procedure takes a few weeks; if you use postal IMOs you must allow for this delay.

BANK DRAFTS, or TRANSFER CHECKS, are the closest you can come to sending cash to a foreign firm through the mail. You pay the order amount, a mailing fee, and a service charge to your bank, then send one copy of the draft form to the firm and another to the firm's bank. The name of the bank may be given in the catalog; if not, your teller will give you the name and address of one in the area. Upon receipt of the form, the firm takes it to the bank, matches it to the other copy, and collects the funds. It will take five to ten days for the forms to reach the foreign country, provided you send them via airmail. Most banks charge $3 and up for bank drafts, depending on the amount of the check. All foreign firms accept them.

CABLE TRANSFERS are for the rich and impatient; they cost from $8 to $12 and result in payment to the firm within two days after you arrange them. You pay your bank the order amount and service fee, and it cables the money directly into the firm's bank account (if you're able to supply the name of the bank). If not, the teller chooses a bank nearby and cables the money there. The bank notifies the firm of the credit, at which point the firm is able to ship your goods. Cable transfers are used primarily when dealing with foreign firms, but can be used for U.S. orders as well.

Credit, Charge, and Debit Cards. Those wafers of plastic in your wallet have been important factors in the mail-order boom, and the pairing of

WATS lines and credit cards has proven an irresistible combination for millions of consumers, creating phenomenal growth in the phone-order industry. (See "Phone Orders," p. 463, for more information.)

Using plastic to pay for an order is simplicity itself—you make sure the firm accepts the card you're using, make out the order form, and provide your account number, card expiration date, phone number, and signature in the blanks. When you're ordering from a catalog without the form, supply the same data on the paper where you've written the item names, code numbers, prices, units, etc. Using a card is especially practical when shipping costs are omitted or difficult to calculate—they'll be added to the order total and appear on your itemized statement, and the order won't be held up as it might be if you paid by check or with a money order. Always check the minimum-order requirements before ordering when using a card, since they're usually higher than those imposed on prepaid orders.

If you're low on cash but determined to order from a firm that doesn't accept cards, you can have Western Union send the company a money order and charge it to your MasterCard or VISA account. This service is limited to the U.S. and to foreign cities with Western Union offices. The surcharge is high—$12.95 for amounts up to $100, $25.95 for orders up to $500—and costlier when the order is sent outside the U.S. But it can be a worthwhile expense if you might otherwise miss out on the buy of a lifetime.

The fact that there are differences in payment structure, membership fees, and services has led some writers on consumer issues to claim that there are two categories of cards, "charge" and "credit." The distinction is based on the erroneous notion that one type of card permits you to borrow money and the other doesn't. In truth, you can borrow money—in the form of cold cash, traveler's checks, or money orders—on almost every card, provided you have the proper credit line and fulfill the conditions set by the card issuer. And, although some card firms request payment in full each month, they usually offer programs that permit you to spread payments over several billing periods on specific types of payments. These payments are assessed finance charges, further blurring the distinctions between the "charge" and "credit" cards.

However, "debit" cards are another category altogether; strictly speaking, they should be listed in the "prepaid" section. Debit cards *look* like regular credit cards, but when the issuing bank receives the invoices for purchases, it deducts those amounts from your depository account—checking, savings, or money management—instead of *charging* your account and billing you. As electronic transmittal networks develop and replace the paper system, the debiting process will occur in nanoseconds at the point of authorization, and the debit card will become electronic cash. At this writing, the problem of applying the existing terms of the FTC Mail Order Rule to a means of payment that appears to be a credit card but acts like a check is being discussed. It's important to know that the FTC views debit-card payments as *cash* payments. Since the card firms foresee extensive growth in their debit-card divisions, we hope that the FTC will be able to define its regulations further to include provisos for debit cards, or promulgate new rules. Until then, we recommend that, if you're using a debit card to pay for an order, you write on the order form, under the account number: "THIS IS A DEBIT ACCOUNT. THIS PAYMENT MUST BE TREATED AS CASH." See p. 484 for a complete discussion of the FTC Mail Order Rule and more information on the debit-card issue.

The card companies, banks, and financial institutions that issue cards consider your past credit history, your current salary, and the length of time you've been at your current job when reviewing your application for a card. Minimums are raised when the interest rate climbs, but at this writing a salary of $18,000 and two years' employment with the same firm should net you a MasterCard or VISA account, provided you're credit-worthy in other respects. Getting an American Express, Diners Club, or debit card usually requires a higher salary and an excellent credit rating, as do the "gold" accounts that offer larger credit lines and special programs geared for business and travel use.

MASTERCARD had 58 million cards in circulation in the U.S. and Canada in 1983, and 29 million in other countries. MasterCards are issued by financial institutions—most large banks offer the card. If you get your MasterCard through your bank, you'll probably enjoy the convenience of one-stop banking—deposits, balance information, payments—on all your accounts through automated teller machines. But consider shopping around. Some states have lower usury ceilings than others, which is why interest rates on these accounts can range from about 12% to 21% per annum. And fees for the cards themselves vary, although most banks charge $20 a year for "membership." You don't have to be a resident of another state to get a card from a bank there, so if you're in a high-interest area, you'd be wise to check rates elsewhere before you apply at your home bank.

The MasterCard International umbrella includes *Access,* in the United Kingdom; the affiliate *Eurocard,* on the Continent; and *Diamond Million* and *Union* cards, in Japan.

VISA, with 106 million cards in circulation, is similar to MasterCard in its structure and services. The VISA International network includes *Barclaycard,* in the United Kingdom; *Carte Bleue,* in France, and *VISA Japan,* in that country. You can apply for a VISA card at any issuing bank. The advice about shopping for a low annual percentage rate applies to VISA as well as MasterCard. Yearly membership fees average about $20.

AMERICAN EXPRESS has 18.8 million cards in circulation and issues them directly to consumers. Unlike MasterCard and VISA, this account must be paid in full when it's billed. The American Express Company does offer special services, such as its "Sign and Travel" program, which enable you to pay off travel and entertainment expenses over several billing periods. Finance charges are imposed on unpaid balances. The membership fee is $35, and there's a $20 charge for each additional card issued on the same account.

Applications for an American Express account can be picked up at restaurants, hotels, and stores that accept the card, or can be obtained by writing to The American Express Co., 125 Broad St., New York, NY 10004.

DINERS CLUB has just under five million cards in circulation worldwide. It's similar to American Express in its programs and billing structure, and in the fact that, in the U.S., it issues cards directly to consumers. Diners Club International is part of Citicorp, whose aggressive marketing programs should make the Diners Club card serious competition for American Express, since they're both geared for "T&E" (travel and entertainment). Like American Express, Diners Club charges a yearly membership fee that's higher than MasterCard and VISA—$45 at this writing—and additional cards on the same account are $20 each. Applications are available from Diners Club International, 183 Inverness Drive, West Englewood, CO 80112.

CARTE BLANCHE, with just over one million cards in use, is also owned by Citicorp. It's a T&E card accepted by most establishments that honor Diners Club, and the annual fee is $40 (additional cards are $20 each). Write to the Diners Club address for an application.

CHOICE, the newest entry in the credit-card market, is owned by Citibank (Maryland) N.A. The card is issued by that institution and other banks. At this writing, there are over one million CHOICE card-holders, chiefly in the mid–Atlantic area, but the number is expected to rise rapidly.

CHOICE offers consumers some attractive features: no annual fee, a rebate of .5% of their total annual billings if these exceed $600, and annual percentage rates comparable to those of other cards. The billing structure is similar to that of MasterCard or VISA, and cash advances and savings programs are part of its package of services. CHOICE is being promoted as the "consumer's card," and the fact that there's no membership fee makes it very attractive. But remember to shop around for the most favorable interest rate as the card becomes available in areas with low usury ceilings. Until then, you can obtain an application for the card (at an annual percentage rate of 21%) from CHOICE, 7720 York Rd., Towson, MD 21204.

ACCESS is MasterCard's United Kingdom card; see *MasterCard* p. 470, for more information.

EUROCARD is a MasterCard affiliate used on the Continent; see *MasterCard* for more information.

Paying for Goods from Foreign Firms. The most commonly used methods of paying for goods from foreign firms are personal checks, certified checks, bank drafts, and credit cards. These are described in detail in the preceding section, "Payment."

If you use a credit card, be aware that you'll be charged for the currency-conversion expense by the card issuer. When the card firm receives the receipt for your purchase from the store, it converts the foreign currency to dollars at a rate determined daily, and then adds a surcharge of anywhere from .25% to 1% to the total. Your statement should tell you the date the conversion was made and the surcharge. Some card firms also state the total in foreign currency that was converted. The methods used by card companies to determine the rate of exchange vary widely, and are subject to the regulations existing in each foreign country. When you get your statement, check it carefully. The foreign currency total should be the same as your original order total, unless there was a price increase, short shipment, or shipping costs were higher than originally calculated. Check the *interbank* rate of exchange valid on the day the money was converted or the invoice was processed by the card company (your bank should be able to quote this). If there's a significant discrepancy between the interbank rate and the one the card firm used, write to the customer-service department and ask for an explanation.

Be sure to read "Ordering from Foreign Firms," p. 466, *before* you order.

RETURN POLICIES. Approaches to returns vary from firm to firm, from "no returns accepted under any circumstances" to "no-questions-asked" policies honored years after the product has been purchased. Most catalog firms guarantee satisfaction and accept returns within 10, 14, or 30 days after you're received the order. Firms selling on a price-quote basis usually accept returns *only* if the product is defective.

Some goods—personalized or monogrammed, custom-made, surplus, and sale items—are routinely exempted from full return policies. Health regulations usually prohibit returns on intimate apparel and bathing suits, but some companies do accept such returns. (We presume that those goods are not returned to stock.)

Check the firm's return policy before you order. If you're shopping for a product that also carries a manufacturer's warranty, obtain a copy of that *before* you buy.

For more information, see "Returns," p. 489.

RESALE NUMBERS AND LETTERHEAD. In order to get really low prices and discounts from some firms, it may be necessary to write to them on business letterhead and/or provide a resale or tax-exemption number.

To be eligible for a resale number, you must have a business using that number to buy goods for resale, not for personal use. Some states require you to post bond in amounts from $50 to $150 against the taxes you collect when you resell goods. These taxes are turned over to the state periodically. By forming a cooperative, you can legitimately hold a resale number, buy and sell goods to members, collect taxes, and still get tremendous discounts on all kinds of goods. To apply for a resale number, write or call your department of taxation and finance and ask for application forms and information on regulations. Please note that abuse of resale numbers is illegal. Before you go into business you should be sure the entire venture is worth the endeavor.

You can also obtain a license for doing business as a firm (a "DBA") from the same agency. You're then able to "do business as" a given name—e.g.

John and Mary Smith might get a license to do business as "MaryJo Interiors." The license enables you to use a business letterhead legitimately, but you aren't required to *do* any business, as you are if you hold a resale number. Remember that rules vary from state to state on all these matters. Investigate the laws before getting a resale number or DBA.

If you want to place an order with a firm that requires a resale number or letterhead and you have neither, ask the firm whether you can place a *sample order*. This is a small order not subject to the minimums that firms usually have to meet when buying from wholesalers. U.S. firms often fill sample orders in the hope of developing new dealers and retailers for their products; European and Asian firms often play a little game in which they want you to request a sample order so they can sell retail at wholesale prices without risking the wrath of their regular dealer accounts. In many cases, you'll be able to place a sample order only once, but you may be able to get what you need in that order, at great savings.

If you do establish some kind of business (and it can be very, very small), you'll be able to go beyond the scope of this catalog and buy merchandise directly from wholesalers in your area who do not sell to the public. Again, a cooperative as a business with a resale number can be extremely useful in accomplishing this.

CANCELING YOUR ORDER: Do you have the right to cancel your order once you've placed it? The answer is no.

When you order goods or services from a firm, whether by phone or mail, you enter into a contract of sale. You do not have the right to call the firm and rescind an order, nor do you have the right to stop payment on a check or money order on the basis of what an FTC staffer described as "buyer's remorse." (This terms seems almost poetic in an industry that thrives on ill-considered impulse purchases.) Different states have different laws governing matters of contract, but your second thoughts could give the firm cause to bring legal action against you. This is especially true if the company has undertaken action on an order, in what is termed "constructive acceptance of payment."

However, if you send an order to a firm on Monday and read on Tuesday that it's commencing bankruptcy proceedings or reorganization, stopping payment might be worth the possible risks. And a firm in such a position is probably too absorbed in its own problems to take action against you for reneging on your obligation. In any case, if you do decide to try to cancel, check the terms of the offer first. Magazine and book subscriptions are often sent on an approval basis, giving you a cancellation option. Goods offered with an unconditional guarantee of satisfaction can be sent back when they arrive. If these terms aren't offered and you're determined to cancel, write to the firm, request permission to cancel, and state your reasons. If you've stopped payment on a check or money order or taken any other action to default on payment, mention that as well.

SHIPPING, INSURANCE, HANDLING, SALES TAX, AND DUTY

When you compare prices on goods from firm to firm, you must consider the costs of shipping, insurance, tax or duty, and handling as part of the total. (See "Cost Comparisons," p. 462, for more information.)

SHIPPING: This section addresses the concerns of those buying from U.S. firms who are having goods delivered to addresses in the U.S. and its possessions. If you're ordering from a firm in another country, see "Shipments from Foreign Countries," p. 478.

Shipping Computations. The largest ancillary cost in an order is shipping. Mail-order firms use a variety of methods in figuring shipping charges. It's helpful to know how each works so you can shop intelligently.

POSTPAID item prices, which appear to be "free" of shipping charges, are beloved by mail-order shoppers because they eliminate extra computation. However, the shipping and packing costs are passed along in the item price, and if the order is taxed, consumers should remember that they're paying sales tax on the shipping fee as well as the item cost. Although the majority of states and localities *require* payment of sales tax on delivery and handling, not all do. And very few firms collect the tax, even when they're required by law to do so. If the departments of revenue concerned begin cracking down, you may see more complicated order forms in the future and find yourself paying a bit more when you order from certain companies.

ITEMIZED shipping costs are often seen as amounts in parentheses following the price or code number of the product. If you compare the UPS or USPS tape on the delivered parcel, you'll often find that the price you paid the firm for shipping was higher. That's because it includes the costs of packing and materials. The price may also be prorated. For example, a California firm will compute all shipping charges based on the price of sending goods to Kansas, midway across the country. The profits made on local deliveries wind up subsidizing the losses on shipments to the East Coast. Some firms simply charge the maximum possible shipping cost. For example, if you bought a beach outfit—tank suit, sleeveless coverup, sunglasses, "fun" chunky earrings and choker, sun hat, and mesh tote bag—from one upscale catalog we perused, you'd pay $17 in shipping costs. Some firms deal with consumers' outrage with this situation by limiting the maximum amount of shipping charges per order to $10 to $15. But remember—even if the price you pay the firm is much higher than the actual shipping cost, don't ask the firm for the difference. Instead, suggest that it change its method of computing the charges, or at least place a ceiling on the shipping costs.

NUMERIC charges are based on the number of items you're ordering, as in "$2.50 for the first item; 75¢ each additional item." Firms structuring charges in this way often limit shipping to $7 to $12, so additional purchases made after you reach that limit are exempted from shipping charges entirely.

FLAT ORDER FEES are simple dollar amounts charged on all orders, usually regardless of the number of items or weight. (The firm often imposes an additional fee if part of the order is shipped to another address.) A flat fee represents a bargain if you're placing a large order, but resist the temptation to order extra products just to make the shipping charge proportionately lower. And note that some firms selling on this basis do charge extra for heavy, outsized, or fragile items. Check the catalog carefully *before* you order.

FREE shipping is offered, often by smaller companies, on large orders. Customarily, orders under a certain dollar or item amount *are* charged shipping on some basis, but if your order exceeds a certain amount, you pay no shipping at all. The fact is often noted on the order blank—"on orders $100 and over, WE pay postage," or "free shipping on three dozen pairs or more same size, style, & color"—usually with the proviso that the order must be sent to one address.

Don't order more than you need just to meet the minimum, unless the extra item costs less than the postage and you're sure it can be used at a later date.

SLIDING SCALES, tied to the cost of the order, are used by many firms. For example, if the goods total $15.00, you pay $2.75 for shipping; from $15.01 to $30.00, the charge is $3.50, etc. This is advantageous when you're ordering many inexpensive, heavy products, but it seems inequitable when you're buying a single, costly item. Some firms remedy this by using itemized shipping charges for small, high-ticket goods. Most limit the shipping charges to a maximum dollar amount, usually $7 to $12. Again, avoid padding your order to get the "most" out of your shipping charges—you'll spend many more dollars on dubious purchases than you "save" on postage.

TABLES, based on the weight and sometimes delivery distance of the order, are used by a number of companies, including Spiegel and Sears, Roebuck and Co. Tables require the most effort on the part of the shopper, since you must tally the shipping weights given with the item prices separately, locate your zone or area on the chart, and then find the shipping charges. Large, nonmailable goods will have to be shipped by truck; their catalog code numbers often have a suffix letter indicating this.

The advantage to table computation is fairness of price. While you won't get the shipping "bargains" possible with firms using other methods to calculate those costs, neither will you find yourself paying exorbitant sums to ship small, light orders.

Saving on Shipping Costs. When you have a chance to save on shipping by placing a large order, consult friends and neighbors to see if they want to combine orders with you. But unless you can view conferring, consolidating orders, and distributing the goods when they arrive as a "social activity," you'll have to count it as part of the cost of the order. You know that time is money—that's one of the reasons you shop by mail!

Carriers. No matter which method a firm uses to calculate shipping, it's going to send your goods by the USPS, UPS, or truck. Some firms, especially those selling highly perishable goods, also use overnight delivery services. Goods are sent by truck when they exceed the size/weight restrictions of UPS and the USPS.

UNITED PARCEL SERVICE (UPS): UPS is the delivery system businesses prefer for mail order. UPS is cheaper, on the whole, than USPS; it automatically insures up to $100 in value on each package; it's considered more reliable than the USPS and more prompt in delivery; and it also picks up the packages at the firm's office or warehouse.

Under its Common Carrier Service, UPS handles packages weighing up to 70 pounds that have a combined girth and length measurement of up to 108 inches (with some qualifications). UPS offers overnight delivery to certain states and ZIP codes through its NEXT DAY AIR service, and 2ND DAY AIR delivery to the 48 contiguous states and some parts of Hawaii. Residents of Hawaii should note that UPS uses its 2ND DAY AIR service for deliveries to that state; not all parts of Hawaii are served, and charges are higher than those for its standard Common Carrier Service. UPS no longer delivers to Alaska. Most mail-order firms are accommodating this change in policy by offering USPS deliveries, but some do not. Check the firm's provisions before ordering. UPS cannot deliver your order anywhere without a street address.

The amount of postage charged by UPS is determined by the delivery address, the location of the firm shipping the goods, the service used, and the dimensions and weight of the package.

UPS has divided the country into 63 sections. Each section has a zoning chart that breaks the rest of the country into seven zones, which run from "Zone 2" through "Zone 8," according to distance, via the first three digits of the ZIP code. A firm located in Manhattan uses a zone chart that lists Manhattan ZIP codes (generally prefix 100) as 2, or the closest zone; and California ZIP codes (prefix 900) as 8, or the farthest zone. In California, 900 prefix ZIP codes are in zone 2, while Manhattan ZIP code prefixes are in zone 8.

To translate these zone numbers into shipping costs, consult a current Common Carrier Rate Chart (see the sample chart on p. 8). This chart lists rates for packages weighing up to 70 pounds from zone 2 to zone 8. Naturally, the lowest charge is on a shipment of up to one pound to zone 2; the highest rate is on a shipment of 70 pounds to zone 8. The rate chart also lists surcharges for additional services, such as C.O.D. delivery, address correction, and acknowledgment of delivery. If your package exceeds the size/weight restrictions, it will be transported by a private trucking firm.

Some firms include in their catalogs all the rate charts you will ever need to figure exact shipping costs; others state at the bottom of the order form,

"Add enough for postage and insurance. We will refund overpayment." When faced with this, you can consult a catalog that lists the weight of a comparable item both before *and* after packing, add the difference to the weight of the item you're ordering, and then call your local UPS office for the rates. You can also call the firm itself and ask the shipping department to give you a quick calculation over the phone. You could send in the order without adding anything for shipping and ask the firm to bill you, but this may delay delivery. UPS rate charts are reproduced on p. 8 to give you an idea of costs, but be sure to check with your local UPS office for the most recent rates and regulations if you're doing calculations yourself.

UNITED STATES POSTAL SERVICE (USPS)—PARCEL POST (PP): The costs for Parcel Post, or fourth-class mail, are somewhat higher than UPS charges, but PP offers one distinct advantage: *only packages sent by Parcel Post can be delivered to a post-office box.* (UPS must have a street address to deliver goods, although carriers will usually deliver to rural routes.) If you're having a package sent to a post-office box, you can avoid delays and the possibility that the package will be returned to the company if sent via UPS. Just write "DELIVERY BY PARCEL POST ONLY; UPS NOT ACCEPTABLE" in bold red letters on the order form, unless there's a box to check to indicate your preference. On the check, write "GOODS TO BE DELIVERED BY PARCEL POST ONLY." Once the firm endorses or cashes the check, it agrees implicitly to this arrangement and must send the goods by Parcel Post.

While postal rates have escalated by leaps and bounds, the size/weight restrictions remain relatively constant. USPS accepts parcels with a combined girth and length measurement of up to 84 inches that weigh up to 70 pounds (40 pounds in some locations). Packages weighing under 15 pounds that have a combined girth/length of between 84 and 100 inches are accepted at rates for 15-lb packages. See p. 8 for more information and rate charts.

PRIVATE TRUCKING FIRMS. When the firm specifies that the goods must be sent by truck, or if you have ordered both mailable (could be sent by UPS or PP) and nonmailable goods, the entire order may be sent by truck. Firms indicate that goods are to be trucked with the term "FOB," followed by the word "warehouse," "manufacturer," or the name of the city from which the goods are trucked. "FOB" stands for "free on board," and it means that the trucking charges will be billed from that point. When the word "manufacturer" follows FOB in the catalog, it means that the firm is probably having that item "drop-shipped," or taking orders for the product and sending the orders to the manufacturer rather than maintaining warehouse inventories. If you want to order nonmailable goods that you have reason to believe will be drop-shipped, you should find out where the manufacturer's warehouse is located so you can estimate trucking costs. If you want the item quickly, you should also ask the firm that takes the order to verify that the manufacturer has the product in stock.

Truck charges are usually collected upon delivery. Since these charges are based on weight and distance, the additional expense is a real factor to consider when ordering very heavy items from a firm that's located far from you. A typical minimum charge for a 100-pound order is $35. Truckers usually make "dump deliveries," which means they unload the goods on the sidewalk in front of your home. For an additional fee (usually $10 to $20), you can have the goods delivered inside your house or apartment. This charge may escalate if there are stairs—we know of at least one firm that charges $1 extra per step. Additional fees may be incurred if your order happens to be the only one the trucker is picking up from the firm that day, or if the driver has to notify you of delivery. You can always arrange to pick up your order at the truck terminal and save some money. Before you decide to purchase anything you know will have to be trucked, get the final cost of the item *plus* trucking charges and compare it to the cost of the same item if bought locally and delivered.

Remember that when the carrier arrives, you must be able to pay the charges with cash or a certified check—personal checks and credit cards are seldom accepted.

SHIPMENTS FROM FOREIGN COUNTRIES: After your payment has been authorized or has cleared the bank, the firm should ship your order. Depending on the dimensions and weight of the package, it may be shipped by mail, or sent by sea or air freight.

Mailable Orders. If the package weighs up to 20kgs. (about 44 pounds), has a length of up to 1.5m (about 59″), and a length/girth measurement of up to 3m (about 118″) for surface mail or up to 2m (about 79″) for airmail, it can be mailed. Almost everything you buy from a foreign country will be mailable. Your decision when ordering will be choosing air, surface, or accelerated-surface shipment (provided the firm offers all three). Mailed packages are delivered by your postal carrier, regardless of the service used by the company. Duty is collected by the carrier upon delivery.

AIRMAIL is the most expensive service; airmailed packages generally take a week to ten days to arrive after they're posted, although some firms ask you to allow two to three weeks for delivery.

SURFACE MAIL, which includes both overland and boat shipment, is the cheapest service, but orders shipped by surface mail can take up to two months to reach you.

ACCELERATED SURFACE MAIL is now available in some countries; it's priced between standard surface and airmail rates, and hastens delivery time to about three weeks. It's known as "Fastmail" in some British catalogs, and represents the best shipping buy if you're neither desperate for an item nor prepared to wait a season for it. Please note that some firms are offering only Fastmail and standard surface. These firms will usually arrange to ship via airmail, but if you're paying by anything other than a credit card, this doesn't make sense. It will take at least a week to request the added postage costs, at least a week for that information to reach you, another week for your order to get to the firm with correct payment, and at least a week for the goods to arrive. That's a total of four weeks, the same length of time you might expect to wait if you were ordering using the Fastmail prices stated in the catalog (a week for the order to reach the firm, and three weeks for the order to be delivered). If you pay by credit card, however, you can send the order, and ask the firm to ship by air and bill your account for the extra charges. Do this *only* when you're frantic to get something, since the shipping charges for airmail will be from 50% to 100% higher than those for surface mail.

Nonmailable Orders. If the package exceeds mail weight and/or size restrictions, it will have to be sent by an air or ship carrier.

AIR FREIGHT is the best choice when the item or order just exceeds mail restrictions. Charges are based on the weight and size of the order, as well as the flight distance. The firm arranges to have the order sent to the airport with a U.S. customs office that's closest to your delivery address. You pay the firm for the air-freight charges, it sees the order to the airport, and sends you a customs declaration form and invoice. When the airport apprises you of arrival, get right over with the forms, since most airports will charge a holding fee on goods still unclaimed five to ten days after delivery. In addition, you should make arrangements to have the package trucked to your home if it's too large to transport yourself. Once you clear customs you can take the goods home, or release them to the truckers you've hired and they'll make delivery.

SEA FREIGHT is much less expensive than air, but it can take months for an order to reach you. If you live near a port, you may want to handle customs clearance yourself and engage a trucking firm to deliver the goods to your home. You may also hire an agent (customs broker) to clear customs and arrange inland trucking. This service will cost from $75 to $125, but it's the only practical way to deal with the process if you live far from the docking site, and the foreign firm that sent the goods doesn't have arrangements with a U.S. agent who could take care of these details for you.

The procedure is similar to that of clearing an air shipment: You present the forms the firm has provided to the shipper and customs officer, pay duty charges, and transport the goods home or release them to the truckers you've hired.

For information on duty rates, trademark regulations, and shipment of problematical or prohibited goods, see "Duty," p. 481. For information on payment of duty on mailed goods, see "Deliveries from Foreign Firms," p. 487.

HANDLING CHARGES: Some firms charge an extra fee for handling or packing your order. The fee, which is usually not more than one or two dollars, may be included in a flat shipping fee. Handling is often waived on orders over a certain dollar amount. The handling fee helps to cover the costs of labor and materials used in preparing your order for shipment. This surcharge, along with the shipping fee, may be taxed in certain states.

You can recoup part of the handling cost, whether paid as a fee or included in the item markup, by reusing the carton and plastic peanuts or excelsior when you send gifts or pack fragile things for storage. If you're mailing the box, be sure to black out any marks made by the carrier, remove postage tapes, and delete addresses printed on the sides or top. It won't be pretty, but resourcefulness has its own style.

INSURANCE: Most firms insure orders as a matter of course. Shipments worth up to $100 sent by UPS are automatically insured by UPS; you should not have to pay extra insurance on those orders. UPS charges 25¢ per each additional $100 in value on the same package. The USPS does not insure automatically, so if you're having your package delivered by the USPS be sure to request insurance. Charges for postal insurance range from 45¢ for goods worth up to $20, to $4.70 for package contents worth from $300.01 to $400. Goods valued at more than $400 but under $25,000 must be registered as well as insured. Some types of goods cannot be insured. If the product you're purchasing is not insurable, have the firm arrange shipping with a carrier that will insure it.

Most insurance claims arise as a result of damage to or loss of goods. Procedures for claiming and reimbursement vary according to the carrier's rules and the firm's policy. Under any circumstances, you should contact the firm as soon as you discover any damage to your shipment and ask the customer service department what you should do. If there is documentation (signature of receipt on the UPS carrier's log or USPS insurance receipt), the claim can be verified, processed, and you should be reimbursed eventually or receive replacement goods. If there is no documentation and the worst happens—the goods never arrive—the firm may absorb the loss and send a replacement order. It may also refuse to do so, especially if its records indicate that the order was shipped. In such cases, it will be almost impossible to prove that you *didn't* receive the order. If repeated entreaties for a refund, credit, or duplicate order meet resistance, state your case to the agencies listed in "Obtaining Help," p. 496. And be sure to tell us—see "Feedback," p. 500, for more information.

If you have any doubts about whether the firm, domestic or foreign, will have your goods insured, *ask before you order.* The small fee is a worthwhile expense, something you know if you've ever had something go awry with an uninsured shipment. See "Accepting Deliveries from U.S. Firms," p. 483, and "Deliveries from Foreign Firms," p. 487, for more information.

SALES TAX: You have to pay sales tax on an order if 1) you're having goods delivered to an address in the same state in which the mail-order firm, a branch office, or representative is located, and 2) the laws governing the state or locality of the delivery address require payment of tax on the ordered goods. You pay the rate of sales tax prevailing in your area, whether it's none (in New Hampshire) or 8.25% (in New York City), according to the laws of your area. As previously stated in this guide, most states require payment of sales tax on handling, packing, and shipping charges.

Those are the general rules. However, the right of a state to create its own definition of "doing business" in that state, or "establishing nexus," has raised the ire of both consumers who have to pay tax on what they perceive as out-of-state orders, and businesses that have the headaches of tax collection and accounting. The issue of nexus is no stranger to the Supreme Court; one energetic individual took on both Sears and Montgomery Ward over 40 years ago and lost, and other mail-order firms have done battle with state governments and lost as well.

The good news is that many firms neglect to collect all the sales tax they're required to, and very few request tax on the shipping and handling charges as required by state laws. That's good for you. But some states may be losing hundreds of thousands of dollars yearly as a result; if they should undertake enforcement, more mail-order purchases will be taxed. While you may enjoy saving some money now, please add the sales tax you *know* you should pay even if the firm doesn't request it. And if the firm asks you to pay a rate lower than the one you should, pay at the proper rate.

DUTY: Orders from foreign firms are not charged state sales taxes, but make up for it with duty charges. You cannot prepay duty to foreign firms. Duty is paid to the postal carrier who delivers your package, or the customs agent if the order is delivered by air or sea freight.

Assessment of Duty. U.S. duty was once charged on the wholesale value of the goods (about a third less than the actual price), but the method of assessment has changed. The rate of duty is now calculated on the transaction value, or actual price, of the goods being imported, on an *ad valorem* (percentage) or *specific* (per-unit) basis, and sometimes a combination of the two. To add to the confusion, U.S. Customs Service classifies foreign countries in one of three categories, each of which has a different rate of duty. Goods made in Communist-bloc countries are charged the highest rates of duty, up to 110%—with the exception of Roumania, Yugoslavia, Poland, and Hungary. These rates apply to any goods made in the bloc countries, even if they're not sold there. Next, Customs designates other countries as "most favored," with much lower rates of duty. These rates are being reduced in equal increments yearly through 1987. Note that there are some goods—such as certified antiques, postage stamps, truffles, and original paintings—that are imported duty-free from countries in both categories. The third rate of duty applies to what are known as "developing countries." U.S. Customs has instituted a Generalized System of Preferences (G.S.P.) affecting about 2,700 items from 139 countries and territories, known as Beneficiary Developing Countries (B.D.C.). Under G.S.P., these items are classified as duty-free, but there are some exceptions. For example, Hong Kong, a B.D.C., qualifies for G.S.P. rates, but gold jewelry and radio receivers from Hong Kong are subject to duty. In order to qualify under G.S.P., an item must be sold directly from the B.D.C. in which it was grown, manufactured, or produced. Some items are excluded from G.S.P. status, even though they're produced by a B.D.C. Check your local U.S. Customs office for current regulations, since rates and classifications may change.

Prohibitions and Restrictions. Before you order from a foreign firm, you should know that there are some goods that can be imported only under certain conditions, and others that are prohibited altogether. You can't import narcotics, pornography, fireworks, switchblade knives, absinthe, poison, or dangerous toys—and to our knowledge, none of the firms listed in this book sells them. If ordered, these items will be confiscated by U.S. Customs. If you want to import animals, animal products, biologicals, petroleum products, plants, or seeds, you must make prior arrangements with certain agencies and obtain the necessary permits. And if you want to buy name-brand goods, you should be sure to check trademark restrictions. The manufacturers of certain goods register the trademarks with Customs, which limits the number of those items an individual may import. Sometimes the manufacturers allow importation of more than one of the item, as long as the trademarked symbols or names are removed. This is done either by the firm selling the goods or by the customs agent. If you want to exceed the limits the manufacturer has set, you may write to the firm and apply for consent. The letter of permission should be presented to the customs agent, or left on file at the customs office. Types of goods that may fall under trademark restrictions include cameras, lenses, opticals, tape recorders, perfumes, cosmetics, musical instruments, jewelry, flatware, and timepieces. Note that many foreign firms offer trademark-restricted goods in their catalogs, but don't inform you of conditions of importation of these products.

Obtaining Information. If you plan to order from a foreign firm and want to know more about duty rates and classifications, import restrictions, permits, and prohibitions, request the free booklet, "Rates of Duty for Popular Tourist Items" from the Office of Information and Publication, Bureau of Customs, 1301 Constitution Ave. N.W., Rm. 6303, Washington, DC 20226. Use it as a general guide only—contact your local customs office for the latest rates. Be sure you are able to provide a description of the goods you're ordering, including materials, composition, decoration or ornamentation, etc., since the classification of goods is more specific than indicated by the brochure. For example, loose pearls and permanently strung pearls are assessed at different rates, and spoons have a rate different from that of knives and forks. In addition, rates may change in response to the protectionist attitude prevailing in the current administration. At this writing, the number of goods imported duty-free under G.S.P. has been cut, and rates for dutiable goods may rise. The affected countries don't like this, U.S. businesses applaud it, and many consumers are torn between anger at paying higher prices and faith in the belief that such changes will strengthen the U.S. economy. Let your congressional representative know how you feel about policy changes.

If you want to import fruits, vegetables, or plants from abroad, write to Quarantines, The Department of Agriculture, Federal Center Building, Hyattsville, MD 20782, and ask for an import permit application.

For more information on related matters, see "Ordering from Foreign Firms," p. 466; "Paying for Goods from Foreign Firms," p. 471; "Shipments from Foreign Countries," p. 478; and "Deliveries from Foreign Firms," p. 487.

RECEIVING YOUR ORDER

What do you do when your order arrives? What steps do you take if it doesn't? You have certain rights and responsibilities in this respect, and as an intelligent consumer, you should understand both.

ACCEPTING DELIVERIES FROM U.S. FIRMS: When the postal clerk, UPS carrier, or trucker delivers your order, check the carton, bag, or crate before signing for it. If you're having someone else accept the package, instruct that person to do the same. If there is damage to the packaging extensive enough that the contents could be affected, you can refuse to sign for or accept the goods. However, this is not a procedure we wholly recommend, and the reasons are explained in "Returns," p. 489.

If the box, bag, or carton is in good condition, accept it and open it as soon as possible. Unpack the goods carefully, putting aside the packing materials and any inserts until you've examined the contents. Most firms include a copy of your order form or a computerized invoice itemizing the order. If it's a printout or there's no invoice at all, get your file copy of the order you sent or phoned in, and check to make sure you've received what you ordered. Remember to check the outside of the box, since some firms insert packing slips in adhesive plastic envelopes that are affixed to the top or side of the carton.

Check your order for the following: short shipments, unauthorized substitutions, wrong sizes, colors, styles, or models; warranty forms if the products carry manufacturers' warranties; missing parts; and instruction sheets if a product requires assembly. Since some firms return clothing modeled for catalog layouts to stock, examine the insides of collars for traces of makeup. Make sure ensembles are complete—that scarves, belts, hats, vests, ties, ascots, and other components have been included. Test electronic goods as soon as possible to make sure they function properly, and *do not* fill out the warranty card unless you're satisfied. Try on clothing and shoes to make sure they fit. Check printed, engraved, or monogrammed goods for accuracy. If you decide to return a product, see "Returns," p. 489, for information.

If you've received a short shipment (one or more item you ordered not included in the package), the firm may have inserted a notice that the product is being shipped separately or an option notice if the product is out of stock. (See "The Option Notice," p. 485, for information on the latter.)

Some companies do not back order, and include a refund check with the order or under separate cover when a product is out of stock, or bill your account with the adjusted total if you used a credit card. If you've received a short shipment without an explanatory enclosure, first check the catalog from which you ordered to see whether that item is shipped from the manufacturer or shipped separately by the firm. If there's no mention of special shipping conditions or delays in shipment in the catalog, contact the customer-service department of the firm immediately.

Don't let the moment of delivery become the moment you realize that doors are only three feet wide. *Prior* to ordering, measure all the doorways through which the article must pass, allowing for narrow hallways, stairs, and the like. Some savvy shoppers even construct a carton dummy of the item by taping boxes together, and maneuver that through a dry-run delivery before they place the order. Our editor wishes she had done this before buying a semi-antique desk on impulse a few years ago. She was forced to saw off half the legs so it would fit through the front door. This won't work with refrigerators or pianos, so measure, measure, measure *before* you buy.

DELAYED SHIPMENTS FROM U.S. FIRMS: The editor of this book once received a letter from a lawyer representing a woman in the midwest who'd purchased a refrigerator from a firm listed in one of the editor's books. The customer had engaged the lawyer because, three weeks after phoning the order the firm, the appliance had not arrived. Did the woman have a case against the company?

Absolutely not, and once you've read this section you should understand why.

The FTC Mail Order Rule. The Federal Trade Commission's "Mail Order Rule," promulgated in 1975, addresses the biggest problem in the mail-order industry: late delivery and nondelivery of goods. Every person buying goods from a U.S. firm should understand the principles of the Rule, know what types of transactions are exempt from its protection, and understand what actions a consumer is obliged to take to ensure protection under the regulations.

Please note: when a state or county has enacted laws similar in purpose to the functions of the FTC Mail Order Rule, the laws affording the consumer more protection take precedence.

GENERAL TERMS OF THE RULE. The Rule specifies that a firm, or "seller," must ship goods within 30 days of receipt of a properly completed order, unless the firm gives another date in its catalog, advertisements, or promotional literature. The operative term here is "ship"—the firm does not have to have *delivered* the goods within 30 days, under the terms of the Rule. And it must have received a *properly completed order:* Your check or money order must be good, your credit must be good if you're charging the order, and the firm must have all the information necessary to process the order. The 30-day clock begins ticking when the firm gets your check or money order made out in the proper amount, but stops if it's dishonored. If you're paying with a credit card, it begins when the firm charges your account.

If your check or money order is insufficient to cover the order total or is dishonored by the bank, if your credit card payment is refused authorization and if you neglect to include data necessary to the processing of your order (which could include size or color information, your address, etc.), the 30-day clock will not start until the problems are remedied—the firm receives complete payment, payment is honored by the bank, the credit card purchase is authorized, or you supply the missing data.

Again, the 30-day limit applies only when a firm does not ask you to allow more time for shipment (and most such qualifiers request extra time for *delivery,* which only confuses the issue. One luxury linens catalog requests an allowance of two years for delivery of some of its Madeira tablecloths; this is not only legal but intelligent, since it takes well over a year to have the cloths made by hand, and customers feel they're worth the wait.)

Certain types of goods and purchases are not protected by the Rule. These include: mail-order photo finishing; seeds and growing plants; C.O.D. orders; purchases made under negative-option plans (such as book and record clubs); magazine subscriptions and like "serial deliveries," except for the first issue; and orders placed by phone which are paid by credit card.

Catalogs for which payment or compensation is requested fall under the terms of the Rule. See "Delayed Shipment of Catalogs," p. 459; "Catalog Shipment Conditions of WBMC Firms," p. 460; and the rest of this section for more information.

The typical phone order is not protected by the Rule. See "The Rule and Phone Orders," p. 486, for more information.

Assuming your order is covered under the Rule, the firm from which you're ordering must follow a specific procedure if it's unable to ship your order within 30 days. You must respond under the terms of the Rule if you want to retain all your rights. Read on.

THE OPTION NOTICE. When the firm knows it will be unable to ship within 30 days of receiving your properly completed order, or by the deadline it's given in its literature, it must send you an option notice. An option notice written in compliance with the Rule will inform you that there is a delay in shipping the item, and may include a revised shipping date. If it does and that date is up to 30 days later than the original deadline (either 30 days or a date specified by the firm), it should offer you the option of consenting to the delay or canceling the order and receiving a refund. The option notice must also state that *lack of response* on your part is *implied consent* to the delay. If you decide to cancel the order, the firm must receive the cancellation *before* it ships the order.

If the new shipping deadline is over 30 days after the original date, or the firm can't provide a revised shipping date, the option notice must say so. The notice should also state that your order will be automatically canceled unless the firm receives consent to the delay from you within 30 days of the original shipping date, and unless it's able to ship the order *within* 30 days after the original deadline and has not received an order cancellation from you as of the time of shipping.

The firm is required to send notices by first-class mail and provide you with a cost-free means of response—a prepaid business-mail reply or post card. Accepting collect calls or cancellations over WATS lines is acceptable as long as the operators are trained to take them. If you want to cancel an order, get the response back to the firm as quickly as possible after you receive the option notice. We recommend that you photocopy the card, form, or letter, and send it return receipt requested if you want absolute proof of the date of delivery. (Remember, if the firm ships your order the day after you can prove it received your cancellation, you have the right to refuse delivery, have the order returned to the firm at its expense, and claim a prompt refund or credit.)

THE RENEWED OPTION NOTICE. When a firm is unable to meet its revised shipping deadline, it must issue you a renewal option notice in advance of the revised deadline. Unlike the first notice, second and subsequent notices must state that if you don't agree *in writing* to a new shipping date or indefinite delay, the order will be canceled. And the consent to a second delay must be received before the first delay period ends, or the order must be cancelled, according to the Rule.

If you consent to an indefinite delay, you retain the right to cancel the order at any time before the goods are shipped. And the firm itself may cancel the order if it's unable to ship the goods within the delay period, and *must* cancel the order under a variety of circumstances.

THE RULE AND REFUNDS. Under the terms of the Rule, when you or the firm cancel the order, you're entitled to a prompt refund. "Prompt" means that, if your order was prepaid, the firm must send you a refund check or money order by first-class mail within seven working days after the cancellation is made. If you paid with a debit card, inform the firm when you cancel or when it notifies you that it's canceling the order that it must treat the payment as if were cash, a check, or a money order and reimburse your account within seven working days. If you used a credit card, the Rule states that refunds must be made within one billing cycle. (We assume that these "refunds" are credits to your account, which will void the charge made for the goods.) The firm is *not* permitted to substitute credit vouchers for its own goods instead of making a reimbursement.

THE RULE AND PHONE ORDERS. As mentioned previously in "Phone Orders," orders placed by phone and paid by credit card are not protected by the Rule. When the Rule was promulgated ten years ago, phone orders comprised a much smaller proportion of the direct-mail industry than they do today.

The FTC is aware of consumers' concern and will be working on extending the Rule to cover phone orders. Because the hearing and review process is quite time-consuming, we can't realistically expect to see new rules or amendments enacted until 1986 or later.

Until then remember that, if your state has laws protecting phone orders, those regulations apply to your transactions. If you order goods by phone and charge a deposit or partial payment to your credit card, but finalize the sale (complete payment) by *mailing* a check, money order, or card data to the company, the purchase is protected. (This practice is common in the furniture industry.) But you cannot trigger protection by simply confirming a phone order in writing after you've called it in.

THE RULE AND THE TRUTH. It's our belief, from experience with some of the biggest names in mail order as well as small specialty firms, that very few companies abide fully by the requirements of the FTC Mail Order Rule. In the industry parlance, the option notice is known as a "delay notice," and that's usually what you receive. "The Wonder Duz-All you ordered is temporarily out of stock and will be sent as soon as it's available." How soon? As soon as the patent fight is over? As soon as the Hong Kong firm that makes the gadget rebuilds its factory after that devastating fire? As soon as the boat docks? The wording on the "Duz-All" notice was lifted from one our editor actually received, and that was from one of the most prestigious mail-order houses in the country. Another notice, from a respected kitchenware catalog, was dated October 27th and was enclosed with a short shipment. It declared that the missing item was "temporarily out of stock" but was expected to arrive "shortly." The product arrived in mid-January, which is "shortly" if you're thinking in terms of the following Christmas.

We have never seen a notice with an anticipated delivery date, nor one with a cost-free response mechanism, but we'd like to. As a reader, you can be immensely helpful to us by sending us copies of option notices of approximations of same that you have received. If a survey of such forms confirms our suspicion that very few firms are complying with the Rule in anything but a marginal fashion, we will present the results to the FTC's Division of Enforcement with our recommendations. Send copies of the forms and any comments you may have to The Wholesale-by-Mail Catalog, III; P.O. Box 505, Varick St. Sta., New York, NY 10014–0505.

See "Complaint Procedures," p. 496, for information on dealing with unresolved delivery problems.

DELIVERIES FROM FOREIGN FIRMS: The general guidelines outlined in "Accepting Deliveries from U.S. Firms," p. 483, apply to deliveries from foreign firms. Please note, however, that the FTC regulations do not apply to non-U.S. firms.

The delivery procedure for foreign orders is determined by the shipping method the firm has used. For a complete discussion of carriers, see "Shipments from Foreign Countries," p. 478.

You usually pay duty, or customs charges, at the time you take possession of your order. The amount you pay is based on the value, type, and origin of the goods. See "Duty," p. 481, for more information.

Most orders from foreign firms are mailable, and are delivered by your postal carrier. Before your goods reach you, they're sent through Customs. Orders processed with the least delay are those with goods designated as duty-free, which qualify under G.S.P. provisions, or those worth under $50 that are marked "unsolicited gift." Some firms mark mail-order packages as gifts to save you money; this is not in keeping with Customs regulations, unless the order originates outside the U.S. Do *not* ask a firm to send your order as an unsolicited gift—evasion of duty is a serious offence.

· The clearance procedure on dutiable goods includes entry, inspection, valuation, appraisal, and "liquidation," another term for determination of duty. Provided the necessary permits and entry papers have been filed with U.S. Customs and shipment of the goods violates no regulations, the Customs department will attach an entry form listing a tariff item number, rate of duty, and the amount of duty owed on the goods to the package. It will be sent to the post office, and delivered to you by your postal carrier. He or she will collect the amount of duty and a handling fee, currently $2.50, as "postage due." The use of this term annoys some foreign firms, since customers assume that the charge is for insufficient postage and complain to the company. Postal authorities have told us that the handling fee is not charged unless the order is assessed duty. But even if your order has dutiable goods, you may not have to pay any customs charges—a high proportion of small orders are delivered fee-free.

If your parcel is held at the post office and you don't collect it within 30 days, it will be returned to the firm. Should you disagree with the duty charge, you can challenge it within 90 days of receiving the order by sending the yellow copy of the mail-entry form to the Customs office named on the form, along with a statement explaining your reasons for contesting the charge.

DELAYED SHIPMENTS FROM FOREIGN FIRMS: You can reasonably expect your goods to arrive within six weeks, provided you sent the order by air, are having it shipped by airmail or air freight, didn't order custom-made goods, and paid the correct amount,—as long as the country concerned is not at war. If you sent the order via surface mail and/or are having the goods shipped that way, are having any custom work done, or the country is in turmoil, don't hold your breath. We know of one shopkeeper who buys much of his stock from foreign firms. He usually places relatively small orders with many firms, and says that, on the average, goods take three to six months to arrive when sent by surface mail. He never orders from a country afflicted by a major strike, since it can affect the entire economy and further slow order processing. In questionable situations, it is best to send a personal check or credit-card data.

Transactions with foreign firms generally come under the jurisdiction of international law. Before taking any official action if an order does not arrive, give the firm every possible chance to inform you of the status of the order. Write to the company, including photocopies of your order and proof of payment, and send the letter by registered airmail. Allow at least one month for a response, then try again. If you still haven't heard from the firm and the check you sent hasn't been cashed, put a stop on it. Put a tracer and a stop on any money orders you used. If the check or money order has been cashed, proceed to the post office and fill out an "International Inquiry" form. It will be forwarded to the postal service in the country concerned, which should investigate the matter. Where possible, retain copies of all correspondence related to the affair, since you may need them at a later date.

For more information on resolving problems with foreign companies, see "Complaints About Foreign Firms," p. 499.

RETURNS, GUARANTEES, AND WARRANTIES

Your right to return goods is determined by the policy of the firm, the problem with the order, the conditions under which you make the return, and state the federal laws. See "Return Policies," p. 472, and "Accepting Deliveries from U.S. Firms," p. 483, for general information. Product warranties, whether written or implied, apply to many goods bought by mail. "Guarantees and Warranties," beginning on p. 490, provides a comprehensive discussion of all types of warranties.

RETURNS: Return policies are often extensions of a firm's pledge of satisfaction. The wording of the policy determines how quickly you must return the product after receipt (if there's a time limit), what is acceptable cause for return, and what the firm will do to remedy the problem. A few companies will take anything back, but most exclude custom-made goods, personalized items, special orders, intimate apparel, bathing suits, and hats. Some also exempt sale or reduced goods. The most bare-bones policy usually makes provisions for exchanges when the firm has erred or the product is defective. It's important to read "Implied Warranties," p. 492, for information on laws concerning product performance and rights you may have that are *not* stated in the catalog.

Obtaining Authorization. Before returning a product for any reason, check the inserts that may have been packed with the order as well as the catalog for instructions on return procedures. If none are given, write to the firm for return authorization. State the reason you want to return the product, the item price and order number, date delivered, and the action you'd like taken. Depending on the firm's policy, you may request repairs or replacement of the item, an exchange, refund check, credit to your charge account, or scrip for future purchases from the firm. Keep a photocopy or carbon of the letter for your files.

Restocking Fees. Some firms impose a charge on returned goods to offset the labor and incidental costs of returning the item to inventory. Restocking fees are most commonly charged by firms selling furniture, appliances, and electronics.

Sending the Item. Follow the mailing procedure outlined in the catalog, order insert, or authorization notice from the firm. When you send the goods back, include a dated letter with your name and address, the order number, authorization number or name of the person approving the return (if applicable), and a statement of what you'd like done. Depending on the circumstances, you may have to enclose invoices, sales slips, and a check for a restocking fee as well. Keep photocopies of your letter and invoices for your files.

Pack the item in the original box and padding material if requested, and be sure to insure it for the full value of its contents. (We know of at least one case in which a consumer returned an appliance without authorization or insurance, and the firm maintained it had never arrived. The shopper lost both the product and any chance for compensation—a $150 lesson he'll never forget.) Allow the firm at least 30 days to process the return or respond before writing again.

Refunds and Credits. If you want your charge account credited for the return, be sure to provide the relevant data. Not every firm will issue a refund check or credit your account; some will offer replacement or repair of the product, an exchange, or catalog credit only.

Exchanges. If you're exchanging the product for something entirely different, state the catalog code number, size, color, price, unit, etc. of the item you want in the letter you enclose with the return.

Postage Reimbursement. Some firms permit you to return goods postage-collect, or will reimburse you for the shipping and insurance charges on a return. Most will not. Businesses are not required by federal law to refund the cost, even when you're returning goods as a result of the firm's error. However, state laws may make provisions for this; check your state and local laws to see whether they do.

GUARANTEES AND WARRANTIES: Although the terms "guarantee" and "warranty" are virtually synonymous, this guide makes a distinction between the two for the purpose of clarity. Here, a "guarantee" is the general pledge of satisfaction or service a firm offers on sales. Guarantees and related matters are discussed in "Return Policies," p. 472; "Returns," p. 489; and "Implied Warranties," p. 492. A "warranty" is, generally, the written policy covering the performance of a particular product. Both guarantees and warranties are free; a paid policy is a service contract.

Warranties are regulated by state and federal law. Understanding policy terms will help you shop for the best product/warranty value; knowing your rights may mean the difference between paying for repairs or a replacement product, and having the firm or manufacturer do it.

The Magnuson-Moss Warranty—Federal Trade Commission Improvement Act: Also known as the Warranty Act, this law was enacted in 1975. It regulates warranties that are in print. And note well—a spoken warranty is worth the wind it's written on when it comes to getting service.

The Warranty Act requires that warranties be written in "simple and readily understood language" and that all terms and conditions must be stated in the warranty. If the product costs more than $15, a copy of the warranty must be available *before* purchase. In a store, it should be posted on or near the product, or filed in a catalog of warranties kept on the premises with a notice posted concerning its location. (In our many forays into department, discount, and specialty stores, none of our staff remembers having seen any of the above.) Mail-order firms comply with the law by making copies of warranties available upon request. A survey of current catalogs indicates that most are diligent in this respect.

The Warranty Act requires the warrantor to use the term "full" or "limited" in describing the policy. A single product can have several warranties covering different parts, and each can be labeled separately as "full" or "limited." For example, a TV set may have a full one-year policy on the set and a limited 90-day policy on the picture tube. Generally speaking, the conditions stated here apply to warranties on goods costing over $15.

FULL WARRANTIES provide for repair or replacement of the product at no cost to you, including the removal and reinstallation of the item, if necessary. The warranty may be limited to a certain length of time, and must state the period plainly. Full warranties can't be limited to the original purchaser—the warrantor must honor the policy for the full term even if the item has changed hands. Implied warranties may not be limited in duration by the terms of the full warranty, and in some states may last up to four years.

The item should be repaired within a "reasonable" length of time after you've notified the firm of the problem. If, after a "reasonable" number of attempts to repair, the product is still not functioning properly, you may invoke the "lemon provision." This entitles you to a replacement or refund for the product.

Registering your product with the warrantor under a full warranty is voluntary, and that fact must be stated clearly in the terms. You may return the card supplied with the policy to the firm, but this is at your discretion and not necessary to maintain the protection of the warranty.

LIMITED WARRANTIES provide less coverage than full warranties. Warrantors using the "limited" designation can require you to remove, transport, and reinstall a product; pay for labor on repairs; and return the warranty card to the firm in order to validate the policy. They can also limit the warranty to the original purchaser and give you prorated refunds or credits for the product. (The "lemon provision" is not included in a limited warranty.)

They may also limit implied warranties to the length of time their policies run, but no less. If they limit the implied-warranty time, they must also state that "Some states do not allow limitations on how long an implied warranty lasts, so the above limitation may not apply to you." The warrantor may not limit the extent of protection you have under implied warranties, however.

OTHER PROVISIONS of the Warranty Act include the following:

—As long as you've complained within the warranty period, the firm has to act to remedy the problem within the terms of the warranty.

—If a *written* warranty is provided with the product, the warrantor cannot exclude it from protection under implied warranties.

—A warrantor *can* exclude or limit consequential damages from coverage under both full and limited policies. If this is done, the warranty must also state: "Some states do not allow the exclusion or limitation of incidental or consequential damages, so the above limitation or exclusion may not apply to you."

—All warranties must include information on whom to contact, where to bring or mail the product, the name of the warrantor, and the address or toll-free number of same.

—All warranties, full and limited, must state: "This warranty gives you specific legal rights, and you may have other rights that vary from state to state."

Implied Warranties. Implied warranties are state laws that offer protection against major hidden defects in products. Every state has these laws, and they cover every sale unless the seller states that no warranties or guarantees are offered; that goods are sold "as is." But if a particular product sold by a firm with a no-guarantee policy carries a *written* warranty, the implied warranty is valid on that item. The terms of implied warranties differ from state to state, but many have similar sorts of provisions.

THE WARRANTY OF MERCHANTABILITY is a common implied warranty. It means that the product must function properly for conventional use—a freezer must freeze, a knife must cut, etc. If the product does not function properly and your state has a warranty of merchantability, you're probably entitled to a refund for that item.

THE WARRANTY OF FITNESS FOR A PARTICULAR PURPOSE covers cases in which the seller cites or recommends special uses of the product. For example, if a seller says that a coat is "all-weather," it should offer protection in rain and snow. If it claims a glue will "bond any two materials together," the glue should be able to do that. When a salesperson offers you these assurances orally, check the printed product information to verify the recommendation. If no such use is included in the application of the product, ask the salesperson to put the pledge *in writing*. And if the product information contradicts the clerk's suggestion, ask for another product—and a more ethical or better-informed salesperson.

Consequential Damages. Incidental or consequential damages occur when the malfunction of a product causes damage to or loss of other property. The FTC uses the example of an engine block cracking when the antifreeze is faulty. Less extreme is the food spoilage caused by a refrigerator breakdown, or the damage resulting from a leaky waterbed mattress.

Written warranties usually entitle you to consequential damages, but warrantors may exempt this coverage under both full and limited warranties. If the warrantor excludes consequential damages from coverage, the warranty must state: "Some states do not allow exclusion or limitation of incidental or consequential damages, so the above limitation or exclusion may not apply to you."

Provisions for consequential damages entitle you to compensation for the property damage or loss, as well as repair or replacement of the defective product. In the engine block example, the exemption of damages must be considered as a definite disadvantage when evaluating the product/warranty value.

Evaluating Warranties. Develop the habit of appraising the written warranty as thoroughly as you do the product's other features *before* you buy. In reading the warranty, keep in mind any past experiences with products and warranty service from that manufacturer or seller, experiences with similar products, and your actual needs. Know that the first few models of a new product, especially in electronics, are seldom as trouble-free or well-designed as subsequent models. New products often carry higher price tags than their descendants—remember color TVs and pocket calculators?

In evaluating a warranty, ask yourself these questions:

- Is the warranty full or limited?
- Does it cover the whole product, or specific parts?
- How long is the warranty period?
- Do you contact the manufacturer, seller, or a service center for repairs?
- Will you have to remove, deliver, and reinstall the product yourself?
- Do you have to have repairs done by an authorized service center or representative? If so, how close is the nearest facility?
- Will the warrantor provide a temporary replacement for use while your product is being serviced?
- Are consequential damages excluded? If the product proved defective, would the consequential damages entail a significant loss?
- If reimbursement is offered on a pro-rata basis, is it computed on a time, use, or price schedule?
- Do you have a choice of a refund or replacement product if the item is not repairable?

Envision a worst-case scenario in which the product breaks down or malfunctions completely. What expenses might you incur in terms of consequential damages, supplying a substitute product or service, transporting the product to the service center or seller, and repair bills? Will returning the product be troublesome, and living without it while it's being repaired inconvenient? Your answers determine the value the warranty has for *you*. Consider that quotient along with the price and features of the product when comparison shopping, and you'll find your best buy.

Complying with Warranty Terms. Understanding and fulfilling the conditions of a warranty should be simple, but we've outlined a few tips that may make it easier:

- Keep the warranty and dated receipt or proof of payment in a readily accessible file.
- If the manufacturer offers a rebate on the product that requires sending the proof of payment, photocopy the receipt and keep the copy with the warranty.
- Return the warranty card as requested.
- Read the instructions or operations manual before using the product, and follow directions for use.
- Abuse, neglect, and mishandling usually void the warranty. Other practices that may invalidate the policy include improper installation, repair or service by an unauthorized person or agency, use of the product on the wrong voltage, and commercial use. If other people will be using the product, be sure they know how to operate it and understand what restrictions there may be on its functions or use.
- Perform routine maintenance (oiling, cleaning, dusting, replacement of worn components) as required by the manual, but attempt no repairs or maintenance that is not required or permitted in the warranty or guide.

If you have a question about maintenance or use, call the seller or manufacturer. If you void the warranty by violating its terms, you'll have to absorb the cost of repairs or replacement.

Obtaining Service. If your product breaks down or malfunctions, you'll find you resolve the problem faster and more easily if you follow these guidelines:

- Read the operating manual or instructions. The problem may be covered in a troubleshooting section, or you may find that you expected the product to do something for which it wasn't designed.
- Contact the warrantor, whose name, address, and/or phone number appear on the warranty, unless the seller offers service under warranty.
- Call, write, or visit as appropriate. State the nature of the problem, the date it occurred, and whether you want a repair, replacement, refund, and/or consequential damages. Bring a copy of the warranty and proof of payment when you visit, and include copies if you write. (Remember that your rights in respect to the nature and extent of compensation depend upon the terms of the warranty and your state's laws.)
- If you leave the product for repairs or have it picked up, get a signed receipt that includes the date on which it should be ready, an estimate of the bill if you have to pay for repairs, and the serial number of the product, if one is given.
- If you send the product, insure it for the full value. Include a letter stating the nature of the problem, the date on which it occurred, and how you'd like it resolved.
- After a call or visit, the FTC recommends sending a follow-up letter

reiterating the conversation. Keep a photocopy, and send it by certified mail to the person or agency with which you spoke.

- Keep a log of all actions you take in having the warranty honored, the dates actions, visits, and calls were made, and a record of the expenses you incur in the process.
- If you've written to the seller or manufacturer concerning the problem and received no response after three to four weeks, write again. Include a photocopy of the first letter, ask for an answer within three weeks, and send the second letter by certified mail (keep a photocopy). Direct the letter to the head of customer relations or the warranty department, unless you've been dealing with an individual.
- If you've written to the manufacturer, it may help to contact the seller (or vice versa). A reputable firm doesn't want to merchandise through a seller who won't maintain good customer relations, and an intelligent seller knows that marketing shoddy goods is bad for business. Bilateral appeals should be made after you've given the responsible party an opportunity to resolve the problem.
- If you have repairs done, ask to see the product demonstrated *before* you accept it, especially if you're paying for repairs. If there are indications that the problem may recur (e.g. it exhibits the same "symptoms" it had before it broke or malfunctioned), tell the service representative—it may be due to something that wasn't noticed during the repair.
- If you're paying for repairs, ask for a guarantee on parts and/or labor so you won't face another bill if the product breaks down shortly after you begin using it again.
- If the product keeps malfunctioning after it's repaired and it's under full warranty, you can probably get a replacement or refund under the "lemon provision." Write to the manufacturer or seller, provide a history of the problems and repairs, plus a copy of the warranty, and ask for a replacement or refund. If the warranty is limited, the terms may entitle you to a replacement or refund. Write to the manufacturer or seller with the product history and a copy of the warranty, and ask for a new product or compensation if you're entitled to same.
- Don't neglect to investigate your rights under your state's implied-warranty and consequential-damages laws. They may offer you protections not given in the warranty.
- If you've been physically injured by a malfunctioning product, contact your lawyer.
- If, after acting in good faith and allowing the manufacturer or seller time to resolve the problem, you are still dissatisfied, contact your local consumer-protection agency for advice.

You may also report problems to other agencies and organizations. For more information, see "Obtaining Help," p. 496.

COMPLAINTS

COMPLAINT PROCEDURES: You make a formal complaint to a firm after you've informed it of a problem and asked for resolution, following procedures outlined in the catalog, warranty, or this guide. Generally, you give the firm one last chance to remedy the situation, and then you ask for help from outside agencies. However, if your problem concerns nondelivery of or dissatisfaction with goods and you paid with a credit card, you may be able to withold payment under the Fair Credit Billing Act. See "The Federal Trade Commission," p. 497, for more information.

The Complaint Letter. State your complaint clearly and concisely with a history of the problem and all the appropriate documentation: photocopies of previous letters, proof of payment, the warranty, repair receipts, etc. Do not send original documents—send photocopies and keep the originals in your file. Make sure your letter includes your name and address, the order or product number or code and descriptive information about the product, and the method of payment you used. *Do not* use abusive language or profanity, and be sure to type or print the letter. Tell the firm exactly what you want done. Give a deadline of 30 days for a reply or resolution of the problem, and state that if you don't receive a response by that time, you'll report the firm to the Better Business Bureau, DMA, FTC, or other agency. (See "Obtaining Help," following, for information on whom to contact.)

If the firm doesn't acknowledge the request or you're not satisfied by the response, take action.

OBTAINING HELP: There are several agencies and organizations that can help you with different types of problems. Some undertake investigations on a case-by-case basis, while others compile files on firms and act when the volume of complaints reaches a certain level.

When you seek help, provide a copy of your final complaint letter to the firm, as well as the documentation as described in the preceding section, "Complaint Procedures."

Consumer Action Panels (CAPs). CAPs are third-party dispute resolution programs established by the industries they represent. They investigate consumer complaints, provide service information to consumers, and give their members suggestions on improving service to consumers.

FICAP represents the furnishings industry. Write to Furniture Industry Consumer Advisory Panel, P.O. Box 951, High Point, NC 27261 for information on its services.

MACAP helps with problems concerning major appliances. Write to Major Appliance Consumer Action Panel, 20 N. Wacker Dr., Chicago, IL 60606, or call (800) 621–0477 for information.

Better Business Bureaus (BBBs). Supported by funding of business and professional firms, BBBs are self-regulatory agencies that monitor advertising and selling practices, maintain files on firms, help resolve consumer complaints, and disseminate service information to consumers. BBBs also perform the vital service of responding to inquiries about a firm's selling history, although they can't make recommendations.

Most of the Bureaus have mediation and arbitration programs, and are empowered to make awards (binding arbitration).

Whether you want to check a firm's record before ordering or file a complaint, you must contact the BBB nearest the company, not the office in your area. You can obtain a directory of BBB offices by requesting a copy from the Council of Better Business Bureaus, Inc., 1515 Wilson Blvd., Arlington, VA 22209. (Include a SASE with the request.) Write to the appropriate office, and ask for a "consumer complaint" or "consumer inquiry" form, depending on your purpose.

Direct Marketing Association (DMA). The DMA is the largest and oldest trade organization of direct marketers and mail-order companies in existence. Over half its members are non-U.S. firms; this gives it some clout in dealing with problematical foreign orders placed with member firms.

The DMA's *Mail Order Action Line (MOAL),* established fifteen years ago, helps resolve nondelivery problems with any direct-marketing firm. Upon receiving your *written* complaint, the DMA contacts the firm, attempts to resolve the problem, notifies you that it's involved, and asks you to allow 30 days for the firm to solve or act on the problem. To get help, send a copy of your complaint letter and documentation to Mail Order Action Line, DMA, 6 E. 43rd St., New York, NY 10017.

Consumers may also have their names added to or removed from mailing lists through the DMA's Mail Preference Service. Write to the DMA at the above address and ask for an "MPS" form.

The Federal Trade Commission (FTC). The FTC is a law-enforcement agency that protects the public against anticompetitive, unfair, and deceptive business practices. While it does not act upon individual complaints, it does use your complaint letters to build files on firms. When the volume or nature of problems indicates an investigation is warranted, the FTC will act. Several levels of action are possible, including court injunctions and fines of up to $10,000 for each day the violation is occurring. Do report deviations from FTC regulations; your letter may be the one that prompts an investigation.

THE FAIR CREDIT BILLING ACT (FCBA), passed in 1975 under the FTC's Consumer Credit Protection Act, offers mail-order shoppers, who use credit cards as payment some real leverage if they have a problem with nondelivery. The act established a settlement procedure for *billing errors* that include, among other discrepancies, charges for goods or services not accepted or not delivered as agreed. The procedure works as follows:

- You must *write* to the creditor (phoning will not trigger FCBA protection) at the "billing error" address given on the bill.

- The letter must include your name and account number, the dollar amount of the error, and a statement of why you believe an error exists.
- The letter must be received by the creditor within 60 days after the first bill with the error was mailed to you. The FTC recommends sending it via certified mail, return receipt requested.
- The creditor has to acknowledge your letter, in writing, within 30 days of receipt, unless the problem is resolved within that time.
- The creditor must investigate the problem within two billing cycles (not more than 90 days), and correct the error or justify the charge.
- You do not have to pay the disputed amount, the related portion of the minimum payment, or its finance charges while it's being disputed.
- If an error is found, the creditor must write to you, explaining the corrections—the amount must be credited to your account, late fees and finance charges removed, etc. If the creditor finds that you owe part of the amount, it must be explained in writing.
- If the creditor finds that the bill is correct, the reasons must be explained in writing and the amount owed stated. You will be liable for finance charges accrued during the dispute and missed minimum payments.
- You may continue to dispute at this point, but only if your state's laws give you the right to take action against the *seller* rather than the creditor. Write to the creditor within ten days of receiving the justification of the charge, and state that you still refuse to pay the disputed amount. If you continue to challenge, contact your local consumer-protection agency, since the creditor can begin collection proceedings against you and the agency may be able to recommend other means of handling the problem that don't jeopardize your credit rating.

Disputes over the quality of goods or services are covered under the FCBA if state law permits you to withold payment from a *seller*. This applies to credit-card purchases over $50 that are made in your home state or within 100 miles of your mailing address. (The limits do not apply if the seller is also the card issuer, as is often the case with department stores.) Contact your local consumer-protection agency for advice before taking action.

The United States Postal Service (USPS). The USPS takes action on every complaint it receives and resolves about 85% of the problems, partly because it has the power to withhold mail delivery to a company that doesn't cooperate. Don't expect quick results with the USPS, though—you may wait months for any action at all. Send a copy of your final complaint letter and documentation to the Chief Postal Inspector, U.S. Postal Service, Washington, DC 20260–2161.

If you're receiving unsolicited, sexually oriented ads or offers, and would rather not, you can fill out Form 2201, *Application for Listing Pursuant to 39 USC 3010,* at your local post office. If, 30 days after your name has been added to the Postal Service list, you're still receiving such mail, report this to your post office.

Form 2150, *Notice for Prohibitory Order Against Sender of Pandering Advertisement in the Mail,* should put a stop to the mailing of anything you consider erotically arousing or sexually provocative. You can fill out this form at your local post office as well.

Bankruptcy courts. These courts may offer information, if no actual compensation, on errant orders and refunds. If you've written to the company and received no response and its phones have been disconnected, you may want to contact the U.S. Bankruptcy Court nearest the firm. State the nature of your complaint and ask whether the company has filed for reorganization under Chapter 11. If it has filed, request the case number and information on filing a claim. Chapter 11 protects a business against the claims of its creditors; all you can do is file and hope. As a customer, your claim comes after those of the firm's suppliers, utilities, banks, etc. The "take a ticket" approach is no guarantee that you'll get anything back, but if it's your only shot, take the trouble to file.

COMPLAINTS ABOUT FOREIGN FIRMS: For general information on handling complaints regarding foreign firms, first see "Delayed Shipments from Foreign Firms," p. 488.

The DMA may be able to undertake an investigation on your behalf. See p. 497 for information on the organization and its address.

The Council of Better Business Bureaus has affiliates in Canada, Mexico, Israel, and Venezuela. If the firm is located in any of those countries, write to the Council for the address of the office nearest the company, and contact that office with the complaint. See p. 496 for more information and the Council's address.

The foreign trade council representing the firm's country may be able to provide information that could prove helpful. Contact the council and briefly describe the problem you have. Ask whether the organization can supply the name of a regulatory agency or trade organization in that country that might be of help. The councils have offices in New York City, and directory assistance can provide you with their phone numbers. You may also contact us (see the following) for their names, numbers, and addresses.

We'll do everything we can to help you resolve problems with all the firms, domestic and foreign, listed in this book. See "Feedback," p. 500, for more information and our mailing address.

Feedback

Consumers and business, *we want to hear from you!* Your suggestions, complaints, and comments have helped shape this edition of *The Wholesale-by-Mail Catalog III,* and are highly valued. We thank every reader who's written in the past, and urge you to keep those cards and letters coming in. You can help us by using the guidelines that follow.

Firms. if you'd like to have your company included in the next edition of WBMC, send us a copy of your current literature, with prices and the name of your publicity or marketing director. Firms are listed at the discretion of the editors, and must meet our basic criteria to qualify for inclusion.

Consumers. If you're writing a letter of complaint, please read the sections of "The Complete Guide to Buying by Mail" that may apply to your problem, and attempt to work it out yourself. If you can't remedy the situation on your own, write to us and include:

- a brief history of the transaction,
- copies (not originals) of all letters and documents related to the problem,
- a list of dates on which events occurred, if applicable (the date a phone order was placed, goods were received, account charged, etc.),
- a description of what you want done (goods delivered, warranty honored, return accepted, money refunded or credited, etc.).

We will begin investigating the matter when we receive your letter. While we cannot *guarantee* resolution, we may be able to help.

If you just want to sound off, we'd like to hear from you too. If you're moved to sing the praises of any mail-order company, please do so—and tell us what has impressed you. And if you have suggestions for the next edition of WBMC, we're all ears. Remember to include your name and address in all correspondence, and send to:

The Wholesale-by-Mail Catalog™ III
P.O. Box 505, Varick St. Sta.
New York, NY 10014–0505

Index

AAA-A1 Factory, Inc., 33–34
ABC Photo Service, 109
ABC Vacuum Cleaner Warehouse, 34
A. Benjamin & Co., Inc., 309–310
A.B. Schou, 318–319
Ace Leather Products, Inc., 347
Ad-Libs Astronomics, 109–110
A.E.S., 428
A. Goto, 63–64
Airborne Sales Co., The, 422
American Discount Wallcoverings, 261–262
A.L.A.S. Accordion-O-Rama, 362–363
Albert S. Smyth Co., Inc., 322
Alfax Mfg., 375
All Electronics Corp., 429
Allyn Air Seat Co., 400–401
Altman Luggage, 347–348
American Educational Services, Inc., 90
American Family Publishers, 91
American Marine Electronics, 77
American Stationery Co., Inc., The, 91–92
American Vacuum & Sewing Machine Corp., 35
America's Hobby Center, 174–175
Amity Hallmark, Ltd., 376
Animal City Wholesale, 21
Animal Veterinary Products, Inc., 21–22
Annex Outlet Ltd., 35–36
Antique Imports Unlimited, 60–61
Arctic Glass Supply, Inc., 303–304
Argus Radio & Appliances, Inc., 36
A. Rosenthal, Inc., 159
Athletes' Corner, 401
Audio Video Center, Inc., 37
Austad Company, The, 401–402
A. Van Moppes & Zoon (Diamant) B.V., 342–343
A to Z Luggage Co., Inc., 348

Babouris Handicrafts, 175
Bailey's, Inc., 430–431
Barnes & Blackwelder, Inc., 272–273
Barnes & Noble Bookstores, Inc., 92–93
Bazaar's Beauty Collection, 244–245
Bear Meadow Farm, 198–199
Beautiful Beginnings, 245–246
Beautiful Visions, Inc., 246
Beauty Buy Book, 246–247
Beauty by Spector, Inc., 247–248
Bedpost, Inc., The, 273–274
Beitman Co., Inc., 175–176
Belle Tire Distributors, Inc., 77

Bell Yarn Co., Inc., 176–177
Bernie's Discount Center, Inc., 37–38
Berry Scuba Co., 402–403
Best Choice, The, 403–404
Best Products Co., Inc., 224
Bettinger's Luggage Shop, 348–349
Bevers, The, 431–432
B & H Photo, 110
Bike Nashbar, 404–405
Blackwelder's Industries, Inc., 274–275
Bondy Export Corp., 38–39
Bowhunters Discount Warehouse, Inc., 405
Boycan's Craft, Art, Needlework & Floral Supplies, 177–178
Brass Bed Shoppe, A., 275–276
Breck's, 199
Briart Services, 93
Bruce Medical Supply, 354–355
Business & Institutional Furniture Company, 377
Buy Direct, Inc., 378

California Digital, 378–379
Cambridge Camera Exchange, Inc., 110–11
Cambridge Wools, Ltd., 178
Camelot Enterprises, 432
Camera World of Oregon, 111
Campmor, 405–406
Cannondale's, 276–277
Capital Cycle Corporation, 78
Capriland's Herb Farm, 200
Carry-on Luggage, Inc., 349
Carvin, 364
Cascio Music Company, Inc., 364–365
Catherine, S.A., 248–249
Caviarteria Inc., 212–213
Central Michigan Tractor & Parts, 78
Central Skindivers of Nassau, Inc., 406
Chanute Iron & Supply Co., Inc., 304
Charles Weiss & Sons, Inc., 169–170
Charlie's Place, 135
Cheese of All Nations, 213–214
Cherry Auto Parts, 79
Cherry Hill Furniture, Carpet & Interiors, 277–278
Chesterfield Music Shops, Inc., 93–94
Chock Catalog Corp., 135–136
Clark's Corvair Parts, Inc., 79–80
Clinton Cycle & Salvage, Inc., 80
Clothcrafters, Inc., 225
Colorchrome, 111–112
Company Store, Inc., The, 294–295

Comp-U-Card, 225–226
Computer Connection, 379
Computer Hut of New England, Inc., 379–380
Computer Warehouse, 380–381
Conroy-LaPointe, Inc., 381–382
Cook's Wares, A, 287–288
Craft Products Company, 179–180
Craftsman Wood Service Co., 180–181
Crown Art Products Co., Inc., 71
Crutchfield, 39
Current, Inc., 94
Custom Coat Company, Inc., 136–137
Custom Golf Clubs, Inc., 407
Cycle Goods Corp., 407–408

Daedalus Books, Inc., 95
Dairy Association Co., Inc., 22
D & A Merchandise Co., Inc., 137–138
Danley's, 112–113
Decor Prints, 62
Deepak's Rokjemperl Products, 327–328
Deerskin Place, The, 138
Defender Industries, Inc., 80–81
De Joger Bulbs, Inc., 200–201
D'Elia's Designs, 96
Del-Mar Co., 328–329
Dial-A-Brand, 40
Diamonds by Rennie Ellen, 330
Dick Blick Co., 70
Dinosaur Catalog, 446–447
Discount Parts & Tires, 81
D. MacGillivray & Coy., 187–188
Doll House & Toy Factory Outlet, 447–448
Dollsville Dolls and Bearsville Bears, 448–449
Down Outlet, The, 295
Down Town, 296
Dreamy Down Fashions, Inc., 296–297
D.R.I. Industries, Inc., 433
Duk Kwong Optical Centre, 356
Dutch Gardens Inc., 201–202
Dyker Heights Sports Shop, Inc., 408

Eastern Cycle Salvage, Inc., 82
E.B.A. Wholesale Corp., 41
E & B Marine, Inc., 81–82
Echo Pet Supplies, 23
E.C. Kraus, 185–186
Economy Software, 383
Ecotech, Inc., 434
Edgar B. Furniture Plantation, 278
Edward R. Hamilton, Bookseller, 98
800-Software Inc., 383–384
Eileen's Handknits, 139
Eisner Bros., 139–140
Elbridge C. Thomas & Sons, 220–221
Eldridge Textile Co., 297–298
Emerald, 310–311
Envelope Sales Company, 384
Erewhon Trading Co., 214
Essential Products Co., Inc., 250
ETCO Electronics Corp., 434–435
E33 Typewriter & Electronics, 40–41
Euro-Tire, Inc., 82–83
Euston Gallery, 62
Executive Photo & Supply Corp., 113–114
Ezra Cohen Corp., 293

Fabric Center, The, 262
Famous Smoke Shop, Inc., 127–128
Father Time, 181–182
Federal/Getz Pharmacy Service, 356–357
Finals, The, 140–141
Fiveson Food Equipment, Inc., 288–289
FixMaster, 435
Focus Electronics, Inc., 42–43
Fortunoff, 311
47st. Computing, 385
47st. Photo, 114–115
Foto Electric Supply Co., 43
Frank Eastern Co., 382
Frank's Highland Park Camera, 115
Franz Roozen B.V., 206
Fred's String Warehouse, 365
Fred Stoker Farms, 130–131
Freeport Music, 365–366
Friar's House, The, 63
F.R. Knitting Mills, Inc., 141–142
Front Row Photos, 96–97
Furniture Barn of Forest City, Inc., The, 278–279

Gailin Collection, The, 312
Garden Corner, 116
George Channing Enterprises, 61–62
George and Son's Co., 279
Gered, 313
Gettinger Feather Corp., 182
G. Hencke and Co., 449
Ginger Schlote, 342
Glorybee Bee Box, Inc., 202
Glorybee Honey, Inc., 214–215
G.M. Trahos & Sons, Fur House, 167–168
Gohn Bros., 142–143
Goldberg's Marine, 83
Goldman & Cohen Inc., 143
Gold N' Stone, 330–331
Golf Haus, 409
Good 'N' Lucky Promotions, 331–332
Good Shepheard's Store, 236
Grand Finale, 227
Grayarc, 385–386
Great American Magazines, Inc., 97
Greater New York Trading Co., 313–314
Great Tracers, 182–183
Guitar Trader, 366–367
Gurian Fabrics Inc., 263

Haber's, 386–387
Handart Embroideries, 144
Hanover House, 227–228
Harbor Freight Salvage Co., 423
Hardware, Software, Anyware, 387
Harris Levy, 298
Harry's Discounts & Appliances Corp., 44
Harvest of Values, 251
Hayim Pinhas, 130
Heritage Clock and Brassmiths, 184
Holabird Sports Discounters, 409–410
Hong Kong Lapidaries, Inc., 332–333
House of Onyx, 333–334
Hunter Audio-Photo, Inc., 44–45

I. Buss & Co., 134–135
Illinois Audio, Inc., 45–46
Innovation Luggage, 349–350
International Import Co., 334–335

International Solgo, Inc., 46
Irish Cottage Industries Ltd., 145
Irv Wolfson Company, 57

James Roy Furniture Co., Inc., 283
J B Jewelry, 335
J.C. Whitney & Co., 87
J. E. Miller Nurseries, Inc., 203
Jems Sounds, Ltd., 47
Jerry's Artarama, Inc., 71–72
Jilor Discount Office Machines, Inc., 387–388
J. Richelle Parfums Ltd., 253–254
J-R Tobacco Co., 129–130
J. Schachter Corp., 300–301
J.W. Chunn Perfumes, 249

Kansas City Vaccine Company, 23–24
Kaplan Bros. Blue Flame Corp., 289
Kennedy of Ardara, 145–146
Kennelly Keys Music and Dance, Inc., 367
King's Chandelier Company, 263–264
Kountry Bear Company, 450

Lamp Warehouse/New York Ceiling Fan
    Center, 264–265
Landis House, 314–315
La Piñata, 237
Las Vegas Discount Golf & Tennis, 410–411
Laurence Corner, 146–147
L&D Press, 98–99
Leather School, 340–341
Lee-McClain Co., 147–148
L'eggs Showcase of Savings, 148–149
Lewi Supply, 47
LHL Enterprises, 186–187
Liberty Leather Manufacturers, 24
Lincoln House, Inc., 228
Lingerie for Less, 357
Lion Photo Supply, Inc., 116–117
Love's Inc., 336
LVT Price Quote Hotline, Inc., 48
Lyben Computer Systems, 388
Lyle Cartridges, 48–49
Lynn Dairy, Inc., 215–216

Magazine Buyers' Service, 99
Magazine Marketplace Inc., 99–100
Mail Order Bride, Inc., The, 149
Maine Discount Hardware, 436
M.A. Knutsen Inc., 290
Mandolin Brothers Ltd., 368
Manny's Musical Instruments & Accessories,
    Inc., 368–369
Manufacturer's Supply, 437
Mardiron Optics, 117
Mass Army & Navy Store, 423–424
Mast Abeam, 84
Mexican Kitchen, The/La Cocina Mexicana,
    216–217
Michel Swiss, 255–256
Mickey Thompson Tires, 85
Micro Mart, Inc., 389
Mid America Vacuum Cleaner Supply Co.,
    49–50
M & I Haberman, Inc., 337
Miscellaneous Man, 64
Mogish String Co., 369
Mr. Spiceman, 217–218

Murrow Furniture Galleries, Inc., 280
Museum Editions New York Ltd., 65

National Business Furniture, Inc., 389–390
National Contact Lens Center, 357–358
National Educational Music Company, Ltd.,
    369–370
National Wholesale Company, Inc., 150
Nat Schwartz & Co., Inc., 319–320
Newark Dressmaker Supply, Inc., 188
North Country Leather, 351
Northern Hydraulics, Inc., 438
Northern Wholesale Veterinary Supply,
    24–25
N. Pintchik, Inc., 265
Nurhan Cevahir, 127

Offshore Imports, 84
Olden Camera & Lens Co., Inc., 117–118
Omaha Vaccine Company, 25
Opticon Laboratories, Inc., 118–119
Oreck Corporation, 50–51
Oregon Bulb Farms, 203–204
Orion Telescope Center, 119
Otten & Son, 237–238

Pacific Exchanges, 390
Pagano Gloves, Inc., 151
Paradise Products, Inc., 450–451
Parfumeries Grillot, 252
Paris International Inc., 290–291
PBS Livestock Drugs, 25–26
Pearl Brothers Office Machinery &
    Equipment, 390–391
Pearl Equipment, 72
Pedal Pushers, Inc., 411
Percy's Inc., 51–52
Petticoat Express, The, 152
Pharmaceutical Services, 358
Pizazz, Inc., 338–339
P & J Company, 338
Plastic Bagmart, 305
Plexi-Craft Quality Products Corp., 280–281
Prentiss Court Ground Covers, 204–205
Prescription Delivery Systems, 358–359
Prince Fashions Ltd., 152–153
Prismatic, 154
Professional Golf Suppliers, Inc., 413
Professional Golf & Tennis Suppliers, Inc.,
    412–413
Professional Marketing Consultants, 339
Professional Racquetball Suppliers, Inc., 413
Pro Photo Labs, 119
Protecto-Pak, 305–306
Publishers Central Bureau, 100
Publishers Clearing House, 101
Puritan Pride, Inc., 252–253

Quality Furniture Market of Lenoir, Inc.,
    281–282
Quilts Unlimited, 65–66

Rachel's for Kids, 154–155
Rainbow Gardens Nursery & Bookshop,
    205–206
Rainbow Music, 370
Rama Jewelry Ltd., Part., 340
Rammagerdin, H.F., 189–190
Rapidforms, Inc., 391–392

R.D. Associates, 439
Reborn Maternity, 155
Regal Greetings & Gifts, Inc., 228–229
Rein Furs, 155–156
Reject China Shops, 315–316
R/E Kane Enterprises, 340–341
Renovator's Supply, Inc., The, 306–307
Ric Clark Company, 355
Richard P. Zarbin and Associates, 285–286
Riteway HAC, 359
Road Runner Sports, 414
Roberts Brass Company, 282–283
Robin Importers, 316–317
Robinson's Wallcoverings, 266
Rocky Mountain Stationery, 238
Rogers & Rosenthal, Inc., 317
Romanes & Paterson Ltd., 157–158
Romni Wools and Fibres Ltd., 190–191
Roussels, 191
Royal Gardens Inc., 207
Royal Silk, Ltd., 159–160
RSP Distributing Co., 229–230
Rubens Babywear Factory, 160–161
Rubin & Green Inc., 299
Rudi's Pottery, Silver, & China, 318
Ruvel and Company, Inc., 424

Saint Laurie Ltd., 161–162
Sales Citi, Inc., 53
Samarth Gem Stones, 341–342
Sam Ash Music Corp., 363
Sanz International, Inc., 266–267
Saw Chain H & H Manufacturing & Supply
    Co., 439–440
Saxkjaers, 66–67
S & C Huber, Accoutrements, 239
Sears, Roebuck and Co., 230
Self-Sufficiency and Smallholding Supplies,
    26–27
7th Heaven Fashions, Inc., 162–163
Sewin' in Vermont, 53–54
SGF, 231
Shama Imports, Inc., 267
Shannon Mail Order, 320–321
Sharp Photo, 120
Shaw Furniture Galleries, 284
Shibui Wallcoverings, 268
Shorland Textile Co., 301
Sierra Fitness Distributers, 415
Silk Plants Ltd., 268–269
Silver & Horland, Inc., 370–371
Simpson & Vail, Inc., 218–219
16 Plus Mail Order, 163
Soccer International, Inc., 416
Sock Shop, The, 164
Solar Cine Products, Inc., 120–121
Southeastern Insulated Glass, 307
Specialty Leathers of California, 164–165
Spiegel, Inc., 231–232
Sports America, Inc., 416–417
Squash Services, Inc., 417
S & S Sound City, 52
Star Pharmaceutical, Inc., 254–255
Stavros Kouyoumoutzakis, 184–185
Stecher's Limited, 323
Stereo Corporation of America, 54
Stereo Discounters Electronic World, 54–55
St. Patrick's Down, 299–300
Strand Book Store, Inc., 101–102
Straw Into Gold, Inc., 191–192

Stu-Art Supplies, Inc., 73
Stuckey Brothers Furniture Co., Inc., 285
Stuyvesant Bicycle & Toy Inc., 418
Subtle Dynamics, 85
Sultan's Delight Inc., 219
Sunburst Biorganics, 255
Sunco Products Corp., 165–166
SuperSave Music, 371
Surplus Center, The, 425
Sussex Clothes, Ltd., 166–167

Tai Inc., 167
Tartan Book Sales, 102–103
Tastefully Yours, 220
Tennis Co., The, 418–419
Terminal Musical Supply, Inc., 371–372
Thai Silks, 192–193
Tibetan Refugee Self Help Centre, 239–240
Tomahawk Live Trap Co., 27–28
Tool Warehouse, The, 440
Toy Balloon Corp., 451–452
Trade Exchange Ceylon, Ltd., 240–241
Trade-Mark Business Barter Exchange of
    New York, 232
Treasure Traders Ltd., 323–324
Triple A Scale & Mfg., Co., 392
Tugon Chemical Corp., 86
Tuli-Latus Perfumes, Ltd., 256–257
Turnbaugh Printers Supply Co., 393–394
Turnkey Material Handling, Inc., 441
Typex Business Machines, Inc., 394

United Pharmaceutical Company, Inc., 28–29
United States Postal Service, 394–395
United Subscription Service, 103
U.S. General Supply Corp., 442
Utex Trading Enterprises, 193–194
Utrecht Art and Drafting Supply, 73–74

Valray International, Inc., 257–258
Van Bourgondien Bros., 207–208
Videotime Corp., The, 55
Vitamin Specialties Co., 258–259

Wall Street Camera Exchange, Inc., 121
Wally Frank, Ltd., 128–129
Walter Drake & Sons, Inc., 226
Warehouse Marine Discount, 86
Wear-Guard Work Clothes, 168–169
Weiss & Mahoney, 425–426
Wells Interiors Inc., 269–270
Western Natural Products, 259–260
West Side Camera Inc., 122
Whole Earth Access, 233
Wholesale Veterinary Supply, Inc., 29
Windfall Lists, 395–396
Wisan TV & Appliance Inc., 56
Wisconsin Discount Stereo, 56
Wolff Office Equipment Corp., 396
Workmen's Garment Co., 170–171
World Abrasives Co., Inc., 442–443
World's Fare, 291
World of 35mm, The, 122
W.S. Robertson (Outfitters) Ltd., 157

Yachtmail Co. Ltd., 87
Yankee Ingenuity, 194

Zabar's, 221–222
Zip-Penn, Inc., 443